3rd Edition

STRATEGIC MANAGEMENT
ESSENTIALS

Gareth R. Jones
Texas A&M University

Charles W. L. Hill
University of Washington

SOUTH-WESTERN
CENGAGE Learning

Australia • Brazil • Japan • Korea • Mexico • Singapore • Spain • United Kingdom • United States

BRIEF CONTENTS

PART ONE   INTRODUCTION TO STRATEGIC MANAGEMENT

1   Developing the Competitive Strategic Process   1
2   Governing Stakeholders and Business Ethics   27

PART TWO   THE NATURE OF COMPETITIVE ADVANTAGE

3   Identifying Opportunities and Threats
    Through External Analysis   55
4   Building Competitive Advantage   83

PART THREE   BUILDING AND SUSTAINING LONG-RUN
COMPETITIVE ADVANTAGE

5   Positioning for Competitive Business-Level Strategy   117
6   Global Strategy   145
7   Long-Run Profitability Through Corporate-Level Strategy   172

PART FOUR   STRATEGY IMPLEMENTATION

8   Strategic Change   200
9   Implementing Strategy Through Organizational Design   226

CONTENTS

Preface   xi

PART ONE   INTRODUCTION TO STRATEGIC MANAGEMENT

Chapter 1   **Developing the Competitive Strategic Process**   1

Competitive Advantage and Superior Performance   2

Running Case: Walmart's Competitive Advantage   3

Strategic Managers   5
   Corporate-Level Managers   6
   Business-Level Managers   6
   Functional-Level Managers   7
The Strategy-Making Process   7
   A Model of the Strategic Planning Process   7
   The Feedback Loop   11
Strategy as an Emergent Process   11
   Strategy Making in an Unpredictable World   11
   Autonomous Action: Strategy Making by Lower-Level Managers   12
   Serendipity and Strategy   12

Strategy in Action 1.1: A Strategic Shift at Microsoft   13

   Intended and Emergent Strategies   14
Strategic Planning in Practice   15
   Scenario Planning   15
   Decentralized Planning   16
Strategic Decision Making   17
   Cognitive Biases   17
   Improving Decision Making   18
Strategic Leadership   19
   Vision, Eloquence, and Consistency   19
   Commitment   20
   Being Well Informed   20
   Willingness to Delegate and Empower   20
   The Astute Use of Power   21
   Emotional Intelligence   21

Closing Case: Planning for the Chevy Volt   23

Chapter 2   **Governing Stakeholders and Business Ethics**   27

Stakeholders   28
The Mission Statement   29
   The Mission   30

Vision   31
Values   32
Major Goals   32
Corporate Governance and Strategy   33
The Agency Problem   34

Strategy In Action 2.1: The Agency Problem at Tyco   35
Governance Mechanisms   38
Ethics and Strategy   42
Ethical Issues in Strategy   42

Running Case: Working Conditions at Walmart   45
The Roots of Unethical Behavior   46
Behaving Ethically   47
Final Words   49

Closing Case: Google's Mission, Ethical Principles, and Involvement in China   51

PART TWO   THE NATURE OF COMPETITIVE ADVANTAGE

Chapter 3   **Identifying Opportunities and Threats Through External Analysis**   **55**

Analyzing Industry Structure   56
Risk of Entry by Potential Competitors   58

Strategy in Action 3.1: Circumventing Entry Barriers into the Soft Drink Industry   59
Rivalry among Established Companies   61
The Bargaining Power of Buyers   63
The Bargaining Power of Suppliers   64
Substitute Products   65
Porter's Model Summarized   66
Strategic Groups within Industries   66

Running Case: Walmart's Bargaining Power over Suppliers   67
Implications of Strategic Groups   68
The Role of Mobility Barriers   69
Industry Life Cycle Analysis   69
Embryonic Industries   70
Growth Industries   70
Industry Shakeout   71
Mature Industries   72
Declining Industries   72
Summary   73
The Macroenvironment   73
Macroeconomic Forces   73
Global Forces   75

Technological Forces 75
Demographic Forces 75
Social Forces 76
Political and Legal Forces 76

Closing Case: The Pharmaceutical Industry   78

Chapter 4   **Building Competitive Advantage**   **83**

Competitive Advantage: Value Creation, Low Cost,
and Differentiation   84
The Generic Building Blocks of Competitive Advantage   86
Efficiency 87
Quality as Excellence and Reliability 88
Innovation 89
Customer Responsiveness 90
The Value Chain   90
Primary Activities 91
Support Activities 92
Functional Strategies and The Generic Building Blocks of Competitive
Advantage   93
Increasing Efficiency 93

Strategy in Action 4.1: Learning Effects in Cardiac Surgery   95

Running Case: Human Resource Strategy and Productivity
at Walmart   99

Increasing Quality 100
Increasing Innovation 103
Achieving Superior Customer Responsiveness 106
Distinctive Competencies and Competitive Advantage   108
Resources and Capabilities 108
The Durability of Competitive Advantage 110

Closing Case: Starbucks   112

PART THREE   BUILDING AND SUSTAINING LONG-RUN
                COMPETITIVE ADVANTAGE

Chapter 5   **Positioning for Competitive Business-Level Strategy**   **117**

The Nature of Competitive Positioning   118
Customer Needs and Product Differentiation 118
Customer Groups and Market Segmentation 119
Distinctive Competencies 119

Running Case: Walmart's Business Model and Competitive
Positioning   120

Choosing a Business-Level Strategy   120
    Cost-Leadership Strategy   *121*
    Differentiation Strategy   *122*
    Cost Leadership and Differentiation   *124*
    Focus Strategy   *125*
    Stuck in the Middle   *128*
Competitive Positioning in Different Industry Environments   129
    Strategies in Fragmented and Growing Industries   *129*
    Strategy in Mature Industries   *131*
    Strategies in Declining Industries   *137*

Closing Case: Nike's Business-Level Strategies   141

Chapter 6   **Global Strategy**   **145**

The Global Environment   146
Increasing Profitability through Global Expansion   148
    Expanding the Market: Leveraging Products and Competencies   *148*
    Realizing Economies of Scale   *149*
    Realizing Location Economies   *149*

Running Case: Walmart's Global Expansion   150
    Leveraging the Skills of Global Subsidiaries   *152*
Cost Pressures and Pressures for Local Responsiveness   152
    Pressures for Cost Reductions   *153*
    Pressures for Local Responsiveness   *154*
Choosing a Global Strategy   156
    Global Standardization Strategy   *156*
    Localization Strategy   *157*

Strategy in Action 6.1: The Evolution of Strategy at Procter &
Gamble   158
    Transnational Strategy   *159*
    International Strategy   *159*
    Changes in Strategy Over Time   *160*
Choices of Entry Mode   161
    Exporting   *161*
    Licensing   *162*
    Franchising   *163*
    Joint Ventures   *164*
    Wholly Owned Subsidiaries   *165*
    Choosing an Entry Strategy   *166*

Closing Case: IKEA—The Global Retailer   169

Chapter 7   **Long-Run Profitability Through Corporate-Level Strategy 172**

Concentration on a Single Industry   173
    Horizontal Integration   *174*
    Benefits and Costs of Horizontal Integration   *175*

Running Case: Walmart's Growing Chain of "Neighborhood Markets" 176

Outsourcing Functional Activities 178
Vertical Integration 180
Arguments for Vertical Integration 182
Arguments against Vertical Integration 184
Vertical Integration and Outsourcing 186
Entering New Industries Through Diversification 186
Creating Value Through Diversification 187

Strategy in Action 7.1: Diversification at 3M: Leveraging Technology 190

Related versus Unrelated Diversification 191
Restructuring and Downsizing 192
Why Restructure? 193
Exit Strategies 194

Closing Case: United Technologies Has an "ACE in Its Pocket" 196

PART FOUR   STRATEGY IMPLEMENTATION

Chapter 8   **Strategic Change**   **200**

Strategic Change 201
Types of Strategic Change 201
A Model of the Change Process 202
Analyzing a Company as a Portfolio of Core Competencies 205
Fill in the Blanks 206
Premier Plus 10 207
White Spaces 207
Mega-Opportunities 207
Implementing Strategy Through Internal New Ventures 208
Pitfalls with Internal New Ventures 209
Guidelines for Successful Internal New Venturing 211
Implementing Strategy Through Acquisitions 212
Pitfalls with Acquisitions 213
Guidelines for Successful Acquisition 214
Implementing Strategy Through Strategic Alliances 215

Strategy in Action 8.1: News Corp's Successful Acquisition Strategy 216

Advantages of Strategic Alliances 217
Disadvantages of Strategic Alliances 217
Making Strategic Alliances Work 218

Closing Case: Oracle's Growing Portfolio of Businesses 222

Chapter 9   **Implementing Strategy Through Organizational Design**   **226**

The Role of Organizational Structure 227
Building Blocks of Organizational Structure 228

Vertical Differentiation   229
  Problems with Tall Structures   230
  Centralization or Decentralization?   232

Strategy in Action 9.1: To Centralize or Decentralize?
That Is the Question   233

Horizontal Differentiation   234
  Functional Structure   234
  Product Structure   236
  Product-Team Structure   237
  Geographic Structure   238
  Multidivisional Structure   240
Integration and Organizational Control   244
  Forms of Integrating Mechanisms   244
  Differentiation and Integration   247
The Nature of Organizational Control   247
  Strategic Controls   248
  Financial Controls   250
  Output Controls   251
  Behavior Control   252

Running Case: How Sam Walton Created Walmart's Culture   255

Closing Case: Strategy Implementation at Dell Computer   257

Introduction: Analyzing a Case Study and Writing a Case Study Analysis   C1

What Is Case Study Analysis?
Analyzing a Case Study
Writing a Case Study Analysis
The Role of Financial Analysis in Case Study Analysis
  Profit Ratios
  Liquidity Ratios
  Activity Ratios
  Leverage Ratios
  Shareholder-Return Ratios
  Cash Flow
Conclusion

Cases

Analyzing a Case Study and Writing a Case Study Analysis   C1

Section A: Business Level Cases: Domestic and Global

Case 1: SGI Versus Dell: Competition in Server and Cloud
Computing   C13

Case 2: The Home Video Game Industry: Atari Pong
to the Nintendo Wii   C21

Case 3: The Global Automobile Industry in 2009   C40

Section B: Corporate Level Cases: Domestic and Global

Case 4: IKEA: Furniture Retailer to the World   C52

Case 5: The Rise of IBM   C60

Case 6: The Fall of IBM   C71

Case 7: IBM in 2009   C84

Index   I1

PREFACE

In framing and writing *Strategic Management Essentials,* our goal is to inform and familiarize students with what strategic management means to today's global world. Often people are unaware of how the strategy-making process affects them. We are all used to going to work and going into companies such as restaurants, stores, and banks, and buying the goods and services we need to satisfy our many needs. However, the actual strategic management activities and processes that are required to make these goods and services available to us commonly go unappreciated. Similarly, we might know that companies exist to make a "profit," but what is profit, how is it created, and what is profit used for? Moreover, what are the actual strategic management activities involved in the creation of goods and services, and why is it that some companies seem to be more effective and more "profitable" than others?

Strategic Management Essentials, Third Edition, has been structured and written to address these issues. The goal of this revision is to explain in a clear, comprehensive, but concise way why strategic management is important to people, the companies they work for, and the society in which they live. Our objective in writing this book has been to provide the overall "big picture" of what strategic management is, what strategic managers do, and how the strategy-making process affects company performance. The book provides a focused, integrated approach that gives students a solid understanding of the nature, functions, and main building blocks of strategic management.

ORGANIZATION OF THE BOOK

The book presents a broad overview of the nature and functions of strategic management in nine chapters. Part 1, *Introduction to Strategic Management,* explains what strategic management is and provides a framework to understand what strategic managers do. Chapter 1 discusses the relationship between strategic management and strategic leadership and shows how competitive advantage results in superior performance. It also describes the plan of this book and discusses the principal functions of strategic managers. Chapter 2 discusses the way companies affect their stakeholders, and why it is necessary to create corporate governance mechanisms that ensure strategic managers work to further the interests of stakeholders and behave ethically.

In Part 2, *The Nature of Competitive Advantage,* we discuss the factors and forces both external and internal to an organization that determine its choice of strategies to create a competitive advantage and achieve above-average profitability. Chapter 3 discusses opportunities, threats, and competition in the external environment. Chapter 4 examines how a company can build competitive advantage by achieving superior efficiency, quality, innovation, and responsiveness to customers. It also discusses how managers can craft functional-level strategies that will allow an organization to achieve these goals.

In Part 3, *Building and Sustaining Long-Run Competitive Advantage,* we provide a streamlined discussion of the different level of strategy that must be developed to build and sustain a long-term competitive advantage. Chapter 5 discusses how to use business-level strategies to optimize competitive positioning and outperform industry rivals. Chapter 6 discusses how to strengthen competitive advantage by expanding globally into new national markets. Chapter 7 then examines the various corporate-level strategies such as vertical integration, diversification, and outsourcing that are used to protect and strengthen competitive advantage and sustain long-run profitability.

Part 4, *Strategy Implementation,* we examine the many operational issues involved in putting all these strategies into action simultaneously. Chapter 8 first discusses the importance of strategic change in today's fast-changing global environment and the issues and problems involved in managing the change process effectively. Then, it outlines how to build and develop a company's business through the use of internal new venturing, acquisitions, and strategic alliances and considers the pros and cons of these different methods. Chapter 9 discusses how to implement strategy through the design of organizational structure and the operational issues involved in selecting structures to match the needs of particular strategies. It also discusses the organizational control systems necessary to fit strategy to structure and the role of organizational culture in developing competitive advantage.

And, finally, in *Part 5* we provide a collection of cases that will appeal to students and instructors alike. We selected cases based both on the intrinsically interesting and timely topics, such as the global auto industry and the gaming industry, and the strategic management issues they illuminate. Through the cases and the guidelines on analyzing a case, students can further investigate the successes and challenges presented throughout the strategic management process. All seven cases are new to this edition and strive to introduce students to well-known global corporations such as Dell, IKEA, and IBM.

As you can see by perusing the table of contents, our essentials book parallels the approach we take in our other book, *Strategic Management: An Integrated Approach.* Our goal is to offer a contemporary, integrated account of strategic management, but one that is streamlined and focused only on the essentials of this complex and fascinating subject.

LEARNING FEATURES

Nothing makes the practice of strategic management come alive more than vivid stories and examples about people and companies that demonstrate clearly the meaning of the chapter material. Hands-on exercises offer students the opportunity to actively think about and engage in strategic management issues and decision making. This book pays considerable attention to creating and developing both in-chapter and end-of-chapter features and exercises to offer the most learning value to students while economizing on their valuable learning time.

Each chapter contains *Strategy in Action* insight boxes that have been carefully selected and written to raise students' interest and are integrated seamlessly into the text so as not to disrupt its flow. Many books have examples that disrupt students' thought processes or distract them with enormous amounts of unnecessary detail; this book avoids these pitfalls.

Each chapter also contains a *Running Case* featuring Walmart as the focus corporation. In this edition, the Running Case examples illustrating continuous real-world changes in strategic management practices such as the increased use of cost reduction strategies like global outsourcing, ethical issues, and lean production are at the heart of the revision.

In midst of ever-present corporate scandals and economic turbulence, educators are faced with the critical and difficult task of teaching ethical decision-making practices. As an instructional tool to broach this task, each chapter contains the new marginal feature—*Ethical Dilemma*—that asks students to make sound management decisions while considering ethical ramifications in business.

The online learning features contained in *Practicing Strategic Management* are composed of exercises designed to offer additional insight into the chapter material to build students' learning experience. They are designed to create lively discussion either at the level of the whole class, or in small groups, or at the individual level. In practice, an instructor will have to decide which of these exercises to select and use in any particular class period or which to use as homework assignments. Frequently, instructors find that varying the particular exercises they use over the semester is the best way to engage students.

- *Discussion Questions.* A set of chapter-related questions and points for reflection, some of which ask students to research actual management issues and learn firsthand from practicing managers.
- *Small-Group Exercise.* This exercise is designed to allow instructors to utilize interactive experiential exercises in groups of three to four students. Each chapter contains a chapter-related issue guaranteed to lead to debate among students. The instructor calls on students to break up into small groups—simply by turning to people around them—and all students participate in the exercise in class. A mechanism is provided for the different groups to share what they have learned with each other.
- *Exploring the Web.* This exercise asks the student to visit the Web site of a company and then to use the information contained on that Web site to answer a series of chapter-related questions.
- *Closing Case.* Each chapter ends with a short case that can be used for further analysis of chapter issues. They have been carefully chosen to reflect contemporary issues and problems in strategic management, and to offer further information on chapter issues. The accompanying discussion questions encourage students to read about and to analyze how managers approach real problems in the strategic management world.

TEACHING AND LEARNING AIDS

For the Instructor

- **The Instructor's Resource Manual (available on the companion Web site, www .cengage.com/international.)** For each chapter, we provide a clearly focused synopsis, a list of teaching objectives, a comprehensive lecture outline, teaching notes for the *Ethical Dilemma* feature, suggested answers to discussion questions, and comments on the end-of-chapter activities. Each Opening Case, Strategy in Action boxed feature, and Closing Case has a synopsis and a corresponding teaching note to help guide class discussion.

- ExamView Test Bank (available on the companion Web site, www.cengage.com/international) offers a set of comprehensive true/false, multiple-choice, and essay questions for each chapter in the book. The mix of questions has been adjusted to provide fewer fact-based of simple memorization items and to provide more items that rely on synthesis or application. Every question contains AACSB standardized tags, is keyed to text Learning Objective, and includes an answer.
- Case Teaching Notes (available on the companion Web site, www.cengage.com/international) include a complete list of case discussion questions as well as a comprehensive teaching note for each case, which gives a complete analysis of case issues.
- PowerPoint (available on the companion Web site, www.cengage.com/international) offer value to enhance your in-class lecture.
- DVD program highlights many issues of interest and can be used to spark class discussion. It features extensive footage from "The Age of Walmart" series, CNBC's "Innovate or Die," "The Execution Plan," as well as other highly valuable segments that will enrich your students' understanding and learning experience.
- Online Resources: To access the online course materials, including CourseMate (the text-specific Web site), visit www.cengagebrain.com. At the CengageBrain.com home page, search for the ISBN of your title (from the back cover of your book) using the search box at the top of the page. This will take you to the product page where these resources can be found.

   Specific online resources to aid instructors include, the Instructor's Manual, a DVD guide, instructor-based PowerPoint, and access to the student protected resources.

For the Student

- CourseMate: Engaging, trackable, and affordable, the new Understanding Business Strategy CourseMate Web site offers a dynamic way to bring course concepts to life with interactive learning, study, and exam preparation tools that support this printed edition of the text. Watch comprehension soar with all-new flash cards, engaging games, streaming videos, and more in this textbook-specific Web site. A complete e-book provides the choice of an entire online learning experience. CourseMate goes beyond the book to deliver what you need!
- CengageBrain.com: Cengage Learning is excited to offer CengageBrain.com. Students can choose to purchase the format that suits them best—print or digital. **To access additional course materials and companion resources, please visit the home page and enter the ISBN of your title (from the back cover) using the search box at the top of the page. This will take you to the product page where these resources can be found.**

ACKNOWLEDGMENTS

Finding a way to integrate and present an overview of the rapidly changing world of strategic management and strategic management activities and make it interesting and meaningful for students is not an easy task. In writing *Strategic Management Essentials*, we have been fortunate to have had the assistance of several people who contributed greatly to the book's final form.

We are indebted to the many colleagues and reviewers who provided us with useful and detailed feedback, perceptive comments, valuable suggestions for improving the manuscript. As well as those individuals have helped create and shape our support package.

Kevin Banning, *Auburn University*
Robert D'Intino, *Rowan University*
Scott Droege, *Western Kentucky University*
Deborah Francis, *Brevard College*
Sanjay Goel, *University of Minnesota*
Leslie Haugen, *University of St. Thomas*
Todd Hostager, *University of Wisconsin–Eau Claire*
John Humphreys, *Eastern New Mexico University*
Deborah Johnson, *Franklin University*
Kevin L. Johnson, *Baylor University*
Elene Kent, *Capital University*
Subodh Kulkarni, *Howard University*
Kamalesh Kumar, *University of Michigan–Dearborn*
Paul Mallette, *Colorado State University*
Josetta McLaughlin, *Roosevelt University*
Tom Morris, *Radford University*
David Olson, *California State–Bakersfield*
William Ritchie, *Florida Gulf Coast University*
Tim Rogers, *Ozarks Technical College*
Stuart Rosenberg, *Dowling College*
Manjula Salimath, *University of North Texas*
Thomas Sgritta, *University of North Carolina–Charlotte*
ChanChai Tangpong, *North Dakota State University*
Michael Wakefield, *Colorado State University–Pueblo*
Edward Ward, *St. Cloud State University*
Kenneth Wendeln, *University of San Diego*
Garland Wiggs, *Hamline University*
Jun Zhao, *Governors State University*

We are grateful to the individuals at Cengage Learning for their support and commitment to *Strategic Management Essentials, Third Edition.* Specifically, we'd like to thank Michele Rhoades, our acquisitions editor, Suzanna Bainbridge, our development editor, Jana Lewis, Rob Ellington, Jonathan Monahan, and all the other individuals that so ably coordinate the book's progress. All these people have been instrumental in creating a product we hope will meet its goal of helping students better understand strategic management and the many ways in which it affects companies and the people who work in them.

Gareth R. Jones, *College Station, Texas*
Charles W. L. Hill, *Seattle, Washington*

DEVELOPING THE COMPETITIVE STRATEGIC PROCESS

1

CHAPTER OUTLINE

Competitive Advantage and Superior Performance

Strategic Managers

Corporate-Level Managers
Business-Level Managers
Functional-Level Managers

The Strategy Making Process

A Model of the Strategic Planning Process
The Feedback Loop

Strategy as an Emergent Process

Strategy Making in an Unpredictable World
Autonomous Action: Strategy Making by Lower-Level Managers
Serendipity and Strategy
Intended and Emergent Strategies

Strategic Planning in Practice

Scenario Planning
Decentralized Planning
Strategic Intent

Strategic Decision Making

Cognitive Biases
Improving Decision Making

Strategic Leadership

Vision, Eloquence, and Consistency
Commitment
Being Well Informed
Willingness to Delegate and Empower
The Astute Use of Power
Emotional Intelligence

LEARNING OBJECTIVES

After reading this chapter you should be able to:

- Explain what is meant by "competitive advantage."
- Discuss the strategic role of managers at different levels in an organization.
- Identify the main steps in a strategic planning process.

- Discuss the main pitfalls of planning, and how those pitfalls can be avoided.
- Outline the cognitive biases that might lead to poor strategic decisions, and explain how these biases can be overcome.
- Discuss the role played by strategic leaders in the strategy-making process.

OVERVIEW

Why do some companies succeed while others fail? In the fast evolving world of the Internet, for example, how is it that companies like Yahoo, Amazon.com, eBay, and Google have managed to attract millions of customers, others like online grocer Webvan, software retailer Egghead.com, and the online pet supplies retailer, pets.com, all went bankrupt? Why has Walmart been able to do so well in the fiercely competitive retail industry, while others like Kmart have struggled? In the personal computer industry, what distinguishes Dell from less successful companies such as Gateway? In the airline industry, how is it that Southwest Airlines has managed to keep increasing its revenues and profits through both good times and bad, while rivals such as US Airways and United Airlines have had to seek bankruptcy protection? What explains the persistent growth and profitability of Nucor Steel, now the largest steel market in America, during a period when many of its once larger rivals disappeared into bankruptcy?

In this book, we argue that the strategies a company's managers pursue have a major impact on its performance relative to rivals. A **strategy** is a set of actions that managers take to increase their company's performance relative to rivals. If a company's strategy does result in superior performance, it is said to have a *competitive advantage*.

Much of this book is about identifying and describing the strategies that managers can pursue to achieve superior performance. A central aim of this book is to give you a thorough understanding of the analytical techniques and skills necessary to identify and implement strategies successfully. The first step toward achieving this objective is to describe in more detail what *superior performance* and *competitive advantage* mean.

COMPETITIVE ADVANTAGE AND SUPERIOR PERFORMANCE

Superior performance is typically thought of in terms of one company's profitability relative to that of other companies in the same or a similar kind of business or industry. The **profitability** of a company can be measured by the return that it makes on the capital invested in the enterprise.[1] The return on invested capital that a company earns is defined as its profit over the capital invested in the firm (profit/capital invested). By *profit*, we mean after-tax earnings. By *capital*, we mean the sum of money invested in the company, that is, stockholders' equity plus debt owed to creditors. This capital is used to buy the resources a company needs to produce and sell goods and services. A company that uses its resources efficiently makes a positive return on invested capital. The more efficient a company is, the higher are its profitability and return on invested capital.

A company's profitability—its return on invested capital—is determined by the strategies its managers adopt. For example, Walmart's strategy of focusing on the realization of cost savings from efficient logistics and information systems, and then passing on the bulk of these cost savings on to customers in the form of lower prices, has enabled the company to gain evermore market share, reap significant economies of scale, and further lower its cost structure, thereby boosting profitability (for details, see the *Running Case* on Walmart).

Strategy

A set of actions that managers take to increase their company's performance relative to rivals.

Profitability

The return that a company makes on the capital invested in the enterprise.

RUNNING CASE

Walmart's Competitive Advantage

Walmart is one of the most extraordinary success stories in business history. Started in 1962 by Sam Walton, Walmart has grown to become the world's largest corporation. In 2008, the discount retailer, whose mantra is "everyday low prices," had sales of $410 billion, 7,400 stores in 15 countries, and 2 million employees. Some 8% of all retail sales in the United States are made at a Walmart store. Walmart is not only large; it is also very profitable. In 2008, the company earned a return on invested capital of 14.5%, better than its well-managed rivals Costco and Target, which earned 11.7% and 9.5% respectively. As shown in the accompanying figure, Walmart has been consistently more profitable than its rivals for years, although, of late, its rivals have been closing the gap.

Walmart's persistently superior profitability reflects a competitive advantage that is based upon a number of strategies. Back in 1962, Walmart was one of the first companies to apply the self-service supermarket business model developed by grocery chains to general merchandise. Unlike its rivals such as Kmart and Target who focused on urban and suburban locations, Sam

Walton's Walmart concentrated on small southern towns that were ignored by its rivals. Walmart grew quickly by pricing lower than local retailers, often putting them out of business. By the time its rivals realized that small towns could support large discount general merchandise stores, Walmart had already preempted them. These towns, which were large enough to support one discount retailer, but not two, provided a secure profit base for Walmart.

The company was also an innovator in information systems, logistics, and human resource practices. These strategies resulted in higher productivity and lower costs than rivals, which enabled the company to earn a high profit while charging low prices. Walmart led the way among American retailers in developing and implementing sophisticated product tracking systems using bar code technology and checkout scanners. This information technology enabled Walmart to track what was selling and adjust its inventory accordingly so that the products found in a store matched local demand. By avoiding overstocking, Walmart did not have to hold periodic sales to shift unsold inventory.

Profitability of Walmart and Competitors

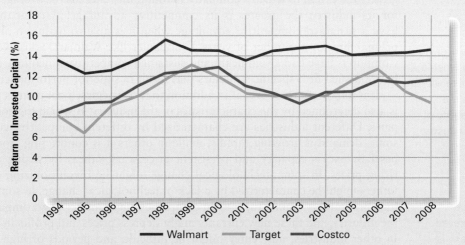

Source: Value Line Calculations. Data for 2008 are estimates based on three quarters.

(continued)

Over time, Walmart linked this information system to a nationwide network of distribution centers where inventory was stored and then shipped to stores within a 400-mile radius on a daily basis. The combination of distribution centers and information centers enabled Walmart to reduce the amount of inventory it held in stores, thereby devoting more of that valuable space to selling and reducing the amount of capital it had tied up in inventory.

With regard to human resources, the tone was set by Sam Walton. He had a strong belief that employees should be respected and rewarded for helping to improve the profitability of the company. Underpinning this belief, Walton referred to employees as "associates." He established a profit-sharing strategy for all employees and after the company went public in 1970, a program that allowed employees to purchase Walmart stock at a discount to its market value. Walmart was rewarded for this approach by high employee productivity, which translated into lower operating costs and higher profitability.

As Walmart grew larger, the sheer size and purchasing power of the company enabled it to drive down the prices that it paid suppliers, passing on those savings to customers in the form of lower prices,

which enabled Walmart to gain more market share and hence demand even lower prices. To take the sting out of the persistent demands for lower prices, Walmart shared its sales information with suppliers on a daily basis, enabling them to gain efficiencies by configuring their own production schedules to sales at Walmart.

By the 1990s, Walmart was already the largest seller of general merchandise in America. To keep its growth going, Walmart started to diversify into the grocery business, opening 200,000-square-foot super-center stores that sold groceries and general merchandise under the same roof. Walmart also diversified into the warehouse club business with the establishment of Sam's Club. The company began expanding internationally in 1991 with its entry into Mexico.

For all its success, however, Walmart is now encountering very real limits to profitable growth. The U.S. market is approaching saturation, and growth overseas has proved more difficult than the company hoped. The company was forced to exit Germany and South Korea after losing money there, and has found it tough going into several other developed nations such as Britain. Moreover, rivals Target and Costco have continued to improve their performances and are now snapping at Walmart's heels.[2]

Competitive Advantage

The advantage over rivals achieved when a company's profitability is greater than the average profitability of all firms in its industry.

Sustained Competitive Advantage

The competitive advantage achieved when a company is able to maintain above-average profitability for a number of years.

A company is said to have a **competitive advantage** over its rivals when its profitability is greater than the average profitability for all firms in its industry. The greater the extent to which a company's profitability exceeds the average profitability for its industry, the greater is its competitive advantage. A company is said to have a **sustained competitive advantage** when it is able to maintain above-average profitability for a number of years. Companies like Walmart, Southwest, and Dell Computers have had a significant and sustained competitive advantage because they have pursued firm-specific strategies that result in superior performance.

It is important to note that in addition to its strategies, a company's performance is also determined by the characteristics of the industry in which the company competes. Different industries are characterized by different competitive conditions. In some, demand is growing rapidly, while in others it is contracting. Some might be beset by excess capacity and persistent price wars, others by strong demand and rising prices. In some, technological change might be revolutionizing competition. Others might be characterized by a lack of technological change. In some industries, high profitability among incumbent companies might induce new companies to enter the industry, and these new entrants might depress prices and profits in the industry. In other industries, new entry might be difficult, and periods of high profitability might persist for a considerable time. Thus, the average profitability is higher in some industries and lower in other industries because competitive conditions vary from industry to industry.[3]

STRATEGIC MANAGERS

Managers are the lynch pin in the strategy-making process. It is individual managers who must take responsibility for formulating strategies to attain a competitive advantage and putting those strategies into effect. They must lead the strategy-making process. Here we look at the strategic roles of different managers. Later in the chapter we discuss strategic leadership, which is how managers can effectively lead the strategy-making process.

In most companies, there are two main types of managers: **general managers**, who bear responsibility for the overall performance of the company or for one of its major self-contained subunits or divisions, and **functional managers**, who are responsible for supervising a particular function, that is, a task, activity, or operation, like accounting, marketing, Research & Development, information technology, or logistics.

A company is a collection of functions or departments that work together to bring a particular product or service to the market. If a company provides several different kinds of products or services, it often duplicates these functions and creates a series of self-contained divisions (each of which contains its own set of functions) to manage each different product or service. The general managers of these divisions then become responsible for their particular product line. The overriding concern of general managers is for the health of the whole company or division under their direction; they are responsible for deciding how to create a competitive advantage and achieve high profitability with the resources and capital they have at their disposal. Figure 1.1 shows the organization of a **multidivisional company**, that is, a company that competes in several different businesses and has created a separate self-contained division to manage each of these. As you can see, there are three main levels of management: corporate, business, and functional. General managers are found at the first two of these levels, but their strategic roles differ depending on their sphere of responsibility.

General Managers

Managers who bear responsibility for the overall performance of the company or for that of one of its major self-contained subunits or divisions.

Functional Managers

Managers responsible for supervising a particular function—that is, a task, activity, or operation, like accounting, marketing, Research & Development, information technology, or logistics.

Multidivisional Company

A company that competes in several different businesses and has created a separate, self-contained division to manage each of them.

Figure 1.1 Levels of Strategic Management

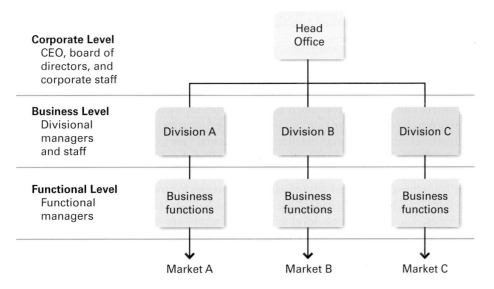

Corporate Level
CEO, board of directors, and corporate staff

Head Office

Business Level
Divisional managers and staff

Division A   Division B   Division C

Functional Level
Functional managers

Business functions   Business functions   Business functions

Market A   Market B   Market C

Corporate-Level Managers

The corporate level of management consists of the chief executive officer (CEO), other senior executives, the board of directors, and corporate staff. These individuals occupy the apex of decision making within the organization. The CEO is the principal general manager. In consultation with other senior executives, the role of *corporate-level managers* is to oversee the development of strategies for the whole organization. This role includes defining the goals of the organization, determining what businesses it should be in, allocating resources among the different businesses, formulating and implementing strategies that span individual businesses, and providing leadership for the entire organization.

Consider General Electric as an example. GE is active in a wide range of businesses, including lighting equipment, major appliances, motor and transportation equipment, turbine generators, construction and engineering services, industrial electronics, medical systems, aerospace, aircraft engines, and financial services. The main strategic responsibilities of its CEO, Jeffrey Immelt, are setting overall strategic goals, allocating resources among the different business areas, deciding whether the firm should divest itself of any of its businesses, and determining whether it should acquire any new ones. In other words, it is up to Immelt to develop strategies that span individual businesses; his concern is with building and managing the corporate portfolio of businesses to maximize corporate profitability.

It is *not* his specific responsibility to develop strategies for competing in the individual business areas, such as financial services. The development of such strategies is the responsibility of the general managers in these different businesses or *business-level managers*. However, it is Immelt's responsibility to probe the strategic thinking of business-level managers to make sure that they are pursuing strategies that will contribute toward the maximization of GE's long-run profitability, to coach and motivate those managers, to reward them for attaining or exceeding goals, and to hold them to account for poor performance.

Corporate-level managers also provide a link between the people who oversee the strategic development of a firm and those who own it (the shareholders). Corporate-level managers, and particularly the CEO, can be viewed as the agents of shareholders.[4] It is their responsibility to ensure that the corporate and business strategies that the company pursues are consistent with maximizing profitability and profit growth. If they are not, then ultimately the CEO is likely to be called to account by the shareholders.

Business-Level Managers

Business Unit

A self-contained division that provides a product or service for a particular market.

A **business unit** is a self-contained division (with its own functions—for example, finance, purchasing, production, and marketing departments) that provides a product or service for a particular market. The principal general manager at the business level, or the business-level manager, is the head of the division. The strategic role of these managers is to translate the general statements of direction and intent that come from the corporate level into concrete strategies for individual businesses. Thus, corporate-level general managers are concerned with strategies that span individual businesses, whereas business-level general managers are concerned with strategies that are specific to a particular business. At GE, a major corporate goal is to be first or second in every business in which the corporation competes. Then the general managers in each division work out for their business the details of a business model that is consistent with this objective.

Functional-Level Managers

Functional-level managers are responsible for the specific business functions or operations (human resources, purchasing, product development, customer service, etc.) that constitute a company or one of its divisions. Thus, a functional manager's sphere of responsibility is generally confined to *one* organizational activity, whereas general managers oversee the operation of a *whole* company or division. Although they are not responsible for the overall performance of the organization, functional managers nevertheless have a major strategic role: to develop functional strategies in their area that help fulfill the strategic objectives set by business- and corporate-level general managers.

In GE's aerospace business, for instance, manufacturing managers are responsible for developing manufacturing strategies consistent with the corporate objective of being first or second in that industry. Moreover, functional managers provide most of the information that makes it possible for business- and corporate-level general managers to formulate realistic and attainable strategies. Indeed, because they are closer to the customer than the typical general manager is, functional managers themselves may generate important ideas that subsequently may become major strategies for the company. Thus, it is important for general managers to listen closely to the ideas of their functional managers. An equally great responsibility for managers at the operational level is strategy implementation: the execution of corporate- and business-level plans.

THE STRATEGY-MAKING PROCESS

Now that we know something about the strategic roles of managers, we can turn our attention to the process by which managers formulate and implement strategies. Many writers have emphasized that strategy is the outcome of a formal planning process and that top management plays the most important role in this process.[5] Although this view has some basis in reality, it is not the whole story. As we shall see later in the chapter, valuable strategies often emerge from deep within the organization without prior planning. Nevertheless, a consideration of formal, rational planning is a useful starting point for our journey into the world of strategy. Here we consider what might be described as a typical formal strategic planning model for making strategy.

A Model of the Strategic Planning Process

The formal strategic planning process has five main steps:

1. Select the corporate mission and major corporate goals.
2. Analyze the organization's external competitive environment to identify *opportunities* and *threats*.
3. Analyze the organization's internal operating environment to identify the organization's *strengths* and *weaknesses*.
4. Select strategies that build on the organization's strengths and correct its weaknesses in order to take advantage of external opportunities and counter external threats. These strategies should be consistent with the mission and major goals of the organization. They should be congruent and constitute a viable business model.
5. Implement the strategies.

The task of analyzing the organization's external and internal environment and then selecting appropriate strategies is known as **strategy formulation**. In contrast, **strategy implementation** involves putting the strategies (or plans) into action. This includes taking actions consistent with the selected strategies of the company at the corporate, business, and functional level, allocating roles and responsibilities among managers (typically through the design of organization structure), allocating resources (including capital and people), setting short-term objectives, and designing the organization's control and reward systems. These steps are illustrated in Figure 1.2 (which can also be viewed as a plan for the rest of this book).

Each step in Figure 1.2 constitutes a *sequential* step in the strategic planning process. At step 1, each round or cycle of the planning process begins with a statement of the corporate mission and major corporate goals. As shown in Figure 1.2, this statement is shaped by the existing business model of the company. The mission statement is followed by the foundation of strategic thinking: external analysis, internal analysis, and strategic choice. The strategy-making process ends with the design of the organizational structure, culture, and control systems necessary to implement the organization's chosen strategy.

Some organizations go through a new cycle of the strategic planning process every year. This does not necessarily mean that managers choose a new strategy each year. In many instances, the result is simply to modify and reaffirm a strategy and structure already in place. The strategic plans generated by the planning process generally look out over a period of 1 to 5 years, with the plan being updated, or *rolled forward*, every year. In most organizations, the results of the

Figure 1.2 A Model of the Strategic Management Process

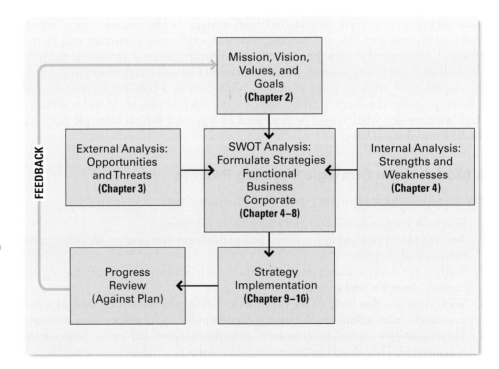

Strategy Formulation

Analyzing the organization's external and internal environments and then selecting appropriate strategies.

Strategy Implementation

Putting strategies into action.

annual strategic planning process are used as input into the budgetary process for the coming year so that strategic planning is used to shape resource allocation within the organization.

Mission Statement   The first component of the strategic management process is crafting the organization's mission statement, which provides the framework or context within which strategies are formulated. A mission statement has four main components: a statement of the *raison d'être* of a company or organization—its reason for existence—which is normally referred to as the *mission*; a statement of some desired future state, usually referred to as the *vision*; a statement of the key *values* that the organization is committed to; and a statement of *major goals*.

For example, the current mission of Microsoft is to "to enable people and business throughout the world to realize their full potential." The vision of the company—the overarching goal—is to be the major player in the software industry. The key values that the company is committed to include "integrity and honesty," "passion for our customers, our partners, and out technology," "openness and respectfulness," and "taking on big challenges and seeing them through." Microsoft's mission statement has absolutely set the context for strategy formulation within the company. Thus, the company's perseverance first with Windows, and now with X-box, both of which took a long time to bear fruit, exemplifies the idea of "taking on big challenges and seeing them through."[6]

We shall return to this topic and discuss it in depth in the next chapter.

External Analysis   The second component of the strategic management process is an analysis of the organization's external operating environment. The essential purpose of the external analysis is to identify strategic *opportunities* and *threats* in the organization's operating environment that will affect how it pursues its mission. Three interrelated environments should be examined at this stage: the *industry environment* in which the company operates, the country or *national environment*, and the wider socioeconomic or *macro-environment*.

Analyzing the industry environment requires an assessment of the competitive structure of the company's industry, including the competitive position of the company and its major rivals. It also requires analysis of the nature, stage, dynamics, and history of the industry. Because many markets are now global markets, analyzing the industry environment also means assessing the impact of globalization on competition within an industry. Such an analysis may reveal that a company should move some production facilities to another nation, that it should aggressively expand in emerging markets such as China, or that it should beware of new competition from emerging nations. Analyzing the macro-environment consists of examining macroeconomic, social, government, legal, international, and technological factors that may affect the company and its industry. We consider these issues in Chapters 3 and 6 (where we discuss global issues).

Internal Analysis   Internal analysis, the third component of the strategic planning process, serves to pinpoint the *strengths* and *weaknesses* of the organization. Such issues as identifying the quantity and quality of a company's resources and capabilities and ways of building unique skills and company-specific or distinctive competencies are considered here when we probe the sources of competitive advantage. Building and sustaining a competitive advantage requires a company to achieve superior efficiency, quality, innovation, and responsiveness to its customers.

Ethical Dilemma

You are the general manager of a home mortgage issuing business within a large diversified financial services firm. In the firm's mission statement, there is a value that emphasizes the importance of acting with integrity at all times. When you asked the CEO what this means, she told you that you should "do the right thing, and not try to do all things right." This same CEO has also set you challenging profitability and growth goals for the coming year. The CEO has told you that the goals are "nonnegotiable." If you hit those goals, you stand to earn a big bonus and may get promoted. If you fail to hit the goals, it may hurt your career at the company. You know however, that hitting those goals will require you to lower lending standards, and it is possible that your unit will end up lending money to some people whose ability to meet their mortgage payments is questionable. If people do default on their loans, however, your company will be able to seize their homes and resell them, which mitigates the risk. What should you do?

Company strengths lead to superior performance in these areas, whereas company weaknesses translate into inferior performance. We discuss these issues in Chapter 4.

SWOT Analysis   The next component of strategic thinking requires the generation of a series of strategic alternatives, or choices of future strategies to pursue, given the company's internal strengths and weaknesses and its external opportunities and threats. The comparison of strengths, weaknesses, opportunities, and threats is normally referred to as a **SWOT analysis**.[7] Its central purpose is to identify the strategies that will create a company-specific business model that will best *align, fit,* or *match* a company's resources and capabilities to the demands of the environment in which it operates. Managers compare and contrast the various alternative possible strategies against each other with respect to their ability to achieve a competitive advantage. Thinking strategically requires managers to identify the set of *strategies* that will create and sustain a competitive advantage:

- *Functional-level strategy,* directed at improving the effectiveness of operations within a company, such as manufacturing, marketing, materials management, product development, and customer service. We consider functional-level strategies in Chapter 4.
- *Business-level strategy,* which encompasses the business's overall competitive theme, the way it positions itself in the marketplace to gain a competitive advantage, and the different positioning strategies that can be used in different industry settings—for example, *cost leadership, differentiation, focusing on a particular niche or segment of the industry,* or some *combination* of these. We consider business-level strategies in Chapter 5.
- *Global strategy,* addressing how to expand operations outside the home country to grow and prosper in a world where competitive advantage is determined at a global level. We consider global strategies in Chapter 6.
- *Corporate-level strategy,* which answers the primary questions: What business or businesses should we be in to maximize the long-run profitability and profit growth of the organization, and how should we enter and increase our presence in these businesses to gain a competitive advantage? We consider corporate-level strategies in Chapters 7 and 8.

The set of strategies identified through a SWOT analysis should be congruent with each other. Thus, functional-level strategies should be consistent with, or support, the business-level strategy and global strategy of the company. Moreover, as we explain later in this book, corporate-level strategies should support business-level strategies.

Strategy Implementation   Having chosen a set of congruent strategies to achieve a competitive advantage and increase performance, managers must put those strategies into action: strategy has to be implemented. Strategy implementation involves taking actions at the functional, business and corporate level to execute a strategic plan. Thus implementation can include, for example, putting quality improvement programs into place, changing the way a product is designed, positioning the product differently in the marketplace, segmenting the marketing and offering different versions of the product to different consumer groups, implementing price increases, or decreases, expanding through mergers and acquisitions, or downsizing the company by closing down or selling off parts of the company. All of this and much more is discussed in detail in Chapters 4–8.

SWOT Analysis

The comparison of strengths, weaknesses, opportunities, and threats.

Strategy implementation also entails designing the best organization structure, culture, and control systems to put a chosen strategy into action. We discuss the organization structure, culture, and controls required to implement strategy in Chapters 8 and 9.

The Feedback Loop

The feedback loop in Figure 1.2 indicates that strategic planning is ongoing: it *never* ends. Once a strategy has been implemented, its execution must be monitored to determine the extent to which strategic goals and objectives are actually being achieved and to what degree competitive advantage is being created and sustained. This information and knowledge is passed back up to the corporate level through feedback loops and become the input for the next round of strategy formulation and implementation. Top managers can then decide whether to reaffirm existing strategies, and goals, or suggest changes for the future. For example, a strategic goal may prove to be too optimistic, and so the next time a more conservative goal is set. Or feedback may reveal that the strategy is not working, so managers may seek ways to change it.

STRATEGY AS AN EMERGENT PROCESS

The basic planning model suggests that a company's strategies are the result of a plan, that the strategic planning process itself is rational and highly structured, and that the process is orchestrated by top management. Several scholars have criticized the formal planning model for three main reasons: the unpredictability of the real world, the role that lower-level managers can play in the strategic management process, and the fact that many successful strategies are often the result of serendipity, not rational strategizing. They have advocated an alternative view of strategy making.[8]

Strategy Making in an Unpredictable World

Critics of formal planning systems argue that we live in a world in which uncertainty, complexity, and ambiguity dominate, and in which small chance events can have a large and unpredictable impact on outcomes.[9] In such circumstances, they claim, even the most carefully thought-out strategic plans are prone to being rendered useless by rapid and unforeseen change. In an unpredictable world, there is a premium on being able to respond quickly to changing circumstances, altering the strategies of the organization accordingly.

A dramatic example of this occurred in 1994 and 1995 when Microsoft's CEO Bill Gates shifted the company strategy after the unanticipated emergence of the World Wide Web (see the Strategy in Action feature). According to critics of formal systems, such a flexible approach to strategy making is not possible within the framework of a traditional strategic planning process, with its implicit assumption that an organization's strategies need to be reviewed only during the annual strategic planning exercise.

Autonomous Action: Strategy Making by Lower-Level Managers

Another criticism leveled at the rational planning model of strategy is that too much importance is attached to the role of top management, and particularly the CEO.[10] An alternative view now widely accepted is that individual employees deep within an organization can and often do exert a profound influence over the strategic direction of the firm.[11] Writing with Robert Burgelman of Stanford University, Andy Grove, the former CEO of Intel, noted that many important strategic decisions at Intel were initiated not by top managers but by the **autonomous action** of lower-level managers deep within Intel—that is, by lower-level managers, who on their own initiative, formulated new strategies and worked to persuade top-level managers to alter the strategic priorities of the firm.[12] At Intel, strategic decisions that were initiated by the autonomous action of lower-level managers included the decision to exit an important market (the DRAM memory chip market) and develop a certain class of microprocessors (RISC-based microprocessors) in direct contrast to the stated strategy of Intel's top managers. The Strategy in Action feature tells how autonomous action by two young employees drove the evolution of Microsoft's strategy toward the Internet. In addition, the prototype for another Microsoft product, the X-box video game system, was developed by four lower-level engineering employees on their own initiative. They subsequently successfully lobbied top managers to dedicate resources to commercialize their prototype.

Autonomous action may be particularly important in helping established companies to deal with the uncertainty created by the arrival of a radical new technology that changes the dominant paradigm in an industry.[13] Top managers usually rise to preeminence by successfully executing the established strategy of the firm. As such, they may have an emotional commitment to the status quo and are often unable to see things from a different perspective. In this sense, they are a conservative force that promotes inertia. Lower-level managers, however, are less likely to have the same commitment to the status quo and have more to gain from promoting new technologies and strategies within the firm. As such, they may be the ones to first recognize new strategic opportunities (as was the case at Microsoft) and lobby for strategic change.

Serendipity and Strategy

Business history is replete with examples of accidental events that help to push companies in new and profitable directions. What these examples suggest is that many successful strategies are not the result of well-thought-out plans but of serendipity, that is, stumbling across good things unexpectedly. One such example occurred at 3M during the 1960s. At that time, 3M was producing fluorocarbons for sale as coolant liquid in air-conditioning equipment. One day, a researcher working with fluorocarbons in a 3M lab spilled some of the liquid on her shoes. Later that day when she spilled coffee over her shoes, she watched with interest as the coffee formed into little beads of liquid and then ran off her shoes without leaving a stain. Reflecting on this phenomenon, she realized that a fluorocarbon-based liquid might turn out to be useful for protecting fabrics from liquid stains, and so the idea for Scotch Guard was born. Subsequently, Scotch Guard became one of 3M's

Autonomous Action

Action taken by lower-level managers who, on their own initiative, formulate new strategies and work to persuade top-level managers to alter the strategic priorities of a company.

1.1 STRATEGY IN ACTION

A Strategic Shift at Microsoft

The Internet has been around since the 1970s, but prior to the early 1990s, it was a drab place, lacking the color, content, and richness of today's environment. What changed the Internet from a scientific tool to a consumer-driven media environment was the invention of hypertext markup language (HTML) and the related invention of a browser for displaying graphics-rich Web pages based on HTML. The combination of HTML and browsers effectively created the World Wide Web (WWW). This was a development that was unforeseen.

A young programmer at the University of Illinois in 1993, Mark Andreesen, had developed the first browser, known as Mosaic. In 1994, he left Illinois and joined a start-up company, Netscape, which produced an improved browser, the Netscape Navigator, along with software that enabled organizations to create Web pages and host them on computer servers. These developments led to a dramatic and unexpected growth in the number of people connecting to the Internet. In 1990, the Internet had 1 million users. By early 1995, the number had exceeded 80 million and was growing exponentially.

Prior to the emergence of the Web, Microsoft did have a strategy for exploiting the Internet, but it was one that emphasized set-top boxes, video on demand, interactive TV, and an online service, MSN, modeled after AOL and based on proprietary standards. In early 1994, Gates received emails from two young employees, Jay Allard and Steve Sinofsky, who argued that Microsoft's current strategy was misguided and ignored the rapidly emerging Web. In companies with a more hierarchical culture, such action might have been ignored, but in Microsoft, which operates as a meritocracy in which good ideas trump hierarchical position, it produced a very different response. Gates convened a meeting of senior executives in April 1994, then wrote a memo to senior executives arguing that the Internet represented a sea change in computing, and that Microsoft had to respond.

What ultimately emerged was a 180 degree shift in Microsoft's strategy. Interactive TV was placed on the back burner, and MSN was relaunched as a Web service based on HTML. Microsoft committed to developing its own browser technology and within a few months had issued Internet Explorer to compete with Netscape's Navigator (the underlying technology was gained by an acquisition). Microsoft licensed Java, a computer language designed to run programs on the Web, from a major competitor, Sun Microsystems. Internet protocols were built into Windows 95 and Windows NT, and Gates insisted that henceforth Microsoft's applications, such as the ubiquitous Office, embrace the WWW and have the ability to convert documents into an HTML format. The new strategy was given its final stamp on December 7, 1995, Pearl Harbor Day, when Gates gave a speech arguing that the Internet was now pervasive in everything Microsoft was doing. By then, Microsoft had been pursuing the new strategy for a year. In short, Microsoft quickly went from a proprietary standards approach to one that embraced the public standards on the WWW.[14]

most profitable products and took the company into the fabric protection business, an area it had never planned to participate in.[15]

Serendipitous discoveries and events can open up all sorts of profitable avenues for a company. But some companies have missed out on profitable opportunities because serendipitous discoveries or events were inconsistent with their prior (planned) conception of what their strategy should be. In one of the classic examples of such myopia, a century ago the telegraph company Western Union turned down an opportunity to purchase the rights to an invention made by Alexander Graham Bell. The invention was the telephone, a technology that subsequently made the telegraph obsolete.

Intended and Emergent Strategies

Henry Mintzberg has proposed a model of strategy development that provides a more encompassing view of what strategy actually is. According to this model, illustrated in Figure 1.3, a company's *realized strategy* is the product of whatever planned strategies are actually put into action (the company's deliberate strategies) *and* of any unplanned, or emergent, strategies.[16] In Mintzberg's view, many planned strategies are not implemented due to unpredicted changes in the environment (they are unrealized). **Emergent strategies** are the unplanned responses to unforeseen circumstances. They arise from autonomous action by individual managers deep within the organization, from serendipitous discoveries or events, or from an unplanned strategic shift by top-level managers in response to changed circumstances. They are *not* the product of formal top-down planning mechanisms. Mintzberg maintains that emergent strategies are often successful and may be more appropriate than intended strategies. Moreover, as Mintzberg has noted, strategies can take root virtually wherever people have the capacity to learn and the resources to support that capacity.

In practice, the strategies of most organizations are probably a combination of the intended (planned) and the emergent. The message for management is that it needs to recognize the process of emergence and to intervene when appropriate, killing off bad, emergent strategies but nurturing potentially good ones.[17] To make such decisions, managers must be able to judge the worth of emergent strategies. *They must be able to think strategically.* Although emergent strategies arise from within the organization without prior planning—that is, without going through the steps illustrated in Figure 1.3 in a *sequential* fashion—top management still has to evaluate emergent strategies. Such evaluation involves comparing each emergent strategy with the organization's goals, external environmental opportunities and threats, and internal strengths and weaknesses. The objective is to assess whether the

Figure 1.3   Emergent and Deliberate Strategies

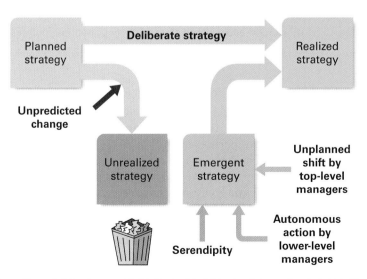

Emergent Strategies

Strategies that "emerge" in the absence of planning.

Source: Adapted from H. Mintzberg and A. McGugh, *Administrative Science Quarterly*, Vol. 30. No. 2, June 1985.

emergent strategy fits the company's needs and capabilities. In addition, Mintzberg stresses that an organization's capability to produce emergent strategies is a function of the kind of corporate culture that the organization's structure and control systems foster. In other words, the different components of the strategic management process are just as important from the perspective of emergent strategies as they are from the perspective of intended strategies.

STRATEGIC PLANNING IN PRACTICE

Despite criticisms, research suggests that formal planning systems do help managers make better strategic decisions.[18] For strategic planning to work, however, it is important that top-level managers plan not just in the context of the *current* competitive environment but also try to find the strategy that will best allow them to achieve a competitive advantage in the *future* competitive environment. To try to forecast what that future will look like, managers can use scenario planning techniques to plan for different possible futures. They can also involve operating managers in the planning process and seek to shape the future competitive environment by emphasizing strategic intent.

Scenario Planning

One reason that strategic planning may fail over the long run is that managers, in their initial enthusiasm for planning techniques, may forget that the future is inherently unpredictable. Even the best-laid plans can fall apart if unforeseen contingencies occur, and that happens all the time in the real world. Scenario planning is based upon the realization that the future is inherently unpredictable, and that an organization should plan for not just one future, but a range of possible futures. Scenario planning involves formulating plans that are based upon "what if" scenarios about the future. In the typical scenario planning exercise, some scenarios are optimistic and some pessimistic. Teams of managers are asked to develop specific strategies to cope with each scenario. A set of indicators is chosen which are used as "signposts" to track trends and identify the probability that any particular scenario is coming to pass. The idea is to get managers to understand the dynamic and complex nature of their environment, to think through problems in a strategic fashion, and to generate a range of strategic options that might be pursued under different circumstances.[19] The scenario approach to planning has spread rapidly among large companies. One survey found that over 50% of the *Fortune* 500 companies use some form of scenario planning methods.[20]

The oil company Royal Dutch Shell has perhaps done more than most to pioneer the concept of scenario planning, and its experience demonstrates the power of the approach.[21] Shell has been using scenario planning since the 1980s. Today it uses two main scenarios to refine its strategic planning, which relate to future demand for oil. One, called "Dynamics as Usual," sees a gradual shift from carbon fuels such as oil, through natural gas, to renewable energy. The second scenario, "The Spirit of the Coming Age," looks at the possibility that a technological revolution will lead to a rapid shift to new energy sources.[22] Shell is making investments that will ensure the profitability of the company whichever scenario comes to pass, and it is carefully tracking technological and market trends for signs of which scenario is becoming more likely over time.

Scenario Planning

Formulating plans that are based on "what if" scenarios about the future.

The great virtue of the scenario approach to planning is that it can push managers to think outside of the box, to anticipate what they might have to do in different situations, and to learn that the world is a complex and unpredictable place which places a premium on flexibility, rather than inflexible plans based on assumptions about the future that may turn out to be incorrect. In many cases, as a result of scenario planning organizations might pursue one dominant strategy, related to the scenario that is judged to be most likely, but make some investments that will pay off if other scenarios come to the fore (see Figure 1.4). Thus the current strategy of Shell is based on the assumption that the world will only gradually shift way from carbon-based fuels (its "Dynamics as Usual" scenario), but the company is also hedging its bets by investing in new energy technologies and mapping out a strategy to pursue should its second scenario come to pass.

Decentralized Planning

A mistake that some companies have made in constructing their strategic planning process has been to treat planning as an exclusively top management responsibility. This *ivory tower* approach can result in strategic plans formulated in a vacuum by top managers who have little understanding or appreciation of current operating realities. Consequently, top managers may formulate strategies that do more harm than good. For example, when demographic data indicated that houses and families were shrinking, planners at GE's appliance group concluded that smaller appliances were the wave of the future. Because they had little contact with homebuilders and retailers, they did not realize that kitchens and bathrooms were the two rooms that were *not* shrinking. Nor did they appreciate that when couples both worked, they wanted big refrigerators to cut down on trips to the supermarket. GE ended up wasting a lot of time designing small appliances with limited demand.

The ivory tower concept of planning can also lead to tensions between corporate-, business-, and functional-level managers. The experience of GE's appliance group is

Figure 1.4 Scenario Planning

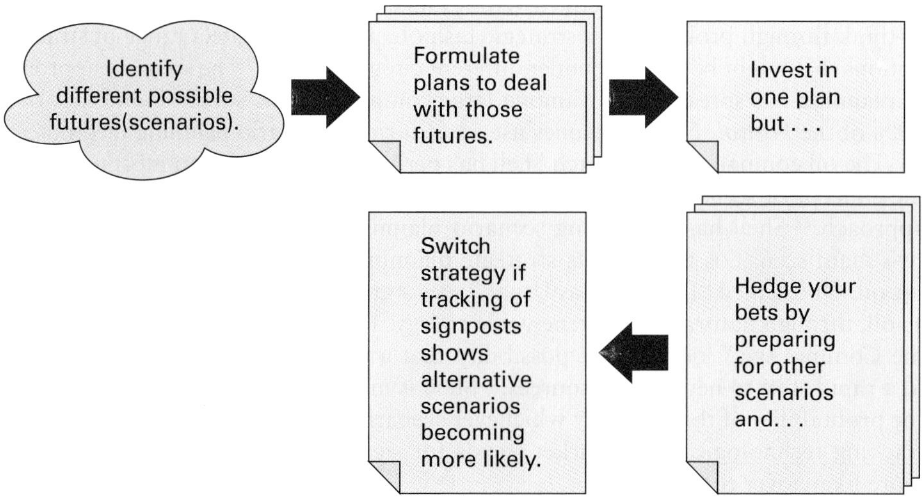

again illuminating. Many of the corporate managers in the planning group were recruited from consulting firms or top-flight business schools. Many of the functional managers took this pattern of recruitment to mean that corporate managers did not think they were smart enough to think through strategic problems for themselves. They felt shut out of the decision-making process, which they believed to be unfairly constituted. Out of this perceived lack of procedural justice grew an "us-versus-them" mind-set that quickly escalated into hostility. As a result, even when the planners were right, operating managers would not listen to them. For example, the planners correctly recognized the importance of the globalization of the appliance market and the emerging Japanese threat. However, operating managers, who then saw Sears Roebuck as the competition, paid them little heed.

Finally, ivory tower planning ignores the important strategic role of autonomous action by lower-level managers and serendipity.

Correcting the ivory tower approach to planning requires recognizing that successful strategic planning encompasses managers at *all* levels of the corporation. Much of the best planning can and should be done by business and functional managers who are closest to the facts—planning should be decentralized. The role of corporate-level planners should be that of *facilitators* who help business and functional managers do the planning by setting the broad strategic goals of the organization and providing the resources required to identify the strategies that might be required to attain those goals.

STRATEGIC DECISION MAKING

Even the best-designed strategic planning systems will fail to produce the desired results if managers do not use the information at their disposal effectively. Consequently, it is important that strategic managers learn to make better use of the information they have and understand the reasons why they sometimes make poor decisions. One important way in which managers can make better use of their knowledge and information is to understand and manage their emotions during the course of decision making.[23]

Cognitive Biases

The rationality of human decision makers is bounded by our own cognitive capabilities.[24] It is difficult for us absorb and process large amounts of information effectively. As a result, when making decisions we tend to fall back on certain rules of thumb, or *heuristics*, that help us to make sense out of a complex and uncertain world. These heuristics can be quite useful, but sometimes their application can result in severe and systematic errors in the decision-making process.[25] Systematic errors are those that appear time and time again. They seem to arise from a series of **cognitive biases** in the way that human decision makers process information and reach decisions. Because of cognitive biases, many managers end up making poor decisions, even when they have good information at their disposal and use a good decision-making process that is consistent with the rational decision-making model.

Several biases have been verified repeatedly in laboratory settings, so we can be reasonably sure that they exist and that we are all prone to them.[26] The **prior hypothesis bias** refers to the fact that decision makers who have strong prior beliefs

Cognitive Biases

Systematic errors in human decision making that arise from the way people process information.

Prior Hypothesis Bias

A cognitive bias that occurs when decision-makers who have strong prior beliefs tend to make decisions on the basis of these beliefs, even when presented with evidence that their beliefs are wrong.

about the relationship between two variables tend to make decisions on the basis of these beliefs, even when presented with evidence that their beliefs are wrong. Moreover, they tend to seek and use information that is consistent with their prior beliefs, while ignoring information that contradicts these beliefs. To put this bias in a strategic context, it suggests that a CEO who has a strong prior belief that a certain strategy makes sense might continue to pursue that strategy, despite evidence that it is inappropriate or failing.

Another well-known cognitive bias, **escalating commitment**, occurs when decision-makers, having already committed significant resources to a project, commit even more resources if they receive feedback that the project is failing.[27] This may be an irrational response; a more logical response would be to abandon the project and move on (i.e., to cut your losses and run), rather than escalate commitment. Feelings of personal responsibility for a project apparently induce decision-makers to stick with a project despite evidence that it is failing.

A third bias, **reasoning by analogy**, involves the use of simple analogies to make sense out of complex problems. The problem with this heuristic is that the analogy may not be valid. A fourth bias, **representativeness**, is rooted in the tendency to generalize from a small sample or even a single vivid anecdote. This bias violates the statistical law of large numbers, which says that it is inappropriate to generalize from a small sample, let alone from a single case. In many respects, the dot-com boom of the late 1990s was based on reasoning by analogy and representativeness. Prospective entrepreneurs saw some of the early dot-com companies such Amazon and Yahoo achieve rapid success, at least judged by some metrics. Reasoning by analogy from a very small sample, they assumed that any dot-com could achieve similar success. Many investors reached similar conclusions. The result was a massive wave of start-ups that jumped into the Internet space in an attempt to capitalize on the perceived opportunities. That the vast majority of these companies subsequently went bankrupt is testament to the fact that the analogy was wrong and the success of the small sample of early entrants was no guarantee that other dot-coms would succeed.

Another cognitive bias is known as the **illusion of control**: this is the tendency to overestimate one's ability to control events. People seem to have tendency to attribute their success in life to their own good decision making and their failures to bad luck.[28] General or top managers seem to be particularly prone to this bias: having risen to the top of an organization, they tend to be overconfident about their ability to succeed.[29] According to Richard Roll, such overconfidence leads to what he has termed the *hubris hypothesis* of takeovers.[30] Roll argues that top managers are typically overconfident about their abilities to create value by acquiring another company. Hence, they end up making poor acquisition decisions, often paying far too much for the companies they acquire. Subsequently, servicing the debt taken on to finance such an acquisition makes it all but impossible to make money from the acquisition.

Improving Decision Making

The existence of cognitive biases raises the issue of how to bring critical information to bear on the decision mechanism so that a company's strategic decisions are realistic and based on thorough evaluation. Two techniques known to enhance strategic thinking and counteract groupthink and cognitive biases are devil's advocacy and dialectic inquiry.[31] **Devil's advocacy** requires the generation of both a plan and a critical analysis of the plan. One member of the decision-making group acts as the devil's

Escalating Commitment

A cognitive bias that occurs when decision makers, having already committed significant resources to a project, commit even more resources after receiving feedback that the project is failing.

Reasoning by Analogy

A cognitive bias that involves the use of simple analogies to make sense out of complex problems.

Representativeness

A cognitive bias rooted in the tendency to generalize from a small sample or even a single vivid anecdote.

Illusion of Control

A cognitive bias rooted in the tendency to overestimate one's ability to control events.

Devil's Advocacy

A technique in which one member of a decision-making group acts as a devil's advocate, bringing out all the considerations that might make the proposal unacceptable.

advocate, bringing out all the reasons that might make the proposal unacceptable. In this way, decision makers can become aware of the possible perils of recommended courses of action.

Dialectic inquiry is more complex, for it requires the generation of a plan (a thesis) and a counterplan (an antithesis) that reflect *plausible but conflicting* courses of action.[32] Strategic managers listen to a debate between advocates of the plan and counterplan and then make a judgment of which plan will lead to the higher performance. The purpose of the debate is to reveal problems with definitions, recommended courses of action, and assumptions of both plans. As a result of this exercise, strategic managers are able to form a new and more encompassing conceptualization of the problem, which becomes the final plan (a synthesis). Dialectic inquiry can promote thinking strategically.

Another technique for countering cognitive biases, championed by Nobel Prize winner Daniel Kahneman and his associates, is known as the outside view.[33] The outside view requires planners to identify a reference class of analogous past strategic initiatives, determine whether those initiatives succeeded or failed, and evaluate the project at hand against those prior initiatives. According to Kahneman, this technique is particularly useful for countering biases such as the illusion of control (hubris), reasoning by analogy and representativeness. Thus, for example, when considering a potential acquisition planners should look at the track record of acquisitions made by other enterprises (the reference class), determine whether they succeeded or failed, and objectively evaluate the potential acquisition against that reference class. Kahneman argues that such a "reality check" against a large sample of prior events tends to constrain the inherent optimism of planners and produce more realistic assessments and plans.

STRATEGIC LEADERSHIP

One of the key strategic roles of both general and functional managers is to use all their knowledge, energy, and enthusiasm to provide strategic leadership for their subordinates and develop a high-performing organization. Several authors have identified a few key characteristics of good strategic leaders that do lead to high performance: (1) vision, eloquence, and consistency, (2) commitment, (3) being well informed, (3) willingness to delegate and empower, (5) astute use of power, and (6) emotional intelligence.[34]

Vision, Eloquence, and Consistency

One of the key tasks of leadership is to give an organization a sense of direction. Strong leaders seem to have clear and compelling visions of where their organizations should go, are eloquent enough to communicate their visions to others within their organization in terms that energize people, and consistently articulate their visions until they become part of the organization's culture.[35]

Examples of strong business leaders include Microsoft's Bill Gates, Jack Welch, the former CEO of GE and Sam Walton, Walmart's founder. For years, Bill Gates' vision of a world in which there would be a Windows-based personal computer on every desk was a driving force at Microsoft. More recently, the vision has evolved into one of a world in which Windows-based software can be found on any computing

Dialectic Inquiry

The generation of a plan (a thesis) and a counterplan (an antithesis) that reflect *plausible but conflicting* courses of action.

device—from PCs and servers to video game consoles (X-Box), cell phones, and handheld computers. At GE, Jack Welch was responsible for articulating the simple but powerful vision that GE should be first or second in every business in which it competed, or exit from that business. Similarly, it was Sam Walton who established and articulated the vision that has been central to Walmart's success—passing on cost savings from suppliers and operating efficiencies to customers in the form of everyday low prices.

Commitment

Strong leaders demonstrate their commitment to their vision and business model by actions and words, and they often lead by example. Consider Nucor's former CEO, Ken Iverson. Nucor is a very efficient steelmaker with perhaps the lowest cost structure in the steel industry. It has turned in 30 years of profitable performance in an industry where most other companies have lost money because of a relentless focus on cost minimization. In his tenure as CEO, Iverson set the example: he answered his own phone, employed only one secretary, drove an old car, flew coach class, and was proud of the fact that his base salary was the lowest in the Fortune 500 (Iverson made most of his money from performance-based pay bonuses). This commitment was a powerful signal to employees that Iverson was serious about doing everything possible to minimize costs. It earned him the respect of Nucor employees, which made them more willing to work hard. Although Iverson has retired, his legacy lives on in the cost-conscious organization culture that has been built at Nucor, and, like all other great leaders, his impact will go beyond his tenure as a leader.

Being Well Informed

Effective strategic leaders develop a network of formal and informal sources who keep them well informed about what is going on within their company. Herb Kelleher at Southwest Airlines, for example, was able to find out a lot about the health of his company by dropping in unannounced on aircraft maintenance facilities and helping workers there to perform their tasks; McDonald's Ray Kroc and Walmart's Sam Walton routinely dropped in unannounced to visit their restaurants and stores. Using informal and unconventional ways to gather information is wise because formal channels can be captured by special interests within the organization or by gatekeepers, managers who may misrepresent the true state of affairs within the company to the leader, such as may have happened at Enron. People like Kelleher who constantly interact with employees at all levels are better able to build informal information networks than leaders who closet themselves and never interact with lower-level employees.

Willingness to Delegate and Empower

High-performance leaders are skilled at delegation. They recognize that unless they learn how to delegate effectively they can quickly become overloaded with responsibilities. They also recognize that empowering subordinates to make decisions is a good motivation tool. Delegating also makes sense when it results in decisions being made by those who must implement them. At the same time, astute leaders recognize that they need to maintain control over certain key decisions. Thus, although they will delegate many *important* decisions to lower-level employees, they will not delegate those that they judge to be of *critical importance* to the future success of the organization under their leadership—such as articulating the vision and business model.

The Astute Use of Power

In a now classic article on leadership, Edward Wrapp noted that effective leaders tend to be very astute in their use of power.[36] He argued that strategic leaders must often play the power game with skill and attempt to build consensus for their ideas rather than use their authority to force ideas through; they act as members or democratic leaders of a coalition rather than as dictators. Jeffery Pfeffer has articulated a similar vision of the politically astute manager who gets things done in organizations by the intelligent use of power.[37] In Pfeffer's view, power comes from control over resources: budgets, capital, positions, information, and knowledge that is important to the organization. Politically astute managers use these resources to acquire another critical resource: critically placed allies who can help a manager attain preferred strategic objectives. Pfeffer stresses that one does not need to be a CEO to assemble power in an organization. Sometimes quite junior functional managers can build a surprisingly effective power base and use it to influence organizational outcomes.

Emotional Intelligence

Emotional intelligence is a term that Daniel Goldman coined to describe a bundle of psychological attributes that many strong and effective leaders exhibit:[38]

- Self-awareness—the ability to understand one's own moods, emotions, and drives, as well as their effect on others
- Self-regulation—the ability to control or redirect disruptive impulses or moods, that is, to think before acting
- Motivation—a passion for work that goes beyond money or status and a propensity to pursue goals with energy and persistence
- Empathy—understanding the feelings and viewpoints of subordinates and taking those into account when making decisions
- Social skills—friendliness with a purpose

According to Goldman, leaders who possess these attributes—who exhibit a high degree of emotional intelligence—tend to be more effective than those who lack these attributes. Their self-awareness and self-regulation help to elicit the trust and confidence of subordinates. In Goldman's view, people respect leaders who, because they are self-aware, recognize their own limitations and because they are self-regulating consider decisions carefully. Goldman also argues that self-aware and self-regulating individuals tend to be more self-confident and therefore better able to cope with ambiguity and more open to change. A strong motivation exhibited in a passion for work can also be infectious, helping to persuade others to join together in pursuit of a common goal or organizational mission. Finally, strong empathy and social skills can help leaders earn the loyalty of subordinates. Empathetic and socially adept individuals tend to be skilled at managing disputes between managers, better able to find common ground and purpose among diverse constituencies, and better able to move people in a desired direction than leaders who lack these skills. In short, Goldman's arguments are that the psychological makeup of a leader matters.

SUMMARY OF CHAPTER

1. A strategy is an action that a company takes to attain one or more of its goals.

2. A company has a competitive advantage over its rivals when it is more profitable than the average for all firms in its industry. It has a sustained competitive advantage when it is able to maintain above-average profitability over a number of years. In general, a company with a competitive advantage will grow its profits more rapidly than rivals.

3. General managers are responsible for the overall performance of the organization or for one of its major self-contained divisions. Their overriding strategic concern is for the health of the total organization under their direction.

4. Functional managers are responsible for a particular business function or operation. Although they lack general management responsibilities, they play a very important strategic role.

5. Formal strategic planning models stress that an organization's strategy is the outcome of a rational planning process. The major components of the strategic management process are defining the mission, vision, and major goals of the organization; analyzing the external and internal environments of the organization; choosing strategies that align or fit an organization's strengths and weaknesses with external environmental opportunities and threats; and adopting organizational structures and control systems to implement the organization's chosen strategy.

6. Strategy can emerge from deep within an organization in the absence of formal plans as lower-level managers respond to unpredicted situations.

7. Strategic planning often fails because executives do not plan for uncertainty and because ivory-tower planners lose touch with operating realities.

8. The fit approach to strategic planning has been criticized for focusing too much on the degree of fit between existing resources and current opportunities, and not enough on building new resources and capabilities to create and exploit future opportunities.

9. Strategic intent refers to an obsession with achieving an objective that stretches the company and requires it to build new resources and capabilities.

10. In spite of systematic planning, companies may adopt poor strategies if their decision-making processes are vulnerable, if individual cognitive biases are allowed to intrude into the decision-making process.

11. Devil's advocacy, dialectic inquiry, and the outside view are techniques for enhancing the effectiveness of strategic decision making.

12. Good leaders of the strategy-making process have a number of key attributes: vision, eloquence, and consistency; commitment; being well informed; a willingness to delegate and empower; political astuteness; and emotional intelligence.

DISCUSSION QUESTIONS

1. What do we mean by *strategy?* How is a business model different from a strategy?

2. What are the strengths of formal strategic planning? What are its weaknesses?

3. Pick the current or a past President of the United States and evaluate his performance against the leadership characteristics discussed in the text. On the basis of this comparison, do you think that the President was/is a good strategic leader? Why?

C L O S I N G   C A S E

Planning for the Chevy Volt

General Motors is a company in deep trouble. As car sales in North America collapsed in 2008, GM, which had already lost money in 2007, plunged deeply into the red. With losses estimated at $14 billion, the company was forced to go cap in hand to the government to beg for public funds to help it stave off bankruptcy. Fearing the economic consequences of a collapse of GM, the government agreed to loan funds to GM, but it insisted that the company have a clear plan charting its way back to profitability. Ironically, such a plan was already in place at GM. At the heart of it was a potentially huge gamble on a new type of car: the Chevy Volt.

The Chevy Volt, which was introduced in 2010, is a compact, four-door electric car with a reserve gasoline-powered engine. The primary power source is a large lithium ion battery (lithium ion batteries are typically found in small electric appliances such as cell phones). The battery can be charged by plugging it into a wall socket for 6 hours; when fully charged, it will fuel the car for 40 miles, which is less than most people's daily commute. After that, a gasoline engine kicks in, providing both drive power and recharging the lithium ion battery. GM estimated fuel economy will be over 100 miles per gallon, and charging the car overnight from a power outlet would cost about 80% less than filling it with gas at $3 per gallon. The car will have a starting cost of around $41,000; however, because it uses a battery-powered technology, buyers will be able to take $7,500 tax credit.

The Volt was the brainchild of two men, Bob Lutz, GM's vice-chairman, and Larry Burns, the head of Research & Development and strategic planning at GM. Although Lutz in particular had always championed large gas-hungry muscle cars, GM's planning told them that the market would probably move away from the SUVs that had been a profitable staple at GM for most of the 1990s. A number of trends were coming together to make this scenario likely.

First, oil prices, and by extension, gas prices, were increasing sharply. Although driving an SUV that gets 12 miles to the gallon might make economic sense when gas was priced at $1 a gallon, it did not for most people when gas was $4 per gallon. GM's planning suggested that due to growing demand in developed nations, including China and India, and limited new supplies, the days of cheap oil were over. Second, global warming was becoming an increasing concern, and it seemed possible that tighter regulations designed to limit carbon emissions would be introduced in the future. As a major source of greenhouses gases, such as carbon dioxide, automobiles powered by internal combustion engines could hardly escape this trend. Third, the cost of manufacturing lithium ion batteries was falling, and new technology was promising to make them more powerful. Finally, GM's major competitor, Toyota, with its best selling hybrid, the Prius, had demonstrated that there was demand for fuel-efficient cars that utilized new battery technology (the Prius, however, uses a conventional fuel cell as opposed to a lithium ion battery).

Despite their analysis, when Lutz and Burns first proposed making the Volt in 2003, other managers at GM beat them down. For one thing, GM had already invested billions in developing fuel cells, and many in the company did not want to suddenly switch gears and focus on lithium ion batteries instead. Besides, said the critics, technologically it would be difficult to produce a large lithium ion battery. Others were skeptical given that GM had already had one failure with an electric car, the ill-fated EV1 introduced in the 1990s. Powered by a fuel cell, the EV1 had not sold well (according to many because the company had not put its weight behind it).

By 2006, however, the tide had started to turn. Not only were oil prices surging, as predicted by the strategic planning group, but also a small Silicon Valley start-up, Telsa Motors, had announced that it would be bringing a lithium ion sports car to market. Lutz's reaction was, "if a start-up can do it, GM can too!" So Lutz and Burns formed a skunk works within GM and quickly put together a Chevy Volt concept car, which they unveiled at the 2007 Detroit auto show. The concept car gained a lot of positive feedback, and Lutz used this to argue within the company that GM needed to commit to the project. Moreover, he argued, Toyota was gaining major benefits from its Prius, both in terms of sales and the halo effect associated with making a green car. This time Lutz and Burns were able to persuade other senior managers to back the project, and it was officially launched in early 2007 with an aggressive goal of market introduction in 2010.

Case Discussion Questions

1. What does the Chevy Volt case tell you about the nature of strategic decision making at a large complex organization like GM?
2. What trends in the external environment favored the pursuit of the Chevy Volt project?
3. What impediments to pursuing this project do you think existed within GM?
4. The plan for the Chevy Volt seems to be based partly on the assumption that oil prices would remain high, and yet, in late 2008, oil prices collapsed in the wake of a sharp global economic slowdown.
   a. What does this tell you about the nature of strategic plans?
   b. What do falling oil prices mean for the potential success of the Chevy Volt?
   c. Do you think oil prices will remain low?
5. What will it take for the Chevy Volt to be a successful car? In light of your analysis, how risky do you think this venture is for GM? What are the costs of failure? What are the costs of not pursuing the project?

NOTES

1. There are several different ratios for measuring profitability, such as return on invested capital, return on assets, and return on equity. Although these different measures are highly correlated with each other, finance theorists argue that the return on invested capital is the most accurate measure of profitability. See Tom Copeland, Tim Koller, and Jack Murrin, *Valuation: Measuring and Managing the Value of Companies* (New York: Wiley, 1996).
2. "How Big Can it Grow?" *The Economist*, April 17, 2004, 4–78; "Trial by Checkout," *The Economist*, June 26, 2004, 74–76; Walmart 10K, 200; Information at Walmart's Web site (www.walmartstores.com); Robert Slater, *The Walmart Triumph*, Portfolio Trade Books, 2004. "The bulldozer from Bentonville slows; Wal-Mart," *The Economist*, February 17, 2007, 70.
3. Trying to estimate the relative importance of industry effects and firm strategy on firm profitability has been one of the most important areas of research in the strategy literature during the past decade. See Y. E. Spanos and S. Lioukas, "An Examination of the Causal Logic of Rent Generation," *Strategic Management Journal* 22, no. 10 (October 2001): 907–934 and R. P. Rumelt, "How Much Does Industry Matter?" *Strategic Management Journal* 12 (1991): 167–185. See also A. J. Mauri and M. P. Michaels, "Firm and Industry Effects within Strategic Management: An Empirical Examination," *Strategic Management Journal* 19 (1998): 211–219.
4. This view is known as "agency theory." See M. C. Jensen and W. H. Meckling, "Theory of the Firm: Managerial Behavior, Agency Costs and Ownership Structure," *Journal of Financial Economics* 3 (1976): 305–360 and E. F. Fama, "Agency Problems and the Theory of the Firm," *Journal of Political Economy* 88 (1980): 375–390.
5. K. R. Andrews, *The Concept of Corporate Strategy* (Homewood, Ill.: Dow Jones Irwin, 1971); H. I. Ansoff, *Corporate Strategy* (New York: McGraw-Hill, 1965); C. W. Hofer and D. Schendel, *Strategy Formulation: Analytical Concepts* (St. Paul, Minn.: West, 1978). Also see P. J. Brews and M. R. Hunt, "Learning to Plan and Planning to Learn," *Strategic Management Journal* 20 (1999): 889–913; R. W. Grant, "Planning in a Turbulent Environment," *Strategic Management Journal* 24 (2003): 491–517.
6. Taken from Micrsoft's Web site at http://www.micro-soft.com/mscorp/mission/
7. Andrews, *The Concept of Corporate Strategy*; Ansoff, *Corporate Strategy*; Hofer and Schendel, *Strategy Formulation*.
8. For details, see R. A. Burgelman, "Intraorganizational Ecology of Strategy Making and Organizational Adaptation: Theory and Field Research," *Organization Science* 2 (1991): 239–262; H. Mintzberg, "Patterns in Strategy Formulation," *Management Science* 24 (1978): 934–948; S. L. Hart, "An Integrative Framework for Strategy Making Processes," *Academy of Management Review* 17 (1992): 327–351; G. Hamel, "Strategy as Revolution," *Harvard Business Review*, 74, July–August 1996, 69–83; Grant, "Planning in a Turbulent Environment," and G. Gaveti, D. A. Levinthal, and J. W. Rivkin, "Strategy Making in Novel and Complex Worlds: The Power of Analogy," *Strategic Management Journal* 26 (2005): 691–712.

9. This is the premise of those who advocate that complexity and chaos theory should be applied to strategic management. See S. Brown and K. M. Eisenhardt, "The Art of Continuous Change: Linking Complexity Theory and Time Based Evolution in Relentlessly Shifting Organizations," *Administrative Science Quarterly* 29 (1997): 1–34; R. Stacey and D. Parker, *Chaos, Management and Economics* (London: Institute for Economic Affairs, 1994). See also H. Courtney, J. Kirkland, and P. Viguerie, "Strategy Under Uncertainty," *Harvard Business Review,* 75, November–December 1997, 66–79.

10. Hart, "Integrative Framework"; Hamel, "Strategy as Revolution."

11. See Burgelman, "Intraorganizational Ecology of Strategy Making and Organizational Adaptation," and Mintzberg, "Patterns in Strategy Formulation."

12. R. A. Burgelman and A. S. Grove, "Strategic Dissonance," *California Management Review* (Winter 1996): 8–28.

13. C. W. L. Hill and F. T. Rothaermel, "The Performance of Incumbent Firms in the Face of Radical technological Innovation," *Academy of Management Review* 28 (2003): 257–274.

14. Interviews by Charles Hill.

15. This story was related to the author by George Rathmann, who at one time was head of 3M's research activities.

16. H. Mintzberg and A. McGugh, *Administrative Science Quarterly*, Vol. 30. No 2, June 1985.

17. This viewpoint is strongly emphasized by Burgelman and Grove, "Strategic Dissonance."

18. C. C. Miller and L. B. Cardinal, "Strategic Planning and Firm Performance: A Synthesis of More Than Two Decades of Research," *Academy of Management Journal* 37 (1994): 1649–1665. Also see P. R. Rogers, A. Miller, and W. Q. Judge, "Using Information Processing Theory to Understand Planning/Performance Relationships in the Context of Strategy," *Strategic Management Journal* 20 (1999): 567–577 and Brews and Hunt, Learning to Plan and Planning to Learn.

19. Courtney, Kirkland, and Viguerie. "Strategy under uncertainty."

20. P. J. H. Schoemaker, "Multiple Scenario Development: Its Conceptual and Behavioral Foundation," *Strategic Management Journal* 14 (1993): 193–213.

21. P. Schoemaker, P. J. H. van der Heijden, and A. J. M. Cornelius, "Integrating scenarios into strategic planning at Royal Dutch Shell," *Planning Review* 20, no. 3 (1992): 41–47. I. Wylie, "There is no alternative to……" *Fast Company,* July 2002, 106–111.

22. "The Next Big Surprise: Scenario Planning," *The Economist,* October 13, 2001, 71.

23. See C. R. Schwenk, "Cognitive Simplification Processes in Strategic Decision Making," *Strategic Management Journal* 5 (1984): 111–128 and K. M. Eisenhardt and M. Zbaracki, "Strategic Decision Making," *Strategic Management Journal* 13 (Special Issue, 1992): 17–37.

24. H. Simon, *Administrative Behavior* (New York: McGraw-Hill, 1957).

25. The original statement of this phenomenon was made by A. Tversky and D. Kahneman, "Judgment Under Uncertainty: Heuristics and Biases," *Science* 185 (1974): 1124–1131. Also see D. Lovallo and D. Kahneman, "Delusions of Success: How Optimism Undermines Executives' Decisions," *Harvard Business Review,* 81, July 2003, 56–67; J. S. Hammond, R. L. Keeny, and H. Raiffa, "The Hidden Traps in Decision Making," *Harvard Business Review,* 76, September-October 1998, 25–34 and N. N. Taleb, *Fooled by Randomness* (New York: Random House, 2005).

26. Schwenk, "Cognitive Simplification Processes," pp. 111–128.

27. B. M. Staw, "The Escalation of Commitment to a Course of Action," *Academy of Management Review* 6 (1981): 577–587.

28. Taleb, *Fooled by Randomness.*

29. N. J. Hiller and D. C. Hambrick, "Conceptualizing Executive Hubris: The Role of (Hyper) Core Self-Evaluations in Strategic Decision Making," *Strategic Management Journal* 26 (2005): 297–320.

30. R. Roll, "The Hubris Hypotheses of Corporate Takeovers," *Journal of Business* 59 (1986): 197–216.

31. See R. O. Mason, "A Dialectic Approach to Strategic Planning," *Management Science* 13 (1969): 403–414; R. A. Cosier and J. C. Aplin, "A Critical View of Dialectic Inquiry in Strategic Planning," *Strategic Management Journal* 1 (1980): 343–356; and I. I. Mintroff and R. O. Mason, "Structuring III—Structured Policy Issues: Further Explorations in a Methodology for Messy Problems," *Strategic Management Journal* 1 (1980): 331–342.

32. Mason, "A Dialectic Approach," pp. 403–414.

33. Lovallo and Kahneman, "Delusions of Success."

34. For a summary of research on strategic leadership, see D. C. Hambrick, "Putting Top Managers Back into the Picture," *Strategic Management Journal* 10 (Special Issue, 1989): 5–15. See also D. Goldman, "What Makes a Leader?" *Harvard Business Review,* November–December 1998, 92–105; H. Mintzberg, "Covert Leadership," *Harvard Business Review,* November–December 1998, 140–148 and R. S. Tedlow, "What Titans Can Teach Us," *Harvard Business Review,* December 2001, 70–79.

35. N. M. Tichy and D. O. Ulrich, "The Leadership Challenge: A Call for the Transformational Leader," *Sloan Management Review* (Fall 1984): 59–68 and F. Westley and H. Mintzberg, "Visionary Leadership and Strategic Management," *Strategic Management Journal* 10 (Special Issue, 1989): 17–32.

36. E. Wrapp, "Good Managers Don't Make Policy Decisions," *Harvard Business Review,* September–October 1967, 91–99.

37. J. Pfeffer, *Managing with Power* (Boston, Mass.: Harvard Business School Press, 1992).

38. Goldman, "What Makes a Leader?"

GOVERNING STAKEHOLDERS AND BUSINESS ETHICS

2

CHAPTER OUTLINE

Stakeholders

The Mission Statement

The Mission
Vision
Values
Major Goals

Corporate Governance and Strategy

The Agency Problem
Governance Mechanisms

Ethics and Strategy

Ethical Issues in Strategy
The Roots of Unethical Behavior
Behaving Ethically
Final Words

LEARNING OBJECTIVES

After reading this chapter you should be able to:

- Explain why managers need to take stakeholder claims into account.
- Discuss the components of a corporate mission statement.
- Explain the role played by corporate governance mechanisms in the management of a company.

- Review the causes of poor business ethics.
- Discuss how managers can ensure that the strategic decisions they make are consistent with good ethical principles.

OVERVIEW

An important part of the strategy making process is ensuring that the company maintains the support of the key constituencies—or stakeholders—upon which it depends for its functioning and ultimate survival. A company's **stakeholders** are individuals or groups with an interest, claim, or stake in the company, in what it does, and in how well it performs.[1] We begin by looking at the relationship between stakeholders and a company. Then we move on to consider the corporate mission statement, which is the first key indicator of how an organization views the claims of its stakeholders. The purpose of the mission statement is to establish the guiding principles for strategic decision making. As we shall see, these guiding principles should recognize the claims of important stakeholder groups. Next we explore the issue of corporate governance.

By **corporate governance**, we mean the mechanisms that exist to ensure that managers pursue strategies that are in the interests of an important stakeholder group—shareholders. The chapter closes with a discussion of the ethical implications of strategic decisions. We consider how managers can make sure that their strategic decisions are founded on strong principles that treat all stakeholders in an ethical manner.

Stakeholders

Individuals or groups with an interest, claim, or stake in the company, in what it does, and in how well it performs.

Corporate Governance

The mechanisms that exist to ensure that managers pursue strategies in the interests of an important stakeholder group, the shareholders.

Internal Stakeholders

Stockholders and employees, including executive officers, other managers, and board members.

External Stakeholders

Individuals and groups outside the company that have some claim on the company.

STAKEHOLDERS

A company's stakeholders can be divided into internal stakeholders and external stakeholders (see Figure 2.1). **Internal stakeholders** are stockholders and employees, including executive officers, other managers, and board members. **External stakeholders** are all other individuals and groups that have some claim on the company. Typically, this group comprises customers, suppliers, creditors (including banks and bondholders), governments, unions, local communities, and the general public.

All stakeholders are in an exchange relationship with the company. Each stakeholder group supplies the organization with important resources (or contributions), and in exchange each expects its interests to be satisfied (by inducements).[2] Stockholders provide the enterprise with risk capital and in exchange expect management to try to maximize the return on their investment. Creditors such as bondholders provide the company with capital in the form of debt, and they expect to be repaid on time with interest. Employees provide labor and skills and in exchange expect

Figure 2.1 Stakeholders and the Enterprise

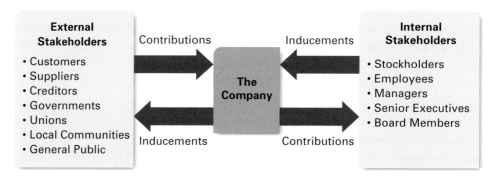

commensurate income, job satisfaction, job security, and good working conditions. Customers provide a company with its revenues and in exchange want high-quality reliable products that represent value for money. Suppliers provide a company with inputs and in exchange seek revenues and dependable buyers. Governments provide a company with rules and regulations that govern business practice and maintain fair competition. In exchange they want companies that adhere to these rules and pay their taxes. Unions help to provide a company with productive employees and in exchange they want benefits for their members in proportion to their contributions to the company. Local communities provide companies with local infrastructure and in exchange want companies that are responsible citizens. The general public provides companies with national infrastructure and in exchange seeks some assurance that the quality of life will be improved as a result of the company's existence.

A company should take these claims into account when formulating its strategies. If it does not stakeholders may withdraw their support. Stockholders may sell their shares, bondholders demand higher interest payments on new bonds, employees leave their jobs, and customers buy elsewhere. Suppliers may seek more dependable buyers. Unions may engage in disruptive labor disputes. Government may take civil or criminal action against the company and its top officers, imposing fines and in some cases jail terms. Communities may oppose the company's attempts to locate its facilities in their area, and the general public may form pressure groups, demanding action against companies that impair the quality of life. Any of these reactions can have a damaging impact on an enterprise.

Managers cannot always satisfy the claims of all stakeholders. The goals of different groups may conflict, and in practice few organizations have the resources to satisfy all stakeholder claims.[3] For example, union claims for higher wages can conflict with consumer demands for reasonable prices and stockholder demands for acceptable returns. Often, the company must make choices. To do so, it must identify the most important stakeholders and give highest priority to pursuing strategies that satisfy their needs. Stakeholder impact analysis can provide such identification. Typically, stakeholder impact analysis follows these steps:

1. Identify stakeholders
2. Identify stakeholders' interests and concerns
3. As a result, identify what claims stakeholders are likely to make on the organization
4. Identify the stakeholders who are most important from the organization's perspective
5. Identify the resulting strategic challenges[4]

Such an analysis enables a company to identify the stakeholders most critical to its survival and to make sure that the satisfaction of their needs is paramount. Most companies that have gone through this process quickly come to the conclusion that three stakeholder groups must be satisfied above all others if a company is to survive and prosper: customers, employees, and stockholders.[5]

THE MISSION STATEMENT

As noted above, a company's mission statement is a key indicator of how an organization views the claims of its stakeholders. You will also recall that in Chapter 1 we stated that the mission statement represented the starting point of the strategic planning process. Although corporate mission statements vary, the most comprehensive include four main elements; the mission, vision, values, and goals of a corporation.

The Mission

The mission describes what it is that the company does. For example, the mission of Kodak is to provide "customers with the solutions they need to capture, store, process, output, and communicate images—anywhere, anytime."[6] Kodak is a company that exists to provide imaging solutions to consumers. This missions focuses on the customer need that the company is trying to satisfy (the need for imaging), as opposed to the products that the company produces (film and cameras). This is a customer-oriented rather than product-oriented mission.

An important first step in the process of formulating a mission is to come up with a definition of the organization's business. Essentially, the definition should answer these questions: "What is our business? What will it be? What should it be?"[7] The responses guide the formulation of the mission. To answer the question, "What is our business?" a company should define its business in terms of three dimensions: who is being satisfied (what customer groups), what is being satisfied (what customer needs), and how customers' needs are being satisfied (by what skills, knowledge, or competencies).[8] Figure 2.2 illustrates these dimensions.

This approach stresses the need for a *customer-oriented* rather than a *product-oriented* business definition. A product-oriented business definition focuses on the

....

Figure 2.2   Defining the Business

Mission

What it is that the company exists to do.

Source: D. F. Abell, *Defining the Business: The Starting Point of Strategic Planning* (Englewood Cliffs, Prentice-Hall, 1980), 7.

characteristics of the products sold and markets served, not on which kinds of customer needs the products are satisfying. Such an approach obscures the company's true mission because a product is only the physical manifestation of applying a particular skill to satisfy a particular need for a particular customer group. In practice, that need may be served in many different ways, and a broad customer-oriented business definition that identifies these ways can safeguard companies from being caught unaware by major shifts in demand.

By helping anticipate demand shifts, a customer-oriented mission statement can also assist companies to capitalize on changes in their environment. It can help answer the question, "What will our business be?" Recall that Kodak's mission emphasizes the company's desire to provide *customers* with the *solutions* they need to capture, store, process, output, and communicate images. This is a customer-oriented mission statement that focuses on customer needs, as opposed to a particular product (or solution) for satisfying those needs. This customer-oriented business definition has helped drive Kodak's investments in digital imaging technologies, since the early 1990s, which have replaced much of Kodak's traditional business based on chemical film processing.

The need to take a customer-oriented view of a company's business has often been ignored. History is littered with the wreckage of once-great corporations that did not define their business or defined it incorrectly so that ultimately they declined. In the 1950s and 1960s, there were many office equipment companies such as Smith Corona and Underwood that defined their businesses as being the production of typewriters. This product-oriented definition ignored the fact that they were really in the business of satisfying customers' information processing needs. Unfortunately for those companies, when a new technology came along that better served customer needs for information processing (computers), demand for typewriters plummeted. The last great typewriter company, Smith Corona, went bankrupt in 1996, a victim of the success of computer-based word processing technology.

In contrast, IBM correctly foresaw what its business would be. In the 1950s, IBM was a leader in the manufacture of typewriters and mechanical tabulating equipment using punch card technology. However, unlike many of its competitors, IBM defined its business as *providing a means for information processing and storage,* rather than just supplying mechanical tabulating equipment and typewriters.[9] Given this definition, the company's subsequent moves into computers, software systems, office systems, and printers seem logical.

Vision

The vision of a company lays out some desired future state—it articulates, often in bold terms, what the company would like to achieve. For example, Nokia, the world's largest manufacturer of mobile (wireless) phones, has been operating with a very simple but powerful vision for some time: "If it can go mobile, it will!" This vision implied that not only would voice telephony go mobile, but also a host of other services based on data, such as imaging and Internet browsing. This vision led Nokia to become one of the early leaders in developing "smart" mobile handsets that not only can be used for voice communication but that also take pictures, browse the Internet, play games, and manipulate personal and corporate information. Good vision statements are meant to stretch a company by articulating some ambitious, but attainable future state that will help to motivate employees at all levels and drive strategies.[10]

Vision

The desired future state of a company.

Values

The **values** of a company state how managers and employees should conduct themselves, how they should do business, and what kind of organization they should build to help a company achieve its mission. Insofar as they help drive and shape behavior within a company, values are commonly seen as the bedrock of a company's **organizational culture**: the set of values, norms, and standards that control how employees work to achieve an organization's mission and goals. An organization's culture is often seen as an important source of its competitive advantage.[11] (We discuss the issue of organization culture in depth in Chapter 9.) For example, Nucor Steel is one of the most productive and profitable steel firms in the world. Its competitive advantage is based in part on the extremely high productivity of its workforce, something, the company maintains, that is a direct result of its cultural values, which shape how it treats its employees. These values are as follow:

- "Management is obligated to manage Nucor in such a way that employees will have the opportunity to earn according to their productivity."
- "Employees should be able to feel confident that if they do their jobs properly, they will have a job tomorrow."
- "Employees have the right to be treated fairly and must believe that they will be."
- "Employees must have an avenue of appeal when they believe they are being treated unfairly."[12]

At Nucor, values emphasizing pay for performance, job security, and fair treatment for employees help to create an atmosphere within the company that leads to high employee productivity. In turn, this has helped to give Nucor one of the lowest cost structures in its industry, which helps to explain the company's profitability in a very price-competitive business.

Major Goals

Having stated the mission, vision, and key values, strategic managers can take the next step in the formulation of a mission statement: establishing major goals. A **goal** is a *precise* and *measurable* desired future state that a company attempts to realize. In this context, the purpose of goals is to specify with precision what must be done if the company is to attain its mission or vision.

Well-constructed goals have four main characteristics:[13]

1. They are *precise and measurable*. Measurable goals give managers a yardstick or standard against which they can judge their performance.
2. They *address crucial issues*. To maintain focus, managers should select a limited number of major goals to assess the performance of the company. The goals that are selected should be crucial or important ones.
3. They are *challenging but realistic*. They give all employees an incentive to look for ways of improving the operations of an organization. If a goal is unrealistic in the challenges it poses, employees may give up; a goal that is too easy may fail to motivate managers and other employees.[14]
4. They *specify a time period* in which they should be achieved when that is appropriate. Time constraints tell employees that success requires a goal to be attained by a given date, not after that date. Deadlines can inject a sense of urgency into goal attainment and act as a motivator. However, not all goals require time constraints.

Values

Statements of how managers and employees of a company should conduct themselves, how they should do business, and what kind of organization they should build to help a company achieve its mission.

Organizational Culture

The set of values, norms, and standards that control how employees work to achieve an organization's mission and goals.

Goal

A precise and measurable desired future state that a company attempts to realize.

Well-constructed goals also provide a means by which the performance of managers can be evaluated.

Although most companies operate with a variety of goals, the central goal of most corporations is to maximize shareholder returns, and maximizing shareholder returns requires high profitability and profit growth.[15] Thus, most companies operate with goals for profitability and profit growth. However, it is important that top managers do not make the mistake of overemphasizing current profitability to the detriment of long-term profitability and profit growth.[16] The overzealous pursuit of current profitability to maximize short-term performance can encourage such misguided managerial actions as cutting expenditures judged to be nonessential in the short run—for instance, expenditures for research and development, marketing, and new capital investments. Although cutting current expenditure increases current profitability, the resulting underinvestment, lack of innovation, and diminished marketing can jeopardize long-run profitability and profit growth. These expenditures are vital if a company is to pursue its long-term mission and sustain its competitive advantage and profitability over time. Despite these negative consequences, managers may make such decisions because the adverse effects of a short-run orientation may not materialize and become apparent to shareholders for several years or because they are under extreme pressure to hit short-term profitability goals.[17]

It is also worth noting that pressures to maximize short-term profitability may result in managers' acting in an unethical manner. This apparently occurred during the late 1990s at a number of companies including Enron Corporation, Tyco, WorldCom, and Computer Associates. In these companies, profits were systematically inflated by managers who manipulated financial accounts in a manner that misrepresented the true performance of the firm to shareholders.

To guard against short-run behavior, managers need to ensure that they adopt goals whose attainment will increase the *long-run* performance and competitiveness of their enterprise. Long-term goals are related to such issues as product development, customer satisfaction, and efficiency, and they emphasize specific objectives or targets concerning such things as employee and capital productivity, product quality, and innovation.

> ### Ethical Dilemma
>
> You work for a U.S.-based textile company struggling with overseas competitors that have access to low-cost labor. While you pay your factory workers $14 an hour plus benefits, you know that a similar textile mill in Vietnam is paying its employees about $0.50 an hour, and the mill does not have to comply with the same safety and environmental regulations that your company does. Although your mill is marginally profitable, the Vietnamese factory clearly has a cost advantage. Your CEO wants to move production to Vietnam where labor and compliance costs are lower, resulting in mill closure and employee lay-offs. Your mill is the only large employer in a small community. Many of the employees have worked there their entire working lives. What is the right action to take for stockholders? What is the most ethical course of action? Is there a conflict here?

CORPORATE GOVERNANCE AND STRATEGY

We noted that a central goal of most companies is to provide its stockholders a good rate of return on their investment. There are good reasons for this. Stockholders are the legal owners of a company and the providers of risk capital. The capital that stockholders provide to a company is seen as **risk capital** because there is no guarantee that stockholders will ever recoup their investment or earn a decent return (publicly held corporations can and go bankrupt, in which case stockholders will lose their capital investment).

In publicly held corporations, stockholders delegate the job of controlling the company and selecting its strategies to professional managers, who become the *agents* of the stockholders.[18] As the *agents* of stockholders, managers should pursue strategies that maximize *long-run* returns to stockholders (subject to the constraint that they do so in a manner that is both legal and ethical). Although most managers are diligent about doing so, not all act in this fashion. This failure gives rise to what is known as the **agency problem**, where managers pursue strategies that are not in the interests of stockholders.

Risk Capital

Equity capital for which there is no guarantee that stockholders will ever recoup their investment or earn a decent return.

Agency Problem

A problem that arises when managers pursue strategies that are not in the interests of stockholders.

The Agency Problem

A branch of economics known as **agency theory** looks at the agency problems that can arise in a business relationship when one person delegates decision-making authority to another. Agency theory offers a way of understanding why managers do not always act in the best interests of stakeholders, and also why they might sometimes engage in actions that are unethical, and perhaps also illegal.[19] Although agency theory was originally formulated to capture the relationship between management and stockholders, the basic principles have also been extended to cover the relationship with other key stakeholders, such as employees, as well as between different layers of management within a corporation.[20] While the focus of attention in this section is on the relationship between senior management and stockholders, it should not be forgotten that some of the same language can be applied to the relationship between other stakeholders and top managers and between top management and lower levels of management.

The basic propositions of agency theory are relatively straightforward. First, an **agency relationship** is held to arise whenever one party delegates decision-making authority or control over resources to another. The **principal** is the person delegating authority, and the **agent** is the person to whom authority is delegated. The relationship between stockholders and senior managers is the classic example of an agency relationship. Stockholders, who are the *principals*, provide the company with risk capital, but they delegate control over that capital to senior managers, and particularly the CEO, who as their *agent* is expected to use that capital in a manner that is consistent with the best interests of stockholders. This means using that capital to maximize the company's long-run profitability and profit growth rate.

While agency relationships often work well, problems arise if agents and principals have different goals, and if agents take actions that are not in the best interests of their principals. Agents may be able to do this because there is an **information asymmetry** between the principal and the agent; agents almost always have more information about the resources they are managing than the principal does. Unscrupulous agents can take advantage of any information asymmetry to mislead principals and maximize their own interests at the expense of principals.

In the case of stockholders, the information asymmetry arises because they delegate decision-making authority to the CEO, their agent, who by virtue of his or her position inside the company is likely to know far more than stockholders do about the company's operations. The information asymmetry between principals and agents is not necessarily a bad thing, but it can make it difficult for principals to measure how well an agent is performing, and thus hold the agent accountable for how well he or she is using the entrusted resources. There is a certain amount of performance ambiguity inherent in the relationship between a principal and agent: the principal cannot know for sure if the agent is acting in his or her best interests. The principal cannot know for sure if the agent is using the resources to which he or she has been entrusted as effectively and efficiently as possible. To an extent, principal has to *trust* the agent to do the right thing.

This trust is not blind: principals do put *governance mechanisms* in place whose purpose is to monitor agents, evaluate their performance, and if necessary, take corrective action. As we shall see shortly, the board of directors is one such governance mechanism, for in part the board exists to monitor and evaluate senior managers on behalf of stockholders. Other mechanisms serve a similar purpose. In the United States, the requirement that publicly owned companies regularly file detailed

Agency Theory

A theory dealing with the problems that can arise in a business relationship when one person delegates decision-making authority to another.

Agency Relationship

A relationship that arises whenever one party delegates decision-making authority or control over resources to another.

Principal

A person delegating authority to an agent, who acts on the principal's behalf.

Agent

A person to whom authority is delegated by a principal.

Information Asymmetry

A situation in which one party to an exchange has more information about the exchange than the other party.

financial statements with the Securities and Exchange Commission (SEC) that are in accordance with generally agreed accounting principles (GAAP) exists to give stockholders consistent and detailed information about how well management is using the capital to which they have been entrusted.

Despite the existence of governance mechanisms and comprehensive measurement and control systems, a degree of information asymmetry will always remain between principals and agents, and there is always an element of trust involved in the relationship. Unfortunately, not all agents are worthy of this trust. A minority will deliberately mislead principals for personal gain, sometimes behaving unethically or breaking laws in the process. The interests of principals and agents are not always the same; they diverge, and some agents may take advantage of information asymmetries to maximize their own interests at the expense of principals, and to engage in behaviors that the principals would never condone.

For example, some authors have argued that like many other people, senior managers are motivated by desires for status, power, job security, and income.[21] By virtue of their position within the company, certain managers, such as the CEO, can use their authority and control over corporate funds to satisfy these desires at the cost of returns to stockholders. CEOs might use their position to invest corporate funds in various perks that enhance their status—executive jets, lavish offices, and expense-paid trips to exotic locations—rather than investing those funds in ways that increase stockholder returns. Economists have termed such behavior *on-the-job*

2.1 STRATEGY IN ACTION

The Agency Problem at Tyco

Under the leadership of Dennis Kozlowski, who became CEO of Tyco in 1990, the company's revenues expanded from $3.1 billion in 1992 to $38 billion in 2001. Most of this growth was due to a series of acquisitions that took Tyco into a diverse range of unrelated businesses. Tyco finance the acquisitions by taking on significant debt commitments, which by 2002 exceeded $23 billion. As Tyco expanded, some questioned Tyco's ability to service its debt commitments, and claimed that the company was engaging in "accounting tricks" to pad its books and make the company appear more profitable than it actually was. These criticisms, which were ignored for several years, were finally shown to have some validity in 2002 when Kozlowski was forced out by the board and subsequently charged with tax evasion by federal authorities.

Among other charges, federal authorities claimed that Kozlowski treated Tyco as his personal treasury, drawing on company funds to purchase an expensive Manhattan apartment and a world class art collection that he obviously thought were befitting of the CEO of a major corporation. Kozlowski even used company funds to help pay for an expensive birthday party for his wife—which

included toga-clad ladies, gladiators, a naked-woman-with-exploding-breasts birthday cake and a version of Michelangelo's David that peed vodka! Kozlowski was replaced by a company outsider, Edward Breen. In 2003 Tyco took a $1.5 billion charge against earnings for accounting errors made during the Kozlowski era (i.e., Tyco's profits had been overstated by $1.5 billion during Kozlowski's tenure). Breen also set about dismantling parts of the empire that Kozlowski had built, divesting several businesses.

After a lengthy criminal trial, in June 2005 Dennis Kozlowski and Mark Swartz, the former chief financial officer of Tyco, were convicted of 23 counts of grand larceny, conspiracy, securities fraud, and falsifying business records in connection with what prosecutors described as the systematic looting of millions of dollars from the conglomerate (Kozlowski was found guilty of looting $90 million from Tyco). Both were set to serve significant jail time. As for Tyco, in 2006 CEO Ed Breen announced that the company would be broken up into three parts, a testament to the strategic incoherence of the conglomerate that Kozlowski built.[22]

consumption.[23] For an example, see Strategy in Action, which describes the on-the-job consumption that occurred at Tyco under the leadership of Dennis Kozlowski.

Besides engaging in on-the-job-consumption, CEOs, along with other senior managers, might satisfy their desires for greater income by using their influence or control over the board of directors to get the compensation committee of the board to grant them substantial pay increases. Critics of U.S. industry claim that extraordinary pay has now become an endemic problem and that senior managers are enriching themselves at the expense of stockholders and other employees. They point out that CEO pay has been increasing far more rapidly than the pay of average workers, primarily because of very liberal stock option grants that enable a CEO to earn huge pay bonuses in a rising stock market, even if the company underperforms the market and competitors.[24] In 1950, when *Business Week* started its annual survey of CEO pay, the highest-paid executive was General Motors CEO Charles Wilson, whose $652,156 pay packet translated into $4.7 million in inflation-adjusted dollars in 2005. In contrast, the highest-paid executive in 2009, Ray Irani of Occidental Petroleum earned $31 million.[25] However, CEO pay in 2009 was fairly constrained compared with earlier years, reflecting the impact of the global financial crisis and public reaction to high CEO pay checks at many struggling financial institutions. In 2005, before the crisis, Lee Raymond of Exxon, earned $405 million![26] In 1980, the average CEO in *Business Week*'s survey of CEO's of the largest 500 American companies earned 42 times what the average blue-collar worker earned. By 1990, this figure had increased to 85 times. By 2005, the average CEO in the survey was earning more than 350 times the pay of the average blue-collar worker.[27]

What rankles critics is the size of some CEO pay packages and their apparent lack of relationship to company performance.[28] For example, in May 2006, shareholders of Home Depot complained bitterly about the compensation package for CEO Bob Nardelli at the company's annual meeting. Nardelli, who was appointed in 2000, had received $124 million in compensation, despite mediocre financial performance at Home Depot and a 12% decline in the company's stock price since he joined. When unexercised stock options were included, his compensation exceeded $250 million.[29] Another target of complaints was Pfizer CEO, Hank McKinnell, who garnered an $83 million lump sum pension, and $16 million in compensation in 2005, despite a 40 plus percentage decline in Pfizer's stock price since he took over as CEO.[30] Critics feel that the size of pay awards such as these is out of all proportion to the achievement of the CEOs. If so, this represents a clear example of the agency problem. It is of note, however, that CEO pay has dropped in 2009 and 2010, reflecting the aftermath of the global financial crisis, In 2009, average pay of CEOs in the S&P 500 was around $9 million, a 40% drop from 2000 and about 260 times average pay of blue collar workers (which still represents a major increase since 1990).[31]

A further concern is that in trying to satisfy a desire for status, security, power, and income, a CEO might engage in *empire building*, buying many new businesses in an attempt to increase the size of the company through diversification.[32] Although such growth may depress the company's long-run profitability, and thus stockholder returns, it increases the size of the empire under the CEO's control and, by extension, the CEO's status, power, security, and income (there is a strong relationship between company size and CEO pay).

Instead of trying to maximizing stockholder returns by seeking to maximize profitability, some senior managers may trade long-run profitability for greater company growth by buying new businesses. Figure 2.3 graphs long-run profitability against the rate of growth in company revenues. A company that does not grow is probably

Figure 2.3 The Tradeoff Between Profitability and Revenue Growth Rates

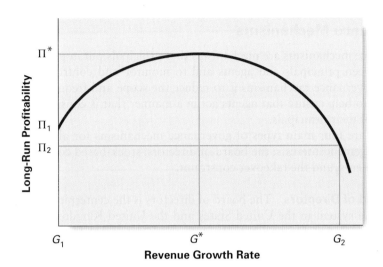

missing out on some profitable opportunities.[33] A moderate revenue growth rate of G^* allows a company to maximize long-run profitability, generating a return of Π^*. Thus, a growth rate of $G1$ in Figure 2.3 (zero growth) is not consistent with maximizing profitability ($\Pi_1 < \Pi^*$). By the same token however, attaining growth *greater than G^** requires diversification into areas that the company knows little about. Consequently, it can be achieved only by sacrificing profitability (i.e., past G^*, the investment required to finance further growth does not produce an adequate return and the company's profitability declines). Yet $G2$ may be the growth rate favored by an empire-building CEO, for it will increase his or her power, status, and income. At this growth rate, profitability is equal only to Π_2. Because $\Pi^* > \Pi_2$, a company growing at this rate is clearly not maximizing its long-run profitability or the wealth of its stockholders. However, a growth rate of $G2$ may be consistent with attaining managerial goals of power, status, and income. Tyco International, which is profiled in the Strategy in Action feature, provides us with an example of this kind of growth.

Just how serious agency problems can be was emphasized in the early 2000s when a series of scandals swept through the corporate world, many of which could be attributed to self-interest seeking by senior executives, and a failure of corporate governance mechanisms to hold the largest of those executives in check. Between 2001 and 2004, accounting scandals unfolded at a number of major corporations, including Enron, World Com, Tyco, Computer Associates, Health South, Adelphia Communications, Dynergy, Royal Dutch Shell, and the major Italian food company, Parmalat. At Enron, for example, some $27 billion in debt was hidden from shareholders, employees, and regulators in special partnership that were kept off the balance sheet. In all of these cases, the prime motivation seems to have been an effort to present a more favorable view of corporate affairs to shareholders than was actually the case, thereby securing senior executives significantly higher pay packets.[34]

Confronted with agency problems, the challenge for principals is to (1) shape the behavior of agents so that they act in accordance with the goals set by principals, (2) reduce the information asymmetry between agents and principals, and (3) develop mechanisms for removing agents who do not act in accordance with the goals of principals, and mislead principals. Principals try to deal with these challenges through a series of governance mechanisms.

Governance Mechanisms

Governance mechanisms are mechanisms that principals put in place to align incentives between principals and agents and to monitor and control agents. The purpose of governance mechanisms is to reduce the scope and frequency of the agency problem: to help ensure that agents act in a manner that is consistent with the best interests of their principals.

There are four main types of governance mechanisms for aligning stockholder and management interests: the board of directors, stock-based compensation, financial statements, and the takeover constraint.

The Board of Directors   The board of directors is the centerpiece of the corporate governance system in the United States and the United Kingdom. Board members are directly elected by stockholders, and under corporate law they represent the stockholders' interests in the company. Hence, the board can be held legally accountable for the company's actions. Its position at the apex of decision-making within the company allows it to monitor corporate strategy decisions and ensure that they are consistent with stockholder interests. If the board's sense is that a company's strategies are not in the best interest of stockholders, it can apply sanctions, such as voting against management nominations to the board of directors or submitting its own nominees. In addition, the board has the legal authority to hire, fire, and compensate corporate employees, including, most importantly, the CEO.[35] The board is also responsible for making sure that audited financial statements of the company present a true picture of its financial situation. Thus, the board exists to reduce the information asymmetry between stockholders and managers and to monitor and control management actions on behalf of stockholders, ensuring that managers pursue strategies that are in the best interests of stockholders.

The typical board of directors is composed of a mix of inside and outside directors. *Inside directors* are senior employees of the company, such as the CEO. They are required on the board because they have valuable information about the company's activities. Without such information, the board cannot adequately perform its monitoring function. But because insiders are full-time employees of the company, their interests tend to be aligned with those of management. Hence, outside directors are needed to bring objectivity to the monitoring and evaluation processes. *Outside directors* are not full-time employees of the company. Many of them are full-time professional directors who hold positions on the boards of several companies. The need to maintain a reputation as competent outside directors gives them an incentive to perform their tasks as objectively and effectively as possible.[36]

There is little doubt that many boards perform their assigned functions admirably, but not all perform as well as they should. The board of now bankrupt energy company Enron signed off on that company's audited financial statements, which were later shown to be grossly misleading.

Critics of the existing governance system charge that inside directors often dominate the outsiders on the board. Insiders can use their position within the management hierarchy to exercise control over what kind of company-specific information the board receives. Consequently, they can present information in a way that puts them in a favorable light. In addition, insiders have the advantage of intimate

Governance Mechanisms

Mechanisms that principals put in place to align incentives between principals and agents and to monitor and control agents.

knowledge of the company's operations. Because of their superior knowledge and control over information are sources of power, they may be better positioned than outsiders to influence boardroom decision making. The board may become the captive of insiders and merely rubber-stamp management decisions instead of guarding stockholder interests.

Some observers contend that many boards are dominated by the company CEO, particularly when the CEO is also the chairman of the board.[37] To support this view, they point out that both inside and outside directors are often the personal nominees of the CEO. The typical inside director is subordinate to the CEO in the company's hierarchy and therefore unlikely to criticize the boss. Because outside directors are frequently the CEO's nominees as well, they can hardly be expected to evaluate the CEO objectively. Thus, the loyalty of the board may be biased toward the CEO, not the stockholders. Moreover, a CEO who is also chairman of the board may be able to control the agenda of board discussions in such a manner as to deflect any criticisms of his or her leadership.

In the aftermath of a wave of corporate scandals that hit the corporate world in the early 2000s, there are clear signs that many corporate boards are moving away from merely rubber-stamping top management decisions and are beginning to play a much more active role in corporate governance. In part they have been prompted by new legislation, such as the 2002 Sarbanes-Oxley Act in the United States which tightened rules governing corporate reporting and corporate governance. Also important has been a growing trend on the part of the courts to hold directors liable for corporate misstatements. Powerful institutional investors such as pension funds have also been more aggressive in exerting their power, often pushing for more outside representation on the board of directors, and for a separation between the roles of chairman and CEO, with the chairman role going to an outsider. As a result, over 50% of big companies had outside directors in the chairman's role by the mid-2000s, up from less than half of that number in 1990.

Stock-Based Compensation   According to agency theory, one of the best ways to reduce the scope of the agency problem is for principals to establish incentives for agents to behave in their best interest through pay-for-performance systems. In the case of stockholders and top managers, stockholders can encourage top managers to pursue strategies that maximize a company's long-run profitability and profit growth, and thus the gains from holding its stock, by linking the pay of those managers to the performance of the stock price.

The most common pay-for-performance system has been to give managers stock options: the right to buy the company's shares at a predetermined (strike) price at some point in the future, usually within 10 years of the grant date. Typically, the strike price is the price that the stock was trading at when the option was originally granted. The idea behind stock options is to motivate managers to adopt strategies that increase the share price of the company, for in doing so they will also increase the value of their own stock options.

Some research studies suggest that stock-based compensation schemes for executives, such as stock options, can align management and stockholder interests. For instance, one study found that managers were more likely to consider the effects of their acquisition decisions on stockholder returns if they themselves were significant shareholders.[38] According to another study, managers who were significant stockholders were less likely to pursue strategies that would maximize the size of the company rather than its profitability.[39] More generally, it is difficult to argue with the proposition that the chance to get rich from exercising stock options is the primary reason for the 14-hour days and 6-day work weeks that many employees of fast-growing companies put in.

However, the practice of granting stock options in particular has become increasingly controversial. Many top managers often earn huge bonuses from exercising stock options that were granted several years previously. While not denying that these options do motivate managers to improve company performance, critics claim that they are often too generous. A particular cause for concern is that stock options are often granted at such low strike prices that senior managers can hardly fail to make a significant amount of money by exercising them, even if the company underperforms the stock market by a significant margin. Indeed, serious examples of the agency problem emerged in 2005 and 2006 when the Securities and Exchange Commission started to investigate a number of companies where stock options granted to senior executives had apparently been "backdated" to a time when the stock price was lower, enabling the executive to earn more money than if those options had simply been dated on the day they were granted.[40] By 2007, the SEC was investigating some 130 companies for possible fraud relating to stock option dating. Included in the list were some major corporations including Apple Computer, Jabil Circuit, United Health, and Home Depot.[41]

Other critics of stock options, including the famous investor Warren Buffett, complain that huge stock option grants increase the outstanding number of shares in a company and therefore dilute the equity of stockholders; accordingly, they should be shown in company accounts as an expense against profits (a practice that was not required until mid-2005).

To summarize, in theory, stock options and other stock-based compensation methods are a good idea; in practice, they have been abused. To limit the abuse, accounting rules now require that stock options be treated as an expense that must be charged against profits. Some companies took matters into their own hands even before the change in accounting rules. Microsoft, for example, stopped issuing options to employees in 2003, replacing them with smaller stock grants. Since 2002, Boeing has expensed options in its accounts. The aerospace company has also gone an important step further in an effort to align management and stockholder interests, issuing what it calls "performance share" units that are convertible into common stock only if its stock appreciates at least 10% annually for 5 years. What these companies are trying to do in their own way is to limit the free ride that many holders of stock options enjoyed during the boom of the 1990s, while continuing to maintain a focus on aligning management and stockholder interests through stock-based compensation schemes.[42]

Financial Statements and Auditors   Publicly trading companies in the United States are required to file quarterly and annual reports with the SEC that are prepared according to Generally Agreed Accounting Principles (GAAP). The purpose of this requirement is to give consistent, detailed, and accurate information about how efficiently and effectively the agents of stockholders, the managers, are running the company. To make sure that managers do not misrepresent this financial information, the SEC also requires that the accounts be audited by an independent and accredited accounting firm. Similar regulations exist in most other developed nations. If the system works as intended, stockholders can have a lot of faith that the information contained in financial statements accurately reflects the state of affairs at a company. Among other things, such information can enable a stockholder to calculate the profitability of a company in which she invests and to compare its profitability against that of competitors.

Unfortunately, in the United States at least, this system has not been working as intended. Although the vast majority of companies do file accurate information in their financial statements and although most auditors do a good job of reviewing that information, there is evidence that a minority of companies have abused the system, aided in part by the compliance of auditors. This was clearly an issue at bankrupt energy trader Enron, where the CFO and others misrepresented the true financial state of the company to investors by creating off-balance-sheet partnerships that hid the true state of Enron's indebtedness from public view. Enron's auditor, Arthur Andersen, also apparently went along with this deception in direct violation of its fiduciary duty. The complacency of Arthur Andersen with financial fraud at Enron appears to have been due to the fact that Arthur Anderson also had lucrative consulting contracts with Enron that it did not want to jeopardize by questioning the accuracy of the company's financial statements. The losers in this mutual deception were shareholders who had to rely upon inaccurate information to make their investment decisions.

There have been numerous examples in recent years of managers gaming financial statements to present a distorted picture of their company's finances to investors. The typical motive has been to inflate the earnings or revenues of a company, thereby generating investor enthusiasm and propelling the stock price higher, which gives managers an opportunity to cash in stock option grants for huge personal gain, obviously at the expense of stockholders who have been mislead by the reports.

The gaming of financial statements by companies raises serious questions about the accuracy of the information contained in audited financial statements. In response, in 2002 the United States passed the Sarbanes-Oxley bill into law, which represents the biggest overall of accounting rules and corporate governance procedures since the 1930s. Among other things, Sarbanes-Oxley set up a new oversight board for accounting firms, required CEOs and CFOs to endorse their company's financial statements, and barred companies from hiring the same accounting firm for auditing and consulting services.

The Takeover Constraint Given the imperfections in corporate governance mechanisms, it is clear that the agency problem may still exist at some companies. However, stockholders still have some residual power, for they can always sell their shares. If they start doing so in large numbers, the price of the company's shares will decline. If the share price falls far enough, the company might be worth less on the stock market than the book value of its assets. At this point, it may become an attractive acquisition target and runs the risk of being purchased by another enterprise, against the wishes of the target company's management.

The risk of being acquired by another company is known as the **takeover constraint**. The takeover constraint limits the extent to which managers can pursue strategies and take actions that put their own interests above those of stockholders. If they ignore stockholder interests and the company is acquired, senior managers typically lose their independence and probably their jobs as well. So the threat of takeover can constrain management action and limit the worst excesses of the agency problem.

Takeover Constraint

The risk of being acquired by another company.

ETHICS AND STRATEGY

The term ethics refers to accepted principles of right or wrong that govern the conduct of a person, the members of a profession, or the actions of an organization. Business ethics are the accepted principles of right or wrong governing the conduct of business people. Ethical decisions are those that are in accordance with those accepted principles of right and wrong, whereas an unethical decision is one that violates accepted principles. This is not as straightforward as it sounds. Managers may be confronted with ethical dilemmas, which are situations where there is no agreement over exactly what the accepted principles of right and wrong are, or where none of the available alternatives seems ethically acceptable.

In our society, many accepted principles of right and wrong are not only universally recognized, but are also codified into law. In the business arena there are laws governing product liability (*tort laws*), contracts and breaches of contract (*contract law*), the protection of intellectual property (*intellectual property law*), competitive behavior (*antitrust law*), and the selling of securities (*securities law*). Not only is it unethical to break these laws, it is illegal.

It is important to realize, however, that behaving ethically goes beyond staying within the bounds of the law. There are many cases of strategies and actions that while legal, do not seem to be ethical. For example, in their quest to boost profitability, during the 1990s managers at Nike contracted out the production of sports shoes to producers in the developing world. Unfortunately for Nike, the working conditions at several of these producers were very poor and the company was subsequently attacked for using "sweatshop labor". Typical of the allegations were those detailed in the CBS news program "48 hours." The report told of young women at a Vietnamese subcontractor who worked 6 days a week, in poor working conditions with toxic materials, for only 20 cents an hour. The report also stated that a living wage in Vietnam was at least $3 a day, an income that could not be achieved without working substantial overtime. Nike was not breaking any laws, nor were its subcontractors, but this report, and others like it, raised questions about the ethics of using "sweatshop labor." It may have been legal. It may have helped the company to increase its profitability. But was it ethical to use subcontractors who by Western standards exploited their workforce? Nike's critics thought not, and the company found itself the focus of a wave of demonstrations and consumer boycotts.[43]

In this section, we take a closer look at the ethical issues that managers may confront when developing strategy, and at the steps managers can take to ensure that strategic decisions are not only legal, but also ethical.

Ethical Issues in Strategy

The ethical issues that managers confront cover a wide range of topics but most arise due to a potential conflict between the goals of the enterprise, or the goals of individual managers, and the fundamental rights of important stakeholders including stockholders, customers, employees, suppliers, competitors, communities, and the general public. Stakeholders have basic rights that should be respected, and it is unethical to violate those rights.

Stockholders have the right to timely and accurate information about their investment (in accounting statements), and it is unethical to violate that right. Customers have the right to be fully informed about the products and services they purchase, including the right to information about how those products might cause harm

Ethics

Accepted principles of right or wrong that govern the conduct of a person, the behavior of members of a profession, or the actions of an organization.

Business Ethics

Accepted principles of right or wrong governing the conduct of business-people.

Ethical Dilemmas

Situations where there is no agreement over exactly what the accepted principles of right and wrong are, or where none of the available alternatives seems ethically acceptable.

to them or others, and it is unethical to restrict their access to such information. Employees have the right to safe working conditions, fair compensation for the work they perform, and to be treated in a just manner by managers. Suppliers have the right to expect contracts to be respected, and the firm should not take advantage of a power disparity between themselves and a supplier to opportunistically rewrite a contract. Competitors have the right to expect that the firm will abide by the rules of competition and not violate the basic principles of antitrust laws. Communities and the general public, including their political representatives in government, have the right to expect that a firm will not violate the basic expectations that society places on enterprises—for example, by dumping toxic pollutants into the environment or overcharging for work performed on government contracts.

Those who take the stakeholder view of business ethics often argue that it is in the enlightened self-interest of managers to behave in an ethical manner that recognizes and respects the fundamental rights of stakeholders, because doing so will ensure the support of stakeholders, which ultimately benefits the firm and its managers. Others go beyond this instrumental approach to ethics to argue that in many cases, acting ethically is simply the right thing to do. They argue that businesses need to recognize their *noblesse oblige* and give something back to the society that made their success possible. *Noblesse oblige* is a French term that refers to honorable and benevolent behavior considered the responsibility of people of high (noble) birth. In a business setting, it is taken to mean benevolent behavior that is the moral responsibility of successful enterprises.

Oftentimes, unethical behavior arises in a corporate setting when managers decide to put the attainment of their own personal goals, or the goals of the enterprise, above the fundamental rights of one or more stakeholder groups (in other words, unethical behavior may arise from agency problems). The most common examples of such behavior involve self-dealing, information manipulation, anticompetitive behavior, opportunistic exploitation of other players in the value chain in which the firm is embedded (including suppliers, complement providers, and distributors), the maintenance of substandard working conditions, environmental degradation, and corruption.

Self-dealing occurs when managers find a way to feather their own nests with corporate monies, and we have already discussed several examples in this chapter (e.g., at Tyco and Computer Associates). **Information manipulation** occurs when managers use their control over corporate data to distort or hide information in order to enhance their own financial situation, or the competitive position of the firm. As we have seen, many of the recent accounting scandals involved the deliberate manipulation of financial information. Information manipulation can also occur with regard to nonfinancial data. This occurred when managers at the tobacco companies suppressed internal research that linked smoking to health problems, violating the rights of consumers to accurate information about the dangers of smoking. When evidence of this came to light, lawyers bought class action suits against the tobacco companies, claiming that they had intentionally caused harm to smokers—they had broken tort law by promoting a product that they knew did serious harm to consumers. In 1999, the tobacco companies settled a lawsuit brought by the states who sought to recover health care costs associated with tobacco related illnesses; the total payout to the states—$260 billion!

Anticompetitive behavior covers a range of actions aimed at harming actual or potential competitors, most often by using monopoly power, thereby enhancing the long-run prospects of the firm. For example, in the 1990s the Justice Department

Self-Dealing

Occurs when managers find a way to feather their own nests with corporate monies.

Information Manipulation

Occurs when managers use their control over corporate data to distort or hide information in order to enhance their own financial situation or the competitive position of the firm.

Anticompetitive Behavior

Actions aimed at harming actual or potential competitors, most often by using monopoly power, thereby enhancing the long-run prospects of the firm.

claimed that Microsoft used its monopoly in operating systems to force PC manufacturers to bundle Microsoft's Web browser, Internet Explorer, with Windows and to display Internet Explorer prominently on the computer desktop (the screen you see when you start a personal computer). Microsoft reportedly told PC manufacturers that it would not supply them with Windows unless they did this. Since the PC manufacturers had to have Windows to sell their machines, this was a powerful threat. This alleged action, an example of "tie in sales," is illegal under antitrust laws, and, purportedly, aimed to drive competing browser maker, Netscape, out of business. The courts ruled that Microsoft was indeed abusing its monopoly power in this case, and under a 2001 consent decree the company agreed to stop the practice.

Putting the legal issues aside, actions such as those allegedly undertaken by managers at Microsoft are unethical on at least three counts—first, they violate the rights of end consumers by unfairly limiting their choices; second, they violate the rights of downstream participants in the industry value chain, in this case PC manufacturers, by forcing them to incorporate a particular product in their design; and third, they violate the rights of competitors to free and fair competition.

Opportunistic exploitation of other players in the value chain in which the firm is embedded is another example of unethical behavior. **Opportunistic exploitation** of this kind typically occurs when the managers of a firm seek to unilaterally rewrite the terms of a contract with suppliers, buyers, or complement providers in a way that is more favorable to the firm, often using their power to force the revision through. For example, in the late 1990s Boeing entered into a $2 billion contract with Titanium Metals Corp to buy certain amounts of titanium annually for 10 years. In 2000, after Titanium Metals Corp had already spent $100 million to expand its production capacity to fulfill the contract, Boeing demanded that the contract be renegotiated, asking for lower prices and an end to minimum purchase agreements. As a major purchaser of titanium, managers at Boeing probably thought they had the power to push this contract revision through, and the investment by Titanium meant that they would be unlikely to walk away from the deal. Titanium Metals Corp promptly sued Boeing for breach of contract. The dispute was settled out of court, and under a revised agreement Boeing agreed to pay monetary damages to Titanium Metals (reported to be in the $60 million range) and entered into an amended contract to purchase titanium. Irrespective of the legality of this action, it is arguably unethical since it violates the rights of suppliers to have buyers who deal with them in a fair and open way.

Substandard working conditions arise when managers underinvest in working conditions, or pay employees below market rates, in order to reduce their costs of production. The most extreme examples of such behavior occur when a firm establishes operations in countries that lack the workplace regulations found in developed nations such as the United States. The example of Nike falls into this category. However, examples of substandard working conditions also occur within developed nations. As documented in the Running Case, for example, Walmart has been accused of promoting substandard working conditions in its U.S. operations.

Environmental degradation occurs when the firm takes actions that directly or indirectly result in pollution or other forms of environmental harm. Environmental degradation can violate the rights of local communities and the general public for clean air and water, land that is free from pollution by toxic chemicals, excessive deforestation that results in land erosion and floods (forests absorb rainfall and limit flooding), and so on.

Finally, **corruption** can arise in a business context when managers pay bribes to gain access to lucrative business contracts. Corruption is clearly unethical since it

Opportunistic Exploitation

Occurs when the managers of a firm seek to unilaterally rewrite the terms of a contract with suppliers, buyers, or complement providers in a way that is more favorable to the firm, often using their power to force the revision through.

Substandard working conditions

Occurs when managers underinvest in working conditions, or pay employees below market rates, in order to reduce their costs of production.

Environmental degradation

Occurs when a firm takes actions that directly or indirectly result in pollution or other forms of environmental harm.

Corruption

Arises in a business context when managers pay bribes to gain access to lucrative business contracts.

RUNNING CASE

Working Conditions at Walmart

When Sam Walton founded Walmart, one of his core values was that if the company treated employees with respect, tied compensation to the performance of the enterprise, trusted them with important information and decisions, and provided ample opportunities for advancement, they would repay the company with dedication and hard work. For years the formula seemed to work. Employees were called "associates" to reflect their status within the company; even the lowest hourly employee was eligible to participate in profit-sharing plans and could use profit-sharing bonuses to purchase company stock at a discount to its market value. The company made a virtue of promoting from within (two-thirds of managers at Walmart started as hourly employees). At the same time, Walton and his successors always demanded loyalty and hard work from employees—managers for example, were expected to move to a new store on very short notice—and base pay for hourly workers was very low. Still, as long as the up side was there, little grumbling was heard from employees.

However, more recently the relationships between the company and its employees has been strained by a succession of lawsuits claiming that Walmart pressures hourly employees to work overtime without compensating them; systematically discriminates against women; and knowingly uses contractors who hire undocumented immigrant workers to clean its stores, paying them below minimum wage.

For example, a class-action lawsuit in Washington State claimed that Walmart routinely (1) pressured hourly employees not to report all their time worked; (2) failed to keep true time records, sometimes shaving hours from employee logs; (3) failed to give employees full rest or meal breaks; (4) threatened to fire or demote employees who would not work off the clock; and (5) required workers to attend unpaid meetings and computer training. Moreover, the suit claimed that Walmart has a strict "no overtime" policy, punishing employees who work more than 40 hours a week, yet the company also gives employees more work than can be completed in a 40-hour week. The Washington suit is one of more than 30 suits that have been filed around the nation in recent years.

With regard to discrimination against women, complaints date back to a 1996, when an assistant manager in a California store, Stephanie Odle, came across the W-2 of a male assistant manager who worked in the

same store. The W-2 showed that he was paid $10,000 more than Odle. When she asked her boss to explain the disparity, she was told that her coworker had "a wife and kids to support." When Odle, a single mother, protested, she was asked to submit a personal household budget. She was then granted a $2,080 raise. Subsequently, Odle was fired, she claims for speaking up. In 1998, she filed a discrimination suit against the company. Others began to file suits around the same time, and by 2004 the legal action had evolved into a class action suit that covered 1.6 million current and former female employees at Walmart. The suit claims that Walmart did not pay female employees the same as their male counterparts and did not provide them with equal opportunities for promotion.

In the case of both undocumented overtime and discrimination, Walmart admits to no wrongdoing. The company does recognize that with more than 2 million employees, some problems are bound to arise, but it claims that there is no systematic company-wide effort to get hourly employees to work without pay or to discriminate against women. Indeed, the company claims that this could not be the case because hiring and promotion decisions are made at the store level.

For their part, critics charge that while the company may have no policies that promote undocumented overtime or discrimination, the hard driving cost containment culture of the company had created an environment in which abuses can thrive. Store managers, for example, are expected to meet challenging performance goals, and, in an effort to do so, they may be tempted to pressure subordinates to work additional hours without pay. Similarly, company policy requiring managers to move to different stores at short notice unfairly discriminates against women, who lack the flexibility to uproot their families and move them to another state at short notice.

While the lawsuits are ongoing and may take years to resolve, Walmart has taken steps to change its employment practices. For example, the company has created a director of diversity, a diversity compliance team, and restructured its pay scales to promote equal pay regardless of gender. Walmart has also taken action to stop employees working overtime without pay. For example, it programmed cash registers to shut down after an employee had exceeded a certain number of hours, and has told managers to make sure that employees take lunch and rest breaks.[44]

violates a bundle of rights, including the right of competitors to a level playing field when bidding for contracts, and when government officials are involved, the right of citizens to expect that government officials act in the best interest of the local community or nation, and not in response to corrupt payments that feather their own nests.

The Roots of Unethical Behavior

Why do some managers behave unethically? Although there is no simple answer to this question a few generalizations that can be made. First, it is important to recognize that the business ethics are not divorced from *personal ethics*—which are the generally accepted principles of right and wrong governing the conduct of individuals. As individuals, we are taught that it is wrong to lie and cheat—it is unethical—and that it is right to behave with integrity and honor, and to stand up for what we believe to be right and true. The personal ethical code that guides our behavior comes from a number of sources, including our parents, our schools, our religion, and the media. Our personal ethical code will exert a profound influence on the way we behave as business people. An individual with a strong sense of personal ethics is less likely to behave in an unethical manner in a business setting, and in particularly, they are less likely to engage in self-dealing and more likely to behave with integrity.

Second, many studies of unethical behavior in a business setting have come to the conclusion that business people sometimes do not realize that they are behaving unethically, primarily because they simply fail to ask the relevant question—is this decision or action ethical? Instead, they apply a straightforward business calculus to what they perceive to be a business decision, forgetting that the decision may also have an important ethical dimension. The fault here lies in processes that do not incorporate ethical considerations into business decision making. This may have been the case at Nike when managers originally made subcontracting decisions. Those decisions were probably made on the basis of good economic logic. Subcontractors were probably chosen on the basis of business variables such as cost, delivery, and product quality, and the key managers simply failed to ask, "How does this subcontractor treat their workforce"? If they thought about the question at all, they probably reasoned that it was the subcontractor's concern, not theirs.

Unfortunately, the climate in some businesses does not encourage people to think through the ethical consequences of business decisions. This brings us to the third cause of unethical behavior in businesses—an organizational culture that deemphasizes business ethics, reducing all decisions to the purely economic. A fourth cause of unethical behavior that is related to this may be pressure from top management to meet performance goals that are unrealistic, and can only be attained by cutting corners or acting in an unethical manner. An organizational culture can "legitimize" behavior that society would judge as unethical, particularly when this is mixed with a focus on unrealistic performance goals, such as maximizing short-term economic performance, no matter what the costs. In such circumstances, there is a greater than average probability that managers will violate their own personal ethics and engage in behavior that is unethical. By the same token, an organization culture can do just the opposite and reinforce the need for ethical behavior. At HP, for example, Bill Hewlett and David Packard, the company's founders, propagated a set of values known as The HP Way. These values, which shape the way business is conducted both within and by the corporation, have an important ethical component. Among other things, they stress the need for confidence in and respect for people, open communication, and concern for the individual employee.

This brings us to a fifth root cause of unethical behavior—*leadership*. Leaders help to establish the culture of an organization, and they set the example that others follow. Other employees in a business often take their cue from business leaders and if those leaders do not behave in an ethical manner, nor might they. It is not what leaders say that matters, but what they do.

Behaving Ethically

What is the best way for managers to make sure that the ethical considerations are taken into account when making business decisions? There is no easy answers to this question, for many of the most vexing ethical problems arise because there are very real dilemmas inherent in them and no obvious right course of action. Nevertheless, there are many things that managers can and should do to make sure that basic ethical principles are adhered to, and that ethical issues are routinely inserted into business decisions. However, as discussed below, there are a number of things that managers can do to make sure that ethical issues are considered in business decision.

Hiring and Promotion   It seems obvious that businesses should strive to hire people who have a strong sense of personal ethics, and would not engage in unethical or illegal behavior. Similarly, you would rightly expect a business to not promote people, and perhaps fire people, whose behavior does not match generally accepted ethical standards. But when you think about it, doing so is actually very difficult. After all, how do you know that someone has a poor sense of personal ethics? In our society, immoral individuals have an incentive to hide a lack of personal ethics from public view. Once people realize that you are unethical they will no longer trust you.

Is there anything that businesses can do to make sure that they do not hire people who subsequently turn out to have poor personal ethics, particularly given that people have an incentive to hide this from public view (indeed, the unethical person may well lie about their nature)? Businesses can give potential employees psychological tests to try and discern their ethical predisposition and they can check with prior employees regarding someone's reputation (e.g., by asking for letters of reference, and talking to people who have worked with the prospective employee). The latter is certainly not uncommon and does indeed influence the hiring process. As for promoting people who have displayed poor ethics, that should not occur in a company where the organization culture places a high value on the need for ethical behavior, and where leaders act accordingly.

Organization Culture and Leadership   To foster ethical behavior, businesses need to build an organization culture that places a high value on ethical behavior. Three things are particularly important in building an organization culture that emphasizes ethical behavior. First, the businesses must explicitly articulate values that place a strong emphasis on ethical behavior. Many companies now do this by drafting a code of ethics, which is a formal statement of the ethical priorities a business adheres to. Others have incorporated ethical statements into documents that articulate the values or mission of the business. The food and consumer products giant Unilever has a code of ethics that includes the following points "We will not use any form of forced, compulsory or child labor" and "No employee may offer, give or receive any gift or payment which is, or may be construed as being, a bribe. Any demand for, or offer of, a bribe must be rejected immediately and reported to management." Unilever's

Code of Ethics

A formal statement of the ethical principles a business adheres to.

principles send a very clear message about the appropriate ethics to managers and employees within the organization.

Having articulated values in a code of ethics or some other document, it is important that leaders in the business give life and meaning to those words by repeatedly emphasizing their importance, *and then acting on them*. This means using every relevant opportunity to stress the importance of business ethics and making sure that key business decisions not only make good economic sense, but also are ethical. Many companies have gone a step further, hiring independent firms to audit the company and make sure that they are behaving in a manner consistent with their ethical code. Nike, for example, has in recent years hired independent auditors to make sure that subcontractors used by the company are living up to Nike's code of conduct.

Finally, building an organization culture that places a high value on ethical behavior requires incentive and promotional systems that reward people who engage in ethical behavior and sanction those who do not.

Decision-Making Processes   In addition to establishing the right kind of ethical culture in an organization, business people must be able to think through the ethical implications of decisions in a systematic way. To do this, they need a moral compass. Some experts on ethics have proposed a straightforward practical guide—or ethical algorithm—to determine whether a decision is ethical. A decision is acceptable on ethical grounds if a business person can answer "yes" to each of these questions:

1. Does my decision fall within the accepted values or standards that typically apply in the organizational environment (as articulated in a code of ethics or some other corporate statement)?
2. Am I willing to see the decision communicated to all stakeholders affected by it—for example, by having it reported in newspapers or on television?
3. Would the people with whom I have a significant personal relationship, such as family members, friends, or even managers in other businesses, approve of the decision?

Ethics Officers   To make sure that a business behaves in an ethical manner, a number of firms now have ethics officers. These are individuals who are responsible for making sure that all employees are trained to be ethically aware, that ethical considerations enter the business decision-making process, and that the company's code of ethics is adhered to. Ethics officers may also be responsible for auditing decisions to make sure that they are consistent with this code. In many businesses, ethics officers act as an internal ombudsperson with responsibility for handling confidential inquiries from employees, investigating complaints from employees or others, reporting findings and making recommendations for change.

United Technologies, a large aerospace company with worldwide revenues of over $28 billion, has had a formal code of ethics since 1990. There are now some 160 "business practice officers" within United Technologies (this is the company's name for ethics officers) who are responsible for making sure that the code is adhered to. United Technologies also established an ombudsperson program in 1986 that lets employees inquire anonymously to business practice officers about ethics issues. The program has received some 56,000 inquiries since 1986 and 8,000 cases have been handled by an ombudsperson.

Strong Corporate Governance Strong corporate governance procedures are needed to make sure that managers adhere to ethical norms, and in particular, to make sure that senior managers do not engage in self-dealing or information manipulation. The key to strong corporate governance procedures is an independent board of directors that is willing to hold top managers into account for self-dealing, and is able to question the information provided to them by managers. If companies like Tyco, WorldCom, and Enron had a strong board of directors, it is unlikely that they would have been subsequently racked by accounting scandals, and top managers would not have been able to view the funds of these corporations as their own personal treasuries.

Moral Courage It is important to recognize that on occasion, managers may need significant *moral courage*. It is moral courage that enables a manager to walk away from a decision that is profitable, but unethical. It is moral courage that gives an employee the strength to say no to a superior instructing her to pursue unethical actions. And, it is moral courage that gives employees the integrity to go public to the media and blow the whistle on persistent unethical behavior in a company. Moral courage does not come easily—there are well known cases where individuals have lost their jobs because they blew the whistle on corporate behaviors they thought unethical, telling the media about what was occurring.

Companies can strengthen the moral courage of employees by committing themselves to not take retribution on employees that exercise moral courage, say no to superiors or otherwise complain about unethical actions. For example, consider the following extract from Unilever's code of ethics:

> Any breaches of the Code must be reported in accordance with the procedures specified by the Joint Secretaries. The Board of Unilever will not criticize management for any loss of business resulting from adherence to these principles and other mandatory policies and instructions. The Board of Unilever expects employees to bring to their attention, or to that of senior management, any breach or suspected breach of these principles. Provision has been made for employees to be able to report in confidence and no employee will suffer as a consequence of doing so.

This statement gives "permission" to employees to exercise moral courage. Companies can also set up ethics hotlines that allow employees to anonymously register complaints with a corporate ethics officer.

Final Words

All of the steps discussed in this chapter can help to make sure that when managers make business decisions, they are fully cognizant of the ethical implications, and do not violate basic ethical prescripts. At the same time, it must be recognized that not all ethical dilemmas have clean and obvious solutions—indeed, that is why they are dilemmas. At the end of the day, there are clearly things that a business should not do, and there are things that they should do, but there are also actions that present managers with true dilemmas. In these cases, a premium is placed on the ability of managers to make sense out of complex messy situations, and make balanced decisions that are as just as possible.

Summary of Chapter

1. Stakeholders are individuals or groups that have an interest, claim, or stake in the company, in what it does, and in how well it performs.

2. A company cannot always satisfy the claims of all stakeholders. The goals of different groups may conflict. The company must identify the most important stakeholders and give highest priority to pursuing strategies that satisfy their needs.

3. The mission statement can be used to incorporate stakeholder demands into the strategy making process of a company. The mission statement includes the mission, and statements of corporate vision, values, and goals.

4. A company's stockholders are its legal owners and the providers of risk capital, a major source of the capital resources that allow a company to operate its business. Maximizing long-run profitability is the route to maximizing returns to stockholders.

5. An agency relationship is held to arise whenever one party delegates decision-making authority or control over resources to another.

6. The essence of the agency problem is that the interests of principals and agents are not always the same, and some agents may take advantage of information asymmetries to maximize their own interests at the expense of principals.

7. A number of governance mechanisms serve to limit the agency problem. These include the board of directors, stock-based compensation schemes, and the threat of a takeover.

8. The term **ethics** refers to accepted principles of right or wrong that govern the conduct of a person, the members of a profession, or the actions of an organization. **Business ethics** are the accepted principles of right or wrong governing the conduct of business people, and an **ethical strategy** is one that does not violate these accepted principles.

9. Unethical behavior is rooted in poor personal ethics, the psychological and geographical distances of a foreign subsidiary from the home office, a failure to incorporate ethical issues into strategic and operational decision making, a dysfunctional culture and failure of leaders to act in an ethical manger.

10. To make sure that ethical issues are considered in business decisions, managers should (a) favor hiring and promoting people with a well grounded sense of personal ethics; (b) build an organizational culture that places a high value on ethical behavior; (c) make sure that leaders within the business not only articulate the rhetoric of ethical behavior, but also act in a manner that is consistent with that rhetoric; (d) put decision-making processes in place that require people to consider the ethical dimension of business decisions; (e) be morally courageous and encourage others to do the same.

Discussion Questions

1. How prevalent was the agency problem in corporate America during the late 1990s?

2. How might a company configure its strategy-making processes to reduce the probability that managers will pursue their own self-interest, at the expense of stockholders?

3. Under what conditions is it ethically defensible to outsource production to producers in the developing world who have much lower labor costs when such actions also involve laying off long-term employees in the firm's home country?

C L O S I N G   C A S E

Google's Mission, Ethical Principles, and Involvement in China

Google, the fast growing Internet search engine company, was established with a clear mission in mind: *to organize the world's information and make it universally acceptable and useful.* This mission has driven Google to create a search engine that on the basis of key words entered by the user will scan the Web for text, images, videos, news articles, books, and academic journals, among other things. Google has built a highly profitable advertising business on the back of its search engine, which is by far the most widely used in the world. Under the pay-per-click business model, advertisers pay Google every time a user of its search engine clicks on one of the paid links typically listed on the right hand side of Google's results page.

Google has long operated with the mantra "don't be evil!" When this phrase was originally formulated, the central message was that Google should never compromise the integrity of its search results. For example, Google decided not to let commercial considerations bias its ranking. This is why paid links are not included in its main search results, but listed on the right hand side of the results page. The mantra "don't be evil," however, has become more than that at Google; it has become a central organizing principle of the company and an ethical touchstone by which managers judge all of its strategic decisions.

Google's mission and mantra raised hopes among human rights activities that the search engine would be an unstoppable tool for circumventing government censorship, democratizing information, and allowing people in heavily censored societies to gain access to information that their governments were trying to suppress, including the largest country on earth, China.

Google began a Chinese language service in 2000, although the service was operated from the United States. In 2002, the site was blocked by the Chinese authorities. Would be users of Google's search engine were directed to a Chinese rival. The blocking took Google's managers totally by surprise. Reportedly, cofounder Sergey Brin immediately ordered half a dozen books on China and quickly read them in an effort to understand this vast country.

Two weeks later, for reasons that have never been made clear, Google's service was restored. Google said that it did not change anything about its service, but Chinese users soon found that they could not access politically sensitive sites that appeared in Google's search results, suggesting that the government was censoring more aggressively. (The Chinese government has essentially erected a giant firewall between the Internet in China and the rest of the world, allowing its censors to block sites outside of China that are deemed subversive.)

By late 2004, it was clear to Google that China was a strategically important market. To exploit the opportunities that China offered, however, the company realized that it would have to establish operations in China, including its own computer servers and a Chinese home page. Serving Chinese users from the United States was too slow, and the service was badly degraded by the censorship imposed. This created a dilemma for the company given the "don't be evil" mantra. Once it established Chinese operations, it would be subject to Chinese regulations, including those censoring information. For perhaps 18 months, senior managers inside the company debated the pros and cons of entering China directly, as opposed to serving the market from its U.S. site. Ultimately, they decided that the opportunity was too large to ignore. With over 100 million users, and that number growing fast, China promised to become the largest Internet market in the world and a major source of advertising revenue for Google. Moreover, Google was at a competitive disadvantage relative to its U.S. rivals, Yahoo and Microsoft's MSN, which had already established operations in China, and relative to China's homegrown company, Baidu, which leads the market for Internet search in China (in 2006, Baidu had around 40% of the market for search in China, compared to Google's 30% share).

In mid-2005, Google established a direct sales presence in China. In January 2006, Google rolled out its Chinese home page, which is hosted on servers based in China and maintained by Chinese employees in Beijing and Shanghai. Upon launch, Google stated that its objective was to give Chinese users "the greatest amount of information possible." It was immediately apparent that this was not the same as "access to all information." In accordance with Chinese regulations, Google had decided to engage in self-censorship, excluding results on such politically sensitive topics as democratic reform, Taiwanese independence, the banned Falun Gong movement, and references to the notorious Tiananmen Square massacre of democratic protestors that occurred in 1989. Human rights activists quickly protested, arguing that Google had abandoned its principles in order to make greater profits. For its part, Google's managers claimed that it was better to give Chinese users access to a limited amount of information, than to none at all, or to serve the market from the United States and allow the government to continue proactively censoring its search results, which would result in a badly degraded service. Sergey Brin justified the Chinese decision by saying that "it will be better for Chinese Web users, because ultimately they will get more information, though not quite all of it." Moreover, Google argued that it was the only search engine in China that let users know if search results had been censored (which is done by the inclusion of a bullet at the bottom of the page indicating censorship).[45]

Case Discussion Questions

1. How does Google's mission drive strategy at the company?
2. Is Google's stance toward Internet search in China consistent with its mission?
3. Do you think that Google should have entered China and engaged in self-censorship, given the company's long-standing mantra "Don't be evil"? Is it better to engage in self-censorship than have the government censor for you?
4. If all foreign search engine companies declined to invest directly in China due to concerns over censorship, what do you think the results would be? Who would benefit most from this action? Who would lose the most?

NOTES

1. E. Freeman, *Strategic Management: A Stakeholder Approach* (Boston, Mass.: Pitman Press, 1984).
2. C. W. L. Hill and T. M. Jones, "Stakeholder-Agency Theory," *Journal of Management Studies* 29 (1992): 131–154 and J. G. March and H. A. Simon, *Organizations* (New York: Wiley, 1958).
3. Hill and Jones, "Stakeholder-Agency Theory."
4. I. C. Macmillan and P. E. Jones, *Strategy Formulation: Power and Politics* (St. Paul, Minn.: West, 1986).
5. John P. Kotter and James L. Heskett, *Corporate Culture and Performance* (New York: Free Press, 1992).
6. http://www.kodak.com/US/en/corp/careers/why/newvaluesmission.jhtml?pq-path=2217/923/10669/10677.
7. These three questions were first proposed by P. F. Drucker, *Management—Tasks, Responsibilities, Practices* (New York: Harper & Row, 1974), 74–94.
8. Derek F. Abell, *Defining the Business: The Starting Point of Strategic Planning* (Englewood Cliffs, NJ: Prentice-Hall, 1980).
9. P. A. Kidwell and P. E. Ceruzzi, *Landmarks in Digital Computing* (Washington, DC: Smithsonian Institute, 1994).
10. See G. Hamel and C. K. Prahalad, "Strategic Intent," *Harvard Business Review*, May–June 1989, 64.
11. J. C. Collins and J. I. Porras, "Building Your Company's Vision," *Harvard Business Review*, September–October 1996, 65–77.
12. http://www.nucor.com/.
13. M. D. Richards, *Setting Strategic Goals and Objectives* (St. Paul, Minn.: West, 1986).
14. E. A. Locke, G. P. Latham, and M. Erez, "The Determinants of Goal Commitment," *Academy of Management Review* 13 (1988): 23–39.
15. C. Y. Baldwin, "Fundamental Enterprise Valuation: Return on Invested Capital," *Harvard Business School Note* 9-801-125, July 3, 2004; and T. Copeland et al., *Valuation: Measuring and Managing the Value of Companies* (New York: Wiley, 2000).
16. R. E. Hoskisson, M. A. Hitt, and C. W. L. Hill, "Managerial Incentives and Investment in R&D in Large Multiproduct Firms," *Organization Science* 3 (1993): 325–341.
17. Robert H. Hayes and William J. Abernathy, "Managing Our Way to Economic Decline," *Harvard Business Review*, July–August 1980, 67–77.
18. M. C. Jensen and W. H. Meckling, "Theory of the Firm: Managerial Behavior, Agency Costs and Ownership Structure," *Journal of Financial Economics* 3 (1976): 305–360.

19. Jensen and Meckling, "Theory of the Firm." and E. F. Fama, "Agency Problems and the Theory of the Firm," *Journal of Political Economy* 88 (1980): 375–390.

20. Hill and Jones, "Stakeholder-Agency Theory."

21. For example, See R. Marris, *The Economic Theory of Managerial Capitalism* (London: Macmillan, 1964) and J. K. Galbraith, *The New Industrial State* (Boston, Mass.: Houghton Mifflin, 1970).

22. "Money Well Spent: Corporate Parties," *The Economist*, November 1, 2003, 79; "Tyco Pair Sentencing Expected on September 19th," *Wall Street Journal*, August 2, 2005, 1; "Off the Jail: Corporate Crime in America," *The Economist*, June 25, 2005, 81; and N. Varchaver, "What's Ed Breen Thinking?," *Fortune*, March 20, 2006, 135–139.

23. Fama, "Agency Problems and the Theory of the Firm."

24. A. Rappaport, "New Thinking on How to Link Executive Pay with Performance," *Harvard Business Review*, March–April 1999, 91–105.

25. J. S. Greenberg, "CEO Pay Drops but Cash is King," *Bloomberg Business Week*, March 25, 2010.

26. R. Kirkland, "The Real CEO Pay Problem," *Fortune*, July 10, 2006, 78–82.

27. D. Henry and D. Stead, "Worker vs CEO: Room to Run," *Business Week*, October 30, 2006, 13.

28. For academic studies that look at the determinants of CEO pay, See M. C. Jensen and K. J. Murphy, "Performance Pay and Top Management Incentives," *Journal of Political Economy* 98 (1990): 225–264; Charles W. L. Hill and Phillip Phan, "CEO Tenure as a Determinant of CEO Pay," *Academy of Management Journal* 34 (1991): 707–717; H. L. Tosi and L. R. Gomez-Mejia, "CEO Compensation Monitoring and Firm Performance," *Academy of Management Journal* 37 (1994): 1002–1016; and Joseph F. Porac, James B. Wade, and Timothy G. Pollock, "Industry Categories and the Politics of the Comparable Firm in CEO Compensation," *Administrative Science Quarterly* 44 (1999): 112–144.

29. Andrew Ward, "Home Depot Investors Stage a Revolt," *Financial Times*, May 26, 2006, p. 20.

30. R. Kirklad, "The Real CEO Pay Problem," *Fortune*, July 10, 2006, 78–82.

31. Data is from AFLCIO Web site, http://www.aflcio.org/corporatewatch/paywatch/pay/.

32. For recent research on this issue, See Peter J. lane, A. A. Cannella, and M. H. Lubatkin, "Agency Problems as Antecedents to Unrelated Mergers and Diversification: Amihud and Lev Reconsidered," *Strategic Management Journal* 19 (1998): 555–578.

33. E. T. Penrose, *The Theory of the Growth of the Firm* (London: Macmillan, 1958).

34. G. Edmondson and L. Cohn, "How Parmalat Went Sour," *Business Week*, January 12, 2004, 46–50 and "Another Enron? Royal Dutch Shell," *The Economist*, March 13, 2004, 71.

35. O. E. Williamson, *The Economic Institutions of Capitalism* (New York: Free Press, 1985).

36. Fama, "Agency Problems and the Theory of the Firm."

37. S. Finkelstein and R. D'Aveni, "CEO Duality as a Double Edged Sword," *Academy of Management Journal* 37 (1994): 1079–1108; B. Ram Baliga and R. C. Moyer, "CEO Duality and Firm Performance," *Strategic Management Journal* 17 (1996): 41–53; M. L. Mace, *Directors: Myth and Reality* (Cambridge, Mass.: Harvard University Press, 1971); and S. C. Vance, *Corporate Leadership: Boards of Directors and Strategy* (New York: McGraw-Hill, 1983).

38. W. G. Lewellen, C. Eoderer, and A. Rosenfeld, "Merger Decisions and Executive Stock Ownership in Acquiring Firms," *Journal of Accounting and Economics* 7 (1985): 209–231.

39. C. W. L. Hill and S. A. Snell, "External Control, Corporate Strategy, and Firm Performance," *Strategic Management Journal* 9 (1988): 577–590.

40. The phenomenon of back dating stock options was uncovered by academic research, and then picked up by the SEC. See Erik Lie, "On the Timing of CEO Stock Option Awards," *Management Science* 51 (2005): 802–812.

41. G. Colvin, "A Study in CEO Greed," *Fortune*, June 12, 2006, 53–55.

42. D. Henry and M. Conlin, "Too Much of a Good Incentive?" *Business Week*, March 4, 2002, 38–39.

43. "Boycott Nike" *CBS News 48 Hours*, October 17, 1996. D. Jones, "Critics Tie Sweatshop Sneakers to "Air Jordan," *USA Today*, June 6, 1996, 1B and S. Greenhouse. "Nike Shoeplant in Vietnam is Called Unsafe for Workers," *New York Times*, November 8, 1997.

44. S. Holt, "Walmart Workers Suit Wins Class Action Status," *Seattle Times*, October 9, 2004, E1, E4; C. Daniels, "Women versus Walmart," *Fortune*, July 21, 2003, 79–82; C. R. Gentry, "Off the Clock," *Chain Store Age*, February 2003, 33–36; M. Grimm, "WalMart Uber Alles," *American Demographic*, October 2003, 38–42; and S. Rosenbloom and M. Barbaro, "Green Light Specials, Now at Walmart," *New York Times*, January 25, 2009, B1, B4.

45. Andy Kessler, "Sellout.com," *Wall Street Journal*, January 31, 2006, A14; D. Henninger, "Wonderland: Google in China," *Wall Street Journal*, March 10, 2006, p. A18; J. Dean, "Limited Search: As Google Pushes into China it Faces Clashes with Censors," *Wall Street Journal*, December 16, 2005, p. A1; and Anonymous, "The party, the people, and the power of cyber talk: China and the Internet," *The Economist*, April 29, 2006, 28–30.

IDENTIFYING OPPORTUNITIES AND THREATS THROUGH EXTERNAL ANALYSIS

3

CHAPTER OUTLINE

Analyzing Industry Structure

Risk of Entry by Potential
Competitors
Rivalry Among Established
Companies
The Bargaining Power
of Buyers
The Bargaining Power
of Suppliers
Substitute Products
Porter's Model Summarized

Strategic Groups within Industries

Implications of Strategic Groups
The Role of Mobility Barriers

Industry Life Cycle Analysis

Embryonic Industries
Growth Industries
Industry Shakeout
Mature Industries
Declining Industries
Summary

The Macroenvironment

Macroeconomic Forces
Global Forces
Technological Forces
Demographic Forces
Social Forces
Political and Legal Forces

LEARNING OBJECTIVES

After reading this chapter you should be able to:

- Review the main technique used to analyze competition in an industry environment, the five forces model.
- Explore the concept of strategic groups and illustrate its implications for industry analysis.

- Discuss how industries evolve over time, with reference to the industry life cycle model.
- Show how trends in the macroenvironment can shape the nature of competition in an industry.

OVERVIEW

The starting point of strategy formulation is an analysis of the forces that shape competition in the industry in which a company is based. The goal of such an analysis is to gain an understanding of the opportunities and threats confronting the firm and to use this understanding to identify strategies that will enable the company to outperform its rivals. **Opportunities** arise when a company can take advantage of conditions in its environment to formulate and implement strategies that enable it to become more profitable. **Threats** arise when conditions in the external environment endanger the integrity and profitability of the company's business.

This chapter begins with an analysis of the industry environment. First, it examines concepts and tools for analyzing the competitive structure of an industry and identifying industry opportunities and threats. Second, it analyzes the competitive implications that arise when groups of companies *within* an industry pursue similar and different kinds of competitive strategies. Third, it explores the way an industry evolves over time and the accompanying changes in competitive conditions. Fourth, it looks at the way in which forces in the macroenvironment affect industry structure and influence opportunities and threats. By the end of the chapter, you will understand that to succeed, a company must either fit its strategy to the external environment in which it operates or must be able to reshape the environment to its advantage through its chosen strategy.

Analyzing Industry Structure

An **industry** can be defined as a group of companies offering products or services that are close substitutes for each other, that is, products or services that satisfy the same basic customer needs. A company's closest **competitors**, its rivals, are those that serve the same basic customer needs. For example, carbonated drinks, fruit punches, and bottled water can be viewed as close substitutes for each other because they serve the same basic customer needs for refreshing and cold nonalcoholic beverages. Thus, we can talk about the soft drink industry, whose major players are Coca-Cola, PepsiCo, and Cadbury Schweppes. Similarly, desktop computers and notebook computers satisfy the same basic need that customers have for computer hardware on which to run personal productivity software; browse the Internet; send e-mail; play games; and store, display, and manipulate digital images. Thus, we can talk about the personal computer industry, whose major players are Dell, HP, Lenovo (the Chinese company that purchased IBM's personal computer business), and Apple Computer.

The starting point of external analysis is to identify the industry that a company competes in. To do this, managers must begin by looking at the basic customer needs their company is serving—that is, they must take a customer-oriented view of their business as opposed to a product-oriented view (see Chapter 2). *The basic customer needs that are served by a market define an industry's boundary.* It is important for managers to realize this, for if they define industry boundaries incorrectly, they may be caught flat-footed by the rise of competitors that serve the same basic customer needs with different product offerings. For example, Coca-Cola long saw itself as being in the *carbonated* soft drink industry, whereas in fact it was in the soft drink industry, which includes noncarbonated soft drinks. In the mid-1990s, Coca-Cola was caught by surprise by the rise of customer demand for bottled water and fruit

Opportunities

Opportunities arise when a company can take advantage of conditions in its environment to formulate and implement strategies that enable it to become more profitable.

Threats

Threats arise when conditions in the external environment endanger the integrity and profitability of the company's business.

Industry

A group of companies offering products or services that are close substitutes for each other—that is, products or services that satisfy the same basic customer needs.

Competitors

Enterprises that serve the same basic customer needs.

Figure 3.1 Porter's Five Forces Model

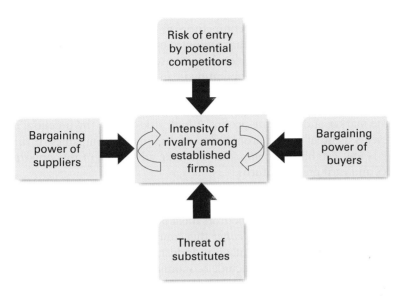

drinks, which began to cut into the demand for sodas. Coca-Cola moved quickly to respond to these threats, introducing its own brand of water, Dasani, and acquiring orange juice maker Minute Maid. By defining its industry boundaries too narrowly, Coca-Cola almost missed the rapid rise of the noncarbonated soft drinks segment of the soft drinks market.

Once the boundaries of an industry have been identified, the task facing managers is to analyze competitive forces in the industry environment to identify opportunities and threats. Michael E. Porter's well-known framework, known as the five forces model, helps managers with this analysis.[1] His model, shown in Figure 3.1, focuses on five forces that shape competition within an industry: (1) the risk of entry by potential competitors, (2) the intensity of rivalry among established companies within an industry, (3) the bargaining power of buyers, (4) the bargaining power of suppliers, and (5) the closeness of substitutes to an industry's products.

Porter argues that the stronger each of these forces, the more limited the ability of established companies to raise prices and earn greater profits. Within Porter's framework, a *strong* competitive force can be regarded as a *threat* because it depresses profits. A *weak* competitive force can be viewed as an *opportunity* because it allows a company to earn greater profits. The strength of the five forces may change through time as industry conditions change. The task facing managers is to recognize how changes in the five forces give rise to new opportunities and threats and to formulate appropriate strategic responses. In addition, it is possible for a company, *through its choice of strategy*, to alter the strength of one or more of the five forces to its advantage.

Risk of Entry by Potential Competitors

Potential competitors are companies that are not currently competing in an industry but have the capability to do so if they choose. For example, cable TV companies have recently emerged as potential competitors to traditional phone companies. This is because new digital technologies have allowed cable companies to offer consumers telephone service over the same cables that are used to transmit TV shows.

Established companies already operating in an industry often attempt to discourage potential competitors from entering the industry because the more companies that enter, the more difficult it becomes for established companies to protect their share of the market and generate profits. A high risk of entry by potential competitors represents a threat to the profitability of established companies. If the risk of new entry is low, established companies can take advantage of this opportunity to raise prices and earn greater returns.

The risk of entry by potential competitors is a function of the height of **barriers to entry**, that is, factors that make it costly for companies to enter an industry. The greater the costs that potential competitors must bear to enter an industry, the greater are the barriers to entry and the *weaker* this competitive force. High entry barriers may keep potential competitors out of an industry even when industry profits are high. Important barriers to entry include economies of scale, brand loyalty, absolute cost advantages, strategic preemption, customer switching costs, and government regulation.[2] It should be noted that a significant aspect of strategy is about building barriers to entry (in the case of incumbent firms), or finding ways to circumvent those barriers (in the case of new entrants). We shall discuss this in more detail in subsequent chapters.

Economies of Scale   Economies of scale arise when unit costs fall as a firm expands its output. Sources of scale economies include (1) cost reductions gained through mass-producing a standardized output, (2) discounts on bulk purchases of raw material inputs and component parts, (3) the advantages gained by spreading fixed production costs over a large production volume, and (4) the cost savings associated with spreading marketing and advertising costs over a large volume of output. If the cost advantages from economies of scale are significant, a new company that enters the industry and produces on a small scale suffers a significant cost disadvantage relative to established companies. If the new company decides to enter on a large scale in an attempt to obtain these economies of scale, it has to raise the capital required to build large scale production facilities and bear the high risks associated with such an investment. A further risk of large-scale entry is that the increased supply of products will depress prices and result in vigorous retaliation by established companies. For these reasons, the threat of entry is reduced when established companies have economies of scale.

Brand Loyalty   Brand loyalty exists when consumers have a preference for the products of established companies. A company can create brand loyalty through continuous advertising of its brand-name products and company name, patent protection of products, product innovation achieved through company research and development programs, an emphasis on high product quality, and good after-sales service. Significant brand loyalty makes it difficult for new entrants to take market share away from established companies. Thus, it reduces the threat of entry by potential competitors since they may see the task of breaking down well-established

Potential Competitors

Companies that are not currently competing in an industry but have the capability to do so if they choose.

Barriers to Entry

Factors that make it costly for companies to enter an industry.

Economies of Scale

Reductions in unit costs attributed to a larger output.

Brand Loyalty

Preference of consumers for the products of established companies.

3.1 STRATEGY IN ACTION

Circumventing Entry Barriers into the Soft Drink Industry

The soft drink industry has long been dominated by two companies, Coca-Cola and PepsiCo. Both companies have historically spent large sums of money on advertising and promotion, which has created significant brand loyalty and made it very difficult for prospective new competitors to enter the industry and take market share away from these two giants. When new competitors do try and enter, both companies have shown themselves capable of responding by cutting prices, forcing the new entrant to curtail expansion plans.

However, in the early 1990s, the Cott Corporation, then a small Canadian bottling company, worked out a strategy for entering the soft drink market. Cott's strategy was deceptively simple. The company initially focused on the cola segment of the soft drink market. Cott signed a deal with Royal Crown Cola for exclusive global rights to its cola concentrate. RC Cola was a small player in the U.S. cola market. Its products were recognized as having a high quality, but RC Cola had never been able to effectively challenge Coke or Pepsi. Next, Cott signed a deal with a Canadian grocery retailer, Loblaw's, to provide the retailer with its own private label brand of cola. Priced low, the Loblaw's private label brand, known as President's Choice, was very successful, taking share from both Coke and Pepsi.

Emboldened by this success, Cott decided to try and convince other retailers to carry private label cola. To retailers, the value proposition was simple—unlike its major rivals, Cott spent almost nothing on advertising and promotion. This constituted a major source of cost savings, which it passed onto retailers in the form of lower prices. For their part, the retailers found that they could significantly undercut the price of Coke and Pepsi colas, and still make better profit margins on private label brands than on branded colas.

Cott's breakthrough came in 1992 when it signed a deal with Walmart to supply the retailing giant with a private label cola, called "Sam's Choice." Walmart proved to be the perfect distribution channel for Cott. The retailer was just starting to get into the grocery business, and consumers went to the stores not to buy branded merchandise, but to get low prices.

As Walmart's grocery business grew, so did Cott's sales. Cott soon added other flavors to its offering, such as lemon lime soda that would compete with Seven Up and Sprite. Moreover, pressured by Walmart, by the late 1990s, other U.S. grocers also started to introduce private label sodas, often turning to Cott to supply their needs. By 2006, Cott had grown to become a $1.8 billion company. Its volume growth in an otherwise stagnant U.S. market for sodas has averaged around 12.5% between 2001 and 2006. Cott captured over 5% of the U.S. soda market in 2005, up from almost nothing a decade earlier, and held onto a 16% share of sodas in grocery stores, its core channel. The losers in this process have been Coca-Cola and PepsiCo, who are now facing the steady erosion of their brand loyalty and market share as consumers increasingly came to recognize the high quality and low price of private-label sodas.[3]

customer preferences as too costly. In the market for colas, for example, consumers have a strong preference for the products of Coca-Cola and PepsiCo which makes it difficult for other enterprises to enter this market (despite this, the Cott Corporation has succeeded in entering the soft drink market—see the Strategy in Action).

Absolute Cost Advantages   Sometimes established companies have an absolute cost advantage relative to potential entrants, meaning that entrants cannot expect to match the established companies' lower cost structure. Absolute cost advantages arise from three main sources (1) superior production operations and processes due to accumulated experience in an industry, patents, or secret processes; (2) control of particular inputs required for production, such as labor, materials, equipment, or management skills, that are limited in their supply; and (3) access to cheaper funds because existing companies represent lower risks than new entrants, and therefore

Absolute Cost Advantage

A cost advantage that is enjoyed by incumbents in an industry and that new entrants cannot expect to match.

face a lower cost of capital.[4] If established companies have an absolute cost advantage, the threat of entry as a competitive force is weaker.

Customer Switching Costs   Switching costs arise when it costs a customer time, energy, and money to switch from the products offered by one established company to the products offered by a new entrant. When switching costs are high, customers can be *locked in* to the product offerings of established companies, even if new entrants offer better products.[5] A familiar example of switching costs concerns the costs associated with switching from one computer operating system to another. If a person currently uses Microsoft's Windows operating system and has a library of related software applications (e.g., word processing software, spreadsheet, games) and document files, it is expensive for that person to switch to another computer operating system. To effect the change, this person would have to buy a new set of software applications and convert all existing document files to run with the new system. Faced with such an expense of money and time, most people are unwilling to make the switch *unless* the competing operating system offers a *substantial* leap forward in performance. Thus, the higher the switching costs are, the higher is the barrier to entry for a company attempting to promote a new computer operating system.

Government Regulation   Historically, government regulation has constituted a major entry barrier into many industries. For example, until the mid-1990s, U.S. government regulation prohibited providers of long-distance telephone service from competing for local telephone service and vice versa. Other potential providers of telephone service, including cable television service companies such as Time Warner and Comcast (which could in theory use their cables to carry telephone traffic as well as TV signals), were prohibited from entering the market altogether. These regulatory barriers to entry significantly reduced the level of competition in both the local and long-distance telephone markets, enabling telephone companies to earn higher profits than might otherwise have been the case. All this changed in 1996 when the government deregulated the industry significantly. In the months that followed this announcement, local, long-distance, and cable TV companies all announced their intention to enter each other's markets, and a host of new players entered the market. The five forces model predicts that falling entry barrier due to government deregulation would result in significant new entry, an increase in the intensity of industry competition, and lower industry profit rates. And, indeed, that is what occurred.

In summary, if established companies have built brand loyalty for their products, have an absolute cost advantage with respect to potential competitors, have significant economies of scale, are the beneficiaries of high switching costs, or enjoy regulatory protection, the risk of entry by potential competitors is greatly diminished; it is a weak competitive force. Consequently, established companies can charge higher prices, and industry profits are higher. Evidence from academic research suggests that the height of barriers to entry is one of the most important determinants of profit rates in an industry.[6] Clearly, it is in the interest of established companies to pursue strategies consistent with raising entry barriers to secure these profits. By the same token, potential new entrants have to find strategies that allow them to circumvent barriers to entry. Research suggests that the best way to do this is *not* to compete head-to-head with incumbents, but to look for customers who are poorly served by incumbents, and to go after those customers using new distribution channels and new business models.[7]

Switching Costs

Costs that consumers must bear to switch from the products offered by one established company to the products offered by a new entrant.

Rivalry among Established Companies

The second of Porter's five competitive forces is the intensity of rivalry among established companies within an industry. **Rivalry** refers to the competitive struggle between companies in an industry to gain market share from each other. The competitive struggle can be fought using price, product design, advertising and promotion spending, direct selling efforts, and after-sales service and support. More intense rivalry implies lower prices or more spending on non–price-competitive weapons, or both. Because intense rivalry lowers prices and raises costs, it squeezes profits out of an industry. Thus, intense rivalry among established companies constitutes a strong threat to profitability. Alternatively, if rivalry is less intense, companies may have the opportunity to raise prices or reduce spending on non–price-competitive weapons, which leads to a higher level of industry profits. The intensity of rivalry among established companies within an industry is largely a function of four factors: (1) industry competitive structure, (2) demand conditions, (3) cost conditions, and (4) the height of exit barriers in the industry.

Industry Competitive Structure   The *competitive structure* of an industry refers to the number and size distribution of companies in it, something that strategic managers determine at the beginning of an industry analysis. Industry structures vary, and different structures have different implications for the intensity of rivalry. A **fragmented industry** consists of a large number of small- or medium-sized companies, none of which is in a position to determine industry price. A **consolidated industry** is dominated by a small number of large companies (an oligopoly), or in extreme cases, by just one company (a monopoly) in which companies often are in a position to determine industry prices. Examples of fragmented industries are agriculture, dry cleaning, video rental, health clubs, real estate brokerage, and sun tanning parlors. Consolidated industries include the aerospace, soft drink, automobile, pharmaceutical, and stockbrokerage industries.

Many fragmented industries are characterized by low entry barriers and commodity-type products that are hard to differentiate. The combination of these traits tends to result in boom-and-bust cycles as industry profits rise and fall. Low entry barriers imply that whenever demand is strong and profits are high, new entrants will flood the market, hoping to profit from the boom. The explosion in the number of video stores, health clubs, and tanning parlors during the 1980s and 1990s exemplifies this situation.

Often the flood of new entrants into a booming fragmented industry creates excess capacity, so companies start to cut prices in order to use their spare capacity. The difficulty companies face when trying to differentiate their products from those of competitors can exacerbate this tendency. The result is a price war, which depresses industry profits, forces some companies out of business, and deters potential new entrants. For example, after a decade of expansion and booming profits, many health clubs are now finding that they have to offer large discounts in order to hold onto their membership. In general, the more commodity-like an industry's product is, the more vicious will be the price war. This bust part of the cycle continues until overall industry capacity is brought into line with demand (through bankruptcies), at which point prices may stabilize again.

A fragmented industry structure, then, constitutes a threat rather than an opportunity. Most booms are relatively short-lived because of the ease of new entry and will be followed by price wars and bankruptcies. Because it is often difficult to

Rivalry

The competitive struggle between companies in an industry to gain market share from each other.

Fragmented Industry

An industry that consists of a large number of small- or medium-sized companies, none of which is in a position to determine industry prices.

Consolidated Industry

An industry dominated by a small number of large companies or, in extreme cases, by just one company, which are in a position to determine industry prices.

differentiate products in these industries, the best strategy for a company is to try to minimize its costs so it will be profitable in a boom and survive any subsequent bust. Alternatively, companies might try to adopt strategies that change the underlying structure of fragmented industries and lead to a consolidated industry structure in which the level of industry profitability is increased. How companies can do this is something we shall consider in later chapters.

In consolidated industries, companies are interdependent, because one company's competitive actions or moves (with regard to price, quality, and so on) directly affect the market share of its rivals, and thus their profitability. When one company makes a move, this generally "forces" a response from its rivals, and the consequence of such competitive interdependence can be a dangerous competitive spiral. Rivalry increases as companies attempt to undercut each other's prices or offer customers more value in their products, pushing industry profits down in the process. The fare wars that have periodically created havoc in the airline industry provide a good illustration of this process.

Companies in consolidated industries sometimes seek to reduce this threat by following the prices set by the dominant company in the industry.[8] However, companies must be careful, for explicit face-to-face price-fixing agreements are illegal. (Tacit, indirect agreements, arrived at without direct or intentional communication, are legal). Instead, companies set prices by watching, interpreting, anticipating, and responding to each other's behavior.

Industry Demand   The level of industry demand is a second determinant of the intensity of rivalry among established companies. Growing demand from new customers or additional purchases by existing customers tend to moderate competition by providing greater scope for companies to compete for customers. Growing demand tends to reduce rivalry because all companies can sell more without taking market share away from other companies. High industry profits are often the result. Conversely, declining demand results in more rivalry as companies fight to maintain market share and revenues. Demand declines when customers are leaving the marketplace or each customer is buying less. Now a company can grow only by taking market share away from other companies. Thus, declining demand constitutes a major threat for it increases the extent of rivalry between established companies.

Cost Conditions   The cost structure of firms in an industry is a third determinant of rivalry. In industries where fixed costs are high, profitability tends to be highly leveraged to sales volume, and the desire to grow volume can spark off intense rivalry. Fixed costs refer to the costs that must be born before the firm makes a single sale. For example, before they can offer service, cable TV companies have to lay cable in the ground—the costs of doing so is a fixed cost. Similarly, in order to offer air express service a company like FedEx has to invest in planes, package sorting facilities, and delivery trucks. These all represent fixed costs that require significant capital investments. In industries where the fixed costs of production are high, if sales volume is low firms cannot cover their fixed costs and they will not be profitable. This creates an incentive for firms to cut their prices and/or increase promotion spending in order to drive up sales volume, thereby covering fixed costs. In situations where demand is not growing fast enough and too many companies are engaged in the same actions, cutting prices and/or raising promotion spending in an attempt to cover fixed costs, the result can be intense rivalry and lower profits. Research suggests that often the weakest firms in an industry initiate such actions precisely because they are the ones struggling to cover their fixed costs.[9]

Fixed Costs

Costs that must be borne before the firm makes a single sale.

Exit Barriers Exit barriers are economic, strategic, and emotional factors that prevent companies from leaving an industry.[10] If exit barriers are high, companies become locked into an unprofitable industry where overall demand is static or declining. The result is often excess productive capacity, which leads to even more intense rivalry and price competition as companies cut prices in the attempt to obtain the customer orders needed to use their idle capacity and cover their fixed costs.[11] Common exit barriers include the following:

- Investments in assets such as specific machines, equipment, and operating facilities that are of little or no value in alternative uses or cannot be sold off. If a company wishes to leave the industry, it has to write off the book value of these assets.
- High fixed costs of exit, such as the severance pay, health benefits, and pensions that have to be paid to workers who are being made redundant when a company ceases to operate.
- Emotional attachments to an industry, as when a company's owners or employees are unwilling to exit from an industry for sentimental reasons or because of pride.
- Economic dependence on an industry because a company relies on a single industry for its revenue and profit.
- The need to maintain an expensive collection of assets at or above some minimum level in order to participate effectively in the industry.
- Bankruptcy regulations, particularly in the United States, where Chapter 11 bankruptcy provisions allow insolvent enterprises to continue operating and reorganize themselves under bankruptcy protection. These regulations can keep unprofitable assets in the industry, result in persistent excess capacity, and lengthen the time required to bring industry supply in line with demand.

As an example of the effect of exit barriers in practice, consider the express mail and parcel delivery industry. The key players in this industry such as FedEx and UPS rely on the delivery business entirely for their revenues and profits. They have to be able to guarantee their customers that they will deliver packages to all major localities in the United States, and much of their investment is specific to this purpose. To meet this guarantee, they need a nationwide network of air routes and ground routes, an asset that is required in order to participate in the industry. If excess capacity develops in this industry, as it does from time to time, FedEx cannot incrementally reduce or minimize its excess capacity by deciding not to fly to and deliver packages in, say, Miami because that proportion of its network is underused. If it did that, it would no longer be able to guarantee that it would be able to deliver packages to all major locations in the United States, and its customers would switch to some other carrier. Thus, the need to maintain a nationwide network is an exit barrier that can result in persistent excess capacity in the air express industry during periods of weak demand. Finally, both UPS and FedEx managers and employees are emotionally tied to this industry because they both were first movers in the ground and air segments of the industry, respectively; their employees are also major owners of their companies' stock; and, they are financially dependent on the fortunes of the delivery business.

The Bargaining Power of Buyers

The third of Porter's five competitive forces is the bargaining power of buyers. An industry's buyers may be the individual customers who ultimately consume its products (its end users) or the companies that distribute an industry's products to end

Exit Barriers

The economic, strategic, and emotional factors that prevent companies from leaving an industry.

users, such as retailers and wholesalers. For example, while soap powder made by Procter & Gamble and Unilever is consumed by end users, the principal buyers of soap powder are supermarket chains and discount stores, which resell the product to end users. The **bargaining power of buyers** refers to the ability of buyers to bargain down prices charged by companies in the industry or to raise the costs of companies in the industry by demanding better product quality and service. By lowering prices and raising costs, powerful buyers can squeeze profits out of an industry. Thus, powerful buyers should be viewed as a threat. Alternatively, when buyers are in a weak bargaining position, companies in an industry can raise prices, and perhaps reduce their costs by lowering product quality and service, and increase the level of industry profits. Buyers are most powerful in the following circumstances:

- When the industry that is supplying a particular product or service is composed of many small companies and the buyers are large and few in number. These circumstances allow the buyers to dominate supplying companies.
- When the buyers purchase in large quantities. In such circumstances, buyers can use their purchasing power as leverage to bargain for price reductions.
- When the supply industry depends on the buyers for a large percentage of its total orders.
- When switching costs are low so that buyers can play off the supplying companies against each other to force down prices.
- When it is economically feasible for buyers to purchase an input from several companies at once so that buyers can play off one company in the industry against another.
- When buyers can threaten to enter the industry and produce the product themselves and thus supply their own needs, also a tactic for forcing down industry prices.

The auto component supply industry, whose buyers are large automobile manufacturers such as GM, Ford, and Toyota, has historically been a good example of an industry in which buyers have had a strong bargaining power and thus constituted a strong competitive threat. Why? The suppliers of auto component are numerous and typically small in scale; their buyers, the auto manufacturers, are large in size and few in number. Additionally, to keep component prices down, both Ford and GM have used the threat of manufacturing a component themselves rather than buying it from auto component suppliers. The automakers have used their powerful position to play off suppliers against each other, forcing down the price they have to pay for component parts and demanding better quality. If a component supplier objects, the automaker can use the threat of switching to another supplier as a bargaining tool.

Another issue is that the relative power of buyers and suppliers tends to change in response to changing industry conditions. For example, because of changes now taking place in the pharmaceutical and health care industries, major buyers of pharmaceuticals (hospitals and health maintenance organizations) are gaining power over the suppliers of pharmaceuticals and have been able to demand lower prices.

The Bargaining Power of Suppliers

The fourth of Porter's five competitive forces is the bargaining power of suppliers—the organizations that provide inputs into the industry, such as materials, services, and labor (which may be individuals, organizations such as labor unions, or companies

Bargaining Power of Buyers

The ability of buyers to bargain down prices charged by companies in the industry or to raise the costs of companies in the industry by demanding better product quality and service.

that supply contract labor). The **bargaining power of suppliers** refers to the ability of suppliers to raise input prices, or to raise the costs of the industry in other ways—for example, by providing poor-quality inputs or poor service. Powerful suppliers squeeze profits out of an industry by raising the costs of companies in the industry. Thus, powerful suppliers are a threat. Alternatively, if suppliers are weak, companies in the industry have the opportunity to force down input prices and demand higher-quality inputs (e.g., more productive labor). As with buyers, the ability of suppliers to make demands on a company depends on their power relative to that of the company. Suppliers are most powerful in the following situations:

- The product that suppliers sell has few substitutes and is vital to the companies in an industry.
- The profitability of suppliers is not significantly affected by the purchases of companies in a particular industry, in other words, when the industry is not an important customer to the suppliers.
- Companies in an industry would experience significant switching costs if they moved to the product of a different supplier because a particular supplier's products are unique or different. In such cases, the company depends on a particular supplier and cannot play suppliers off against each other to reduce price.
- Suppliers can threaten to enter their customers' industry and use their inputs to produce products that would compete directly with those of companies already in the industry.
- Companies in the industry cannot threaten to enter their suppliers' industry and make their own inputs as a tactic for lowering the price of inputs.

An example of an industry in which companies are dependent on a powerful supplier is the personal computer industry. Personal computer firms are heavily dependent on Intel, the world's largest supplier of microprocessors for PCs. The industry standard for personal computers runs on Intel's microprocessor chips. Intel's competitors, such as Advanced Micro Devices (AMD), must develop and supply chips that are compatible with Intel's standard. Although AMD has developed competing chips, Intel still supplies about 85% of the chips used in PCs primarily because only Intel has the manufacturing capacity required to serve a large share of the market. It is beyond the financial resources of Intel's competitors, such as AMD, to match the scale and efficiency of Intel's manufacturing systems. This means that while PC manufacturers can buy some microprocessors from Intel's rivals, most notably AMD, they still have to turn to Intel for the bulk of their supply. Because Intel is in a powerful bargaining position, it can charge higher prices for its microprocessors than would be the case if its competitors were more numerous and stronger (i.e., if the microprocessor industry were fragmented).

Bargaining Power of Suppliers

The ability of suppliers to raise the price of inputs or to raise the costs of the industry in other ways.

Substitute Products

The final force in Porter's model is the threat of **substitute products**: the products of different businesses or industries that can satisfy similar customer needs. For example, companies in the coffee industry compete indirectly with those in the tea and soft drink industries because all three serve customer needs for nonalcoholic drinks. The existence of close substitutes is a strong competitive threat because this limits the price that companies in one industry can charge for their product, and thus industry profitability. If the price of coffee rises too much relative to that of tea or soft drinks, coffee drinkers may switch to those substitutes.

Substitute Products

The products of different businesses or industries that can satisfy similar customer needs.

Ethical Dilemma

You are a strategic analyst at a successful hotel enterprise that has been generating substantial excess cash flow. Your CEO instructed you to analyze the competitive structure of closely related industries to find one that the company could enter, using its cash reserve to build a sustainable position. Your analysis, using Porter's five forces model, suggests that the highest profit opportunities are to be found in the gambling industry. You realize that it might be possible to add casinos to existing hotels, lowering entry costs into this industry. However, you personally have strong moral objections to gambling. Should your own personal beliefs influence your recommendations to the CEO?

If an industry's products have few close substitutes, so that substitutes are a weak competitive force, then, other things being equal, companies in the industry have the opportunity to raise prices and earn additional profits. For example, there is no close substitute for microprocessors, which gives companies like Intel and AMD the ability to charge higher.

Porter's Model Summarized

The systematic analysis of forces in the industry environment using the Porter framework is a powerful tool that helps managers to think strategically. It is important to recognize that one competitive force often affects the others, so that all forces need to be considered and thought about when performing industry analysis. Indeed, industry analysis leads managers to think systematically about the way their strategic choices will both be affected by the forces of industry competition and how their choices will affect the five forces and change conditions in the industry. For an example of industry analysis using Porter's framework, see the Running Case.

STRATEGIC GROUPS WITHIN INDUSTRIES

Companies in an industry often differ significantly from each other with respect to the way they strategically position their products in the market in terms of such factors as the distribution channels they use, the market segments they serve, the quality of their products, technological leadership, customer service, pricing policy, advertising policy, and promotions. As a result of these differences, within most industries, it is possible to observe groups of companies in which each company follows a strategy that is similar to that pursued by other companies in the group, but *different* from the strategies followed by companies in other groups. These different groups of companies are known as **strategic groups**.[12]

Strategic Groups

Groups of companies in which each company follows a strategy that is similar to that pursued by other companies in the group, but different from the strategies followed by companies in other groups.

Normally, the basic differences between the strategies that companies in different strategic groups use can be captured by a relatively small number of strategic factors. For example, in the pharmaceutical industry, two main strategic groups stand out (see Figure 3.2).[13] One group, which includes such companies as Merck, Eli Lilly, and Pfizer, is characterized by a business model based on heavy R&D spending and a focus on developing new, proprietary, blockbuster drugs. The companies in this *proprietary* strategic group are pursuing a high-risk, high-return strategy. It is a high-risk strategy because basic drug research is difficult and expensive. Bringing a new drug to market can cost up to $800 million in R&D money and a decade of research and clinical trials. The risks are high because the failure rate in new drug development is very high: only one out of every five drugs entering clinical trials is ultimately approved by the U.S. Food and Drug Administration. However, the strategy is also a high-return one because a single successful drug can be patented, giving the innovator a 20-year monopoly on its production and sale. This lets these proprietary companies charge a high price for the patented drug, allowing them to earn millions, if not billions, of dollars over the lifetime of the patent.

The second strategic group might be characterized as the *generic drug* strategic group. This group of companies, which includes Forest Labs, Mylan Labs and Watson Pharmaceuticals focuses on the manufacture of generic drugs: low-cost

RUNNING CASE

Walmart's Bargaining Power over Suppliers

When Walmart and other discount retailers began in the 1960s, they were small operations with little purchasing power. To generate store traffic, they depended in large part on stocking nationally branded merchandise from well-known companies such as Procter & Gamble and Rubbermaid. Since the discounters did not have high sales volume, the nationally branded companies set the price. This meant that the discounters had to look for other ways to cut costs, which they typically did by emphasizing self-service in stripped-down stores located in the suburbs where land was cheaper (in the 1960s, the main competitors for discounters were full-service department stores such as Sears that were often located in downtown shopping areas).

Discounters such as Kmart purchased their merchandise through wholesalers, who in turned bought from manufacturers. The wholesaler would come into a store and write an order, and when the merchandise arrived, the wholesaler would come in and stock the shelves, saving the retailer labor costs. However, Walmart was located in Arkansas and placed its stores in small towns. Wholesalers were not particularly interested in serving a company that built its stores in such out-of-the-way places. They would do it only if Walmart paid higher prices.

Walmart's Sam Walton refused to pay higher prices. Instead he took his fledgling company public and used the capital raised to build a distribution center to stock merchandise. The distribution center would serve all stores within a 300-mile radius, with trucks leaving the distribution center daily to restock the stores. Because the distribution center was serving a collection of stores and thus buying in larger volumes, Walton found that he was able to cut the wholesalers out of the equation and order directly from manufacturers. The cost savings generated by not having to pay profits to wholesalers were then passed on to consumers in the form of lower prices, which helped Walmart continue growing. This growth increased its buying power and thus its ability to demand deeper discounts from manufacturers.

Today Walmart has turned its buying process into an art form. Since 8% of all retail sales in the United States are made in a Walmart store, the company has enormous bargaining power over its suppliers. Suppliers of nationally branded products, such as Procter & Gamble, are no longer in a position to demand high prices. Instead, Walmart is now so important to Procter & Gamble that it is able to demand deep discounts from them. Moreover, Walmart has itself become a brand that is more powerful than the brands of manufacturers. People do not go to Walmart to buy branded goods; they go to Walmart for the low prices. This simple fact has enabled Walmart to bargain down the prices it pays, always passing on cost savings to consumers in the form of lower prices.

Since the early 1990s, Walmart has provided suppliers with real-time information on store sales through the use of individual Stock Keeping Units (SKUs). These have allowed suppliers to optimize their own production processes, matching output to Walmart's demands and avoiding under- or overproduction and the need to store inventory. The efficiencies that manufacturers gain from such information are passed on to Walmart in the form of lower prices, which then passes on those cost savings to consumers.[14]

copies of drugs that were developed by companies in the proprietary group whose patents have now expired. Low R&D spending, production efficiency, and an emphasis on low prices characterize the business models of companies in this strategic group. They are pursuing a low-risk, low-return strategy. It is low risk because they are not investing millions of dollars in R&D. It is low return because they cannot charge high prices.

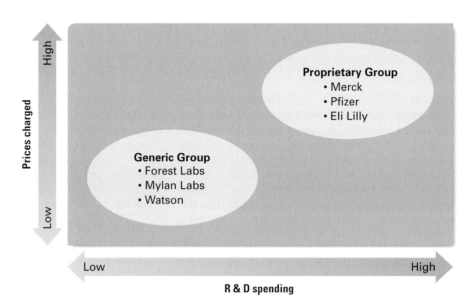

Figure 3.2   Strategic Groups in the Pharmaceutical Industry

Implications of Strategic Groups

The concept of strategic groups has a number of implications for the identification of opportunities and threats within an industry. First, because all the companies in a strategic group are pursuing similar business models, customers tend to view the products of such enterprises as *direct substitutes* for each other. Thus, a company's *closest* competitors are those in its strategic group, not those in other strategic groups in the industry. The most immediate threat to a company's profitability comes from rivals within its own strategic group. For example, in the retail industry, there is a group of companies that might be characterized as discounters. Included in this group are Walmart, Kmart, Target, Costco and Fred Meyer. These companies compete most vigorously with each other, as opposed to with other retailers in different groups, such as Nordstrom or The Gap. Kmart, for example, was driven into bankruptcy in the early 2000s, not because Nordstrom or The Gap took business from it, but because Walmart and Target gained share in the discounting group by virtue of their superior strategic execution of the discounting business model.

A second competitive implication is that different strategic groups can have a different standing with respect to each of the competitive forces; thus, *each strategic group may face a different set of opportunities and threats.* The risk of new entry by potential competitors, the degree of rivalry among companies within a group, the bargaining power of buyers, the bargaining power of suppliers, and the competitive force of substitute and complementary products can each be a relatively strong or weak competitive force depending on the competitive positioning approach adopted by each strategic group in the industry. For example, in the pharmaceutical industry, companies in the proprietary group have historically been in a very powerful position in relation to buyers because their products are patented and there are no substitutes. Also, rivalry based on price competition within this group has been low because competition in the industry revolves around being the first to patent a new drug (so-called patent races), not around drug prices. Thus, companies in this group have been able to charge high prices and earn high profits. In contrast, companies in the generic group have been in much weaker positions because many companies are able to produce different versions of the same generic drug after patents expire. In the strategic group, products are close substitutes, rivalry has been high, and price competition has led to lower profits for this group as compared to companies in the proprietary group.

The Role of Mobility Barriers

It follows from these two issues that some strategic groups are more desirable than others because competitive five forces open up greater opportunities and present fewer threats for those groups. Managers, after analyzing their industry, might identify a strategic group where competitive forces are weaker and higher profits can be made. Sensing an opportunity, they might contemplate changing their business models and move to compete in that strategic group. However, taking advantage of this opportunity may be difficult because of mobility barriers between strategic groups.

Mobility barriers are within-industry factors that inhibit the movement of companies between strategic groups. They include the barriers to entry into a group and the barriers to exit from a company's existing group. For example, Forest Labs would encounter mobility barriers if it attempted to enter the proprietary group in the pharmaceutical industry because it lacks R&D skills, and building these skills would be an expensive proposition. Over time, companies in different groups develop different cost structures and skills and competencies that give them different pricing options and choices. A company contemplating entry into another strategic group must evaluate whether it has the ability to imitate, and indeed outperform, its potential competitors in that strategic group. Managers must determine if it is cost-effective to overcome mobility barriers before deciding whether the move is worthwhile.

In summary, an important task of industry analysis is to determine the sources of the similarities and differences among companies in an industry and to work out the broad themes that underlie competition in an industry. This analysis often reveals new opportunities to compete in an industry by developing new kinds of products to meet the needs of customers better. It can also reveal emerging threats that can be countered effectively by changing competitive strategy.

INDUSTRY LIFE CYCLE ANALYSIS

An important determinant of the strength of the competitive forces in an industry is the changes that take place in it over time. The strength and nature of each of the competitive forces change as an industry evolves, particularly the two forces of risk of entry by potential competitors and rivalry among existing firms.[15]

A useful tool for analyzing the effects of industry evolution on competitive forces is the industry life cycle model, which identifies five sequential stages in the evolution of an industry that lead to five distinct kinds of industry environment: embryonic, growth, shakeout, mature, and decline (see Figure 3.3). The task facing managers is to *anticipate* how the strength of competitive forces will change as the industry environment evolves and to formulate strategies that take advantage of opportunities as they arise and that counter emerging threats.

Mobility Barriers

Within-industry factors that inhibit the movement of companies between strategic groups.

....

Figure 3.3   Stages in the Industry Life Cycle

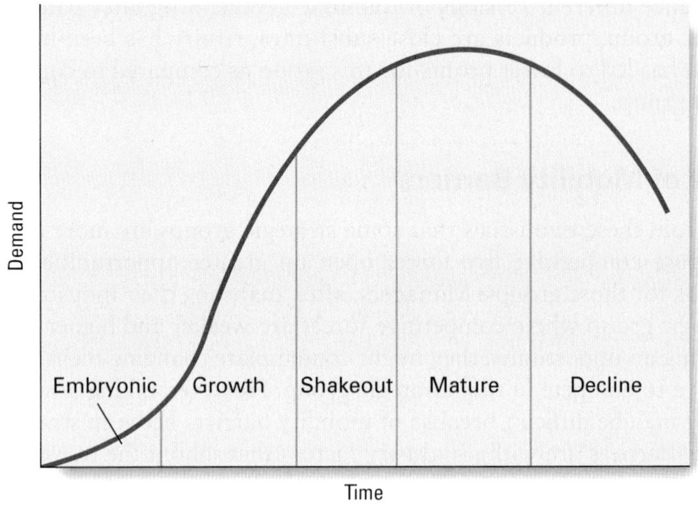

Embryonic Industries

An **embryonic industry** is just beginning to develop (e.g., personal computers and biotechnology in the 1970s, and nanotechnology today). Growth at this stage is slow because of buyers' unfamiliarity with the industry's product, high prices due to the inability of companies to reap any significant scale economies, and poorly developed distribution channels. Barriers to entry tend to be based on access to key technological know-how rather than cost economies or brand loyalty. If the core know-how required to compete in the industry is complex and difficult to grasp, barriers to entry can be quite high, and established companies will be protected from potential competitors. Rivalry in embryonic industries is based not so much on price as on educating customers, opening up distribution channels, and perfecting the design of the product. Such rivalry can be intense, and the company that is the first to solve design problems often has the opportunity to develop a significant market position. An embryonic industry may also be the creation of one company's innovative efforts, as happened with microprocessors (Intel) and photocopiers (Xerox). In such circumstances, the company has a major opportunity to capitalize on the lack of rivalry and build a strong hold on the market.

Growth Industries

Embryonic Industry

An industry that is just beginning to develop.

Growth Industry

An industry where demand is expanding as first-time consumers enter the market.

Once demand for the industry's product begins to take off, the industry develops the characteristics of a growth industry. In a **growth industry**, first-time demand is expanding rapidly as many new customers enter the market. An industry grows when customers become familiar with the product, prices fall because experience and scale economies have been attained, and distribution channels develop. The U.S. cellular telephone industry was in the growth stage for most of the 1990s. In 1990, there were only 5 million cellular subscribers in the nation. By 2006, this figure had increased to over 160 million, and overall demand was still expanding.

Normally, the importance of control over technological knowledge as a barrier to entry has diminished by the time an industry enters its growth stage. Because few companies have yet achieved significant scale economies or built brand loyalty, other entry barriers tend to be relatively low as well, particularly early in the growth stage. Thus, the threat from potential competitors generally is highest at this point. Paradoxically, however, high growth usually means that new entrants can be absorbed into an industry without a marked increase in the intensity of rivalry. Thus, rivalry tends to be relatively low. Rapid growth in demand enables companies to expand their revenues and profits without taking market share away from competitors. A strategically aware company takes advantage of the relatively benign environment of the growth stage to prepare itself for the intense competition of the coming industry shakeout.

Industry Shakeout

Explosive growth cannot be maintained indefinitely. Sooner or later, the rate of growth slows, and the industry enters the shakeout stage. In the shakeout stage, demand approaches saturation levels: most of the demand is limited to replacement because there are few potential first-time buyers left.

As an industry enters the shakeout stage, rivalry between companies becomes intense. Typically, companies that have become accustomed to rapid growth continue to add capacity at rates consistent with past growth. However, demand is no longer growing at historic rates, and the consequence is the emergence of excess productive capacity. This condition is illustrated in Figure 3.4, where the solid curve indicates the growth in demand over time and the broken curve indicates the growth in productive capacity over time. As you can see, past point t_1, demand growth becomes slower as the industry becomes mature. However, capacity continues to grow until time t_2. The gap between the solid and the broken lines signifies excess capacity. In an attempt to use this capacity, companies often cut prices. The result can be a price war, which drives many of the most inefficient companies into bankruptcy, which is enough to deter any new entry.

Figure 3.4 Growth in Demand and Capacity

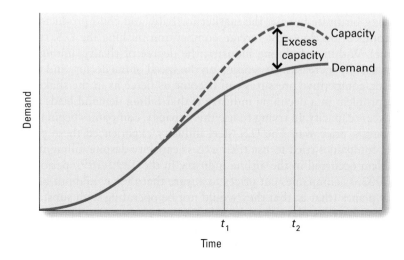

Mature Industries

The shakeout stage ends when the industry enters its **mature stage**: the market is totally saturated, demand is limited primarily to replacement demand, and growth is low or zero. What growth there is comes from population expansion that brings new customers into the market or an increase in replacement demand.

As an industry enters maturity, barriers to entry increase, and the threat of entry from potential competitors decreases. As growth slows during the shakeout, companies can no longer maintain historic growth rates merely by holding on to their market share. Competition for market share develops, driving down prices. Often the result is a price war, as has happened in the airline industry for example. To survive the shakeout, companies begin to focus on cost minimization and building brand loyalty. The airlines, for example, tried to cut operating costs by hiring nonunion labor and to build brand loyalty by introducing frequent-flyer programs. By the time an industry matures, the surviving companies are those that have brand loyalty and efficient low-cost operations. Because both these factors constitute a significant barrier to entry, the threat of entry by potential competitors is greatly diminished. High entry barriers in mature industries give companies the opportunity to increase prices and profits.

As a result of the shakeout, most industries in the maturity stage have consolidated and become oligopolies. In mature industries, companies tend to recognize their interdependence and try to avoid price wars. Stable demand gives them the opportunity to enter into price leadership agreements. The net effect is to reduce the threat of intense rivalry among established companies, thereby allowing greater profitability. Nevertheless, the stability of a mature industry is always threatened by further price wars. A general slump in economic activity can depress industry demand. As companies fight to maintain their revenues in the face of declining demand, price leadership agreements break down, rivalry increases, and prices and profits fall. The periodic price wars that occur in the airline industry seem to follow this pattern.

Declining Industries

Eventually, most industries enter a **decline stage**: growth becomes negative for a variety of reasons, including technological substitution (e.g., air travel for rail travel), social changes (greater health consciousness hitting tobacco sales), demographics (the declining birthrate hurting the market for baby and child products), and international competition (low-cost foreign competition pushing the U.S. steel industry into decline). Within a declining industry, the degree of rivalry among established companies usually increases. Depending on the speed of the decline and the height of exit barriers, competitive pressures can become as fierce as in the shakeout stage.[16] The main problem in a declining industry is that falling demand leads to the emergence of excess capacity. In trying to use this capacity, companies begin to cut prices, thus sparking a price war. The U.S. steel industry experienced these problems because steel companies tried to use their excess capacity despite falling demand. The same problem occurred in the airline industry in the 1990–1992 period and again in 2001–2002, as companies cut prices to ensure that they would not be flying with half-empty planes (that is, that they would not be operating with substantial excess capacity). Exit barriers play a part in adjusting excess capacity. The greater the exit barriers, the harder it is for companies to reduce capacity and the greater is the threat of severe price competition.

Mature Stage

The stage in which the market is saturated, demand is limited to replacement demand, and growth is slow.

Decline Stage

The stage in which primary demand is declining.

Summary

In summary, a third task of industry analysis is to identify the opportunities and threats that are characteristic of different kinds of industry environments in order to develop an effective business model and competitive strategy. Managers have to tailor their strategies to changing industry conditions. And they have to learn to recognize the crucial points in an industry's development so that they can forecast when the shakeout stage of an industry might begin or when an industry might be moving into decline. This is also true at the level of strategic groups, for new embryonic groups may emerge because of shifts in customer needs and tastes or some groups may grow rapidly because of changes in technology and others will decline as their customers defect. Thus, for example, companies in the upscale retail group such as Macy's, Dillard's, and Nordstrom are facing declining sales as customers defect to discount retailers like Target and Walmart and online companies like amazon.com and landsend.com.

THE MACROENVIRONMENT

Just as the decisions and actions of strategic managers can often change an industry's competitive structure, so too can changing conditions or forces in the wider **macroenvironment**, that is, the broader economic, global, technological, demographic, social, and political context in which companies and industries are embedded (see Figure 3.5). Changes in the forces in the macroenvironment can have a direct impact on any or all of the forces in Porter's model, thereby altering the relative strength of these forces and, with it, the attractiveness of an industry.

Macroeconomic Forces

Macroeconomic forces affect the general health and well-being of a nation or the regional economy of an organization, which in turn affect companies' and industries' ability to earn an adequate rate of return. Four most important factors in the macroeconomic are the growth rate of the economy, interest rates, currency exchange rates, and price inflation. Economic growth, because it leads to an expansion in customer expenditures, tends to produce a general easing of competitive pressures within an industry. This gives companies the opportunity to expand their operations and earn higher profits. Because economic decline (a recession) leads to a reduction in customer expenditures, it increases competitive pressures. Economic decline frequently causes price wars in mature industries.

The level of interest rates can determine the demand for a company's products. Interest rates are important whenever customers routinely borrow money to finance their purchase of these products. The most obvious example is the housing market, where mortgage rates directly affect demand. Interest rates also have an impact on the sale of autos, appliances, and capital equipment, to give just a few examples. For companies in such industries, rising interest rates are a threat and falling rates an opportunity.

Currency exchange rates define the value of different national currencies against each other. Movement in currency exchange rates has a direct impact on the competitiveness of a company's products in the global marketplace. For example, when

Macroenvironment

The broader economic, global, technological, demographic, social, and political context in which an industry is embedded.

Figure 3.5 The Role of the Macroenvironment

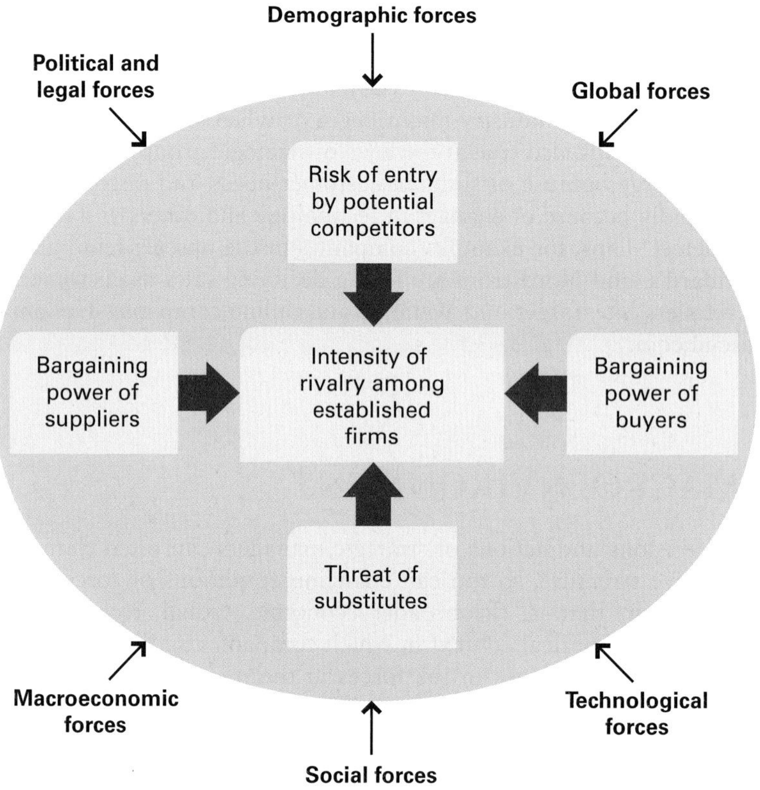

the value of the dollar is low compared with the value of other currencies, products made in the United States are relatively inexpensive and products made overseas are relatively expensive. A low or declining dollar reduces the threat from foreign competitors while creating opportunities for increased sales overseas. Thus the fall in the dollar against the Euro during 2006 and 2007 enabled American companies to export more goods and services to Europe. The fall in the value of the dollar against the Japanese yen that occurred between 1985 and 1995, when the dollar-to-yen exchange rate declined from 240 yen per dollar to 85 yen per dollar, sharply increased the price of imported Japanese cars, giving U.S. car manufacturers some protection against those imports.

Price inflation can destabilize the economy, producing slower economic growth, higher interest rates, and volatile currency movements. If inflation keeps increasing, investment planning becomes hazardous. The key characteristic of inflation is that it makes the future less predictable. In an inflationary environment, it may be impossible to predict with any accuracy the real value of returns that can be earned from a project 5 years hence. Such uncertainty makes companies less willing to invest. Their holding back in turn depresses economic activity and ultimately pushes the economy into a slump. Thus, high inflation is a threat to companies.

Global Forces

Over the last half of a century there have been enormous changes in the world economic system. We review these changes in detail in Chapter 6 when we discuss global strategy. For now, the important points to note are that barriers to international trade and investment have tumbled, and an increasing number of countries are enjoying sustained economic growth. Economic growth in places like Brazil, China and India is creating large new markets for the goods and services of companies, and gives companies an opportunity to grow their profits faster by entering these nations. Falling barriers to international trade and investment have made it much easier to enter foreign nations. Twenty years ago, it was almost impossible for a Western company to set up operations in China. Today, Western and Japanese companies are investing over $50 billion a year in China. By the same token, however, falling barriers to international trade and investment have made it easier for foreign enterprises to enter the domestic markets of many companies (by lowering barriers to entry), thereby increasing the intensity of competition and lowering profitability. Because of these changes, many formally isolated domestic markets have now become part of a much larger, and more competitive, global market place, creating a myriad of threats and opportunities for companies.

Technological Forces

Since World War II, the pace of technological change has accelerated.[17] This has unleashed a process that has been called a "perennial gale of creative destruction."[18] Technological change can make established products obsolete overnight and simultaneously create a host of new product possibilities. Thus, technological change is both creative and destructive—both an opportunity and a threat.

One of the most important impacts of technological change is that it can affect the height of barriers to entry and therefore radically reshape industry structure. The Internet, because it is so pervasive, has the potential for changing the competitive structure of many industries. It often lowers barriers to entry and reduces customer switching costs, changes that tend to increase the intensity of rivalry in an industry and lower both prices and profits.[19] For example, the Internet has lowered barriers to entry into the news industry. Providers of financial news now have to compete for advertising dollars and customer attention with new Internet-based media organizations that sprung up during the 1990s such as TheStreet.com, the Motley Fool, and Yahoo's financial section. The resulting increase in rivalry has given advertisers more choices, enabling them to bargain down the prices that they must pay to media companies.

Demographic Forces

Demographic forces are outcomes of changes in the characteristics of a population, such as age, gender, ethnic origin, race, sexual orientation, and social class. Like the other forces in the general environment, demographic forces present managers with opportunities and threats and can have major implications for organizations. Changes in the age distribution of a population are an example of a demographic force that affects managers and organizations. Currently, most industrialized nations are experiencing the aging of their populations as a consequence of falling birth and death rates and the aging of the baby boom generation. In Germany, for example, the percentage of the population over age 65 is expected to rise from 15.4% in 1990 to 20.7% in 2010. Comparable figures for Canada are 11.4 and 14.4%; for Japan, 11.7 and 19.5%; and for the United States, 12.6 and 13.5%.[20]

The aging of the population is increasing opportunities for organizations that cater to older people; the home health care and recreation industries, for example, are seeing an upswing in demand for their services. As the baby boom generation from the late 1950s to the early 1960s has aged, it has created a host of opportunities and threats. During the 1980s, many baby boomers were getting married and creating an upsurge in demand for the customer appliances normally bought by couples marrying for the first time. Companies such as Whirlpool Corporation and General Electric capitalized on the resulting upsurge in demand for washing machines, dishwashers, dryers, and the like. In the 1990s, many of these same baby boomers were starting to save for retirement, creating an inflow of money into mutual funds and creating a boom in the mutual fund industry. In the next 20 years, many of these same baby boomers will retire, creating a boom in retirement communities.

Social Forces

Social forces refer to the way in which changing social mores and values affect an industry. Like other macroenvironmental forces discussed here, social change creates opportunities and threats. One major social movement of recent decades has been the trend toward greater health consciousness. Its impact has been immense, and companies that recognized the opportunities early have often reaped significant gains. Philip Morris, for example, capitalized on the growing health consciousness trend when it acquired Miller Brewing Company and then redefined competition in the beer industry with its introduction of low-calorie beer (Miller Lite). Similarly, PepsiCo was able to gain market share from its rival, Coca-Cola, by being the first to introduce diet colas and fruit-based soft drinks. At the same time, the health trend has created a threat for many industries. The tobacco industry, for example, is in decline as a direct result of greater customer awareness of the health implications of smoking.

Political and Legal Forces

Political and legal forces are outcomes of changes in laws and regulations. They result from political and legal developments within society and significantly affect managers and companies. Political processes shape a society's laws, which constrain the operations of organizations and managers and thus create both opportunities and threats.[21] For example, throughout much of the industrialized world, there has been a strong trend toward deregulation of industries previously controlled by the state and privatization of organizations once owned by the state. In the United States, deregulation of the airline industry in 1979 allowed 29 new airlines to enter the industry between 1979 and 1993. The increase in passenger carrying capacity after deregulation led to excess capacity on many routes, intense competition, and fare wars. To respond to this more competitive task environment, airlines have had to look for ways to reduce operating costs. The development of hub-and-spoke systems, the rise of nonunion airlines, and the introduction of no-frills discount service are all responses to increased competition in the airlines' task environment. Despite these innovations, the airline industry still experiences intense fare wars, which have lowered profits and caused numerous airline company bankruptcies. The global tele-communications service industry is now experiencing the same kind of turmoil fol-lowing the deregulation of that industry in the United States and elsewhere.

In most countries, the interplay between political and legal forces, on the one hand, and industry competitive structure, on the other, is a two-way process in which the government sets regulations that influence competitive structure, and firms in an industry often seek to influence the regulations that governments enact by a number of means. First, when permitted, they may provide financial support to politicians or political parties that espouse views favorable to the industry and lobby govern-ment legislators directly to shape government regulations. For example, in 2002, the United States Steel Industry Association was a prime mover in persuading President Bush to enact a 30% tariff on imports of foreign steel into the United States. The purpose of the tariff was to protect American steel makers from foreign competitors, thereby reducing the intensity of rivalry in the United States steel markets.

SUMMARY OF CHAPTER

1. The main technique used to analyze competi-tion in the industry environment is the five forces model. The five forces are (1) the risk of new entry by potential competitors, (2) the extent of rivalry among established firms, (3) the bargain-ing power of buyers, (4) the bargaining power of suppliers, and (5) the threat of substitute prod-ucts. The stronger each force is, the more com-petitive the industry and the lower the rate of return that can be earned.

2. The risk of entry by potential competitors is a function of the height of barriers to entry. The higher the barriers to entry are, the lower is the risk of entry and the greater are the profits that can be earned in the industry.

3. The extent of rivalry among established com-panies is a function of an industry's competi-tive structure, demand conditions, and barriers to exit. Strong demand conditions moderate the competition among established companies and create opportunities for expansion. When de-mand is weak, intensive competition can develop, particularly in consolidated industries with high exit barriers.

4. Buyers are most powerful when a company de-pends on them for business but they themselves are not dependent on the company. In such cir-cumstances, buyers are a threat.

5. Suppliers are most powerful when a company de-pends on them for business but they themselves are not dependent on the company. In such cir-cumstances, suppliers are a threat.

6. Substitute products are the products of compa-nies serving customer needs similar to the needs served by the industry being analyzed. The more similar the substitute products are to each other, the lower is the price that companies can charge without losing customers to the substitutes.

7. Most industries are composed of strategic groups: groups of companies pursuing the same or a similar strategy. Companies in different stra-tegic groups pursue different strategies.

8. Industries go through a well-defined life cycle: from an embryonic stage, through growth, shake-out, and maturity, and eventually decline. Each stage has different implications for the competi-tive structure of the industry, and each gives rise to its own set of opportunities and threats.

9. The macroenvironment affects the intensity of rivalry within an industry. Included in the mac-roenvironment are the macroeconomic environ-ment, the global environment, the technological environment, the demographic and social envi-ronment, and the political and legal environment.

DISCUSSION QUESTIONS

1. Under what environmental conditions are price wars most likely to occur in an industry? What are the implications of price wars for a company? How should a company try to deal with the threat of a price war?

2. Discuss Porter's five forces model with reference to what you know about the U.S. beer industry (see the Opening case). What does the model tell you about the level of competition in this industry?

3. Assess the impact of macroenvironmental factors on the likely level of enrollment at your university over the next decade. What are the implications of these factors for the job security and salary level of your professors?

C L O S I N G   C A S E

The Pharmaceutical Industry

Historically, the pharmaceutical industry has been a profitable one. Between 2002 and 2006 the average rate of return on invested capital (ROIC) for firms in the industry was 16.45%. Put differently, for every dollar of capital invested in the industry, the average pharmaceutical firm generated 16.45 cents of profit. This compares with an average return on invested capital of 12.76% for firms in the computer hardware industry, 8.54% for grocers, and 3.88% for firms in the electronics industry. However, the average level of profitability in the pharmaceutical industry has been declining of late. In 2002, the average ROIC in the industry was 21.6%; by 2006, it had fallen to 14.5%.

The profitability of the pharmaceutical industry can be best understood by looking at several aspects of its underlying economic structure. First, demand for pharmaceuticals has been strong and has grown for decades. Between 1990 and 2003, there was a 12.5% annual increase in spending on prescription drugs in the United States. This growth was driven by favorable demographics. As people grow older, they tend to need and consume more prescription medicines, and the population in most advanced nations has been growing older as the post–World War II baby boom generation ages. Looking forward, projections suggest that spending on prescription drugs will increase at between 10 and 11% annually through till 2013.

Second, successful new prescription drugs can be extraordinarily profitable. Lipitor, the cholesterol-lowering drug sold by Pfizer, was introduced in 1997, and by 2006, this drug had generated a staggering $12.5 billion in annual sales for Pfizer. The costs of manufacturing, packing, and distributing Lipitor amounted to only about 10% of revenues. Pfizer spent close to $500 million on promoting Lipitor and perhaps as much again on maintaining a sales force to sell the product. That still left Pfizer with a gross profit of perhaps $10 billion. Since the drug is protected from direct competition by a 20-year patent, Pfizer has a temporary monopoly and can charge a high price. Once the patent expires, which is scheduled to occur in 2010, other firms will be able to produce "generic" versions of Lipitor and the price will fall—typically by 80% within a year.

Competing firms can produce drugs that are similar (but not identical) to a patent-protected drug. Drug firms patent a specific molecule, and competing firms can patent similar, but not identical, molecules that have a similar pharmacological effect. Thus Lipitor does have competitors in the market for cholesterol-lowering drugs, such as Zocor sold by Merck and Crestor sold by AstraZeneca. But these competing drugs are also patent protected. Moreover, the high costs and risks associated with developing a new drug and bringing it to market limit new competition. Out of every 5,000 compounds tested in the laboratory by a drug company, only five enter clinical trials, and only one of these will ultimately make it to the market. On average, estimates suggest that it costs some $800 million and takes anywhere from 10 to 15 years to bring a new drug to market. Once on the market, only three out of 10 drugs ever recoup their R&D and marketing costs and turn a profit. Thus the high profitability of the pharmaceutical industry rests on a handful of blockbuster drugs. At Pfizer, the world's largest pharmaceutical company, 55% of revenues were generated from just eight drugs.

To produce a blockbuster, a drug company must spend large amounts of money on research, most of which fails to produce a product. Only very large companies can shoulder the costs and risks of doing this, making it difficult for new companies to enter the industry. Pfizer, for example, spent some $7.44 billion on R&D in 2005 alone, equivalent to 14.5% of its total revenues. In a testament to just how difficult it is to get into the industry, although a large number of companies have been started in the last 20 years in the hope that they might develop new pharmaceuticals, only two of these companies, Amgen and Genentech, were ranked among the top 20 in the industry in terms of sales in 2005. Most have failed to bring a product to market.

In addition to R&D spending, the incumbent firms in the pharmaceutical industry spend large amounts of money on advertising and sales promotion. While the $500 million a year that Pfizer spends promoting Lipitor is small relative to the drug's revenues, it is a large amount for a new competitor to match, making market entry difficult unless the competitor has a significantly better product.

There are also some big opportunities on the horizon for firms in the industry. New scientific breakthroughs in genomics are holding out the promise that within the next decade pharmaceutical firms might be able to bring new drugs to market that treat some of the most intractable medical conditions, including Alzheimer's, Parkinson's disease, cancer, heart disease, stroke, and AIDS.

However, there are some threats to the long-term dominance and profitability of industry giants like Pfizer. First, as spending on health care rises, politicians are looking for ways to limit health care costs, and one possibility is some form of price control on prescription drugs. Price controls are already in effect in most developed nations, and although they have not yet been introduced in the United States, they could be.

Second, between 2006 and 2009, 12 of the top 35 selling drugs in the industry will lose their patent protection. By one estimate some 28% of the global drug industry's sales of $307 billion will be exposed to generic challenge in America alone, due to drugs going of patent between 2006 and 2012. It is not clear to many industry observers whether the established drug companies have enough new drug prospects in their pipelines to replace revenues from drugs going off patent. Moreover, generic drug companies have been aggressive in challenging the patents of proprietary drug companies, and in pricing their generic offerings. As a result, their share of industry sales has been growing. In 2005, they accounted for more than half of all drugs prescribed by volume in the United States, up from one third in 1990.

Third, the industry has come under renewed scrutiny following studies which showed that some FDA approved prescription drugs, known as COX-2 inhibitors, were associated with a greater risk of heart attacks. Two of these drugs, Vioxx and Bextra, were pulled from the market in 2004.[22]

Case Discussion Questions

1. Drawing on the five forces model, explain why the pharmaceutical industry has historically been a very profitable industry.
2. After 2002, the profitability of the industry, measured by ROIC, started to decline. Why do you think this occurred?
3. What are the prospects for the industry going forward? What are the opportunities, what are the threats? What must pharmaceutical firms do to exploit the opportunities and counter the threats?

NOTES

1. M. E. Porter, *Competitive Strategy* (New York: Free Press, 1980).
2. J. E. Bain, *Barriers to New Competition* (Cambridge, Mass.: Harvard University Press, 1956). For a review of the modern literature on barriers to entry, see R. J. Gilbert, "Mobility Barriers and the Value of Incumbency," in *Handbook of Industrial Organization*, eds. R. Schmalensee and R. D. Willig, vol. 1 (Amsterdam, The Netherlands: North-Holland, 1989). Also see R. P. McAfee, H. M. Mialon, and M. A. Williams, "What is a Barrier to Entry?" *American Economic Review* 94 (May 2004): 461–468 and A. V. Mainkar, M. Lubatkin,

and W. S. Schulze, "Towards a Product Proliferation Theory of Entry Barriers," *Academy of Management Review* 31 (2006): 1062–1082.

3. *Sources*: A. Kaplan, "Cott Corporation," *Beverage World*, June 15, 2004, 32; J. Popp, "2004 Soft Drink Report," *Beverage Industry*, March 2004, 13L–18L; Sparks, "From Coca-Colinization to Copy Catting: The Cott Corporation and Retailers Brand Soft Drinks in the UK and US," *Agribusiness* 13, no. 2 (March 1997): 153–127; E. Cherney, "After Flat Sales, Cott Challenges Pepsi, Coca-Cola," *Wall Street Journal*, January 8, 2003, B1, B8; and Anonymous, "Cott Corporation: Company Profile," *Just—Drinks*, August 2006, 19–22.

4. N. Cetorelli and P. E. Strahan, "Finance as a Barrier to Entry," *Journal of Finance* 61 (2006): 437–456.

5. A detailed discussion of switching costs and lock in can be found in C. Shapiro and H. R. Varian, *Information Rules: A Strategic Guide to the Network Economy* (Boston, Mass.: Harvard Business School Press, 1999).

6. Most of this information on barriers to entry can be found in the industrial organization economics literature. See especially the following works: Bain, *Barriers to New Competition*; M. Mann, "Seller Concentration, Barriers to Entry and Rates of Return in 30 Industries," *Review of Economics and Statistics* 48 (1966): 296–307; W. S. Comanor and T. A. Wilson, "Advertising, Market Structure and Performance," *Review of Economics and Statistics* 49 (1967): 423–440; Gilbert, "Mobility Barriers"; and K. Cool, L.-H. Roller, and B. Leleux, "The Relative Impact of Actual and Potential Rivalry on Firm Profitability in the Pharmaceutical Industry," *Strategic Management Journal* 20 (1999): 1–14.

7. D. J. Bryce and J. H. Dyer, "Strategies to crack well guarded markets," *Harvard Business Review*, 85, May 2007, 84–95.

8. For a discussion of tacit agreements, see T. C. Schelling, *The Strategy of Conflict* (Cambridge, Mass.: Harvard University Press, 1960).

9. M. Busse, "Firm Financial Condition and Airline Price Wars," *Rand Journal of Economics* 33 (2002): 298–318.

10. For a review see F. Karakaya, "Market Exit and Barriers to Exit: Theory and Practice," *Psychology and Marketing* 17 (2000): 651–668. Also see C. Decker and T. Mellewight, "Thirty years after Michael E. Porter: What do We Know About Business Exit," *Academy of Management Review* 21 (2007): 41–60.

11. P. Ghemawat, *Commitment: The Dynamics of Strategy* (Boston, Mass.: Harvard Business School Press, 1991).

12. The development of strategic group theory has been a strong theme in the strategy literature. Important contributions include the following: R. E. Caves and Michael E. Porter, "From Entry Barriers to Mobility Barriers," *Quarterly Journal of Economics* (May 1977): 241–262; K. R. Harrigan, "An Application of Clustering for Strategic Group Analysis," *Strategic Management Journal* 6 (1985): 55–73; K. J. Hatten and D. E. Schendel, "Heterogeneity Within an Industry: Firm Conduct in the U.S. Brewing Industry, 1952–71," *Journal of Industrial Economics* 26 (1977): 97–113; Michael E. Porter, "The Structure Within Industries and Companies' Performance," *Review of Economics and Statistics* 61 (1979): 214–227. Also see K. Cool and D. Schendel, "Performance Differences among Strategic Group Members," *Strategic Management Journal* 9 (1988): 207–233; A. Nair and S. Kotha, "Does Group Membership Matter? Evidence from the Japanese Steel Industry," *Strategic Management Journal* (2001): 221–235; G. McNamara, D. L. Deephouse, and R. A. Luce, "Competitive Positioning Within and Across a Strategic Group Structure," *Strategic Management Journal* (2003): 161–180; and J. C. Short, T. B. Palmer, and G. M. Hult, "Firm, Strategic Group, and Industry Influences on Performance," *Strategic Management Journal* 28 (2007): 147–165.

13. For details on the strategic group structure in the pharmaceutical industry, see K. Cool and I. Dierickx, "Rivalry, Strategic Groups, and Firm Profitability," *Strategic Management Journal* 14 (1993): 47–59.

14. "How Big Can It Grow? Walmart," *Economist*, April 17, 2004, 74–76; H. Gilman, "The Most Underrated CEO Ever," Fortune, April 5, 2004, 242–247; K. Schaffner, "Psst! Want to Sell to Walmart?" *Apparel Industry Magazine*, August 1996, 18–20.

15. Charles W. Hofer argued that life cycle considerations may be the most important contingency when formulating business strategy. See Hofer, "Towards a Contingency Theory of Business Strategy," *Academy of Management Journal* 18 (1975): 784–810. There is empirical evidence to support this view. See C. R. Anderson and C. P. Zeithaml, "Stages of the Product Life Cycle, Business Strategy, and Business Performance," *Academy of Management Journal* 27 (1984): 5–24; and D. C. Hambrick and D. Lei, "Towards an Empirical Prioritization of Contingency Variables for Business Strategy," *Academy of Management Journal* 28 (1985): 763–788. Also see G. Miles, C. C. Snow, and M. P. Sharfman, "Industry Variety and Performance," *Strategic Management Journal* 14 (1993): 163–177 and G. K. Deans, F. Kroeger, and S. Zeisel, "The Consolidation Curve," *Harvard Business Review*, December 2002, 2–3.

16. The characteristics of declining industries have been summarized by K. R. Harrigan, "Strategy Formulation in Declining Industries," *Academy of Management Review* 5 (1980): 599–604. Also see J. Anand and H. Singh, "Asset Redeployment, Acquisitions and Corporate Strategy in Declining Industries," *Strategic Management Journal* 18 (1997): 99–118.

17. See M. Gort and J. Klepper, "Time Paths in the Diffusion of Product Innovations," *Economic Journal* (September 1982): 630–653. Looking at the history of forty-six products, Gort and Klepper found that the length of time before other companies entered the markets created by a few inventive companies declined from an average

of 14.4 years for products introduced before 1930 to 4.9 years for those introduced after 1949.

18. The phrase was originally coined by J. Schumpeter, *Capitalism, Socialism and Democracy* (London: Macmillan, 1950), 68.

19. M. E. Porter, "Strategy and the Internet," *Harvard Business Review,* March 2001, 62–79.

20. *Economist, The Economist Book of Vital World Statistics* (New York: Random House, 1990).

21. For a detailed discussion of the importance of the structure of law as a factor explaining economic change and growth, see D. C. North, Institutions, *Institutional Change and Economic Performance* (Cambridge, Mass.: Cambridge University Press, 1990).

22. *Sources:* Staff Reporter, "Pharm Exec 50," *Pharmaceutical Executive*, May 2004, 61–68; J. A. DiMasi, R. W. Hansen, and H. G. Grabowski, "The Price of Innovation: New Estimates of Drug Development Costs," *Journal of Health Economics* 22 (March 2003): 151–170; Staff Reporter, "Where the Money Is: The Drug Industry," *Economist,* April 26, 2003, 64–65; Value Line Investment Survey, various issues. Staff reporter, "Heartburn: Pharmaceuticals," *Economist*, August 19, 2006, 57; and P. B. Ginsberg et al., "Tracking Health Care Costs," *Health Affairs*, October 3, 2006, published online at www.healthaffairs.org.

BUILDING COMPETITIVE ADVANTAGE

4

CHAPTER OUTLINE

Competitive Advantage: Value Creation, Low Cost, and Differentiation

The Generic Building Blocks of Competitive Advantage

Efficiency
Quality as Excellence and Reliability
Innovation
Customer Responsiveness

The Value Chain

Primary Activities
Support Activities

Functional Strategies and the Generic Building Blocks of Competitive Advantage

Increasing Efficiency
Increasing Quality
Increasing Innovation
Achieving Superior Customer Responsiveness

Distinctive Competencies and Competitive Advantage

Resources and Capabilities
The Durability of Competitive Advantage

LEARNING OBJECTIVES

After reading this chapter you should be able to:

- Discuss the source of competitive advantage.
- Identify and explore the role of efficiency, quality, innovation, and customer responsiveness in building and maintaining a competitive advantage.

- Introduce the concept of the value chain.
- Explore how functional level strategies can be used to build superior efficiency, quality, innovation and customer responsiveness.
- Explain the nature of distinctive competencies.

OVERVIEW

In Chapter 3, we discussed the elements of the external environment that determine an industry's attractiveness. However, industry structure is not the only force that affects company's performance. Within any given industry some companies are more profitable than others. For example, in the global auto industry, Toyota has consistently outperformed General Motors for most of the last 20 years. In the steel industry, Nucor has consistently outperformed U.S. Steel. And in the U.S. retail industry, Walmart has consistently outperformed Kmart. The question, therefore, is why within a particular industry do some companies outperform others? What is the basis of their competitive advantage?

As you will see in this chapter, the answer is that companies which outperform their rivals do so because they are more efficient, have higher product quality, are more innovative or are more responsive to their customers than their rivals. We refer to *efficiency*, *quality*, *innovation*, and *customer responsiveness* as the four generic building blocks of competitive advantage. For a company to outperform its rivals, it must have unique strengths, or distinctive competencies, in at least one of these building blocks. Walmart, for example, outperforms its rivals in the discount retail industry because it is more efficient, and more responsive to its customers, than its rivals.

COMPETITIVE ADVANTAGE: VALUE CREATION, LOW COST, AND DIFFERENTIATION

As noted in Chapter 1, a company has a *competitive advantage* when its profitability is higher than the average for its industry, and it has a *sustained competitive advantage* when it is able to maintain superior profitability over a number of years. In the U.S. retail industry, for example, Walmart has had a sustained competitive advantage that has persisted for decades. This has been translated into higher profitability.

Two basic conditions determine a company's profitability: first, the amount of value customers place on the company's goods or services, and second, the company's costs of production. In general, the more value customers place on a company's products, the higher the price the company can charge for those products. Note, however, that the price a company charges for a good or service is typically less than the value placed on that good or service by the average customer. This is so because the average customer captures some of that value in the form of what economists call a consumer surplus.[1] The customer is able to do this because the company is competing with other companies for the customer's business, so the company must charge lower prices than it could were it a monopoly supplier. Moreover, it is normally impossible to segment the market to such a degree that the company can charge each customer a price that reflects that individual's assessment of the value of a product—which economist refer to as a customer's reservation price. For these reasons the price that gets charged tends to be less than the value placed on the product by many customers.

These concepts are illustrated in Figure 4.1. There you can see that the value of a product to a consumer may be V, the price that the company can charge for that product given competitive pressures may be P, and the costs of producing that product are C. The company's profit margin is equal to $P - C$, while the consumer surplus is equal to $V - P$. The company makes a profit as long as $P > C$, and its profit rate

....

Figure 4.1 Value Creation

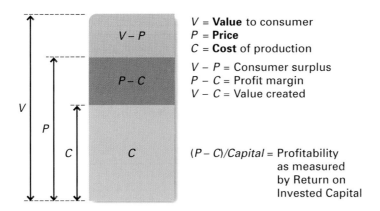

V = **Value** to consumer
P = **Price**
C = **Cost** of production

$V - P$ = Consumer surplus
$P - C$ = Profit margin
$V - C$ = Value created

$(P - C)$/*Capital* = Profitability
as measured
by Return on
Invested Capital

will be greater the lower is C *relative* to P. Bear in mind that the difference between V and P is in part determined by the intensity of competitive pressure in the market place. The lower the intensity of competitive pressure, the higher the price that can be charged relative to V.[2]

Note also that the value created by a company is measured by the difference between V and C $(V - C)$. A company creates value by converting inputs that cost C into a product on which consumers place a value of V. A company can create more value for its customers either by lowering C, or by making the product more attractive through superior design, functionality, quality, and the like, so that consumers place a greater value on it (V increases) and, consequently, are willing to pay a high price (P increases). This discussion suggests that a company has high profitability, and thus a competitive advantage, when it creates more value for its customers than rivals do. Put differently, *the concept of value creation lies at the heart of competitive advantage.*[3]

For a more concrete example, compare Toyota with General Motors. Consider the automobile industry. According to a study by Harbour & Associates, in 2005 Toyota made $1,200 in profit on every vehicle it manufactured in North America. General Motors, in contrast, lost $2,496 on every vehicle it made.[4] What accounts for the difference? First, Toyota has the best reputation for quality in the industry. According to annual surveys issued by J.D. Power and Associates, Toyota consistently tops the list in terms of quality, while GM cars are at best in the middle of the pack. The higher quality translates into a higher utility and allows Toyota to charge 5%–10% higher prices than General Motors for equivalent cars. Second, Toyota has a lower cost per vehicle than General Motors, in part because of its superior labor productivity. For example, in Toyota's North American plants, it took an average of 29.40 employee hours to build a car, compared to 33.19 at GM plants in North America. That 3.49 hour productivity advantage translates into much lower labor costs for Toyota and, hence, a lower overall cost structure. Therefore, as summarized in Figure 4.2 Toyota's advantage over GM derives from greater utility (U), which has allowed the company to charge a higher price (P) for its cars, and from a lower cost structure (C), which taken together implies significantly greater profitability per vehicle ($P - C$).

Figure 4.2 Comparing Toyota and General Motors

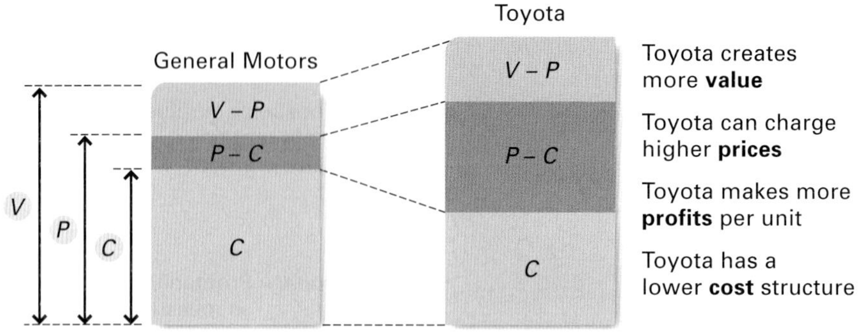

> **Ethical Dilemma**
>
> Your friend manages a highly profitable retailer. She attributes the principle source of competitive advantage to low labor costs, which are a result of her hiring minimum wage workers, denying worker benefits, and her consistent opposition to unionization at the company. Although she acknowledges that this approach leads to high employee turnover, she argues that the jobs are low skilled and easily refilled. Is your friend's approach to doing business ethical? Are there ways of achieving low labor costs without relying on placement of minimum wage workers? Would you council your friend to use an alternative approach?

Superior value creation does not necessarily require a company to have the lowest cost structure in an industry, or to create the most valuable product in the eyes of consumers, but it does require that the gap between perceived value (V) and costs of production (C) be greater than the gap attained by competitors. For example, Nordstrom has a strong competitive position among apparel retailers. Although Nordstrom has a higher cost structure than many of its competitors, it has been able to create more value because it successfully differentiated its service by offering a selection of high quality merchandise, and by being superior in store customer service. Indeed, Nordstrom is legendary for the attention that its sales people devote to individual customers. Thus consumers assigned a higher V to products purchased at Nordstrom, which enables Nordstrom to charge a higher price (P) for the products it sells than many competing full service department stores. The higher price translates into a greater profit margin ($P - C$) and greater profitability for Nordstrom relative to many of its rivals.

Michael Porter has argued that *low cost* and *differentiation* are two basic strategies for creating value and attaining a competitive advantage in an industry.[5] According to Porter, competitive advantage (and higher profitability) goes to those companies that can create superior value—and the way to create superior value is to drive down the cost structure of the business and/or differentiate the product in some way so that consumers value it more and are prepared to pay a premium price. This is all well and good, but it rather begs the question of exactly how a company can drive down its cost structure and differentiate its product offering from that of competitors so that it can create superior value. In this chapter and the next we explain just how companies can do these two things. We shall return to Porter's notions of low cost and differentiation strategies in Chapter 5, when we examine his idea in significantly more depth.

The Generic Building Blocks of Competitive Advantage

Four factors build competitive advantage: efficiency, quality, innovation, and customer responsiveness. They are the generic building blocks of competitive advantage that any company can adopt, regardless of its industry or the products or services it

Figure 4.3 Generic Building Blocks of Competitive Advantage

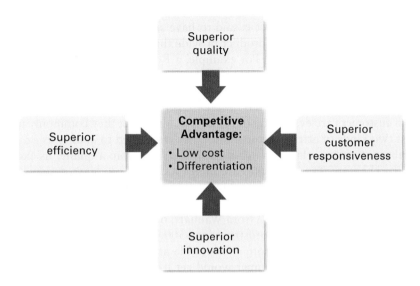

produces (Figure 4.3). Although we discuss them separately below, they are interrelated. For example, superior quality can lead to superior efficiency, while innovation can enhance efficiency, quality, and customer responsiveness.

Efficiency

In one sense, a business is simply a device for transforming inputs into outputs. Inputs are basic factors of production such as labor, land, capital, management, and technological know-how. Outputs are the goods and services that the business produces. The simplest measure of efficiency is the quantity of inputs that it takes to produce a given output, that is, efficiency = outputs/inputs. The more efficient a company is, the fewer the inputs required to produce a given output. For example, if it takes General Motors 30 hours of employee time to assemble a car and it takes Ford 25 hours, we can say that Ford is more efficient than GM. And as long as other things are equal, such as wage rates, we can assume from this information that Ford will have a lower cost structure than GM. Thus, efficiency helps a company attain a competitive advantage through a lower cost structure.

Two of the most important components of efficiency for many companies are employee productivity and capital productivity. **Employee productivity** is usually measured by output per employee and **capital productivity** by output per unit of invested capital. Holding all else constant, the company with the highest labor and capital productivity in an industry will typically have the lowest cost structure and therefore a cost-based competitive advantage. The concept of productivity is not limited to employee and capital productivity. Pharmaceutical companies, for example, often talk about the productivity of their R&D spending, by which they mean how many new drugs they develop from their investment in R&D. Other companies talk about their sales force productivity, which means how many sales they generate from every sales call, and so on. The important point to remember is that high productivity leads to greater efficiency and lower costs.

Efficiency

The quantity of inputs that it takes to produce a given output (that is, efficiency = outputs/inputs).

Employee Productivity

Output per employee.

Capital Productivity

Output per unit of invested capital.

Quality as Excellence and Reliability

A product can be thought of as a bundle of attributes.[6] The attributes of many physical products include the form, features, performance, durability, reliability, style, and design of the product.[7] A product is said to have *superior quality* when customers perceive that the attributes of a product provide them with higher value than attributes of products sold by rivals. For example, a Rolex watch has attributes—such as design, styling, performance, and reliability—that customers perceive as being superior to the same attributes in many other watches. Thus, we can refer to a Rolex as a high-quality product: Rolex has *differentiated* its watches by these attributes.

When customers are evaluating the quality of a product they commonly measure it against two kinds of attributes; attributes that are related to *quality as excellence*, and attributes that are related to *quality as reliability*. From a quality as excellence perspective, the important attributes are things such as a product's design and styling, its aesthetic appeal, its features and functions, the level of service associated with the delivery of the product, and so on. For example, a customer can purchase a pair of imitation leather boots for $20 from Walmart, or they can buy a handmade pair of genuine leather boots from Nordstrom for $500. The boots from Nordstrom will have far superior styling, feel more comfortable and look much better than those from Walmart. The value a consumer would get from the Nordstrom boots would in all probability be much greater than the value derived from the Walmart boots, but of course, they have to pay far more for them. That is the point of course; when excellence is built into a product offering, consumers have to pay more to own or consume them.

With regard to *quality as reliability*, a product can be said to be *reliable* when it consistently does the job it was designed for, does it well, and rarely, if ever, breaks down. As with excellence, reliability increases the value a consumer gets from a product, and thus the price the company can charge for that product. Toyota's cars, for example, have the highest reliability ratings in the automobile industry, and as a consequence consumers are prepared to pay more for them than cars that are very similar with regard to their other attributes.

The position of a product against these two dimensions, reliability and other attributes, can be plotted on a figure similar to Figure 4.4. For example, a Lexus has attributes—such as design, styling, performance, and safety features—that customers perceive as demonstrating excellence in quality, and is viewed as being superior to those of most other cars. Lexus is also a very reliable car. Thus, the overall level of quality of the Lexus is very high, which means that the car offers consumers significant utility, and that gives Toyota the option of charging a premium price for the Lexus. Toyota also produces another very reliable vehicle, the Toyota Corolla, but this is aimed at less wealthy customers and it lacks many of the superior attributes of the Lexus. Thus, although this is also a high-quality car in the sense of being reliable, it is not as high quality as a Lexus in the sense of being an excellent product. At the other end of the spectrum, we can find poor-quality products that have both low reliability and inferior attributes, such as poor design, performance, and styling. An example is the Proton, which is built by the Malaysian car firm of the same name. The design of the car is over a decade old and has a dismal reputation for styling and safety. Moreover, Proton's quality record is one of the worst offerings according to J.D. Power.[8]

The concept of quality applies whether we are talking about Toyota automobiles, clothes designed and sold by the Gap, the customer service department of Citibank, or the ability of airlines to arrive on time. Quality is just as relevant to services as it is to goods.[9]

Figure 4.4 A Quality Map for Automobiles

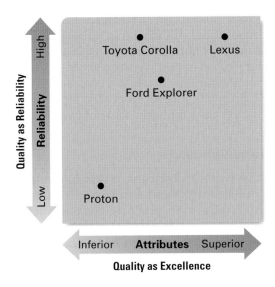

The impact of high product quality on competitive advantage is twofold.[10] First, providing high quality products increase the value those products provide to customers which gives the company the option of charging a higher price for them. The second impact of high quality on competitive advantage comes from the greater efficiency and the lower unit costs associated with *reliable* products. When products are reliable, less employee time is wasted making defective products or providing substandard services and less time has to be spent fixing mistakes, which translates into higher employee productivity and lower unit costs. Thus, high product quality not only enables a company to differentiate its product from that of rivals, but if the product is reliable, it also lowers costs.

Innovation

Innovation refers to the act of creating new products or processes. There are two main types of innovation: product innovation and process innovation. **Product innovation** is the development of products that are new to the world or have superior attributes to existing products. Examples are Intel's invention of the microprocessor in the early 1970s, Cisco's development of the router for routing data over the Internet in the mid-1980s, and Palm's development of the PalmPilot, the first commercially successful hand-held computer, in the mid-1990s. **Process innovation** is the development of a new process for producing products and delivering them to customers. An example would be Toyota which developed a range of new techniques collectively known as the Toyota *lean production system* for making automobiles which included just-in-time inventory systems, self-managing teams, and reduced setup times for complex equipment.

Product innovation creates value by creating new products, or enhanced versions of existing products, that customers perceive as having more value, thus giving the company the option to charge a higher price. Process innovation often allows a company to create more value by lowering production costs. Toyota's lean production

Innovation

The creation of new products or processes.

Product Innovation

The development of products that are new to the world or have attributes superior to those of existing products.

Process Innovation

The development of a new process for producing products and delivering them to customers.

system, for example, helped to boost employee productivity, thus giving Toyota a cost-based competitive advantage.[11]

In the long run, innovation of products and processes is perhaps the most important building block of competitive advantage.[12] Competition can be viewed as a process driven by innovations. Although not all innovations succeed, those that do can be a major source of competitive advantage because, by definition, they give a company something *unique*—something its competitors lack (at least until they imitate the innovation). Uniqueness can allow a company to differentiate itself from its rivals and charge a premium price for its product or, in the case of many process innovations, reduce its unit costs far below those of competitors.

Customer Responsiveness

To achieve superior customer responsiveness, a company must be able to do a better job than competitors of identifying and satisfying its customers' needs. Customers will then attribute more value to its products, creating a differentiation based on competitive advantage. Improving the quality of a company's product offering is consistent with achieving responsiveness, as is developing new products with features that existing products lack. In other words, achieving superior quality and innovation is integral to achieving superior responsiveness to customers.

Another factor that stands out in any discussion of customer responsiveness is the need to customize goods and services to the unique demands of individual customers or customer groups. For example, the proliferation of soft drinks and beers can be viewed partly as a response to this trend. Similarly, automobile companies have become more adept at customizing cars to the demands of individual customers, often allowing a wide range of colors and options to choose from.

An aspect of customer responsiveness that has drawn increasing attention is **customer response time**: the time that it takes for a good to be delivered or a service to be performed.[13] For a manufacturer of machinery, response time is the time it takes to fill customer orders. For a bank, it is the time it takes to process a loan or that a customer must stand in line to wait for a free teller. For a supermarket, it is the time that customers must stand in checkout lines. Survey after survey have shown slow response time to be a major source of customer dissatisfaction.[14]

Other sources of enhanced customer responsiveness include superior design, service, and after-sales service and support. All of these factors enhance customer responsiveness and allow a company to differentiate itself from its competitors. In turn, differentiation enables a company to build brand loyalty and charge a premium price for its products. Consider how much more people are prepared to pay for next-day delivery of express mail, as opposed to delivery in 3–4 days. In 2009, a two-page letter sent overnight by Express Mail within the United States cost about $13, compared with 44 cents for regular mail. Thus, the price premium for express delivery (reduced response time) was $12.60, or a premium of 2.757% over the regular price.

Customer Response Time

The time that it takes for a good to be delivered or a service to be performed.

THE VALUE CHAIN

In this section we will take a look at the role played by the different functions of a company—such as production, marketing, R&D, service, information systems, materials management, and human resources—in the value creation process. Specifically,

Figure 4.5 The Value Chain

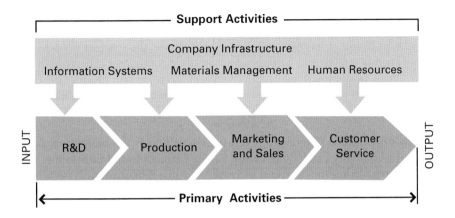

we shall review how the different functional of a company can help in the process of driving down costs and increasing the perception of value through differentiation. As a first step toward doing this, consider the concept of the value chain, which is illustrated in Figure 4.5.[15] The term **value chain** refers to the idea that a company is a chain of activities for transforming inputs into outputs valued by customers' value. The process of transforming inputs into outputs is composed of a number of primary activities and support activities. Each activity adds value to the product.

Primary Activities

Primary activities have to do with the design, creation, and delivery of the product, its marketing, and its support and after-sales service. In the value chain illustrated in Figure 4.5, the primary activities are broken down into four functions: research and development, production, marketing and sales, and customer service.

Research and Development Research and development (R&D) is concerned with the design of products and production processes. Although we think of R&D as being associated with the design of physical products and production processes in manufacturing enterprises, many service companies also undertake R&D. For example, banks compete with each other by developing new financial products and new ways of delivering those products to customers. Online banking and smart debit cards are two recent examples of the fruits of new product development in the banking industry. Earlier examples of innovation in the banking industry were ATM machines, credit cards, and debit cards.

By superior product design, R&D can increase the functionality of products, which makes them more attractive to customers, thereby adding value. Alternatively, the work of R&D may result in more efficient production processes, thereby lowering production costs. Either way, the R&D function can help to lower costs or raise the value of a product and permit a company to charge higher prices. At Intel, for example, R&D creates value by developing ever more powerful microprocessors and helping to pioneer ever more efficient manufacturing processes (in conjunction with equipment suppliers).

Value Chain

The idea that a company is a chain of activities for transforming inputs into outputs that customers value.

Primary Activities

Activities related to the design, creation, and delivery of the product, its marketing, and its support and after-sale service.

Production   Production is concerned with the creation of a good or service. For physical products, when we talk about production, we generally mean manufacturing. For services such as banking or retail operations, "production" typically takes place when the service is delivered to the customer, as when a bank makes a loan to a customer. By performing its activities efficiently, the production function of a company helps to lower its cost structure. For example, the efficient production operations of Honda and Toyota help those automobile companies achieve higher profitability relative to competitors such as General Motors. The production function can also perform its activities in a way that is consistent with high product quality, which leads to differentiation (and higher value) and lower costs.

Marketing and Sales   There are several ways in which the *marketing and sales* functions of a company can help to create value. Through brand positioning and advertising, the marketing function can increase the value that customers perceive to be contained in a company's product (and thus the utility they attribute to the product). Insofar as these help to create a favorable impression of the company's product in the minds of customers, they increase perceived value. For example, in the 1980s, the French company Perrier persuaded U.S. customers that slightly carbonated bottled water was worth $1.50 per bottle rather than a price closer to the $0.50 that it cost to collect, bottle, and distribute the water. Perrier's marketing function essentially increased the perception of utility that customers ascribed to the product.

Marketing and sales can also create value by discovering customer needs and communicating them back to the R&D function of the company, which can then design products that better match those needs.

Customer Service   The role of the *service* function of an enterprise is to provide after-sales service and support. This function can create superior utility by solving customer problems and supporting customers after they have purchased the product. For example, Caterpillar, the U.S.-based manufacturer of heavy earthmoving equipment, can get spare parts to any point in the world within 24 hours, thereby minimizing the amount of downtime its customers have to face if their Caterpillar equipment malfunctions. This is an extremely valuable support capability in an industry where downtime is expensive. It has helped to increase the utility that customers associate with Caterpillar products, and thus the price that Caterpillar can charge for its products.

Support Activities

The **support activities** of the value chain provide inputs that allow the primary activities to take place. These activities are broken down into four functions: materials management (or logistics), human resources, information systems, and company infrastructure (see Figure 4.5).

Support Activities

Activities of the value chain that provide inputs that allow the primary activities to take place.

Materials Management (Logistics)   The *materials management* (or logistics) function controls the transmission of physical materials through the value chain, from procurement through production and into distribution. The efficiency with which this is carried out can significantly lower cost, thereby creating more value. Walmart, for example, has a very efficient materials management setup. By tightly controlling the flow of goods from its suppliers through its stores and into the hands of customers, Walmart has eliminated the need to hold large inventories of goods. Lower inventories mean lower costs, and hence greater value creation.

Human Resources   There are a number of ways in which the *human resource* function can help an enterprise to create more value. This function ensures that the company has the right mix of skilled people to perform its value-creation activities effectively. It is also the job of the human resource function to ensure that people are adequately trained, motivated, and compensated to perform their value-creation tasks. If the human resources are functioning well, employee productivity rises (which lowers costs) and customer service improves (which raises utility), thereby enabling the company to create more value.

Information Systems   *Information systems* refer largely to the electronic systems for managing inventory, tracking sales, pricing products, selling products, dealing with customer service inquiries, and so on. Information systems, when coupled with the communications features of the Internet, are holding out the promise of being able to improve the efficiency and effectiveness with which a company manages its other value-creation activities. Walmart uses information systems to alter the way it does business. By tracking the sale of individual items very closely, its materials management function has enabled it to optimize its product mix and pricing strategy. Walmart is rarely left with unwanted merchandise on its hands, which saves on costs, and the company is able to provide the right mix of goods to customers, which increases the utility that customers associate with Walmart.

Company Infrastructure   Company infrastructure is the companywide context within which all the other value creation activities take place: the organizational structure, control systems, and company culture. Because top management can exert considerable influence in shaping these aspects of a company, top management should also be viewed as part of the infrastructure of a company. Indeed, through strong leadership, top management can shape the infrastructure of a company and, through that, the performance of all other value-creation activities that take place within it.

FUNCTIONAL STRATEGIES AND THE GENERIC BUILDING BLOCKS OF COMPETITIVE ADVANTAGE

Now that we have reviewed the generic building blocks of competitive advantage and discussed how the different functions of a company fit together into the value chain, we can look at some of the functional level strategies managers pursue improve the efficiency, quality, innovation, and customer responsiveness of their organization. Since this topic is a vast one worthy of a book in its own right, we not attempt an exhaustive review of functional level strategies. Instead, we shall illustrate the role of functional level strategies in building competitive advantage by focusing on a limited number of important functional level strategies.

Increasing Efficiency

Actions can be taken by functional managers at every step in the value chain to increase the efficiency of a company.

Company Infrastructure

The companywide context within which all the other value creation activities take place: the organizational structure, control systems, and company culture.

R&D and Efficiency   Managers in the R&D function might look for ways to simplify the design of a product, reducing the number of parts it contains. By doing so, R&D can dramatically decrease the required assembly time, which translates into higher employee productivity, lower costs, and higher profitability. For example, after Texas Instruments redesigned an infrared sighting mechanism that it supplies to the Pentagon, it found that it had reduced the number of parts from 47 to 12, the number of assembly steps from 56 to 13, the time spent fabricating metal from 757 minutes per unit to 219 minutes per unit, and unit assembly time from 129 minutes to 20 minutes. The result was a substantial decline in production costs. Design for manufacturing requires close coordination between the production and R&D functions of the company, of course. Cross-functional teams that contain production and R&D personnel who work jointly on the problem best achieve this.

Production and Efficiency   Managers in the production function of a company might look for ways to increase the productivity of capital and labor. One common strategy is to pursue economies of scale—driving down unit costs by mass producing output. A major source of economies of scale is the ability to spread fixed costs over a large production volume. *Fixed costs* are costs that must be incurred to produce a product whatever the level of output. For example, Microsoft spends perhaps $5 billion to develop its latest Windows operating system. It can realize substantial scale economies by spreading the fixed costs associated with developing the new operating system over the enormous unit sales volume it expects for this system (over 90% of the world's personal computers use a Microsoft operating system). These scale economies are significant because of the trivial incremental (or marginal) cost of producing additional copies of a Windows operating system: once the master copy has been produced, additional CDs containing the operating system can be produced for a few cents. The key to Microsoft's efficiency and profitability (and that of other companies with high fixed costs and trivial incremental or marginal costs) is to increase sales rapidly enough that fixed costs can be spread out over a large unit volume and substantial scale economies can be realized.

Another source of scale economies is the ability of companies producing in large volumes to achieve a greater division of labor and specialization. Specialization is said to have a favorable impact on productivity, mainly because it enables employees to become very skilled at performing a particular task. The classic example of such economies is Ford's Model T car. The world's first mass-produced car, the Model T Ford was introduced in 1923. Until then, Ford had made cars using an expensive hand-built craft production method. By introducing mass-production techniques, the company achieved greater division of labor (it split assembly into small, repeatable tasks) and specialization, which boosted employee productivity. Ford was also able to spread the fixed costs of developing a car and setting up production machinery over a large volume of output. As a result of these economies, the cost of manufacturing a car at Ford fell from $3,000 to less than $900 (in 1958 dollars).

In addition to scale effects, production managers might seek to boost efficiency by pursuing strategies that help to maximize learning effects. **Learning effects** are cost savings that come from learning by doing. Labor, for example, learns by repetition how best to carry out a task. Therefore, labor productivity increases over time, and unit costs fall as individuals learn the most efficient way to perform a particular task. Equally important, management in new manufacturing facilities typically learns over time how best to run the new operation. Hence, production costs decline because of increasing labor productivity and management efficiency.

Learning Effects

Cost savings that come from learning by doing.

Although learning effects are normally associated with the manufacturing process, there is every reason to believe that they are just as important in service industries. For example, one famous study of learning in the context of the health care industry found that more experienced medical providers posted significantly lower mortality rates for a number of common surgical procedures, suggesting that learning effects are at work in surgery.[16] The authors of this study used the evidence to argue for establishing regional referral centers for the provision of highly specialized medical care. These centers would perform many specific surgical procedures (such as heart surgery), replacing local facilities with lower volumes and presumably higher mortality rates (for another study showing learning effects in surgery see the next Strategy in Action feature). Another recent study found strong evidence of learning effects in a financial institution. The study looked at a newly established document processing unit with 100 staff and found that over time, documents were processed much more rapidly as the staff learned the process. Overall, the study concluded that unit costs fell every time the cumulative number of documents processed since the unit was established doubled.[17]

4.1 STRATEGY IN ACTION

Learning Effects in Cardiac Surgery

A study carried out by researchers at the Harvard Business School tried to estimate the importance of learning effects in the case of a specific new technology for minimally invasive heart surgery that was approved by federal regulators in 1996. The researchers looked at 16 hospitals and obtained data on the operations for 660 patients. They examined how the time required to undertake the procedure varied with cumulative experience. Across the 16 hospitals, they found that average time fell from 280 minutes for the first procedure with the new technology to 220 minutes by the time a hospital had performed 50 procedures. (Note that not all of the hospitals performed 50 procedures, and the estimates represent an extrapolation based on the data.)

Next they looked at differences across hospitals. They found evidence of very large differences in learning effects. One hospital, in particular, stood out. This hospital, which they called "Hospital M," reduced its net procedure time from 500 minutes on case 1 to 132 minutes by case 50. Hospital M's 88-minute procedure time advantage over the average hospital at case 50 translated into a cost saving of approximately $2,250 per case and allowed surgeons at the hospital to do one more revenue-generating procedure per day.

The researchers tried to find out why Hospital M was superior. They noted that all hospitals had similar state-of-the-art operating rooms and used the same set of FDA approved devices. All adopting surgeons went through the same training courses, and all surgeons came from highly respected training hospitals. Follow-up interviews, however, suggested that Hospital M differed in how it implemented the new procedure. The team was handpicked by the adopting surgeon to perform the surgery. It had significant prior experience working together (that was apparently a key criterion for team members). The team was trained together to perform the new surgery. Before undertaking a single procedure, they met with the operating room nurses and anesthesiologists to discuss the procedure. Moreover, the adopting surgeon mandated that the surgical team and surgical procedure was stable in the early cases. The initial team went through 15 procedures, and new members were added or substituted 20 cases before the procedures were modified. The adopting surgeon also insisted that the team meet prior to each of the first 10 cases, and they also met after the first 20 cases to debrief.

The picture that emerges is one of a core team that was selected and managed to maximize the gains from learning. Unlike other hospitals in which there was less stability of team members and procedures, and less attention to briefing, debriefing, and learning, surgeons at Hospital M both learned much faster, and ultimately achieved higher productivity than their peers in other institutions. Clearly, differences in the implementation of the new procedure were very important.[18]

An important source of greater efficiency has been the introduction of flexible manufacturing technology by managers in the production function of an enterprise. The term **flexible manufacturing technology**—or **lean production**, as it is sometimes called—covers a range of manufacturing technologies designed to reduce setup times for complex equipment, increase the use of individual machines through better scheduling, and improve quality control at all stages of the manufacturing process.[19] Flexible manufacturing technologies allow the company to produce a wider variety of end products at a unit cost that at one time could be achieved only through the mass production of a standardized output. Indeed, research suggests that the adoption of flexible manufacturing technologies may increase efficiency and lower unit costs relative to what can be achieved by the mass production of a standardized output, while at the same time enabling the company to customize its product offering to a much greater extent than was once thought possible. The term **mass customization** has been coined to describe the ability of companies to use flexible manufacturing technology to reconcile two goals that were once thought to be incompatible: *low cost* and *differentiation through product customization*.[20]

Marketing and Efficiency   The marketing strategy that a company adopts can have a major impact on efficiency and cost structure. **Marketing strategy** refers to the position that a company takes with regard to pricing, promotion, advertising, product design, and distribution. Some of the steps leading to greater efficiency are fairly obvious. For example, attaining economies of scale and learning effects can be facilitated by aggressive pricing, promotions, and advertising, all of which build sales volume rapidly and allow for the cost reductions that come from scale and learning effects. Other aspects of marketing strategy have a less obvious but no less important impact on efficiency. For many companies, one important strategy involves reducing customer defection rates.[21]

Customer defection rates are the percentage of a company's customers who defect every year to competitors. Defection rates are determined by customer loyalty, which in turn is a function of the ability of a company to satisfy its customers. Because acquiring a new customer entails certain one-time fixed costs for advertising, promotions, and the like, there is a direct relationship between defection rates and costs. The longer a company holds on to a customer, the greater the volume of unit sales generated by a customer that can be set against customer acquisition costs. Thus, lowering customer defection rates allows a company to amortize its customer acquisition costs and achieve a lower overall cost structure.

For example, in the wireless telecommunications industry it can cost between $300 and $400 to acquire a customer (this includes the costs of advertising and promotion, providing a customer with a wireless phone, and the cost of service activation). With monthly bills in the United States averaging $50-$100, it can take six to a year just to recoup the fixed costs of customer acquisition. If customer defection rates are high, costs are driven up by the costs of acquiring customers to replace those who left. In fact, many wireless service providers have customer defection rates approaching 25% per annum, which drives up their costs and reduces their profitability.

To reduce customer defection rates, marketing managers take steps to build brand loyalty, and to make it more expensive for customers to defect. In the wireless telecommunications industry Verizon Wireless has invested heavily in customer service and coverage to try and build brand loyalty. In addition, it has progressively moved customers toward 2 year contracts, with penalty clauses attached if

Flexible Manufacturing Technology , or Lean Production

A range of manufacturing technologies designed to reduce setup times for complex equipment, increase the use of individual machines through better scheduling, and improve quality control at all stages of the manufacturing process. Also known as lean production.

Mass Customization

The ability of companies to use flexible manufacturing technology to customize output at costs normally associated with mass production.

Marketing Strategy

The position that a company takes with regard to pricing, promotion, advertising, product design, and distribution.

Customer Defection Rate

The percentage of a company's customers who defect every year to competitors.

customers switch to another service provider within 2 years. These strategies have been quite successful; at around 17% in 2010, Verizon's customer defection rate is the lowest in the industry.[22]

Materials Management and Efficiency   The contribution of materials management (logistics) to boosting the efficiency of a company can be just as dramatic as the contribution of production and marketing. For a typical manufacturing company, materials and transportation costs account for 50%–70% of its revenues, so even a small reduction in these costs can have a substantial impact on profitability. According to one estimate, for a company with revenues of $1 million, a return on invested capital of 5%, and materials management costs that amount to 50% of sales revenues (including purchasing costs), increasing total profits by $15,000 would require either a 30% increase in sales revenues or a 3% reduction in materials costs.[23] In a typical competitive market, reducing materials costs by 3% is usually much easier than increasing sales revenues by 30%.

Improving the efficiency of the materials management function often requires the adoption of a just-in-time (JIT) inventory system, designed to economize on inventory holding costs by having components arrive at a manufacturing plant just in time to enter the production process or goods at a retail store only when stock is almost depleted. The major cost saving comes from increasing inventory turnover, which reduces inventory holding costs, such as warehousing and storage costs, and the company's need for working capital.

For example, through efficient logistics Walmart can replenish the stock in its stores at least twice a week; many stores receive daily deliveries if they are needed. The typical competitor replenishes its stock every 2 weeks so that they have to carry a much higher inventory and need more working capital per dollar of sales. Compared to its competitors, Walmart can maintain the same service levels with a lower investment in investment, a major source of its lower cost structure. Thus, faster inventory turnover has helped Walmart achieve an efficiency-based competitive advantage in the retailing industry.[24]

The drawback of JIT systems is that they leave a company without a buffer stock of inventory. Although buffer stocks are expensive to store, they can help tide a company over shortages on inputs brought about by disruption among suppliers (for instance, a labor dispute at a key supplier) and help a company respond quickly to increases in demand. However, there are ways around these limitations. For example, to reduce the risks linked to dependence on just one supplier for an important input, a company might decide to source inputs from multiple suppliers.

Human Resource Strategy and Efficiency   As noted earlier, employee productivity is one of the key determinants of an enterprise's efficiency, cost structure, and profitability.[25] Many companies well known for their productive employees devote considerable attention to their hiring strategy. Southwest Airlines hires people who have a positive attitude and work well in teams because it believes that people who have a positive attitude will work hard and interact well with customers, therefore helping to create customer loyalty. Nucor hires people who are self-reliant and goal oriented, because its employees work in self-managing teams where they have to be self-reliant and goal oriented to perform well. As these examples suggest, it is important to make sure that the hiring strategy of the company is consistent with its own internal organization, culture, and strategic priorities. The people a company hires should have attributes that match the strategic objectives of the company. The

Running case looks at the steps Walmart has taken to boost the productivity of its workforce through human resource strategy.

Organizing the workforce into self-managing teams is a popular human resource strategy for boosting productivity. In a **self-managing team**, members coordinate their own activities, which might include making their own hiring, training, work, and reward decisions. The typical team comprises 5 to 15 employees who produce an entire product or undertake an entire task. Team members learn all team tasks and rotate from job to job. Because a more flexible work force is one result, team members can fill in for absent coworkers and take over managerial duties such as work and vacation scheduling, ordering materials, and hiring new members. The greater responsibility thrust on team members and the empowerment it implies are seen as motivators. People often respond well to being given greater autonomy and responsibility. Performance bonuses linked to team production and quality targets can work as an additional motivator. The effect of introducing self-managing teams is reportedly an increase in productivity of 30% or more and also a substantial increase in product quality. Further cost savings arise from eliminating supervisors and creating a flatter organizational hierarchy, which also lowers the cost structure of the company.[26]

Implementing pay for performance compensation systems is another common human resource strategy for boosting efficiency. It is hardly surprising that linking pay to performance can help increase employee productivity. However, it is important to define what kind of job performance is to be rewarded and how. Some of the most efficient companies in the world, mindful that cooperation among employees is necessary to realize productivity gains, link pay to group or team (rather than individual) performance. Nucor divides its work force into teams of 30 or so, with bonus pay, which can amount to 30% of base pay, linked to the ability of the team to meet productivity and quality goals. This link creates a strong incentive for individuals to cooperate with each other in pursuit of team goals; that is, it facilitates teamwork.

Information Systems and Efficiency   With the rapid spread of computers, the explosive growth of the Internet and corporate intranets (internal corporate computer networks based on Internet standards), and the spread of high-bandwidth fiber optics and digital wireless technology, the information systems function is moving to center stage in the quest for operating efficiencies and a lower cost structure.[27] The impact of information systems on productivity is wide ranging and potentially affects all other activities of a company. For example, Cisco Systems has been able to realize significant cost savings by moving its ordering and customer service functions online. The company has just 300 service agents handling all of its customer accounts, compared to the 900 it would need if sales were not handled online. The difference represents an annual saving of $20 million a year. Moreover, without automated customer service functions, Cisco calculates that it would need at least 1,000 additional service engineers, which would cost around $75 million.[28]

Like Cisco, many companies are using web-based information systems to reduce the costs of coordination between the company and its customers and the company and its suppliers. By using web-based programs to automate customer and supplier interactions, the number of people required to manage these interfaces can be substantially reduced, thereby reducing costs. This trend extends beyond high-tech companies. Banks and financial service companies are finding that they can substantially reduce

Self-Managing Team

A team wherein members coordinate their own activities, which might include making their own decisions about hiring, training, work, and rewards.

RUNNING CASE

Human Resource Strategy and Productivity at Walmart

Walmart has one of the most productive workforces of any retailer. The roots of Walmart's high productivity go back to the company's early days and the business philosophy of the company's founder, Sam Walton. Walton started off his career as a management trainee at JCPenney. There he noticed that all employees were called associates, and, moreover, that treating them with respect seemed to reap dividends in the form of high employee productivity.

When he founded Walmart, Walton decided to call all employees "associates" to symbolize their importance to the company. He reinforced this by emphasizing that at Walmart, "Our people make the difference." Unlike many managers who have stated this mantra, Walton believed it and put it into action. He believed that if he treated people well, they would return the favor by working hard, and that if he empowered them, ordinary people could work together to achieve extraordinary things. These beliefs formed the basis for a decentralized organization that operated with an open-door policy and open books. This allowed associates to see just how their store and the company were doing.

Consistent with the open-door policy, Walton continually emphasized that management needed to listen to associates and their ideas. As he noted:

> The folks on the front lines—the ones who actually talk to the customer—are the only ones who really know what's going on out there. You'd better find out what they know. This really is what total quality is all about. To push responsibility down in your organization, and to force good ideas to bubble up within it, you must listen to what your associates are trying to tell you.

For all of his belief in empowerment, however, Walton was notoriously tight on pay. Walton opposed unionization, fearing that it would lead to higher pay and restrictive work rules that would sap productivity. The culture of Walmart also encouraged people to work hard. One of Walton's favorite homilies was the "sundown rule," which stated that one should never put off until tomorrow what can be done today. The sundown rule was enforced by senior managers, including Walton, who would drop in unannounced at a store, peppering store managers and employees with questions, but at the same time praising them for a job well done and celebrating the "heroes" who took the sundown rule to heart and did today what could have been put off for tomorrow.

The key to getting extraordinary effort out of employees, while paying them meager salaries, was to reward them with profit-sharing plans and stock-ownership schemes. Long before it became fashionable in American business, Walton was placing a chunk of Walmart's profits into a profit-sharing plan for associates, and the company put matching funds into employee stock-ownership programs. The idea was simple: reward associates by giving them a stake in the company, and they will work hard for low pay because they know they will make it up in profit sharing and stock price appreciation.

For years, this formula worked extraordinarily well, but there are now signs that Walmart's very success is creating problems. In 2008, the company had a staggering 2.1 million associates, making it the largest private employer in the world. As the company has grown, it has become increasingly difficult to hire people that Walmart has traditionally relied on—those willing to work long hours for low pay based on the promise of advancement and reward through profit sharing and stock ownership. The company has come under attack for paying its associates low wages and pressuring them to work long hours without overtime pay. Labor unions have made a concerted but so far unsuccessful attempt over time to unionize stores, and the company itself is the target of lawsuits from employees alleging sexual discrimination. Walmart claims that the negative publicity is based on faulty data, and perhaps that is right, but if the company has indeed become too big to put Walton's principles into practice, the glory days may be over.[29]

costs by moving customer accounts and support functions online. Such a move reduces the need for customer service representatives, bank tellers, stockbrokers, insurance agents, and others. For example, it costs an average of about $1.07 to execute a transaction at a bank, such as shifting money from one account to another; executing the same transaction over the Internet costs $0.01.[30]

Infrastructure and Efficiency   A company's infrastructure—that is, its structure, culture, style of strategic leadership, and control system—determines the context within which all other value creation activities take place. It follows that improving infrastructure can help a company increase efficiency and lower its cost structure. Above all, an appropriate infrastructure can help foster a companywide commitment to efficiency and promote cooperation among different functions in pursuit of efficiency goals. These issues are addressed at length in later chapters.

For now, it is important to note that strategic leadership is especially important in building a companywide commitment to efficiency. The leadership task is to articulate a vision that recognizes the need for *all* functions of a company to focus on improving efficiency. It is not enough to improve the efficiency of production, or of marketing, or of R&D in a piecemeal fashion. Achieving superior efficiency requires a companywide commitment to this goal that must be articulated by general and functional managers. A further leadership task is to facilitate cross-functional cooperation needed to achieve superior efficiency. For example, designing products that are easy to manufacture requires that production and R&D personnel communicate; integrating JIT systems with production scheduling requires close communication between material management and production; designing self-managing teams to perform production tasks requires close cooperation between human resources and production; and so on.

Summary: Increasing Efficiency   Table 4.1 summarizes the primary roles that various functions must take in order to achieve superior efficiency. Bear in mind that achieving superior efficiency is not something that can be tackled on a function-by-function basis. It requires an organization-wide commitment and an ability to ensure close cooperation among functions. Top management, by exercising leadership and influencing the infrastructure, plays a major role in this process.

Increasing Quality

Earlier we noted that quality can be thought of in terms of two dimensions: *quality as reliability* and *quality as excellence*. High-quality products are reliable, in the sense that they do the job they were designed for and do it well, and are also perceived by consumers to have superior attributes. Superior quality gives a company two advantages; first a strong reputation for quality allows a company to *differentiate* its products from those offered by rivals, and second, eliminating defects or errors from the production process reduces waste, increases efficiency, and lowers the cost structure of the company and increases its profitability.

Attaining Superior Reliability   The principal tool that most managers now use to increase the reliability of their product offering is the Six Sigma quality improvement methodology. The Six Sigma methodology is a direct descendent of the Total Quality Management (TQM) philosophy that was widely adopted, first by Japanese

Table 4.1 Primary Roles of Value Creation Functions in Achieving Superior Efficiency

Value Creation Function	Primary Roles
Infrastructure (leadership)	1. Provide companywide commitment to efficiency. 2. Facilitate cooperation among functions.
Production	1. Where appropriate, pursue economies of scale and learning economics. 2. Implement flexible manufacturing systems.
Marketing	1. Where appropriate, adopt aggressive marketing to ride down the experience curve. 2. Limit customer defection rates by building brand loyalty.
Materials management	1. Implement JIT systems. 2. Supply chain coordination.
R&D	1. Design products for ease of manufacture. 2. Seek process innovations.
Information systems	1. Use information systems to automate processes. 2. Use information systems to reduce costs of coordination.
Human resources	1. Institute training programs to build skills. 2. Implement self-managing teams. 3. Implement pay for performance.

companies and then American companies during the 1980s and early 1990s.[31] The basic philosophy underlying quality improvement methodologies is as follows:

1. Improved quality means that costs decrease because of less rework, fewer mistakes, fewer delays, and better use of time and materials.
2. As a result, productivity improves.
3. Better quality leads to higher market share and allows the company to raise prices.
4. This increases the company's profitability and allows it to stay in business.

Among companies that have successfully adopted quality improvement methodologies, certain imperatives stand out. First, it is important that senior managers buy into a quality improvement program and communicate its importance to the organization. Second, if a quality improvement program is to be successful, individuals must be identified to lead the program. Under the Six Sigma methodology, exceptional employees are identified and put through a "black belt" training course on the Six Sigma methodology. The black belts are taken out of their normal job roles, and assigned to work solely on Six Sigma projects for the next 2 years. In effect, the black belts become internal consultants and project leaders. Because they are dedicated to Six Sigma programs, the black belts are not distracted from the task at hand by day-to-day operating responsibilities. To make a black belt assignment attractive, many companies now use it as a step in a career path. Successful black belts may not return to their prior job after 2 years, but instead are promoted and given more responsibility.

Third, quality improvement methodologies preach the need to identify defects that arise from processes, trace them to their source, find out what caused them, and make corrections so that they do not recur. Production and materials management typically have primary responsibility for this task. To uncover defects, quality improvement methodologies rely upon the use of statistical procedures to pinpoint variations in the quality of goods or services. Once variations have been identified, they must be traced to their source and eliminated.

One technique that greatly helps in tracing defects to their source is reducing lot sizes for manufactured products. With short production runs, defects show up immediately. Consequently, they can be quickly traced to the source, and the problem can be addressed. Reducing lot sizes also means that when defective products are produced, their number will not be large, thus decreasing waste. Flexible manufacturing techniques can be used to reduce lot sizes without raising costs. JIT inventory systems also play a part. Under a JIT system, defective parts enter the manufacturing process immediately; they are not warehoused for several months before use. Hence, defective inputs can be quickly spotted. The problem can then be traced to the supply source and corrected before more defective parts are produced. Under a more traditional system, the practice of warehousing parts for months before they are used may mean that large numbers of defects are produced by a supplier before they enter the production process.

Fourth, another key to any quality improvement program is to create a metric that can be used to measure quality. In manufacturing companies quality can be measured by criteria such as defects per million parts. In service companies, with a little creativity suitable metrics can be devised. For example, one of the metrics Florida Power & Light uses to measure quality is meter-reading errors per month.

Fifth, once a metric has been devised, the next step is to set a challenging quality goal and create incentives for reaching it. Under Six Sigma programs the goal is 3.4 defects per million units. One way of creating incentives to attain such a goal is to link rewards, like bonus pay and promotional opportunities, to the goal.

Sixth, shop floor employees can be a major source of ideas for improving product quality, so their participation needs to be incorporated into a quality-improvement program.

Seventh, a major source of poor-quality finished goods is poor-quality component parts. To decrease product defects, a company has to work with its suppliers to improve the quality of the parts they supply.

Eighth, the more assembly steps a product requires, the more opportunities there are for making mistakes. Thus, designing products with fewer parts is often a major component of any quality improvement program.

Finally, implementing quality-improvement methodologies requires organization-wide commitment and substantial cooperation among functions. R&D has to cooperate with production to design products that are easy to manufacture; marketing has to cooperate with production and R&D so that customer problems identified by marketing can be acted on; human resource management has to cooperate with all the other functions of the company in order to devise suitable quality-training programs; and so on.

Improving Quality as Excellence   As we stated earlier, a product is a bundle of different attributes. In addition to reliability, these attributes include the form, features, performance, durability, and styling of a product. A company can also create quality as excellence by emphasizing attributes of the *service* associated with the product, such as ordering ease, prompt delivery, easy installation, the availability of customer training and consulting, and maintenance services. Singapore Airlines, for example, enjoys an excellent reputation for quality service, largely because passengers perceive their flight attendants as competent, courteous, and responsive to their needs.

For a product to be regarded as high quality on the excellence dimension, its offering must be seen as superior to that of rivals. Achieving a perception of high quality on key attributes requires specific actions by managers. First, it is important for managers to collect marketing intelligence indicating which of these attributes are most important to customers. Second, once the company has identified important attributes, it needs to design its products, and the associated services, so that those attributes are embodied in the product, and it needs to make sure that personnel in the company are appropriately trained so that the correct attributes are emphasized. This requires close coordination between marketing and product development, and the involvement of the human resource management function in employee selection and training.

Third, the company must decide which of the significant attributes to promote and how best to position them in the minds of consumers, that is, how to tailor the marketing message so that it creates a consistent image in the minds of customers.[32] At this point, it is important to recognize that although a product might be differentiated on the basis of six attributes, covering all of those attributes in the company's communication messages may lead to an unfocused message. Many marketing experts advocate promoting only one or two central attributes to customers. For example, Volvo consistently emphasizes the safety and durability of its vehicles in all marketing messages, creating the perception in the minds of consumers (backed by product design) that Volvo cars are safe and durable. Volvo cars are also very reliable and have high performance, but the company does not emphasize these attributes in its marketing messages.

Finally, it must be recognized that competition does not stand still, but instead produces continual improvement in product attributes and often the development of new product attributes. This is obvious in fast-moving high-tech industries where product features that were considered leading edge just a few years ago are now obsolete, but the same process is also at work in more stable industries. For example, the rapid diffusion of microwave ovens during the 1980s required food companies to build new attributes into their frozen food products: they had to maintain their texture and consistency while being microwaved. A product could not be considered high quality unless it could do that. This speaks to the importance of having a strong R&D function in the company that can work with marketing and manufacturing to continually upgrade the quality of the attributes that are designed into the company's product offerings.

Increasing Innovation

In many ways, innovation is the most important source of competitive advantage. This is because innovation can result in new products that better satisfy customer needs, can improve the quality (attributes) of existing products, or can reduce the costs of making products that customers want. The ability to develop innovative new products or processes gives a company a major competitive advantage that allows it to (1) *differentiate* its products and charge a premium price and/or (2) *lower its cost structure* below that of its rivals. Competitors, however, attempt to imitate successful innovations and often succeed. Therefore, maintaining a competitive advantage requires a continuing commitment to innovation.

Successful new product launches are major drivers of superior profitability. Robert Cooper looked at more than 200 new product introductions and found that of those classified as successes, some 50% achieve a return on investment in excess of 33%, half have a payback period of 2 years or less, and half achieve a market share in excess of 35%.[33] Many companies have established a track record for successful innovation. Among them Sony, whose successes include the Walkman, the Compact Disc, and the PlayStation; Nokia, which has been a leader in the development of wireless phones; Pfizer, a drug company that during the 1990s and early 2000s produced eight blockbuster new drugs; 3M, which has applied its core competency in tapes and adhesives to developing a wide range of new products; Intel, which has consistently managed to lead in the development of innovative new microprocessors to run personal computers; and Cisco Systems, whose innovations helped to pave the way for the rapid growth of the Internet.

The High Failure Rate of Innovation   Although promoting innovation can be a source of competitive advantage, the failure rate of innovative new products is high. Research evidence suggests that only 10%–20% of major R&D projects give rise to commercial products.[34] Well-publicized product failures include Apple Computer's Newton, a personal digital assistant, Sony's Betamax format in the video player and recorder market, and Sega's Dreamcast videogame console. While many reasons have been advanced to explain why so many new products fail to generate an economic return, five explanations for failure appear on most lists.[35]

First, many new products fail because the demand for innovations is inherently uncertain. It is impossible to know prior to market introduction whether the new product has tapped an unmet customer need, and if there is sufficient market demand to justify making the product. While good market research can likely reduce the uncertainty about the future demand for a new technology, it cannot be completely eradicated, so a certain failure rate is to be expected.

Second, new products often fail because the technology is poorly commercialized. This occurs when there is definite customer demand for a new product, but the product is not well adapted to customer needs because of factors such as poor design and poor quality. For instance, the failure of Apple Computer to establish a market for the Newton, a hand-held personal digital system that Apple introduced in the summer of 1993, can be traced to poor commercialization of a potentially attractive technology. Apple predicted a $1 billion market for the Newton, but sales failed to materialize when it became clear that the Newton's handwriting software, an attribute that Apple chose to emphasize in its marketing promotions, could not adequately recognize messages written on the Newton's message pad.

Positioning Strategy

The specific set of options a company adopts for a product on four main dimensions of marketing: price, distribution, promotion and advertising, and product features.

Third, new products may fail because of poor positioning strategy. **Positioning strategy** is the specific set of options a company adopts for a product on four main dimensions of marketing: price, distribution, promotion and advertising, and product features. Apart from poor product quality, another reason for the failure of the Apple Newton was poor positioning strategy. The Newton was introduced at such a high initial price (close to $1,000) that there would probably have been few buyers even if the technology had been adequately commercialized.

Another reason that many new product introductions fail is that companies often make the mistake of marketing a technology for which there is not enough demand. A company can gets blinded by the wizardry of a new technology and fail to examine whether there is customer demand for the product. Finally, companies fail when they are slow to get their products to market. The more time that elapses between initial development and final marketing—the slower "cycle time"—the more likely it is that someone else will beat the company to market and gain a first-mover advantage.[36] In the car industry, General Motors has suffered from being a slow innovator. Its product development cycle has been about 5 years, compared with 2–3 years at Honda, Toyota, and Mazda and 3–4 years at Ford. Because they are based on 5-year-old technology and design concepts, GM cars are already out of date when they reach the market.

Reducing Innovation Failures   One of the most important things that managers can do to reduce the high failure rate associated with innovation is to make sure that there is tight integration between R&D, production and marketing.[37] Tight cross-functional integration can help a company to ensure that:

1. Product development projects are driven by customer needs.
2. New products are designed for ease of manufacture.
3. Development costs are kept in check.
4. Time to market is minimized.
5. Close integration between R&D and marketing is achieved to ensure that product development projects are driven by the needs of customers.

A company's customers can be one of its primary sources of new product ideas. The identification of customer needs, and particularly unmet needs, can set the context within which successful product innovation takes place. As the point of contact with customers, the marketing function can provide valuable information. Moreover, integrating R&D and marketing is crucial if a new product is to be properly commercialized. Otherwise, a company runs the risk of developing products for which there is little or no demand.

Integration between R&D and production can help a company to ensure that products are designed with manufacturing requirements in mind. Design for manufacturing lowers manufacturing costs and leaves less room for mistakes and thus can lower costs and increase product quality. Integrating R&D and production can help lower development costs and speed products to market. If a new product is not designed with manufacturing capabilities in mind, it may prove too difficult to build, given existing manufacturing technology. In that case, the product will have to be redesigned, and both overall development costs and time to market may increase significantly. Making design changes during product planning can increase overall development costs by 50% and add 25% to the time it takes to bring the product to market.[38]

One of the best ways to achieve cross-functional integration is to establish cross-functional product development teams, composed of representatives from R&D, marketing, and production. The objective of a team should be to take a product development project from the initial concept development to market introduction. A number of attributes seem to be important in order for a product development team to function effectively and meet all its development milestones.[39]

First, a **heavyweight project manager**—one who has high status within the organization and the power and authority required to get the financial and human resources that the team needs to succeed—should lead the team and be dedicated

Heavyweight Project Manager

A project manager who has high status within the organization and the power and authority required to get the financial and human resources that a project team needs to succeed.

primarily, if not entirely, to the project. The leader should believe in the project (a champion) and be skilled at integrating the perspectives of different functions and helping personnel from different functions work together for a common goal. The leader should also be able to act as an advocate of the team to senior management.

Second, the team should be composed of at least one member from each key function. The team members should have a number of attributes, including an ability to contribute functional expertise, high standing within their function, a willingness to share responsibility for team results, and an ability to put functional advocacy aside. It is generally preferable if core team members are 100% dedicated to the project for its duration. This makes sure that their focus is on the project, not on the ongoing work of their function.

Third, the team members should be physically co-located to create a sense of camaraderie and facilitate communication. Fourth, the team should have a clear plan and clear goals, particularly with regard to critical development milestones and development budgets. The team should have incentives to attain those goals; for example, pay bonuses when major development milestones are hit. Fifth, each team needs to develop its own processes for communication and conflict resolution. For example, one product development team at Quantum Corporation, a California-based manufacturer of disk drives for personal computers, instituted a rule that all major decisions would be made and conflicts resolved at meetings that were held every Monday afternoon. This simple rule helped the team to meet its development goals.[40]

Achieving Superior Customer Responsiveness

Customer responsiveness is an important *differentiating* attribute that can help to build brand loyalty. Achieving superior responsiveness means giving customers value for money. Taking steps to improve the efficiency of a company's production process and the quality of its products is consistent with this aim. Responding to customers needs may also require the development of new products with new features. *In other words, achieving superior efficiency, quality, and innovation are all part of achieving superior responsiveness to customers.* In addition, there are two other prerequisites for attaining this goal; a tight customer focus and an ongoing effort to seek better ways to satisfy those needs.

Customer Focus A company cannot be responsive to its customers' needs unless it knows what those needs are. The first step to building superior responsiveness is to motivate the whole company to focus on the customer. Customer focus must start at the top of the organization. A commitment to superior customer responsiveness brings attitudinal changes throughout a company that ultimately can be built only through strong leadership. A mission statement that puts customers first is one way to send a clear message to employees about the desired focus. Another avenue is top management's own actions. For example, Tom Monaghan, the founder of Domino's Pizza, stayed close to the customer by visiting as many stores as possible every week, running some deliveries himself, insisting that other top managers do the same, and eating Domino's pizza regularly.[41]

Leadership alone is not enough to attain a superior customer focus. All employees must see the customer as the focus of their activity and be trained to focus on the customer, whether their function is marketing, manufacturing, R&D, or accounting. The objective should be to make employees think of themselves as customers—to put themselves in customers' shoes. At that point, employees will be better able to identify ways to improve the quality of a customer's experience with the company.

To reinforce this mindset, incentive systems within the company should reward employees for satisfying customers. For example, senior managers at the Four Seasons hotel chain, who pride themselves on their customer focus, like to tell the story of Roy Dyment, a doorman in Toronto who neglected to load a departing guest's briefcase into his taxi. The doorman called the guest, a lawyer, in Washington D.C., and found that he desperately needed the briefcase for a morning meeting. Dyment hopped on a plane to Washington and returned it—without first securing approval from his boss. Far from punishing Dyment for making a mistake and for not checking with management before going to Washington, the Four Seasons responded by naming Dyment Employee of the Year.[42] This action sent a powerful message to Four Seasons employees about the importance of satisfying customer needs.

Satisfying Customer Needs   Another key to superior responsiveness is to satisfy customer needs that have been identified. As already noted, efficiency, quality, and innovation are crucial competencies that help a company satisfy customer needs. Beyond that, companies can provide a higher level of satisfaction if they differentiate their products by (1) customizing them, where possible, to the requirements of individual customers and (2) reducing the time it takes to respond to or satisfy customer needs.

Customization entails varying the features of a good or service to tailor it to the unique needs or tastes of groups of customers or, in the extreme case, individual customers. Although extensive customization can raise costs, the development of flexible manufacturing technologies has made it possible to customize products to a much greater extent than was feasible 10–15 years ago without experiencing a prohibitive rise in cost structure (particularly when flexible manufacturing technologies are linked with web-based information systems). For example, online retailers such as Amazon. com have used Web-based technologies to develop a home page customized for each individual user. When a customer accesses Amazon.com, he or she is offered a list of recommendations for books or music to purchase based on an analysis of prior buying history, a powerful competency that gives Amazon.com a competitive advantage.

In addition, to gain a competitive advantage a company must often respond to customer demands very quickly, whether the transaction is a furniture manufacturer's delivery of a product once it has been ordered, a bank's processing of a loan application, an automobile manufacturer's delivery of a spare part for a car that broke down, or the wait in a supermarket checkout line. We live in a fast-paced society, where time is a valuable commodity. Companies that can satisfy customer demands for rapid response build brand loyalty, differentiate their products, and can charge higher prices for them.

A good example of the value of rapid response time is Caterpillar, the manufacturer of heavy earth-moving equipment, which can get a spare part to any point in the world within 24 hours. Downtime for heavy construction equipment is very costly, so Caterpillar's ability to respond quickly in the event of equipment malfunction is of prime importance to its customers. As a result, many of them have remained loyal to Caterpillar despite the aggressive low-price competition from Komatsu of Japan.

In general, reducing response time requires (1) a marketing function that can quickly communicate customer requests to production, (2) production and materials management functions that can quickly adjust production schedules in response to unanticipated customer demands, and (3) information systems that can help production and marketing in this process.

Customization

Varying the features of a good or service to tailor it to the unique needs or tastes of groups of customers or, in the extreme case, of individual customers.

DISTINCTIVE COMPETENCIES AND COMPETITIVE ADVANTAGE

Distinctive Competency

A unique, firm-specific strength that enables a company to better *differentiate* its products and/or achieve substantially *lower costs* than its rivals and thus gain a competitive advantage.

If managers are successful in their efforts to improve the efficiency, quality, innovation and customer responsiveness of their organization, they may lower the cost structure of the company and/or better differentiate its product offering, either of which can be the basis for a competitive advantage. When a company is uniquely skilled at a value chain activity that underlies superior efficiency, quality, innovation, or customer responsiveness relative to its rivals, we say that it has a *distinctive competency* in this activity. A **distinctive competency** is a unique firm-specific strength that allows a company to better *differentiate* its products and/or achieve substantially *lower costs* than its rivals and thus gain a competitive advantage. For example, 3M has a distinctive competency in innovation that has enabled the company to generate 30% of its sales from differentiated products introduced within the last 5 years. Distinctive competencies can be viewed as the bedrock of a company's competitive advantage. Distinctive competencies arise from two complementary sources: *resources* and *capabilities*.[43]

Resources and Capabilities

Resources

Financial, physical, social or human, technological, and organizational factors that allow a company to create value for its customers. Company resources can be divided into two types: tangible and intangible resources.

Resources are financial, physical, social or human, technological, and organizational factors that allow a company to create value for its customers. Company resources can be divided into two types: tangible and intangible resources. **Tangible resources** are something physical, such as land, buildings, plant, equipment, inventory, and money. **Intangible resources** are nonphysical entities that are the creation of managers and other employees, such as brand names, the reputation of the company, the knowledge that employees have gained through experience, and the intellectual property of the company, including that protected through patents, copyrights, and trademarks.

Tangible Resources

Physical resources, such as land, buildings, plant, equipment, inventory, and money.

The more *firm specific* and *difficult to imitate* is a resource, the more likely a company is to have a distinctive competency. For example, Polaroid's distinctive competency in instant photography was based on a firm-specific and valuable intangible resource: technological know-how in instant film processing that was protected from imitation by a thicket of patents. Once a process can be imitated, as when patents expire, or a superior technology, such as digital photography, comes along, the distinctive competency disappears, as has happened to Polaroid. Another important quality of a resource that leads to a distinctive competency is that it is *valuable*: in some way, it helps to create strong *demand* for the company's products. Thus, Polaroid's technological know-how was valuable while it created strong demand for its photographic products; it became far less valuable when superior digital technology came along.

Intangible Resources

Nonphysical entities that are the creation of managers and other employees, such as brand names, the reputation of the company, the knowledge that employees have gained through experience, and the intellectual property of the company, including that protected through patents, copyrights, and trademarks.

Capabilities refer to a company's skills at coordinating its resources and putting them to productive use. These skills reside in an organization's rules, routines, and procedures, that is, the style or manner through which it makes decisions and manages its internal processes to achieve organizational objectives. More generally, a company's capabilities are the product of its organizational structure, processes, and control systems. They specify how and where decisions are made within a company, the kind of behaviors the company rewards, and the company's cultural norms and values. (We discuss how organizational structure and control systems help a company obtain capabilities in Chapters 7 and 8.) Capabilities are intangible. They reside not so much in individuals as in the way individuals interact, cooperate, and make decisions within the context of an organization.[44]

The distinction between resources and capabilities is critical to understanding what generates a distinctive competency. A company may have firm-specific and valuable resources, but unless it has the capability to use those resources effectively, it may not be able to create a distinctive competency. It is also important to recognize that a company may not need firm-specific and valuable resources to establish a distinctive competency so long as it *does have* capabilities that no competitor possesses. For example, the steel mini-mill operator Nucor is widely acknowledged to be the most cost-efficient steel maker in the United States. Its distinctive competency in low-cost (efficient) steel making does not come from any firm-specific and valuable resources. Nucor has the same resources (plant, equipment, skilled employees, know-how) as many other mini-mill operators. What distinguishes Nucor is its unique capability to manage its resources in a highly productive way. Specifically, Nucor's structure, control systems, and culture promote efficiency at all levels within the company.

In sum, for a company to have a distinctive competency it must at a minimum have either (1) a firm-specific and valuable resource and the capabilities (skills) necessary to take advantage of that resource (as illustrated by Polaroid) or (2) a firm-specific capability to manage resources (as exemplified by Nucor). A company's distinctive competency is strongest when it possesses *both* firm-specific and valuable resources and firm-specific capabilities to manage those resources.

Figure 4.6 illustrates the relationship of a company's strategies, distinctive competencies, and competitive advantage. Distinctive competencies shape the strategies that the company pursues, which build superior efficiency, quality, innovation or customer responsiveness. In turn, this leads to competitive advantage and superior profitability. However, it is also very important to realize that the strategies a company adopts can build new resources and capabilities or strengthen the existing resources and capabilities of the company, thereby enhancing the distinctive competencies of the enterprise. Thus, the relationship between distinctive competencies and strategies is not a linear one; rather, it is a reciprocal one in which distinctive competencies shape strategies, and strategies help to build and create distinctive competencies.[45]

Capabilities

A company's skills at coordinating its resources and putting them to productive use.

Figure 4.6 Strategy, Resources, Capabilities, and Competencies

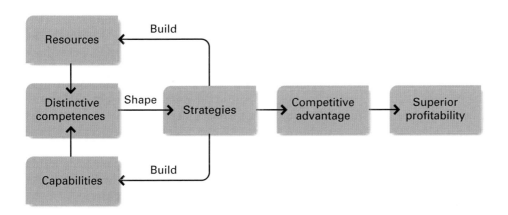

The Durability of Competitive Advantage

A company with a competitive advantage will have superior profitability. This sends a signal to rivals that the company has some valuable distinctive competency that allows it to create superior value. Competitors will try to identify and imitate that competency, and insofar as they are successful, ultimately the imitators may compete away the company's superior profitability.[46] The speed at which this process occurs depends upon the height of barriers to imitation.

Barriers to imitation are factors that make it difficult for a competitor to copy a company's distinctive competencies; the greater the barriers to imitation, the more sustainable are a company's competitive advantage.[47] Barriers to imitation differ depending on whether a competitor is trying to imitate resources or capabilities.

In general, the easiest distinctive competencies for prospective rivals to imitate tend to be those based on possession of firm-specific and valuable tangible resources, such as buildings, plant, and equipment. Such resources are visible to competitors and can often be purchased on the open market. For example, if a company's competitive advantage is based on sole possession of efficient-scale manufacturing facilities, competitors may move fairly quickly to establish similar facilities. Although Ford gained a competitive advantage over General Motors in the 1920s by being the first to adopt an assembly line manufacturing technology to produce automobiles, General Motors quickly imitated that innovation, competing away Ford's distinctive competence in the process.

Intangible resources can be more difficult to imitate. This is particularly true of brand names, which are important because they symbolize a company's reputation. In the heavy earthmoving equipment industry, for example, the Caterpillar brand name is synonymous with high quality and superior after-sales service and support. Customers often display a preference for the products of such companies because the brand name is an important guarantee of high quality. Although competitors might like to imitate well-established brand names, the law prohibits them from doing so.

Marketing and technological know-how are also important intangible resources and can be relatively easy to imitate. Successful marketing strategies are relatively easy to imitate because they are so visible to competitors. Thus, Coca-Cola quickly imitated PepsiCo's Diet Pepsi brand with the introduction of its own brand, Diet Coke.

With regard to technological know-how, the patent system in theory should make technological know-how relatively immune to imitation. Patents give the inventor of a new product a 20-year exclusive production agreement. However, it is often possible to invent around patents—that is, produce a product that is functionally equivalent, but does not rely upon the patented technology. One study found that 60% of patented innovations were successfully invented around in 4 years.[48] This suggests that in general, distinctive competencies based on technological know-how can be relatively short-lived.

Imitating a company's capabilities tends to be more difficult than imitating its tangible and intangible resources, chiefly because capabilities are based on the way in which decisions are made and processes managed deep within a company. It is hard for outsiders to discern them.

On its own, the invisible nature of capabilities would not be enough to halt imitation; competitors could still gain insights into how a company operates by hiring people away from that company. However, a company's capabilities rarely reside in a

Barriers to Imitation

Factors that make it difficult for a competitor to copy a company's distinctive competencies.

single individual. Rather, they are the product of how numerous individuals interact within a unique organizational setting.[49] It is possible that no one individual within a company may be familiar with the totality of a company's internal operating routines and procedures. In such cases, hiring people away from a successful company in order to imitate its key capabilities may not be helpful.

In sum, a company's competitive advantage tends to be more secure when it is based upon intangible resources and capabilities, as opposed to tangible resources. Capabilities can be particularly difficult to imitate, since doing so requires the imitator to change its own internal management processes—something that is never easy due to organization inertia. Even in such a favorable situation, however, a company is never totally secure. The reason for this is that rather than imitating a company with a competitive advantage, competitors may invent their way around the source of competitive advantage. The decline of once dominant companies like IBM, General Motors, and Sears has not been due to imitation of their distinctive competencies, but to the fact that rivals such as Dell, Toyota, and Walmart developed new and better ways of competing which nullified the competitive advantage once enjoyed by these enterprises. Herein lies the rationale for the statement popularized by the former CEO of Intel, Andy Grove that "only the paranoid survive!" Even if a company's distinctive competencies are protected by high barriers to imitation, it should act as if rivals are continually trying to nullify its source of advantage either by imitation, *or* by developing new ways of doing business—for in reality, that is exactly what they are trying to do.

SUMMARY OF CHAPTER

1. To have superior profitability, a company must lower its costs or differentiate its product so that it creates more value and can charge a higher price, or do both simultaneously.

2. The four building blocks of competitive advantage are efficiency, quality, innovation, and customer responsiveness. Superior efficiency enables a company to lower its costs; superior quality allows it to charge a higher price and lower its costs; and superior customer service lets it charge a higher price. Superior innovation can lead to higher prices, particularly in the case of product innovations, or lower unit costs, particularly in the case of process innovations.

3. The term value chain refers to the idea that a company is a chain of activities for transforming inputs into outputs valued by customers' value. The process of transforming inputs into outputs is composed of a number of primary activities and support activities. Each activity adds value to the product.

4. Actions taken by functional managers at every step in the value chain—functional level strategies—can increase the efficiency, quality, innovation, and customer responsiveness of a company.

5. Distinctive competencies are the firm-specific strengths of a company. Valuable distinctive competencies enable a company to generate superior profitability.

6. The distinctive competencies of an organization arise from its resources and capabilities.

7. In order to achieve a competitive advantage, a company needs to pursue strategies that build on its existing resources and capabilities and formulate strategies that build additional resources and capabilities (develop new competencies).

8. The durability of a company's competitive advantage depends on the height of barriers to imitation.

DISCUSSION QUESTIONS

1. When is a company's competitive advantage most likely to endure over time?
2. What role can top management play in helping a company achieve superior efficiency, quality, innovation, and responsiveness to customers?

3. How are the four generic building blocks of competitive advantage related to each other?

C L O S I N G   C A S E

Starbucks

In 2006, Starbucks', the ubiquitous coffee retailer, closed a decade of astounding financial performance. Sales had increased from $697 million to $7.8 billion and net profits from $36 million to $540 million. In 2006, Starbucks' was earning a return on invested capital of 25.5%, which was impressive by any measure, and the company was forecasted to continue growing earnings and maintain high profits through to the end of the decade. How did this come about?

Thirty years ago Starbucks was a single store in Seattle's Pike Place Market selling premium roasted coffee. Today it is a global roaster and retailer of coffee with more than 12,000 retail stores, some 3,000 of which are to be found in 40 countries outside the United States. Starbucks Corporation set out on its current course in the 1980s when the company's director of marketing, Howard Schultz, came back from a trip to Italy enchanted with the Italian coffeehouse experience. Schultz, who later became CEO, persuaded the company's owners to experiment with the coffeehouse format—and the Starbucks experience was born.

Schultz's basic insight was that people lacked a "third place" between home and work where they could have their own personal time out, meet with friends, relax, and have a sense of gathering. The business model that evolved out of this was to sell the company's own premium roasted coffee, along with freshly brewed espresso-style coffee beverages, a variety of pastries, coffee accessories, teas, and other products, in a coffeehouse setting. The company devoted, and continues to devote, considerable attention to the design of its stores, so as to create a relaxed, informal and comfortable atmosphere.

Underlying this approach was a belief that Starbucks was selling far more than coffee—it was selling an experience. The premium price that Starbucks charged for its coffee reflected this fact.

From the outset, Schultz also focused on providing superior customer service in stores. Reasoning that motivated employees provide the best customer service, Starbucks executives developed employee hiring and training programs that were the best in the restaurant industry. Today, all Starbucks employees are required to attend training classes that teach them not only how to make a good cup of coffee, but also the service oriented values of the company. Beyond this, Starbucks provided progressive compensation policies that gave even part-time employees stock option grants and medical benefits—a very innovative approach in an industry where most employees are part time, earn minimum wage, and have no benefits.

Unlike many restaurant chains, which expanded very rapidly through franchising arrangement once they have established a basic formula that appears to work, Schultz believed that Starbucks needed to own its stores. Although it has experimented with franchising arrangements in some countries, and some situations in the United States such as at airports, the company still prefers to own its own stores wherever possible.

This formula met with spectacular success in the United States, where Starbucks went from obscurity to one of the best known brands in the country in a decade. As it grew, Starbucks found that it was generating an enormous volume of repeat business. Today the average customer comes into a Starbucks' store around 20 times a month. The customers themselves are a fairly well-healed group—their average income is about $80,000.

As the company grew, it started to develop a very sophisticated location strategy. Detailed demographic analysis was used to identify the best locations for Starbuck's stores. The company expanded rapidly to capture as many premium locations as possible before imitators. Astounding many observers, Starbucks would even sometimes locate stores on opposite corners of the same busy street—so that it could capture traffic going different directions down the street.

By 1995 with almost 700 stores across the United States, Starbucks began exploring foreign opportunities. First stop was Japan, where Starbucks proved that the basic value proposition could be applied to a different cultural setting (there are now 600 stores in Japan). Next, Starbucks embarked upon a rapid development strategy in Asia and Europe. By 2001, the magazine *Brandchannel* named Starbucks 1 of

the 10 most impactful global brands, a position it has held ever since. But this is only the beginning. In late 2006, with 12,000 stores in operation, the company announced that its long term goal was to have 40,000 stores worldwide. Looking forward, it expects 50% of all new store openings to be outside of the United States.[50]

Case Discussion Questions

1. What functional strategies at Starbucks' help the company to achieve superior financial performance?
2. Identify the resources, capabilities, and distinctive competencies of Starbucks?
3. How do Starbucks' resources, capabilities, and distinctive competencies translate into superior financial performance?
4. Why do you think Starbucks' prefers to own its own stores wherever possible?
5. How secure is Starbucks' competitive advantage? What are the barriers to imitation here?

NOTES

1. The concept of consumer surplus is an important one in economics. For a more detailed exposition see D. Besanko, D. Dranove, and M. Shanley, *Economics of Strategy* (New York: John Wiley & Sons, 1996).
2. However, $P = V$ only in the special case where the company has a perfect monopoly, and where it can charge each customer a unique price that reflects the value of the product to that customer (i.e., where perfect price discrimination is possible). More generally, except in the limiting case of perfect price discrimination even a monopolist will see most consumers capture some of the value of a product in the form of a consumer surplus.
3. This point is central to the work of Michael Porter. See M. E. Porter, *Competitive Advantage* (New York: Free Press, 1985). See also Chapter 4 in P. Ghemawat, *Commitment: The Dynamic of Strategy* (New York: Free Press, 1991).
4. Harbour Consulting, "Productivity Gap Among North American Auto Makers Narrows in Harbour Report 2006," *Harbour Consulting Press Release*, July 1, 2006.
5. M. E. Porter, *Competitive Strategy* (New York: Free Press, 1980).
6. This approach goes back to the pioneering work by K. Lancaster, *Consumer Demand: A New Approach* (New York: Columbia University Press, 1971).
7. D. Garvin, "Competing on the Eight Dimensions of Quality," *Harvard Business Review,* November–December 1987, 101–119; P. Kotler, *Marketing Management* (Millennium ed.) (Upper Saddle River, N.j.: Prentice-Hall, 2000).
8. J.D. Power Asia Pacific 2010 Malaysia Initial Quality Studysm (IQS), October 29, 2010, http://businesscenter.jdpower.com/news/pressrelease.aspx?ID=2010208 (accessed January 6, 2011); and "Proton Bomb," *The Economist,* May 8, 2004, 77.
9. C. K. Prahalad and M. S. Krishnan, "The New Meaning of Quality in the Information Age," *Harvard Business Review,* September–October 1999, 109–118.
10. See D. Garvin, "What Does Product Quality Really Mean," *Sloan Management Review,* Fall 1984, 26, 25–44; P. B. Crosby, *Quality is Free* (New York: Mentor, 1980); and A. Gabor, *The Man Who Discovered Quality* (New York: Times Books, 1990).
11. M. Cusumano, *The Japanese Automobile Industry* (Cambridge, Mass.: Harvard University Press, 1989); and S. Spear and H. K. Bowen, "Decoding the DNA of the Toyota Production System," *Harvard Business Review*, September–October 1999, 96–108.
12. W. Chan Kim and R. Mauborgne, "Value Innovation: The Strategic Logic of High Growth," *Harvard Business Review*, January–February 1997, 102–115.

13. G. Stalk and T. M. Hout, *Competing Against Time* (New York: Free Press, 1990).

14. Ibid.

15. M. E. Porter, *Competitive Advantage*.

16. H. Luft, J. Bunker, and A.C. Enthoven, "Should Operations Be Regionalized?" *New England Journal of Medicine* 301 (1979): 1364–1369.

17. S. Chambers and R. Johnston, "Experience Curves in Services," *International Journal of Operations and Production Management* 20 (2000): 842–860.

18. Source: G. P. Pisano, R. M. J. Bohmer, and A. C. Edmondson, "Organizational Differences in Rates of Learning: Evidence from the Adoption of Minimally Invasive Cardiac Surgery," *Management Science* 47 (2001): 752–768.

19. See P. L. Nemetz and L. W. Fry, "Flexible Manufacturing Organizations: Implications for Strategy Formulation," *Academy of Management Review* 13 (1988): 627–638; N. Greenwood, *Implementing Flexible Manufacturing Systems* (New York: Halstead Press, 1986); J. P. Womack, D. T. Jones, and D. Roos, *The Machine That Changed the World* (New York: Rawson Associates, 1990); and R. Parthasarthy and S. P. Seith, "The Impact of Flexible Automation on Business Strategy and Organizational Structure," *Academy of Management Review* 17 (1992): 86–111.

20. B. J. Pine, *Mass Customization: The New Frontier in Business Competition* (Boston, Mass.: Harvard Business School Press, 1993); S. Kotha, "Mass Customization: Implementing the Emerging Paradigm for Competitive Advantage," *Strategic Management Journal* 16 (1995): 21–42; and J. H. Gilmore and B. J. Pine II, "The Four Faces of Mass Customization," *Harvard Business Review*, January–February 1997, 91–101.

21. F. F. Reichheld and W. E. Sasser, "Zero Defections: Quality Comes to Service," *Harvard Business Review*, September–October 1990, 105–111.

22. A. Z. Cuneo, "Call Verizon Victorious," *Advertising Age*, March 8, 2004, 3–5.

23. H. F. Busch, "Integrated Materials Management," *International Journal of Physical. Distribution and Materials Management* 18 (1990): 28–39.

24. Stalk and Hout, *Competing Against Time*.

25. See P. Bamberger and I. Meshoulam, *Human Resource Strategy: Formulation, Implementation, and Impact* (Thousand Oaks, Calif.: Sage, 2000); and P. M. Wright and S. Snell, "Towards a Unifying Framework for Exploring Fit and Flexibility in Human Resource Management," *Academy of Management Review,* 23 October 1998, 756–772.

26. J. Hoerr, "The Payoff from Teamwork," *Business Week,* July 10, 1989, 56–62.

27. T. C. Powell and A. Dent-Micallef, "Information Technology as Competitive Advantage: The Role of Human, Business, and Technology Resource," *Strategic Management Journal* 18 (1997): 375–405; and B. Gates, *Business @ the Speed of Thought* (New York: Warner Books, 1999).

28. "Cisco@speed," *Economist,* June 26, 1999, 12; S. Tully, "How Cisco Mastered the Net," *Fortune,* August 17, 1997, 207–210; and C. Kano, "The Real King of the Internet," *Fortune,* September 7, 1998, 82–93.

29. Sources: S. Walton and J. Huey, *Sam Walton: Made in America* (New York: Bantam, 1993). S. Maich, "Walmart's Mid Life Crisis," *Maclean's,* August 23, 2004, 45; and "The People Make It All Happen," *Discount Store News,* October 1999, 103–106. http://www.walmartstores.com.

30. Gates, *Business @ the Speed of Thought.*

31. See the articles published in the special issue of the *Academy of Management Review on Total Quality Management* 19 (1994): 3. The following article provides a good overview of many of the issues involved from an academic perspective: J. W. Dean and D. E. Bowen, "Management Theory and Total Quality," *Academy of Management Review* 19 (1994): 392–418. Also see T. C. Powell, "Total Quality Management as Competitive Advantage," *Strategic Management Journal* 16 (1995): 15–37.

32. A. Ries and J. Trout, *Positioning: The Battle for Your Mind* (New York: Warner Books, 1982).

33. R. G. Cooper, *Product Leadership* (Reading, Mass.: Perseus Books, 1999).

34. See: Cooper, *Product Leadership*. A. L. Page PDMA's New product development practices survey: Performance and best practices. PDMA 15th Annual International Conference, Boston, Mass., October 16, 1991; and E. Mansfield, "How Economists See R&D," *Harvard Business Review*, November–December 1981, 98–106.

35. S. L. Brown and K. M. Eisenhardt, "Product Development: Past Research, Present Findings, and Future Directions," *Academy of Management Review* 20 (1995): 343–378; M. B. Lieberman and D. B. Montgomery, "First Mover Advantages," Special Issue, *Strategic Management Journal* 9 (Summer 1988): 41–58; D. J. Teece, "Profiting from Technological Innovation: Implications for Integration, Collaboration, Licensing and Public Policy," *Research Policy* 15 (1987): 285–305; G. J. Tellis and P. N. Golder, "First to Market, First to Fail?" *Sloan Management Review,* Winter 1996, 65–75; and G. A. Stevens and J. Burley, "Piloting the Rocket of Radical Innovation," *Research Technology Management,* 46 (2003): 16–26.

36. Stalk and Hout, *Competing Against Time.*

37. K. B. Clark and S. C. Wheelwright, *Managing New Product and Process Development* (New York: Free Press, 1993); and M. A. Schilling and C. W. L. Hill, "Managing the New Product Development Process," *Academy of Management Executive* 12, no. 3 (August 1998): 67–81.

38. O. Port, "Moving Past the Assembly Line," Special Issue, *Business Week,* Reinventing America, 1992, 177–180.

39. K. B. Clark and T. Fujimoto, "The Power of Product Integrity," *Harvard Business Review,* November–December 1990, 107–118; Clark and Wheelwright, *Managing New Product and Process Development*; Brown and Eisenhardt, "Product Development"; and Stalk and Hout, *Competing Against Time.*

40. C. Christensen, "Quantum Corporation—Business and Product Teams," *Harvard Business School Case,* #9-692-023.

41. S. Caminiti, "A Mail Order Romance: Lands' End Courts Unseen Customers," *Fortune,* March 13, 1989, 43–44.

42. P. Sellers, "Getting Customers to Love You," *Fortune,* March 13, 1989, 38–42.

43. The material in this section relies on the resource-based view of the company. For summaries of this perspective, see J. B. Barney, "Company Resources and Sustained Competitive Advantage," *Journal of Management* 17 (1991): 99–120; J. T. Mahoney and J. R. Pandian, "The Resource-Based View Within the Conversation of Strategic Management," *Strategic Management Journal* 13 (1992): 63–380; R. Amit and P. J. H. Schoemaker, "Strategic Assets and Organizational Rent," *Strategic Management Journal* 14 (1993): 33–46; M. A. Peteraf, "The Cornerstones of Competitive Advantage: A Resource-Based View," *Strategic Management Journal* 14 (1993): 179–191; B. Wernerfelt, "A Resource Based View of the Company," *Strategic Management Journal* 15 (1994): 171–180; and K. M. Eisenhardt and J. A. Martin, "Dynamic Capabilities: What are They?" *Strategic Management Journal*, 21 (2000): 1105–1121.

44. For a discussion of organizational capabilities, see R. R. Nelson and S. G. Winter, *An Evolutionary Theory of Economic Change* (Cambridge, Mass.: Belknap Press, 1982).

45. Kim and Mauborgne, "Value Innovation: The Strategic Logic of High Growth."

46. This is the nature of the competitive process. For more detail, see C. W. L. Hill and D. Deeds, "The Importance of Industry Structure for the Determination of Company Profitability: A Neo-Austrian Perspective," *Journal of Management Studies,* 33 (1996): 429–451.

47. As with resources and capabilities, so the concept of barriers to imitation is also grounded in the resource-based view of the company. For details, see R. Reed and R. J. DeFillippi, "Causal Ambiguity, Barriers to Imitation, and Sustainable Competitive Advantage," *Academy of Management Review* 15 (1990): 88–102.

48. E. Mansfield, "How Economists See R&D."

49. S. L. Berman, J. Down, and C. W. L. Hill, "Tacit Knowledge as a Source of Competitive Advantage in the National Basketball Association," *Academy of Management Journal* (2002): 13–33.

50. Sources: Starbucks 10K, various years; C. McLean, "Starbucks Set to Invade Coffee-Loving Continent," *Seattle Times,* October 4, 2000, E1; J. Ordonez, "Starbucks to Start Major Expansion in Overseas Market," *Wall Street Journal*, October 27, 2000, B10; S. Homes and D. Bennett, "Planet Starbucks," *Business Week,* September 9, 2002, 99–110; J. Batsell, "A Bean Counters Dream," *Seattle Times,* March 28, 2004, E1; Staff Reporter, "Boss Talk: it's a Grande Latte World," *Wall Street Journal*, December 15, 2003, B1. S. C. Harris, "Starbucks beats estimates, outlines expansion plans," *Seattle Post Intelligencer,* October 5, 2006, C1.

POSITIONING FOR COMPETITIVE BUSINESS-LEVEL STRATEGY

5

CHAPTER OUTLINE

The Nature of Competitive Positioning

*Customer Needs and Product
   Differentiation*
*Customer Groups and Market
   Segmentation*
Distinctive Competencies

Choosing a Business-Level Strategy

Cost-Leadership Strategy
Differentiation Strategy

*Cost Leadership and Differentiation
Focus Strategy
Stuck in the Middle*

**Competitive Positioning in Different
Industry Environments**

*Strategies in Fragmented and
   Growing Industries
Strategy in Mature Industries
Strategies in Declining Industries*

LEARNING OBJECTIVES

After reading this chapter, you should be able to:

- Discuss the nature of competitive positioning in reference to the three main factors that underlie the choice of a successful business-level strategy.
- Differentiate between the principal kinds of generic business-level strategies

and appreciate their advantages and disadvantages.
- Appreciate the competitive positioning issues involved in fragmented, growing, mature, and declining industry environments.

OVERVIEW

This chapter examines the various strategies a company can adopt to maximize its competitive advantage and profitability in a business or industry. Chapter 3, on the industry environment, provides concepts for analyzing industry opportunities and threats. Chapter 4 discusses how a company develops functional-level strategies to build distinctive competencies to achieve a competitive advantage. In this chapter, we first examine the principal business-level strategies that a company can use to achieve a competitive advantage against rivals in an industry. Second, we discuss a separate but related issue: how to choose appropriate competitive tactics, and maneuvers to build a company's competitive advantage over time in different kinds of industry environments. By the end of this chapter, you will be able to identify and distinguish among the business-level strategies and tactics that strategic managers use to give their companies a competitive advantage over their industry rivals.

THE NATURE OF COMPETITIVE POSITIONING

In order to maximize its competitive advantage, a company must find the best way to position itself against its rivals. It does this by using business-level strategy. Business-level strategy is the plan of action that strategic managers adopt to use a company's resources and distinctive competencies to gain a competitive advantage over its rivals in a market or industry. In Chapter 2 we discuss how the process of defining a business involves decisions about (1) customer needs, or *what* is to be satisfied; (2) customer groups, or *who* is to be satisfied; and (3) distinctive competencies, or *how* customer needs are to be satisfied.[1] These three decisions are the basis of the choice of a business-level strategy because they determine how a company will compete in an industry. Consequently, we need to look at the ways in which a company makes these three decisions in an effort to gain a competitive advantage over its rivals.

Customer Needs and Product Differentiation

Customer needs are desires, wants, or cravings that can be satisfied by means of the characteristics of a product (a good or service). For example, a person's craving for something sweet can be satisfied by a carton of Godiva chocolates, a Snickers bar, or a spoonful of sugar. Product differentiation is the process of creating a competitive advantage by designing products—goods or services—to satisfy customer needs. All companies must differentiate their products to a certain degree in order to attract customers and satisfy some minimal level of need. However, some companies differentiate their products to a much greater degree than others, and this difference can give them a competitive edge.

Some companies offer the customer a low-priced product without engaging in much product differentiation. Others seek to endow their product with some unique attribute(s) so that it will satisfy customers' needs in ways that other products cannot. The uniqueness may be related to the physical characteristics of the product, such as quality or reliability, or it may lie in the product's appeal to

---

Business-Level Strategy

The plan of action strategic managers adopt to use a company's resources and distinctive competencies to gain a competitive advantage.

Customer Needs

Desires, wants, or cravings that can be satisfied by means of the characteristics of a product or service.

Product Differentiation

The process of creating a competitive advantage by designing goods or services to satisfy customer needs.

customers' psychological needs, such as the need for prestige or status.[2] Thus, a Japanese car may be differentiated by its reputation for reliability, and a Corvette or a Porsche may be differentiated by its ability to satisfy customers' needs for status.

Customer Groups and Market Segmentation

Market segmentation is the way a company decides to group customers, based on important differences in their needs or preferences, in order to gain a competitive advantage.[3] For example, General Motors groups its customers according to the amount of money they want to spend, and can afford to spend, to buy a car, and for each group it builds different cars, which range from the low-priced Chevrolet Aveo to the high-priced Cadillac DTS.

In general, a company can adopt one of three alternative strategies for market segmentation.[4] First, it can choose not to recognize that different groups of customers have different needs and can instead adopt the approach of serving the average customer. Second, a company can choose to recognize the differences between customer groups and make a product targeted toward most or all of the different market segments. For example, Toyota offers over 20 different kinds of vehicles, such as family cars, luxury vehicles, SUVs, and trucks, each targeted at a different market segment. Third, a company can choose to recognize that the market is segmented but concentrate on servicing only one market segment—an example is the luxury-car niche chosen by Mercedes-Benz.

Why would a company want to make complex product/market choices and create a different product tailored to each market segment, rather than creating a single product for the whole market? The answer is that the decision to provide many products for many market niches allows a company to satisfy customers' needs better. As a result, customer demand for a company's products rises and generates more revenue than would be the case if the company offered just one product for the whole market.[5] Sometimes, however, the nature of the product or the nature of the industry does not allow much differentiation; this is the case, for example, with bulk chemicals or cement.[6] In these industries, there is little opportunity to obtain a competitive advantage through product differentiation and market segmentation, because there is little opportunity for serving customers' needs and customer groups in different ways. Instead, price is the main criterion that customers use to evaluate the product, and the competitive advantage lies with the company that has superior efficiency and can provide the lowest-priced product.

Distinctive Competencies

The third issue in business-level strategy is to decide which distinctive competencies to pursue to satisfy customers' needs and customer groups.[7] In Chapter 4 we discuss four ways in which companies can obtain a competitive advantage: superior efficiency, quality, innovation, and responsiveness to customers. The Four Seasons hotel chain, for example, attempts to do all it can to provide its customers with the highest-quality accommodations and the best customer service possible. In making business strategy choices, a company must decide how to organize and combine its distinctive competencies to gain a competitive advantage.

Market Segmentation

The way a company decides to group customers based on important differences in their needs or preferences, to gain a competitive advantage.

RUNNING CASE

Walmart's Business Model and Competitive Positioning

Walmart's business model is based on buying goods from suppliers as inexpensively as possible and then selling them to customers at the lowest possible prices. Sam Walton, the company's founder, developed strategies to allow the company to position itself to keep operating costs to a minimum so that he could offer customers everyday low prices and continuous price rollbacks. Walton chose strategies to increase efficiency, such as having low product differentiation (Walmart chooses minimal advertising and low responsiveness to customers) and targeting the mass market. His discount retail business model was based on the idea that lower costs mean lower prices.

Having devised a way to compete for customers, Walton's task was now to implement the business model in ways that would create a low-cost structure to allow him to charge lower prices. One business-level strategy he implemented was to locate his stores in small towns where there were no low-cost competitors; a second was to find ways to manage the value chain to reduce the costs of getting products from manufacturers to customers; and a third was to design and staff store operations to increase efficiency. The task of all functional managers in logistics, materials management, sales and customer service, store management, and so on, was to implement specific functional-level strategies that supported the low-cost/low-price business model. Walmart has made thousands of specific strategic choices to allow it to implement its low-price business model successfully.

CHOOSING A BUSINESS-LEVEL STRATEGY

Companies pursue a business-level strategy to gain a competitive advantage that enables them to outperform rivals and achieve above-average returns. They can choose from three basic generic competitive approaches: cost leadership, differentiation, and focus, although, as we will see, these can be combined in different ways.[8] These strategies are called *generic* because all businesses or industries can pursue them, regardless of whether they are manufacturing, service, or nonprofit enterprises. Each of the generic strategies results from a company's making consistent choices on product, market, and distinctive competencies—choices that reinforce each other. Table 5.1 summarizes the choices appropriate for each of the three generic strategies.

Table 5.1   Product/Market/Distinctive-Competency Choices and Generic Competitive Strategies

	Cost Leadership	Differentiation	Focus
Product Differentiation	Low (principally by price)	High (principally by uniqueness)	Low to high (price or uniqueness)
Market Segmentation	Low (mass market)	High (many market segments)	Low (one or few segments)
Distinctive Competency	Manufacturing and materials management	Research and development, sales and marketing	Any kind of distinctive competency

Cost-Leadership Strategy

A company's goal in pursuing a cost-leadership strategy is to outperform competitors by doing everything it can to produce goods or services at a cost lower than those competitors. Two advantages accrue from a cost-leadership strategy. First, because the company has lower costs, it will be more profitable than its closest competitors—the companies that compete for the same set of customers and charge similar low prices for their products. If companies in the industry charge similar prices for their products, the cost leader still makes a higher profit than its competitors because of its lower costs. Second, if rivalry within the industry increases and companies start to compete on price, the cost leader will be able to withstand competition better than the other companies because of its lower costs. For both of these reasons, cost leaders are likely to earn above-average profits. How does a company become the cost leader? It achieves this position by means of the product/market/distinctive-competency choices that it makes to gain a low-cost competitive advantage (see Table 5.1).

Strategic Choices The cost leader chooses a low to moderate level of product differentiation. Differentiation is expensive; if the company expends resources to make its products unique, then its costs rise.[9] The cost leader aims for a level of differentiation not markedly inferior to that of the differentiator (a company that competes by spending resources on product development), but a level obtainable at low cost.[10] The cost leader does not try to be the industry leader in differentiation; it waits until customers want a feature or service before providing it. For example, a cost leader does not introduce stereo sound in television sets. It adds stereo sound only when consumers clearly want it or after competitors do it first.

The cost leader also normally ignores the different market segments and positions its product to appeal to the average customer. This is because developing a line of products tailored to the needs of different market segments is an expensive proposition. A cost leader normally engages in only a limited amount of market segmentation. Even though no customer may be totally happy with the product, the fact that the company normally charges a lower price than its competitors attracts customers to its products.

In developing distinctive competencies, the overriding goal of the cost leader must be to increase its efficiency and lower its costs compared with its rivals. The development of distinctive competencies in manufacturing and materials management is central to achieving this goal. Companies pursuing a low-cost strategy may attempt to ride down the experience curve so that they can lower their manufacturing costs.

Achieving a low-cost position may also require that the company develop skills in flexible manufacturing and adopt efficient materials-management techniques. (As you may recall, Table 4.1 outlines the ways in which a company's functions can be used to increase efficiency.) Consequently, the reduction of operating costs of manufacturing and materials-management functions are the center of attention for a company pursuing a cost-leadership strategy, and the other functions shape their distinctive competencies to meet this objective.[11] For example, the sales function may develop the competency of capturing large, stable sets of customers' orders. This, in turn, allows manufacturing to make longer production runs and so achieve economies of scale and reduce costs. The human resource function may focus on instituting training programs and compensation systems that lower costs by enhancing employees' productivity, and the research and development function may specialize in process improvements to lower the manufacturing costs.

Cost-Leadership Strategy

A strategy of trying to outperform competitors by doing everything possible to produce goods or services at a cost lower than they do.

Many cost leaders gear all their strategic choices to the single goal of squeezing out every cent of costs to sustain their competitive advantage. A company such as H. J. Heinz is another excellent example of a cost leader. Because beans and canned vegetables do not permit much of a markup, the profit comes from the large volume of cans sold. Therefore, Heinz goes to extraordinary lengths to reduce costs—by even one-twentieth of a cent per can, because this will lead to large cost savings and thus bigger profits over the long-run.

Advantages and Disadvantages   The advantages of each generic strategy are best discussed in terms of Porter's five forces model introduced in Chapter 3.[12] The five forces are threats from competitors, powerful suppliers, powerful buyers, substitute products, and new entrants. The cost leader is protected from *industry competitors* because it has a lower cost structure. Its lower costs also mean that it will be less affected than its competitors by increases in the price of inputs if there are *powerful suppliers* and less affected by the lower prices it can charge for its products if *powerful buyers* exist. Moreover, because cost leadership usually requires a big market share, the cost leader purchases in relatively large quantities, increasing its bargaining power over suppliers. If *substitute products* start to come into the market, the cost leader can reduce its price to compete with them and retain its market share. Finally, the leader's cost advantage constitutes a *barrier to entry*, because other companies are unable to enter the industry and match the leader's low costs or prices. The cost leader is therefore relatively safe as long as it can maintain its cost advantage, and price is the key for a significant number of buyers.

The principal dangers of the cost-leadership approach arise when competitors are able to develop new strategies that lower their cost structure and beat the cost leader at its own game. For instance, if technological change makes experience-curve economies obsolete, new companies may apply lower-cost technologies that give them a cost advantage over the cost leader. The steel mini-mills discussed in Chapter 4 gained this advantage. Competitors may also draw a cost advantage from labor-cost savings. Competitors in many Asian countries, for example, have very low labor costs, and U.S. companies now assemble many of their products abroad as part of their low-cost strategy.

Competitors' ability to imitate the cost leader's methods is another threat to the cost-leadership strategy. For example, the ability of Dell's major competitors HP, Acer, and Lenovo to imitate Dell's low-cost materials management practices has eroded its competitive advantage and Dell is struggling to find new ways to compete.

Finally, the cost-leadership strategy carries a risk that the cost leader, in its single-minded desire to reduce costs, may lose sight of changes in customers' tastes. Thus, a company might make decisions that decrease costs but drastically affect demand for the product. For example, Joseph Schlitz Brewing lowered the quality of its beer's ingredients, substituting inferior grains to reduce costs. Consumers immediately caught on, and demand for the product dropped dramatically. As mentioned earlier, the cost leader cannot abandon product differentiation, and even low-priced products, such as Timex watches, cannot be too inferior to the more expensive watches made by Seiko if the low-cost, low-price policy is to succeed.

Differentiation Strategy

A strategy of trying to achieve a competitive advantage by creating a product that is perceived by customers as unique in some important way.

Differentiation Strategy

The objective of the generic **differentiation strategy** is to achieve a competitive advantage by creating a product that is perceived by customers to be *unique* in some important way. The differentiated company's ability to satisfy a customer's need in a way that its competitors cannot means that it can charge a *premium price*— a price considerably above the industry average. The ability to increase revenues by charging premium prices (rather than by reducing costs as the cost leader does) allows the differentiator to outperform its competitors and gain above-average profits. The premium price is usually substantially above the price charged by the cost leader, and customers pay it because they believe the product's differentiated qualities are worth the difference. Consequently, the product is priced on the basis of what customers are willing to pay for it.[13]

Cars made by Mercedes-Benz, BMW, and Lexus command premium prices because customers perceive that the luxury and prestige of owning these vehicles are something worth paying for. In watches, the name of Rolex stands out; in jewelry, Tiffany; in airplanes, Learjet. All these products command premium prices because of their differentiated qualities.

Strategic Choices As Table 5.1 shows, a differentiator chooses a high level of product differentiation to gain a competitive advantage. Product differentiation can be achieved in three principal ways, which are discussed in detail in Chapter 4: quality, innovation, and responsiveness to customers. For example, Procter & Gamble claims that its product quality is high and that Ivory soap is 99.44% pure. IBM promotes the quality service provided by its well-trained sales force.

Innovation is very important for high-tech products for which new features are the source of differentiation, and many people pay a premium price for new and innovative products, such as a state-of-the-art computer, videogame console, or car.

When differentiation is based on responsiveness to customers, a company offers comprehensive after-sale service and product repair. This is an especially important consideration for complex products such as cars and domestic appliances, which are likely to break down periodically. Companies such as Whirlpool, Dell, and BMW all excel in responsiveness to customers. In service organizations, quality-of-service attributes are also very important. Why can Neiman Marcus, Nordstrom's, and FedEx charge premium prices? They offer an exceptionally high level of service. Similarly, law firms and accounting firms emphasize to clients the service aspects of their operations: their knowledge, professionalism, and reputation.

Finally, a product's appeal to customers' psychological desires can become a source of differentiation. The appeal can be prestige or status, as it is with Rolls-Royce cars and Rolex watches; patriotism, as with Chevrolet; safety of home and family, as with Prudential Insurance; or value for money, as with Bed, Bath, & Beyond and The Gap. Differentiation can also be tailored to age groups and to socio-economic groups. Indeed, the bases of differentiation are endless.

A company that pursues a differentiation strategy strives to differentiate itself along as many dimensions as possible. The less it resembles its rivals, the more it is protected from competition and the wider its market appeal. Thus, BMWs do not offer prestige alone. They also offer technological sophistication, luxury, reliability, and good (though very expensive) repair service. All these bases of differentiation help increase sales.

Generally, a differentiator chooses to segment its market into many niches. Now and then a company offers a product designed for each market niche and decides to be a **broad differentiator**, but a company might choose to serve just those niches in which it has a specific differentiation advantage. For example, Sony produces over 20 different kinds of high-definition, flat-screen televisions, filling all the niches from mid-priced to high-priced sets. However, its lowest-priced models are always priced hundreds of dollars above that of its competitors, bringing into

Broad Differentiator

A company that offers a product designed for each market niche.

play the premium-price factor. You have to pay extra for a Sony. Similarly, although Mercedes-Benz has filled niches below its old high-priced models with its S and C series, it has made no attempt to produce a car for every market segment.

Finally, in choosing which distinctive competency to pursue, a differentiated company concentrates on the organizational function that provides the sources of its differentiation advantage. Differentiation on the basis of innovation and techno-logical competency depends on the R&D function, as we noted in Chapter 4. Efforts to improve service to customers depend on the quality of the sales function. A focus on a specific function does not mean, however, that the control of costs is not impor-tant for a differentiator. A differentiator does not want to increase costs unnecessar-ily and tries to keep them somewhere near those of the cost leader. However, because developing the distinctive competency needed to provide a differentiation advantage is often expensive, a differentiator usually has higher costs than the cost leader. Still, it must control all costs that do not contribute to its differentiation advantage so that the price of the product does not exceed what customers are willing to pay. Because bigger profits are earned by controlling costs and by maximizing revenues, it pays to control costs but not to minimize them to the point of losing the source of differentiation.[14]

Advantages and Disadvantages   Differentiation safeguards a company against competitors to the degree that customers develop *brand loyalty* for its products. Brand loyalty is a very valuable asset that protects the company on all fronts. For example, *powerful suppliers* are rarely a problem because the differentiated com-pany's strategy is geared more toward the price it can charge than toward the costs of production. Thus, a differentiator can tolerate moderate increases in the prices of its inputs better than the cost leader can. Differentiators are unlikely to experience problems with *powerful buyers* because the differentiator offers the buyer a unique product. Only it can supply the product, and it commands brand loyalty. Differentiation and brand loyalty also create a *barrier to entry* for other companies seeking to enter the industry. New companies are forced to develop their own distinctive competency to be able to compete, and doing so is very expensive. Finally, the threat of *substitute products* depends on the ability of competitors' products to meet the same customer needs as the differentiator's products and to break the differentiator's customers' brand loyalty. The main problems with a differentiation strategy center on the com-pany's long-term ability to maintain its perceived uniqueness in customers' eyes. We have seen in the last 10 years how quickly competitors move to imitate and copy successful differentiators. This has happened in many industries, such as computers, autos, and electronics. Patents and first-mover advantages (the advantages of being the first to market a product or service) last only so long, and as the overall quality of products made by all companies increases, brand loyalty declines.

Cost Leadership and Differentiation

Recently, changes in production techniques—in particular, the development of flex-ible manufacturing technologies (discussed in Chapter 4)—have made the choice between cost-leadership and differentiation strategies less clear-cut. With techno-logical developments, companies have found it easier to obtain the benefits of both strategies. The reason is that the new flexible technologies allow firms to pursue a differentiation strategy at a low cost; that is, companies can combine these two generic strategies.

Traditionally, differentiation was obtainable only at high cost, because the necessity of producing different models for different market segments meant that firms had to have short production runs, which raised manufacturing costs. In addition, the differentiated firm had to bear higher marketing costs than the cost leader because it was servicing many market segments. As a result, differentiators had higher costs than cost leaders, which produced large batches of standardized products. However, flexible manufacturing may enable a firm pursuing differentiation to manufacture a range of products at a cost comparable to that of the cost leader. The use of flexible manufacturing cells reduces the costs of retooling the production line and the costs associated with small production runs. Indeed, a factor promoting the current trend toward market fragmentation and niche marketing in many consumer goods industries, such as mobile phones, computers, and appliances, is the substantial reduction of the costs of differentiation achieved via flexible manufacturing.

Another way that a differentiated producer may be able to realize significant economies of scale is by standardizing many of the component parts used in its end products. In the late 2000s, for example, Fiat-Chrysler introduced more than 20 different models of cars and minivans to different segments of the auto market. However, despite their different appearances, all 20 models are based on only three different platforms. Moreover, most of the cars used many of the same components, including axles, drive units, suspensions, and gear boxes. As a result, Fiat-Chrysler was able to realize significant economies of scale in the manufacture and bulk purchase of standardized component parts.

A company can also reduce both production and marketing costs if it limits the number of models in the product line by offering packages of options rather than letting consumers decide exactly what options they require. It is increasingly common for auto manufacturers, for example, to offer an economy auto package, a luxury package, and a sports package to appeal to the principal market segments. Package offerings substantially lower manufacturing costs because long production runs of the various packages are possible. At the same time, the firm is able to focus its advertising and marketing efforts on particular market segments so that these costs are also decreased. Once again, the firm is reaping gains from differentiation and low cost at the same time.

Taking advantage of new developments in production and marketing, some companies are managing to reap the gains from cost-leadership and differentiation strategies simultaneously. Because they can charge a premium price for their products compared with the price charged by the pure cost leader, and because they have lower costs than the pure differentiator, they obtain at least an equal, and probably a higher, level of profit than firms pursuing only one of the generic strategies. Companies have moved quickly to take advantage of new production and marketing techniques because the combined strategy is the most profitable to pursue, as the example of Dell Computer suggests.

Focus Strategy

The third generic competitive strategy, the **focus strategy**, differs from the other two chiefly in that it is directed toward serving the needs of a *limited customer group or segment*. A focus strategy concentrates on serving a particular market niche, which can be defined geographically, by type of customer, or by a segment of the product line.[15] For example, a geographic niche can be defined by region or even by locality. Selecting a niche by type of customer might mean serving only the very rich, the very

Focus Strategy

A strategy of serving the needs of one or a few customer groups or segments.

young, or the very adventurous. A company that concentrates on a segment of the product line focuses only on vegetarian foods, for example, or on very fast cars, or on designer clothes or sunglasses. In following a focus strategy, a company is *specializing* in some way.

Once it has chosen its market segment, a company pursues a focus strategy through either a differentiation or a low-cost approach. Figure 5.1 shows these two different kinds of focused strategies and compares them with a pure cost-leadership or pure differentiation strategy.

In essence, a focused company is a specialized differentiator *or* a cost leader. If a company uses a focused low-cost approach, it competes against the cost leader in the market segments in which it has no cost disadvantage. For example, in local lumber or cement markets, the focuser has lower transportation costs than the low-cost national company. The focuser may also have a cost advantage because it is producing complex or custom-built products that do not lend themselves easily to economies of scale in production and, therefore, offer few experience-curve advantages. With a focus strategy, a company concentrates on small-volume custom products, for which it has a cost advantage, and leaves the large-volume standardized market to the cost leader.

If a company uses a focused differentiation approach, then all the means of differentiation that are open to the differentiator are available to the focused company. The point is that the focused company competes with the differentiator in only one or a few segments. For example, Porsche, a focused company, competes against BMW and Lexus in the sports car, luxury-SUV, and most recently luxury sedan segments of the auto market, not in other segments. Focused companies are likely to be able to differentiate their products successfully because of their detailed knowledge of a small customer set (such as sports car buyers) or of a region.

Furthermore, concentration on a small range of products sometimes allows a focuser to develop innovations faster than a large differentiator can. However, the focuser does not attempt to serve all market segments, because doing so would bring it into direct competition with the differentiator. Instead, a focused company concentrates on building market share in one or a few market segments and, if successful, may begin to serve more and more market segments and chip away at the differentiator's competitive advantage over time.

Figure 5.1 Types of Business-Level Strategies

Strategic Choices Table 5.1 illustrated the specific product/market/distinctive-competency choices made by a focused company. Differentiation can be high or low because the company can pursue a low-cost or a differentiation approach. As for customer groups, a focused company chooses specific niches in which to compete rather than going for a whole market, as a cost leader does, or filling a large number of niches, as a broad differentiator does. The focused firm can pursue any distinctive competency because it can seek any kind of differentiation or low-cost advantage. Thus, it might find a cost advantage and develop superior efficiency in low-cost manufacturing within a region. Alternatively, it might develop superior skills in responsiveness to customers, based on its ability to serve the needs of regional customers in ways that a national differentiator would find very expensive.

The many avenues that a focused company can take to develop a competitive advantage explain why there are so many more small companies than large ones. A focused company has enormous opportunity to develop its own niche and compete against larger low-cost and differentiated companies. A focus strategy provides an opportunity for an entrepreneur to find and then take advantage of a gap in the market by developing an innovative product that customers cannot do without.[16] The steel mini-mills discussed in Chapter 4 are a good example of how focused companies specializing in one market can grow so efficient that they become the cost leaders. Many large companies started with a focus strategy, and, of course, one means by which companies can expand is to take over other focused companies.

Advantages and Disadvantages A focused company's competitive advantages stem from the source of its distinctive competency: efficiency, quality, innovation, or responsiveness to customers. The firm is protected from *rivals* to the extent that it can provide a good or service that they cannot. This ability also gives the focuser power over its *buyers* because they cannot get the same product from anyone else. With regard to *powerful suppliers,* however, a focused company is at a disadvantage because it buys inputs in small volume and thus is in the suppliers' power. However, as long as it can pass on price increases to loyal customers, this disadvantage may not be a significant problem. *Potential entrants* have to overcome the customer loyalty the focuser has generated, which also reduces the threat from substitute products. This protection from the five forces allows the focuser to earn above-average returns on its investment. A further advantage of the focus strategy is that it permits a company to stay close to its customers and to respond to their changing needs.

Because a focuser produces a small volume, its production costs often exceed those of a low-cost company. Higher costs can also reduce profitability if a focuser is forced to invest heavily in developing a distinctive competency, such as expensive product innovation, in order to compete with a differentiated firm. However, once again, flexible manufacturing systems are opening up new opportunities for focused firms because small production runs become possible at a lower cost. Increasingly, small, specialized firms are competing with large companies in specific market segments in which their cost disadvantage is much reduced.

Finally, there is the prospect that differentiators will compete for a focuser's niche by offering a product that can satisfy the demands of the focuser's customers; for example, GM's and Ford's new luxury cars are aimed at Lexus, BMW, and Mercedes-Benz buyers. A focuser is vulnerable to attack and, therefore, has to defend its niche constantly.

Stuck in the Middle

Each generic strategy requires a company to make consistent product/market/ distinctive-competency choices to establish a competitive advantage. Thus, for example, a low-cost company cannot strive for a high level of market segmentation, as a differentiator does, and provide a wide range of products, because doing so would raise production costs too much and the company would lose its low-cost advantage. Similarly, a differentiator with a competency in innovation that tries to reduce its expenditures on research and development, or one with a competency in responsiveness to customers through after-sale service that seeks to economize on its sales force to decrease costs, is asking for trouble because it will lose its competitive advantage as its distinctive competency disappears.

Choosing a business-level strategy successfully means giving serious attention to all elements of the competitive plan. Many companies, through ignorance or error, do not do the planning necessary for success in their chosen strategy. Such companies are said to be **stuck in the middle** because they have made product/market choices in such a way that they have been unable to obtain or sustain a competitive advantage.[17] As a result, they have no consistent business-level strategy, experience below-average performance, and suffer when industry competition intensifies.

Some companies that find themselves stuck in the middle may have started out pursuing one of the three generic strategies but then have made wrong resource allocation decisions or have experienced a hostile, changing environment. It is very easy to lose control of a generic strategy unless strategic managers keep close track of the business and its environment, constantly adjusting product/market choices to suit changing conditions within the industry. There are many paths to getting stuck in the middle. Quite commonly, a focuser gets stuck in the middle when it becomes over-confident and starts to act like a broad differentiator.

People Express, a now defunct airline, exemplifies a company in this situation. It started out as a specialized air carrier serving a narrow market niche: low-priced travel on the eastern seaboard. In pursuing this focus strategy based on cost leadership, it was very successful. But when it tried to expand to other geographic regions and began taking over other airlines to gain a larger number of planes, it lost its niche. People Express became just one more carrier in an increasingly competitive market where it had no competitive advantage against other national carriers. The result was financial disaster, and People Express was incorporated into Continental Airlines. By contrast, Southwest Airlines, a focused low-cost company, continued to focus on this strategy and has grown successfully to become a national low-cost leader—in 2010 it bought another cost leader Air Tran for $1.4 billion to gain access to profitable markets in Boston and the East Coast.

Differentiators, too, can fail in the market and end up stuck in the middle if competitors attack their markets with more specialized or low-cost products that blunt their competitive edge. This happened to IBM in the mainframe computer market as PCs grew more powerful and became able to do the job of the much more expensive mainframes. The increasing movement toward flexible manufacturing systems aggravates the problems faced by cost leaders and differentiators. Many large firms will become stuck in the middle unless they make the investment needed to pursue both strategies simultaneously. No company is safe in a highly-competitive global environment and each must be constantly on the lookout to take advantage of competitive advantages as they arise and to defend the advantages it already has.

To sum up, successful management of a generic competitive strategy requires that strategic managers attend to two main issues. First, they must ensure that their

Stuck in the Middle

The fate of a company whose strategy fails because it has made product/market choices in a way that does not lead to a sustained competitive advantage.

product/market/distinctive-competency decisions are oriented toward one specific competitive strategy. Second, they need to monitor the environment so that they can keep the firm's sources of competitive advantage in tune with changing opportunities and threats—the issue we turn to now.

COMPETITIVE POSITIONING IN DIFFERENT INDUSTRY ENVIRONMENTS

If strategic managers succeed in developing a successful generic business-level strategy, they immediately face another crucial issue: how to choose appropriate competitive tactics and maneuvers to position their company to sustain its competitive advantage over time in different kinds of industry environments. In this section we first focus on how companies in fragmented and growing industries try to develop competitive strategies to support their generic strategies. Second, we consider the challenges of maintaining a competitive advantage in mature industries. Finally, we assess the problems of managing a company's generic competitive strategy in declining industries, in which rivalry between competitors is high because market demand is slowing or falling.

Strategies in Fragmented and Growing Industries

Many industries are fragmented, which means they are composed of a large number of small and medium-sized companies. The restaurant industry is fragmented, for example, as is the health club industry and the legal-services industry. There are several reasons why an industry may consist of many small companies rather than a few large ones. In some industries there are few economies of scale, so large companies do not have an advantage over smaller ones. Indeed, in some industries there are advantages to staying small, which enables companies to get closer to their customers. Many home buyers, for example, have a preference for dealing with local real estate agents, whom they perceive as having better local knowledge than national chains. Similarly, in the restaurant business, many customers prefer the unique style of a local restaurant. In addition, many industries are fragmented because there are few barriers to entry (such as in the restaurant industry, where a single entrepreneur can often bear the costs of opening a restaurant). High transportation costs, too, can keep an industry fragmented, for regional production may be the only efficient way to satisfy customers' needs, as in the cement business. Finally, an industry may be fragmented because customers' needs are so specialized that only small job lots of products are required, and thus there is no room for a large, mass-production operation to satisfy the market.

For some fragmented industries, these factors dictate the competitive strategy to pursue, and the focus strategy stands out as a principal choice. Companies may specialize by customer group, customer need, or geographic region, so that many small specialty companies operate in local or regional market segments. All kinds of custom-made products—furniture, clothing, hats, boots, and so on—fall into this category, as do all small service operations that cater to particular customers' needs, such as laundries, restaurants, health clubs, and furniture rental stores.

Strategic managers, however, are eager to gain the cost advantages of pursuing a low-cost strategy or the sales-revenue-enhancing advantages of differentiation by circumventing the problems of a fragmented industry. Returns from consolidating a fragmented industry are often huge—especially when industry sales and revenues are growing. Thus, over the past decades many companies have developed competitive strategies to consolidate fragmented industries. These companies include large retailers such as Walmart and Target; fast-food chains such as McDonald's and Subway; and chains of health clubs, repair shops, and even lawyers and consultants. As illustrated in Figure 5.2, to grow and consolidate their industries, and to become the dominant companies in them, strategic managers utilize three main competitive strategies: (1) chaining, (2) franchising, and (3) horizontal merger.

Chaining   Companies such as Walmart and Midas International pursue a chaining strategy to obtain the advantages of cost leadership. They establish networks of linked merchandising outlets that are so interconnected that they function as one large business entity. The amazing buying power that these companies possess through their nationwide store chains enables them to negotiate large price reductions with their suppliers, which in turn promotes their competitive advantage. They overcome the barrier of high transportation costs by establishing sophisticated regional distribution centers, which can economize on inventory costs and maximize responsiveness to the needs of stores and customers. (This is Walmart's specialty.) Last but not least, they realize economies of scale from sharing managerial skills across the chain and from placing nationwide, rather than local, advertising.

Franchising   For differentiated companies in fragmented industries, such as McDonald's and Century 21 Real Estate, the competitive advantage comes from a business strategy that employs franchise agreements. In franchising, the franchisor (parent) grants the franchisee the right to use the parent's name, reputation, and business skills in a particular location or area. If the franchisee also acts as the manager, he or she is strongly motivated to control the business closely and make sure that quality and standards are consistently high so that customer needs are always satisfied. Such motivation is particularly critical in a strategy of differentiation, where it is vital that a company maintain its uniqueness. One reason why industries are fragmented is the difficulty of maintaining control over the many small outlets that they must operate, while at the same time retaining their uniqueness. Franchising solves this problem. In addition, franchising lessens the financial burden of swift expansion and so permits rapid growth of the company. Finally, a differentiated large company can reap the advantages of large-scale advertising, as well as

Figure 5.2   Strategies for Consolidating a Fragmented Industry

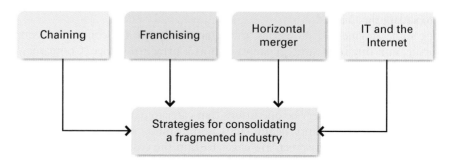

economies in purchasing, management, and distribution, as McDonald's does very efficiently. Indeed, McDonald's is able to pursue cost leadership and differentiation simultaneously only because franchising allows costs to be controlled locally and differentiation to be achieved by marketing on a national level.

Horizontal Merger   Companies such as Anheuser-Busch and Macy's Inc. chose a strategy of horizontal merger to consolidate their respective industries. For example, Macy's arranged the merger of many regional store chains in order to form a national company. By pursuing horizontal merger, companies are able to obtain economies of scale or secure a national market for their products. As a result, they are able to pursue a cost-leadership strategy, or a differentiation strategy, or both. We discuss merger in more detail in Chapter 7.

Using the Internet   The latest way in which companies have been able to consolidate a fragmented industry is by using the Internet. eBay is a good example of how a company can accomplish this. Before eBay, the auction business was extremely fragmented, with local auctions, fairs, or garage sales in cities being the principal way people could dispose of their antiques and collectibles. Now, using eBay, sellers can be assured that they are getting global visibility for their collectibles so that they are likely to receive a higher price for their product. Similarly, Amazon.com's success in the online book market led to the closing of thousands of small bookstores that simply could not compete on either price or selection. The trend toward using the Internet seems likely to further consolidate even relatively oligopolistic industries.

The challenge in fragmented and growing industries is to choose the most appropriate means—franchising, chaining, horizontal merger, or the Internet—to consolidate the market and grow sales so that the competitive advantages gained from pursuing the generic business-level strategies can be realized. It is difficult to think of any major service activities—from consulting and accounting firms to businesses satisfying the smallest consumer need, such as beauty parlors and car repair shops—that have not been merged or consolidated by chaining or franchising. In addition, the Internet has brought into being many new industries, such as those that make computer and digital products, and many of these are growing at a rapid pace as Internet broadband service expands.

Strategy in Mature Industries

As a result of fierce competition in the growth and shakeout stages, an industry becomes consolidated, so a mature industry is often dominated by a small number of large companies. Although a mature industry may also contain many medium-sized companies and a host of small, specialized ones, the large companies determine the nature of the industry's competition because they can influence the five competitive forces. Indeed, these are the companies that developed the most successful generic business-level strategies in the industry.

By the end of the shakeout stage, companies in an industry have learned how important it is to analyze each other's business-level strategies continually. This competitive analysis helps them determine how to modify their competitive positioning to maintain and build their competitive advantage. At the same time, however, they also know that if they move aggressively to change their strategies to attack competitors, this will stimulate a competitive response from rivals threatened by the change in strategy.

For example, a differentiator that starts to lower its prices because it has adopted a more cost-efficient technology threatens other differentiators. It also threatens low-cost companies that see their competitive edge being eroded. All these companies may now change their strategies in response, most likely by reducing their prices, too, as often occurs in the PC and car industries. Thus, the way one company changes or fine-tunes its business-level strategy over time affects the way the other companies in the industry pursue theirs. Hence, by the mature stage of the industry life cycle, companies have learned just how *interdependent* their strategies are.

In fact, the main challenge facing companies in a mature industry is to adopt a competitive strategy that simultaneously allows each individual company to protect its competitive advantage *and* preserves industry profitability. No generic strategy will generate above-average profits if competitive forces in an industry are so strong that companies are at the mercy of each other, of potential entrants, of powerful suppliers, of powerful customers, and so on. As a result, in mature industries, competitive strategy revolves around understanding how large companies try *collectively* to reduce the strength of the five forces of industry competition to preserve both company and industry profitability.

Interdependent companies can help protect their competitive advantage and profitability by adopting competitive moves and tactics to reduce the threat of each competitive force. In the next sections, we examine the various price and nonprice competitive moves and tactics that companies use—first, to deter entry into an industry, and second, to reduce the level of rivalry within an industry.

Strategies to Deter Entry in Mature Industries   Companies can utilize three main methods to deter entry by potential rivals and hence maintain and increase industry profitability. As Figure 5.3 shows, these methods are product proliferation, price cutting, and maintaining excess capacity.

Product Proliferation   Companies seldom produce just one product. Most commonly, they produce a range of products aimed at different market segments so that they have broad product lines. Sometimes, to reduce the threat of entry, companies expand the range of products they make to fill a wide variety of niches. This creates a barrier to entry because potential competitors now find it harder to break into an industry in which all the niches are filled.[18] This strategy of pursuing a broad product line to deter entry is known as *product proliferation*.

Figure 5.3   Strategies for Deterring Entry of Rivals

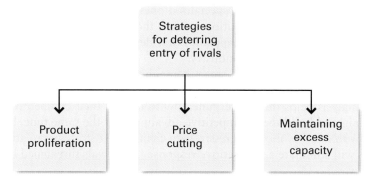

Because the Big Three U.S. carmakers were so slow to fill the small-car niches in the 1980s (they did *not* pursue a product proliferation strategy), they allowed Japanese companies to enter these segments, which they now dominate in the 2000s. U.S. carmakers really had no excuse for this lack of foresight, for in their European operations they had a long history of successful small-car manufacturing. They should have seen the danger of leaving this market segment open and filled it 10 years earlier, but their view was that "small cars mean small profits." In the breakfast cereal industry, on the other hand, competition is based on continually producing new kinds of cereal, or improving existing cereals, to satisfy consumer desires or create new desires. Thus the number and kind of breakfast cereals and snacks proliferate, making it very difficult for prospective entrants to find an empty market segment to fill. Filling all the product "spaces" in a particular market creates a barrier to entry and makes it much more difficult for a new company to gain a foothold and differentiate itself.

Price Cutting In some situations, pricing strategies that involve price cutting can be used to deter entry by other companies, thus protecting the profit margins of companies already in an industry. One price-cutting strategy, for example, is initially to charge a high price for a product and seize short-term profits but then to cut prices aggressively in order to build market share *and* deter potential entrants simultaneously.[19] The incumbent companies thus signal to potential entrants that if they enter the industry, the incumbents will use their competitive advantage to drive down prices to a level at which new companies will be unable to cover their costs.[20] This pricing strategy also allows a company to ride down the experience curve and obtain substantial economies of scale. Because costs fall with increasing sales, profit margins can still be maintained.

Still, this strategy is unlikely to deter a strong potential competitor—an established company that is trying to find profitable investment opportunities in other industries. It is difficult, for example, to imagine that IBM or 3M would be afraid to enter an industry because incumbent companies threaten to drive down prices. Companies such as IBM and 3M have the resources to withstand any short-term losses. Hence, it may be in the interests of incumbent companies to accept new entry gracefully, giving up market share gradually to the new entrants to prevent price wars from developing, and thus maintain their profit margins, if this is feasible.

Most evidence suggests that companies first skim the market and charge high prices during the growth stage, maximizing short-run profits.[21] Then they move to increase their market share and charge a lower price to expand the market rapidly; develop a reputation; and obtain economies of scale, driving down costs and barring entry. As competitors do enter, incumbent companies reduce prices to retard entry and give up market share to create a stable industry context—one in which they can use nonprice competitive tactics, such as product differentiation, to maximize long-run profits. At that point, nonprice competition becomes the main basis of industry competition, and prices are quite likely to rise as competition stabilizes. Thus, competitive tactics such as pricing and product differentiation are linked in mature industries; competitive decisions are taken to maximize the returns from a company's generic strategy.

Maintaining Excess Capacity A third competitive technique that allows companies to deter entry involves maintaining excess capacity—that is, producing more of a product than customers currently demand. Existing industry companies may deliberately develop some limited amount of excess capacity because it serves to warn potential entrants that if they do enter the industry, existing firms will retaliate by increasing output and forcing down prices, so entry would be unprofitable. However, the threat to increase output has to be *credible*; that is, companies in an industry must collectively be able to raise the level of production quickly if entry appears likely.

Strategies to Manage Rivalry in Mature Industries   Beyond seeking to deter entry, incumbent companies also need to develop a competitive strategy to manage *their* competitive interdependence and decrease rivalry. As we noted earlier, unrestricted industry price competition reduces both company and industry profitability. Several competitive tactics and gambits are available to companies to prevent price wars and manage industry relations. The most important are price signaling, price leadership, nonprice competition, and capacity control.

Price Signaling   Most industries start out fragmented, with small companies battling for market share. Then, over time, the leading players emerge, and companies start to interpret each other's competitive moves. Price signaling is the first means by which companies attempt to structure competition within an industry in order to control rivalry.[22] Price signaling is the process by which companies increase or decrease product prices to convey their competitive intentions to other companies and so influence the way competitors price *their* products.[23] There are two ways in which companies can use price signaling to help defend their generic competitive strategies.

First, companies use price signaling to make a clear announcement that they will respond vigorously to hostile competitive moves that threaten them. For example, companies may signal that if one company starts to cut prices aggressively, they will respond in kind; hence, the term **tit-for-tat strategy** is often used to describe this kind of market signaling. The outcome of a tit-for-tat strategy is that nobody gains and everybody loses. Similarly, as we noted in the last section, companies may signal to potential entrants that if the latter do enter the market, they will fight back by reducing prices, so that new entrants may incur significant losses.

A second, and very important, use of price signaling is to allow companies indirectly to coordinate their actions and avoid costly competitive moves that lead to a breakdown in pricing policy within an industry. One company may signal that it intends to lower prices because it wishes to attract customers who are switching to the products of another industry, not because it wishes to stimulate a price war. On the other hand, signaling can be used to improve profitability within an industry. The PC industry is a good example of the power of price signaling. In the 1990s, signals of lower prices set off price wars, but in the 2000s, PC makers have used price signaling to prevent price wars and keep prices steady. In sum, price signaling allows companies to give one another information that enables them to understand each other's competitive product/market strategy and make coordinated, competitive moves to protect industry profitability.

Price Leadership   Price leadership, the process by which one company informally takes the responsibility for setting industry prices, is a second tactic used to enhance the profitability of companies in a mature industry.[24] Formal price leadership, or price setting by companies jointly, is *illegal* under antitrust laws, so the process of price leadership is often very subtle. In the auto industry, for example, vehicle prices are set by imitation. The price set by the weakest company—the one with the highest costs—is often used as the basis for competitors' pricing. Thus, U.S. carmakers set their prices, and Japanese carmakers then set theirs with reference to the U.S. prices. The Japanese are

Price Signaling

The process by which companies increase or decrease product prices to convey their competitive intentions to other companies.

Tit-for-Tat Strategy

A form of market signaling in which one company starts to cut prices aggressively, and then competitors respond in a similar way; when this occurs, nobody gains and everybody loses.

Price Leadership

The process by which one company informally takes the responsibility for setting industry prices.

happy to do this because they have lower costs than U.S. companies and are making higher profits than U.S. carmakers without competing with them by price. Pricing is done by market segment. The prices of different vehicles in a company's model range indicate the customer segments that it is aiming for and the price range it believes the market segment can tolerate. Each manufacturer prices a model in the segment with reference to the prices charged by its competitors, not by reference to costs. Price leadership allows differentiators to charge a premium price and also helps low-cost companies by increasing their margins.

Although price leadership can stabilize industry relationships by preventing head-to-head competition and thus raise the level of profitability within an industry, it has its dangers. Price leadership helps companies with higher costs by allowing them to survive without becoming more productive or more efficient. In the long term, such behavior makes them vulnerable to companies that continually develop new production techniques to lower costs. That is what happened in the U.S. auto industry after the Japanese entered the market. After years of tacit price fixing, with GM as the price leader, the carmakers were subjected to growing low-cost Japanese competition. By the 2000s, Japanese carmakers such as Toyota and Honda had become so popular that they were setting the prices, and U.S. carmakers were forced to offer incentive price discounts, often around $3,000–4,000, to get their cars off the lot, while the Japanese did not drop theirs significantly. Even so, the market share of Japanese carmakers continued to increase, and by 2006 Toyota was selling more cars than Ford in the United States and by 2010 it became the largest global automaker 2008.

Nonprice Competition A third very important aspect of product/market strategy in mature industries is the use of nonprice competition to manage rivalry within an industry. Using various tactics and maneuvers to try to prevent costly price cutting and price wars does *not* preclude competition by product differentiation. Indeed, in many industries, product differentiation is the principal competitive tactic used to prevent rivals from stealing a company's customers and reducing its market share. In other words, companies rely on product differentiation to deter potential entrants and manage rivalry within their industry.

Product differentiation allows industry rivals to compete for market share by offering products with *different or superior features* or by utilizing different *marketing* techniques. In Figure 5.4, product and market segment dimensions are used to identify four nonprice competitive strategies based on product differentiation. (Note that this model applies to new market *segments*, not to new *markets*.)[25]

Figure 5.4 Four Nonprice Competitive Strategies

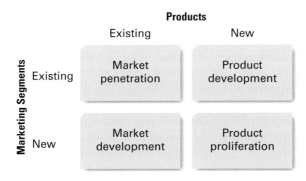

- When a company concentrates on expanding market share in its existing product markets, it is engaging in a strategy of **market penetration**.[26] Market penetration involves heavy advertising to promote and build product differentiation. In a mature industry, the thrust of advertising is to influence consumers' brand choice and create a brand-name reputation for the company and its products. In this way, a company can increase its market share by attracting the customers off its rivals. Because brand-name products often command premium prices, building market share in this situation is very profitable.

- In some mature industries (for example, soap and detergent, disposable diapers, and brewing), a market-penetration strategy becomes a way of life.[27] In these industries, all companies engage in intensive advertising and battle for market share. Each company fears that by not advertising, it will lose market share to rivals. Consequently, in the soap and detergent industry, for instance, Procter & Gamble spends more than 20% of sales revenues on advertising, with the aim of maintaining and increasing market share. These huge advertising outlays constitute a barrier to entry for prospective entrants.

- **Product development** is the creation of new or improved products to replace existing ones, such as occurs in the fast-food industry.[28] The wet-shaving industry is another industry that depends on product replacement to create successive waves of consumer demand, which then creates new sources of revenue for companies in the industry. Gillette, for example, periodically comes out with a new and improved razor, such as the Sensor, the Mach3, and the Fusion shaving system, to boost its market share and profitability. Similarly, each major global car-maker replaces its models every 3–5 years to encourage customers to trade in their old models and buy the new one that has the latest styling and technology.

- Product development is important for maintaining product differentiation and building market share.[29] For instance, the laundry detergent Tide has gone through more than 50 different changes in formulation during the past 40 years to improve its performance. The product is always advertised as Tide, but it is a different product each year. The battle over diet and flavored colas is another interesting example of competitive product differentiation by product development. Royal Crown Cola developed Diet Rite, the first diet cola. However, Coca-Cola and PepsiCo responded quickly with their versions of the diet drink, and by massive advertising they soon achieved dominance. Today, there are dozens of variations of diet colas on the market. Refining and improving products is an important competitive tactic in defending a company's generic competitive strategy in a mature industry. However, this kind of competition can be as vicious as a price war because it is expensive and raises costs dramatically.

- **Market development** involves searching for new market segments, and therefore uses, for a company's products. A company pursuing this strategy wants to capitalize on the brand name it has developed in one market segment by locating new market segments in which to compete. In this way, it can exploit the product differentiation advantages of its brand name. Japanese carmakers provide an interesting example of the use of market development. When they first entered the market, each Japanese manufacturer offered a car, such as the Toyota Corolla and the Honda Accord, aimed at the economy segment of the auto market. However, the Japanese upgraded each car over time, and now each is directed at a more expensive market segment. The Accord and Toyota Camry are the leading contenders in the mid-size car segment, while the Honda Civic, and Toyota Corolla, and Prius compete to lead the small-car segment. By redefining their product offerings, Japanese manufacturers have profitably developed their market segments

Market Penetration

A strategy in which a company concentrates on expanding market share in its existing product markets.

Product Development

A strategy involving the constant creation of new or improved products to replace existing ones.

Market Development

A strategy involving a search for new market segments, and therefore new uses, for a company's products.

and successfully attacked their U.S. rivals, continually wresting market share from these companies. Although the Japanese used to compete primarily as low-cost producers, market development has allowed them to become leading differentiators as well. Toyota is an example of a company that has used market development to pursue simultaneously a low-cost and a differentiation strategy, and its Lexus brand competes in the luxury segment of the global car market.

- Product proliferation can be used to manage rivalry within an industry and to deter entry. The strategy of product proliferation generally means that the leading companies in an industry all have a product in each market segment, or niche, and compete head-to-head for customers. If a new niche develops (such as SUVs, designer sunglasses, or Internet Web sites), then the leader gets a first-mover advantage, but soon all the other companies catch up, and once again competition is stabilized and rivalry within the industry is reduced. Product proliferation thus allows the development of stable industry competition based on product differentiation, not price—that is, nonprice competition based on the development of new products. The battle is over a product's perceived quality and uniqueness, *not* over its price.

Strategies in Declining Industries

Sooner or later many industries enter into a decline stage, in which the size of the total market starts to shrink. Examples include the railroad industry, the tobacco industry, and the steel industry. Industries start declining for a number of reasons, including technological change, social trends, and demographic shifts. The railroad and steel industries began to decline when technological changes brought viable substitutes for the products these industries offered. The advent of the internal combustion engine drove the railroad industry into decline, and the steel industry fell into decline with the rise of plastics and composite materials. The decline of the tobacco industry was caused by changing social attitudes toward smoking because of concerns about its health effects.

When the size of the total market is shrinking, competition tends to intensify in a declining industry, and profit rates tend to fall. The intensity of competition in a declining industry depends on four critical factors, which are indicated in Figure 5.5.

Product Proliferation

A strategy in which leading companies in an industry all make a product in each market segment or niche and compete head-to-head for customers.

Figure 5.5   Factors That Determine the Intensity of Competition in Declining Industries

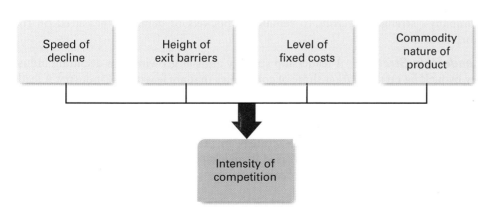

First, the intensity of competition is greater in industries where decline is rapid than in industries, such as tobacco, where decline is gradual.

Second, the intensity of competition is greater in declining industries in which exit barriers are high. As you recall from Chapter 3, high exit barriers keep companies locked into an industry even when demand is falling. The result is the emergence of excess productive capacity—and hence an increased probability of fierce price competition.

Third, and related to the previous point, the intensity of competition is greater in declining industries in which fixed costs are high (as in the steel industry). This is because the need to cover fixed costs, such as the costs of maintaining productive capacity, can make companies try to utilize any excess capacity they have by slashing prices—an action that can trigger a price war.

Finally, the intensity of competition is greater in declining industries where the product is perceived as a commodity (as it is in the steel industry) than in industries where differentiation gives rise to significant brand loyalty, as was true until very recently of the declining tobacco industry.

Not all segments of an industry typically decline at the same rate. In some segments, demand may remain reasonably strong, despite decline elsewhere. The steel industry illustrates this situation. Although bulk steel products, such as sheet steel, have suffered a general decline, demand has actually risen for specialty steels, such as those used in high-speed machine tools. Vacuum tubes provide another example. Although demand for them collapsed when transistors replaced them as a key component in many electronics products, for years afterward vacuum tubes still had some limited applications in radar equipment. Consequently, demand in this vacuum tube segment remained strong despite the general decline in the demand for vacuum tubes. The point is that in an industry, there may be pockets of demand in which demand is declining more slowly than in the industry as a whole or, indeed, is not declining at all. Price competition may be far less intense among the companies serving such pockets of demand than within the industry as a whole.

Choosing a Strategy   There are four main strategies that companies can adopt to deal with decline: (1) a leadership strategy, by which a company seeks to become the dominant player in a declining industry; (2) a niche strategy, which focuses on pockets of demand that are declining more slowly than demand in the industry as a whole; (3) a harvest strategy, which optimizes cash flow; and (4) a divestment strategy, by which a company sells off the business to others. The choice of strategy depends in part on the *intensity* of the competition. Figure 5.6 provides a framework for guiding choice or strategy on the basis of two factors: (1) the intensity of competition in the declining industry, measured on the vertical axis, and (2) a company's strengths *relative* to remaining pockets of demand, measured on the horizontal axis.

Leadership Strategy   A leadership strategy aims at growing in a declining industry by picking up the market share of companies that are leaving the industry. A leadership strategy makes the most sense (1) when the company has distinctive strengths that enable it to capture market share in a declining industry and (2) when the speed of decline and the intensity of competition in the declining industry are moderate. Philip Morris has pursued such a strategy in the tobacco industry. By aggressive marketing, Philip Morris has increased its market share in a declining industry and earned enormous profits in the process.

Leadership Strategy

A strategy through which a company seeks to become the dominant player in a declining industry.

Figure 5.6　Strategy Selection in a Declining Industry

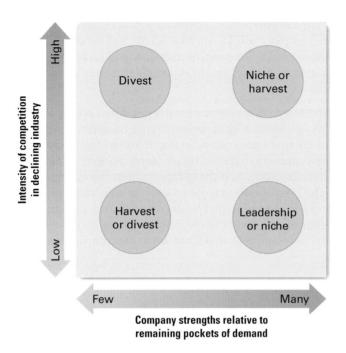

The tactical steps companies might use to achieve a leadership position include aggressive pricing and marketing to build market share; acquiring established competitors to consolidate the industry; and raising the stakes for other competitors—for example, by making new investments in productive capacity. Such competitive tactics signal to other competitors that the company is willing and able to stay and compete in the declining industry. These signals may persuade other companies to exit the industry, which would further enhance the competitive position of the industry leader.

Niche Strategy　A niche strategy focuses on those pockets of demand in the industry in which demand is stable or is declining less rapidly than demand in the industry as a whole. The strategy makes sense when the company has some unique strengths relative to those niches where demand remains relatively strong. As an example, consider Naval, a company that manufactures whaling harpoons and small guns to fire them and makes money doing so. This might be considered rather odd, given that most whaling has been outlawed by the world community. However, Naval survived the terminal decline of the harpoon industry by focusing on the one group of people who are still allowed to hunt whales in very limited numbers: the North American Inuit tribe. Inuit are permitted to hunt bowhead whales, provided that they do so only for food and not for commercial purposes. Naval is the sole supplier of small harpoon whaling guns to Eskimo communities, and its monopoly position allows it to earn a healthy return in this small market.[30]

Harvest Strategy　A harvest strategy is the best choice when a company wishes to get out of a declining industry and perhaps optimize cash flow in the process.

Niche Strategy

The strategy of focusing on pockets of demand that are declining more slowly than demand in the industry as a whole.

Harvest Strategy

A strategy that optimizes cash flow.

This strategy makes the most sense when the company foresees a steep decline and intense future competition or when it lacks strengths relative to remaining pockets of demand in the industry. A harvest strategy requires the company to cut all new investments in capital equipment, advertising, R&D, and the like. The inevitable result is that the company will lose market share, but because it is no longer investing in this business, initially its positive cash flow will increase. Ultimately, however, cash flows will start to decline, and at this stage it makes sense for the company to liquidate the business.

Divestment Strategy   A **divestment strategy** is based on the idea that a company can maximize its net investment recovery from a business by selling it early, before the industry has entered into a steep decline. This strategy is appropriate when the company has few strengths relative to whatever pockets of demand are likely to remain in the industry and when the competition in the declining industry is likely to be intense. The best option may be to sell out to a company that is pursuing a leadership strategy in the industry. The drawback of the divestment strategy is that its success depends on the ability of the company to notice its industry's decline before it becomes serious and thus to sell out while the company's assets are still valued by others.

Divestment Strategy

A strategy in which a company sells off its business assets and resources to other companies.

Summary of Chapter

1. Companies can use various generic competitive strategies in different industry environments to protect and enhance their competitive advantage. Companies must first develop a successful generic competitive strategy in order to gain a secure position in an industry. Then they must choose industry-appropriate competitive tactics and maneuvers to position their company successfully over time. Companies must always be on the alert for changes in conditions within their industry and in the competitive behavior of their rivals if they are to respond to these changes in a timely manner.

2. Business-level strategy consists of the way strategic managers devise a plan of action to use a company's resources and distinctive competencies to gain a competitive advantage over rivals in a market or industry.

3. At the heart of developing a generic business-level strategy are choices concerning product differentiation, market segmentation, and distinctive competency. The combination of those three choices results in the specific form of generic business-level strategy employed by a company.

4. The three pure generic competitive strategies are cost leadership, differentiation, and focus. Each has advantages and disadvantages. A company must constantly manage its strategy; otherwise, it risks being stuck in the middle.

5. Increasingly, developments in manufacturing technology are allowing firms to pursue both a cost-leadership and a differentiation strategy and thus obtain the economic benefits of both strategies simultaneously. Technical developments also enable small firms to compete with large firms on an equal footing in particular market segments; thus these developments increase the number of firms pursuing a focus strategy.

6. Companies can also adopt either of two forms of focus strategy: a focused low-cost strategy or a focused differentiation strategy.

7. In fragmented and growing industries composed of a large number of small and medium-sized companies, the principal forms of competitive strategy are chaining, franchising, and horizontal merger.

8. Mature industries are composed of a few large companies whose actions are so highly interdependent that the success of one company's strategy depends on the responses of its rivals.

9. The principal competitive tactics used by companies in mature industries to deter entry are product proliferation, price cutting, and maintaining excess capacity.

10. The principal competitive tactics used by companies in mature industries to manage rivalry are price signaling, price leadership, nonprice competition, and capacity control.
11. There are four main strategies a company can pursue when demand is falling: leadership, niche, harvest, and divestment strategies. The choice of strategy is determined by the severity of industry decline and the company's strengths relative to the remaining pockets of demand.

DISCUSSION QUESTIONS

1. Why does each generic competitive strategy require a different set of product/market/distinctive-competency choices? Give examples of pairs of companies in (a) the computer industry and (b) the auto industry that pursue different competitive strategies.

2. Why are industries fragmented? What are the main ways in which companies can turn a fragmented industry into a consolidated one?
3. Discuss how companies can use (a) product differentiation and (b) capacity control to manage rivalry and increase an industry's profitability.

C L O S I N G   C A S E

Nike's Business-Level Strategies

Nike, headquartered in Beaverton, Oregon, was founded over 30 years ago by Bill Bowerman, a former University of Oregon track coach, and Phil Knight, an entrepreneur in search of a profitable business opportunity. Bowerman's goal was to dream up a new kind of sneaker tread that would enhance a runner's traction and speed, and he came up with the idea for Nike's "waffle tread" after studying the waffle iron in his home. Bowerman and Knight made their shoe and began by selling it out of the trunks of their car at track meets. From this small beginning Nike has grown into a company that sold over $12 billion worth of shoes in the $35 billion athletic footwear and apparel industries in 2004.[31]

Nike's amazing growth came from its business model, which has always been based on two original functional strategies: to innovate state-of-the-art athletic shoes and then to publicize the qualities of its shoes through dramatic "guerrilla" marketing. Nike's marketing is designed to persuade customers that its shoes are not only superior but also a high fashion statement and a necessary part of a lifestyle based on sporting or athletic interests. A turning point came in 1987 when Nike increased its marketing budget from $8 million to $48 million to persuade customers its shoes were the best. A large part of this advertising budget soon went to pay celebrities like Michael Jordan millions of dollars to wear and champion its products. The company has consistently pursued this strategy and many other sporting stars, such as Tiger Woods and Serena Williams who are part of its charmed circle.

Nike's strategy to emphasize the uniqueness of its product paid off; its market share soared and its revenues hit $9.6 billion in 1998. However, 1998 was also a turning point, for in that year sales began to fall. Nike's $200 Air Jordans no longer sold like they used to, and inventory built up in stores and warehouses. Suddenly it seemed much harder to design new shoes that customers perceived to be significantly better and Nike's stunning growth in sales was actually reducing its profitability—somehow it had lost control of its business strategy. Phil Knight, who had resigned his management position, was forced to resume the helm and lead the company out of its troubles. He recruited a team of talented top managers from leading consumer products companies to help him improve Nike's business model. As a result, Nike has changed its business strategies in some fundamental ways.

In the past, Nike shunned sports like golf, soccer, rollerblading, and so on and focused most of its efforts on making shoes for the track and basketball market to build its market share in this area. However, when its sales started to fall, it realized that using marketing to increase sales in a particular market segment can only grow sales and profits so far; it needed to start to sell more types of shoes to more segments of the athletic shoe market. So Nike took its design and marketing competencies and began to craft new lines of shoes for new market segments. For example, it launched a line of soccer shoes and perfected their design over time, and by 2004 it had won the biggest share of the soccer market from its archrival Adidas.[32] In addition, in 2004 it launched its Total 90 III shoes, which are aimed at the millions of casual soccer players throughout the world who want a shoe they can just "play" in. Once more, Nike's dramatic marketing campaigns aim to make their shoes part of the "soccer lifestyle," to persuade customers that traditional sneakers do not work because soccer shoes are sleeker and fit the foot more snugly.[33]

To take advantage of its competencies in design and marketing, Nike then decided to enter new market segments by purchasing other footwear companies that offered shoes that extended or complemented its product lines. For example, it bought Converse, the maker of retro-style sneakers; Hurley International, which makes skateboards and Bauer in-line and hockey skates; and Official Starter, a licensor of athletic shoes and apparel whose brands include the low-priced Shaq brand. Allowing Converse to take advantage of Nike's in-house competencies has resulted in dramatic increases in the sales of its sneakers, and Converse has made an important contribution to Nike's profitability.[34]

Nike had also entered another market segment when it bought Cole Haan, the dress shoemaker, in the 1980s. Now it is searching for other possible acquisitions. It decided to enter the athletic apparel market to use its skills there, and by 2004 sales were over $1 billion. Nike made all these changes to its product line to increase its market share and profitability. Its new focus on developing new and improved products for new market segments is working. Nike's profits have soared from 14% in 2000 to 25% in 2007, it makes over $1 billion profit a year.

Case Discussion Questions
1. What business-level strategies is Nike pursuing?
2. How have Nike's business-level strategies changed the nature of industry competition?

NOTES

1. Derek F. Abell, *Defining the Business: The Starting Point of Strategic Planning* (Englewood Cliffs, N.j.: Prentice-Hall, 1980), 169.
2. R. Kotler, *Marketing Management*, 5th. ed. (Englewood Cliffs, N.j.: Prentice-Hall, 1984) and M. R. Darby and E. Karni, "Free Competition and the Optimal Amount of Fraud," *Journal of Law and Economics* 16 (1973): 67–86.
3. Abell, *Defining the Business*, p. 8.
4. Michael E. Porter, *Competitive Advantage: Creating and Sustaining Superior Performance* (New York: Free Press, 1985).
5. R. D. Buzzell and F. D. Wiersema, "Successful Share Building Strategies," *Harvard Business Review*, January–February 1981, 135–144 and L. W. Phillips, D. R. Chang, and R. D. Buzzell, "Product Quality, Cost Position, and Business Performance: A Test of Some Key Hypotheses," *Journal of Marketing* 47 (1983): 26–43.
6. Michael E. Porter, *Competitive Strategy: Techniques for Analyzing Industries and Competitors* (New York: Free Press, 1980), 45.
7. Abell, *Defining the Business*, p. 15.
8. Although many other authors have discussed cost leadership and differentiation as basic competitive approaches [e.g., F. Scherer, *Industrial Market Structure and Economic Performance*, 2nd ed. (Boston, Mass.: Houghton Mifflin, 1980)], Porter's model (Porter, *Competitive Strategy*) has become the dominant approach. Consequently, this model is the one developed here, and the discussion draws heavily on his definitions. The basic cost-leadership/differentiation dimension has received substantial empirical support (e.g., D. C. Hambrick, "High Profit Strategies in Mature Capital Goods Industries: A Contingency Approach," *Academy of Management Journal* 26 (1983): 687–707.
9. Porter, *Competitive Advantage*, p. 37.
10. Ibid., pp. 13–14.
11. D. Miller, "Configurations of Strategy and Structure: Towards a Synthesis," *Strategic Management Journal* 7 (1986): 217–231.
12. Porter, *Competitive Advantage*, pp. 44–46.

13. Charles W. Hofer and D. Schendel, *Strategy Formulation: Analytical Concepts* (St. Paul, Minn.: West, 1978).

14. W. K. Hall, "Survival Strategies in a Hostile Environment," *Harvard Business Review* 58 (1980): 75–85 and Hambrick, "High Profit Strategies.".

15. Porter, *Competitive Strategy*, p. 46.

16. Peter F. Drucker, *The Practice of Management* (New York: Harper, 1954).

17. Porter, *Competitive Advantage*, pp. 44–46.

18. J. Brander and J. Eaton, "Product Line Rivalry," *American Economic Review* 74 (1985): 323–334.

19. P. Milgrom and J. Roberts, "Predation, Reputation, and Entry Deterrence," *Journal of Economic Theory* 27 (1982): 280–312.

20. Sharon M. Oster, *Modern Competitive Analysis* (New York: Oxford University Press, 1990), 262–264.

21. Donald A. Hay and Derek J. Morris, *Industrial Economics: Theory and Evidence* (New York: Oxford University Press, 1979), 192–193.

22. Porter, *Competitive Strategy*, pp. 76–86.

23. O. Heil and T. S. Robertson, "Towards a Theory of Competitive Market Signaling: A Research Agenda," *Strategic Management Journal* 12 (1991): 403–418.

24. Scherer, *Industrial Market Structure and Economic Performance*, Ch. 8.

25. The model differs from Ansoff's model for this reason.

26. H. Igor Ansoff, *Corporate Strategy* (London: Penguin Books, 1984), 97–100.

27. Robert D. Buzzell, Bradley T. Gale, and Ralph G. M. Sultan, "Market Share—A Key to Profitability," *Harvard Business Review*, January–February 1975, 97–103 and Robert Jacobson and David A. Aaker, "Is Market Share All That It's Cracked Up to Be?" *Journal of Marketing* 49 (1985): 11–22.

28. Ansoff, *Corporate Strategy*, pp. 98–99.

29. S. L. Brown, and K. M. Eisenhardt, "Product Development: Past Research, Present Findings, and Future Directions," *Academy of Management Review* 20 (1995): 343–378.

30. Jack Willoughby, "The Last Iceman," *Forbes*, July 13, 1987, 183–202.

31. www.nike.com, 2008.

32. www.nike.com (2004), press release; "The New Nike," *yahoo.com* September 12, 2004.

33. A. Wong, "Nike: Just Don't Do It," *Newsweek*, November 1, 2004, 84.

34. www.nike.com, 2008.

GLOBAL STRATEGY

6

CHAPTER OUTLINE

The Global Environment

Increasing Profitability
Through Global Expansion

*Expanding the Market: Leveraging
    Products and Competencies*
Realizing Economies of Scale
Realizing Location Economies
*Leveraging the Skills of Global
    Subsidiaries*

Cost Pressures and Pressures
for Local Responsiveness

Pressures for Cost Reductions
Pressures for Local Responsiveness

Choosing a Global Strategy

Global Standardization Strategy
Localization Strategy
Transnational Strategy
International Strategy
Changes in Strategy over Time

Choices of Entry Mode

Exporting
Licensing
Franchising
Joint Ventures
Wholly Owned Subsidiaries
Choosing an Entry Strategy

LEARNING OBJECTIVES

After reading this chapter you should be
able to:

- Understand the process of globalization
  and how that impacts upon a company's
  strategy.
- Discuss the motives for expanding
  internationally.

- Review the different strategies that
  companies use to compete in the global
  market place.
- Explain the pros and cons of different
  modes for entering foreign markets.

OVERVIEW

This chapter looks at the process of globalization in the world economy and the strategic response required from companies that compete across national borders. The chapter opens with a discussion of ongoing changes in the global competitive environment and discusses models managers can use for analyzing competition in different national markets. Next, we look at the various ways in which international expansion can increase a company's profitability and profit growth. Then we discuss the different strategies companies can pursue to gain a competitive advantage in the global marketplace and discuss the advantages and disadvantages of each. This is followed by a discussion of two related strategic issues: (1) how managers decide which foreign markets to enter, when to enter them, and on what scale and (2) what kind of vehicle or means a company should use to expand globally and enter a foreign country. By the time you have completed this chapter, you will have a good understanding of the various strategic issues that companies face when they decide to expand their operations internationally to achieve competitive advantage and superior profitability.

THE GLOBAL ENVIRONMENT

Fifty years ago most national markets were isolated from each other by significant barriers to international trade and investment. In those days, managers could focus on analyzing just those national markets in which their company competed. They did not need to pay much attention to entry by global competitors, for there were few and entry was difficult. Nor did they need to pay much attention to entering foreign markets, since that was often prohibitively expensive. All of this has now changed. Barriers to international trade and investment have tumbled. Huge global markets for goods and services have been created. Companies from different nations are entering each others home markets on a hitherto unprecedented scale, increasing the intensity of competition. Rivalry can no longer be understood merely in terms of what happens within the boundaries of a nation; managers now need to consider how globalization is impacting the environment in which their company competes, and what strategies their company should adopt to exploit opportunities, and counter competitive threats.

Consider barriers to international trade and investment. The average tariff rate on manufactured goods traded between advanced nations has fallen from around 40% to under 4%. Similarly, in nation after nation, regulations prohibiting foreign companies from entering domestic markets and establishing production facilities, or acquiring domestic companies, have been removed. As a result of these two developments, there has been a surge in both the volume of international trade and the value of foreign direct investment. The volume of world merchandise trade has grown faster than the world economy since 1950 (see Figure 1.1).[1] From 1970 to 2007, the volume of world merchandise trade expanded 28-fold, outstripping the expansion of world production, which grew about eight times in real terms. Moreover, between 1992 and 2007, the total flow of foreign direct investment from all countries increased by more than 500% while world trade by value grew by some 145% and world output by about 40%.[2] These two trends have led to the globalization of production and the globalization of markets.[3]

The globalization of production has been increasing as companies take advantage of lower barriers to international trade and investment to disperse important parts of their production process around the globe. Doing so enables them to take advantage of national differences in the cost and quality of factors of production such as labor, energy, land, and capital, which allow them to lower their cost structures and boost profits. For example, the Boeing Company's commercial jet aircraft, the 777, uses 132,500 engineered parts that are produced around the world by 545 suppliers. Eight Japanese suppliers make parts of the fuselage, doors, and wings; a supplier in Singapore makes the doors for the nose landing gear; three suppliers in Italy manufacture wing flaps; and so on. In total, some 30% of the 777, by value, is built by foreign companies. For its most recent jet airliner, the 787, Boeing has pushed this trend even further, with some 65% of the total value of the aircraft scheduled to be outsourced to foreign companies, 35% of which is going to three major Japanese companies.[4] Part of Boeing's rationale for outsourcing so much production to foreign suppliers is that these suppliers are the best in the world at performing their particular activity. Therefore, the result of having foreign suppliers build specific parts is a better final product and higher profitability for Boeing.[5]

As for the globalization of markets, it has been argued that the world's economic system is moving from one in which national markets are distinct entities, isolated from each other by trade barriers and barriers of distance, time, and culture, toward a system in which national markets are merging into one huge global marketplace. Increasingly, customers around the world demand and use the same basic product offerings. Consequently, in many industries, it is no longer meaningful to talk about the German market, the U.S. market, or the Japanese market; there is only the global market. The global acceptance of Coca-Cola, Citigroup credit cards, blue jeans, the Sony PlayStation and Nintendo Wii, McDonald's hamburgers, the Nokia wireless phone, and Microsoft's Windows operating system are examples of this trend.[6]

The trend toward the globalization of production and markets has several important implications for competition within an industry. First, industry boundaries do not stop at national borders. Because many industries are becoming global in scope, actual and potential competitors exist not only in a company's home market but also in other national markets. Managers who analyze only their home market can be caught unprepared by the entry of efficient foreign competitors. The globalization of markets and production implies that companies around the globe are finding their home markets under attack from foreign competitors. For example, in Japan, American financial institutions such as JP Morgan have been making inroads against Japanese financial service institutions. In the United States, Finland's Nokia has taken the lead from Motorola in the market for wireless phone handsets.

Second, the shift from national to global markets has intensified competitive rivalry in industry after industry. National markets that once were consolidated oligopolies, dominated by three or four companies and subjected to relatively little foreign competition, have been transformed into segments of fragmented global industries where a large number of companies battle each other for market share in country after country. This rivalry has threatened to drive down profitability and made it all the more critical for companies to maximize their efficiency, quality, customer responsiveness, and innovative ability. The painful restructuring and downsizing that has been going on at companies such as Motorola and Kodak is as much a response to the increased intensity of global competition as it is to anything else. However, not all global industries are fragmented. Many remain consolidated oligopolies, except that now they are consolidated *global*, rather than *national*, oligopolies. In the video game industry, for example, three companies are battling for global dominance, Microsoft from the U.S. and Nintendo and Sony from Japan. In the market for wireless handsets, Nokia of Finland does global battle against Motorola of the U.S. and Samsung from South Korea, and, most recently, Apple with its iPhone; and Research in Motion of Canada with its Blackberry.

Finally, although globalization has increased both the threat of entry and the intensity of rivalry within many formerly protected national markets, it has also created enormous opportunities for companies based in those markets. The steady decline in barriers to cross-border trade and investment has opened up many once protected markets to companies based outside them. Thus in recent years, Western European, Japanese, and U.S. companies have accelerated their investments in the nations of Eastern Europe, Latin America, and Southeast Asia as they try to take advantage of growth opportunities in those areas.

INCREASING PROFITABILITY THROUGH GLOBAL EXPANSION

There are a number of ways in which expanding globally can enable companies to increase their profitability and grow their profits more rapidly. At the most basic level, global expansion increases the size of the market a company is addressing, thereby boosting profit growth. Moreover, global expansion offers opportunities for reducing the cost structure of the enterprise, or adding value through differentiation, thereby potentially boosting profitability.

Expanding the Market: Leveraging Products and Competencies

A company can increase its growth rate by taking goods or services developed at home and selling them internationally. Indeed, almost all multinationals started out doing just this. Procter and Gamble, for example, developed most of its best selling products at home, and then sold them around the world. Similarly, from its earliest days, Microsoft has always focused on selling its software around the world. Automobile companies like Ford, Volkswagen and Toyota also grew by developing products at home, and then selling them in international markets. The returns from such a strategy are likely to be greater if indigenous competitors in the nations a company enters lack comparable products. Thus Toyota has grown its profits by entering the large automobile markets of North America and Europe, offering products that are differentiated from those offered by local rivals (Ford and GM) by their superior quality and reliability.

It is important to note that the success of many multinational companies is based not just upon the goods or services that they sell in foreign nations, but also upon the distinctive competencies (unique skills) that underlie the production and marketing of those goods or services. Thus Toyota's success is based upon its distinctive competence in manufacturing automobiles, and expanding internationally can be seen as a way of generating greater returns from this competence. Similarly, Procter & Gamble's global success was based on more than its portfolio of consumer products; it was also based on the company's skills in mass marketing consumer goods. P&G grew rapidly in international markets between 1950 and 1990 because it was one of the most skilled mass marketing enterprises in the world, and could "out market" indigenous competitors in the nations it entered. Global expansion was thus a way of generating higher returns from its competency in marketing.

Pushing this further, one could say that since distinctive competencies are in essence the most valuable aspects of a company's business, successful global expansion by manufacturing companies like Toyota and P&G was based upon their ability to take their distinctive competencies and apply them to foreign markets.

The same can be said of companies engaged in the service sectors of an economy—such as financial institutions, retailers, restaurant chains and hotels. Expanding the market for their services often means replicating their basic business model in foreign nations (albeit with some changes to account for local differences—which we will discuss in more detail shortly). Starbucks, for example, is expanding rapidly outside of the United States by taking the basic business model it developed at home, and using that as a blue print for establishing international operations. As detailed in the Running Case, Walmart has done the same thing, establishing stores in nine other nations since 1992 following the blue print it developed in the United States. Similarly, McDonalds is famous for its international expansion strategy which has taken the company into more than 120 nations that collectively generate over half of the company's revenues.

Realizing Economies of Scale

In addition to growing profits more rapidly, by expanding its sales volume through international expansion a company can realize cost savings from economies of scale, thereby boosting profitability. Such scale economies come from several sources. First, by spreading the fixed costs associated with developing a product and setting up production facilities over its global sales volume, a company can lower its average unit cost. Thus, Microsoft can garner significant scale economies by spreading the $5 billion it cost to develop Windows Vista over global demand.

Second, by serving a global market, a company can potentially utilize its production facilities more intensively, which leads to higher productivity, lower costs and greater profitability. For example, if Intel only sold microprocessors in the United States, it may only be able to keep its factories open for one shift, 5 days a week. But by serving a global market from the same factories, it may be able to utilize those assets for two shifts, 7 days a week. In other words, the capital invested in those factories is used more intensively if Intel sells to a global as opposed to national market, which translated into higher capital productivity and a higher return on invested capital.

Third, as global sales increase the size of the enterprise, so its bargaining power with suppliers increases, which may allow it to bargain down the cost of key inputs and boost profitability that way. Walmart has been able to use its enormous sales volume as a lever to bargain down the price it pays suppliers for merchandise sold through its stores.

Realizing Location Economies

Earlier in this chapter we discussed how countries differ from each other along a number of dimensions, including differences in the cost and quality of factors of production. These differences imply that some locations are more suited than others for producing certain goods and services.[7] **Location economies** are the economic benefits that arise from performing a value creation activity in the optimal location for that

Location Economies

Economic benefits that arise from performing a value creation activity in the optimal location for that activity.

RUNNING CASE

Walmart's Global Expansion

In the early 1990s, managers at Walmart realized that the company's opportunities for growth in the United States were becoming more limited. By 1995, the company would be active in all 50 states. Management calculated that by the early 2000s, domestic growth opportunities would be constrained due to market saturation. So the company decided to expand globally. The critics scoffed. Walmart, they said, was too American a company. Although its business model was well suited to America, it would not work in other countries where infrastructure was different, consumer tastes and preferences varied, and where established retailers already dominated.

Unperturbed, in 1991, Walmart started to expand internationally with the opening of its first stores in Mexico. The Mexican operation was established as a joint venture with Cifera, the largest local retailer. Initially, Walmart made a number of missteps that seemed to prove the critics right. Walmart had problems replicating its efficient distribution system in Mexico. Poor infrastructure, crowded roads, and a lack of leverage with local suppliers, many of whom could not or would not deliver directly to Walmart's stores or distribution centers, resulted in stocking problems and raised costs and prices. Initially, prices at Walmart in Mexico were some 20% above prices for comparable products in the company's United States stores, which limited Walmart's ability to gain market share. There were also problems with merchandise selection. Many of the stores in Mexico carried items that were popular in the United States. These included ice skates, riding lawn mowers, leaf blowers, and finishing tackle. Not surprisingly, these items did not sell well in Mexico, so managers would slash prices to move inventory, only to find that the company's automated information systems would immediately order more inventory to replenish the depleted stock.

By the mid-1990s, however, Walmart had learned from its early mistakes and adapted its operations in Mexico to match the local environment. A partnership with a Mexican trucking company dramatically improved the distribution system, while more careful stocking practices meant that the Mexican stores sold merchandise that appealed more to local tastes and preferences. As Walmart's presence grew, many of Walmart's suppliers built factories close by its Mexican distribution centers so that they could better serve the company, which helped to drive down inventory and logistics costs. In 1998, Walmart acquired a controlling interest in Cifera. Today, Mexico is a leading light in Walmart's international operations, where the company is more than twice the size of its nearest rival.

The Mexican experience proved to Walmart that it could compete outside the United States. It subsequently expanded into 15 other countries. In Canada, Britain, Germany, Japan, and South Korea, Walmart entered by acquiring existing retailers and then transferring its information systems, logistics, and management expertise. In Puerto Rico, Brazil, Argentina, and China, Walmart established its own stores (although it added to its Chinese operations with a major acquisition in 2007). As a result of these moves, by 2008, the company had more than 3,000 stores outside the United States, 600,000 associates, and generated international revenues of more than $80 billion.

In addition to greater growth, expanding internationally has brought Walmart two other major benefits. First, Walmart has also been able to reap significant economies of scale from its global buying power. Many of Walmart's key suppliers have long been international companies; for example, GE (appliances), Unilever (food products), and P&G (personal care products) are all major Walmart suppliers that have long had their own global operations. By building international reach, Walmart has been able to use its enhanced size to demand deeper discounts from the local operations of its global suppliers, increasing the company's ability to lower prices to consumers, gain market share and ultimately earn greater profits. Second, Walmart has found that it is benefiting from the flow of ideas across the countries in which it now competes. For example, Walmart's Argentina team worked with Walmart's Mexican management to replicate a Walmart store format developed first in Mexico and to adopt the best practices in human resources and real estate that had been developed in Mexico. Other ideas, such as wine departments in its stores in Argentina, have now been integrated into layouts worldwide.

Moreover, Walmart realized that if it did not expand internationally, other global retailers would beat them to the punch. In fact, Walmart does face significant global competition from Carrefour of France, A hold of Holland, and Tesco of the United Kingdom. Carrefour, the world's second-largest retailer, is perhaps the most global of the lot. The pioneer of the hypermarket concept now operates in 26 countries and generates more than 50% of its sales outside France. Compared to this, Walmart is a laggard with just 25% of its sales in 2008 generated from international operations. However, there is still room for significant global expansion. The global retailing market is still very fragmented. The top-25 retailers controlled only about a quarter of retail sales in 2008.

Still, for all of its success Walmart has hit some significant speed bumps in its drive for global expansion. In 2006, the company pulled out of two markets, South Korea—where it failed to decode the shopping habits of local customers—and Germany—where it could not beat incumbent discount stores on price. It is also struggling in Japan, where the company does not seem to have grasped the market's cultural nuances. One example was Walmart's decision to sell lower-priced gift fruits at Japanese holidays. It failed because customers felt spending less would insult the recipient. Interestingly, the markets where Walmart has struggled were all developed markets that it entered through acquisitions, where it faced long-established and efficient local competitors, and where shopping habits were very different than in the United States. In contrast, many of those markets where it has done better have been developing nations that lacked strong local competitors, and where Walmart has built operations from the ground up (e.g., Mexico, Brazil, and, increasingly, China).[8]

activity, wherever in the world that might be (transportation costs and trade barriers permitting). Locating a value creation activity in the optimal location for that activity can have one of two effects: (1) it can lower the costs of value creation, helping the company achieve a low-cost position, or (2) it can enable a company to differentiate its product offering, which gives it the option of charging a premium price or keeping price low and using differentiation as a means of increasing sales volume. Thus, efforts to realize location economies are consistent with the business-level strategies of low cost and differentiation. In theory, a company that realizes location economies by dispersing each of its value creation activities to the optimal location for that activity should have a competitive advantage over a company that bases all of its value creation activities at a single location. It should be able to differentiate its product offering better and lower its cost structure more than its single-location competitor. In a world where competitive pressures are increasing, such a strategy may well become an imperative for survival.

For illustration, consider IBM's ThinkPad X31 laptop computer (this business was acquired by China's Lenova in 2005).[9] The ThinkPad was designed in the United States by IBM engineers because IBM believed that the U.S. was the best location in the world to do the basic design work. The case, keyboard and hard drive were made in Thailand, the display screen and memory was made in South Korea, the built in wireless card was made in Malaysia; and the microprocessor was manufactured in the United States. In each case, these components were manufactured in the optimal location given manager's assessment of the relative costs of performing each activity at different locations. These components were shipped to an IBM operation in Mexico, where the product was assembled, before being shipped to the United States for final sale. IBM assembled the ThinkPad in Mexico because IBM's managers calculated that due to low labor costs, the costs of assembly could be minimized there. The marketing and sales strategy for North America was developed by IBM personnel in the United States, primarily because IBM believed that due to their knowledge of the local marketplace, U.S. personnel would add more value to the product through their marketing efforts than personnel based elsewhere.

Leveraging the Skills of Global Subsidiaries

Initially, many multinational companies develop the valuable competencies and skills that underpin their business in their home nation then expand internationally, primarily by selling products and services based on those competencies. Thus, Walmart honed its retailing skills in the United States before transferring them to foreign locations. However, for more mature multinationals enterprises that have already established a network of subsidiary operations in foreign markets, the development of valuable skills can just as well occur in foreign subsidiaries.[10] Skills can be created anywhere within a multinational's global network of operations, wherever people have the opportunity and incentive to try new ways of doing things. The creation of skills that help to lower the costs of production, or to enhance perceived value and support higher product pricing, is not the monopoly of the corporate center.

Leveraging the skills created within subsidiaries and applying them to other operations within the firm's global network may create value. For example, McDonald's increasingly is finding that its foreign franchisees are a source of valuable new ideas. Faced with slow growth in France, its local franchisees have begun to experiment not only with the menu, but also with the layout and theme of restaurants. Gone are the ubiquitous Golden Arches, gone too are many of the utilitarian chairs and tables and other plastic features of the fast-food giant. Many McDonald's restaurants in France now have hardwood floors, exposed brick walls, and even armchairs. Half of the 930 or so outlets in France have been upgraded to a level that would make them unrecognizable to an American. The menu, too, has been changed to include premier sandwiches, such as a chicken on focaccia bread, priced some 30% higher than the average hamburger. In France at least, the strategy seems to be working. Following the change, increases in same store sales rose from 1% annually to 3.4%. Impressed with the impact, McDonald's executives are now considering adopting similar changes at other McDonald's restaurants in markets where same store sales growth is sluggish, including the United States.[11]

COST PRESSURES AND PRESSURES FOR LOCAL RESPONSIVENESS

Companies that compete in the global marketplace typically face two types of competitive pressures: *pressures for cost reductions* and *pressures to be locally responsive* (see Figure 6.2).[12] These competitive pressures place conflicting demands on a company. Responding to pressures for cost reductions requires that a company try to minimize its unit costs. To attain this goal, it may have to base its productive activities at the most favorable low-cost location, wherever in the world that might be. It may also have to offer a standardized product to the global marketplace in order to realize the cost savings that come from economies of scale and learning effects. On the other hand, responding to pressures to be locally responsive requires that a company differentiate its product offering and marketing strategy from country to country in an effort to accommodate the diverse demands arising from national differences in consumer tastes and preferences, business practices, distribution channels, competitive conditions, and government policies. Because differentiation across countries can involve significant duplication and a lack of product standardization, it may raise costs.

Figure 6.1 Pressures for Cost Reductions and Local Responsiveness

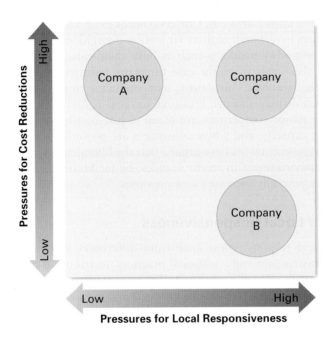

While some companies, such as Company A in Figure 6.1, face high pressures for cost reductions and low pressures for local responsiveness, and others, such as Company B, face low pressures for cost reductions and high pressures for local responsiveness, many companies are in the position of Company C. They face high pressures for *both* cost reductions and local responsiveness. Dealing with these conflicting and contradictory pressures is a difficult strategic challenge, primarily because being locally responsive tends to raise costs.

Pressures for Cost Reductions

In competitive global markets, international businesses often face pressures for cost reductions. Responding to pressures for cost reduction requires a firm to try to lower the costs of value creation. A manufacturer, for example, might mass producing a standardized product at the optimal location in the world, wherever that might be, to realize economies of scale and location economies. Alternatively, they might outsource certain functions to low cost foreign suppliers in an attempt to reduce costs. Thus, many computer companies have outsourced their telephone based customer service functions to India, where qualifies technicians who speak English can be hired for a lower wage rate than in the United States. In the same vein, a retailer like Walmart might push its suppliers (who are manufacturers) to do the same. (In fact, the pressure that Walmart's has placed on its suppliers to reduce prices has been cited as a major cause of the trend among North American manufacturers to shift production to China).[13] A service business, such as a bank, might move some back office functions, such as information processing, to developing nations were wage rates are lower.

Universal Needs

Needs arising from the similar, if not identical, tastes and preferences of consumers in different nations.

Cost reduction pressures can be particularly intense in industries producing commodity-type products where meaningful differentiation on nonprice factors is difficult and price is the main competitive weapon. This tends to be the case for products that serve universal needs. **Universal needs** exist when the tastes and preferences of consumers in different nations are similar if not identical. This is the case for conventional commodity products such as bulk chemicals, petroleum, steel, sugar, and the like. It also tends to be the case for many industrial and consumer products; for example, handheld calculators, semiconductor chips, personal computers, and liquid crystal display screens. Pressures for cost reductions are also intense in industries where major competitors are based in low-cost locations, where there is persistent excess capacity, and where consumers are powerful and face low switching costs. Many commentators have argued that the liberalization of the world trade and investment environment in recent decades, by facilitating greater international competition, has generally increased cost pressures.[14]

Pressures for Local Responsiveness

Pressures for local responsiveness arise from differences in consumer tastes and preferences, infrastructure and traditional practices, distribution channels, and host government demands. Recall that responding to pressures to be locally responsive requires that a company differentiate its products and marketing strategy from country to country to accommodate these factors, all of which tends to raise a company's cost structure.

Differences in Consumer Tastes and Preferences   Strong pressures for local responsiveness emerge when customer tastes and preferences differ significantly between countries, as they may for historic or cultural reasons. In such cases, a multinational company's products and marketing message have to be customized to appeal to the tastes and preferences of local customers. This typically creates pressures for the delegation of production and marketing responsibilities and functions to a company's overseas subsidiaries.

For example, the automobile industry in the 1980s and early 1990s moved toward the creation of "world cars." The idea was that global companies such as General Motors, Ford, and Toyota would be able to sell the same basic vehicle the world over, sourcing it from centralized production locations. If successful, the strategy would have enabled automobile companies to reap significant gains from global scale economies. However, this strategy frequently ran aground upon the hard rocks of consumer reality. Consumers in different automobile markets seem to have different tastes and preferences, and these require different types of vehicles. North American consumers show a strong demand for pickup trucks. This is particularly true in the South and West where many families have a pickup truck as a second or third car. But in European countries, pickup trucks are seen purely as utility vehicles and are purchased primarily by firms rather than individuals. As a consequence, the product mix and marketing message needs to be tailored to take into account the different nature of demand in North America and Europe.

Differences in Infrastructure and Traditional Practices   Pressures for local responsiveness arise from differences in infrastructure or traditional practices among countries, creating a need to customize products accordingly. Fulfilling this need may require the delegation of manufacturing and production functions to foreign subsidiaries. For example, in North America, consumer electrical systems are based on 110 volts, whereas in some European countries, 240-volt systems are standard. Thus, domestic electrical appliances have to be customized to take this difference in infrastructure into account. Traditional practices also often vary across nations. For example, in Britain, people drive on the left-hand side of the road, creating a demand for right-hand-drive cars, whereas in France (and the rest of Europe), people drive on the right-hand side of the road and therefore want left-hand-drive cars. Obviously, automobiles have to be customized to take this difference in traditional practices into account.

Although many of the country differences in infrastructure are rooted in history, some are quite recent. For example, in the wireless telecommunications industry, different technical standards are found in different parts of the world. A technical standard known as GSM is common in Europe, and an alternative standard, CDMA, is more common in the United States and parts of Asia. The significance of these different standards is that equipment designed for GSM will not work on a CDMA network, and vice versa. Thus, companies such as Nokia, Motorola, and Ericsson, which manufacture wireless handsets and infrastructure such as switches, need to customize their product offering according to the technical standard prevailing in a given country.

Differences in Distribution Channels A company's marketing strategies may have to be responsive to differences in distribution channels among countries, which may necessitate the delegation of marketing functions to national subsidiaries. In the pharmaceutical industry, for example, the British and Japanese distribution system is radically different from the U.S. system. British and Japanese doctors will not accept or respond favorably to a U.S.-style high-pressure sales force. Thus, pharmaceutical companies have to adopt different marketing practices in Britain and Japan compared with the United States—soft sell versus hard sell.

Differences in Host Government Demands Economic and political demands imposed by host country governments may require local responsiveness. For example, pharmaceutical companies are subject to local clinical testing, registration procedures, and pricing restrictions, all of which make it necessary that the manufacturing and marketing of a drug should meet local requirements. Moreover, because governments and government agencies control a significant proportion of the health care budget in most countries, they are in a powerful position to demand a high level of local responsiveness.

More generally, threats of protectionism, economic nationalism, and local content rules (which require that a certain percentage of a product should be manufactured locally) dictate that international businesses manufacture locally. As an example, consider Bombardier, the Canadian-based manufacturer of railcars, aircraft, jet boats, and snowmobiles. Bombardier has twelve railcar factories across Europe. Critics of the company argue that the resulting duplication of manufacturing facilities leads to high costs and helps explain why Bombardier makes lower profit margins on its railcar operations than on its other business lines. In reply, managers at Bombardier argue that in Europe, informal rules with regard to local content favor people who use local workers. To sell railcars in Germany, they claim, you must manufacture in Germany. The same goes for Belgium, Austria, and France. To try and address its cost structure in Europe, Bombardier has centralized its engineering and purchasing functions, but it has no plans to centralize manufacturing.[15]

CHOOSING A GLOBAL STRATEGY

Pressures for local responsiveness imply that it may not be possible for a firm to realize the full benefits from economies of scale and location economies. It may not be possible to serve the global marketplace from a single low-cost location, producing a globally standardized product, and marketing it worldwide to achieve economies of scale. In practice, the need to customize the product offering to local conditions may work against the implementation of such a strategy. For example, automobile firms have found that Japanese, American, and European consumers demand different kinds of cars, and this necessitates producing products that are customized for local markets. In response, firms like Honda, Ford, and Toyota are pursuing a strategy of establishing top-to-bottom design and production facilities in each of these regions so that they can better serve local demands. Although such customization brings benefits, it also limits the ability of a firm to realize significant scale economies and location economies.

In addition, pressures for local responsiveness imply that it may not be possible to leverage skills and products associated with a firm's distinctive competencies wholesale from one nation to another. Concessions often have to be made to local conditions. Despite being depicted as "poster boy" for the proliferation of standardized global products, even McDonald's has found that it has to customize its product offerings (i.e., its menu) in order to account for national differences in tastes and preferences.

Given the need to balance the cost and differentiation (value) sides of a company's business, how do differences in the strength of pressures for cost reductions versus those for local responsiveness affect the choice of a company's strategy? Companies typical make a choice among four main strategic postures when competing internationally. These can be characterized as a global standardization strategy, a localization strategy, a transnational strategy, and an international strategy.[16] The appropriateness of each strategy varies given the extent of pressures for cost reductions and local responsiveness. Figure 6.2 illustrates the conditions under which each of these strategies is most appropriate.

Global Standardization Strategy

Global Standardization Strategy

A strategy that focuses on increasing profitability by reaping the cost reductions derived from economies of scale and location economies.

Companies that pursue a **global standardization strategy** focus on increasing profitability by reaping the cost reductions that come from economies of scale and location economies; that is, their strategy is to pursue a low-cost strategy on a global scale. The production, marketing, and R&D activities of companies pursuing a global strategy are concentrated in a few favorable locations. Companies pursuing a global standardization strategy try not to customize their product offering and marketing strategy to local conditions because customization, which involves shorter production runs and the duplication of functions, can raise costs. Instead, they prefer to market a standardized product worldwide so that they can reap the maximum benefits from economies of scale. They also tend to use their cost advantage to support aggressive pricing in world markets.

This strategy makes most sense when there are strong pressures for cost reductions and demand for local responsiveness is minimal. Increasingly, these conditions prevail in many industrial goods industries, whose products often serve universal needs. In the semiconductor industry, for example, global standards have emerged,

Figure 6.2 Four Basic Strategies

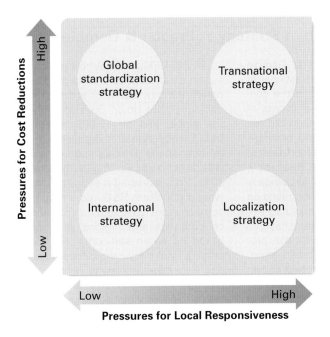

creating enormous demands for standardized global products. Accordingly, companies such as Intel, Texas Instruments, and Motorola all pursue a global strategy. These conditions are not always found in many consumer goods markets, where demands for local responsiveness remain high. However, even some consumer goods companies are moving towards a global standardization strategy in an attempt to drive down their costs. Procter & Gamble, which is featured in the next Strategy in Action feature, is one example of such a company.

Localization Strategy

A localization strategy focuses on increasing profitability by customizing the company's goods or services so that they provide a good match to tastes and preferences in different national markets. Localization is most appropriate when there are substantial differences across nations with regard to consumer tastes and preferences, and where cost pressures are not too intense. By customizing the product offering to local demands, the company increases the value of that product in the local market. On the downside, because it involves some duplication of functions and smaller production runs, customization limits the ability of the company to capture the cost reductions associated with mass producing a standardized product for global consumption. The strategy may make sense, however, if the added value associated with local customization supports higher pricing, which enables the company to recoup its higher costs, or if it leads to substantially greater local demand, enabling the company to reduce costs through the attainment of some scale economies in the local market.

Localization Strategy

A strategy that focuses on increasing profitability by customizing the company's goods or services so that they provide a good match to tastes and preferences in different national markets.

6.1 *STRATEGY IN ACTION*

The Evolution of Strategy at Procter & Gamble

Founded in 1837, Cincinnati-based Procter & Gamble has long been one of the world's most international of companies. Today P&G is a global colossus in the consumer products business with annual sales in excess of $50 billion, some 54% of which are generated outside the United States. P&G sells more than 300 brands—including Ivory soap, Tide, Pampers, Iams pet food, Crisco, and Folgers—to consumers in 160 countries. Historically, the strategy at P&G was well established. The company developed new products in Cincinnati and then relied on semiautonomous foreign subsidiaries to manufacture, market, and distribute those products in different nations. In many cases, foreign subsidiaries had their own production facilities and tailored the packaging, brand name, and marketing message to local tastes and preferences. For years this strategy delivered a steady stream of new products and reliable growth in sales and profits. By the 1990s, however, profit growth at P&G was slowing.

The essence of the problem was simple; P&G's costs were too high because of extensive duplication of manufacturing, marketing, and administrative facilities in different national subsidiaries. The duplication of assets made sense in the world of the 1960s, when national markets were segmented from each other by barriers to cross-border trade. Products produced in Great Britain, for example, could not be sold economically in Germany due to high tariff duties levied on imports into Germany. By the 1980s, however, barriers to cross-border trade were falling rapidly worldwide, and fragmented national markets were merging into larger regional or global markets. Also, the retailers through which P&G distributed its products were growing larger and more global, such as Walmart, Tesco from the United Kingdom, and Carrefour from France. These emerging global retailers were demanding price discounts from P&G.

In the 1990s, P&G embarked on a major reorganization in an attempt to control its cost structure and recognize the new reality of emerging global markets. The company shut down 30 manufacturing plants around the globe, laid off 13,000 employees, and concentrated production in fewer plants that could better realize economies of scale and serve regional markets. It was not enough. Profit growth remained sluggish, so in 1999, P&G launched a second reorganization. The goal was to transform P&G into a truly global company. The company tore up its old organization, which was based on countries and regions, and replaced it with one based on seven self-contained global business units, ranging from baby care to food products. Each business unit was given complete responsibility for generating profits from its products, and for manufacturing, marketing, and product development. Each business unit was told to rationalize production, concentrating it in fewer larger facilities; to try to build global brands wherever possible, thereby eliminating marketing difference between countries; and to accelerate the development and launch of new products. P&G announced that as a result of this initiative, it would close another 10 factories and lay off 15,000 employees, mostly in Europe where there was still extensive duplication of assets. The annual cost savings were estimated to be about $800 million. P&G planned to use the savings to cut prices and increase marketing spending in an effort to gain market share, and thus further lower costs through the attainment of economies of scale. This time the strategy seemed to be working. Between 2003 and 2007, P&G reported strong growth in both sales and profits. Significantly, P&G's global competitors, such as Unilever, Kimberly-Clark, and Colgate-Palmolive, were struggling in 2003 to 2007.[17]

MTV is a good example of a company that has had to pursue a localization strategy. MTV has varied its programming to match the demands of viewers in different nations. If MTV had not done this, it would have lost market share to local competitors, its advertising revenues would have fallen and its profitability would have declined. Thus, even though it raised costs, localization became a strategic imperative at MTV.

At the same time, it is important to realize that companies like MTV still have to keep a close eye on costs. Companies pursuing a localization strategy still need to be efficient and whenever possible, to capture some scale economies from their global reach. As noted earlier, many automobile companies have found that they have to customize some of their product offerings to local market demands—for example, producing large pickup trucks for US consumers and small fuel efficient cars for Europeans and Japanese. At the same time, these companies try to get some scale economies from their global volume by using common vehicle platforms and components across many different models, and manufacturing those platforms and components at efficiently scaled factories that are optimally located. By designing their products in this way, these companies have been able to localize their product offering, yet simultaneously capture some scale economies.

Transnational Strategy

We have argued that a global standardization strategy makes most sense when cost pressures are intense, and demands for local responsiveness limited. Conversely, a localization strategy makes most sense when demands for local responsiveness are high, but cost pressures are moderate or low. What happens, however, when the company simultaneously faces both strong cost pressures, and strong pressures for local responsiveness? How can managers balance out the competing and inconsistent demands such divergent pressures place on the company? According to some researchers, the answer is by pursuing what has been called a transnational strategy.

According to some, today's global environment, competitive conditions are so intense that to survive, companies must do all they can to respond to pressures for cost reductions and local responsiveness. They must try to realize location economies and economies of scale from global volume, transfer distinctive competencies and skills within the company, and simultaneously pay attention to pressures for local responsiveness.[18] Moreover, in the modern multinational enterprise, distinctive competencies and skills do not reside just in the home country but can develop in any of the company's worldwide operations. Thus, the flow of skills and product offerings should not be all one way, from home company to foreign subsidiary. Rather, the flow should also be from foreign subsidiary to home country and from foreign subsidiary to foreign subsidiary. Transnational companies, in other words, must also focus on leveraging subsidiary skills.

In essence, companies that pursue a transnational strategy are trying to simultaneously achieve low-costs, differentiate the product offering across geographic markets, and foster a flow of skills between different subsidiaries in the company's global network of operations. As attractive as this may sound, the strategy is not an easy one to pursue since it places conflicting demands on the company. Differentiating the product to respond to local demands in different geographic markets raises costs, which runs counter to the goal of reducing costs. Companies like Ford and ABB (one of the world's largest engineering conglomerates) have tried to embrace a transnational strategy, and found it difficult to implement in practice.

International Strategy

Sometimes it is possible to identify multinational companies that find themselves in the fortunate position of being confronted with low cost pressures and low pressures for local responsiveness. Typically these are enterprises that are selling a product that serves universal needs, but who do not face significant competitors, and thus are not

Transnational Strategy

A strategy in which firms try to simultaneously achieve low costs, differentiate the product offering across geographic markets, and foster a flow of skills among different subsidiaries in the company's global network of operations.

confronted with pressures to reduce their cost structure. Xerox found itself in this position in the 1960s after its invention of the photocopier. The technology underlying the photocopier was protected by strong patents, so for several years Xerox did not face competitors—it had a monopoly. The product was highly valued in most developed nations, and so Xerox was able to sell the same basic product the world over, charge a relatively high price for that product, and because it did not face direct competitors, the company did not have to deal with strong pressures to minimize its costs.

Historically, companies like Xerox have followed a similar developmental pattern as they build their international operations. Companies pursuing an international strategy tend to centralize product development functions such as R&D at home. However, they also tend to establish manufacturing and marketing functions in each major country or geographic region in which they do business. Although they may undertake some local customization of product offering and marketing strategy, this tends to be rather limited in scope. Ultimately, in most international companies, the head office retains tight control over marketing and product strategy.

Other companies that have pursues this strategy include Procter & Gamble, which historically always developed innovative new products in Cincinnati, and then transferred them wholesale to local markets (see the Strategy in Action feature). Another company that has followed a similar strategy is Microsoft. The bulk of Microsoft's product development work takes place in Redmond, Washington, where the company is headquartered. Although some localization work is undertaken elsewhere, this is limited to producing foreign language versions of popular Microsoft programs such as Office.

Changes in Strategy Over Time

The Achilles heal of the international strategy is that over time, competitors inevitably emerge, and if managers do not take proactive steps to reduce their cost structure, their company may be rapidly outflanked by efficient global competitors. This is exactly what happened to Xerox. Japanese companies such as Canon ultimately invented their way around Xerox's patents, produced their own photocopies in very efficient manufacturing plants, priced them below Xerox's products, and rapidly took global market share from Xerox. Xerox's demise was not due to the emergence of competitors, for ultimately that was bound to occur, but due to its failure to proactively reduce its cost structure in advance of the emergence of efficient global competitors. The message in this story is that an international strategy may not be viable in the long term, and to survive companies that are able to pursue it need to shift towards a global standardization strategy, or perhaps a transnational strategy, in advance of competitors (see figure 6.3).

The same can be said about a localization strategy. Localization may give a company a competitive edge, but if it is simultaneously facing aggressive competitors, the company will also have to reduce its cost structure, and the only way to do that may be to adopt more of a transnational strategy. Thus, as competition intensifies, international and localization strategies tend to become less viable, and managers need to orientate their companies towards either a global standardization strategy, or a transnational strategy. Procter & Gamble, for example, has moved from a localization strategy to more of a transnational strategy in recent years (see the Strategy in Action feature).

International Strategy

A strategy in which firms try to centralize product development functions such as R&D at home but establish manufacturing and marketing functions in each major country or geographic region in which they do business.

Figure 6.3 Changes Over Time

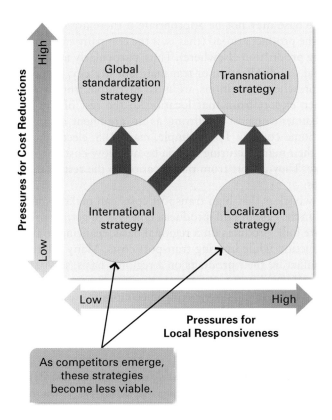

CHOICES OF ENTRY MODE

Another key strategic issue confronting managers in a multinational enterprise is deciding upon the best strategy for entering a market. There are five main choices of entry mode: exporting, licensing, franchising, entering into a joint venture with a host country company, and setting up a wholly owned subsidiary in the host country. Each mode has its advantages and disadvantages, and managers must weigh these carefully when deciding which mode to use.[19]

Exporting

Most manufacturing companies begin their global expansion as exporters and only later switch to one of the other modes for serving a foreign market. Exporting has two distinct advantages: it avoids the costs of establishing manufacturing operations in the host country, which are often substantial, and it may be consistent with scale economies and location economies. By manufacturing the product in a centralized location and then exporting it to other national markets, the company may be able to realize substantial scale economies from its global sales volume. That is how Sony came to dominate the global television market, how Matsushita came to dominate the VCR market, and how many Japanese auto companies originally made inroads into the U.S. auto market.

There are also a number of drawbacks to exporting. First, exporting from the company's home base may not be appropriate if there are lower-cost locations for manufacturing the product abroad (that is, if the company can realize location economies by moving production elsewhere). Thus, particularly in the case of a company pursuing a global standardization or transnational strategy, it may pay to manufacture in a location where conditions are most favorable from a value creation perspective and then export from that location to the rest of the globe. This is not so much an argument against exporting as an argument against exporting from the company's home country. For example, many U.S. electronics companies have moved some of their manufacturing to Asia because low-cost but highly skilled labor is available there. They export from that location to the rest of the globe, including the United States.

Another drawback is that high transport costs can make exporting uneconomical, particularly in the case of bulk products. One way of getting around this problem is to manufacture bulk products on a regional basis, realizing some economies from large-scale production while limiting transport costs. Many multinational chemical companies manufacture their products on a regional basis, serving several countries in a region from one facility.

Tariff barriers, too, can make exporting uneconomical, and a government's threat to impose tariff barriers can make the strategy very risky. Indeed, the implicit threat from the U.S. Congress to impose tariffs on Japanese cars imported into the United States led directly to the decision by many Japanese auto companies to set up manufacturing plants in the United States.

Finally, a common practice among companies that are just beginning to export also poses risks. A company may delegate marketing activities in each country in which it does business to a local agent, but there is no guarantee that the agent will act in the company's best interest. Often foreign agents also carry the products of competing companies and thus have divided loyalties. Consequently, they may not do as good a job as the company would if it managed marketing itself. One way to solve this problem is to set up a wholly owned subsidiary in the host country to handle local marketing. In this way, the company can reap the cost advantages that arise from manufacturing the product in a single location and exercise tight control over marketing strategy in the host country.

Licensing

International Licensing

An arrangement whereby a foreign licensee buys the rights to produce a company's product in the licensee's country for a negotiated fee.

International licensing is an arrangement whereby a foreign licensee buys the rights to produce a company's product in the licensee's country for a negotiated fee (normally, royalty payments on the number of units sold). The licensee then puts up most of the capital necessary to get the overseas operation going.[20] The advantage of licensing is that the company does not have to bear the development costs and risks associated with opening up a foreign market. Licensing therefore can be a very attractive option for companies that lack the capital to develop operations overseas. It can also be an attractive option for companies that are unwilling to commit substantial financial resources to an unfamiliar or politically volatile foreign market where political risks are particularly high.

Licensing has three serious drawbacks, however. First, it does not give a company the tight control over manufacturing, marketing, and strategic functions in foreign countries that it needs to have in order to realize scale economies and location economies—as companies pursuing both global standardization and transnational strategies try to do. Typically, each licensee sets up its own manufacturing operations. Hence, the company stands little chance of realizing scale economies and location economies by manufacturing its product in a centralized location. When these economies are likely to be important, licensing may not be the best way of expanding overseas.

Second, competing in a global marketplace may make it necessary for a company to coordinate strategic moves across countries so that the profits earned in one country can be used to support competitive attacks in another. Licensing, by its very nature, severely limits a company's ability to coordinate strategy in this way. A licensee is unlikely to let a multinational company take its profits (beyond those due in the form of royalty payments) and use them to support an entirely different licensee operating in another country.

A third problem with licensing is the risk associated with licensing technological know-how to foreign companies. For many multinational companies, technological know-how forms the basis of their competitive advantage, and they would want to maintain control over the use to which it is put. By licensing its technology, a company can quickly lose control over it. RCA, for instance, once licensed its color television technology to a number of Japanese companies. The Japanese companies quickly assimilated RCA's technology and then used it to enter the U.S. market. Now the Japanese have a bigger share of the U.S. market than the RCA brand does.

Franchising

Franchising is similar to licensing, although franchising tends to involve longer-term commitments than licensing. **Franchising** is basically a specialized form of licensing in which the franchiser not only sells intangible property to the franchisee (normally a trademark), but also insists that the franchisee agree to abide by strict rules as to how it does business. The franchiser will also often assist the franchisee to run the business on an ongoing basis. As with licensing, the franchiser typically receives a royalty payment, which amounts to some percentage of the franchisee revenues.

Whereas licensing is a strategy pursued primarily by manufacturing companies, franchising, which resembles it in some respects, is a strategy employed chiefly by service companies. McDonald's provides a good example of a firm that has grown by using a franchising strategy. McDonald's has set down strict rules as to how franchisees should operate a restaurant. These rules extend to control over the menu, cooking methods, staffing policies, and restaurant design and location. McDonald's also organizes the supply chain for its franchisees and provides management training and financial assistance.[21]

The advantages of franchising are similar to those of licensing. Specifically, the franchiser does not have to bear the development costs and risks of opening up a foreign market on its own, for the franchisee typically assumes those costs and risks. Thus, using a franchising strategy, a service company can build up a global presence quickly and at a low cost.

The disadvantages are less pronounced than in the case of licensing. Because franchising is a strategy used by service companies, a franchiser does not have to consider the need to coordinate manufacturing in order to achieve scale economies and location economies. Nevertheless, franchising may inhibit a company's ability to achieve global strategic coordination.

Franchising

A specialized form of licensing in which the franchiser sells the franchisee intangible property (normally a trademark) and insists that the franchisee agree to abide by strict rules about how it does business.

A more significant disadvantage of franchising is the lack of quality control. The foundation of franchising arrangements is the notion that the company's brand name conveys a message to consumers about the quality of the company's product. Thus, a traveler booking into a Four Seasons hotel in Hong Kong can reasonably expect the same quality of room, food, and service as he or she would receive in New York; the Four Seasons name is a guarantee of the consistency of product quality. However, foreign franchisees may not be as concerned about quality as they should be, and poor quality may mean not only lost sales in the foreign market but also a decline in the company's worldwide reputation. For example, if the traveler has a bad experience at the Four Seasons in Hong Kong, he or she may never go to another Four Seasons hotel and steer her colleagues away as well. The geographic distance separating it from its foreign franchisees and the sheer number of individual franchisees—tens of thousands in the case of McDonald's—can make it difficult for the franchiser to detect poor quality. Consequently, quality problems may persist.

To reduce this problem, a company can set up a subsidiary in each country or region in which it is expanding. The subsidiary, which might be wholly owned by the company or a joint venture with a foreign company, then assumes the rights and obligations to establish franchisees throughout that particular country or region. The combination of proximity and the limited number of independent franchisees that have to be monitored reduces the quality control problem. Besides, since the subsidiary is at least partly owned by the company, the company can place its own managers in the subsidiary to ensure the kind of quality monitoring it wants. This organizational arrangement has proved very popular in practice. It has been used by McDonald's, KFC, and Hilton Hotels Corp. to expand their international operations, to name just three examples.

Joint Ventures

Establishing a joint venture with a foreign company has long been a favored mode for entering a new market. A **joint venture** is a separate corporate entity in which two or more companies have an ownership stake. One of the most famous long-term joint ventures is the Fuji-Xerox joint venture to produce photocopiers for the Japanese market. The most typical form of joint venture is a fifty-fifty venture, in which each party takes a 50% ownership stake and operating control is shared by a team of managers from both parent companies. Some companies have sought joint ventures in which they have a majority shareholding (for example, a 51% to 49% ownership split), which permits tighter control by the dominant partner.[22]

Joint ventures have a number of advantages. First, a company may feel that it can benefit from a local partner's knowledge of a host country's competitive conditions, culture, language, political systems, and business systems. Second, when the development costs and risks of opening up a foreign market are high, a company might gain by sharing these costs and risks with a local partner. Third, in some countries, political considerations make joint ventures the only feasible entry mode.[23] For example, historically many U.S. companies found it much easier to get permission to set up operations in Japan if they went in with a Japanese partner than if they tried to enter on their own. This is why Xerox originally teamed up with Fuji to sell photocopiers in Japan.

Despite these advantages, joint ventures can be difficult to establish and run because of two main drawbacks. First, as in the case of licensing, a company that enters

Joint Venture

A separate corporate entity in which two or more companies have an ownership stake.

into a joint venture risks losing control over its technology to its venture partner. To minimize this risk, it can seek a majority ownership stake in the joint venture, for as the dominant partner it would be able to exercise greater control over its technology. The trouble with this strategy is that it may be difficult to find a foreign partner willing to accept a minority ownership position.

The second disadvantage is that a joint venture does not give a company the tight control over its subsidiaries that it might need in order to realize scale economies or location economies—as both global standardization and transnational companies try to do—or to engage in coordinated global attacks against its global rivals.

Wholly Owned Subsidiaries

A **wholly owned subsidiary** is one in which the parent company owns 100% of the subsidiary's stock. To establish a wholly owned subsidiary in a foreign market, a company can either set up a completely new operation in that country or acquire an established host country company and use it to promote its products in the host market.

Setting up a wholly owned subsidiary offers three advantages. First, when a company's competitive advantage is based on its control of a technological competency, a wholly owned subsidiary will normally be the preferred entry mode, since it reduces the company's risk of losing this control. Consequently, many high-tech companies prefer wholly owned subsidiaries to joint ventures or licensing arrangements. Wholly owned subsidiaries tend to be the favored entry mode in the semiconductor, computer, electronics, and pharmaceutical industries.

Second, a wholly owned subsidiary gives a company the kind of tight control over operations in different countries that it needs if it is going to engage in global strategic coordination—taking profits from one country to support competitive attacks in another.

Third, a wholly owned subsidiary may be the best choice if a company wants to realize location economies and the scale economies that flow from producing a standardized output from a single or limited number of manufacturing plants. When pressures on costs are intense, it may pay a company to configure its value chain in such a way that value added at each stage is maximized. Thus, a national subsidiary may specialize in manufacturing only part of the product line or certain components of the end product, exchanging parts and products with other subsidiaries in the company's global system. Establishing such a global production system requires a high degree of control over the operations of national affiliates. Different national operations have to be prepared to accept centrally determined decisions as to how they should produce, how much they should produce, and how their output should be priced for transfer between operations. A wholly owned subsidiary would have to comply with these mandates, whereas licensees or joint venture partners would most likely shun such a subservient role.

On the other hand, establishing a wholly owned subsidiary is generally the most costly method of serving a foreign market. The parent company must bear all the costs and risks of setting up overseas operations—in contrast to joint ventures, where the costs and risks are shared, or licensing, where the licensee bears most of the costs and risks. But the risks of learning to do business in a new culture diminish if the company acquires an established host country enterprise. Acquisitions, though, raise a whole set of additional problems, such as trying to marry divergent corporate cultures, and these problems may more than offset the benefits.

Wholly Owned Subsidiary

A subsidiary where the parent company owns 100% of the subsidiary's stock.

Choosing an Entry Strategy

The advantages and disadvantages of the various entry modes are summarized in Table 6.1. Inevitably, there are trade-offs in choosing one entry mode over another. For example, when considering entry into an unfamiliar country with a track record of nationalizing foreign-owned enterprises, a company might favor a joint venture with a local enterprise. Its rationale might be that the local partner will help it establish operations in an unfamiliar environment and speak out against nationalization should the possibility arise. But if the company's distinctive competency is based on proprietary technology, entering into a joint venture might mean risking loss of control over that technology to the joint venture partner, which would make this strategy unattractive. Despite such hazards, some generalizations can be offered about the optimal choice of entry mode.

Distinctive Competencies and Entry Mode   When companies expand internationally to earn greater returns from their differentiated product offerings, entering markets where indigenous competitors lack comparable products, the companies are pursuing an international strategy. The optimal entry mode for such companies depends to some degree on the nature of their distinctive competency. In particular, we

Table 6.1   The Advantages and Disadvantages of Different Entry Modes

Entry Mode	Advantages	Disadvantages
Exporting	• Ability to realize location and scale based economies	• High transport costs • Trade barriers • Problems with local marketing agents
Licensing	• Low development costs and risks	• Inability to realize location and scale based economies • Inability to engage in global strategic coordination • Lack of control over technology
Franchising	• Low development costs and risks	• Inability to engage in global strategic coordination • Lack of control over quality
Joint ventures	• Access to local partner's knowledge • Shared development costs and risks • Political dependency	• Inability to engage in global strategic coordination • Inability to realize location scale based economies • Lack of control over technology
Wholly owned subsidiaries	• Protection of technology • Ability to engage in global strategic coordination • Ability to realize location and scale based economies	• High costs and risks

need to distinguish between companies with a distinctive competency in technological know-how and those with a distinctive competency in management know-how.

If a company's competitive advantage—its distinctive competency—derives from its control of proprietary *technological know-how,* licensing and joint venture arrangements should be avoided if possible in order to minimize the risk of losing control of that technology. Thus, if a high-tech company is considering setting up operations in a foreign country in order to profit from a distinctive competency in technological know-how, it should probably do so through a wholly owned subsidiary.

However, this rule should not be viewed as a hard and fast one. For instance, a licensing or joint venture arrangement might be structured in such a way as to reduce the risks that a company's technological know-how will be expropriated by licensees or joint venture partners. We consider this kind of arrangement in more detail later in the chapter when we discuss the issue of structuring strategic alliances. To take another exception to the rule, a company may perceive its technological advantage as being only transitory and expect rapid imitation of its core technology by competitors. In this situation, the company might want to license its technology as quickly as possible to foreign companies in order to gain global acceptance of its technology before imitation occurs.[24] Such a strategy has some advantages. By licensing its technology to competitors, the company may deter them from developing their own, possibly superior, technology. It also may be able to establish its technology as the dominant design in the industry (as Matsushita did with its VHS format for VCRs), ensuring a steady stream of royalty payments. Such situations apart, however, the attractions of licensing are probably outweighed by the risks of losing control of technology, and therefore licensing should be avoided.

The competitive advantage of many service companies, such as McDonald's or Hilton Hotels, is based on *management know-how.* For such companies, the risk of losing control of their management skills to franchisees or joint venture partners is not that great. The reason is that the valuable asset of such companies is their brand name, and brand names are generally well protected by international laws pertaining to trademarks. Given this fact, many of the issues that arise in the case of technological know-how do not arise in the case of management know-how. As a result, many service companies favor a combination of franchising and subsidiaries to control franchisees within a particular country or region. The subsidiary may be wholly owned or a joint venture. In most cases, however, service companies have found that entering into a joint venture with a local partner in order to set up a controlling subsidiary in a country or region works best because a joint venture is often politically more acceptable and brings a degree of local knowledge to the subsidiary.

Pressures for Cost Reduction and Entry Mode   The greater the pressures for cost reductions are, the more likely it is that a company will want to pursue some combination of exporting and wholly owned subsidiaries. By manufacturing in the locations where factor conditions are optimal and then exporting to the rest of the world, a company may be able to realize substantial location economies and substantial scale economies. The company might then want to export the finished product to marketing subsidiaries based in various countries. Typically, these subsidiaries would be wholly owned and have the responsibility for overseeing distribution in a particular country. Setting up wholly owned marketing subsidiaries is preferable to a joint venture arrangement or using a foreign marketing agent because it gives the company the tight control over marketing that might be required to coordinate a globally dispersed value chain. In addition, tight control over a local operation enables the company to use the profits generated in one market to improve its competitive position in another market. Hence companies pursuing global or transnational strategies prefer to establish wholly owned subsidiaries.

SUMMARY OF CHAPTER

1. For some companies, international expansion represents a way of earning greater returns by transferring the skills and product offerings derived from their distinctive competencies to markets where indigenous competitors lack those skills.

2. Because of national differences, it pays a company to base each value creation activity it performs at the location where factor conditions are most conducive to the performance of that activity. This strategy is known as focusing on the attainment of location economies.

3. By building sales volume more rapidly, international expansion can assist a company in the process of gain a cost advantage through the realization of scale economies and learning effects.

4. The best strategy for a company to pursue may depend on the kind of pressures it must cope with: pressures for cost reductions or for local responsiveness. Pressures for cost reductions are greatest in industries producing commodity-type products, where price is the main competitive weapon. Pressures for local responsiveness arise from differences in consumer tastes and preferences, as well as from national infrastructure and traditional practices, distribution channels, and host government demands.

5. Companies pursuing an international strategy transfer the skills and products derived from distinctive competencies to foreign markets, while undertaking some limited local customization.

6. Companies pursuing a localization strategy customize their product offering, marketing strategy, and business strategy to national conditions.

7. Companies pursuing a global standardization strategy focus on reaping the cost reductions that come from scale economies and location economies.

8. Many industries are now so competitive that companies must adopt a transnational strategy. This involves a simultaneous focus on reducing costs, transferring skills and products, and local responsiveness. Implementing such a strategy may not be easy.

9. There are five different ways of entering a foreign market: exporting, licensing, franchising, entering into a joint venture, and setting up a wholly owned subsidiary. The optimal choice among entry modes depends on the company's strategy.

DISCUSSION QUESTIONS

1. Plot the position of the following companies on Figure 6.3: Procter & Gamble, IBM, Coca-Cola, Dow Chemicals, Pfizer, and McDonald's. In each case, justify your answer.

2. Discuss how the need for control over foreign operations varies with the strategy and distinctive competencies of a company. What are the implications of this relationship for the choice of entry mode?

3. Licensing proprietary technology to foreign competitors is the best way to give up a company's competitive advantage. Discuss.

C L O S I N G   C A S E

IKEA—The Global Retailer

IKEA may be the world's most successful global retailer. Established by Ingvar Kamprad in Sweden in 1943 when he was just 17 years old, the home furnishing superstore has grown into a global cult brand with 230 stores in 33 countries that host 410 million shoppers a year and generates sales of €15 billion ($18 billion). Kamprad himself, who still owns the private company, is rumored to be the world's richest man.

IKEA's target market is the global middle class who are looking for low priced but attractively designed furniture and household items. The company applies the same basic formula worldwide—open large warehouse stores festooned in the blue and yellow colors of the Swedish flag that offer 8,000 to 10,000 items from kitchen cabinets to candlesticks. Use wacky promotions to drive traffic into the stores. Configure the interior of the stores so that customers have to pass through each department to get to the checkout. Add restaurants and child care facilities so that shoppers stay as long as possible. Price the items as low as possible. Make sure that product design reflects the simple clean Swedish lines that have become IKEA's trademark. And then watch the results—customers who enter the store planning to buy a $40 coffee table and end up spending $500 on everything from storage units to kitchen ware.

IKEA aims to reduce the price of its offerings by 2%–3% per year, which requires relentless attention to cost cutting. With a network of 1,300 suppliers in 53 countries, IKEA devotes considerable attention to finding the right manufacturer for each item. Consider the company's best selling Klippan love seat. Designed in 1980, the Klippan with its clean lines, bright colors, simple legs and compact size has sold some 1.5 million units since its introduction. Originally manufactured in Sweden, IKEA soon transferred production to lower cost suppliers in Poland. As demand for the Klippan grew, IKEA then decided that it made more sense to work with suppliers in each of the company's big markets to avoid the costs associated with shipping the product all over the world. Today there are five suppliers of the frames in Europe, plus three in the United States and two in China. To reduce the cost of the cotton slipcovers, production has been concentrated in four core suppliers in China and Europe. The resulting efficiencies from these global sourcing decisions enabled IKEA to reduce the price of the Klippan by some 40% between 1999 and 2006.

Despite its standard formula, however, IKEA has found that global success requires that it adapt its offerings to the tastes and preferences of consumers in different nations. IKEA first discovered this in the early 1990s when it entered the United States. The company soon found that its European style offerings didn't always resonate with American consumers. Beds were measured in centimeters, not the king, queen and twin sizes that Americans are familiar with. Sofas weren't big enough, wardrobe draws were not deep enough, glasses were too small, curtains too short, and kitchens didn't fit U.S. size appliances. Since then IKEA has redesigned its offerings in the U.S. to appeal to American consumers, and has been rewarded with stronger stores sales. The same process is now unfolding in China where the company plans to have 10 stores by 2010. The store layout in China reflects the layout of many Chinese apartments, and since many Chinese apartments have balconies, IKEA's Chinese stores include a balcony section. IKEA has had to adapt its locations to China, where car ownership is still not widespread. In the West, IKEA stores are generally located in suburban areas and have lots of parking space, but in China they are located near public transportation, and IKEA offers delivery services so that Chinese customers can get their purchases home.[25]

Case Discussion Questions

1. How is IKEA profiting from global expansion? What is the essence of its strategy for creating value by expanding internationally?
2. How would you characterize IKEA's original strategic posture in foreign markets? What were the strengths of this posture? What were its weaknesses?
3. How has the strategic posture of IKEA changed as a result of its experiences in the United States? Why did it change its strategy? How would you characterize the strategy of IKEA today?

NOTES

1. World Trade Organization, *International Trade Trends and Statistics, 2006* (Geneva: WTO, 2007).
2. World Trade Organization, *International Trade Statistics, 2008* (Geneva: WTO, 2008), and United Nations, *World Investment Report, 2008.*
3. P. Dicken, *Global Shift* (New York: Guilford Press, 1992).
4. D. Pritchard, "Are Federal Tax Laws and State Subsidies for Boeing 7E7 Selling America Short?" *Aviation Week,* April 12, 2004, 74–75.
5. I. Metthee, "Playing a Large Part," *Seattle Post Intelligence,* April 9, 1994, 13.
6. T. Levitt, "The Globalization of Markets," *Harvard Business Review* (May–June 1983): 92–102.
7. M. E. Porter, *The Competitive Advantage of Nations* (New York: Free Press, 1990).
8. A. Lillo, "Walmart Says Global Going Good," *Home Textiles Today,* Septmeber 15, 2003, 12–13. A. de Rocha and L. A. Dib, "The Entry of Walmart into Brazil," *International Journal of Retail and Distribution Management,* 30 (2002): 61–73; Anonymous, "Walmart: Mexico's Biggest Retailer," *Chain Store Age,* June 2001, 52–54; M. Flagg, "In Asia, Going to the Grocery Increasingly Means Heading for a European Retail Chain," *Wall Street Journal,* April 24, 2001, A21; "A Long Way from Bentonville," *The Economist,* September 20, 2006, 38–39; and "How Walmart Should Right Itself," *The Wall Street Journal,* April 20, 2007, C1, C5. http://www.walmart.com
9. D. Barboza, "An Unknown Giant Flexes its Muscles," *New York Times,* December 4, 2004, B1, B3.
10. See J. Birkinshaw and N. Hood, "Multinational Subsidiary Evolution: Capability and Charter Change in Foreign Owned Subsidiary Companies;" *Academy of Management Review* 23 (October 1998): 773–95; A. K. Gupta and V. J. Govindarajan, "Knowledge Flows within Multinational Corporations," *Strategic Management Journal* 21 (2000): 473–96; V. J. Govindarajan and A. K. Gupta, *The Quest for Global Dominance* (San Francisco, Calif: Jossey Bass, 2001); T. S. Frost, J. M. Birkinshaw, and P. C. Ensign, "Centers of Excellence in Multinational Corporations," *Strategic Management Journal* 23 (2002), 997–1018; and U. Andersson, M. Forsgren, and U. Holm, "The Strategic Impact of External Networks," *Strategic Management Journal* 23 (2002): 979–96.
11. S. Leung, "Armchairs, TVs and Espresso: Is It McDonald's?" *Wall Street Journal,* August 30, 2002, A1, A6.
12. C. K. Prahalad and Yves L. Doz, *The Multinational Mission: Balancing Local Demands and Global Vision* (New York: Free Press, 1987). Also see J. Birkinshaw, A. Morrison, and J. Hulland, "Structural and Competitive Determinants of a Global Integration Strategy," *Strategic Management Journal* 16 (1995): 637–655.
13. J.E. Garten, "Walmart gives globalization a bad name", *Business Week*, March 8, 2004, 24.
14. C. K. Prahalad and Yves L. Doz, *The Multinational Mission: Balancing Local Demands and Global Vision* (New York: Free Press, 1987). Prahalad and Doz actually talk about local responsiveness rather than local customization.
15. C. J. Chipello, "Local Presence Is Key to European Deals," *Wall Street Journal,* June 30, 1998, A15.
16. Bartlett and Ghoshal, *Managing Across Borders.*
17. J. Neff, "P&G Outpacing Unilever in Five-Year Battle," *Advertising Age,* November 3, 2003, 1–3; G. Strauss, "Firm Restructuring into Truly Global Company," *USA Today,* September 10, 1999, B2; *Procter & Gamble 10K Report, 2005;* and M. Kolbasuk McGee, "P&G Jump-Starts Corporate Change," *Information Week,* November 1, 1999, 30–34.
18. Ibid.
19. This section draws on several studies, including: C. W. L. Hill, P. Hwang, and W. C. Kim, "An Eclectic Theory of the Choice of International Entry Mode," *Strategic Management Journal* 11 (1990): 117–128; C. W. L. Hill and W. C. Kim, "Searching for a Dynamic Theory of the Multinational Company: A Transaction Cost Model," *Strategic Management Journal* 9 (Special Issue on Strategy Content, 1988): 93–104. E. Anderson and H. Gatignon, "Modes of Foreign Entry: A Transaction Cost Analysis and Propositions," *Journal of International Business Studies* 17 (1986): 1–26; F. R. Root, *Entry Strategies for International Markets* (Lexington, Mass.: D. C. Heath, 1980). A. Madhok, "Cost, Value and Foreign Market Entry: The Transaction and the Company," *Strategic Management Journal* 18 (1997): 39–61.
20. F. J. Contractor, "The Role of Licensing in International Strategy," *Columbia Journal of World Business* (Winter 1982): 73–83.
21. Andrew E. Serwer, "McDonald's Conquers the World," *Fortune,* October 17, 1994, 103–116.
22. B. Kogut, "Joint Ventures: Theoretical and Empirical Perspectives," *Strategic Management Journal* 9 (1988): 319–332.
23. D. G. Bradley, "Managing Against Expropriation," *Harvard Business Review* (July–August 1977): 78–90.
24. C. W. L. Hill, "Strategies for Exploiting Technological Innovations," *Organization Science* 3 (1992): 428–441.
25. K. Capell, A. Sains, C. Lindblad and A.T. Palmer, "IKEA", *Business Week,* November 14, 2005, 96–101. K. Capell et al, "What a sweetheart of a love seat", *Business Week,* November 14, 2005, 101. P.M. Miller, "IKEA with Chinese Characterristics," *The Chinese Business Review,* July/August 2004, 36–69. C. Daniels, "Create IKEA, make billions, take bus," *Fortune,* May 3, 2004, 44.

7

LONG-RUN PROFITABILITY THROUGH CORPORATE-LEVEL STRATEGY

CHAPTER OUTLINE

Concentration on a Single Industry

Horizontal Integration
Benefits and Costs of Horizontal Integration
Outsourcing Functional Activities

Vertical Integration

Arguments for Vertical Integration
Arguments Against Vertical Integration
Vertical Integration and Outsourcing

Entering New Industries Through Diversification

Creating Value Through Diversification
Related versus Unrelated Diversification

Restructuring and Downsizing

Why Restructure?
Exit Strategies

LEARNING OBJECTIVES

After reading this chapter, you should be able to:

- Discuss the arguments for and against concentrating a company's resources and competing in just one industry.
- Explain the conditions under which a company is likely to pursue vertical integration as a means to strengthen its position in its core industry.

- Appreciate the conditions under which a company can create more value through diversification and why there is a limit to successful diversification.
- Understand why restructuring a company is often necessary, and discuss the pros and cons of the strategies a company can adopt to exit businesses and industries.

OVERVIEW

The principal concern of corporate-level strategy is to identify the industry or industries a company should participate in to maximize its long-run profitability. A company has several options when choosing which industries to compete in. First, a company can concentrate on only one industry and focus its activities on developing business-level strategies to improve its competitive position in that industry (see Chapter 5). Second, a company may decide to enter *new* industries in adjacent stages of the industry value chain by pursuing a strategy of *vertical integration*, which means it either begins to make its own inputs and/or sell its own products. Third, a company can choose to enter *new* industries that may or may not be connected to its existing industry by pursuing a strategy of *diversification*. Finally, a company may choose to exit businesses and industries to increase its long-run profitability and to shrink the boundaries of the organization by restructuring and downsizing its activities.

In this chapter we explore these different alternatives and discuss the pros and cons of each as a method of increasing a company's profitability over time. The chapter repeatedly stresses that if corporate-level strategy is to increase long-run profitability, it must enable a company, or its different business units, to perform one or more value creation functions at a *lower cost* and/or in a way that leads to increased *differentiation* (and thus a premium price). Thus successful corporate-level strategy works to build a company's distinctive competencies and increase its competitive advantage over industry rivals. There is, therefore, a very important link between corporate-level strategy and creating competitive advantage at the business level.

CONCENTRATION ON A SINGLE INDUSTRY

For many companies the appropriate choice of corporate-level strategy entails **concentration on a single industry**, whereby a company focuses its resources and capabilities on competing successfully within the confines of a particular product market. Examples of companies that currently pursue such a strategy include McDonald's with its focus on the fast-food restaurant market, Starbucks with its focus on the premium coffee shop business, and Walmart with its focus on global discount retailing. These companies have chosen to stay in one industry because there are several advantages to concentrating on the needs of customers in just one product market (and the different segments within it).

A major advantage of concentrating on a single industry is that doing so enables a company to focus all its managerial, financial, technological, and functional resources and capabilities on developing strategies to strengthen its competitive position in just one business. This strategy is important in fast-growing industries that make strong demands on a company's resources and capabilities but also offer the prospect of substantial long-term profits if a company can sustain its competitive advantage. For example, it would make little sense for a company such as Starbucks to enter new industries such as supermarkets or specialty doughnuts when the coffee shop industry is still in a period of rapid growth and when finding new ways to compete successfully would impose significant demands on Starbucks' managerial, marketing, and financial resources and capabilities. In fact, companies that spread their resources too thin, in order to compete in several different product markets, run the risk of starving their fast-growing core business of the resources needed

Concentration on a Single Industry

The strategy a company adopts when it focuses its resources and capabilities on competing successfully within a particular product market.

to expand rapidly. The result is loss of competitive advantage in the core business and—often—failure.

Nor is it just rapidly growing companies that benefit from focusing their resources and capabilities on one business, market, or industry. Many mature companies that expand over time into too many different businesses and markets find out later that they have stretched their resources too far and that their performance declines as a result. For example, Coca-Cola once decided to expand into the movie business and acquired Columbia Pictures; it also acquired a large California winemaker. It soon found it lacked the competencies to compete successfully in these new industries and that it had not foreseen the strong competitive forces that existed in these industries, from movie companies such as Fox and winemakers such as Gallo. Coca-Cola concluded that entry into these new industries had reduced rather than created value and lowered its profitability; it divested or sold off these new businesses at a significant loss.

Concentrating on a single business allows a company to "stick to the knitting"—that is, to focus on doing what it knows best and avoid entering new businesses it knows little about and where it can create little value.[1] This prevents companies from becoming involved in businesses that their managers do not understand and where poor, uninformed decision making can result in huge losses.

On the other hand, concentrating on just one market or industry can result in disadvantages emerging over time. As we discuss later in the chapter, a certain amount of vertical integration may be necessary to strengthen a company's competitive advantage within its core industry. Moreover, companies that concentrate on just one industry may miss out on opportunities to create more value and increase their profitability by using their resources and capabilities to make and sell products in *other* markets or industries.

Horizontal Integration

Horizontal Integration

Acquiring or merging with industry competitors to achieve the competitive advantages that come with large size.

Acquisition

A company's use of capital such as stock, debt, or cash to purchase another company.

Merger

An agreement between two companies to pool their operations and create a new business entity.

For many companies, as we have just noted, profitable growth and expansion often entail concentrating on competing successfully within a single industry. One tactic or tool that has been widely used at the corporate level to help managers position their companies to compete better in an industry is horizontal integration, which we discussed briefly in Chapter 5. **Horizontal integration** is the process of acquiring or merging with industry competitors in an effort to achieve the competitive advantages that come with large size or scale. An **acquisition** occurs when one company uses its capital resources (such as stock, debt, or cash) to purchase another company, and a **merger** is an agreement between two companies to pool their resources in a combined operation. For example, Rupert Murdock, CEO of News Corp, made scores of acquisitions in the newspaper industry so that all his newspapers could reduce costs by taking advantage of the news and stories written by News Corp journalists anywhere in the world.

In industry after industry there have been thousands of mergers and acquisitions over the past decades. In the aerospace industry, Boeing merged with McDonald Douglass to create the world's largest aerospace company; in the pharmaceutical industry, Pfizer acquired Warner-Lambert to become the largest pharmaceutical firm; in the computer hardware industry, Compaq acquired Digital Equipment and then was itself acquired by HP; and in the Internet industry, Yahoo!, Google, and AOL have taken over hundreds of small Internet companies to better position themselves in segments such as streaming video, music downloading, and digital photography.

The result of wave upon wave of global mergers and acquisitions has been to increase the level of concentration in a wide range of industries. Twenty years ago, cable television was dominated by a patchwork of thousands of small, family-owned businesses, but by the 2000s, three companies controlled over two-thirds of the market. In 1990 the three main publishers of college textbooks accounted for 35% of the market; by 2008 they accounted for over 75%. In semiconductor chips, mergers and acquisitions between the industry leaders resulted in the four largest firms controlling 85% of the global market in 2007, up from 45% in 1997. This has occurred because horizontal integration can significantly improve the competitive advantage and profitability of companies whose managers choose to stay inside one industry and focus on managing its competitive forces. The way in which Walmart did this by expanding its presence in the supermarket industry is discussed in the Running Case below.

Benefits and Costs of Horizontal Integration

Managers who pursue horizontal integration have decided that the best way to increase their company's profitability is to invest its capital to purchase the resources and assets of industry competitors. Profitability increases when horizontal integration results in four major benefits: It (1) lowers operating costs, (2) increases product differentiation, (3) reduces rivalry within an industry, and/or (4) increases a company's bargaining power over suppliers and buyers.

Lower Operating Costs Horizontal integration lowers a company's operating costs when it results in increasing economies of scale. Suppose there are five major competitors, each of which owns a manufacturing plant in every region of the United States, but none of these plants is operating at full capacity (so costs are relatively high). If one competitor buys up another and shuts down that competitor's plant, it can then operate its own plant at full capacity and so reduce manufacturing costs.

Achieving economies of scale is very important in industries that have high fixed costs, because large-scale production allows a company to spread its fixed costs over a large volume, which drives down average operating costs. In the telecommunications industry, for example, the fixed costs of building an advanced Internet network are enormous, so to make such an investment pay off, a company needs a large volume of customers. Thus companies such as AT&T and Verizon acquired many large telecommunications companies in order to obtain their customers who would then be "switched" to their network. This drives up network utilization and drives down the cost of serving each customer on the network. Similarly, mergers and acquisitions in the pharmaceutical industry are often driven by the need to realize scale economies in sales and marketing. The fixed costs of building a nationwide pharmaceutical sales force are very high, and pharmaceutical companies need to have a large number of drugs to sell if they are to use their sales force effectively. Thus, for example, Pfizer acquired Warner-Lambert because its combined sales force would then have many more products to sell when they visited physicians—an advantage that increases their productivity. And, again, after Pfizer acquired Wyeth Pharmaceuticals it created a prescription drug company of unprecedented scale; the combined company had almost $70 billion in sales in 2009.

A company can also lower its operating costs when horizontal integration eliminates the need for two sets of corporate head offices, two separate sales forces, and so on, such that the costs of operating the combined company fall.

RUNNING CASE

Walmart's Growing Chain of "Neighborhood Markets"

After its entry into the supermarket industry, Walmart soon recognized that its huge supercenters and discount stores do not serve the needs of customers who want quick and convenient shopping experiences, for example, when they want to pick up food for evening meals. It also recognized that customers spend billions of dollars shopping in local stores such as neighborhood supermarkets, drugstores, and convenience stores and that this was potentially a highly profitable segment of the retail market. Thus, in the 2000s, Walmart decided to enter this segment by opening a new chain of Walmart "Neighborhood Markets." Each of these supermarkets is approximately 40,000 square feet, about one-quarter the size of a Walmart superstore, and stocks 20,000–30,000 items compared to more than 100,000 items available in superstores. Walmart's strategy for the new chain stores was to position them to compete directly with local supermarkets, such as those run by Kroger and Safeway. They would be open 24 hours a day to maximize responsiveness to local customers, and they would also have high-profit-margin departments such as a pharmacy, drugs, health, and beauty products to draw off trade from drugstores such as CVS and Walgreen's. As a result, customers could shop for food while they waited for their prescriptions to be filled or their film to be developed.[2]

To test whether its cost-leadership model would work at this small scale of operations, Walmart opened stores slowly in good locations. Margins are small in the supermarket business, often between 1% and 2%, which is lower than Walmart was accustomed to. To keep costs low, it located its new stores in areas where it had efficient warehouse food preparation and delivery systems. Its strategy was to prepare high-margin items like bakery goods and meat and deli products in central locations and then ship them to supermarkets in prepackaged containers. Each neighborhood market store was also tied in by satellite to Walmart's retail link network so that food service managers would know what kind of food was selling and what was not. They could then customize the food each store sold to customer needs by changing the mix that was trucked fresh each day. Also, because the stores had no onsite butchers or bakers, costs were much lower.

As a result of these strategies the 60-plus United States stores opened by 2004 were able to undercut the prices charged by supermarkets such as Publix, Winn-Dixie, Kroger, and Albertsons by 10%. A typical neighborhood market generates approximately $20 million per year in sales, has a staff of 90, and obtains a 2.3% profit margin, which is significantly higher than average in the supermarket industry. Encouraged by their success, Walmart continued to open more stores and by 2009, had 145 neighborhood markets in operation, most of which are the southern United States.

Walmart is continuing to experiment with new kinds of small supermarkets to increase its share of this market segment. Its "Marketside" store concept is an even smaller "corner-store" format with store size in the 30–25,000 square-feet range. It is also experimenting actively with a chain of stores geared to the needs of Hispanic consumers.[3] One experimental "Hispanic Community" store in Texas is a large-format store at about 160,000 square feet, which in addition to its focus on Hispanic food and grocery also offers a large selection of non-food products tailored toward Hispanic shoppers. Walmart is also looking into small "bodega" supermarkets tailored toward this customer group. Clearly, many profitable opportunities exist in this market segment and just, as at the global level, Walmart's managers are developing strategies to take advantage of them—indeed, in 2010 Walmart announced it would open another 1,000 Neighborhood Markets in the next 5 years.[4]

Increased Product Differentiation   Horizontal integration may also boost profitability when it increases product differentiation, for example, by allowing a company to combine the product lines of merged companies in order to offer customers a wider range of products that can be bundled together. Product bundling involves offering customers the opportunity to buy a complete range of products they need at a single, combined price. This increases the value that customers see in a company's product line, because (1) they often obtain a price discount by purchasing products as a set and (2) they get used to dealing with just one company. For this reason, a company may obtain a competitive advantage from increased product differentiation.

An early example of the value of product bundling is Microsoft Office, which is a bundle of different software programs, including a word processor, spreadsheet, and presentation program. At the beginning of the 1990s, Microsoft was Number two or three in each of these product categories, behind companies such as WordPerfect (which led in the word-processing category), Lotus (which had the best-selling spreadsheet), and Harvard Graphics (which had the best-selling presentation software). When it offered all three programs in a single-price package, however, Microsoft presented consumers with a superior value proposition. Its product bundle quickly gained market share, ultimately accounting for more than 90% of all sales of word-processing, spreadsheet, and presentation software.

Reduced Industry Rivalry   Horizontal integration can help to reduce industry rivalry in two ways. First, acquiring or merging with a competitor helps to eliminate excess capacity in an industry, which, as we saw in Chapter 5, often triggers price wars. By taking excess capacity out of an industry, horizontal integration creates a more benign environment in which prices might stabilize or even increase.

In addition, by reducing the number of competitors in an industry, horizontal integration often makes it easier to use tacit price coordination between rivals. (Recall that tacit coordination is coordination reached without communication, whereas explicit communication to fix prices is illegal.) In general, the larger the number of competitors in an industry, the more difficult it is to establish an informal pricing agreement, such as price leadership by a dominant firm, which reduces the chances that a price war will erupt. Horizontal integration makes it easier for rivals to coordinate their actions because it increases industry concentration and creates an oligopoly.

Both of these motives also seem to have been behind Oracle's many software acquisitions. There was significant excess capacity in the corporate software industry, and major competitors were offering customers discounted prices that had led to a price war and falling profit margins. Oracle hoped to be able to eliminate excess industry that would reduce price competition. By 2009, it was clear that the major corporate software competitors were focusing on finding ways to better differentiate their product suites to prevent a price war and continuing to make major acquisitions to help them build competitive advantage.

Increased Bargaining Power   A final reason for a company to use horizontal integration is to achieve more bargaining power over suppliers or buyers, which strengthens its competitive position and increases its profitability at their expense. By using horizontal integration to consolidate its industry, a company becomes a much larger buyer of a supplier's product; it can use this buying power as leverage to bargain down the price it pays for inputs, and this also lowers its costs. Similarly, a company that acquires its competitors controls a greater percentage of an industry's final product or output, and so buyers become more dependent on it. Other things being equal, the company now has more power to raise prices and profits, because customers have less choice of suppliers from whom to buy. When a company has greater ability to raise prices to buyers or to bargain down the price it pays for inputs, it has increased market power.

Product Bundling

The strategy of offering customers the opportunity to buy a complete range of products at a single, combined price.

Although horizontal integration can strengthen a company's competitive position in several ways, this strategy does have some problems and limitations. As we discuss in detail in Chapter 8, the gains that are anticipated from mergers and acquisitions often are not realized for a number of reasons. These include problems associated with merging very different company cultures, high management turnover in the acquired company when the acquisition was a hostile one, and a tendency for managers to overestimate the benefits to be had from a merger or acquisition and to underestimate the problems involved in merging their operations. For example, there was considerable opposition to the merger between HP and Compaq because critics believed that HP's then CEO, Carly Fiorina, was glossing over the difficulties and costs associated with merging the operations of these two companies, which had very different cultures. As it turned out, she was right and the merger went smoothly, however, it took longer than she expected and she lost her job as CEO before the benefits of her strategy became apparent.

Another problem with horizontal integration is that when a company uses it to become a dominant industry competitor, an attempt to keep using the strategy to grow even larger brings a company into conflict with the Federal Trade Commission (FTC), the government agency responsible for enforcing antitrust law. Antitrust authorities are concerned about the potential for abuse of market power; they believe that more competition is better for consumers than less competition. So the FTC is concerned when a few industry companies try to make acquisitions that will allow them to raise prices to consumers above the level that would exist in a more competitive situation and thus abuse their market power. The FTC wishes to prevent dominant companies from using their market power to crush potential competitors by, for example, cutting prices whenever new competitors enter a market and so forcing them out of business, and then raising prices again once the threat has been eliminated. Because of these concerns, the FTC blocks any merger or acquisition that they decide will create too much industry consolidation and so increase the potential for companies to abuse their market power in the future.

Outsourcing Functional Activities

A second tactic that a company may deploy to improve its competitive position in an industry is to outsource one or more of its own value creation functions and contract with another company to perform that activity on its behalf. In recent years the amount of outsourcing of functional activities, especially manufacturing and information technology (IT) activities, has grown enormously.[5] The expansion of global outsourcing has become one of the most significant trends in modern strategic management, as companies seek not only to improve their competitive advantage at home but also to compete more effectively in today's cutthroat global environment.

We discussed this trend in Chapter 6 and noted that the outsourcing of functions begins with a company identifying those value chain activities that form the basis of its competitive advantage—that give it its distinctive competencies. A company's goal is to nurture and protect these vital functions and competences by performing them internally. The remaining noncore functional activities are then reviewed to see whether they can be performed more efficiently and effectively by specialist companies either at home or abroad. If they can, these activities are outsourced to specialists in manufacturing, distribution, IT, and so on. The relationships between the company and its subcontractors are then structured by a competitive bidding process; subcontractors compete for a company's business for a specified price and length of time. The term **virtual corporation** has been coined to describe companies that outsource most of their functional activities and focus on one or a few core value chain functions.[6]

Xerox is one company that has significantly increased its use of outsourcing in recent years. It decided that its distinctive competencies are in the design and manufacture of photocopying systems. Accordingly, to reduce costs Xerox outsourced the responsibility for performing its noncore value chain activities, such as its IT, to other companies. For example, Xerox has a $3.2 billion contract with Electronic Data Systems (EDS), a global IT consulting company, to manage and maintain all Xerox's internal computer and telecommunications networks. As part of this relationship, 1,700 Xerox employees were transferred to EDS.[7] As another example, Nike, the world's largest maker of athletic shoes, has outsourced all its manufacturing operations to Asian partners, while keeping its core product design and marketing capabilities in-house.

Advantages and Disadvantages of Outsourcing   There are several advantages to outsourcing functional activities.[8] First, outsourcing a particular noncore activity to a specialist company that is more efficient at performing that activity than the company itself lowers a company's operating costs. Second, a specialist often has a distinctive competency in a particular functional activity, so the specialist can help the company better differentiate its products. For example, Convergys, a division spun off by phone company Cincinnati Bell, developed a distinctive competency in the customer care function, which includes activating accounts, billing customers, and dealing with customer inquiries. To take advantage of this competency, other phone companies and global companies such as Orange, Cox, and Logica, decided to outsource their customer care function to Convergys; they recognize that it can provide better customer care service than they can. Thus Convergys helps its client companies to better differentiate their service offerings, and by 2010 it had almost $3 billion in revenues.

A third advantage of outsourcing is that it enables a company to concentrate scarce human, financial, and physical resources on further strengthening its core competencies. Thus Nortel and Wachovia can devote their energies to building wireless networks and providing insurance, secure in the knowledge that Convergys is providing first-class customer care.

On the other hand, there are some disadvantages associated with outsourcing functions. A company that outsources an activity loses both the ability to learn from that activity and the opportunity to transform that activity into one of its distinctive competencies. Thus, although outsourcing customer care activities to Convergys may make sense right now for Nortel, a potential problem is that it will not be building its own internal competency in customer care that may become crucial in the future. A second drawback of outsourcing is that in its enthusiasm for outsourcing, a company may go too far and outsource value creation activities that are central to the maintenance of its competitive advantage. As a result, the company may lose control over the future development of a competency, and its performance may start to decline as a result. Finally, over time a company may become too dependent on a particular subcontractor. This may hurt the company if the performance of that supplier starts to deteriorate or if the supplier starts to use its power to demand higher prices from the company. These problems do not mean that strategic outsourcing should not be pursued, but they do suggest that managers should carefully weigh the pros and cons of the strategy before pursuing it and should negotiate contracts that prevent some of these problems.

Virtual Corporation

A company that outsources most of its functional activities and focuses on one or a few core value chain functions.

In sum, the corporate strategy of concentrating on one industry may enable a company to significantly strengthen its competitive position in that industry because such concentration may help it either to lower costs or to better differentiate its products. Both horizontal integration and outsourcing functional activities are powerful tools that help a company make better use of its resources and capabilities and build its competitive advantage over time. To the extent that a company becomes the dominant industry competitor, it also gains increasing market power that also helps it to increase its long-run profitability.

VERTICAL INTEGRATION

Vertical integration is a corporate-level strategy that involves a company entering new industries to increase its long-run profitability. Once again, the justification for pursuing vertical integration is that a company is able to enter new industries that *add value* to the "core" products it makes and sells because entry into these new industries increases the core products' differentiated appeal or reduces the costs of making them.

Vertical Integration

A strategy in which a company expands its operations either backward into industries that produce inputs for its core products (*backward vertical integration*) or forward into industries that use, distribute, or sell its products (*forward vertical integration*).

When a company pursues a strategy of **vertical integration**, it expands its operations either backward into industries that produce inputs for its core products (*backward vertical integration*) or forward into industries that use, distribute, or sell its products (*forward vertical integration*). To enter a new industry, a company may establish its own operations and create the set of value chain functions it needs to compete effectively in this industry. Alternatively, it may acquire or merge with a company that is already in the industry. A steel company that establishes the value chain operations necessary to supply its iron ore needs from company-owned iron ore mines exemplifies backward integration. A PC maker that sells its laptops through a nationwide chain of company-owned retail outlets illustrates forward integration. For example, Apple Computer entered the retail industry when it decided to set up the value chain functions necessary to retail its products through Apple Stores. IBM is a highly vertically integrated company. It integrated backward and entered the microprocessor and disk drive industries to produce the major components that go into its computers. It also integrated forward and established the value chain functions necessary to compete in the computer software and IT consulting services industries.

Figure 7.1 illustrates four *main* stages in a typical raw-materials-to-customer value-added chain. For a company based in the final assembly stage, backward

Figure 7.1   Stages in the Raw-Materials-to-Customer Value-Added Chain

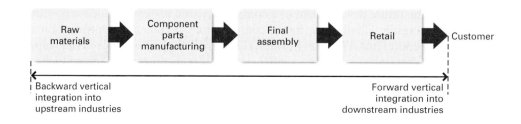

integration means moving into component-parts manufacturing and raw materials production. Forward integration means moving into distribution and sales. At each stage in the chain *value is added* to the product, which means that a company at that stage takes the product produced in the previous stage and transforms it in some way so that it is worth more to a company at the next stage in the chain and, ultimately, to the customer.

It is important to note that each stage of the value-added chain is a *separate industry or industries* in which many different companies may be competing. And within each industry, every company has a value chain composed of the value chain functions we discussed in Chapter 4: R&D, manufacturing, marketing, customer service, and so on. In other words, we can think of a value chain that runs *across* industries, and embedded within that are the value chains of companies *within* each industry.

As an example of the value-added concept, consider the production chain involved in the PC industry illustrated in Figure 7.2. Companies in the raw materials stage of the PC value chain include the manufacturers of specialty ceramics, chemicals, and metals, such as Kyocera of Japan that manufactures the ceramic substrate for semiconductors. Raw materials companies sell their output to the manufacturers of intermediate or component products. Intermediate manufacturers, including companies such as Intel, AMD, and Samsung, transform the ceramics, chemicals, and metals they purchase into computer components such as microprocessors, disk drives, and flash memory chips. In doing so they *add value* to the raw materials they purchase.

In turn, at the final assembly stage, these components are sold to companies such as Apple, Dell, and HP and transformed into PCs—and, hence, adding value to the components they purchase. Many of the completed PCs are then sold to distributors such as Best Buy and Staples that then sell them to final customers. The distributors also add value to the product by making it accessible to customers and by providing PC service and support. Thus value is added by companies at each stage in the raw-materials-to-consumer chain.

As a corporate-level strategy, vertical integration gives companies a choice about which industries in the raw-materials-to-consumer chain they should compete in to maximize their long-run profitability. In the PC industry, most companies have not entered industries in adjacent stages because of the many advantages of specialization and concentration on one industry. However, there are exceptions, such as IBM and HP, who are involved in several different industries.

Figure 7.2 The Raw-Materials-to-Customer Value-Added Chain in the Personal Computer Industry

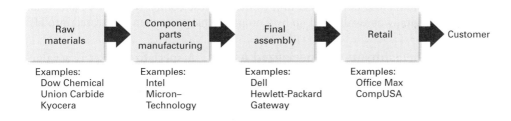

Arguments for Vertical Integration

A company pursues vertical integration to strengthen its competitive position in its original or core business.[9] There are four main reasons for pursuing a vertical integration strategy. It (1) enables the company to build barriers to new competition, (2) facilitates investments in efficiency-enhancing specialized assets, (3) protects product quality, and (4) results in improved scheduling.

Building Barriers to Entry   By vertically integrating backward to gain control over the source of critical inputs or by vertically integrating forward to gain control over distribution channels, a company can build barriers to new entry into its industry. To the extent that this strategy is effective, it limits competition in the company's industry, thereby enabling the company to charge a higher price and make greater profits than it could otherwise.[10] To grasp this argument, consider a famous example of this strategy from the 1930s.

At that time the commercial smelting of aluminum was pioneered by companies such as Alcoa and Alcan. Aluminum is derived from smelting bauxite. Although bauxite is a common mineral, the percentage of aluminum in bauxite is usually so low that it is not economical to mine and smelt. During the 1930s, only one large-scale deposit of bauxite had been discovered where the percentage of aluminum in the mineral made smelting economical. This deposit was on the Caribbean island of Jamaica. Alcoa and Alcan vertically integrated backward and acquired ownership of this deposit. This action created a barrier to entry into the aluminum industry. Potential competitors were deterred from entry because they could not get access to high-grade bauxite; it was all owned by Alcoa and Alcan. Because they had to use lower-grade bauxite, those that did enter the industry found themselves at a cost disadvantage. This situation persisted until the 1950s, when new high-grade deposits were discovered in Australia and Indonesia.

During the 1970s and 1980s, a similar strategy was pursued by vertically integrated companies in the computer industry, such as IBM and Digital Equipment. These companies manufactured the main components of computers (such as microprocessors and memory chips), designed and assembled the computers, produced the software that ran the computers, and sold the final product directly to end users. These companies reasoned that by producing the proprietary technology in-house, they could limit rivals' access to it, thereby building barriers to entry. This strategy worked well until the early 1990s but it has failed since especially in the PC and server computer industries. In the early 1990s, the worst performers in the computer industry were precisely the companies that pursued the vertical integration strategy: IBM and Digital Equipment. Why? The shift to open standards in computer hardware and software nullified the advantages of extensive vertical integration for computer companies. In addition, companies such as Dell took advantage of open standards to search out the world's lowest-cost producer of every computer component in order to drive down costs, effectively circumventing this barrier to entry. In 2005, IBM sold its loss-making PC unit to the Chinese company, Lenovo, and what was left of Digital was swallowed up by Compaq, which was then integrated into HP.

Facilitating Investments in Specialized Assets   A specialized asset is a value-creation tool—machine, computer, or even factory—designed to perform a specific set of activities, but whose value-creation potential is *significantly* lower in its next-best use.[11] A specialized asset may be a piece of equipment used to make only one

Specialized Asset

A value creation tool that is designed to perform a specific set of activities and whose value creation potential is significantly lower in its next-best use.

kind of product, or it may be the know-how or skills that a person or company has acquired through training and experience. Companies invest in specialized assets because these assets allow them to *lower* the costs of value creation and/or to *better* differentiate their products from those of competitors—that permits premium pricing.

A company might invest in specialized equipment because that equipment enables it to lower its manufacturing costs and increase its quality, or it might invest in developing highly specialized technological knowledge because doing so allows it to develop better products than its rivals. Thus specialization can be the basis for achieving a competitive advantage at the business level.

Why does a company have to vertically integrate and invest in the specialized assets itself? Why can't another company perform this function? Because it may be very difficult to persuade other companies in adjacent stages in the raw-materials-to-consumer value-added chain to undertake investments in specialized assets. To realize the economic gains associated with specialized assets, the company may have to vertically integrate into such adjacent stages and make the investments itself.

As an illustration, imagine that Ford has developed a new, high-performance, high-quality, uniquely designed fuel injector. The injector will increase fuel efficiency, which in turn will help differentiate Ford's cars from those of its rivals and give it a competitive advantage. Ford has to decide whether to make the injector in-house (vertical integration) or contract its manufacture out to an independent supplier. Manufacturing these fuel injectors requires substantial investments in equipment that can be used only for this purpose. Because of its unique design, the equipment cannot be used to manufacture any other type of injector for Ford or any other carmaker. Thus the investment in this equipment constitutes an investment in specialized assets.

First consider this situation from the perspective of an independent supplier that has been asked by Ford to make this investment. The supplier might reason that once it has made the investment, it will be dependent on Ford for business because Ford is the only possible customer for this equipment. The supplier perceives this as putting Ford in a strong bargaining position and worries that the carmaker might use this position to force down the price it pays for the injectors. Given this risk, the supplier declines to invest in the specialized equipment.

Now consider Ford's position. Ford might reason that if it contracts out production of these fuel injectors to an independent supplier, it might become too dependent on that supplier for a vital input. Because specialized equipment is needed to produce the injector, Ford cannot easily switch its orders to other suppliers that lack the equipment. Ford perceives this as increasing the bargaining power of the supplier and worries that the supplier might use its bargaining strength to demand higher prices.

The situation of *mutual dependence* that would be created by this investment in specialized assets makes Ford hesitant to contract out and makes any potential suppliers hesitant to undertake the investments in specialized assets required to produce the fuel injectors. The real problem here is a lack of trust: Neither Ford nor the supplier trusts the other to play fair in this situation. The lack of trust arises from the risk of *holdup*—that is, the risk of being taken advantage of by a trading partner after the investment in specialized assets has been made.[12] Because of this risk, Ford might reason that the only safe way to get the new fuel injectors is to manufacture them itself.

To generalize from this example, when achieving a competitive advantage requires one company to make investments in specialized assets in order to trade with another, the risk of holdup may serve as a deterrent, and the investment may not take place. Consequently, the potential gains from lower costs or increased differentiation will not be realized. To obtain these gains, companies must vertically integrate into adjacent stages in the value chain. This consideration has driven automobile companies to vertically integrate backward into the production of component parts, steel companies to vertically integrate backward into the production of iron, computer companies to vertically integrate backward into chip production, and aluminum companies to vertically integrate backward into bauxite mining.

Protecting Product Quality   By protecting product quality, vertical integration enables a company to become a differentiated player in its core business. The banana industry illustrates this situation. Historically, a problem facing food companies that import bananas was the variable quality of delivered bananas, which often arrived on the shelves of American stores either too ripe or not ripe enough. To correct this problem, major U.S. food companies such as General Foods have integrated backward to gain control over supply sources. Consequently, they have been able to distribute bananas of a standard quality at the optimal time for consumption. Knowing they can rely on the quality of these brands, consumers are willing to pay more for them. Thus, by vertically integrating backward into plantation ownership, the banana companies have built consumer confidence, which enables them to charge a premium price for their product. Similarly, when McDonald's decided to open up its first restaurant in Moscow, it found, much to its initial dismay, that in order to serve food and drink indistinguishable from that served in McDonald's restaurants elsewhere, it had to vertically integrate backward and supply its own needs. The quality of Russian-grown potatoes and meat was simply too poor. Thus, to protect the quality of its product, McDonald's set up its own dairy farms, cattle ranches, vegetable plots, and food-processing plant within Russia.

The same kinds of considerations can result in forward integration. Ownership of distribution outlets may be necessary if the required standards of after-sale service for complex products are to be maintained. For example, in the 1920s Kodak owned retail outlets for distributing photographic equipment. The company felt that few established retail outlets had the skills necessary to sell and service its photographic equipment. By the 1930s, however, Kodak decided that it no longer needed to own its retail outlets, because other retailers had begun to provide satisfactory distribution and service for Kodak products. The company then withdrew from retailing. Now, in the 2000s, Kodak has a chain of digital photo-processing booths that it has established to attract people to use its paper, digital cameras, and so on.

Arguments Against Vertical Integration

Over time, however, vertical integration can result in some major disadvantages. Even though it is often undertaken to reduce production costs, vertical integration may actually increase costs when a company has to purchase high-cost inputs from company-owned suppliers despite the existence of low-cost external sources of supply. For example, during the early 1990s General Motors made 68% of the component parts for its vehicles in-house, more than any other major automaker (at Chrysler the figure was 30% and at Toyota 28%). This high level of vertical integration resulted in GM being the highest-cost global carmaker, and despite its attempts to reduce costs, such as spinning off its Delco components division, GM remained in deep trouble and was forced to declare bankruptcy in 2009. Thus, vertical integration can be a major disadvantage when it leads to increases in operating costs.

Frequently, the operating costs of company-owned suppliers become higher than those of outside, independent suppliers when their managers know that they can always sell their components to the company's assembly divisions—that are captive buyers. For example, GM's glass-making division knows it can sell its windows to GM's car-making divisions. Because they do not have to compete for orders, company suppliers have less incentive to be efficient and find ways to reduce operating costs. Indeed, managers of the supply divisions may be tempted to pass on any cost increases to other company divisions in the form of higher prices for components, rather than looking for ways to lower costs! This problem is far less serious, however, when the company pursues taper, rather than full, integration (see Figure 7.3).

A company pursues full integration when it produces *all* of a particular input needed for its processes or when it disposes of *all* its output through its own operations. Taper integration occurs when a company buys some components from independent suppliers and some from company-owned suppliers, or when it sells some of its output through independent retailers and some through company-owned outlets. When a company pursues taper integration, as most companies do today, company-owned suppliers have to compete with independent suppliers. This gives managers a strong incentive to reduce costs; if they do not do so, a company might close down or sell off its component operations, which is what GM did when it spun off its Delco components division.

Another problem is that when technology is changing rapidly, a strategy of vertical integration often ties a company into old, obsolescent, high-cost technology.[13] In general, because a company has to develop value chain functions in each industry stage in which it operates, any significant changes in the environment of each industry, such as major changes in technology, can put its investment at risk. The more industries in which a company operates, the more risk it incurs.

Thus, on the one hand, vertical integration may create value and increase profitability when it lowers operating costs or increases differentiation. On the other hand,

Figure 7.3   Full Integration and Taper Integration

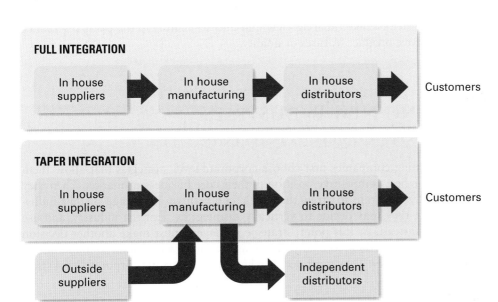

it can reduce profitability if a lack of cost-cutting incentive on the part of company-owned suppliers increases operating costs, or if the inability to change its technology quickly results in lower quality and reduced differentiation. How much vertical differentiation, then, should a company pursue?

In general, a company should pursue vertical integration only if the extra *value created* by entering a new industry in the value chain exceeds the extra costs involved in managing its new operations when it decides to perform additional upstream or downstream value creation activities. Not all vertical integration opportunities have the same potential for value creation. Therefore, strategic managers will first vertically integrate into those industry stages that will realize the *most* value at the least cost. Then, when the extra value created by entering each new industry falls and the costs of managing exchanges along the industry value chain increase, managers stop the vertical integration process. Indeed, if operating costs rise faster, over time, than the value being created in a particular industry, companies will *vertically disintegrate* and exit the industries that are now unprofitable. Clearly, there is a limit to how much a strategy of vertical integration can increase a company's long-run profitability.[14]

Vertical Integration and Outsourcing

Can the advantages associated with vertical integration be obtained if a company makes agreements with specialized suppliers to perform specific upstream or downstream activities on its behalf? Under certain circumstances, companies can realize the advantages of vertical integration, without experiencing problems due to low incentive to contain costs or due to changing technology, by entering into *cooperative outsourcing relationships* with suppliers or distributors. The advantages and disadvantages of outsourcing were discussed earlier in this chapter.

In general, research suggests that outsourcing promotes a company's competitive advantage when the company enters into long-term relationships or strategic alliances with its partners, because trust and goodwill build up between them over time. However, if a company enters into only short-term or "once and for all" contracts with suppliers or distributors, it is often unable to realize the gains associated with vertical integration through outsourcing. This is because its outsourcing partners have no incentive to take the long view and find ways to help the company reduce costs or improve product features or quality.

ENTERING NEW INDUSTRIES THROUGH DIVERSIFICATION

High-performing companies first choose corporate-level strategies that allow them to achieve the best competitive position in their core business or market. Then they may vertically integrate to strengthen their competitive advantage in that industry. Still later, they may decide to vertically disintegrate, exit the industry, and use outsourcing instead. At this point, strategic managers must make another decision about how to invest their company's growing resources and capital to maximize its long-run profitability: They must decide whether to pursue the corporate-level strategy of diversification.

Diversification is the process of entering one or more industries that are distinct or different from a company's core or original industry, in order to find ways to use its distinctive competencies to increase the value of products in those industries to customers. A **diversified company** is one that operates in two or more different or distinct industries (industries *not* in adjacent stages of an industry value chain as in vertical integration) to find ways to increase its long-run profitability. In each industry a company enters, it establishes an operating division or business unit, which is essentially a *self-contained company* that performs a complete set of the value chain functions needed to make and sell products for that particular market. Once again, to increase profitability, a diversification strategy should enable the company, or its individual business units, to perform one or more of the value chain functions either at a *lower cost* or in a way that results in *higher differentiation* and premium prices.

Creating Value Through Diversification

Most companies first consider diversification when they are generating financial resources in excess of those necessary to maintain a competitive advantage in their original business or industry.[15] The question strategic managers must tackle is how to invest a company's excess resources in such a way that they will create the most value and profitability in the long run. Diversification can help a company create greater value in three main ways: (1) by permitting superior internal governance, (2) by transferring competencies among businesses, and (3) by realizing economies of scope.

Superior Internal Governance   The term *internal governance* refers to the manner in which the top executives of a company manage (or "govern") its business units, divisions, and functions. In a diversified company, effective or superior governance revolves around how well top managers can develop strategies that improve the competitive positioning of its business units in the industries where they compete. Diversification creates value when top managers operate the company's different business units so effectively that they perform better than they would if they were *separate and independent companies.*[16]

It is important to recognize that this is *not* an easy thing to do. In fact, it is one of the most difficult tasks facing top managers—and the reason why some CEOs and other top executives are paid tens of millions of dollars a year. Certain senior executives develop superior skills in managing and overseeing the operation of many business units and pushing the managers in charge of these business units to achieve high performance. Examples include Jeffrey Immelt at General Electric, Steve Ballmer at Microsoft, Steve Jobs at Apples, and Michael Dell and Kevin Rollins at Dell.

Research suggests that the top, or corporate, managers who are successful at creating value through superior internal governance seem to make a number of similar kinds of strategic decisions. First, they organize the different business units of the company into self-contained divisions each of which operates separately. For example, GE has over 300 self-contained divisions, including light bulbs, turbines, NBC, and so on. Second, these divisions tend to be managed by corporate executives in a highly decentralized fashion. Corporate executives do *not* get involved in the day-to-day operations of each division. Instead, they set challenging financial goals for each division, probe the general managers of each division about their strategy for attaining these goals, monitor divisional performance, and hold divisional managers accountable for that performance. Third, corporate managers are careful to

Diversification

The process of entering into one or more industries that are distinct or different from a company's core or original industry to find ways to use the company's distinctive competencies to increase the value to customers of the products it offers in those industries.

Diversified Company

A company that operates in two or more industries to find ways to increase long-run profitability.

link their internal monitoring and control mechanisms to incentive pay systems that reward divisional personnel for attaining, and especially for surpassing, performance goals. Although this may sound easy to do, in practice it requires highly skilled corporate executives to pull it off.

An extension of this approach is an **acquisition and restructuring strategy**, which involves corporate managers acquiring inefficient and poorly managed enterprises and then creating value by installing their superior internal governance in these acquired companies and restructuring their operations systems to improve their performance. This strategy can be considered as diversification because the acquired company does not have to be in the same industry as the acquiring company.

The performance of an acquired company can be improved in various ways. First, the acquiring company usually replaces the top management team of the acquired company with a more aggressive top management team—one often drawn from its own ranks of executives who understand the ways to achieve superior governance. Then the new top management team in charge looks for ways to reduce operating costs by, for example, selling off unproductive assets such as executive jets and very expensive corporate headquarters buildings, and by finding ways to reduce the number of managers and employees (badly managed companies frequently let their labor forces grow out of control).

The top management team put in place by the acquiring company then focuses on how the acquired businesses were managed previously and seeks out ways to improve the business unit's efficiency, quality, innovativeness, and responsiveness to customers. In addition, the acquiring company often establishes, for the acquired company, performance goals that cannot be met without significant improvements in operating efficiency. It also makes the new top management aware that failure to achieve performance improvements consistent with these goals within a given amount of time will probably result in losing their jobs. Finally, to motivate the new top management team and the other managers of the acquired unit to undertake such demanding and stressful activities, the acquiring company directly links performance improvements in the acquired unit to pay incentives.

This system of rewards and punishments established by the corporate executives of the acquiring company gives the new managers of the acquired business unit every incentive to look for ways of improving the efficiency of the unit under their charge. GE, Textron, United Technologies, and IBM are good examples of companies that operate in this way.

Acquisition and Restructuring Strategy

A strategy in which a company acquires inefficient and poorly managed enterprises and creates value by putting a superior internal governance structure in place and restructuring the operating systems to improve performance of the acquired companies.

Transferring Competencies   A second way for a company to create value from diversification is to transfer its existing distinctive competencies in one or more value creation functions (for example, manufacturing, marketing, materials management, and R&D) to other industries. Top managers seek out companies in new industries where they believe they can apply these competencies to create value and increase profitability. For example, they may use the superior skills in one or more of their company's value creation functions to improve the competitive position of the new business unit. Alternatively, corporate managers may decide to acquire a company in a different industry because they believe the acquired company possesses superior skills that can improve the efficiency of their existing value creation activities.

If successful, such competency transfers can lower the costs of value creation in one or more of a company's diversified businesses or enable one or more of these businesses to perform their value creation functions in a way that leads to differentiation and a premium price. The transfer of Philip Morris's existing marketing

Figure 7.4 Transfer of Competencies at Philip Morris

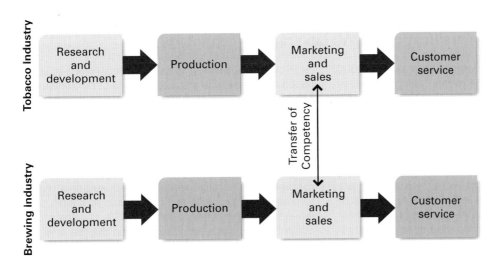

skills to Miller Brewing is one of the classic examples of how value can be created by competency transfers. Drawing on its marketing and competitive positioning skills, Philip Morris pioneered the introduction of Miller Lite, a product that redefined the brewing industry and moved Miller from Number six to Number two in the market (see Figure 7.4).

For such a strategy to work, the competencies being transferred must allow the acquired company to establish a competitive advantage in its industry; that is, they must confer a competitive advantage on the acquired company. All too often, however, corporate executives incorrectly assess the advantages that will result from the competency transfer and overestimate the benefits that will accrue from it. The acquisition of Hughes Aircraft by GM, for example, took place because GM's managers believed cars and car manufacturing were "going electronic," and Hughes was an electronics concern. The acquisition failed to realize any of the anticipated gains for GM, which finally sold the company off in 2005. On the other hand, Yahoo! has taken over many companies in the electronics, media, video, and entertainment industries because it recognized the need to strengthen its competitive position as a web portal. 3M has done the same, as the accompanying Strategy in Action recounts.

Economies of Scope　The phrase "two can live cheaper than one" expresses the idea behind economies of scope. When two or more business units can share resources or capabilities such as manufacturing facilities, distribution channels, advertising campaigns, and R&D costs, total operating costs fall because of economies of scope. Each business unit that shares a common resource has to pay less to operate a particular functional activity.[17] Procter & Gamble's disposable diaper and paper towel businesses offer one of the best examples of the successful realization of economies of scope. These businesses share the costs of procuring certain raw materials (such as paper) and of developing the technology for new products and processes. In addition, a joint sales force sells both products to supermarkets, and both products

7.1 STRATEGY IN ACTION

Diversification at 3M: Leveraging Technology

3M is a 100-year-old industrial colossus that in 2009 generated over $17 billion in revenues and $1.4 billion in profits from a portfolio of more than 50,000 individual products ranging from sandpaper and sticky tape to medical devices, office supplies, and electronic components. The company has consistently created new businesses by leveraging its scientific knowledge to find new applications for its proprietary technology. Today, the company is composed of more than 40 discrete business units grouped into six major sectors: transportation, health care, industrial, consumer and office, electronics and communications, and specialty materials. The company has consistently generated 30% of sales from products introduced within the prior 5 years and currently operates with the goal of producing 40% of sales revenues from products introduced within the previous 4 years.

The process of leveraging technology to create new businesses at 3M can be illustrated by the following quotation from William Coyne, head of R&D at 3M: "It began with sandpaper: mineral and glue on a substrate. After years as an abrasives company, it created a tape business. A researcher left off the mineral, and adapted the glue and substrate to create the first sticky tape. After creating many varieties of sticky tape—consumer, electrical, medical—researchers created the world's first audiotapes and videotapes. In their search to create better tape backings, other researchers happened on multilayer films that, surprise, have remarkable light management qualities. This multiplayer film technology is being used in brightness enhancement films, which are incorporated in the displays of virtually all laptops and palm computers."

How does 3M do it? First, the company is a science-based enterprise with a strong tradition of innovation and risk taking. Risk taking is encouraged, and failure is not punished but seen as a natural part of the process of creating new products and business. Second, 3M's management is relentlessly focused on the company's customers and the problems they face. Many of 3M's products have arisen from efforts to help solve difficult problems. Third, managers set "stretch goals" that require the company to create new products and businesses at a rapid pace (an example is the current goal that 40% of sales should come from products introduced within the last 4 years). Fourth, employees are given considerable autonomy to pursue their own ideas. An employee can spend 15% of his or her time working on a project of his or her own choosing without management approval. Many products have resulted from this autonomy, including the ubiquitous Post-it Notes.

Fifth, although products belong to business units and it is business units that are responsible for generating profits, the technologies belong to every unit within the company. Anyone at 3M is free to try to develop new applications for a technology developed by its business units. Sixth, 3M has implemented an IT system that promotes the sharing of technological knowledge between business units so that new opportunities can be identified. Also, it hosts many in-house conferences where researchers from different business units are brought together to share the results of their work. Finally, 3M uses numerous mechanisms to recognize and reward those who develop new technologies, products, and businesses, including peer-nominated award programs, a corporate hall of fame, and, of course, monetary rewards.[18]

are shipped via the same distribution system (see Figure 7.5). This resource sharing has given both business units a cost advantage that has enabled them to undercut the prices of their less diversified competitors.[19]

Similarly, one of the motives behind the merger of Citicorp and Travelers Insurance to form Citigroup was that the merger would allow Travelers to sell its insurance products and financial services through Citicorp's retail banking network. To put it differently, the merger was intended to allow the expanded group to better utilize a major existing common resource—its retail banking customer network. This merger was a total failure; it turned out that Citicorp's customers had little interest in buying insurance from a bank. Citigroup sold Travelers to MetLife because the

Figure 7.5 Sharing Resources at Procter & Gamble

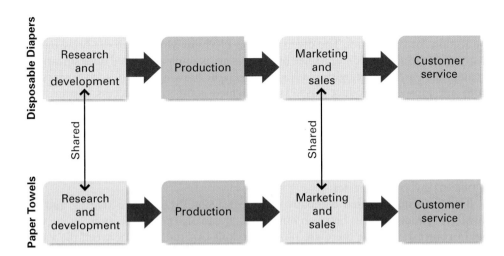

merger had not created value. The decision to diversify, like all corporate strategies, is a complex one, and it is hard to make the right decisions all the time.

Like competency transfers, diversification to realize economies of scope is possible only if there is a real opportunity for sharing the skills and services of one or more of the value creation functions between a company's existing and new business units. Diversification for this reason should be pursued only when sharing is likely to generate a *significant* competitive advantage in one or more of a company's business units. Moreover, managers need to be aware that the costs of managing and coordinating the activities of the newly linked business units to achieve economies of scope are substantial and may outweigh the value that can be created by such a strategy. This is apparently what happened to Citigroup.[20]

Thus, just as in the case of vertical integration, the costs of managing and coordinating the skill and resource exchanges between business units increase substantially as the number and diversity of its business units increase. This places a limit on the amount of diversification that can profitably be pursued. It makes sense for a company to diversify only as long as the extra value created by such a strategy exceeds the increased costs associated with incorporating additional business units into a company. Many companies diversify past this point, acquiring too many new companies, and their performance declines. To solve this problem, a company must reduce the scope of the enterprise through divestments—that is, through the selling of business units and exiting industries, which is discussed at the end of this chapter.

Related versus Unrelated Diversification

One issue that a diversifying company must resolve is whether to diversify into totally new businesses and industries or into those that are related to its existing business because their value chains share something in common. The choices it makes determine whether a company pursues related diversification and/or unrelated diversification.

Related diversification is the strategy of operating a business unit in a new industry that is related to a company's existing business units by some form of linkage or connection between one or more components of each business unit's value chain. Normally, these linkages are based on manufacturing, marketing, or technological connections or similarities. The diversification of Philip Morris into the brewing industry with the acquisition of Miller Brewing is an example of related diversification, because there are marketing similarities between the brewing and tobacco businesses (both are consumer product businesses in which competitive success depends on competitive positioning skills).

Unrelated diversification is diversification into a new business or industry that has *no* obvious value chain connection with any of the businesses or industries in which a company is currently operating. A company pursuing unrelated diversification is often called a *conglomerate*, a term that implies the company is made up of a number of diverse businesses.

By definition, a related company can create value by resource sharing and by transferring competencies between businesses. It can also carry out some restructuring. In contrast, because there are no connections or similarities between the value chains of unrelated businesses, an unrelated company cannot create value by sharing resources or transferring competencies. Unrelated diversifiers can create value *only by pursuing an acquisition and restructuring strategy.*

Related diversification can create value in more ways than unrelated diversification, so one might expect related diversification to be the preferred strategy. In addition, related diversification is normally perceived as involving fewer risks, because the company is moving into businesses and industries about which top management has some knowledge. Probably because of those considerations, most diversified companies display a preference for related diversification.[21] Indeed, in the last decade, many companies pursuing unrelated diversification have decided to split themselves up into totally self-contained companies to increase the value they can create. In 2007, for example, the conglomerate Tyco split into three separate public companies focusing on the electronics, health care, and security and fire protection businesses for this reason—and each separate company has performed at a higher level since.

However, United Technologies (UTC), a conglomerate that pursues unrelated diversification, provides an excellent example of a company that has created a lot of value using this strategy. UTC's CEO George David uses all the kinds of superior governance skills that we have discussed to improve the profitability of his company's business units. The closing case describes how UTC has pursued unrelated diversification successfully and why it is one of the highest performing of the Fortune 500 companies.

Related Diversification

The strategy of operating a business unit in a new industry that is related to a company's existing business units through some commonality in their value chains.

Unrelated Diversification

The strategy of operating a business unit in a new industry that has no value chain connection with a company's existing business units.

RESTRUCTURING AND DOWNSIZING

So far we have focused on strategies for expanding the scope of a company and entering into new business areas. We turn now to their opposite: strategies for reducing the scope of the company by *exiting* business areas. In recent years, reducing the scope of a company through restructuring and downsizing has become an increasingly popular strategy, particularly among the companies that diversified their activities during the 1980s and 1990s. In most cases, companies that are engaged in restructuring are divesting themselves of diversified activities and downsizing in order to concentrate on fewer businesses.[22] For example, in 1996 AT&T spun off its telecommunications equipment business (Lucent), and then, after acquiring two large cable TV companies in the late 1990s, in 2002 AT&T sold its cable unit to rival cable TV provider Comcast for $72 billion. Then, in 2005 a downsized AT&T became a takeover target for SBC Communications that acquired AT&T to strengthen its position in the growing mobile phone business. By 2007 SBC, renamed AT&T, had once again become the largest U.S. global communications company, and by 2010, given that it was the sole supplier of Apple's iPhone, it had once again become the dominant U.S. phone and Internet provider.

The first question to ask is why have so many companies restructured during the last decade. Then, we can examine the different strategies that companies adopt for exiting from business areas. Finally, we discuss the various turnaround strategies that companies employ to revitalize their core profit-making business.

Why Restructure?

A prime reason why extensively diversified companies restructure is that in the last decade, the stock market has assigned a diversification discount to the stock price of these companies.[23] **Diversification discount** refers to the fact that the stock of highly diversified companies are often assigned a lower valuation relative to their earnings than the stock of less diversified companies. There are two reasons for this. First, investors are often put off by the complexity and lack of transparency in the financial statements of highly diversified enterprises that are harder to interpret and may not give them a good picture of how the individual divisions of the company are performing. In other words, they perceive diversified companies as riskier investments than companies that focus on one or a few major industries. In such cases, restructuring can boost the returns to shareholders when it splits the company into a number of parts that can each be divested at a higher price.

A second reason for the diversification discount is that many investors have learned from experience that managers often have a tendency to pursue too much diversification or to diversify for the wrong reasons, such as the pursuit of growth for its own sake, rather than to increase profitability.[24] Some senior managers tend to expand the scope of their company beyond the point where the bureaucratic costs of managing extensive diversification *exceed* the additional value that can be created so that the performance of the company begins to decline. Restructuring in such cases is often a response to declining financial performance.

Restructuring can also be a response to failed acquisitions. This is true whether the acquisitions were made to support a horizontal integration, vertical integration, or diversification strategy. We noted earlier in the chapter that many acquisitions fail to deliver the anticipated gains. When this is the case, corporate managers often respond by cutting their losses and exiting from the acquired business.

A final factor that helps to explain why restructuring is occurring more and more frequently is that innovations in management strategy and in advanced IT have diminished the profit-enhancing advantages of vertical integration and diversification. So, to increase profitability, companies have reduced the scope of their activities through restructuring and exiting businesses. For example, a few decades ago, there was little understanding of how long-term cooperative relationships or strategic alliances between a company and its suppliers could be a viable alternative to vertical integration. Most companies considered only two alternatives for

Diversification Discount

When stock in highly diversified companies is assigned a lower market valuation than stock in less diversified companies.

managing the supply chain: vertical integration or competitive bidding. However, if conditions are right, a third alternative for managing the supply chain, *long-term contracting*, can be a better strategy than either vertical integration or competitive bidding. Like vertical integration, long-term contracting facilitates investments in specialization. But unlike vertical integration, long-term contracting avoids the need to incur bureaucratic costs or dispense with market discipline. As this strategic innovation has spread throughout global business the relative advantages of vertical integration have declined.

Exit Strategies

Companies can choose from three main strategies for exiting business areas: divestment, harvest, and liquidation. Of the three strategies, divestment is usually favored. It represents the best way for a company to recoup as much of its initial investment in a business unit as possible.

Divestment Divestment involves selling a business unit to the highest bidder. Three types of buyers are independent investors, other companies, and the management of the unit to be divested. Selling off a business unit to independent investors is normally referred to as a **spinoff**. A spinoff makes good sense when the unit to be sold is profitable and when the stock market has an appetite for new stock issues (which is normal during market upswings, but *not* during market downswings). However, spinoffs do not work if the unit to be spun off is unprofitable and unattractive to independent investors or if the stock market is slumping and unresponsive to new issues.

Selling off a unit to another company is a strategy frequently pursued when a unit can be sold to a company in the same line of business as the unit. In such cases, the purchaser is often prepared to pay a considerable amount of money for the opportunity to substantially increase the size of its business virtually overnight. For example, as we noted earlier, in 2002 AT&T sold off its cable TV business to Comcast for a hefty $72 billion; SBC then bought AT&T for $16 billion and today it has become the dominant U.S. phone and Internet provider.

Harvest Strategy A harvest strategy involves halting investment in a unit in order to maximize short-to-medium-term cash flow from that unit. Although this strategy seems fine in theory, it is often a poor one to apply in practice. Once it becomes apparent that the unit is pursuing a harvest strategy, the morale of the unit's employees, as well as the confidence of the unit's customers and suppliers in its continuing operation, can sink very quickly. If this occurs, as it often does, the rapid decline in the unit's revenues can make the strategy untenable.

Liquidation Strategy A liquidation strategy involves shutting down the operations of a business unit. A pure liquidation strategy is the least attractive of all to pursue, because it requires that the company write off its investment in a business unit, often at considerable cost. However, for a poorly performing business unit where a selloff or spinoff is unlikely, and where an MBO cannot be arranged, it may be the only viable alternative.

Divestment

The sale a business unit to the highest bidder.

Spinoff

The sale of a business unit to another company or to independent investors.

Harvest Strategy

The halting of investment in a business unit to maximize short-to-medium-term cash flow from that unit.

Liquidation Strategy

The shutting down of the operations of a business unit and the sale of its assets.

SUMMARY OF CHAPTER

1. There are different corporate-level strategies that companies pursue in order to increase their long-run profitability; they may choose to remain in the same industry, to enter new industries, or even to leave industries in order to prosper over time.

2. Corporate strategies should add value to a corporation, enabling it, or one or more of its business units, to perform one or more of the value creation functions at a lower cost or in a way that allows for differentiation and thus a premium price.

3. Concentrating on a single business allows a company to focus its total managerial, financial, technological, and physical resources and competencies on competing successfully in just one area. It also ensures that the company sticks to doing what it knows best.

4. The strategic outsourcing of noncore value creation activities may allow a company to lower its costs, better differentiate its product offering, and make better use of scarce resources, while also enabling it to respond rapidly to changing market conditions. However, strategic outsourcing may have a detrimental effect if the company outsources important value creation activities or if it becomes too dependent on key suppliers of those activities.

5. The company that concentrates on a single business may be missing out on the opportunity to create value through vertical integration and/or diversification.

6. Vertical integration can enable a company to achieve a competitive advantage by helping build barriers to entry, facilitating investments in specialized assets, and safeguarding product quality.

7. The disadvantages of vertical integration include cost disadvantages if a company's internal source of supply is a high-cost one, and lack of strategic flexibility if technology and the environment are changing rapidly.

8. Entering into cooperative long-term outsourcing agreements can enable a company to realize many of the benefits associated with vertical integration without having to contend with these problems.

9. Diversification can create value through the application of superior governance skills, including a restructuring strategy, competency transfers, and the realization of economies of scope.

10. Related diversification is often preferred to unrelated diversification because it enables a company to engage in more value creation activities and is less risky.

11. Restructuring is often a response to excessive diversification, failed acquisitions, and innovations in the management process that have reduced the advantages of vertical integration and diversification.

12. Exit strategies include divestment, harvest, and liquidation. The choice of exit strategy is governed by the characteristics of the business unit involved.

DISCUSSION QUESTIONS

1. Why do you think vertical integration is normally the first strategy to be pursued after concentration on a single business?

2. What value creation activities should a company out-source to independent suppliers? What are the risks involved in outsourcing these activities?

3. Under what conditions might concentration on a single business be inconsistent with the goal?

C L O S I N G   C A S E

United Technologies Has an "ACE in Its Pocket"

United Technologies Corporation (UTC), based in Hartford, Connecticut, is a *conglomerate*, a company that owns a wide variety of other companies that operate in different businesses and industries. Some of the companies in UTC's portfolio are more well known than UTC itself, such as Sikorsky Aircraft Corporation; Pratt & Whitney, the aircraft engine and component maker; Otis Elevator Company; Carrier air conditioning; and Chubb, the security and lock maker that UTC acquired in 2003. Today, investors frown upon companies like UTC that own and operate companies in widely different industries. There is a growing perception that managers can better manage a company's business model when the company operates as an independent or stand-alone entity. How can UTC justify holding all these companies together in a conglomerate? Why would this lead to a greater increase in their long-term profitability than if they operated as separate companies? In the last decade the boards of directors and CEOs of many conglomerates, such as Greyhound-Dial, ITT Industries, and Textron, have realized that by holding diverse companies together they were reducing, not increasing, the profitability of their companies. As a result, many conglomerates have been broken up and their companies spun off to allow them to operate as separate, independent entities.

UTC's CEO George David claims that he has created a unique and sophisticated multibusiness model that adds value across UTC's diverse businesses. David joined Otis Elevator as an assistant to its CEO in 1975, but within one year Otis was acquired by UTC, during a decade when "bigger is better" ruled corporate America and mergers and acquisitions, of whatever kind, were seen as the best way to grow profits. UTC sent David to manage its South American operations and later gave him responsibility for its Japanese operations. Otis had formed an alliance with Matsushita to develop an elevator for the Japanese market, and the resulting "Elevonic 401," after being installed widely in Japanese buildings, proved to be a disaster. It broke down much more often than elevators made by other Japanese

companies, and customers were concerned about its reliability and safety.

Matsushita was extremely embarrassed about the elevator's failure and assigned one of its leading total quality management (TQM) experts, Yuzuru Ito, to head a team of Otis engineers to find out why it performed so poorly. Under Ito's direction all the employees—managers, designers, and production workers—who had produced the elevator analyzed why the elevators were malfunctioning. This intensive study led to a total redesign of the elevator, and when their new and improved elevator was launched worldwide, it met with great success. Otis's share of the global elevator market increased dramatically, and one result was that David was named president of UTC in 1992. He was given the responsibility to cut costs across the entire corporation, including its important Pratt & Whitney division, and his success in reducing UTC's cost structure and increasing its ROIC led to his appointment as CEO in 1994.

Now responsible for all of UTC's diverse companies, David decided that the best way to increase UTC's profitability, which had been falling, was to find ways to improve efficiency and quality in all its constituent companies. He convinced Ito to move to Hartford and take responsibility for championing the kinds of improvements that had by now transformed the Otis division, and Ito began to develop UTC's TQM system, which is known as *Achieving Competitive Excellence,* or ACE.

ACE is a set of tasks and procedures that are used by employees from the shop floor to top managers to analyze all aspects of the way a product is made. The goal is to find ways to improve *quality and reliability,* to *lower the costs* of making the product, and especially to find ways to make the next generation of a particular product perform better—in other words, to encourage *technological innovation.* David makes every employee in every function and at every level take responsibility for achieving the incremental, step-by-step gains that can result in innovative and efficient products that enable a company to dominate its industry—to push back the value creation frontier.

David calls these techniques "process disciplines," and he has used them to increase the performance of all UTC companies. Through these techniques he has created the extra value for UTC that justifies it owning and operating such a diverse set of businesses. David's success can be seen in the performance that his company has achieved in the decade since he took control: he has quadrupled UTC's earnings per share, and in the first 6 months of 1994 profit grew by 25% to $1.4 billion, while sales increased by 26% to $18.3 billion. UTC has been in the top three performers of the companies that make up the Dow Jones industrial average for the last 3 years, and the company has consistently outperformed GE, another huge conglomerate, in its returns to investors.

David and his managers believe that the gains that can be achieved from UTC's process disciplines are never-ending because its own R&D—in which it invests over $2.5 billion a year—is constantly producing product innovations that can help all its businesses. Indeed, recognizing that its skills in creating process improvements are specific to manufacturing companies, UTC's strategy is to only acquire companies that make products that can benefit from the use of its ACE program—hence its Chubb acquisition. At the same time, David only invests in companies that have the potential to remain leading companies in their industries and so can charge above-average prices. His acquisitions strengthen the competencies of UTC's existing businesses. For example, he acquired a company called Sunderstrand, a leading aerospace and industrial systems company, and combined it with UTC's Hamilton aerospace division to create Hamilton Sunderstrand, which is now a major supplier to Boeing and makes products that command premium prices.

Case Discussion Questions

1. In what ways does UTC's corporate-level strategy of unrelated diversification create value?
2. What are the dangers and disadvantages of this strategy?
3. Collect some recent information on UTC from sources like Yahoo! Finance. How successful has it been in pursuing its strategy?

NOTES

1. T. J. Peters and R. H. Waterman, *In Search of Excellence* (New York: Harper & Row, 1982).
2. www.walmart.com, 2009.
3. J. Birchall, "Walmart Looks to Hispanic Market," *ft.com*, March 12, 2009.
4. "Does 'Cool' Matter? A Blogger Compares Tesco and Walmart's 'Neighborhood Market' Offerings," *http:// freshneasybuzz.blogspot.com/2009/01/bloggers-at-large-does-cool-matter.html*.
5. W. H. Davidow and M. S. Malone, *The Virtual Corporation* (New York: Harper & Row, 1992).
6. Ibid.
7. "The Outing of Outsourcing," *Economist*, November 25, 1995, 57–58.
8. Davidow and Malone, *The Virtual Corporation* and H. W. Chesbrough and D. J. Teece, "When Is Virtual Virtuous? Organizing for Innovation," *Harvard Business Review*, January–February 1996, 65–74.
9. This is the essence of Chandler's argument. See Alfred D. Chandler, *Strategy and Structure* (Cambridge, Mass.: MIT Press, 1962). The same argument is made by Jeffrey Pfeffer and Gerald R. Salancik, *The External Control of Organizations* (New York:

Harper & Row, 1978). See also K. R. Harrigan, *Strategic Flexibility* (Lexington, Mass.: Lexington Books, 1985); K. R. Harrigan, "Vertical Integration and Corporate Strategy," *Academy of Management Journal* 28 (1985): 397–425; and F. M. Scherer, *Industrial Market Structure and Economic Performance* (Chicago, Ill.: Rand McNally, 1981).
10. This section is based on the transaction cost approach popularized by Oliver E. Williamson, *The Economic Institutions of Capitalism* (New York: Free Press, 1985).
11. Williamson, *The Economic Institutions of Capitalism*. For recent empirical work that uses this framework, see L. Poppo and T. Zenger, "Testing Alternative Theories of the Firm: Transaction Cost, Knowledge Based, and Measurement Explanations for Make or Buy Decisions in Information Services," *Strategic Management Journal* 19 (1998): 853–878.
12. Williamson, *The Economic Institutions of Capitalism*.
13. Harrigan, *Strategic Flexibility*, pp. 67–87.
14. For a detailed theoretical rationale for this argument, see G. R. Jones and C. W. L. Hill, "A Transaction Cost Analysis of Strategy-Structure Choice," *Strategic Management Journal* 9 (1988): 159–172.

15. This resource-based view of diversification can be traced to Edith Penrose's seminal book *The Theory of the Growth of the Firm* (Oxford: Oxford University Press, 1959).

16. See, for example, Jones and Hill, "A Transaction Cost Analysis" and Williamson, *Markets and Hierarchies* (New York: Free Press), 132–175.

17. D. J. Teece, "Economies of Scope and the Scope of the Enterprise," *Journal of Economic Behavior and Organization* 3 (1980): 223–247. For recent empirical work on this topic, see C. H. St. John and J. S. Harrison, "Manufacturing Based Relatedness, Synergy and Coordination," *Strategic Management Journal* 20 (1999): 129–145.

18. W.E. Coyne, "How 3M Innovated for Long-Term Growth," *Research Technology Management* (March-April 2001): 21–24.

19. Michael E. Porter, *Competitive Advantage: Creating and Sustaining Superior Performance* (New York: Free Press, 1985), 326.

20. For a detailed discussion, see C. W. L. Hill and R. E. Hoskisson, "Strategy and Structure in the Multi-product Firm," *Academy of Management Review* 12 (1987): 331–341.

21. For example, see C. W. L. Hill, "Diversified Growth and Competition," *Applied Economics* 17 (1985): 827–847; R. P. Rumelt, *Strategy, Structure and Economic Performance* (Boston, Mass.: Harvard Business School Press, 1974); and Jones and Hill, "A Transaction Cost Analysis."

22. For a review of the evidence, and some contrary empirical evidence, see D. E. Hatfield, J. P. Liebskind, and T. C. Opler, "The Effects of Corporate Restructuring on Aggregate Industry Specialization," *Strategic Management Journal* 17 (1996): 55–72.

23. O. A. Lamont and C. Polk, "The Diversification Discount: Cash Flows versus Returns," *Journal of Finance* 56 (October 2001): 1693–1721. See also R. Raju, H. Servaes, and L. Zingales, "The Cost of Diversity: The Diversification Discount and Inefficient Investment," *Journal of Finance* 55 (February 2000): 35–80.

24. For example, see A. Schleifer and R. W. Vishny, "Takeovers in the 60s and 80s: Evidence and Implications," *Strategic Management Journal* 12 (Special Issue, Winter 1991): 51–60.

STRATEGIC CHANGE

8

CHAPTER OUTLINE

Strategic Change

Types of Strategic Changes
A Model of the Change Process

Analyzing a Company as a Portfolio of Core Competencies

Fill in the Blanks
Premier Plus 10
White Spaces
Mega-Opportunities

Implementing Strategy Through Internal New Ventures

Pitfalls with Internal New Ventures
Guidelines for Successful Internal New Venturing

Implementing Strategy Through Acquisitions

Pitfalls with Acquisitions
Guidelines for Successful Acquisition

Implementing Strategy Through Strategic Alliances

Advantages of Strategic Alliances
Disadvantages of Strategic Alliances
Making Strategic Alliances Work

LEARNING OBJECTIVES

After reading this chapter, you should be able to:

- Understand the main steps involved in the strategic change process.
- Appreciate the need to analyze a company's set of businesses from a "portfolio of competencies" perspective.
- Review the advantages and risks of implementing strategy through (1) internal new ventures, (2) acquisitions, and (3) strategic alliances.
- Discuss how to limit the risks associated with internal new ventures, acquisitions, and strategic alliances.
- Appreciate the special issues associated with using a joint venture to structure a strategic alliance.

OVERVIEW

In Chapter 7 we examined the different corporate-level strategies that managers can pursue to increase a company's long-run profitability. All these choices of strategy have important implications for a company's future prosperity, and it is vital that managers understand the issues and problems involved in implementing these strategies if the strategies are to be successful. We begin this chapter by examining the nature of strategic change and the obstacles that may hinder managers' attempts to change a company's strategy and structure to improve its future performance. We then focus on the steps managers can take to overcome these obstacles and make their efforts to change a company successful.

Second, we tackle a crucial question: How do managers determine which businesses or industries a company should continue to participate in or exit from, and how do they determine whether a company should enter one or more new businesses? Obviously managers need to have a vision of where their company should be in the future—that is, a vision of its desired future state—and we discuss an important technique, the portfolio of competencies approach, that helps them accomplish this.

Third, we turn our attention to the different methods that managers can use to enter new businesses or industries in order to build and develop their company and improve its performance over time. The choice here is whether to implement a corporate-level strategy through *acquisitions, internal new ventures,* or *strategic alliances* (including joint ventures). Finally, we examine the pros and cons of these different ways of implementing strategy, given the goal of increasing a company's competitive advantage and long-run profitability.

Strategic Change

Strategic change is the movement of a company away from its present state toward some desired future state to increase its competitive advantage and profitability.[1] In the last decade, most large Fortune 500 companies have gone through some kind of strategic change as their managers have tried to strengthen their existing core competencies and build new ones to compete more effectively. Often, because of drastic unexpected changes in the environment, such as the emergence of aggressive new competitors or technological breakthroughs, strategic managers need to develop a new strategy and structure to raise the level of their business's performance.[2]

Types of Strategic Change

One way of changing a company to enable it to operate more effectively is by **reengineering**, a process in which managers focus not on a company's functional activities but on the business processes underlying the value creation process.[3] A **business process** is any activity (such as order processing, inventory control, or product design) that is vital to delivering goods and services to customers quickly or that promotes high quality or low costs.[4] Business processes are not the responsibility of any one function but cut across functions.

Hallmark Cards, for example, reengineered its card design process with great success. Before the reengineering effort, artists, writers, and editors worked in different functions to produce all kinds of cards. After reengineering, these same artists,

Strategic Change

The movement of a company away from its present state toward some desired future state to increase its competitive advantage and profitability.

Reengineering

A process whereby, in their effort to boost company performance, managers focus not on the company's functional activities but on the business processes underlying its value creation operations.

Business Process

Any business activity, such as order processing, inventory control, or product design, that is vital to delivering goods and services to customers quickly or that promotes high quality or low costs.

writers, and editors were organized into cross-functional teams, each of which now works on a specific type of card (such as birthday, Christmas, or Mother's Day). The result was that the time it took to bring a new card to market dropped from years to months, and Hallmark's performance improved dramatically.

Reengineering and total quality management (TQM, discussed in Chapter 4) are highly interrelated and complementary.[5] After reengineering has taken place and the question "What is the best way to provide customers with the goods or service they require?" has been answered, TQM takes over and addresses the question "How can we now continue to improve and refine the new process and find better ways of managing task and role relationships?" Successful companies examine both questions together, and managers continuously work to identify new and better processes for meeting the goals of increased efficiency, quality, and responsiveness to customer needs. Thus managers are always working to improve their vision of their company's desired future state.

Recall from Chapter 7 that *restructuring* is the process through which managers simplify organizational structure by eliminating divisions, departments, or levels in the hierarchy, and downsize by terminating employees, thereby lowering operating costs. Restructuring may also involve *outsourcing,* the process whereby one company contracts with other companies to perform a functional activity such as manufacturing, marketing, or customer service. Restructuring is a second form of strategic change that managers can implement to improve performance. As we noted, there are many reasons why it can become necessary for an organization to streamline, simplify, and downsize its operations. Sometimes a change in the business environment occurs that could not have been foreseen; perhaps a shift in technology renders the company's products obsolete or a worldwide recession reduces the demand for its products. Sometimes an organization has excess capacity because customers no longer want the goods and services it provides, perhaps because they are outdated or offer poor value for the money. Sometimes organizations downsize because they have grown too tall and bureaucratic and operating costs have become excessive. And sometimes they restructure even when they are in a strong position, simply to build and improve their competitive advantage and stay on top.

All too often, however, companies are forced to downsize and lay off employees because managers have *not* continuously monitored the way they operate their basic business processes and have not made the incremental changes to their strategies that would allow them to contain costs and adjust to changing conditions. Paradoxically, because they have not paid attention to the need to reengineer themselves, they are forced into a position where restructuring is the only way they can survive and compete in an increasingly competitive environment.

A Model of the Change Process

In order to understand the issues involved in implementing strategic change, it is useful to focus on the series of distinct steps that strategic managers must follow if the change process is to succeed.[6] These steps are listed in Figure 8.1.

Determining the Need for Change   The first step in the change process is for strategic managers to recognize the need for change. Sometimes this need is obvious, as when divisions are fighting or when competitors introduce a product that is clearly superior to anything the company has in production. More often, however, managers have trouble determining that something is going wrong in the organization.

Figure 8.1   Stages in the Change Process

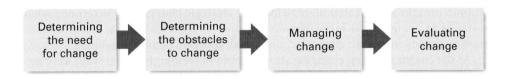

Problems may develop gradually, and organizational performance may slip for a number of years before the decline becomes obvious. Thus, the first step in the change process occurs when strategic managers, or others in a position to take action, such as directors or takeover specialists, recognize that there is a gap between desired company performance and actual performance. Using measures such as a decline in profitability, return on investment (ROI), stock price, or market share as indicators that change is needed, managers can start looking for the source of the problem. To discover it, they conduct a strengths, weaknesses, opportunities, and threats (SWOT) analysis.

Strategic managers examine the company's *strengths* and *weaknesses*. For example, management conducts a strategic audit of all functions and divisions and assesses their contribution to profitability over time. Perhaps some divisions have become relatively unprofitable as innovation has slowed without the management realizing it. Perhaps sales and marketing have failed to keep pace with changes in the competitive environment. Perhaps the company's product is simply outdated. Strategic managers also analyze the company's level of differentiation and integration to make sure that it is appropriate for its strategy. Perhaps a company does not have the integrating mechanisms in place to achieve gains from synergy, or perhaps the structure has become tall and inflexible so that bureaucratic costs have escalated.

Strategic managers then examine environmental *opportunities* and *threats* that might explain the problem, using all the concepts developed in Chapter 3 of this book. For instance, intense competition may have arisen unexpectedly from substitute products, or a shift in technology or consumers' tastes may have caught the company unawares.

Once the source of the problem has been identified via SWOT analysis, strategic managers must determine the desired future state of the company—that is, how it should change its strategy and structure to achieve the new goals they have set for it. In the next section, we discuss one important tool managers can use to work out the best future mission and strategy for maximizing company profitability. Of course, the choices they make are specific to each individual company, because each company has a unique set of skills and competencies. The challenge for managers is that there is no way they can determine in advance, or even reliably estimate, the accuracy of their assumptions about the future. Strategic change always involves considerable uncertainty and risks that must be borne if above-average returns are to be achieved.

Determining the Obstacles to Change   Strategic change is frequently resisted by people and groups inside an organization. Often, for example, the decision to reengineer and restructure a company requires the establishment of a new set of role and authority relationships among managers in different functions and divisions.

Because this change may threaten the status and rewards of some managers, they resist the changes being implemented. Many efforts at change take a long time, and many fail because of the high level of resistance to change at all levels in the organization. Thus, the second step in implementing strategic change is to determine what obstacles to change exist in a company. Obstacles to change can be found at four levels in the organization: corporate, divisional, functional, and individual.

At the corporate level, changing strategy even in seemingly trivial ways may significantly affect a company's behavior. For example, suppose that to reduce costs, a company decides to centralize all divisional purchasing and sales activities at the corporate level. Such consolidation could severely damage each division's ability to develop a unique strategy for its own individual market. Alternatively, suppose that in response to low-cost foreign competition, a company decides to pursue a strategy of increased differentiation. This action would change the balance of power among functions and could lead to problems as functions start fighting to retain their status in the organization. A company's present strategies constitute a powerful obstacle to change. They generate a massive amount of resistance that has to be overcome before change can take place. This is why strategic change is usually a slow process.

Similar factors operate at the divisional level. Change is difficult at the divisional level if divisions are highly interrelated, because a shift in one division's operations affects other divisions. Furthermore, changes in strategy affect different divisions in different ways, because change generally favors the interests of some divisions over those of others. Managers in the different divisions may thus have different attitudes toward change, and some will be less supportive than others. Existing divisions may resist establishing new product divisions, for example, because they will lose resources and their status in the organization will diminish.

The same obstacles to change exist at the functional level. Just like divisions, different functions have different strategic orientations and goals and react differently to the changes management proposes. For example, manufacturing generally has a short-term, cost-directed efficiency orientation; research and development is oriented toward long-term, technical goals; and the sales function is oriented toward satisfying customers' needs. Thus, production may see the solution to a problem as one of reducing costs, sales as one of increasing demand, and research and development as product innovation. Differences in functional orientation make it hard to formulate and implement a new strategy and may significantly slow a company's response to changes in the competitive environment.

At the individual level, too, people are notoriously resistant to change because change implies uncertainty, which breeds insecurity and fear of the unknown. Because managers are people, this individual resistance reinforces the tendency of each function and division to oppose changes that may have uncertain effects on them. Restructuring and reengineering efforts can be particularly stressful for managers at all levels of the organization. All these obstacles make it difficult to change strategy or structure quickly. That is why U.S. carmakers and companies such as IBM, Kodak, and Motorola were so slow to respond to fierce global competition, first from Japan and then from China and other Asian countries.

Paradoxically, companies that experience the greatest uncertainty may become best able to respond to it. When companies have been forced to change frequently, managers often develop the ability to handle change easily. Strategic managers must identify potential obstacles to change as they design and implement new strategies. The larger and more complex the organization, the harder it is to implement change because inertia is likely to be more pervasive.

Managing and Evaluating Change The process of managing and evaluating change raises several questions. For instance, who should actually carry out the change: internal managers or external consultants? Although internal managers may have the most experience or knowledge about a company's operations, they may lack perspective because they are too close to the situation and "can't see the forest for the trees." They also run the risk of appearing to be politically motivated and of having a personal stake in the changes they recommend. This is why companies often turn to external consultants, who can view a situation more objectively. Outside consultants, however, have to spend a lot of time learning about the company and its problems before they can propose a plan of action. It is for both of these reasons that many companies (such as Quaker Oats, Gap, and IBM) bring in new CEOs from outside the company, and even from outside its industry, to spearhead their change efforts. In this way, companies can get the benefits of both inside information and external perspective.

Generally, a company can take one of two main approaches to implementing and managing change: top-down change or bottom-up change.[7] With top-down change, a strong CEO or top management team analyzes what strategies need to be pursued, recommends a course of action, and then moves quickly to restructure and implement change in the organization. The emphasis is on speed of response and prompt management of problems as they occur. Bottom-up change is much more gradual. Top management consults with managers at all levels in the organization. Then, over time, it develops a detailed plan for change, with a timetable of events and stages that the company will go through. The emphasis in bottom-up change is on participation and on keeping people informed about the situation so that uncertainty is minimized.

The advantage of bottom-up change is that it removes some of the obstacles to change by including them in the strategic plan. Furthermore, the purpose of consulting with managers at all levels is to reveal potential problems. The disadvantage of bottom-up change is its slow pace. On the other hand, in the case of the much speedier top-down change, problems may emerge later and may be difficult to resolve. Giants such as GM and Kodak often must apply top-down change because managers are so unaccustomed to and threatened by change that only a radical restructuring effort provides enough momentum to overcome organizational inertia.

The last step in the change process is to evaluate the effects of the changes in strategy on organizational performance. A company must compare the way it operates after implementing change with the way it operated before. Managers use indexes such as changes in stock market price, market share, and higher revenues from increased product differentiation. They also can benchmark their company's performance against market leaders to see how much they have improved, and how much more they need to improve to catch the market leader.

ANALYZING A COMPANY AS A PORTFOLIO OF CORE COMPETENCIES

Earlier we noted that managers must have access to tools that help them determine their companies' desired future state—the businesses and industries that they should compete in to increase long-run competitive advantage. One conceptual tool that helps them do this was developed by Gary Hamel and C. K. Prahalad. It is to analyze a company as a portfolio of core competencies, as opposed to a portfolio of actual businesses.[8] Recall from Chapter 1 the importance of adopting a customer-oriented, rather than a product-oriented, business definition; now the core competency becomes the key competitive variable.

According to Hamel and Prahalad, a core competency is a central value creation capability of a company—that is, a core skill. They argue, for example, that Canon, the Japanese concern best known for its cameras and photocopiers, has core competencies in precision mechanics, fine optics, microelectronics, and electronic imaging. Corporate development is oriented toward maintaining existing competencies, building new competencies, and leveraging competencies by applying them to new business opportunities. For example, Hamel and Prahalad argue that the success of a company such as 3M in creating new business has come from its ability to apply its core competency in adhesives to a wide range of businesses opportunities, from Scotch Tape to Post-it-Notes.

Hamel and Prahalad maintain that identifying current core competencies is the first step a company should take in deciding which business opportunities to pursue. Once a company has identified its core competencies, they advocate using a matrix similar to that illustrated in Figure 8.2 to establish an agenda for building and leveraging core competencies to create new business opportunities. This matrix distinguishes between existing and new competencies, and between existing and new product markets. Each quadrant in the matrix has a title, and the strategic implications of these quadrants are discussed below.

Fill in the Blanks

The lower-left quadrant represents the company's existing portfolio of competencies and products. Twenty years ago, for example, Canon had competencies in precision mechanics, fine optics, and microelectronics and was active in two basic businesses: producing cameras and photocopiers. The competencies in precision mechanics and

Figure 8.2   Establishing a Competency Agenda

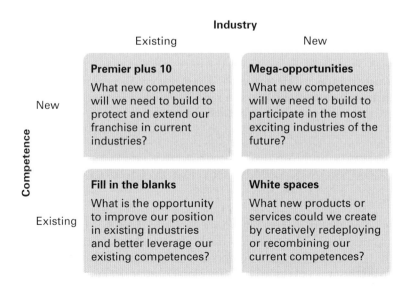

fine optics were used in the production of basic mechanical cameras. These two competencies, plus an additional competency in microelectronics, were needed to produce plain paper copiers. The title for this quadrant of the matrix, *Fill in the blanks*, refers to the opportunity to improve the company's competitive position in existing markets by leveraging existing core competencies. For example, Canon was able to improve the position of its camera business by leveraging microelectronics skills from its copier business to support the development of cameras with electronic features, such as autofocus capabilities.

Premier Plus 10

The upper-left quadrant is referred to as *Premier plus 10*. This title is meant to suggest another important question: What new core competencies must be built today to ensure that the company remains a premier provider of its existing products in 10 years' time? Canon, for example, decided that in order to maintain a competitive edge in its copier business, it was going to have to build a new competency in digital imaging. This new competency subsequently helped Canon to extend its product range to include laser copiers, color copiers, and digital cameras.

White Spaces

The lower-right quadrant is titled *White spaces*. The question to be addressed here is how best to fill the "white space" by creatively redeploying or recombining current core competencies. In Canon's case, the company has been able to recombine its established core competencies in precision mechanics, fine optics, and microelectronics with its more recently acquired competency in digital imaging to enter the market for computer printers and scanners.

Mega-Opportunities

The *Mega-opportunities* represented by the upper-right quadrant of Figure 8.2 do not overlap with the company's current market position or with its current endowment of competencies. Nevertheless, a company may choose to pursue such opportunities if they are particularly attractive, significant, or relevant to the company's existing business opportunities. For example, back in 1979 Monsanto was primarily a manufacturer of chemicals, including fertilizers. However, the company saw that there were enormous opportunities in the emerging field of biotechnology. Specifically, senior research scientists at Monsanto believed it might be possible to produce genetically engineered crop seeds that would produce their own "organic" pesticides. In that year the company embarked upon a massive investment that ultimately amounted to over a billion dollars to build a world-class competency in biotechnology. This investment was funded by cash flows generated from Monsanto's core chemical operations. The investment began to bear fruit after Monsanto introduced a series of genetically engineered crop seeds, including Bollgard, a cotton seed that is resistant to many common pests, including the bollworm; and Roundup-resistant soybean seeds (Roundup is an herbicide produced by Monsanto) that have earned the company hundreds of billions of dollars in profit.[9]

The framework proposed by Hamel and Prahalad helps a company identify business opportunities, and it has clear implications for resource allocation (as exemplified by the Monsanto case just discussed). However, the great advantage of Hamel and Prahalad's framework is that it focuses explicitly on how a company can create value by building new competencies or by recombining existing competencies to enter new business areas (as Canon did with fax machines and bubble jet printers). Whereas traditional portfolio tools treat businesses as independent, Hamel and Prahalad's framework recognizes the interdependencies among businesses and focuses on opportunities to create value by building and leveraging competencies. In this sense, their framework is a useful tool to help strategic managers reconceptualize their company's core competencies, activities, and businesses to determine its desired future state—and so reduce the uncertainty surrounding the investment of its scarce resources.

Having reviewed the different businesses in the company's portfolio, corporate managers might decide to enter a new business area or industry to create more value and profit—something Monsanto did when it decided to enter the biotechnology industry. In the next three sections, we discuss the three main vehicles that companies can use to enter new businesses or industries: internal new ventures, acquisitions, and strategic alliances (including joint ventures).

IMPLEMENTING STRATEGY THROUGH INTERNAL NEW VENTURES

Internal new ventures involve creating the value chain functions necessary to start a new business from scratch. Internal new venturing is typically used to execute corporate-level strategy when a company possesses a set of valuable competencies (resources and capabilities) in its existing businesses that can be leveraged or recombined to enter the new business area. As a rule, science-based companies that use their technology to create market opportunities in related areas tend to favor internal new venturing as an entry strategy. 3M, for example, has a near-legendary knack for shaping new markets from internally generated ideas. HP originally started out making test and measurement instruments and later moved into computers and then printers through an internal new-venture strategy. Microsoft started out making software for PCs, but it developed the Xbox video game business by leveraging its software skills and applying them to this new industry.

Even if it lacks the competencies required to compete in a new business, a company may pursue internal new venturing if the industry it is entering is an emerging or embryonic industry. In such an industry there are no established companies that already possess the competencies required to compete in that industry. Thus a company is at no competitive disadvantage if it starts a new venture. Also, the option of acquiring an established enterprise that possesses those competencies is not available, so a company may have no choice but to enter via an internal new venture.

This was the position in which Monsanto found itself back in 1979 when it contemplated entering the biotechnology field to produce herbicide and seeds yielding pest-resistant crops. The biotechnology field was young at that time, and there were no incumbent companies focused on applying biotechnology to agricultural products. Accordingly, Monsanto established an internal new venture to enter the business, even though at the time it lacked the required competencies. Indeed, Monsanto's whole venturing strategy was built around the notion that it had the ability to build competencies ahead of potential competitors and so gain a strong competitive lead in this newly emerging field.

Internal New Venture

A company's creation of the value chain functions necessary to start a new business from scratch.

Pitfalls with Internal New Ventures

Despite the popularity of internal new venturing, there is a high risk of failure. Research suggests that somewhere between 33% and 60% of all new products that reach the marketplace do not generate an adequate economic return,[10] and most of these products were the result of internal new ventures. Three reasons are often put forward to explain the relatively high failure rate of internal new ventures: (1) market entry on too small a scale, (2) poor commercialization of the new-venture product, and (3) poor corporate management of the new-venture division.[11]

Scale of Entry Research suggests that on average, large-scale entry into a new business is often a critical precondition of success with a new venture. In the short run, this means that a substantial capital investment must be made to support large-scale entry; thus, there is a risk of major losses if the new venture fails. But, in the long run, which can be as long as 5–12 years depending on the industry, such a large investment results in far greater returns than if a company chooses to enter on a small scale in order to limit its investment to reduce potential losses.[12] Large-scale entrants can more rapidly realize scale economies, build brand loyalty, and gain access to distribution channels in the new industry, all of which increase the probability of a new venture's success. In contrast, small-scale entrants may find themselves handicapped by high costs due to a lack of scale economies and market presence that limits their ability to build brand loyalties and gain access to distribution channels. These scale effects are particularly significant when a company is entering an established industry where incumbent companies do have the benefit of scale economies, brand loyalty, and access to distribution channels. In that case, the new entrant has to make a major investment in order to succeed.

Figure 8.3 plots the relationship between scale of entry and profitability over time for successful small-scale and large-scale ventures. The figure shows that successful small-scale entry is associated with lower initial losses but that in the long

Figure 8.3 Scale of Entry and Profitability

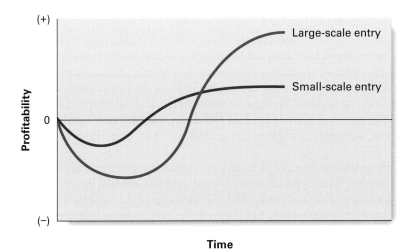

run, large-scale entry generates greater returns. However, because of the high costs and risks associated with large-scale entry, many companies make the mistake of choosing a small-scale entry strategy, which often means they fail to build the market share necessary for long-term success.

Commercialization   Many internal new ventures are driven by the opportunity to use a new or advanced technology to make better products for customers and out-perform competitors. To be commercially successful, science-based innovations must be developed with market requirements in mind. Many internal new ventures fail when a company ignores the basic needs of the market. A company can be blinded by the technological possibilities of a new product and fail to analyze market oppor-tunities properly. Thus, a new venture may fail because of a lack of commercializa-tion or because it is marketing a technology for which there is no demand. One of the most dramatic new-venture failures in recent history, the Iridium satellite com-munications system developed by Motorola, illustrates this well. The Iridium project was breathtaking in its scope. It called for 66 communications satellites to be placed in an orbital network. In theory, this network of flying telecommunications switches would enable anyone with an Iridium satellite phone to place and receive calls, no matter where they were on the planet. Motorola's CEO, Christopher Galvin, called the project the eighth wonder of the world but after spending 5 billion dollars to launch Iridium Motorola declared that Iridium was bankrupt only 9 months after the service began!

To its critics, the Iridium project was a classic case of a company being so blinded by the promise of a technology that it ignored market realities. Several serious short-comings of the Iridium project limited its market acceptance. First, the phones them-selves were large and heavy by current cell phone standards, weighing more than a pound! They were difficult to use, call clarity was poor, the phones themselves cost $3,000 each, and despite the "can be used anywhere" marketing theme, the phones could not be used inside cars or buildings—a major inconvenience for the busy globe-trotting executives at whom the service was aimed! Finally, the rapid ac-ceptance of much cheaper and more convenient cell phones limited the need for the Iridium phone. Why would a customer who had a cheaper, more convenient alterna-tive pay $3,000 for the privilege of owning a phone the size and weight of a brick that would not work in places where other cell phones do?[13]

Poor Corporate Management   Managing the new-venture process and control-ling the new-venture division creates many difficult managerial and organizational issues.[14] For example, one common mistake some companies make to try to increase their chances of making successful products is to establish *too many* different inter-nal new-venture divisions at the same time. It places great demands on a company's cash flow and can result in the best ventures being starved of the cash they need for success. In addition, if a company has too many internal new ventures in progress, management attention is likely to be spread too thin over these ventures, inviting disaster.

Another common mistake is failure by corporate management to establish the strategic context within which new-venture projects should be developed. Simply taking a team of research scientists and allowing them to do research in their favorite field may produce novel results, but these results may have little strategic or commer-cial value. It is necessary to be very clear about the strategic objectives of the venture and to understand exactly how it will seek to establish a competitive advantage.

Failure to anticipate the time and costs involved in the new-venture process is another common mistake. Many companies have unrealistic expectations regarding the time frame involved. Reportedly, some companies operate with a philosophy of killing new businesses if they do not turn a profit by the end of the third year—a most unrealistic view, given the evidence that it can take 5–12 years before a new venture generates substantial profits.

Guidelines for Successful Internal New Venturing

To avoid the pitfalls just discussed, a company should adopt a structured approach to managing internal new venturing.[15] New venturing typically begins with R&D. To make effective use of its R&D capacity, a company must first spell out its strategic objectives and then communicate them to its scientists and engineers. Research, after all, makes sense only when it is undertaken in areas relevant to strategic goals.[16]

To increase the probability of commercial success, a company should foster close links between R&D and marketing personnel, for this is the best way to ensure that research projects address the needs of the market. The company should also foster close links between R&D and manufacturing personnel to ensure that the company has the capability to manufacture any proposed new products.

Many companies successfully integrate different functions by setting up project teams. Such teams comprise representatives of the various functional areas; their task is to oversee the development of new products. Another advantage of such teams is that they can significantly reduce the time it takes to develop a new product. Thus, while R&D personnel are working on the design, manufacturing personnel can be setting up facilities, and marketing can be developing its plans. Because of such integration, Apple needed only 12 months to take the iPad tablet computer from an idea on the drawing board to a marketable product that has been wildly successful.

To use resources to the best effect, a company must also devise a selection process for choosing only the ventures that are most likely to meet with commercial success. Picking future winners is a tricky business; by their very definition, new ventures have an uncertain future. One study found the uncertainty surrounding new ventures to be so great that it usually took a company 4–5 years after launching the venture to reasonably estimate the venture's future profitability.[17] Nevertheless, a selection process is necessary if a company is to avoid spreading its resources over too many projects.

Once a project has been selected, management needs to monitor the progress of the venture closely. Evidence suggests that the most important criterion for evaluating a venture during its first 4–5 years is growth in market share, rather than cash flow or profitability. In the long run, the most successful ventures are those that increase their market share. A company should have clearly defined market share objectives for an internal new venture and should decide whether to retain or kill it in its early years on the basis of its ability to achieve market share goals. Only in the medium term should profitability and cash flow begin to take on greater importance.

Finally, the association of large-scale entry with greater long-term profitability suggests that a company can increase the probability of success for an internal new venture by "thinking big." Thinking big means the construction of efficient-scale production facilities before demand has fully materialized, large marketing expenditures to build a market presence and brand loyalty, and a commitment by corporate management to accept initial losses as long as market share is expanding. Note that it is not just high-tech companies that utilize internal new venturing, any company can take its existing skills and distinctive competencies to develop new ways to gain access to customers such as Walmart did when it developed its chain of Neighborhood Market stores (see Chapter 7, p. 176).

IMPLEMENTING STRATEGY THROUGH ACQUISITIONS

Acquisitions involve one company purchasing another company. A company may use acquisitions in two ways: to strengthen its competitive position in an existing business by purchasing a competitor (horizontal integration) and to enter a new business or industry. Companies may use acquisitions to enter a new business when they lack the distinctive competencies (resources and capabilities) required to compete in that area, but they can purchase, at a reasonable price, an incumbent company that *does* have those competencies.

Companies also have a preference for acquisitions as an entry mode when they feel the need to *move fast*. As we noted above, building a new business through internal venturing can be a relatively slow process. Acquisition is a much quicker way to establish a significant market presence, create value, and increase profitability. A company can purchase a leading company with a strong competitive position in months, rather than waiting years to build a market leadership position by engaging in internal venturing. Thus when speed is important, acquisition is the favored entry mode.

Acquisitions are also often perceived as somewhat *less risky* than internal new ventures, primarily because they involve less commercial uncertainty. It is in the very nature of internal new ventures that large uncertainties are associated with projecting future profitability, revenues, and cash flows. In contrast, when one company acquires another, it knows the profitability, revenues, and market share of the acquired company, so there is considerably less uncertainty. In short, acquisition enables a company to buy an established business with a track record, and for this reason, many companies favor an acquisition strategy.

Finally, acquisitions may be the preferred entry mode when the industry to be entered is well established and incumbent companies enjoy significant protection from barriers to entry. As you recall from Chapter 3, barriers to entry arise from factors associated with product differentiation (brand loyalty), absolute cost advantages, and economies of scale. When such barriers are substantial, a company finds entering an industry through internal new venturing difficult. To enter, a company may have to construct an efficient-scale manufacturing plant, undertake massive advertising to break down established brand loyalties, and quickly build up distribution outlets—all challenging goals likely to involve substantial expenditures.

In contrast, by acquiring an established enterprise, a company can circumvent most entry barriers. It can purchase a market leader that already benefits from substantial scale economies and brand loyalty. Thus the greater the barriers to entry, the more likely it is that acquisition will be the favored entry mode. (We should note, however, that the attractiveness of an acquisition is based on the assumption that an incumbent company can be acquired for less than it would cost to enter the same industry through internal new venturing. As we discuss in the next section, the validity of this assumption is often questionable.)

Acquisition

The purchase of one company by another.

Pitfalls with Acquisitions

For the reasons just noted, acquisitions have long been a popular vehicle for expanding the scope of the organization into new business areas. However, despite their popularity, there is ample evidence that many acquisitions fail to add value for the acquiring company and, indeed, often end up dissipating value. For example, a study of 700 large acquisitions found that although 30% of these resulted in higher profits, 31% led to losses, and the remainder had little impact.[18]

In fact, a wealth of evidence from academic research suggests that many acquisitions fail to realize their anticipated benefits.[19] Not only do profits and market shares often decline following acquisition, but a substantial subset of acquired companies experience traumatic difficulties that ultimately lead to their being sold off by the acquiring company.[20] Thus many acquisitions dilute value rather than create it.[21]

Why do so many acquisitions fail to create value? There appears to be four major reasons: (1) companies often experience difficulties when trying to integrate divergent corporate cultures; (2) companies overestimate the potential economic benefits from an acquisition; (3) acquisitions tend to be very expensive; and (4) companies often do not adequately screen their acquisition targets.

Postacquisition Integration Having made an acquisition, the acquiring company has to integrate the acquired business into its own organizational structure. Integration involves the adoption of common management and financial control systems, the joining together of operations from the acquired and the acquiring company, the establishment of bureaucratic mechanisms to share information and personnel, and the need to create a common culture. When integration is attempted, many unexpected problems can occur. Often they stem from differences in corporate cultures. After an acquisition, many acquired companies experience high management turnover, possibly because their employees do not like the acquiring company's way of doing things.[22] Research evidence suggests that the loss of management talent and expertise, to say nothing of the damage from constant tension between different business units, can harm the performance of the acquired unit.[23]

Overestimating Economic Benefits Even when companies achieve integration, they often overestimate the potential for creating value by marrying different businesses. They overestimate the strategic advantages that can be derived from the acquisition, and thus pay more for the target company than it is probably worth. Why? Top managers typically overestimate their ability to create value from an acquisition, primarily because rising to the top of a corporation gives them an exaggerated sense of their own capabilities.[24] The overestimation of economic benefits seems to have been a factor in the disastrous 2001 acquisition of Time Warner by AOL, for example, that resulted in billions of dollars in losses for Time Warner, which spun AOL off into a separate company in December 2009.

The Expense of Acquisitions Acquisitions of companies whose stock is publicly traded tend to be very expensive, as Time Warner found out. When a company moves to acquire the stock of another company, the stock price frequently gets bid up in the acquisition process. In such cases the acquiring company must often pay a significant premium over the current market value of the target. Often these premiums are 50%–100% above the stock value of the target company before the acquisition was announced. Such a situation is particularly likely to occur in the case of contested bids, where two or more companies simultaneously bid for control of a single target company. For example, in 2010 Dell and HP entered into a bidding war for cloud-computing data storage company 3Par. Dell first offered $1 billion to buy the company but then HP offered $1.5 billion. Dell then offered $1.7 billion but gave up the battle after HP bid over $2 billion for 3Par—over a 150% premium.

The debt taken on in order to finance expensive acquisitions can later become a noose around the acquiring company's neck, particularly if interest rates rise. Moreover, if the market value of the target company prior to an acquisition was a true reflection of that company's worth under its management at that time, a premium of 50% or 100% over this value means that the acquiring company has to improve the performance of the acquired unit by just as much if it is to reap a positive return on its investment! Such performance gains can be very difficult to achieve.

Inadequate Preacquisition Screening　One common reason for the failure of acquisitions is management's inadequate attention to preacquisition screening.[25] Many companies decide to acquire other firms without thoroughly analyzing the potential benefits and costs. After the acquisition has been completed, many acquiring companies discover that instead of buying a well-run business, they have purchased a troubled organization. IBM avoided this situation in 2009 when it was in negotiations to purchase chip maker Sun Microsystems. After spending 1 week examining its books IBM reduced its offer price by 10% after its negotiators had examined Sun's books and found its customer base was not as solid as they had expected. Sun was eventually sold to Oracle for a much lower price.

Guidelines for Successful Acquisition

To avoid pitfalls and make successful acquisitions, companies need to take a structured approach with three main components: (1) target identification and preacquisition screening, (2) bidding strategy, and (3) integration.[26]

Screening　Thorough preacquisition screening increases a company's knowledge about potential takeover targets and lessens the risk of purchasing a problem company—one with a weak business model. It also leads to a more realistic assessment of the problems involved in executing a particular acquisition so that a company can plan how to integrate the new business and blend organizational structures and cultures. The screening should begin with a detailed assessment of the strategic rationale for making the acquisition and with identification of the kind of enterprise that would make an ideal acquisition candidate.

Next, the company should scan a target population of potential acquisition candidates, evaluating each in terms of a detailed set of criteria, focusing on (1) financial position, (2) product market position, (3) competitive environment, (4) management capabilities, and (5) corporate culture. Such an evaluation should enable the company to identify the strengths and weaknesses of each candidate, the extent of potential economies of scope between the acquiring and the acquired companies, potential integration problems, and the compatibility of the corporate cultures of the acquiring and the acquired companies. For example, Microsoft and SAP, the world's leading provider of enterprise resource planning software, sat down together to discuss a possible acquisition by Microsoft. Both companies decided that even though there was a strong strategic rationale for a merger—together they could dominate the software computing market that satisfies the need of large global companies—the problems of creating an organizational structure that could successfully integrate their hundreds of thousands of employees throughout the world, and blend two very different cultures, were insurmountable.

The company should then reduce the list of candidates to the most promising ones and evaluate them further. At this stage, it should sound out third parties, such as investment bankers, whose opinions may be important and who may be able to offer valuable insights into the efficiency of target companies. The company that heads the list after this process should be the acquisition target.

Bidding Strategy   The objective of bidding strategy is to reduce the price that a company must pay for an acquisition candidate. The essential element of a good bidding strategy is timing. For example, Hanson PLC, one of the most successful companies to pursue unrelated diversification, always looked for essentially sound businesses that were suffering from short-term problems due to cyclical industry factors or from problems localized in one division. Such companies are typically undervalued by the stock market and thus can be picked up without payment of the standard 40% or 50% premium over current stock prices. With good timing, a company can make a bargain purchase.

Integration   Despite good screening and bidding, an acquisition will fail unless positive steps are taken to integrate the acquired company into the organizational structure of the acquiring one. Integration should center on the source of the potential strategic advantages of the acquisition—for instance, opportunities to share marketing, manufacturing, procurement, R&D, financial, or management resources. Integration should also be accompanied by steps to eliminate any duplication of facilities or functions. In addition, any unwanted divisions of the acquired company should be sold. Finally, if the different business activities are closely related, they will require a high degree of integration. In the case of a company pursuing unrelated diversification, the level of integration may be a minimal problem. But for a strategy of related diversification, the problem of integrating the two companies' operations is much greater. One company that has succeeded well in its acquisition strategy for these reasons is News Corp., discussed in the following Strategy in Action.

IMPLEMENTING STRATEGY THROUGH STRATEGIC ALLIANCES

Strategic alliances are cooperative agreements between two or more companies to work together and share resources to achieve a common business objective. A joint venture is a formal type of strategic alliance in which two companies jointly create a new, separate company to enter a new business area.

A company may prefer internal new venturing to acquisition as an entry strategy into new business areas and yet hesitate to commit itself to an internal new venture because of the risks and costs of building a new operation "from the ground up." Such a situation is likely when a company sees the advantages of establishing a new business in an embryonic or growth industry, but the risks and costs associated with

Strategic Alliance

A cooperative agreement between two or more companies to work together and share resources to achieve a common business objective.

Joint Venture

A formal type of strategic alliance in which two companies jointly create a new, separate company to enter a new product market or industry.

8.1 STRATEGY IN ACTION

News Corp's Successful Acquisition Strategy

News Corp is a company that has engineered scores of acquisitions to become one of the four largest, and most powerful, entertainment media companies in the world. What kind of strategies has its CEO Rupert Murdock used to create his media empire?

Rupert Murdock was born into a newspaper family; his father owned and ran the *Adelaide News*, an Australian regional newspaper, and when his father died in 1952 he gained control of it. He quickly set his sights on enlarging his customer base. After all, more profit is earned when more customers buy your products, and so he used his financial acumen to acquire more and more Australian newspapers. One of these had connections to a major British "pulp" newspaper the Mirror, which is quite similar to National Enquirer, and Murdock acquired and established the Sun as a leading British tabloid.

His growing reputation as an entrepreneur enabled him to borrow more and more money from investors who saw that he could create a much higher return from the assets he controlled than competitors. Murdock carried on buying well-known newspapers such as the *British Sunday Telegraph*, and then his first U.S. newspaper, the *San Antonio Express*. Then, he launched the *National Star* and his growing profits allowed him to continue to borrow money and he bought the *New York Post* and *The Times* and *Sunday Times*.

Pursuing this strategy of horizontal integration through acquisitions to create one of the world's biggest newspaper empires was just one part of Murdock's corporate strategies, however. He realized that industries in the entertainment and media sector can be divided into those that provide media content, or "software," such as book publishing, movies, and television programming, and those that provide or supply the media channels or "hardware" necessary to get media software to customers such as movie theatres, TV channels, TV cable, and satellite broadcasting. Murdock realized he could create the most profit by getting involved in both the media software *and* media hardware industries, which are essentially adjacent stages in the value chain of the entertainment and media sector. So, Murdock went all out to pursue a strategy of vertical integration and went on a buying spree to purchase global media companies in both the software and hardware stages of the entertainment sector. He paid $1.5 billion for Metromedia, which owned seven stations that reached over 20% of households in the United States. He scored another major coup when he bought Twentieth Century Fox Movie Studios, a premium content provider. Now he had Fox's huge film library and the creative talents the studio possessed to make new films and TV programming. Murdock decided to create the Fox Broadcasting network and buy or create its own U.S. network of Fox affiliates that would show programs developed by its own Fox movie studios. After a slow start, the Fox Network gained popularity with shows like The Simpson's, which became Fox's first blockbuster program. He also engineered another coup when Fox purchased the sole rights to broadcast all NFL games for over $1 billion, shutting out NBC, and making Fox the "fourth network." The Fox network has never looked back and it was one of the first to get into "reality" programming. News Corp has acquired a host of companies in the entertainment value chain that fit with its newspaper, TV station, and movie and broadcasting companies to strengthen its competitive position in these industries.

the business are more than it is willing to assume on its own. In this case, a company may decide to form some kind of strategic alliance with another company.

As noted earlier, strategic alliances are cooperative agreements between companies. The parties to an alliance may be actual or potential competitors; or they may be situated at different stages in an industry's value chain; or they may be in different businesses but have a joint interest in working together to develop distinctive competencies in R&D or marketing that are useful to both parties or decide to cooperate on a particular problem, such as developing a new product or technology.

Strategic alliances run the gamut from informal agreements and short-term contracts, where companies agree to share know-how, to formal contractual agreements such as long-term outsourcing agreements and joint ventures in which both companies establish and assume ownership of a new company. Thus some strategic alliances are meant to be temporary, but others may be a prelude to a permanent relationship. For example, sometimes long-term agreements result in the establishment of a joint venture (they may even lead to a merger through acquisition). Strategic alliances of all kinds are often used as a vehicle that enables companies to share the risks and costs of developing a new business. In any event, strategic alliances are a valuable strategic tool that helps companies maximize their business opportunities, especially in today's competitive global environment.

Advantages of Strategic Alliances

Companies enter into strategic alliances with competitors to achieve a number of strategic objectives.[27] First, strategic alliances may be a way of facilitating entry into a market. For example, Motorola initially found it very difficult to gain access to the Japanese cellular telephone market because of formal and informal Japanese trade barriers. The turning point for Motorola came when it formed its alliance with Toshiba to build microprocessors. As part of the deal, Toshiba provided Motorola with marketing help, including some of its best managers. This helped Motorola win government approval to enter the Japanese market.[28]

Second, many companies enter into strategic alliances to share the fixed costs and associated risks that arise from the development of new products or processes. Motorola's alliance with Toshiba was partly motivated by a desire to share the high fixed costs associated with setting up the capital-intensive operation that manufacturing microprocessors entailed (it cost Motorola and Toshiba close to $1 billion to set up their facility). Few companies can afford the costs and risks of going it alone on such a venture. Similarly, an alliance between Boeing and a number of Japanese companies to build Boeing's latest commercial jet liner, the 787, was motivated by Boeing's desire to share the burden of the estimated $8 billion investment required to develop the aircraft.

Third, many alliances can be seen as a way of bringing together complementary skills and assets that neither company could easily develop on its own. For example, Microsoft and Toshiba established an alliance aimed at developing embedded microprocessors (essentially, tiny computers) that can perform a variety of entertainment functions in an automobile (for example, they can run a backseat DVD player or a wireless Internet connection). The processors will run a version of Microsoft's Windows CE operating system. Microsoft brings its software engineering skills to the alliance, and Toshiba brings its skills in developing microprocessors.[29]

Disadvantages of Strategic Alliances

Strategic alliances have many significant advantages, but there are also several disadvantages that may arise. First, strategic alliances may provide a company's competitors with access to valuable low-cost manufacturing knowledge and a route to gain new technology and market access.[30] For example, some commentators have argued that many strategic alliances between U.S. and Japanese firms facilitated an implicit Japanese strategy to keep higher-paying, higher-value-added jobs in Japan while gaining the project engineering and production process skills that underlie the competitive success of many U.S. companies.[31] These observers maintain that Japanese success in the machine tool and semiconductor industries was the result of knowledge acquired through strategic alliances with U.S. companies. And they contend that U.S. managers aided the Japanese by entering into alliances that channel new inventions to Japan and provide a convenient sales and distribution network for the resulting Japanese products sent back for sale in the United States. Although such agreements may generate short-term profits, in the long run the result is to "hollow out" U.S. firms, leaving them with no competitive advantage in the global marketplace.

Consider, for example, the situation in a joint venture, the formal strategic alliance in which two companies team up and establish a separate company to pool their complementary skills and assets. Such an arrangement enables a company to share the substantial risks and costs involved in developing a new business opportunity and may increase the probability of success in the new business. But there are three main drawbacks to joint venture arrangements.

First, just as a joint venture allows a company to share the risks and costs of developing a new business, it also requires the sharing of profits if the new business succeeds. Second, a company that enters into a joint venture always runs the risk of giving critical know-how away to its joint-venture partner, which might use that know-how to compete directly with the company in the future. Third, the venture partners must share control. If the partners have different business philosophies, time horizons, or investment preferences, substantial problems can arise. Conflicts over how to run the joint venture can tear it apart and result in business failure.

Thus the critics of strategic alliances have a point: Alliances do have risks, and the more formal or extensive the alliance, the greater the possibility that a company may give away more than it gets in return. Nevertheless, there are so many examples of apparently successful alliances between companies, including alliances between U.S. and Japanese companies, that it seems that long-term strategic alliances can and often do result in more advantages than disadvantages. The next section suggests why, and under what conditions, companies can gain these advantages.

Making Strategic Alliances Work

The failure rate for strategic alliances is quite high. For example, one study of 49 global strategic alliances found that two-thirds ran into serious managerial and financial troubles within 2 years of their formation. The same study suggests that although many of these problems are ultimately resolved, 33% of strategic alliances are ultimately rated as failures by the parties involved.[32] The success of a strategic alliance seems to be a function of three main factors: partner selection, alliance structure, and the manner in which the alliance is managed.

Partner Selection   One of the keys to making a strategic alliance work is to select the right kind of partner. A good partner has three principal characteristics. First, a good partner helps the company achieve strategic goals, such as gaining market access, sharing the costs and risks of new-product development, or gaining access to critical core competencies. In other words, the partner must have capabilities that the company lacks and that it values. Second, a good partner shares the firm's vision for the purpose of the alliance. If two companies approach an alliance with radically different agendas, the chances are great that the relationship will not be harmonious and will end in divorce.

Third, a good partner is unlikely to try to exploit the alliance opportunistically for its own ends—that is, to expropriate or even steal the company's technological know-how while giving little in return. In this respect, firms with reputations for fair play to maintain probably make the best partners. For example, IBM is involved in so many strategic alliances that it would not pay the company to cheat on individual alliance partners (in the mid-2000s, IBM reportedly had more than 150 major strategic alliances).[33] Doing so would tarnish IBM's reputation as a good ally and make it difficult for IBM to attract alliance partners in the future. Because IBM attaches great importance to its alliances, it is unlikely to engage in the kind of underhand behavior that critics highlight. Similarly, their reputations make it less likely (though by no means impossible) that such Japanese firms as Sony, Toshiba, and Fuji, which have histories of alliances with non-Japanese firms, would exploit an alliance partner.

To select a partner with these three characteristics, a company needs to thoroughly investigate potential alliance candidates. To increase the probability of selecting a good partner, the company should collect as much relevant publicly available information about potential allies as possible; collect data from informed third parties, including companies that have had alliances with the potential partners, investment bankers who have had dealings with them, and some of their former employees; and get to know potential partners as well as possible before committing to an alliance. This last step should include face-to-face meetings between senior managers to ensure that the "chemistry" is right.

Alliance Structure   Once a partner has been selected, the alliance should be structured so that the company's risk of giving too much away to the partner is reduced to an acceptable level. Figure 8.4 depicts the four safeguards against opportunism of cheating by alliance partners discussed below. First, alliances can be designed to make it difficult or impossible to transfer technology meant to be kept secret and proprietary. Specifically, the design, development, and servicing of a product manufactured by an alliance can be structured so as to "wall off" and protect sensitive technologies from partners. In the alliance between GE and Snecma to build commercial aircraft engines, for example, GE reduced the risk of "excess transfer" by walling off certain sections of the production process. This effectively cut off the transfer of what GE regarded as key competitive technology, while permitting Snecma access to final assembly. Similarly, in the alliance between Boeing and the Japanese to build the 767, Boeing walled off research, design, and marketing functions considered central to its competitive position, while allowing the Japanese to share in production technology. Boeing also walled off new technologies not required for 767 production.[34]

Second, contractual safeguards can be written into an alliance agreement to guard against the risk of being exploited by a partner. For example, TRW Systems,

Figure 8.4   Structuring Alliances to Reduce Opportunism

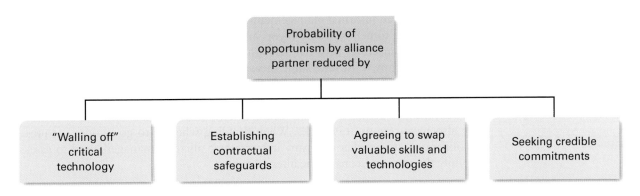

an auto-parts supplier now part of Honeywell, had strategic alliances with large Japanese car component suppliers to produce seat belts, engine valves, and steering gears for sale to Japanese-owned car assembly plants in the United States. TRW ensured that clauses in each of its alliance contracts barred the Japanese firms from competing with TRW to supply U.S.-owned auto companies with component parts. So TRW protected itself against the possibility that the Japanese companies entered the alliances only as a way of gaining access to the U.S. market to compete with TRW on its home turf.

Third, both parties to an alliance can promise in advance to swap important proprietary skills and technologies, thereby ensuring the opportunity for equitable gain. Cross-licensing agreements are one way to achieve this goal. For example, in an alliance between Motorola and Toshiba, Motorola licensed some of its microprocessor technology to Toshiba and in return Toshiba licensed some of its memory chip technology to Motorola.

Fourth, the risk of deceitful behavior by an alliance partner can be reduced if the less powerful firm extracts a significant *credible commitment* from its partner in advance. The purpose of a credible commitment is to send a signal that the company making the commitment will do its best to ensure that the alliance works. Such credible commitments often come in the form of capital investments. For example, in 2004 the small British biotechnology firm Cambridge Antibody Technology entered into a 5-year alliance with the large pharmaceutical company Astra Zeneca to develop new treatments for inflammatory disorders. As part of the deal, Astra Zeneca agreed to invest $140 million, a 20% equity stake in the smaller company. This investment increases the probability that Astra Zeneca will do its best to ensure the alliance achieves its strategic goals.[35]

Managing the Alliance   Once a partner has been selected and an appropriate alliance structure agreed on, the task facing the company is to maximize the benefits from the alliance. One important ingredient of success appears to be sensitivity to cultural differences. Many differences in management style are attributable to cultural differences, and managers need to make allowances for these in dealing with their partner. Beyond this, maximizing the benefits from an alliance seems to involve building trust between partners and learning from partners.[36]

Managing an alliance successfully requires building interpersonal relationships between the firms' managers, or what is sometimes referred to as *relational capital*.[37] This is one lesson that can be learned from a successful strategic alliance between Ford and Mazda. Ford and Mazda set up a framework of meetings within which their managers not only discuss matters pertaining to the alliance but also have time to get to know each other better. The belief is that the resulting friendships help build trust and facilitate harmonious relations between the two firms. Personal relationships also foster an informal management network between the firms. This network can then be used to help solve problems arising in more formal contexts (such as in joint committee meetings between personnel from the two firms). When entering an alliance, a company must take some measures to ensure that it learns from its alliance partner and then puts that knowledge to good use within its own organization.

In sum, although strategic alliances often have a distinct advantage over internal new venturing or acquisitions as a means of establishing a new business operation, they also have certain drawbacks. When deciding whether to go it alone, acquire, or cooperate with another company in a strategic alliance, managers need to assess carefully the pros and cons of the alternatives.

SUMMARY OF CHAPTER

1. Strategic change is the movement of a company from its present state to some desired future state to increase its competitive advantage. Two main types of strategic changes are reengineering and restructuring.

2. Strategic change is implemented through a series of steps. The first step in the change process is determining the need for change. Strategic managers use a SWOT analysis to determine the company's present state and then characterize its desired future state. The second stage in the change process is to identify the obstacles to change at all levels in the organization.

3. An important technique used to identify a company's desired future state is to analyze it as a portfolio of "core competencies"—as opposed to a portfolio of businesses. In this approach, strategic change is oriented toward maintaining existing competencies, building new competencies, and leveraging competencies by applying them to new business opportunities.

4. There are three vehicles that companies use to enter new business areas: internal ventures, acquisitions, and strategic alliances (including joint ventures).

5. Internal new venturing is used as an entry strategy when a company possesses a set of valuable competencies in its existing businesses that can be leveraged or recombined to enter the new business area.

6. Many internal ventures fail because of entry on too small a scale, poor commercialization, and/or poor corporate management of the internal venture process. Guarding against failure involves a structured approach to project selection and management, integration of R&D and marketing to improve commercialization of a venture idea, and entry on a significant scale.

7. Acquisitions are often favored as an entry strategy when the company lacks important competencies (resources and capabilities) required to compete in an area, but when it can purchase, at a reasonable price, an incumbent company that has those competencies. Acquisitions also tend to be favored when the barriers to entry into the target industry are high and when the company is unwilling to accept the time frame, development costs, and risks of internal new venturing.

8. Many acquisitions fail because of poor post-acquisition integration, overestimation of the value that can be created from an acquisition, the high cost of acquisition, and poor preacquisition screening. Guarding against acquisition failure requires structured screening, good bidding strategies, and positive attempts to integrate the acquired company into the organization of the acquiring firm.

9. Strategic alliances may be the preferred entry strategy when (1) the risks and costs associated with setting up a new business unit are more than the company is willing to assume on its own and (2) the company can increase the probability of successfully establishing a new business by teaming up with another company that has skills and assets complementing its own.

10. Strategic alliances are short-term informal or long-term formal cooperative agreements between companies. Alliances can facilitate entry into markets, enable partners to share the fixed costs and risks associated with new products and processes, facilitate the transfer of complementary skills between companies, and help companies establish technical standards.

11. The drawbacks of formal strategic alliances, particularly joint ventures, include the risk that a company may give away technological know-how and market access to its alliance partner without getting much in return.

12. The disadvantages associated with alliances can be reduced if the company selects partners carefully, paying close attention to their reputation, and structures the alliance in such a way as to avoid unintended transfers of know-how.

DISCUSSION QUESTIONS

1. Outline the issues and problems involved in identifying a company's desired future state.
2. Under what circumstances might it be best to enter a new business area by acquisition? Under what circumstances might internal new venturing be the preferred mode of entry?
3. If IBM decides to diversify into the wireless telecommunications business, what entry strategy would you recommend that the company pursue? Why?

C L O S I N G   C A S E

Oracle's Growing Portfolio of Businesses

Oracle Corp., based in Redwood City California, is the world's largest maker of database software and the third largest global software company in terms of sales after Microsoft and IBM. This commanding position is not enough for Oracle, however, which has set its sights on becoming the global leader in the corporate applications software market. Here, Germany's SAP which has 45% of the market is the acknowledged leader and Oracle, with only 19%, is a distant second.[38] Corporate applications is a fast growing and highly profitable market, however, and Oracle has been snapping up leading companies in this segment at a fast pace. Its goal is to quickly build the distinctive competencies it needs to expand the range of products that it can offer to its existing customers and to attract new customers to compete with SAP. Beginning in 2005, Oracle's CEO Larry Ellison spent $19 billion to acquire 14 leading suppliers of corporate software including two of the top five companies: PeopleSoft, a leading Human Resource Management (HRM) software supplier it bought for $10 billion, and Siebel Systems, a leader in customer relationship management (CRM) software which cost Oracle $5.8 billion.

Oracle expects several competitive advantages to result from its use of acquisitions to pursue the corporate strategy of horizontal integration. First, it is now able to meld or bundle the best software applications of these acquired companies—with Oracle's own first-class set of corporate and database software programs—to create a new integrated suite of software that will allow corporations to manage all their functional activities such as accounting, marketing,

sales, HRM, CRM, and supply-chain management. Second, through these acquisitions Oracle obtained access to thousands of new customers—all the companies that currently use the software of the companies it acquired. All these companies now become potential new customers for all of Oracle's other database and corporate software offerings. Third, beyond increasing the range of its products and number of its customers, Oracle's acquisitions have consolidated the corporate software industry. By taking over some of its largest rivals, Oracle has become the second largest supplier of corporate software and so it is better positioned to compete with leader SAP.

Achieving the advantages of its new strategy may not be easy, however. The person in charge of assembling Oracle's new unified software package and selling it to customers is John Wookey, Oracle's senior vice-president in charge of applications, who jokingly says that his "head is the one on the chopping block if this doesn't work." CEO Ellison has been quick to fire executives who don't perform well in the past, however, who expects a lot from his top executives. To grow Oracle's market share and profits Wookey must draw on the best of the technology Oracle obtain from each of the companies it acquired to build its new suite of state-of-the-art corporate software applications. He also has to persuade customers not to switch software vendors, for example, jump ship to SAP, while Oracle builds its package and then to gradually adopt more and more of Oracle's software offerings to run their functional activities.

Wookey is well-placed to implement Oracle's new strategy. However, he is known as a consensus builder and product champion, both inside the company and outside, when interacting with Oracle's customers. He spends his working day sharing information with the top managers of Oracle's various businesses, and meeting with his team of 14 senior staff members, to work out how the whole package should be put together and what it should include. He also regularly visits major customers, especially those that came with its acquisitions, to gain their input into how and what kind of software package Oracle should build. Wookey even formed an advisory council of leading customers to help make sure the final package meets their needs. One of Wookey's notable achievements was retaining the top-rate software engineers who Oracle obtained from its acquired rivals. These people could have easily found high-paying jobs elsewhere, but most of the top engineers Oracle wanted stayed to help it achieve its new goals.

Nevertheless, by the end of 2006 there were signs that all was not going well with Oracle's new strategy. SAP is a powerful competitor, its popular software is fast becoming the industry standard, so unseating SAP in the $23.4 billion corporate software market will not be easy. Moreover, SAP is still the leader in more advanced functional applications incorporating the latest technologies and its proprietary technology is all homegrown, so it doesn't face the huge implementation issue of bringing together the applications from many different acquisitions. Preventing customers from switching to SAP may not be easy now that their loyalty to their old software supplier has been broken because of its acquisition by Oracle. Analysts also say that Oracle runs the risk of stretching itself too thin if it continues to purchase too many companies too quickly because high-tech acquisitions are the most difficult to pull off in terms of management and execution.[39]

Larry Ellison is under pressure to accelerate sales growth and surpass investors' expectations and only if Oracle can put out corporate application software sales numbers that beat expectations will analysts regard its strategy as a success. Still, Oracle's stock gained 47% in 2006 compared to SAP's 15% and in 2007 Oracle announced record revenues and profits. Its stock price jumped as investors now believe he and Wookey have the ability to make its acquisitions pay. In 2008 Oracle announced yet another major acquisition of software supplier BEA Systems; will they be able to continue their track record of success?

Case Discussion Questions

1. In what ways is Oracle seeking to create value from its acquisitions?
2. Based upon the ways it is seeking to increase the value it creates, what is its corporate-level strategy?

NOTES

1. R. Beckhard, *Organizational Development* (Reading, Mass.: Addison-Wesley, 1969); and W. L. French and C. H. Bell, Jr., *Organizational Development*, 2nd ed. (Englewood Cliffs, N.J.: Prentice-Hall, 1978).
2. Beckhard, *Organizational Development*.
3. M. Hammer and J. Champy, *Reengineering the Corporation* (New York: HarperCollins, 1993).
4. Hammer and Champy, *Reengineering the Corporation*, p. 39.
5. J. F. McDonnell, "Learning to Think in Different Terms: TQM & Restructuring at McDonnell Douglas," *Executive Speeches*, June/July 1994, 25–28.
6. L. C. Coch and R. P. French, Jr., "Overcoming Resistance to Change," *Human Relations*, August 1948, 512–532 and P. R. Lawrence, "How to Deal with Resistance to Change," *Harvard Business Review*, January–February 1969, 4–12.
7. P. Kotter and L. A. Schlesinger, "Choosing Strategies for Change," *Harvard Business Review*, March–April 1979, 106–114.
8. G. Hamel and C. K. Prahalad, *Competing for the Future* (Cambridge, Mass.: Harvard Business School Press, 1994).
9. D. Leonard Barton and G. Pisano, "Monsanto's March into Biotechnology," *Harvard Business School Case*, 1990, 690009. See Monsanto's homepage (http://www.monsanto.com) for more information about its genetically engineered seed products.
10. See Booz, Allen, and Hamilton, *New Products Management for the 1980s* (privately published, 1982); A. L. Page, "PDMA's New Product Development Practices Survey: Performance and Best Practices" (presented at the PDMA Fifteenth Annual International Conference, Boston, October 16, 1991); and E. Mansfield, "How

Economists See R&D," *Harvard Business Review*, November–December 1981, 98–106.

11. See R. Biggadike, "The Risky Business of Diversification," *Harvard Business Review*, May–June 1979, 103–111; R. A. Burgelman, "A Process Model of Internal Corporate Venturing in the Diversified Major Firm," *Administrative Science Quarterly* 28 (1983): 223–244; and Z. Block and I. C. MacMillan, *Corporate Venturing* (Boston, Mass.: Harvard Business School Press, 1993).

12. Biggadike, "The Risky Business of Diversification" and Block and Macmillan, *Corporate Venturing*.

13. R. O. Crockett and C. Yang, "Why Motorola Should Hang Up on Iridium," *Business Week*, August 30, 1999, 46; L. Cauley, "Iridium's Downfall: The Marketing Took a Back Seat to the Science," *Wall Street Journal*, August 18, 1999, A1; and J. N. Seth and R. Sisodia, "Why Cell Phones Succeeded Where Iridium Failed," *Wall Street Journal*, August 23, 1999, A14.

14. I. C. Macmillan and R. George, "Corporate Venturing: Challenges for Senior Managers," *Journal of Business Strategy* 5 (1985): 34–43.

15. I. C. MacMillan and R. G. McGrath, "Nine New Roles for Technology Managers," *Research Technology Management* 47 (2004): 16–25.

16. See Block and Macmillan, *Corporate Venturing* (Cambridge, Mass.: Harvard Business School Press, 1993); and Burgelman, Maidique, and Wheelwright, *Strategic Management of Technology and Innovation* (Chicago: Irwin, 1996).

17. G. Beardsley and E. Mansfield, "A Note on the Accuracy of Industrial Forecasts of the Profitability of New Products and Processes," *Journal of Business* 23 (1978): 127–130.

18. For evidence on acquisitions and performance, see R. E. Caves, "Mergers, Takeovers, and Economic Efficiency," *International Journal of Industrial Organization* 7 (1989): 151–174; M. C. Jensen and R. S. Ruback, "The Market for Corporate Control: The Scientific Evidence," *Journal of Financial Economics* 11 (1983): 5–50; R. Roll, "Empirical Evidence on Takeover Activity and Shareholder Wealth," in *Knights, Raiders and Targets*, edited by J. C. Coffee, L. Lowenstein, and S. Rose (Oxford: Oxford University Press, 1989); A. Schleifer and R. W. Vishny, "Takeovers in the 60s and 80s: Evidence and Implications," *Strategic Management Journal* 12 (Special Issue, Winter 1991): 51–60; T. H. Brush, "Predicted Changes in Operational Synergy and Post Acquisition Performance of Acquired Businesses," *Strategic Management Journal* 17 (1996): 1–24; and T. Loughran and A. M. Vijh, "Do Long Term Shareholders Benefit from Corporate Acquisitions?" *Journal of Finance* 5 (1997): 1765–1787.

19. For evidence on acquisitions and performance, see Caves, "Mergers, Takeovers, and Economic Efficiency"; Jensen and Ruback, "The Market for Corporate Control: The Scientific Evidence"; Roll, "Empirical Evidence on Takeover Activity and Shareholder Wealth," in *Knights,*

Raiders and Targets; Schleifer and Vishny, "Takeovers in the 60s and 80s: Evidence and Implications"; and Brush, "Predicted Changes in Operational Synergy and Post Acquisition Performance of Acquired Businesses."

20. D. J. Ravenscraft and F. M. Scherer, *Mergers, Selloffs, and Economic Efficiency* (Washington, D.C.: Brookings Institution, 1987).

21. S. B. Moeller, F. P. Schlingemann, and R. M. Stulz, "Wealth Destruction on a Massive Scale? A Study of Acquiring Firm Returns in the Recent Merger Wave," *Journal of Finance* 60, no. 2 (2005): 757–783.

22. See J. P. Walsh, "Top Management Turnover Following Mergers and Acquisitions," *Strategic Management Journal* 9 (1988): 173–183.

23. See A. A. Cannella and D. C. Hambrick, "Executive Departure and Acquisition Performance," *Strategic Management Journal* 14 (1993): 137–152.

24. R. Roll, "The Hubris Hypothesis of Corporate Takeovers," *Journal of Business* 59 (1986): 197–216.

25. P. Haspeslagh and D. Jemison, *Managing Acquisitions* (New York: Free Press, 1991).

26. For views on this issue, see L. L Fray, D. H. Gaylin, and J. W. Down, "Successful Acquisition Planning," *Journal of Business Strategy* 5 (1984): 46–55; C. W. L. Hill, "Profile of a Conglomerate Takeover: BTR and Thomas Tilling," *Journal of General Management* 10 (1984): 34–50; D. R. Willensky, "Making It Happen: How to Execute an Acquisition," *Business Horizons*, March–April 1985, 38–45; Haspeslagh and Jemison, *Managing Acquisitions*; and P. L. Anslinger and T. E. Copeland, "Growth Through Acquisition: A Fresh Look," *Harvard Business Review*, January–February 1996, 126–135.

27. See K. Ohmae, "The Global Logic of Strategic Alliances," *Harvard Business Review*, March–April 1989, 143–154; G. Hamel, Y. L. Doz, and C. K. Prahalad, "Collaborate with Your Competitors and Win!" *Harvard Business Review*, January–February 1989, 133–139; W. Burgers, C. W. L. Hill, and W. C. Kim, "Alliances in the Global Auto Industry," *Strategic Management Journal* 14 (1993): 419–432; and P. Kale, H. Singh, and H. Perlmutter, "Learning and Protection of Proprietary Assets in Strategic Alliances: Building Relational Capital," *Strategic Management Journal* 21 (2000): 217–237.

28. "Asia Beckons," *Economist*, May 30, 1992, 63–64.

29. C. Souza, "Microsoft Teams with MIPS, Toshiba," *EBN*, February 10, 2003, 4.

30. Kale, Singh, and Perlmutter, "Learning and Protection of Proprietary Assets in Strategic Alliances: Building Relational Capital."

31. R. B. Reich and E. D. Mankin, "Joint Ventures with Japan Give Away Our Future," *Harvard Business Review*, March–April 1986, 78–90.

32. J. Bleeke and D. Ernst, "The Way to Win in Cross-Border Alliances," *Harvard Business Review*, November–December 1991, 127–135.

33. E. Booker and C. Krol, "IBM Finds Strength in Alliances," *B to B*, February 10, 2003, 3, 27.

34. W. Roehl and J. F. Truitt, "Stormy Open Marriages Are Better," *Columbia Journal of World Business* (Summer 1987): 87–95.

35. Staff Reporter, "Cambridge Antibody Technology: Astra Zeneca to Buy 19.9% Stake," *Wall Street Journal*, November 23, 2004, A1.

36. See T. Khanna, R. Gulati, and N. Nohria, "The Dynamics of Learning Alliances: Competition, Cooperation, and Relative Scope," *Strategic Management Journal* 19 (1998): 193–210; and Kale, Singh, and Perlmutter, "Learning and Protection of Proprietary Assets in Strategic Alliances."

37. Kale, Singh, and Perlmutter, "Learning and Protection of Proprietary Assets in Strategic Alliances."

38. www.sap.com, 2010.

39. www.oracle.com, 2010.

9

IMPLEMENTING STRATEGY THROUGH ORGANIZATIONAL DESIGN

CHAPTER OUTLINE

The Role of Organizational Structure

Building Blocks of Organizational Structure

Vertical Differentiation

Problems with Tall Structures
Centralization or Decentralization?

Horizontal Differentiation

Functional Structure
Product Structure
Product-Team Structure
Geographic Structure
Multidivisional Structure

Integration and Organizational Control

Forms of Integrating Mechanisms
Differentiation and Integration

The Nature of Organizational Control

Strategic Controls
Financial Controls
Output Controls
Behavior Controls

LEARNING OBJECTIVES

After reading this chapter, you should be able to:

- Discuss how organizational strategy is implemented through organizational structure.
- Explain the building blocks of organizational structure.

- Distinguish between vertical and horizontal differentiation.
- Discuss the importance of integration and the relationship between differentiation and integration.
- Explain the nature and function of strategic control systems.

OVERVIEW

In this chapter, we examine how a company should organize its activities to create the most value. In Chapter 1, we defined *strategy implementation* as the way a company creates the organizational arrangements that enable it to pursue its strategy most effectively. Strategy is implemented through organizational design.

Organizational design means selecting the combination of organizational structure and control systems that allows a company to pursue its strategy most effectively—that lets it *create and sustain a competitive advantage.* Good organizational design increases profits in two ways. First, it economizes on operating costs and lowers the costs of value creation activities. Second, it enhances the ability of a company's value creation functions to achieve superior efficiency, quality, innovativeness, and customer responsiveness and to obtain a differentiation advantage.

The primary role of organizational structure and control is twofold: (1) to *coordinate* the activities of employees in such a way that they work together most effectively to implement a strategy that increases competitive advantage and (2) to *motivate* employees and provide them with incentives to achieve superior efficiency, quality, innovation, or customer responsiveness. Microsoft's strategy, for example, is to speed decision making and new-product development, and it constantly works to keep its structure as flexible as possible to allow its teams of programmers to respond quickly to the ever-changing nature of competition in the software industry.

Organizational structure and control shape the way people behave and determine how they will act in the organizational setting. If a new CEO wants to know why it takes a long time for people to make decisions in a company, why there is a lack of cooperation between sales and manufacturing, or why product innovations are few and far between, he or she needs to look at the design of the organizational structure and control system and analyze how it coordinates and motivates employees' behavior. An analysis of how structure and control work makes it possible to change them to improve both coordination and motivation. Good organizational design allows an organization to improve its ability to create value and obtain a competitive advantage.

In this chapter we first examine the organizational structures available to strategic managers to coordinate and motivate employees. Then we consider the strategic control systems that companies use in conjunction with their organizational structures to monitor and motivate managers and employees at all levels and encourage them to be responsive to changes in the competitive environment.

THE ROLE OF ORGANIZATIONAL STRUCTURE

After formulating a company's strategies, management must make designing organizational structure its next priority, for strategy is also implemented through organizational structure. The value creation activities of organizational members are meaningless unless some type of structure is used to assign people to tasks and link the activities of different people and functions.[1] As we saw in Chapter 4, each organizational function needs to develop a distinctive competency in a value creation activity in order to increase efficiency, quality, innovation, or customer responsiveness. Thus, each function needs a structure designed to allow it to develop its skills and become more specialized and productive. As functions become

Organizational Design

The process through which managers select the combination of organizational structure and control systems that they believe will enable the company to create and sustain a competitive advantage.

increasingly specialized, however, they often begin to pursue their own goals exclusively and lose sight of the need to communicate and coordinate with other functions. The goals of R&D, for example, center on innovation and product design, whereas the goals of manufacturing often revolve around increasing efficiency. Left to themselves, the various functions may have little to say to one another, and value creation opportunities will be lost.

The role of organizational structure is to provide the vehicle through which managers can coordinate the activities of a company's various functions, divisions, and business units to take advantage of their skills and competencies. To pursue a cost-leadership strategy, for example, a company must design a structure that facilitates close coordination between the activities of manufacturing and those of R&D to ensure that innovative products can be produced reliably and cost-effectively. To achieve gains from economies of scope and resource sharing between divisions, managers must design mechanisms that motivate and encourage divisional managers to communicate and share their skills and knowledge. In pursuing a global or transnational strategy, managers must create the right kind of organizational structure for managing the flow of resources and capabilities between domestic and overseas divisions. Below we examine the basic building blocks of organizational structure to understand how it shapes the behavior of people, functions, and divisions.

Building Blocks of Organizational Structure

The basic building blocks of organizational structure are differentiation and integration. **Differentiation** is the way in which a company allocates people and resources to organizational tasks in order to create value.[2] Generally, the greater the number of different functions or divisions in an organization and the more skilled and specialized they are, the higher is the level of differentiation. For example, a company such as General Electric, which has more than 300 different divisions and a multitude of different sales and R&D departments, has a much higher level of differentiation than a small manufacturing company or a national restaurant chain. In deciding how to differentiate the organization to create value, strategic managers face two choices.

First, strategic managers must choose how to distribute *decision-making authority* in the organization to control value creation activities best; these are **vertical differentiation** choices.[3] For example, corporate managers must decide how much authority to delegate to managers at the divisional or functional level. Second, corporate managers must choose how to divide people and tasks into functions and divisions to increase their ability to create value; these are **horizontal differentiation** choices. Should there be separate sales and marketing departments, for example, or should the two be combined? What is the best way to divide the sales force to maximize its ability to serve customers' needs—by type of customer or by region in which customers are located?

Integration is the means by which a company seeks to coordinate people and functions to accomplish organizational tasks.[4] As we have just noted, when separate and distinct value creation functions exist, they tend to pursue their own goals and objectives. An organization has to create an organizational structure that encourages the different functions and divisions to coordinate their activities. An organization uses integrating mechanisms and control systems to promote coordination and cooperation between functions and divisions. In Microsoft and Google, for instance, to speed innovation and product development, these companies have established teams

---

Differentiation

The way in which a company allocates people and resources to organizational tasks and divides them into functions and divisions so as to create value.

Vertical Differentiation

The process by which strategic managers choose how to distribute decision-making authority over value creation activities in an organization.

Horizontal Differentiation

The process by which strategic managers choose how to divide people and tasks into functions and divisions to increase their ability to create value.

Integration

The means a company uses to coordinate people, functions, and divisions to accomplish organizational tasks.

so that employees could work together to exchange information and ideas and co-operate effectively. Similarly, establishing organizational norms, shared values, and a common culture that supports innovation promotes integration.

In short, differentiation consists of the way a company divides itself into parts (functions and divisions), and integration consists of the way those parts are then combined. Together, the two processes determine how an organizational structure will operate and how successfully strategic managers will be able to create value through their chosen strategies. Consequently, it is necessary to understand the principles behind organizational design. We start by looking at differentiation.

VERTICAL DIFFERENTIATION

The aim of vertical differentiation is to specify the reporting relationships that link people, tasks, and functions at all levels of a company. Fundamentally, this means that management chooses the appropriate number of hierarchical levels and the correct span of control for implementing a company's strategy most effectively.

The organizational hierarchy establishes the authority structure from the top to the bottom of the organization. The **span of control** is defined as the number of subordinates a manager directly manages.[5] The basic choice is whether to aim for a **flat structure**, with few hierarchical levels and thus a relatively wide span of control, or a **tall structure**, with many levels and thus a relatively narrow span of control (see Figure 9.1). Tall structures have many hierarchical levels relative to their size, and flat structures have relatively few.[6] For example, research suggests that the average

Span of Control

The number of subordinates a manager directly manages.

Flat Structure

A structure with few hierarchical levels and a relatively wide span of control.

Tall Structure

A structure with many hierarchical levels and a relatively narrow span of control.

Figure 9.1 Tall and Flat Structures

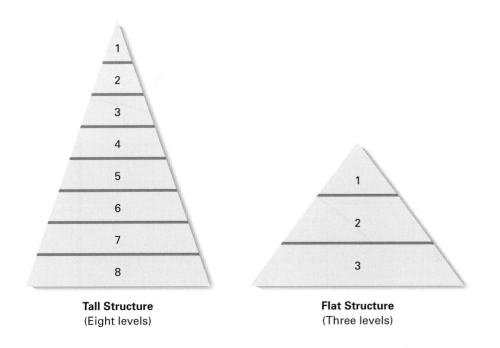

Tall Structure
(Eight levels)

Flat Structure
(Three levels)

number of hierarchical levels for a company employing 3,000 people is seven. Thus, such an organization having nine levels would be called tall, and one having four would be called flat. With its 22,000 employees and five hierarchical levels, Google, for instance, has a relatively flat structure.

Companies choose the number of levels they need on the basis of their strategy and the functional tasks necessary to achieve this strategy.[7] High-tech companies, for example, often pursue a strategy of differentiation based on service and quality. Consequently, these companies usually have flat structures, giving employees wide discretion to meet customers' demands without having to consult constantly with supervisors.[8] The crux of the matter is that the allocation of authority and responsibility in a company must match the needs of its corporate-, business-, and functional-level strategies.[9]

Problems with Tall Structures

As a company grows and diversifies, the number of levels in its hierarchy of authority increases to allow it to monitor and coordinate employee activities efficiently. Research shows that the number of hierarchical levels relative to company size is predictable as the size increases (see Figure 9.2).[10]

Companies with approximately 1,000 employees usually have four levels in the hierarchy: chief executive officer (CEO), departmental vice presidents, first-line supervisors, and shop-floor employees. Those with 3,000 employees normally increase their level of vertical differentiation by raising the number of levels to seven. However, something interesting happens to companies that employ more than 3,000 employees. Even when companies grow to 10,000 employees or more, the number of hierarchical levels rarely increases beyond nine or ten. As organizations grow, managers work to limit the number of hierarchical levels.

Figure 9.2   Relationship Between Company Size
and Number of Hierarchical Levels

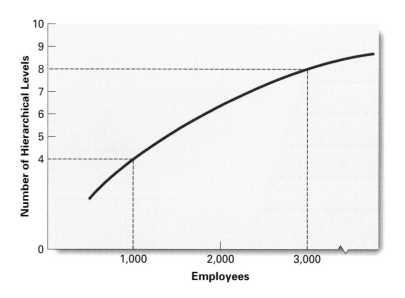

Managers try to keep the organization as flat as possible and follow what is known as the **principle of the minimum chain of command**, which states that an organization should choose a hierarchy with the minimum number of levels of authority necessary to achieve its strategy. Managers try to keep the hierarchy as flat as possible because when companies become too tall, several problems arise that make strategy more difficult to implement.[11]

Coordination Problems   Having too many hierarchical levels impedes communication and coordination between employees and functions and also raises costs. Communication between the top and the bottom of the hierarchy takes much longer as the chain of command lengthens. This leads to inflexibility, and valuable time is lost in bringing a new product to market or in keeping up with technological developments.[12] For FedEx, rapid communication and coordination is vital, so the company allows a maximum of only five layers of management between employees and the CEO.[13] In contrast, Procter & Gamble had a tall hierarchy, and the company needed twice as much time as its competitors to introduce new products. To improve coordination and reduce costs, the company moved to streamline its structure and reduce its number of hierarchical levels.[14] Other companies have also taken measures to flatten their structures to speed communication and decision making.

Information Distortion   More subtle, but just as important, are the problems of information distortion that occur as the hierarchy of authority lengthens. Going down the hierarchy, managers at different levels (for example, divisional or corporate managers) may misinterpret information, either through accidental garbling of messages or on purpose to suit their own interests. In either case, information from the top may not reach its destination intact. For instance, a request to share divisional knowledge to achieve gains from synergy may be overlooked or ignored by divisional managers who perceive it as a threat to their autonomy and power. Information transmitted upward in the hierarchy may also be distorted. Subordinates may transmit to their superiors only the information that enhances their own standing in the organization. The greater the number of hierarchical levels, the more scope subordinates have to distort facts and, as a consequence, the costs of managing the hierarchy increase.

Motivational Problems   As the number of levels in the hierarchy increases, the amount of authority possessed by managers at each hierarchical level diminishes. For example, consider the situation of two organizations of identical size, one of which has three levels in its hierarchy and the other seven. Managers in the flat structure have much more authority, and greater authority increases their motivation to perform effectively and take responsibility for the organization's performance. Besides, when there are fewer managers, their performance is more visible, so they can expect greater rewards when the business does well.

By contrast, the ability of managers in a tall structure to exercise authority is limited, and their decisions are constantly scrutinized by their superiors. As a result, managers tend to pass the buck and refuse to take the risks that are often necessary when new strategies are pursued. This increases the costs of coordination because more managerial time must be spent coordinating task activities. Thus, the shape of the organization's structure strongly affects the motivation of people within it and the way strategy is implemented.[15]

Principle of the Minimum Chain of Command

The principle that managers should choose a hierarchy with the minimum number of levels of authority necessary to achieve its strategy.

Too Many Middle Managers   Another drawback of tall structures is that having many hierarchical levels implies having many middle managers, and employing managers is expensive. As noted earlier, managerial salaries, benefits, offices, and secretaries are a huge expense for an organization. If the average middle manager costs a company a total of $200,000 a year, then employing 100 "surplus" managers costs $20 million a year. Most large U.S. companies have recognized this fact, and in the 2000s, companies such as IBM, HP, and Procter & Gamble have moved to downsize their hierarchies, terminating thousands of managers to reduce billions in operating costs. Also, when companies grow and are successful, they often hire personnel and create new positions without much regard for the effect of these actions on the organizational hierarchy. Later, when managers review that structure, they frequently act to reduce the number of levels because of the disadvantages we have noted.

In sum, when companies become too tall and the chain of command becomes too long, strategic managers tend to lose control over the hierarchy, which means that they lose control over their strategies. Disaster often follows because a tall organizational structure decreases, rather than promotes, motivation and coordination between employees and functions, and operating costs escalate as a result. One way to address such problems and lower costs is to decentralize authority—that is, to vest authority in the hierarchy's lower levels as well as at the top.

Centralization or Decentralization?

Authority is centralized when managers at the upper levels of the organizational hierarchy retain the authority to make the most important decisions. When authority is decentralized, it is delegated to divisions, functions, and managers and workers at lower levels in the organization. By delegating authority in this fashion, managers can avoid communication and coordination problems because information does not have to be constantly sent to the top of the organization for decisions to be made. Decentralization has three main advantages:

1. When strategic managers delegate operational decision-making responsibility to middle and first-level managers, they reduce information overload, enabling strategic managers to spend more time on strategic decision making. Consequently, they can make more effective decisions.
2. When managers in the bottom layers of the organization become responsible for adapting the organization to local conditions, their motivation and accountability increase. The result is that decentralization promotes organizational flexibility because lower-level managers are authorized to make on-the-spot decisions. This can often provide a company with a significant competitive advantage. Companies such as IBM and Dell empower their employees and allow them to make significant decisions so that they can respond quickly to customers' needs and so ensure superior service.
3. When lower-level employees are given the right to make important decisions, fewer managers are needed to oversee their activities and tell them what to do. And fewer managers mean lower costs.

If decentralization is so effective, why don't all companies decentralize decision making and avoid the problems of tall hierarchies? The answer is that centralization has its advantages, too. First, centralized decision making facilitates coordination of the organizational activities needed to pursue a company's strategy. If managers at all levels can make their own decisions, overall planning becomes extremely difficult, and the company may lose control of its decision making. Second, centralization also means that decisions fit broad organizational objectives. When its branch operations were getting out of hand, for example, Merrill Lynch increased centralization by installing more information systems to give corporate managers greater control over branch activities. Similarly, HP centralized R&D responsibility at the corporate level to provide a more directed corporate strategy and to lower operating costs across its growing number of operating divisions.

9.1 STRATEGY IN ACTION

To Centralize or Decentralize? That Is the Question

Union Pacific (UP), one of the biggest rail freight carriers in the United States, was experiencing a crisis in the 1990s. An economic boom had led to a record increase in the amount of freight the railroad had to transport—but, at the same time, the railroad was experiencing record delays in moving the freight. UP's customers were irate and complaining bitterly about the problem, and the delays were costing the company millions of dollars in penalty payments. The problem stemmed from UP's decision to centralize authority high in the organization to cut costs. All scheduling and route planning were handled centrally at its headquarters to promote operating efficiency. The job of regional managers was largely to ensure the smooth flow of freight through their regions. Now, recognizing that efficiency had to be balanced by the need to be responsive to customers, UP's CEO Dick Davidson announced a sweeping reorganization. In the future, regional, not top managers, would have the authority to make operational decisions; they could alter scheduling and routing to accommodate customer requests even if it raised costs. The goal of the organization was to "return to excellent performance by simplifying our processes and becoming easier to deal with." In deciding to decentralize authority, UP was following the lead of its competitors who had already decentralized their operations; its managers, would continue to "decentralize decision making into the field, while fostering improved customer responsiveness, operational excellence, and personal accountability."

Yahoo!, on the other hand, has been forced by circumstances to pursue a different approach to decentralization. In 2009, after the failed merger between Yahoo! and Microsoft, the company's stock price plunged. Jerry

Wang, one of the company' founders, who had come under intense criticism for preventing the merger, resigned as CEO and was replaced by Carol Bartz. Bartz, with a long history of success in managing online companies, had to move quickly to find ways to reduce Yahoo!'s cost structure and simplify its operations to maintain its strong online brand identity. Intense competition from the growing popularity of new online companies such as Facebook, Twitter, and established companies such as Google and Microsoft were threatening its popularity.

Bartz decided the best way to rebuild Yahoo!'s business model was to recentralize authority. To both gain more control over its different business units and reduce operating costs, she decided to centralize functions that had been previously performed by Yahoo!'s different business units, such as product development and marketing activities. For example, all the company's publishing and advertising functions were centralized and put under the control of Hilary Schneider. The control over Yahoo!'s European, Asian, and emerging markets divisions was centralized and another top Yahoo! executive took control. Her goal was to find out how she could make the company work better. While she was centralizing authority, she was also holding many "town hall" meetings. Bartz was asking Yahoo!'s employees, across all departments, "What would you do if you were me?" Even as she centralized authority to help Yahoo! recover its dominant industry position, she was looking for the input of employees at any level in the hierarchy. Once Yahoo! has regained its competitive advantage, she will likely decentralize authority to increase Yahoo!'s profitability, given her general managerial competences.[16]

HORIZONTAL DIFFERENTIATION

Managing the strategy-structure relationship when the number of hierarchical levels becomes too great is difficult and expensive. Depending on a company's situation, the problems of tall hierarchies can be reduced by decentralization. As company size increases, however, decentralization may become less effective. How, then, as firms grow and diversify, can they operate effectively without becoming too tall or decentralized? How can a firm such as Exxon control 300,000 employees without becoming too bureaucratic and inflexible? There must be alternative ways of creating organizational arrangements to achieve corporate objectives.

The first of these ways is to choose the appropriate form of *horizontal differentiation*—that is, to decide how best to group organizational tasks and activities to meet the objectives of a company's strategies.[17] The kinds of structures that companies can choose among are discussed next.

Functional Structure

The issue facing a company is to find the best way to invest its resources to create an infrastructure that allows it to build the distinctive competencies that increase the amount of value a company can create. As a company grows, two things begin to happen. First, the range of tasks that must be performed expands. For example, it suddenly becomes apparent that a professional accountant or a production manager or a marketing expert is needed to perform specialized tasks. Second, no one person can successfully perform more than one organizational task without becoming overloaded. The company's founder, for example, can no longer simultaneously make and sell the product. The question that arises is what grouping of activities—what form of horizontal differentiation—can most efficiently handle the needs of the growing company at least cost? The answer for most companies is a functional structure.

Functional structures arrange and group people on the basis of their common expertise and experience or because they use the same resources.[18] For example, engineers are grouped in a function because they perform the same tasks and use the same skills or equipment. Figure 9.3 shows a typical functional structure. Each of the rectangles represents a different functional specialization (research and development, sales and marketing, manufacturing, etc.), and each function concentrates on its own specialized task.

Advantages of a Functional Structure   Functional structures have several advantages. First, if people who perform similar tasks are grouped together, they can learn from one another and become better—more specialized and productive—at what they do. Second, they can monitor each other to make sure that all are performing their tasks effectively and not shirking their responsibilities. As a result, the work process becomes more efficient, reducing manufacturing costs and increasing operational flexibility.

A third important advantage of functional structures is that they give managers greater control of organizational activities. As already noted, many difficulties arise when the number of levels in the hierarchy increases. If people are grouped into different functions, however, each with their own managers, then *several different hierarchies are created,* and the company can avoid becoming too tall. There will be one hierarchy in manufacturing, for example, and another in accounting and finance. Managing the business is much easier when different groups specialize in different organizational tasks and are managed separately.

Functional Structure

A structure in which people are grouped on the basis of their common expertise and experience or because they use the same resources.

Figure 9.3   Functional Structure

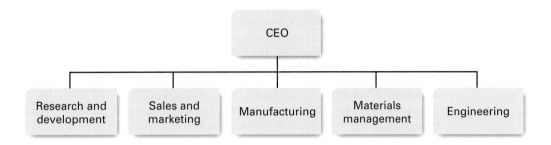

Disadvantages of a Functional Structure   In adopting a functional structure, a company increases its level of horizontal differentiation to handle more complex tasks. The structure enables it to keep control of its activities as it grows. This structure serves the company well until it starts to grow and diversify. If the company becomes geographically diverse and begins operating in many locations, or if it starts producing a wide range of products, control and coordination problems arise that undermine a company's ability to coordinate its activities and reduce costs.[19]

Communications Problems   As separate functional hierarchies evolve, functions grow more remote from one another. As a result, it becomes increasingly difficult to communicate across functions and to coordinate their activities. This communication problem arises because with greater differentiation, the various functions develop different orientations toward the problems and issues facing the organization. Different functions have different time or goal orientations, for example. Some, such as manufacturing, see things in a short time frame and concentrate on achieving short-run goals, such as reducing manufacturing costs. Others, such as R&D, see things from a long-term point of view, and their goals (innovation and product development) may have a time horizon of several years. These factors may cause each function to develop a different view of the strategic issues facing the company. Manufacturing, for example, may see the strategic issue as the need to reduce costs, sales may see it as the need to increase customer responsiveness, and R&D may see it as the need to create new products. In such cases, functions have trouble coordinating with one another, and costs increase.

Measurement Problems   As the number of its products grows, a company may find it difficult to measure the contribution of one or a few products to its overall profitability. Consequently, the company may turn out some unprofitable products without realizing it and so make poor resource allocation decisions. This means that the company's measurement systems are not complex enough to serve its needs. Dell's explosive growth in the early 1990s, for example, caused it to lose control of its inventory management systems; soon it could not accurately project supply and demand for the components that go into its personal computers. Problems with its organizational structure plagued Dell, reducing efficiency and quality. As one manager commented, designing its structure to keep pace with its growth was like building a high-performance car while going around the race track. Dell succeeded until the mid-2000s and it enjoyed a 20% cost advantage over competitors such as HP and Acer because of its innovative organizational design. However, HP and

Acer imitated Dell's innovations and by 2007 they had caught up with Dell and then overtook it to become the lowest cost PC makers.

Location Problems   Location factors may also hamper coordination and control. If a company makes and sells in many different regions, then the centralized system of control provided by the functional structure no longer suits it because managers in the various regions must have the flexibility to respond to the needs of their customers. Thus, the functional structure is not complex enough to handle regional diversity.

Strategic Problems   Sometimes the combined effect of all these factors is that long-term strategic considerations are frequently ignored because management is preoccupied with solving communication and coordination problems. As a result, a company may lose direction and fail to take advantage of new opportunities while costs escalate.

Experiencing these problems is a sign that the company does not have an appropriate form of differentiation to achieve its objectives. A company must change its mix of vertical and horizontal differentiation if it is to perform effectively the organizational tasks that will enhance its competitive advantage. Essentially, these problems indicate that the company has outgrown its structure. It needs to invest resources in developing a more complex structure, one that can meet the needs of its competitive strategy. Once again, this is expensive, but as long as the value a company can create is greater than the costs of operating the structure, it makes sense to adopt a more complex structure. To this end, many companies reorganize, adopting a product, geographic, or product-team structure depending on the source of the coordination problem.

Product Structure

In the product structure, activities are grouped by product line. The manufacturing function is broken down into different product lines based on the similarities and differences among the products. Figure 9.4 presents a product structure typical of an imaging company. In this company, products are grouped in terms of their being consumer, health, or commercial imaging products. Inside each product group, many kinds of similar products are being manufactured.

Because three different product groupings now exist, the degree of horizontal differentiation in this structure is higher than that in the functional structure. The specialized support functions, such as accounting and sales, are centralized at the top of the organization, but each support function is divided in such a way that personnel tend to specialize in one of the different product categories to avoid communication problems. Thus there may be three groups of accountants, one for each of the three product categories. In sales, separate sales forces dealing with the different product lines may emerge, but because maintaining a single sales function brings economies of scale to selling and distribution, these groups will coordinate their activities. Dell, for example, moved to a product structure based on serving the product needs of different customer groups; the commercial and the public sectors are two such groups. Dell's salespeople specialize in one customer group, but all groups coordinate their sales activities to ensure good communication and the transfer of knowledge among product lines.

The use of a product structure reduces the problems of control and coordination associated with the functional structure. It pushes aside barriers among functions because the product line, rather than each individual function, becomes the focus

Figure 9.4   Product Structure

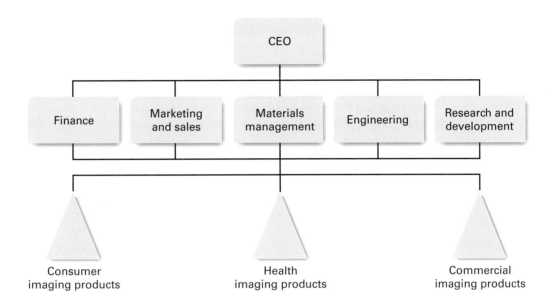

of attention. In addition, the profit contribution of each product line can be clearly identified, and resources can be allocated more efficiently. Note also that this structure has one more level in the hierarchy than the functional structure—that of the product line manager. This increase in vertical differentiation allows managers at the level of the production line to concentrate on day-to-day operations and gives top managers more time to develop the company's competitive advantage. Although operating costs are higher, that expense is warranted by the extra coordination and control the structure provides.

Another example of a company that adopted a product structure to manage its product lines is Maytag. Initially, when it manufactured only washers and dryers, Maytag used a functional structure. In trying to increase its market share, however, Maytag bought two other appliance manufacturers: Jenn-Air, known for its electric ranges, and Hardwick, which made gas ranges. Maytag moved to a product structure, and each company operated as a separate product line, but major specialized support functions were centralized to reduce costs (this is similar to the structure of the imaging company shown in Figure 9.4). Maytag continued to diversify, however, and, as we discuss in the next section, it then needed to move to a multidivisional structure to manage its strategy more effectively.

Product-Team Structure

A major structural innovation in recent years has been the product-team structure. In today's competitive environment, many companies have been forced to find better ways of coordinating their support functions in order to bring their products to market more rapidly and protect their competitive advantage. One way to do this is to use cross functional teams and develop a product-team structure (see Figure 9.5).

Figure 9.5 Product-Team Structure

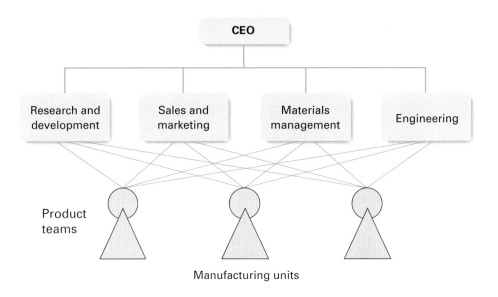

In the product-team structure, as in the product structure, task activities are divided along product lines to reduce costs and increase management's ability to monitor and control the manufacturing process. However, specialists are taken from the various support functions and assigned to work on a product or project, where they are combined into cross-functional teams to serve the needs of the product. These teams are formed right at the beginning of the product development process so that any problems that arise can be ironed out early, before they lead to major redesign problems. When all functions have direct input from the beginning, design costs and subsequent manufacturing costs can be kept low. Moreover, the use of cross-functional teams can speed innovation and responsiveness to customers, because when authority is decentralized to the team, decisions can be made more quickly.

Geographic Structure

When a company is organized geographically, geographic regions become the basis for the grouping of organizational activities. For example, a company may divide up its manufacturing operations and establish manufacturing plants in different regions of the country. This allows it to be responsive to the needs of regional customers and reduces transportation costs. Similarly, service organizations such as store chains and banks may organize their sales and marketing activities on a regional, rather than national, level to get closer to their customers. Like a product structure, a geographic structure provides more control than a functional structure because there are several regional hierarchies carrying out the work previously performed by a single centralized hierarchy. A company like FedEx clearly needs a geographic structure to fulfill its corporate goal: next-day mail. Large merchandising organizations, such as Neiman Marcus, Dillard's, and Walmart, also moved to a geographic structure soon after they started building stores across the country. With a geographic structure,

Figure 9.6   Geographic Structure

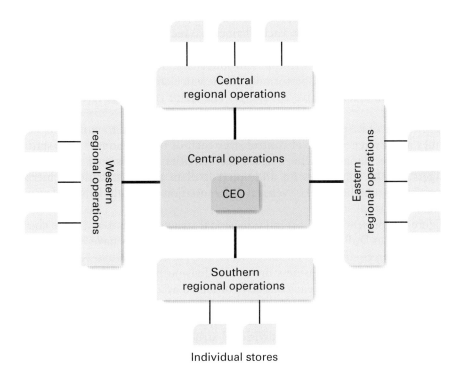

Individual stores

different regional clothing needs—sun wear in the West, down coats in the East—can be handled as required. At the same time, because the purchasing function remains centralized, one central organization can buy for all regions. Thus a company both achieves economies of scale in buying and distribution and reduces coordination and communication problems. For example, Neiman Marcus developed a geographic structure similar to the one shown on Figure 9.6 to manage its nationwide store chain.

In each region, it established a team of regional buyers to respond to the needs of customers in each of the Western, Central, Eastern, and Southern regions. The regional buyers then fed their information to the central buyers at corporate headquarters, who coordinated their demands in order to obtain purchasing economies and to ensure that Neiman Marcus's high-quality standards, on which its differentiation advantage depends, were maintained nationally. Today, it is the most profitable luxury department store chain.

Once again, however, the usefulness of the product or geographic structure depends on the size of the company and its range of products and regions. If a company starts to diversify into unrelated products or to integrate vertically into new industries, the product structure will not be capable of handling the increased diversity. The reason is that it does not allow managers to coordinate the company's value creation activities effectively; it is not complex enough to deal with the needs of the large, multi business company. At this point in its development, the company would normally adopt the multidivisional structure.

Multidivisional Structure

The multidivisional structure possesses two main advantages over a functional structure, innovations that let a company grow and diversify yet overcome problems that stem from loss of control. First, each distinct product line or business unit is placed in its own *self-contained unit or division,* with all support functions. For example, GE competes in more than 150 different industries, and in each industry, all of its divisions are self-contained, performing all the value creation functions necessary to give the division a competitive advantage. The result is a higher level of horizontal differentiation.

Second, the office of *corporate headquarters staff* is created to monitor divisional activities and exercise financial control over each of the divisions.[20] This staff contains corporate managers who oversee the activities of divisional and functional managers, and it constitutes an additional level in the organizational hierarchy. Hence, there is a higher level of vertical differentiation in a multidivisional structure than in a functional structure.

Figure 9.7 presents a typical multidivisional structure found in a large chemical company such as DuPont. Although this company might easily have 70 operating divisions, only three—the oil, pharmaceuticals, and plastics divisions—are represented here. As a self-contained business unit, each division possesses a full array of support services. For example, each has self-contained accounting, sales, and personnel departments. Each division functions as a profit center, which makes it much easier for corporate headquarters staff to monitor and evaluate each division's activities.[21]

The costs of operating a multidivisional structure are very high compared with the costs of a functional structure. The size of the corporate staff is a major expense,

Figure 9.7 Multidivisional Structure

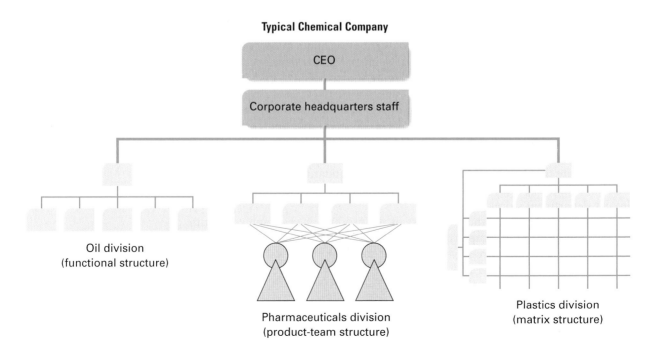

Typical Chemical Company

Oil division
(functional structure)

Pharmaceuticals division
(product-team structure)

Plastics division
(matrix structure)

and while thousands of managers remain on the corporate staff of large companies such as IBM and Ford, all companies today make major efforts to keep their number to a minimum. Similarly, the use of product divisions, each with its own specialist support functions, such as research and development and marketing, is a major expense. Here again, however, if higher operating costs are offset by a higher level of value creation, it makes sense to move to a more complex structure.

Each division is also able to adopt the structure that best suits its needs. Figure 9.7 shows that the oil division has a functional structure because its activities are standardized; the pharmaceuticals division has a product-team structure; and the plastics division has a matrix structure. In a **matrix structure**, functional managers work with project managers in temporary teams to develop a new product. But once the product is completed, functional and project managers move to new teams where they can apply their skills to develop a string of new products.

Similarly, Microsoft operates its corporation through a multidivisional structure, but each division is part of a different product group depending on the kind of software or hardware that it is responsible for developing.

In the multidivisional structure, day-to-day operations of a division are the responsibility of divisional management; that is, divisional management has **operating responsibility**. Corporate headquarters staff, however, which includes members of the board of directors as well as top executives, is responsible for overseeing long-term plans and providing the guidance for interdivisional projects. This staff has **strategic responsibility**. Such a combination of self-contained divisions with a centralized corporate management represents a higher level of both vertical and horizontal differentiation, as noted earlier.

These two innovations provide the extra control necessary to coordinate growth and diversification. Because this structure, despite its high costs, has now been adopted by more than 90% of all large U.S. corporations, we need to consider its advantages and disadvantages in more detail.

Advantages of a Multidivisional Structure   When managed effectively at both the corporate level and the divisional level, a multidivisional structure offers several advantages. Together, they can raise corporate profitability to a new peak because they enable the organization to operate more complex kinds of corporate-level strategies.

Enhanced Corporate Financial Control   The profitability of different business divisions is clearly visible in the multidivisional structure.[22] Because each division is its own profit center, financial controls can be applied to each business on the basis of profit criteria. Corporate managers establish performance goals for each division, monitor their performance on a regular basis, and selectively intervene when problems arise. They can then use this information to identify the divisions in which investment of the company's financial resources will yield the greatest long-term ROIC. As a result, they can allocate the company's funds among competing divisions in a way that will maximize the profitability of the *whole* company. Essentially, managers at corporate headquarters act as "internal investors" who channel funds to high-performing divisions in which they will produce the most profits.

Enhanced Strategic Control   The multidivisional structure frees corporate managers from operating responsibilities. The managers thus gains time for contemplating wider long-term strategic issues and for developing responses to environmental

Matrix Structure

A structure in which functional managers work with project managers in temporary teams to develop new products.

Operating Responsibility

In the multidivisional structure, the responsibility of divisional managers for the day-to-day operations of their divisions.

Strategic Responsibility

In the multidivisional structure, responsibility of managers at corporate headquarters for overseeing long-term plans and providing guidance for divisional managers.

changes. The multidivisional structure also enables corporate headquarters to obtain the information it needs to perform strategic planning functions. For example, separating individual businesses is a necessary prerequisite to portfolio planning.

Growth   The multidivisional structure lets the company overcome an organizational limit to its growth. By reducing information overload at the center, corporate managers can handle a greater number of businesses. They can consider opportunities for further growth and diversification. Communication problems are reduced because the same set of standardized accounting and financial control techniques can be used to evaluate all divisions. Corporate managers are also able to implement a policy of management by exception, which means that they intervene only when problems arise.

Stronger Pursuit of Internal Efficiency   Within a functional structure, the interdependence of functional departments means that the *individual* performance of each function inside a company cannot be measured by objective criteria. For example, the profitability of the finance function, marketing function, or manufacturing function cannot be assessed in isolation, because they are only part of the whole. This often means that within the functional structure, considerable degrees of organizational slack—that is, functional resources that are being used unproductively—can go undetected. For example, in order to reduce work pressure within the department and achieve higher personal status, the head of the finance function might employ a larger staff than was necessary, resulting in relatively inefficient operation.

In a multidivisional structure, however, the individual efficiency of each autonomous division can be directly observed and measured in terms of the profit it generates. Autonomy makes divisional managers accountable; they have no excuses for poor performance. The corporate office is thus in a better position to identify inefficiencies.

Disadvantages of a Multidivisional Structure   Because multidivisional structure has a number of powerful advantages, it seems to be the preferred choice of most large, diversified enterprises today. Indeed, research suggests that large companies that adopt this structure outperform those that retain the functional structure.[23] A multidivisional structure has its disadvantages as well, however. Good management can eliminate some of them, but others are inherent in the way the structure operates. Corporate managers have to continually pay attention to the way they operate to detect problems. These disadvantages are discussed next.

Establishing the Divisional–Corporate Authority Relationship   The authority relationship between corporate headquarters and the divisions must be correctly established. The multidivisional structure introduces a new level in the management hierarchy, the corporate level. The problem for corporate managers is to decide how much authority and control to assign to the operating divisions and how much authority to retain at corporate headquarters.

This problem was first noted by Alfred Sloan, who introduced the multidivisional structure at General Motors (which became the first company to adopt it) and created GM's original five automobile divisions: Chevrolet, Pontiac, Oldsmobile, Buick, and Cadillac.[24] What Sloan found, however, was that when corporate managers retained too much power and authority, the managers of operating divisions lacked sufficient autonomy to develop the business strategy that might best meet the needs of the division. On the other hand, when too much authority is delegated to divisions, managers may start to pursue strategies that benefit their own divisional objectives but add little value to the corporation as a whole. As a result, for example, not all of the potential gains from synergy can be achieved.

Thus, the central issue in managing a multidivisional structure is how much authority should be *centralized* at corporate headquarters and how much should be *decentralized* to the divisions. This issue must be decided by each company, taking into account the nature of its business- and corporate-level strategies. There are no easy answers, and, as the environment changes or a company alters its strategies over time, the optimal balance between centralization and decentralization of authority will also change.

Distortion of Information   If corporate headquarters puts too much emphasis on divisional return on investment—for instance, by setting very high and stringent return-on-investment targets—divisional managers may choose to distort the information they supply top management and paint a rosy picture of the present situation at the expense of future profits. That is, divisions may start to pursue strategies that increase short-run profitability but reduce future profitability. The problem stems from too tight financial control. GM suffered from this problem in recent years, as declining performance prompted divisional managers to try to make their divisions look good to corporate headquarters. Managing the corporate-divisional interface requires coping with subtle power issues. Hence, corporate managers must carefully control their interactions with divisional managers to ensure that both the short- and long-term goals of the business are being met.

Competition for Resources   A third problem of managing a multidivisional structure is that the divisions themselves may compete for resources, and this rivalry prevents synergy gains or economies of scope from emerging. For example, the amount of money that corporate personnel have to distribute to the divisions is fixed. Generally, the divisions that can demonstrate the highest return on investment will get the lion's share of the money. In turn, because they have more money to invest in their business, this usually will raise their performance the next year so strong divisions grow ever stronger. Consequently, divisions may actively compete for resources and, by doing so, reduce interdivisional coordination.

Transfer Pricing   Divisional competition may also lead to battles over transfer pricing. One of the main challenges that vertical integration or related diversification imposes is the need to set the prices at which products are transferred between divisions. Rivalry among divisions increases the problem of setting fair prices. Each supplying division tries to set the highest price for its outputs to maximize its own profitability. Such competition can completely undermine the corporate culture and make the company a battleground. Many companies have a history of competition among divisions. Some, of course, may encourage competition if managers believe that it leads to maximum performance.

Focus on Short-Term Research and Development   If extremely high profitability targets are set by corporate headquarters, the danger arises that the divisions will cut back on research and development expenditures to improve the financial performance of the division. Although this inflates divisional performance in the short term, it reduces a division's ability to develop new products and leads to a fall in the stream of long-term profits. Hence, corporate headquarters personnel must carefully control their interactions with the divisions to ensure that both the short-term and long-term goals of the business are being achieved.

High Operating Costs   As noted earlier, because each division possesses its own specialized functions, such as finance and R&D, multidivisional structures are expensive to run and manage. R&D is especially costly, so some companies centralize

Transfer Pricing

Establishment of the prices at which the products produced by one business unit are sold to other company-owned business units.

such functions at the corporate level to serve all divisions. The duplication of specialist services is not a problem if the gains from having separate specialist functions outweigh the costs. Again, strategic managers must decide whether duplication is financially justified. Activities (particularly advisory services and planning functions) are often centralized in times of downturn or recession; divisions, however, are retained as profit centers.

The advantages of divisional structures must be balanced against their disadvantages, but the disadvantages can be managed by an observant, professional management team that is aware of the issues involved. The multidivisional structure is the dominant one today, which clearly suggests its usefulness as a means of managing the multi business corporation.

INTEGRATION AND ORGANIZATIONAL CONTROL

As we have seen, an organization must choose the appropriate form of differentiation to match its strategy. Greater diversification, for example, requires that a company move from a functional structure to a multidivisional structure. Choosing a type of differentiation, however, is only the first organizational design decision to be made. The second decision concerns the level and type of integration and control necessary to make an organizational structure work effectively.

Forms of Integrating Mechanisms

As noted earlier, a company's level of *integration* is the extent to which it seeks to coordinate its value creation activities and make them interdependent. The design issue can be summed up simply: The higher a company's level of differentiation, the higher the level of integration needed to make organizational structure work effectively.[25] Thus, if a company adopts a more complex form of differentiation, it requires a more complex form of integration to accomplish its goals. FedEx, for example, needs a tremendous amount of integration to fulfill its promise of next-day package delivery. It is renowned for its innovative use of integrating mechanisms, such as customer liaison personnel, to coordinate its activities quickly and efficiently.

There is a series of integrating mechanisms a company can use to increase its level of integration as its level of differentiation increases.[26] Some of these mechanisms—on a continuum from simple to complex—are diagrammed in Figure 9.8. Like increasing the level of differentiation, increasing the level of integration is also expensive. There are high costs associated with using managers to coordinate value creation activities. Hence, a company uses more complex integrating mechanisms to coordinate its activities only to the extent necessary to implement its strategy effectively.

Direct Contact   The aim behind establishing direct contact among managers is to set up a context within which managers from different divisions or functions can work together to solve mutual problems. Managers from different functions have different goals and interests but equal authority, so they may tend to compete rather than cooperate when conflicts arise. In a typical functional structure, for example, the heads of each of the functions have equal authority; the nearest common point of authority is the CEO. Consequently, when disputes arise, no mechanism exists to resolve the conflicts except the authority of the boss.

In fact, one sign of conflict in organizations is the number of problems sent up the hierarchy for upper-level managers to solve. This wastes management time and effort, retards strategic decision making, and makes it difficult to create a cooperative culture in the company. For this reason, companies generally choose more complex integrating mechanisms to coordinate interfunctional and divisional activities.

Interdepartmental Liaison Roles   A company can improve its interfunctional coordination through the interdepartmental liaison role. When the volume of contacts between two departments or functions increases, one of the ways of improving coordination is to give one manager in *each* division or function the responsibility for coordinating with the other function. These managers may meet daily, weekly, monthly, or as needed. Figure 9.8a depicts the nature of the liaison role; the small dot represents the manager inside the functional department who has responsibility for coordinating with the other function. The responsibility for coordination is part of a manager's full-time job, but through these roles a permanent relationship forms between the managers involved, greatly easing strains between departments. Furthermore, liaison roles offer a way of transferring information across the organization, which is important in large, anonymous organizations whose employees may not know anyone outside their immediate department.

Temporary Task Forces   When more than two functions or divisions share common problems, direct contact and liaison roles are of limited value because they do not provide enough coordination. The solution is to adopt a more complex integrating mechanism called a task force. The nature of the task force is represented diagrammatically in Figure 9.8b. One member of each function or division is assigned to a task force created to solve a specific problem. Essentially, task forces are *ad hoc committees,* and members are responsible for reporting to their departments on the issues addressed and the solutions recommended. Task forces are temporary because once the problem has been solved, members return to their normal roles in their own departments or are assigned to other task forces. Task force members also perform many of their normal duties while serving on the task force.

Permanent Teams   In many cases, the issues addressed by a task force recur. To deal with these issues effectively, an organization must establish a permanent integrating mechanism, such as a permanent team. An example of a permanent team is a new-product development committee, which is responsible for the choice, design, and marketing of new products. Such an activity obviously requires a great deal of integration among functions if new products are to be successfully introduced, and establishing a permanent integrating mechanism accomplishes this. Intel, for instance, emphasizes teamwork. It devised a council system based on approximately 90 cross-functional groups, which meet regularly to set functional strategy in areas such as engineering and marketing and to develop business-level strategy.

The importance of teams in the management of the organizational structure cannot be overemphasized. Essentially, permanent teams are the organization's *standing committees,* and much of the strategic direction of the organization is formulated in their meetings. Henry Mintzberg, in a study of how the managers of corporations spend their time, discovered that they spend more than 60% of their time in these committees.[27] The reason is not bureaucracy but rather that integration is possible only in intensive, face-to-face sessions, in which managers can understand others' viewpoints and develop a cohesive organizational strategy. The more complex

Figure 9.8 Types of Integrating Mechanisms

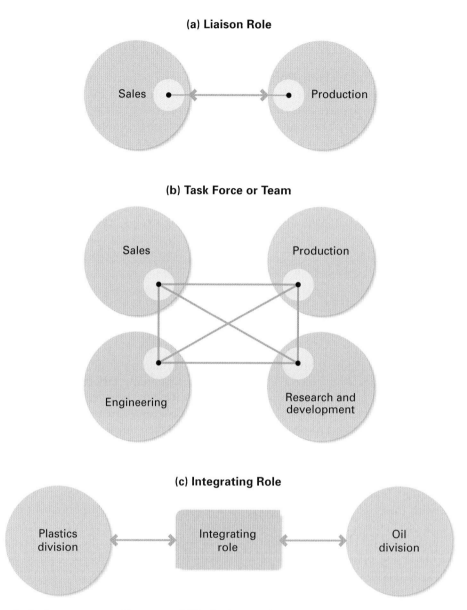

(a) Liaison Role

Sales   Production

(b) Task Force or Team

Sales   Production

Engineering   Research and development

(c) Integrating Role

Plastics division   Integrating role   Oil division

● Indicates manager with responsibility for integration

the company, the more important these teams become. Microsoft, for example, has established a whole new task force and team system to promote integration among divisions and improve corporate performance. As we noted earlier, the product-team structure is based on the use of cross-functional teams to speed products to market. These teams assume the responsibility for all aspects of product development; their goal is to increase coordination and integration among functions.

Integrating Roles   The only function of the integrating role is to prompt integration among divisions or departments; it is a full-time job. As Figure 9.8c indicates, this role is independent of the subunits or divisions being integrated. It is staffed by an independent expert, who is normally a senior manager with a great deal of experience in the joint needs of the two departments. The job is to coordinate the decision process among departments or divisions in order to reap synergetic gains from cooperation. One study found that DuPont had created 160 integrating roles to provide coordination among the different divisions of the company and improve corporate performance.[28] Once again, the more differentiated the company, the more common are these roles. Often people in these roles take the responsibility for chairing task forces and teams, and this provides additional integration. Sometimes the number of integrating roles becomes so high that a permanent integrating department is established at corporate headquarters. Normally, this occurs only in large, diversified corporations that see the need for integration among divisions.

Differentiation and Integration

Clearly, firms have a large number of options available to them when they increase their level of differentiation as a result of increased growth or diversification. The implementation issue is for managers to match differentiation with the level of integration to meet organizational objectives. Note that just as too much differentiation and not enough integration lead to a failure of implementation, the converse is also true. The combination of low differentiation and high integration leads to an over-controlled, bureaucratized organization in which flexibility and speed of response are reduced rather than enhanced by the level of integration. Besides, too much integration is expensive for the company because it raises costs. For these reasons, the goal is to decide on the optimum amount of integration necessary for meeting organizational goals and objectives. A company needs to operate the simplest structure consistent with implementing its strategy effectively.

In practice, integrating mechanisms are only the first means through which a company seeks to increase its ability to coordinate its activities. Control systems are a second.

THE NATURE OF ORGANIZATIONAL CONTROL

Organizational control is the process by which managers monitor the ongoing activities of an organization and its members to evaluate whether activities are being performed efficiently and effectively and to take corrective action to improve performance if they are not. First, strategic managers choose the organizational strategy and structure they hope will allow the organization to use its resources most effectively to create value for its customers. Second, strategic managers create control systems to monitor and evaluate whether, in fact, their organization's strategy and structure are working as managers intended, how they could be improved, and how they should be changed if they are not working.

Organizational control does not just mean reacting to events *after* they have occurred; it also means keeping an organization on track, anticipating events that might occur, and responding swiftly to new opportunities that present themselves. For this reason, control is a strategic process. Companies develop *strategic control systems* that establish ambitious goals and targets for all managers and employees,

Organizational Control

The process by which managers monitor the ongoing activities of an organization and its members to evaluate whether activities are being performed efficiently and effectively and to take corrective action to improve performance if they are not.

and then they develop *performance measures* that stretch and encourage mangers and employees to excel in their quest to raise performance. Thus, control is not just about monitoring how well an organization and its members are achieving current goals or how well the firm is utilizing its existing resources. It is also about keeping employees motivated, focused on the important problems confronting an organization now and for the future, and working together to find ways to change a company so that it will perform better over time.[29]

Strategic Controls

Strategic control systems are developed to measure performance at four levels in an organization: the corporate, divisional, functional, and individual levels. Managers at all levels must develop the most appropriate set of measures to evaluate corporate-, business-, and functional-level performance. These measures should be tied as closely as possibly to the goals of achieving superior efficiency, quality, innovativeness, and responsiveness to customers. Care must be taken, however, to ensure that the standards used at each level do not cause problems at the other levels. Rather, the controls at each level should provide a platform on which managers at the levels below can base their control systems.

Strategic control systems are the formal target-setting, measurement, and feedback systems that allow strategic managers to evaluate whether a company is achieving superior efficiency, quality, innovation, and customer responsiveness and is implementing its strategy successfully. An effective control system should have three characteristics. It should be *flexible* enough to allow managers to respond as necessary to unexpected events; it should provide *accurate information*, giving a true picture of organizational performance; and it should supply managers with the information in a *timely manner* because making decisions on the basis of outdated information is a recipe for failure.[30] As Figure 9.9 shows, designing an effective strategic control system requires four steps.

Strategic Control Systems

The formal target-setting, measurement, and feedback systems that enable strategic managers to evaluate whether a company is implementing its strategy successfully.

Figure 9.9   Steps in Designing an Effective Control System

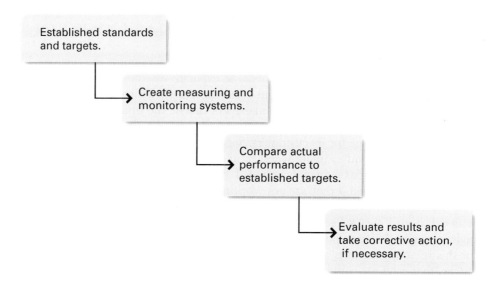

Established standards and targets.

Create measuring and monitoring systems.

Compare actual performance to established targets.

Evaluate results and take corrective action, if necessary.

1. *Establish the standards and targets against which performance is to be evaluated.* The standards and targets that managers select are the ways in which a company chooses to evaluate its performance. General performance standards often derive from the goal of achieving superior efficiency, quality, innovation, or responsiveness to customers. Specific performance targets are derived from the strategy pursued by the company. For example, if a company is pursuing a low-cost strategy, then reducing costs by 7% a year might be a target. If the company is a service organization such as Walmart or McDonald's, then its standards might include time targets for serving customers or guidelines for food quality.

2. *Create the measuring and monitoring systems that indicate whether the standards and targets are being reached.* The company establishes procedures for assessing whether work goals at all levels in the organization are being achieved. In some cases, measuring performance is fairly straightforward. For example, managers can measure quite easily how many customers their employees serve by counting the number of receipts from the cash register. In many cases, however, measuring performance is difficult because the organization is engaged in many complex activities. How can managers judge how well their research and development department is doing when it may take 5 years for products to be developed? How can they measure the company's performance when the company is entering new markets and serving new customers? How can they evaluate how well divisions are integrating their activities? The answer is that managers need to use various types of control systems, which we discuss later in this chapter.

3. *Compare actual performance against the established targets.* Managers evaluate whether and to what extent performance deviates from the standards and targets developed in step one. If performance is higher, management may decide that it has set the standards too low and may raise them for the next time period. The Japanese are renowned for the way they use targets on the production line to control costs. They are constantly trying to raise performance, and they raise the standards to provide a goal for managers to work toward. On the other hand, if performance is too low, managers must decide whether to take remedial action. This decision is easy when the reasons for poor performance can be identified—for instance, high labor costs. More often, however, the reasons for poor performance are hard to uncover. They may stem from external factors, such as a recession. Alternatively, the cause may be internal. For instance, the research and development laboratory may have underestimated the problems it would encounter or the extra costs of doing unforeseen research.

4. *Initiate corrective action when it is determined that the standards and targets are not being achieved.* The final stage in the control process is to take the corrective action that will allow the organization to meet its goals. Such corrective action may mean changing any aspect of strategy or structure discussed in this book. For example, managers may invest more resources in improving R&D, or diversify, or even decide to change their organizational structure. The goal is continuously to enhance the organization's competitive advantage.

Table 9.1 shows the various types of strategic control systems that managers can use to monitor and coordinate organizational activities. Each of these types of control, along with its use at the corporate, divisional, functional, and individual levels, is discussed next.

Table 9.1 Types of Control Systems

Financial Controls	Output Controls	Behavior Controls	Organizational Controls
Stock price	Divisional goals	Budgets	Values
ROI	Functional goals	Standardization	Norms
	Individual goals	Rules and procedures	Socialization

Financial Controls

The measures most commonly used by managers and other stakeholders to monitor and evaluate a company's performance are financial controls. Typically, strategic managers select financial goals they wish their company to achieve (such as goals related to growth, profitability, and/or return to shareholders), and then they measure whether or not these goals have been achieved. One reason for the popularity of financial performance measures is that they are objective. The performance of one company can be compared with that of another in terms of its stock market price, return on investment, market share, or even cash flow so that strategic managers and other stakeholders, particularly shareholders, have some way of judging their company's performance relative to that of other companies.

Stock price, for example, is a useful measure of a company's performance, primarily because the price of the stock is determined competitively by the number of buyers and sellers in the market. The stock's value is an indication of the market's *expectations* for the firm's future performance. Thus, movements in the price of a stock provide shareholders with feedback on a company's and its manager's performance. Stock market price acts as an important measure of performance because top managers watch it closely and are sensitive to its rise and fall—particularly its fall! When Ford's stock price plunged in the 2000s, for example, its then CEO Bill Ford, and present CEO Alan Mulally, heeded its shareholders' complaints that Ford's operating costs were too high. In response, they both took radical steps, such as laying off thousands of employees and closing many plants to reduce costs in order to boost the company's profitability and stock price. Finally, because stock price reflects the long-term future return from the stock, it can be regarded as an indicator of the company's long-run potential.

Return on investment (ROI), a measure of profitability determined by dividing net income by invested capital, is another popular kind of financial control. At the corporate level, the performance of the whole company can be evaluated *against* that of other companies to assess its relative performance. Top managers, for example, can assess how well their strategies have worked by comparing their company's performance against that of similar companies. In the PC industry, companies such as Dell, HP, and Apple use ROI to gauge their performance relative to that of their competitors. A declining ROI signals a potential problem with a company's strategy or structure. When HP's ROI fell in relation to Dell's in the early 2000s because HP could not match the efficiency of Dell's inventory management systems, this signaled to its managers the need to find new and improved materials management strategies. By 2007 they had succeeded and HP overtook Dell to become the largest global PC maker.

ROI can also be used inside the company at the divisional level to judge the performance of an operating division by comparing it to that of a similar freestanding business or other internal division. Indeed, one reason for selecting a multidivisional structure is that each division can be evaluated as a self-contained profit center. Consequently, management can directly measure the performance of one division against that of another. HP moved to a divisional structure partly because it gave corporate managers information about the relative costs of its various divisions, allowing them to base capital allocations on the divisions' relative performance.

Similarly, manufacturing companies often establish production facilities at different locations, domestically and globally, so that they can measure the performance of one against the other. For example, Xerox was able to identify the relative inefficiency of its U.S. division by comparing its profitability with that of its Japanese counterpart. ROI is a powerful form of control at the divisional level, especially if divisional managers are rewarded on the basis of their performance vis-à-vis other divisions. The most successful divisional managers are promoted to become the next generation of corporate executives.

Failure to meet stock price or ROI targets also indicates that corrective action is necessary. It signals the need for corporate reorganization in order to meet corporate objectives, and such reorganization can involve a change in structure or the liquidation and divestiture of businesses. It can also indicate the need for new strategic leadership. In recent years, the CEOs of Merck, Ford, and Motorola have all been ousted by disgruntled boards of directors, dismayed at the declining performance of their companies relative to that of competitors.

Output Controls

Financial goals and controls are important, but it is also necessary to develop goals and controls that tell managers how well their strategies are creating a competitive advantage and building distinctive competences and capabilities that will lead to future success. When strategic managers establish goals and measures to evaluate efficiency, quality, innovation, and responsiveness to customers, they are using output control. In **output control**, strategic managers estimate or forecast appropriate performance goals for each division, department, and employee and then measure actual performance relative to these goals. Often a company's reward system is linked to performance on these goals, so that output control also provides an incentive structure for motivating employees at all levels in the organization.

Divisional Goals   Divisional goals state corporate managers' expectations for each division's performance on such dimensions as efficiency, quality, innovation, and responsiveness to customers. Generally, corporate managers set challenging divisional goals to encourage divisional managers to create more effective strategies and structures in the future. At GE, for example, CEO Jeffrey Immelt sets clear performance goals for GE's more than 150 divisions. He expects each division to be number one or number two in its industry in terms of market share. Divisional managers are given considerable autonomy to formulate a strategy to meet this goal (to find ways to increase efficiency, innovation, etc.), and the divisions that fail are divested.

Functional and Individual Goals   Output control at the functional and individual levels is a continuation of control at the divisional level. Divisional managers set goals for functional managers that will allow the division to achieve *its* goals. As at

Output Control

A system of control in which strategic managers estimate or forecast appropriate performance goals for each division, department, and employee and then measure actual performance relative to these goals.

the divisional level, functional goals are established to encourage development of competencies that give the company a competitive advantage. The same four building blocks of competitive advantage (efficiency, quality, innovation, and customer responsiveness) act as the standards against which functional performance is evaluated. In the sales function, for example, goals related to efficiency (such as cost of sales), quality (such as number of returns), and customer responsiveness (such as the time needed to respond to customer needs) can be established for the whole function.

Finally, functional managers establish goals that individual employees are expected to achieve to allow the function to achieve its goals. Sales personnel, for example, can be given specific goals (related to functional goals) that they in turn are required to achieve. Functions and individuals are then evaluated on the basis of whether they achieve their goals—and in sales, compensation is commonly pegged to achievement. The achievement of these goals is a sign that the company's strategy is working and it is meeting organizational objectives.

Behavior Control

The first step in strategy implementation is for managers to design the right kind of organizational structure. To make the structure work, however, employees must learn the kinds of behaviors they are expected to perform. Using managers to tell employees what to do lengthens the organizational hierarchy, is expensive, and raises costs; consequently, strategic managers rely on behavior controls. **Behavior control** is control through the establishment of a comprehensive system of rules and procedures to direct the actions or behavior of divisions, functions, and individuals.[31]

The objective of using behavior controls is not to specify the goals but to standardize the way of reaching them. Rules standardize behavior and make outcomes predictable. If employees follow the rules, then actions are performed and decisions handled the same way, time and time again. The result is predictability and accuracy, the aim of all control systems. The main kinds of behavior controls are operating budgets, standardization, rules and procedures, and organizational culture.

Behavior Control

A system of control based on the establishment of a comprehensive system of rules and procedures to direct the actions or behavior of divisions, functions, and individuals.

Operating Budget

A blueprint that states how managers intend to use organizational resources to achieve organizational goals most efficiently.

Operating Budgets   Once managers at each level have been given a goal to achieve, operating budgets that regulate how managers and workers are to attain those goals are established. An **operating budget** is a blueprint that states how managers intend to use organizational resources to achieve organizational goals most efficiently. Most often, managers at one level allocate to managers at a lower level a specific amount of resources to use to produce goods and services.

Once they have been given a budget, managers must decide how they will allocate certain amounts of money for different organizational activities. These lower-level managers are then evaluated on the basis of their ability to stay inside the budget and make the best use of it. Thus, for example, managers at GE's washing machine division might have a budget of $50 million to develop and sell a new line of washing machines, and they have to decide how much money to allocate to R&D, engineering, sales, and the other functions so that the division will generate the most revenue and hence make the biggest profit possible. Most commonly, large organizations treat each division as a stand-alone profit center, and corporate managers evaluate each division's performance by its relative contribution to corporate profitability.

Standardization Standardization is the degree to which a company specifies how decisions are to be made so that employees' behavior becomes predictable.[32] In practice, there are three things an organization can standardize: *inputs, conversion activities,* and *output*s. First, an organization can control the behavior of both people and resources by standardizing inputs into the organization. This means that managers screen inputs according to preestablished criteria or standards and then decide which inputs to allow into the organization. If employees are the input in question, one way of standardizing them is to specify which qualities and skills they must possess and then to select only those applicants who possess them. If the inputs in question are raw materials or component parts, the same considerations apply. The Japanese are renowned for the high quality and precise tolerances they demand from component parts to minimize problems with the product at the manufacturing stage. Just-in-time (JIT) inventory systems also help standardize the flow of inputs.

Second, the aim of standardizing conversion activities is to program work activities such that they are done the same way time and time again. The goal is predictability. Behavior controls, such as rules and procedures, are among the chief means by which companies can standardize throughputs. Fast food restaurants such as McDonald's and Burger King, for example, standardize all aspects of their restaurant operations; the result is standardized fast food.

Third, the goal of standardizing outputs is to specify what the performance characteristics of the final product or service should be—what the dimensions or tolerances the product should conform to, for example. To ensure that their products are standardized, companies apply quality control and use various criteria to measure this standardization. One criterion might be the number of goods returned from customers or the number of customers' complaints. On production lines, periodic sampling of products can indicate whether they are meeting performance standards.

Rules and Procedures As with other kinds of controls, the use of behavior control is accompanied by potential pitfalls that must be managed if the organization is to avoid strategic problems. Top management must be careful to monitor and evaluate the usefulness of behavior controls over time. Rules constrain people and lead to standardized, predictable behavior. However, rules are always easier to establish than to get rid of, and over time the number of rules an organization uses tends to increase. As new developments lead to additional rules, often the old rules are not discarded, and the company becomes overly bureaucratized. Consequently, the organization and the people in it become inflexible and are slow to react to changing or unusual circumstances. Such inflexibility can reduce a company's competitive advantage by lowering the pace of innovation and reducing responsiveness to customers.

Similarly, inside the organization, integration and coordination may fall apart as rules impede communication between functions. Managers must therefore be constantly on the alert for opportunities to reduce the number of rules and procedures necessary to manage the business, and they should always prefer to discard a rule rather than add a new one. Hence, reducing the number of rules and procedures to the essential minimum is important. Strategic managers frequently neglect this task, however, and often only a change in strategic leadership brings the company back on course.

Standardization

The degree to which a company specifies how decisions are to be made so that employees' behavior becomes predictable.

Organizational Culture   One important kind of behavioral control that serves this dual function of keeping organizational members goal-directed yet open to new opportunities to use their skills to create value is organizational culture. **Organizational culture** is the specific collection of values and norms that are shared by people and groups in an organization and that control the way they interact with each other and with stakeholders outside the organization.[33] **Organizational values** are beliefs and ideas about what kinds of goals members of an organization *should* pursue and what kinds or standards of behavior employees *should* use to achieve these goals. Bill Gates of Microsoft is famous for the set of organizational values that he created for his company, which include entrepreneurship, ownership, honesty, frankness, and open communication. Gates stressed entrepreneurship and ownership because he wanted Microsoft to operate less like a big bureaucracy and more like a collection of smaller and very adaptive companies. Gates also emphasized giving lower-level managers considerable decision-making autonomy and encouraged them to take risks—that is, to behave more like entrepreneurs and less like corporate bureaucrats. The stress Gates, and its current top managers, place on values such as honesty, frankness, and open communication reflects their belief that an open internal dialogue is necessary for competitive success at Microsoft.

From organizational values develop **organizational norms**, the guidelines or expectations that *prescribe* appropriate kinds of behavior by employees in particular situations and control the behavior of organizational members toward one another. The norms of behavior for software programmers at Microsoft include working long hours and weekends, wearing whatever clothing is comfortable (but never a suit and tie), consuming junk food, and communicating with other employees via electronic mail and the company's state-of-the-art intranet.

Organizational culture functions as a form of control in that strategic managers can influence the values and norms that develop in an organization—values and norms that specify appropriate and inappropriate behaviors and that shape the way its members behave.[34] Strategic managers such as Gates and Michael Dell, for example, deliberately cultivate values that encourage subordinates to perform their roles in innovative and creative ways. They establish and support norms dictating that to be innovative and entrepreneurial, employees should feel free to experiment and go out on a limb even if there is a significant chance of failure.

Managers of other companies, however, might cultivate values that encourage employees always to be conservative and cautious in their dealings with others, to consult their superiors before they make important decisions, and to record their actions in writing so they can be held accountable for what happens. Managers of organizations such as chemical and oil companies, financial institutions, and insurance companies—indeed, any organization in which caution is needed—may encourage such an approach to making decisions.[35] In a bank or mutual fund, the risk of losing all your investors' money makes a cautious approach to investing highly appropriate. Thus, we might expect that managers of different kinds of organizations will deliberately try to cultivate and develop the organizational values and norms that are best suited to their strategy and structure.

Culture and Strategic Leadership   Because both an organization's structure (the design of its task and reporting relationships) and its culture shape employees' behavior, it is crucial to match organizational structure and culture to implement strategy successfully. How do managers design and create their cultures? In general, organizational culture is the product of *strategic leadership* provided by an

---

Organizational Culture

The specific collection of values and norms that are shared by people and groups in an organization and that control the way they interact with each other and with stakeholders outside the organization.

Organizational Values

Beliefs and ideas about what kinds of goals members of an organization should pursue and what behaviors they should use to achieve these goals.

Organizational Norms

Unwritten guidelines or expectations that prescribe the kinds of behavior employees should adopt in particular situations and regulate the way they behave.

organization's founder and top managers. The organization's founder is particularly important in determining culture, because the founder imprints his or her values and management style on the organization. Walt Disney's conservative influence on the company he established continued until well after his death, for example. Managers were afraid to experiment with new forms of entertainment because they were afraid Walt Disney wouldn't have liked it.

The leadership style established by the founder is transmitted to the company's managers, and as the company grows, it typically attracts new managers and employees who share the same values. Moreover, members of the organization typically recruit and select only those who share their values. Thus, a company's culture becomes more and more distinct as its members become more similar.

The virtue of these shared values and common culture is that it *increases integration and improves coordination among organizational members*. For example, the common language that typically emerges in an organization because people share the same beliefs and values facilitates cooperation among managers. Similarly, rules and procedures and direct supervision are less important when shared norms and values regulate behavior and motivate employees. When organizational members subscribe to the organization's cultural norms and values, this bonds them to the organization and increases their commitment to find new ways to help it succeed. That is, such employees are more likely to commit themselves to organizational goals and work actively to develop new skills and competencies to help achieve those goals. Strategic managers need to establish the values and norms that will help them bring their organizations into the future.

Finally, organizational structure contributes to the implementation process by providing the framework of tasks and roles that reduces transaction difficulties and allows employees to think and behave in ways that allow a company to achieve superior performance. The way in which the frugal Sam Walton (he used to drive a 30-year-old pickup truck, for example, and lived in a very modest home) used all the kinds of control systems discussed above to implement Walmart's cost-leadership strategy is very instructive, as discussed in the Running Case.

RUNNING CASE

How Sam Walton Created Walmart's Culture

Walmart, headquartered in Bentonville, Arkansas, is the largest retailer in the world. In 2009, it sold more than $700 billion worth of products. A large part of Walmart's success is due to the nature of the culture that its founder, the late Sam Walton, established for the company. Walton wanted all his managers and workers to take a hands-on approach to their jobs and be totally committed to Walmart's main goal, which he defined as total customer satisfaction. To motivate his employees, Walton created a culture that gave all employees, called "associates," continuous feedback about their performance and the company's performance.

To involve his associates in the business and encourage them to develop work behaviors focused on providing quality customer service, Walton established strong cultural values and norms for his company. One of the norms associates are expected to follow is the

(continued)

"10-foot attitude." This norm encourages associates, in Walton's words, to "promise that whenever you come within 10 feet of a customer, you will look him in the eye, greet him, and ask him if you can help him." The "sundown rule" states that employees should strive to answer customer requests by sundown of the day they are made. The Walmart cheer ("Give me a W, give me an A," etc.) is used in all its stores.

The strong customer-oriented values that Walton created are exemplified in the stories Walmart members tell one another about associates' concern for customers. They include stories like the one about Sheila, who risked her own safety when she jumped in front of a car to prevent a little boy from being struck; about Phyllis, who administered CPR to a customer who had suffered a heart attack in her store; and about Annette, who gave up the Power Ranger she had on layaway for her own son to fulfill the birthday wish of a customer's son. The strong Walmart culture helps to control and motivate employees to achieve the stringent output and financial targets the company sets for itself.

A notable way Walmart builds its culture is through its annual stockholders' meeting, its extravagant ceremony celebrating the company's success. Every year, Walmart flies thousands of its highest performers to its annual meeting at its corporate headquarters in Arkansas for a show featuring famous singers, rock bands, and comedians. Walmart feels that expensive entertainment is a reward its employees deserve and that the event reinforces the company's high-performance values and culture. The proceedings are even broadcast live to all of Walmart's stores so that employees can celebrate the company's achievements together.

Since Sam Walton's death, public attention to Walmart, which has more than 1 million employees, has revealed the "hidden side" of its culture. Critics claim that few Walmart employees receive reasonably priced health care or other benefits, and the company pays employees at little above the minimum wage. They also contend that employees do not question these policies because managers have convinced them into believing that this has to be the case—that the only way Walmart can keep its prices low is by keeping their pay and benefits low. In 2009, Walmart was threatened by proposed changes to health care laws that would force it to pay a much higher percentage of employee benefits. Will its loyal employees decide to follow Sam Walton's 10-foot-attitude rule in the future?[36]

SUMMARY OF CHAPTER

1. Implementing a strategy successfully depends on selecting an organizational structure and control system appropriate to the company's strategy.

2. The basic tool of strategy implementation is organizational design. Good organizational design increases profits in two ways. First, it economizes on operating costs and lowers the costs of value creation activities. Second, it enhances the ability of a company's value creation functions to achieve a differentiation advantage through superior efficiency, quality, innovativeness, and responsiveness to customers.

3. Differentiation and integration are the two design concepts that govern how a structure will work. Differentiation has two aspects: Vertical differentiation reflects how a company chooses to allocate its decision-making authority, and horizontal differentiation reflects the way a company groups organizational activities into functions, departments, or divisions.

4. Tall hierarchies have a number of disadvantages, such as problems with communication and information transfer, motivation, and cost. Decentralization, or delegation of authority, can solve some of these problems, however.

5. Most companies first choose a functional structure. Then, as a company grows and diversifies, it adopts a multidivisional structure. Although a multidivisional structure has higher costs than a functional structure, it overcomes the control problems associated with a functional structure and gives a company the capability to handle its value creation activities effectively.

6. Other kinds of structures include the product, product-team, and geographic structures. Each has a specialized use and, to be effective, must match the needs of the organization.

7. The more complex the company and the higher its level of differentiation, the higher the level of integration needed to manage its structure. The kinds

of integrating mechanisms available to a company range from direct contact to integrating roles. The more complex the mechanism, the greater the costs of using it. A company should take care to match these mechanisms to its strategic needs.

8. Strategic control is the process of setting targets and monitoring, evaluating, and rewarding organizational performance. Managers should develop strategic control systems that measure all important aspects of their organization's performance.

9. Control takes place at all levels in the organization: corporate, divisional, functional, and individual. Effective control systems are flexible,

accurate, and able to provide quick feedback to strategic planners.

10. Control systems range from those directed at measuring outputs to those that measure behaviors or actions. Output controls establish goals for divisions, functions, and individuals. They can be used only when outputs can be objectively measured and are often linked to a "management by objectives" system. Behavior controls are achieved through budgets, standardization, rules and procedures, and organizational culture, the collection of norms and values that govern the way people act and behave inside the organization.

DISCUSSION QUESTIONS

1. What is the difference between vertical differentiation and horizontal differentiation? Rank the various structures discussed in this chapter along these two dimensions.

2. When would a company decide to change from a functional to a multidivisional structure?

3. For each of the structures we discussed in this chapter, outline the most suitable control system.

CLOSING CASE

Strategy Implementation at Dell Computer

Dell Computer was one of the fastest-growing companies of the 1990s, and its stock price increased at the rate of 100% per year, delighting its stockholders. Achieving this high return has been a constant challenge for Michael Dell. One of his biggest battles has been to manage and change Dell's organizational structure, control systems, and culture as his company grows.

Michael Dell was 19 in 1984, when he took $1,000 and spent it on the computer parts he assembled into PCs that he sold over the phone. Increasing demand for his PCs meant that within a few weeks, he needed to hire people to help him. Soon he found himself supervising three employees who worked together around a six-foot table to assemble computers while two more employees took orders over the phone.[37]

By 1993, Dell employed 4,500 workers and was hiring more than 100 new workers each week just

to keep pace with the demand for the computers. When he found himself working 18-hour days managing the company, he realized that he could not lead the company single-handedly. The company's growth had to be managed, and he knew that he had to recruit and hire strategic managers who had experience in managing different functional areas, such as marketing, finance, and manufacturing. He recruited executives from IBM and Compaq. With their help, he created a functional structure, one in which employees were grouped by their common skills or tasks they performed, such as sales or manufacturing, to organize the value chain activities necessary to deliver his PCs to customers. As a part of this organizing process, Dell's structure also became taller, with more levels in the management hierarchy, to ensure that he and his managers had sufficient control over the different activities of his growing business. Michael Dell delegated authority to control Dell's functional value chain activities to his managers, which gave him the time he needed to perform his entrepreneurial task of finding new opportunities for the company.

Dell's functional structure worked well and, under its new management team, the company's growth continued to soar. Moreover, Dell's new structure had given functional managers the control they needed to squeeze out costs, and Dell had become the lowest-cost PC maker. Analysts also reported that Dell had developed a lean organizational culture, meaning that employees had developed norms and values that emphasized the importance of working hard to help each other find innovative new ways of making products to keep costs low and increase their reliability. Indeed, Dell rose to the top of the customer satisfaction rankings for PC makers because few customers complained about its products. Its employees became known for the excellent customer service they gave to PC buyers who were experiencing problems with setting up their computers.

However, Michael Dell realized that new and different kinds of problems were arising. Dell was now selling huge numbers of computers to different kinds of customers, for example, home, business, and educational customers and different branches of government. Because customers were demanding computers with different features or more computing power, the company's product line broadened rapidly. It became more difficult for employees to meet the needs of these customers efficiently because each employee needed information about all product features or all of Dell's thousands of different sales offers across its product range.

By the late 1990s, Michael Dell moved to change his company to a market structure and created separate divisions, each geared to the needs of a different group of customers: a consumer division, a business division, and so on. In each division, teams of employees specialized in servicing the needs of one of these customer groups. This move to a more complex structure also allowed each division to develop a unique subculture that suited its tasks, and employees were able to obtain in-depth knowledge about the needs of their market that helped them to respond better to their customers' needs. So successful was this change in structure and culture that by 2000, Dell's revenues were more than $35 billion

and its profits in excess of $3 billion, a staggering increase from 1984.[38]

Michael Dell has continued to change his company's structure in the 2000s to respond to changing customer needs and increasing competitive challenges from Apple and HP. For example, Michael Dell realized that he could leverage his company's strengths in materials management, manufacturing, and Internet sales over a wider range of computer hardware products. He decided to begin assembling servers, workstations, and storage devices to compete with IBM, Sun, and HP. The increasing importance of the Internet also led him to pay more attention to more specialized groups of customers and find the best way to customize its approach to best meet each group's specific needs over the Internet. Today, for example, Dell can offer large and small companies and private buyers a complete range of computers, workstations, and storage devices that can be customized to their needs.

To help coordinate its growing activities, Dell is increasingly making use of its corporate Intranet to standardize activities across divisions and integrate its activities across functions to reduce costs. Dell's hierarchy is shrinking as managers increasingly delegate decision making to employees who use its advanced IT to access the information they need to provide excellent customer service. To reduce costs, Dell has also outsourced most of its customer service function to India and in June 2010 Dell closed its last U.S. factory and now outsources all its assembly operations to companies in China and Taiwan.[39] As a result of these moves, Dell's smaller U.S. workforce has become even more committed to finding ways to keep costs as low as possible while being responsive to its customers. All members of the organization are working to fight back and regain Dell's low-cost competitive advantage from rivals such as HP and Acer that have imitated its cost-saving strategies.

Case Discussion Questions

1. Why has Dell moved to different kinds of organizational structures over time?
2. Has Dell's performance been improved?
3. Search the Internet to find out how Dell has been trying to increase its performance and how its competitors such as HP and Acer have also been working to improve theirs.

NOTES

1. J. R. Galbraith, *Designing Complex Organizations* (Reading, Mass.: Addison-Wesley, 1973).
2. J. Child, *Organization: A Guide for Managers and Administrators* (New York: Harper & Row, 1977), 50–72.
3. R. H. Miles, *Macro Organizational Behavior* (Santa Monica, Calif.: Goodyear, 1980), 19–20.
4. Galbraith, *Designing Complex Organizations*.
5. V. A. Graicunas, "Relationships in Organizations," in *Papers on the Science of Administration*, ed. L. Gulick and L. Urwick (New York: Institute of Public Administration, 1937), 181–185 and J. C. Worthy, "Organizational Structure and Company Morale," *American Sociological Review* 15 (1950): 169–179.
6. Child, *Organization*, pp. 50–52.
7. G. R. Jones, "Organization-Client Transactions and Organizational Governance Structures," *Academy of Management Journal* 30 (1987): 197–218.
8. H. Mintzberg, *The Structuring of Organizations* (Englewood Cliffs, N.J.: Prentice-Hall, 1979), 435.
9. B. Woolridge and S. W. Floyd, "The Strategy Process, Middle Management Involvement, and Organizational Performance," *Strategic Management Journal* 9 (1990): 231–241.
10. Child, *Organization*, p. 51.
11. R. Carzo Jr. and J. N. Yanousas, "Effects of Flat and Tall Organization Structure," *Administrative Science Quarterly* 14 (1969): 178–191.
12. A. Gupta and V. Govindarajan, "Business Unit Strategy, Managerial Characteristics, and Business Unit Effectiveness at Strategy Implementation," *Academy of Management Journal* 27 (1984): 25–41 and R. T. Lenz, "Determinants of Organizational Performance: An Interdisciplinary Review," *Strategic Management Journal* 2 (1981): 131–154.
13. fedex.com, 2011.
14. www.pg.com, 2011.
15. G. R. Jones, "Task Visibility, Free Riding and Shirking: Explaining the Effect of Organization Structure on Employee Behavior," *Academy of Management Review* 4 (1984): 684–695.
16. http://www.unionpacific.com, 2010; yahoo.com, 2010.
17. R. L. Daft, *Organizational Theory and Design*, 3rd ed. (St. Paul, Minn.: West, 1986), 215.
18. J. R. Galbraith and R. K. Kazanjian, *Strategy Implementation: Structure System and Process*, 2nd ed. (St. Paul, Minn.: West, 1986); Child, *Organization*; and R. Duncan, "What Is the Right Organization Structure?" *Organizational Dynamics*, Winter 1979, 59–80.
19. O. E. Williamson, *Markets and Hierarchies: Analysis and Antitrust Implications* (New York: Free Press, 1975).
20. Alfred D. Chandler, *Strategy and Structure* (Cambridge, Mass.: MIT Press, 1971); Williamson, *Markets and Hierarchies*; and L. Wrigley, *Divisional Autonomy and Diversification* (Ph.D. diss., Harvard Business School, 1970).
21. R. P. Rumelt, *Strategy, Structure, and Economic Performance* (Boston, Mass.: Division of Research, Harvard Business School, 1974); B. R. Scott, *Stages of Corporate Development* (Cambridge, Mass.: Harvard Business School, 1971); and Williamson, *Markets and Hierarchies*.
22. The discussion draws on each of the sources cited in endnotes 10–17 and on G. R. Jones and C. W. L. Hill, "Transaction Cost Analysis of Strategy-Structure Choice," *Strategic Management Journal* 9 (1988): 159–172.
23. H. O. Armour and D. J. Teece, "Organizational Structure and Economic Performance: A Test of the Multidivisional Hypothesis," *Bell Journal of Economics* 9 (1978): 106–122.
24. Alfred Sloan, *My Years at General Motors* (New York: Doubleday, 1983), Ch. 3.
25. P. R. Lawrence and J. Lorsch, *Organization and Environment* (Homewood, Ill.: Irwin, 1967), 50–55.
26. Galbraith, *Designing Complex Organizations*, Ch. 1 and Galbraith and Kazanjian, *Strategy Implementation*, Ch. 7.
27. Henry Mintzberg, *The Nature of Managerial Work* (Englewood Cliffs, N.J.: Prentice-Hall, 1973), Ch. 10.
28. Lawrence and Lorsch, *Organization and Environment*, p. 55.
29. R. Simmons, "Strategic Orientation and Top Management Attention to Control Systems," *Strategic Management Journal* 10 (1991): 49–62.
30. W. G. Ouchi, "The Transmission of Control Through Organizational Hierarchy," *Academy of Management Journal* 21 (1978): 173–192 and W. H. Newman, *Constructive Control* (Englewood Cliffs, N.J.: Prentice-Hall, 1975).
31. O. E. Williamson, *Markets and Hierarchies*; and W. G. Ouchi, "Markets, Bureaucracies, and Clans," *Administrative Science Quarterly* 25 (1980): 109–141.
32. H. Mintzberg, *The Structuring of Organizations* (Englewood Cliffs, N.J.: Prentice-Hall, 1979), 5–9.
33. L. Smircich, "Concepts of Culture and Organizational Analysis," *Administrative Science Quarterly* 28 (1983): 339–358.
34. Ouchi, "Markets, Bureaucracies, and Clans," p. 130.
35. G. R. Jones, *Organizational Theory, Design, and Change*, 6th ed. (Upper Saddle River, N.J.: Prentice Hall, 2007.
36. http:// www.walmart.com, 2009; "Associates Keystone to Structure," *Chain Store Age*, December, 1999, 17; M. Troy, "The Culture Remains the Constant," *Discount Store News*, June 8, 1998, 95–98; S. Voros, "3D Management," *Management Review*, January 2000, 45–47; "Neurosis, Arkansas-Style," *Fortune*, April 17, 2000, 36.
37. http://www.dell.com, 2011.
38. G. McWilliams, "Dell Looks for Ways to Rekindle the Fire It Had as an Upstart," *Wall Street Journal*, August 31, 2000, A.1, A.8 and "Dell Hopes to Lead Firm out of Desert," *Houston Chronicle*, September 3, 2000, 4D.
39. http://www.dell.com, 2011.

ANALYZING A CASE STUDY AND WRITING A CASE STUDY ANALYSIS

WHAT IS CASE STUDY ANALYSIS?

Case study analysis is an integral part of a course in strategic management. The purpose of a case study is to provide students with experience of the strategic management problems that actual organizations face. A case study presents an account of what happened to a business or industry over a number of years. It chronicles the events that managers had to deal with, such as changes in the competitive environment, and charts the managers' response, which usually involved changing the business- or corporate-level strategy. The cases in this book cover a wide range of issues and problems that managers have had to confront. Some cases are about finding the right business-level strategy to compete in changing conditions. Some are about companies that grew by acquisition, with little concern for the rationale behind their growth, and how growth by acquisition affected their future profitability. Each case is different because each organization is different. The underlying thread in all cases, however, is the use of strategic management techniques to solve business problems.

Cases prove valuable in a strategic management course for several reasons. First, cases provide you, the student, with experience of organizational problems that you probably have not had the opportunity to experience firsthand. In a relatively short period of time, you will have the chance to appreciate and analyze the problems faced by many different companies and to understand how managers tried to deal with them.

Second, cases illustrate the theory and content of strategic management. The meaning and implications of this information are made clearer when they are applied to case studies. The theory and concepts help reveal what is going on in the companies studied and allow you to evaluate the solutions that specific companies adopted to deal with their problems. Consequently, when you analyze cases, you will be like a detective who, with a set of conceptual tools, probes what happened and what or who was responsible and then marshals the evidence that provides the solution. Top managers enjoy the thrill of testing their problem-solving abilities in the real world. It is important to remember that no one knows what the right answer is. All that managers can do is to make the best guess. In fact, managers say repeatedly that they are happy if they are right only half the time in solving strategic problems. Strategic management is an uncertain game, and using cases to see how theory can be put into practice is one way of improving your skills of diagnostic investigation.

Third, case studies provide you with the opportunity to participate in class and to gain experience in presenting your ideas to others. Instructors may sometimes call on students as a group to identify what is going on in a case, and through classroom discussion the issues in and solutions to the case problem will reveal themselves. In such a situation, you will have to organize your views and conclusions so that you can present them to the class. Your classmates may have analyzed the issues differently from you, and they will want you to argue your points before they will accept your conclusions, so be prepared for debate. This mode of discussion is an example of the dialectical approach to decision making. This is how decisions are made in the actual business world.

Instructors also may assign an individual, but more commonly a group, to analyze the case before the whole class. The individual or group probably will be responsible for a thirty- to forty-minute presentation of the case to the class. That presentation must cover the issues posed, the problems facing the company, and a series of recommendations for resolving the problems. The discussion then will be thrown open to the class, and you will have to defend your ideas. Through such discussions and presentations, you will experience how to convey your ideas effectively to others. Remember that a great deal of managers' time is spent in these kinds of situations: presenting their ideas and engaging in discussion with other managers who have their own views about what is going on. Thus, you will experience in the classroom the actual process of strategic management, and this will serve you well in your future career.

If you work in groups to analyze case studies, you also will learn about the group process involved in working as a team. When people work in groups, it is often difficult to schedule time and allocate responsibility for the case analysis. There are always group members who shirk their responsibilities and group members who are so sure of their own ideas that they try to dominate the group's analysis. Most of the strategic management takes place in groups, however, and it is best if you learn about these problems now.

ANALYZING A CASE STUDY

The purpose of the case study is to let you apply the concepts of strategic management when you analyze the issues facing a specific company. To analyze a case study, therefore, you must examine closely the issues confronting the company. Most often you will need to read the case several times—once to grasp the overall picture of what is happening to the company and then several times more to discover and grasp the specific problems.

Generally, detailed analysis of a case study should include eight areas:

1. The history, development, and growth of the company over time
2. The identification of the company's internal strengths and weaknesses
3. The nature of the external environment surrounding the company
4. A SWOT analysis
5. The kind of corporate-level strategy that the company is pursuing
6. The nature of the company's business-level strategy
7. The company's structure and control systems and how they match its strategy
8. Recommendations

To analyze a case, you need to apply the concepts taught in this course to each of these areas. To help you further, we next offer a summary of the steps you can take to analyze the case material for each of the eight points we just noted:

1. *Analyze the company's history, development, and growth.* A convenient way to investigate how a company's past strategy and structure affect it in the present is to chart the critical incidents in its history—that is, the events that were

the most unusual or the most essential for its development into the company it is today. Some of the events have to do with its founding, its initial products, how it makes new-product market decisions, and how it developed and chose functional competencies to pursue. Its entry into new businesses and shifts in its main lines of business are also important milestones to consider.

2. *Identify the company's internal strengths and weaknesses.* Once the historical profile is completed, you can begin the SWOT analysis. Use all the incidents you have charted to develop an account of the company's strengths and weaknesses as they have emerged historically. Examine each of the value creation functions of the company, and identify the functions in which the company is currently strong and currently weak. Some companies might be weak in marketing; some might be strong in research and development. Make lists of these strengths and weaknesses. The SWOT Checklist (Table 1) gives examples of what might go in these lists.

3. *Analyze the external environment.* To identify environmental opportunities and threats, apply all the concepts on industry and macroenvironments to analyze the environment the company is confronting. Of particular importance at the industry level are Porter's five forces model and the stage of the life cycle model. Which factors in the macroenvironment will appear salient depends on the specific company being analyzed. Use each factor in turn (for instance, demographic factors) to see whether it is relevant for the company in question.

   Having done this analysis, you will have generated both an analysis of the company's environment and a list of opportunities and threats. The SWOT Checklist table also lists some common environmental opportunities and threats that you may look for, but the list you generate will be specific to your company.

4. *Evaluate the SWOT analysis.* Having identified the company's external opportunities and threats as well as its internal strengths and weaknesses, consider what your findings mean. You need to balance strengths and weaknesses against opportunities and threats. Is the company in an overall strong competitive position? Can it continue to pursue its current business- or corporate-level strategy profitably? What can the company do to turn weaknesses into strengths and threats into opportunities? Can it develop new functional, business, or corporate strategies to accomplish this change? *Never merely generate the SWOT analysis and then put it aside.* Because it provides a succinct summary of the company's condition, a good SWOT analysis is the key to all the analyses that follow.

5. *Analyze corporate-level strategy.* To analyze corporate-level strategy, you first need to define the company's mission and goals. Sometimes the mission and goals are stated explicitly in the case; at other times, you will have to infer them from available information. The information you need to collect to find out the company's corporate strategy includes such factors as its lines of business and the nature of its subsidiaries and acquisitions. It is important to analyze the relationship among the company's businesses. Do they trade or exchange resources? Are there gains to be achieved from synergy? Alternatively, is the company just running a portfolio of investments? This analysis should enable you to define the corporate strategy that the company is pursuing (for example, related or unrelated diversification, or a combination of both) and to conclude whether the company operates in just one core business. Then, using your SWOT analysis, debate the merits of this strategy. Is it appropriate given the environment the company is in? Could a change in corporate strategy provide the company with new opportunities or transform a weakness into a strength? For example, should the company diversify from its core business into new businesses?

Table 1 A SWOT Checklist

Potential Internal Strengths	Potential Internal Weaknesses
Many product lines?	Obsolete, narrow product lines?
Broad market coverage?	Rising manufacturing costs?
Manufacturing competence?	Decline in R&D innovations?
Good marketing skills?	Poor marketing plan?
Good materials management systems?	Poor material management systems?
R&D skills and leadership?	Loss of customer good will?
Information system competencies?	Inadequate human resources?
Human resource competencies?	Inadequate information systems?
Brand name reputation?	Loss of brand name capital?
Portfolio management skills?	Growth without direction?
Cost of differentiation advantage?	Bad portfolio management?
New-venture management expertise?	Loss of corporate direction?
Appropriate management style?	Infighting among divisions?
Appropriate organizational structure?	Loss of corporate control?
Appropriate control systems?	Inappropriate organizational
Ability to manage strategic change?	structure and control systems?
Well-developed corporate strategy?	High conflict and politics?
Good financial management?	Poor financial management?
Others?	Others?
Potential Environmental Opportunities	**Potential Environmental Threats**
Expand core business(es)?	Attacks on core business(es)?
Exploit new market segments?	Increases in domestic competition?
Widen product range?	Increase in foreign competition?
Extend cost or differentiation advantage?	Change in consumer tastes?
Diversify into new growth businesses?	Fall in barriers to entry?
Expand into foreign markets?	Rise in new or substitute products?
Apply R&D skills in new areas?	Increase in industry rivalry?
Enter new related businesses?	New forms of industry competition?
Vertically integrate forward?	Potential for takeover?
Vertically integrate backward?	Existence of corporate raiders?
Enlarge corporate portfolio?	Increase in regional competition?
Overcome barriers to entry?	Changes in demographic factors?
Reduce rivalry among competitors?	Changes in economic factors?
Make profitable new acquisitions?	Downturn in economy?
Apply brand name capital in new areas?	Rising labor costs?
Seek fast market growth?	Slower market growth?
Others?	Others?

Other issues should be considered as well. How and why has the company's strategy changed over time? What is the claimed rationale for any changes? Often, it is a good idea to analyze the company's businesses or products to assess its situation and identify which divisions contribute the most to or detract from its competitive advantage. It is also useful to explore how the company has built its portfolio over time. Did it acquire new businesses, or did it internally venture its own? All of these factors provide clues about the company and indicate ways of improving its future performance.

6. *Analyze business-level strategy.* Once you know the company's corporate-level strategy and have done the SWOT analysis, the next step is to identify the company's business-level strategy. If the company is a single-business company, its business-level strategy is identical to its corporate-level strategy. If the company is in many businesses, each business will have its own business-level strategy. You will need to identify the company's generic competitive strategy—differentiation, low-cost, or focus—and its investment strategy, given its relative competitive position and the stage of the life cycle. The company also may market different products using different business-level strategies. For example, it may offer a low-cost product range and a line of differentiated products. Be sure to give a full account of a company's business-level strategy to show how it competes.

Identifying the functional strategies that a company pursues to build competitive advantage through superior efficiency, quality, innovation, and customer responsiveness and to achieve its business-level strategy is very important. The SWOT analysis will have provided you with information on the company's functional competencies. You should investigate its production, marketing, or research and development strategy further to gain a picture of where the company is going. For example, pursuing a low-cost or a differentiation strategy successfully requires very different sets of competencies. Has the company developed the right ones? If it has, how can it exploit them further? Can it pursue both a low-cost and a differentiation strategy simultaneously?

The SWOT analysis is especially important at this point if the industry analysis, particularly Porter's model, has revealed threats to the company from the environment. Can the company deal with these threats? How should it change its business-level strategy to counter them? To evaluate the potential of a company's business-level strategy, you must first perform a thorough SWOT analysis that captures the essence of its problems.

Once you complete this analysis, you will have a full picture of the way the company is operating and be in a position to evaluate the potential of its strategy. Thus, you will be able to make recommendations concerning the pattern of its future actions. However, first you need to consider strategy implementation, or the way the company tries to achieve its strategy.

7. *Analyze structure and control systems.* The aim of this analysis is to identify what structure and control systems the company is using to implement its strategy and to evaluate whether that structure is the appropriate one for the company. Different corporate and business strategies require different structures. You need to determine the *degree of fit between the company's strategy and structure.* For example, does the company have the right level of vertical differentiation (e.g., does it have the appropriate number of levels in the hierarchy or decentralized control?) or horizontal differentiation (does it use a functional structure when it should be using a product structure?)? Similarly, is the company using the right integration or control systems to

manage its operations? Are managers being appropriately rewarded? Are the right rewards in place for encouraging cooperation among divisions? These are all issues to consider.

In some cases, there will be little information on these issues, whereas in others there will be a lot. In analyzing each case, you should gear the analysis toward its most salient issues. For example, organizational conflict, power, and politics will be important issues for some companies. Try to analyze why problems in these areas are occurring. Do they occur because of bad strategy formulation or because of bad strategy implementation?

Organizational change is an issue in many cases because the companies are attempting to alter their strategies or structures to solve strategic problems. Thus, as part of the analysis, you might suggest an action plan that the company in question could use to achieve its goals. For example, you might list in a logical sequence the steps the company would need to follow to alter its business-level strategy from differentiation to focus.

8. *Make recommendations.* The quality of your recommendations is a direct result of the thoroughness with which you prepared the case analysis. Recommendations are directed at solving whatever strategic problem the company is facing and increasing its future profitability. Your recommendations should be in line with your analysis; that is, they should follow logically from the previous discussion. For example, your recommendation generally will center on the specific ways of changing functional, business, and corporate strategies and organizational structure and control to improve business performance. The set of recommendations will be specific to each case, and so it is difficult to discuss these recommendations here. Such recommendations might include an increase in spending on specific research and development projects, the divesting of certain businesses, a change from a strategy of unrelated to related diversification, an increase in the level of integration among divisions by using task forces and teams, or a move to a different kind of structure to implement a new business-level strategy. Make sure your recommendations are mutually consistent and written in the form of an action plan. The plan might contain a timetable that sequences the actions for changing the company's strategy and a description of how changes at the corporate level will necessitate changes at the business level and subsequently at the functional level.

After following all these stages, you will have performed a thorough analysis of the case and will be in a position to join in class discussion or present your ideas to the class, depending on the format used by your professor. Remember that you must tailor your analysis to suit the specific issue discussed in your case. In some cases, you might completely omit one of the steps in the analysis because it is not relevant to the situation you are considering. You must be sensitive to the needs of the case and not apply the framework we have discussed in this section blindly. The framework is meant only as a guide, not as an outline.

WRITING A CASE STUDY ANALYSIS

Often, as part of your course requirements, you will need to present a written case analysis. This may be an individual or a group report. Whatever the situation, there are certain guidelines to follow in writing a case analysis that will improve the evaluation your work will receive from your instructor. Before we discuss these guidelines and before you use them, make sure that they do not conflict with any directions your instructor has given you.

The structure of your written report is critical. Generally, if you follow the steps for analysis discussed in the previous section, *you already will have a good structure for your written discussion.* All reports begin with an *introduction* to the case. In it, outline briefly what the company does, how it developed historically, what problems it is experiencing, and how you are going to approach the issues in the case write-up. Do this sequentially by writing, for example, "First, we discuss the environment of Company X. . . . Third, we discuss Company X's business-level strategy. . . . Last, we provide recommendations for turning around Company X's business."

In the second part of the case write-up, the *strategic analysis* section, do the SWOT analysis, analyze and discuss the nature and problems of the company's business-level and corporate strategies, and then analyze its structure and control systems. Make sure you use plenty of headings and subheadings to structure your analysis. For example, have separate sections on any important conceptual tool you use. Thus, you might have a section on Porter's five forces model as part of your analysis of the environment. You might offer a separate section on portfolio techniques when analyzing a company's corporate strategy. Tailor the sections and subsections to the specific issues of importance in the case.

In the third part of the case write-up, present your *solutions and recommendations.* Be comprehensive, and make sure they are in line with the previous analysis so that the recommendations fit together and move logically from one to the next. The recommendations section is very revealing because your instructor will have a good idea of how much work you put into the case from the quality of your recommendations.

Following this framework will provide a good structure for most written reports, though it must be shaped to fit the individual case being considered. Some cases are about excellent companies experiencing no problems. In such instances, it is hard to write recommendations. Instead, you can focus on analyzing why the company is doing so well, using that analysis to structure the discussion. Following are some minor suggestions that can help make a good analysis even better:

1. Do not repeat in summary form large pieces of factual information from the case. The instructor has read the case and knows what is going on. Rather, use the in formation in the case to illustrate your statements, defend your arguments, or make salient points. Beyond the brief introduction to the company, you must avoid being *descriptive;* instead, you must be *analytical.*

2. Make sure the sections and subsections of your discussion flow logically and smoothly from one to the next. That is, try to build on what has gone before so that the analysis of the case study moves toward a climax. This is particularly important for group analysis, because there is a tendency for people in a group to split up the work and say, "I'll do the beginning, you take the middle, and I'll do the end." The result is a choppy, stilted analysis; the parts do not flow from one to the next, and it is obvious to the instructor that no real group work has been done.

3. Avoid grammatical and spelling errors. They make your work look sloppy.

4. In some instances, cases dealing with well-known companies end in 1998 or 1999 because no later information was available when the case was written. If possible, do a search for more information on what has happened to the company in subsequent years.

Many libraries now have comprehensive web-based electronic data search facilities that offer such sources as *ABI/Inform, The Wall Street Journal Index,* the *F&S Index,* and the *Nexis-Lexis* databases. These enable you to identify any article that has been written in the business press on the company of your choice within the past few years. A number of nonelectronic data sources are also useful. For example, *F&S Predicasts* publishes an annual list of articles relating to major companies that appeared in the national and international business press. *S&P Industry Surveys* is a great source for basic industry data, and *Value Line Ratings and Reports* can contain good summaries of a firm's financial position and future prospects. You will also want to collect full financial information on the company. Again, this can be accessed from web-based electronic databases such as the *Edgar* database, which archives all forms that publicly quoted companies have to file with the Securities and Exchange Commission (SEC; e.g., 10-K filings can be accessed from the SEC's *Edgar* database). Most SEC forms for public companies can now be accessed from Internet-based financial sites, such as Yahoo's finance site (http://finance.yahoo.com/).

5. Sometimes instructors hand out questions for each case to help you in your analysis. Use these as a guide for writing the case analysis. They often illuminate the important issues that have to be covered in the discussion.

If you follow the guidelines in this section, you should be able to write a thorough and effective evaluation.

THE ROLE OF FINANCIAL ANALYSIS IN CASE STUDY ANALYSIS

An important aspect of analyzing a case study and writing a case study analysis is the role and use of financial information. A careful analysis of the company's financial condition immensely improves a case write-up. After all, financial data represent the concrete results of the company's strategy and structure. Although analyzing financial statements can be quite complex, a general idea of a company's financial position can be determined through the use of ratio analysis. Financial performance ratios can be calculated from the balance sheet and income statement. These ratios can be classified into five subgroups: profit ratios, liquidity ratios, activity ratios, leverage ratios, and shareholder-return ratios. These ratios should be compared with the industry average or the company's prior years of performance. It should be noted, however, that deviation from the average is not necessarily bad; it simply warrants further investigation. For example, young companies will have purchased assets at a different price and will likely have a different capital structure than older companies do. In addition to ratio analysis, a company's cash flow position is of critical importance and should be assessed. Cash flow shows how much actual cash a company possesses.

Profit Ratios

Profit ratios measure the efficiency with which the company uses its resources. The more efficient the company, the greater is its profitability. It is useful to compare a company's profitability against that of its major competitors in its industry to determine whether the company is operating more or less efficiently than its rivals. In addition, the change in a company's profit ratios over time tells whether its performance is improving or declining.

A number of different profit ratios can be used, and each of them measures a different aspect of a company's performance. Here, we look at the most commonly used profit ratios.

Return on Invested Capital This ratio measures the profit earned on the capital invested in the company. It is defined as follows:

$$\text{Return on invested capital (ROIC)} = \frac{\text{Net profit}}{\text{Invested capital}}$$

Net profit is calculated by subtracting the total costs of operating the company away from its total revenues (total revenues − total costs). Total costs are the (1) costs of goods sold, (2) sales, general, and administrative expenses, (3) R&D expenses, and (4) other expenses. Net profit can be calculated before or after taxes, although many financial analysts prefer the before-tax figure. Invested capital is the amount that is invested in the operations of a company—that is, in property, plant, equipment, inventories, and other assets. Invested capital comes from two main sources: interest-bearing debt and shareholders' equity. Interest-bearing debt is money the company borrows from banks and from those who purchase its bonds. Shareholders' equity is the money raised from selling shares to the public, *plus* earnings that have been retained by the company in prior years and are available to fund current investments. ROIC measures the effectiveness with which a company is using the capital funds that it has available for investment. As such, it is recognized to be an excellent measure of the value a company is creating.[1] Remember that a company's ROIC can be decomposed into its constituent parts.

Return on Total Assets (ROA) This ratio measures the profit earned on the employment of assets. It is defined as follows:

$$\text{Return on total assests} = \frac{\text{Net profit}}{\text{Total assets}}$$

Return on Stockholders' Equity (ROE) This ratio measures the percentage of profit earned on common stockholders' investment in the company. It is defined as follows:

$$\text{Return on stockholders equity} = \frac{\text{Net profit}}{\text{Stockholders equity}}$$

If a company has no debt, this will be the same as ROIC.

Liquidity Ratios

A company's liquidity is a measure of its ability to meet short-term obligations. An asset is deemed liquid if it can be readily converted into cash. Liquid assets are current assets such as cash, marketable securities, accounts receivable, and so on. Two liquidity ratios are commonly used.

[1]Tom Copeland, Tim Koller, and Jack Murrin, *Valuation: Measuring and Managing the Value of Companies* (New York: Wiley, 1996).

Current Ratio   The current ratio measures the extent to which the claims of short-term creditors are covered by assets that can be quickly converted into cash. Most companies should have a ratio of at least 1, because failure to meet these commitments can lead to bankruptcy. The ratio is defined as follows:

$$\text{Current ratio} = \frac{\text{Current assets}}{\text{Current liabilities}}$$

Quick Ratio   The quick ratio measures a company's ability to pay off the claims of short-term creditors without relying on selling its inventories. This is a valuable measure since in practice the sale of inventories is often difficult. It is defined as follows:

$$\text{Quick ratio} = \frac{\text{Current assets} - \text{inventory}}{\text{Current liabilities}}$$

Activity Ratios

Activity ratios indicate how effectively a company is managing its assets. Two ratios are particularly useful.

Inventory Turnover   This measures the number of times inventory is turned over. It is useful in determining whether a firm is carrying excess stock in inventory. It is defined as follows:

$$\text{Inventory turnover} = \frac{\text{Cost of goods sold}}{\text{Inventory}}$$

Cost of goods sold is a better measure of turnover than sales because it is the cost of the inventory items. Inventory is taken at the balance sheet date. Some companies choose to compute an average inventory, beginning inventory, and ending inventory, but for simplicity, use the inventory at the balance sheet date.

Days Sales Outstanding (DSO) or Average Collection Period   This ratio is the average time a company has to wait to receive its cash after making a sale. It measures how effective the company's credit, billing, and collection procedures are. It is defined as follows:

$$\text{DSO} = \frac{\text{Accounts receivable}}{\text{Total sales/360}}$$

Accounts receivable is divided by average daily sales. The use of 360 is the standard number of days for most financial analysis.

Leverage Ratios

A company is said to be highly leveraged if it uses more debt than equity, including stock and retained earnings. The balance between debt and equity is called the *capital structure*. The optimal capital structure is determined by the individual company. Debt has a lower cost because creditors take less risk; they know they will get their interest and principal. However, debt can be risky to the firm because if enough profit is not made to cover the interest and principal payments, bankruptcy can result. Three leverage ratios are commonly used.

Debt-to-Assets Ratio   The debt-to-assets ratio is the most direct measure of the extent to which borrowed funds have been used to finance a company's investments. It is defined as follows:

$$\text{Debt-to-assets ratio} = \frac{\text{Total debt}}{\text{Total assets}}$$

Total debt is the sum of a company's current liabilities and its long-term debt, and total assets are the sum of fixed assets and current assets.

Debt-to-Equity Ratio The debt-to-equity ratio indicates the balance between debt and equity in a company's capital structure. This is perhaps the most widely used measure of a company's leverage. It is defined as follows:

$$\text{Debt-to-equity ratio} = \frac{\text{Total debt}}{\text{Total equity}}$$

Times-Covered Ratio The times-covered ratio measures the extent to which a company's gross profit covers its annual interest payments. If this ratio declines to less than 1, the company is unable to meet its interest costs and is technically insolvent. The ratio is defined as follows:

$$\text{Times-covered ratio} = \frac{\text{Profit before interest and tax}}{\text{Total interest charges}}$$

Shareholder-Return Ratios

Shareholder-return ratios measure the return that shareholders earn from holding stock in the company. Given the goal of maximizing stockholders' wealth, providing shareholders with an adequate rate of return is a primary objective of most companies. As with profit ratios, it can be helpful to compare a company's shareholder returns against those of similar companies as a yardstick for determining how well the company is satisfying the demands of this particularly important group of organizational constituents. Four ratios are commonly used.

Total Shareholder Returns Total shareholder returns measure the returns earned by time $t + 1$ on an investment in a company's stock made at time t. (Time t is the time at which the initial investment is made.) Total shareholder returns include both dividend payments and appreciation in the value of the stock (adjusted for stock splits) and are defined as follows:

$$\text{Total shareholder returns} = \frac{\begin{array}{c}\text{Stock price } (t+1) - \text{stock price } (t) \\ + \text{ sum of annual dividends per share}\end{array}}{\text{Stock price } (t)}$$

If a shareholder invests $2 at time t and at time $t + 1$ the share is worth $3, while the sum of annual dividends for the period t to $t + 1$ has amounted to $0.20, total shareholder returns are equal to $(3 - 2 + 0.2)/2 = 0.6$, which is a 60% return on an initial investment of $2 made at time t.

Price-Earnings Ratio The price-earnings ratio measures the amount investors are willing to pay per dollar of profit. It is defined as follows:

$$\text{Price-earnings ratio} = \frac{\text{Market price per share}}{\text{Earnings per share}}$$

Market-to-Book Value Market-to-book value measures a company's expected future growth prospects. It is defined as follows:

$$\text{Market-to-book value} = \frac{\text{Market price per share}}{\text{Earnings per share}}$$

Dividend Yield   The dividend yield measures the return to shareholders received in the form of dividends. It is defined as follows:

$$\text{Dividend yield} = \frac{\text{Dividend per share}}{\text{Market price per share}}$$

Market price per share can be calculated for the first of the year, in which case the dividend yield refers to the return on an investment made at the beginning of the year. Alternatively, the average share price over the year may be used. A company must decide how much of its profits to pay to stockholders and how much to reinvest in the company. Companies with strong growth prospects should have a lower dividend payout ratio than mature companies. The rationale is that shareholders can invest the money elsewhere if the company is not growing. The optimal ratio depends on the individual firm, but the key decider is whether the company can produce better returns than the investor can earn elsewhere.

Cash Flow

Cash flow position is cash received minus cash distributed. The net cash flow can be taken from a company's statement of cash flows. Cash flow is important for what it reveals about a company's financing needs. A strong positive cash flow enables a company to fund future investments without having to borrow money from bankers or investors. This is desirable because the company avoids paying out interest or dividends. A weak or negative cash flow means that a company has to turn to external sources to fund future investments. Generally, companies in strong-growth industries often find themselves in a poor cash flow position (because their investment needs are substantial), whereas successful companies based in mature industries generally find themselves in a strong cash flow position.

A company's internally generated cash flow is calculated by adding back its depreciation provision to profits after interest, taxes, and dividend payments. If this figure is insufficient to cover proposed new investments, the company has little choice but to borrow funds to make up the shortfall or to curtail investments. If this figure exceeds proposed new investments, the company can use the excess to build up its liquidity (that is, through investments in financial assets) or repay existing loans ahead of schedule.

CONCLUSION

When evaluating a case, it is important to be *systematic*. Analyze the case in a logical fashion, beginning with the identification of operating and financial strengths and weaknesses and environmental opportunities and threats. Move on to assess the value of a company's current strategies only when you are fully conversant with the SWOT analysis of the company. Ask yourself whether the company's current strategies make sense given its SWOT analysis. If they do not, what changes need to be made? What are your recommendations? Above all, link any strategic recommendations you may make to the SWOT analysis. State explicitly how the strategies you identify take advantage of the company's strengths to exploit environmental opportunities, how they rectify the company's weaknesses, and how they counter environmental threats. Also, do not forget to outline what needs to be done to implement your recommendations.

SGI versus Dell: Competition in Server and Cloud Computing

SGI, or Silicon Graphics International, was formed by the merger of Rackable Systems and Silicon Graphics in May 2009. Although Silicon Graphics is the company with the longest and most famous history—it was once the industry leader in graphical, supercomputing solutions and worth $7 billion at its peak—it lost its competitive advantage in the last decade to other high-tech companies, such as HP, Nvidia, Dell, and Sun Microsystems. The company was forced to declare Chapter 11 bankruptcy in 2009. In March 2009, Rackable Systems CEO Mark Barrenechea decided to buy Silicon Graphics for $45 million, and managers from both companies are working to combine their technological competences to strengthen the new SGI business model. Barrenechea, now SGI's CEO, is hoping Silicon Graphic's assets and competences can help the new company cope better with an intensely competitive industry environment that emerged after Dell decided to target the same market segment as Rackable Systems. Both companies are competing to sell powerful servers to Internet companies, particularly those building up their capabilities in cloud computing. In May 2009, the strategic task facing Barrenechea was how to use SGI's global assets to better position the company for the upcoming battle against Dell, as well as HP, IBM, and Sun.

THE SERVER COMPUTER INDUSTRY ENVIRONMENT

Server computers (servers) are designed to perform powerful, information-intensive computing that in the past could have been executed only on expensive mainframe computers. Servers are also designed to link to desktop and laptop personal computers (PCs) so that all company employees can access the powerful computing capacity and software applications to gain historical and real-time information about ongoing events. In the late 1990s, the power of servers increased enormously as Intel and AMD developed ever-more advanced microprocessors (chips) that delivered more and more computing capacity, a trend that has continued. A server is fundamentally a PC on steroids. Just as a PC purchased today is much more powerful than one bought just two or three years ago, so today's individual servers usually contain microprocessors from Intel or AMD and other components such as powerful graphical units (GPUs) from Nvidia, enormous storage devices from Samsung or EMC, and powerful networking chips from Cisco Systems. All these components are linked by some brand of software that allows them to work seamlessly together so that they can perform the specific computing application they were designed to do. Today, servers are more or less similar to the

For the most recent financial results of the company discussed in this case, go to http://finance.yahoo.com, input the company's stock symbol, and download the latest company report from its homepage.

"supercomputers" of the past; they can process staggering amounts of data to execute highly complex software applications, and they can access and store enormous amounts of information. As a result, servers are the foundation of most companies' database management centers.

From its beginning, the development of the server industry has been affected by a lack of common industry standards; each server maker has sought to obtain a competitive advantage from its proprietary chips, software, or even server case or chassis. (The server chassis houses and links whatever mix of components, such as storage devices, microprocessor, networking hardware, cooling systems, and motherboard, a server maker chooses and so determines the final server design.) Most major computer companies that make servers—such as IBM, HP, and Dell—use chips based on the x86 computing architecture pioneered by Intel, which it licensed to its main competitor, AMD. However, Sun, which once dominated the server market, uses its own proprietary chips and software to power its servers; in the past, Silicon Graphics was also a competitor in this market, offering a "supercomputing" server solution. The servers made by different companies are also loaded with a wide variety of different software systems, such as Sun's Solaris and Microsoft's NT that are proprietary; and some operate on the Linux open software platform. Because of their different hardware and software configurations, the servers made by different companies cannot easily be combined into one integrated system.

This causes major problems for large or medium-sized companies or organizations that are major buyers of the standardized, "brand name" servers offered by the major computer makers. Each company's IT managers have to select the brand of server that can best perform the specific set of computing applications necessary to manage its company-wide value chain activities and process and store its database. Once a company has chosen one server brand or "platform," for example, Sun's or HP's, it then becomes locked into that server maker because of the enormous problems of making the servers of different companies work seamlessly together. This is especially aggravating to companies. Often, a server made by one computer maker is configured in a way that allows it to perform specific computing applications, such as crunching data, Web site hosting, or massive database management much more efficiently

than the servers available from a company's current server maker; however, the servers of different companies are incompatible.

Over time, this problem has become more and more important; sales of servers have increased enormously (the server market is $25 billion a year) because of their ever-increasing computing power and their low cost compared to mainframe computers. As companies began to buy hundreds and thousands of servers to meet their increasing need to process information, server makers started to design rack-mounted servers or *rack servers*. Rack servers link an individual server to a rack of 10 connected servers; then 10 racks create a network of 100 servers; 100 racks create a network of 1,000 servers, and so on. Using software to link the operations of these server racks, large companies develop what are called "server farms" to manage their information databases. Server farms are "remote," physically separate database centers composed of many thousands of networked server racks that are constantly monitored, maintained, and upgraded by a company's IT engineers.

Also, interconnected systems of powerful servers that in many respects resemble the way a single computer operates are referred to as *cluster computing*. In cluster computing, servers are connected to each other through vast local area networks (LANs) between the different divisions or functions of a company to perform complex software applications, such as enterprise resource planning (ERP), for example. They are also used to handle sophisticated applications, such as computer-aided product design or customer relationship management inside functions such as research and development (R&D) or sales and marketing. Clusters are also deployed to improve computing performance for enormous information-intensive computing tasks; provide backup data capabilities in case of computer failure; or provide the extra information processing or storage capacity power needed to handle peak period user demands on servers, either from in-house users at 9–11 A.M. and 1–3 P.M. or from Internet users between 5–10 P.M. each evening.

As noted previously, huge racks of servers or cluster server solutions are much more flexible and cost-effective than using a single mainframe computer of comparable speed or capacity. However, to deliver the highest quality and most cost-effective solution, they also must be customized to each company's unique requirements by choosing the mix of hardware and software to allow specific computing applications and services to execute most efficiently and effectively. Increasingly, this requires mixing the server hardware and software of different companies so that different brands of servers work together. This complex computing task requires the development of "middleware" computer software that allows different brands or makes of servers to operate seamlessly together. This expensive middleware is provided by companies such as IBM, EDS, and Accenture, which have all expanded their computer consulting services to serve the growing and lucrative server market.

SGI/Rackable Systems, 1999–2009

Rackable Systems (SGI) was founded in 1999 in Milpitas in Silicon Valley, California, as a specialist server company. The question facing the start-up's top management team was how to break into a server market dominated by IBM, HP, and Sun, the principal providers of servers to large and medium-sized companies. The question for SGI was how to offer companies buying servers something unique: How could it find a way to design its servers to find a way to enter the market and avoid head-to-head competition with the Big Three? At this time, SGI's larger competitors still thought of servers as standardized products; they competed by buying the best available server hardware and software—such as Intel's chips or Oracle's database management software—and then embedding them in their servers to offer customers a more powerful computing solution that could be sold by SGI's nationwide force of sale representatives.

SGI could offer customers an equally powerful server, because any server maker can buy the latest AMD chips or Microsoft software. In addition, however, SGI decided to focus on offering a customized solution. Using the competences of its engineers, the strategy SGI's managers developed was to offer customers a server rack\cluster-computing solution that could be custom designed to each company's individual requirements, thus offering its customers maximum flexibility and cost-effectiveness. In other words, SGI's strategy was to offer customers a unique kind of server computing solution that would better meet customer needs than its competitors; in this way it would be able to gain a profitable share of the server market.

What was unique about its strategy? First, SGI focused on custom manufacturing servers that had superior computing *density*, meaning that many more chips could be placed in the same amount of physical space that those of its competitors. Second, it emphasized superior *thermal efficiency* and worked hard to design server racks that operated at lower temperatures, thus reducing a company's energy costs—a major source of cost savings for a large company. Third, its engineers developed a design to compete on the basis of superior reliability and serviceability. They focused on simplifying the components in its servers to reduce the potential for failure; if a breakdown occurred, its servers were configured to make it easier to find and solve the problem.

From the beginning, a major focus of SGI's business model was to publicize its energy-efficiency server solutions and their ability to create "ecologically minded," green database centers that could significantly reduce the electricity costs associated with cooling the hundreds, thousands—or tens of thousands of servers—companies must constantly monitor to protect their data and information systems. For a large company, electricity costs can amount to many hundreds of thousands of dollars a year; SGI was offering companies a significant way to reduce costs—especially Internet companies whose use of servers was increasing exponentially.

Over time, SGI worked to improve its distinctive competences to increase its competitive advantage. One of its earliest innovations was to create half-depth servers that allow back-to-back rack mounting of servers. This means that two servers can operate in the space that formerly was taken up by only one, so it could pack double the computing processing power into a smaller physical "footprint." Second, SGI worked to design "dense server racks," using its highly differentiated and patented server rack chassis and cabinet to house the thousands of individual servers that it custom builds to meet each customer's specific needs for computer processing capacity and performance. Third, SGI worked to improve the physical design of these server racks to reduce heat emissions from the core microprocessors as well as find innovative ways to cool all the other server components. One of the main ways it did this was to reduce the number of individual components in each server. It was one of the first companies to recognize that it is possible to eliminate the storage, networking, and cooling hardware necessary for each server to work as a stand-alone entity. In the design, all of the individual servers in a dense server rack are connected to a single set of storage and networking hardware located in each server rack, and one fan cools all the servers. SGI's design significantly reduces the amount of heat generated by each server rack, and its cooling solution also substantially reduces the energy costs associated with cooling its server racks and server clusters while allowing them to operate at maximum efficiency. In fact, SGI claims it has the most energy efficient solution of any of the major server makers.

Also, its custom-built server racks offer customers unparalleled configuration flexibility and a significantly smaller physical footprint that helps to radically reduce the total costs of managing a company's database center. "Through our unique build-to-order program, SGI servers are configured using best-of-breed, industry-standard components (processors, memory, hard disk, RAID, power supplies, etc.) to provide the ideal configuration for a given data center's application needs and power envelope." Indeed, to provide the best customized solution to each company's or client's needs, SGI partnered with leading hardware component manufacturers and software makers to provide the latest combination of server technology to meet their needs. For example, SGI can custom-build rack servers using either Intel or AMD chips that operate in conjunction with whatever operating system (Linux, Windows, Solaris, and so on) that a particular customer requires to be compatible with its existing server platform.

SGI's ability to provide an energy-efficient server solution that could be customized to a client's specific needs appealed to large and medium-sized companies because they now were no longer locked into the server technology of any particular maker, such as Sun, HP, or IBM. Many large companies were willing to experiment with SGI server solutions, and in a short time, Internet companies such as Amazon.com and Yahoo!; high-tech companies such as Electronic Arts, Microsoft, Nvidia, Oracle; and public institutions such as Lawrence Livermore National Laboratory and large state universities were experimenting with its innovative high-density energy-saving server rack solutions.

New Competitive Issues

SGI's business model led to increasing customer purchases of its dense rack servers, and its revenues increased steadily over time; it seemed as if the company had found a profitable new business model to compete against giants such as HP and IBM. SGI conducted an initial public offering of its stock in June 2005 at $12 a share; by the fall of 2005, it had reached $55, as sales of its racks continued to soar. Investors thought SGI had found a niche in the low-profit, mature rack server market. Its breakthrough designs for dense, compact, and energy-saving rack servers met the needs of Internet companies such as Amazon, Facebook, Yahoo! and Microsoft's online division that were growing at an explosive rate. These companies were all rapidly expanding their bricks-and-mortar database centers to deal with the huge increase in Internet usage but wanted to expand capacity while reducing operating costs by adopting more energy-efficient server racks.

However, the start-up's success was not unnoticed; all the major server companies began to analyze SGI's business model; seeing its advantages, their focus became to beat the company at its own game. IBM, HP, and, especially, Dell began to experiment with new ways to design rack servers to increase their capacity and reduce their power consumption. SGI's committed engineers worked hard to protect its first-mover advantage, but it did not have the resources of the large server makers.

By 2006, the cost-leader Dell recognized the challenge that SGI posed to its continuing leadership in the low-cost segment of the rack server market as it continued to increase its installed customer base. So Dell created a new business unit and hired a new team of skilled engineers to learn how to build customized, energy-efficient servers that could compete with SGI. Dell was especially concerned to protect its advantage in the crucially important Internet company segment of the market that was expanding rapidly because of increasing emphasis on cloud computing. And, because the core of SGI's dense servers were the components it bought from other high-tech companies, such as chips from Intel and AMD, the only thing it had to protect itself from Dell's attack was its propriety server design and cooling technology.

By 2007, Dell had entered the market with its own low-priced, customized servers targeted at Internet companies, as well as its own installed base of customers. In doing so, it created a price war that, by the end of 2007, decimated SGI's profit margins as its server sales plunged. This precipitated a huge plunge in its stock price. Dell's goal was clear: to prevent SGI from gaining a sustained competitive advantage by attracting away its customers with offers of low-priced server racks. As a result, SGI had to accelerate its development of even more efficient rack server and cluster computing solutions for companies' database centers—especially given the growing popularity of cloud computing.

The Growth of Cloud Computing

In 2007, the term *cloud computing* was being popularized by companies like Google, Amazon.com, and IBM to refer to a new, emerging kind of information or computing service that would be available to companies and individuals in the same way that they used utilities like water or electricity. Essentially, the push behind cloud computing was to create (1) a cost-effective, Internet-based global platform of hardware and software provided by (2) a network of thousands of interlinked information technology (IT) companies that have (3) the capability to provide a full range of on-demand software applications, services, database storage, and computing services to millions of companies and billions of individual users. The word *cloud* is used to emphasize that the users of cloud computing often do not even know which specific IT providers are satisfying their computing or information-processing needs; users' principal concern is that they have the ability to send, receive, and process data and information reliably and securely and at low cost.

The two main uses of cloud computing for companies and individual users are applications and infrastructure. Applications such as corporate e-mail systems and powerful on-demand online computing software programs for individual users, such as e-mail, messaging, online document storage, and word processing, along with the ability to access YouTube, search engines, Wikipedia, Facebook, and so on. The infrastructure dimension of cloud computing is most important to the companies providing these Internet applications to users or that use Internet-based applications to manage their own businesses. These companies contract with an application or service IT provider in the cloud network infrastructure to store and access the software resources and database management services they need to manage their in-house value-chain functions or provide Internet applications/services to individual users.

In sum, cloud computing is outsourced, pay-as-you-go, on-demand, Internet software capabilities available to companies for a fee; it is usually free to individual users (because companies supplying Internet services to individuals get their revenues from online advertising). The cloud metaphor is invoked, because, in the future, as more and more software services such as e-mail, data storage, and business software applications come to be located in tens of thousands of physical database centers around the world, the identity of these service providers will be largely unknown to users. Today, for example, most individual users of the Internet have no idea which IT companies actually send them the Web pages they request; usually the Web sites they visit have contracted with Web site hosting and data storage companies to actually supply the Web pages their visitors request.

If the idea of cloud computing takes off in the future, then even the largest companies may cease to operate their own database centers and move all their information and computing operations to Web-based IT providers, because those companies will be able to perform their computing function at a significantly lower cost than the company can itself. For example, in 2009, IBM announced its own cloud computing initiative, called "Blue Cloud." Blue Cloud is intended to show large companies that they do not need to own and operate their own database centers and maintain physical networks of company-wide servers. Instead, IBM would provide powerful cloud-based server racks and mainframes bundled with software that automates, self-manages, and maintains the cloud computing network, thus safeguarding any company's database and applications and making them available on-demand. IBM's cloud infrastructure will be located around the world in huge globally accessible data centers that contain hundreds of thousands of servers with the capacity to drive the real-time data streams required for applications such as search, social networking, and mobile e-commerce. And, IBM claims Blue Cloud will save companies money: It will be a cost-effective energy-saving solution.

Mobile Data Center Storage Capacity

An idea, which originated in Europe, was to offer companies a quick and efficient way to enlarge and upgrade their cluster computing and database center capabilities by housing a server rack storage and processing solution in a standard storage container—the same kind of container hauled on trucks or stacked on cargo ships. The first United States server maker to announce such a mobile database solution was

Sun; in 2006, it launched its "Blackbox" data center containing its proprietary Solaris rack server configuration in a 20-foot shipping container. Its Blackbox would contain a mobile data center that could deliver the computing capability of a 9,000-square-foot physical data center but would only cost about one-fifth of a physical data center. In addition, Sun said it would save about 20% on the power costs necessary to cool the servers.

However, SGI beat Sun to the punch when it announced that its new "Concentro" mobile server container would be available for delivery in the spring of 2007. Sun did not expect to roll out its first container until the summer. SGI's engineers had used all their design capabilities to make the Concentro the market leader. SGI's first self-contained data center is based on its custom-designed, high-density server racks and data storage housed in a larger 40-by-20-foot shipping container. Because SGI's space-saving rack servers are half as deep as standard servers, it can cram in twice as many individual servers into a 40-foot container than its competitors—and four times as many as Sun because Sun's container is smaller. Also, SGI's container design takes advantage of its competence in reducing server power consumption. Each server rack is equipped with one large fan that allowed its engineers to eliminate the need for each individual server to have its own individual fan; across the thousands of servers in a Concentro container, this cut the amount of power needed to cool the servers by 80% compared to a conventional server design. The immense processing power of these Concentro containers allows companies to rethink their need for high-cost brick-and-mortar data centers, especially given the relatively low operating costs of SGI containers compared to physical data centers. Companies will be able to efficiently operate networks of geographically dispersed server containers that allow for a more reliable and secure computing solution—one that will not be subject to local disasters or Internet or power outages that can seriously harm centralized data centers.

SGI's engineers have worked steadily to increase the energy efficiency of its server containers. In 2008, SGI introduced a new advanced class of containers, called the ICE Cube™ Modular Data Center. It is purely air cooled and does not require chilled water from an outside physical data center, which means that mobile data centers can be located in any convenient low-cost location. The ICE Cube system also accepts SGI's customized rack servers or the fast-growing market for *blade servers*. Blade servers are stripped-down servers that are designed to slide into existing rack servers. Server blades are smaller, more cost-efficient, and consume less power than traditional servers. Also, blade servers are inherently different from rack servers because they are used for more general-purpose computing solutions, such as Web hosting and general database management; customized rack servers, as noted earlier, are meant for specific computing applications, where enormous amounts of data must be crunched to provide a user-specific solution. However, introducing blade servers into its new mobile data center puts SGI in a position to offer its customers a broader set of solutions from cloud computing to company-wide applications, such as ERP systems.

In 2008, SGI announced that it would provide the ICE Cube solution—which was claimed to be the most energy efficient on the market—in 20- or 40-foot container sizes. Also, it would allow users to choose either Intel or AMD microprocessors to power the high-performing blade systems. An ICE Cube container can hold up to 1,344 dual-socket blades with quad-core Intel Xeons or 672 quad-socket, dual-core AMD Opteron blades—equivalent to an old 20,000-square-foot bricks-and-mortar database center. To try to attract customers quickly, given competition from Dell, SGI also signed an agreement with IBM to allow its proprietary blade servers to be fitted seamlessly into its ICE Cube containers that provide the energy-efficient power and cooling system SGI claims is the lowest-cost cluster computing server solution on the market.

In 2008, however, IBM announced it was buying another server container start-up company to allow it to enter this market segment, making it a direct competitor to SGI in the mobile blade server market. In 2009, IBM also announced that, like Dell, it was entering the market for customized servers, which would mean it was also going head to head with SGI. By 2009, worldwide blade server revenues had grown to more than $5 billion despite the recession; however, IBM and HP controlled 80% of the market between them.

So, despite its advances in developing state-of-the-art cooling and customizable server solutions, SGI was still struggling to compete with its larger rivals, including Dell, which has targeted SGI's customer base with low-priced products. As Mark

Barrenechea commented in 2008, however, "I certainly don't see Dell as an innovator; I see them more as a price spoiler." Barrenechea singled out Dell because of its increasing strategy to compete with SGI by offering customers lower and lower prices for servers—that it was increasingly customizing to each individual client's needs. As a result, profit margins in the "customizable" segment of the server market became razor thin. Indeed, Dell has been able to use its competence in low-cost supply chain management because of its enormous buying power to offset SGI's competitive advantage from its unique design skills in making dense, compact, energy-efficient servers.

SGI's revenues collapsed to $39 million from $111 million in the last quarter of 2008 compared to 2007, and its gross margins went from a positive 25% to a negative 15%. The company warned that lower orders from its two largest customers had caused a 21% fall in revenues. However, Barrenechea claimed that in the customized server segment of the market, price discounting was not a viable long-term strategy and that SGI would remain a viable competitor, even if it took two, four, or even eight quarters to force Dell to give up its price-cutting policy.

Some analysts thought that Dell might attempt to takeover SGI to gain access to its proprietary technology. However, in December 2008 Dell announced it was also entering the mobile data center container market with a unique, double-decker server design code-named "Humidor." One Dell container stores 1,300 servers and their associated storage and networking systems; the other container stores all the necessary power and cooling devices. Dell has adopted this solution, because it can outfit its twin containers with standard hardware and software and avoid the need to use proprietary technology such as SGI's. Once again, instead of paying for an expensive physical building, a company can order a data center in a container, add power, cooled water, and a network connection and upgrade its existing data center. Some of Dell's first containers would go to a new Microsoft data center near Chicago. Microsoft has been pushing a platform based on its own server software, and Dell is the biggest buyer of Microsoft's software. This was a blow to SGI; having also sold some of the ICE Cube systems to Microsoft, it is competing directly with Dell for the business of its major customers such as Amazon.com and Facebook. Dell is ready and willing to fight with its smaller rival for

orders despite slim profit margins—perhaps to drive SGI out of the market.

Another sign that Dell was not letting up on its smaller rival came in May 2009 when Dell announced it was expanding its range of powerful blade servers to include a new product aimed at Internet businesses, those like Amazon and Google that promote cloud computing. The new Dell XS11-VX8 consumes only about one-tenth of the power of a typical server but has the enormous processing capacity that can handle the millions of Internet user requests for Web pages from Internet-based businesses. This new server uses an energy-saving chip from Via Technologies, a Taiwanese company that is practically the only other maker of the proprietary X86 chips controlled by Intel that had licensed them to AMD and VIA Technologies. Dell's new server will put to the test SGI's claim to be the greenest, most energy-efficient custom server maker on the market. Despite the recession, companies are expected to spend about $100 billion in 2009 on data center hardware and software, so there is a lot at stake for SGI—and Dell.

The Merger between Rackable Systems and Silicon Graphics

In the first quarter of 2009, SGI's sales fell by 35% to $44.3 million. Even though the company had been forced to reduce its cost structure in 2008, to compete with Dell, by lowering its R&D spending and laying off employees in R&D and sales and marketing, the company suffered more than a $13 million loss. However, this was not as bad as the fourth quarter of 2008 when the recession hit so hard that sales fell by 65% to $39 million and the loss was more than $18 million. Indeed, SGI sold its first two ICE Cube systems in the first quarter of 2009 to Yahoo! and Amazon.com. It launched more than 30 different customized server platforms based on Intel's new XEON chips.

Despite its losses, Rackable Systems had $174 million in cash and decided to use $42 million to purchase the failed supercomputer maker Silicon Graphics. Analysts wondered what Rackable Systems or SGI was getting for its money. Mark Barrenechea said that SGI was obtaining all the equity in SGI's overseas subsidiaries, as well as its U.S. federal systems business, and all SG's real estate, core patents, cash on hand, inventories of servers and storage hardware, and a 5,000-strong global customer list.

These are very important assets to a young company with no established foreign operations. In May 2009, a few weeks after the merger, SGI announced that its new UK subsidiary (formerly owned by SG) would begin selling ICE Cube containers in the summer; also, it was currently taking orders from European companies, particularly Internet-oriented companies, to design its customized server platforms to meet their needs.

This appears to be a make-or-break deal for SGI. After the merger, SGI had more than 1,200 employees compared to 270 before, which was down from 350 in the previous year because SGI was forced to lay off employees after its revenues plunged. Nevertheless, SGI announced that the company targets more than $500 million in annual sales and gross margins of more than 20% by 2010. How will the merger help it achieve this?

First, SGI will be able to combine the two main product lines of the former companies: servers and storage products from the Rackable Systems lineup, and storage, visualization, and professional services acquired from Silicon Graphics, including its expertise in super computing. Second, SGI argued that by combining their skills, the new SGI could make superior cluster computing systems and be able to solve large-scale data problems through a combination of hardware, storage, and software solutions. Third, the ability to leverage SGI's new global competence is expected to be very important. Barrenechea claimed that on "day one," SGI would be operational in 25 countries, with the expertise necessary to deliver customized stationary and mobile servers, together with the skills necessary to provide customers with unique solutions and provide on-site services and logistics to provide them with best of breed solutions. As Barrenechea commented, "Innovation, expertise, and service are at the core of SGI. We built our company by listening to our customers, providing unique solutions for the toughest and most demanding technology and business problems, offering mass customization, and being first to market with new component technology in order for our customers to maintain their competitive advantage. This tradition will continue."

The question is, can SGI survive the challenge from Dell, and from the other two major server makers, HP and IBM, that have also developed customizable and mobile server platforms? In the next few crucial years, will the new SGI be able to realize the value in the business model proposed by its CEO? Will it be acquired by a leading company, because it has unique and valuable skills and competences? Will it simply fall by the wayside and end up in bankruptcy itself, and be acquired by some company that recognized the value in the assets of the new SGI? Or will it become a leading server "supercomputer" company that will come to dominate the applications, database storage, and processing needs of leading Internet companies?

THE HOME VIDEO GAME INDUSTRY: ATARI PONG TO THE NINTENDO WII

AN INDUSTRY IS BORN

In 1968, Nolan Bushell, the 24-year-old son of a Utah cement contractor, graduated from the University of Utah with a degree in engineering.[1] Bushnell then moved to California, where he worked briefly in the computer graphics division of Ampex. At home, Bushnell turned his daughter's bedroom into a laboratory. There, he created a simpler version of Space War, a computer game that had been invented in 1962 by an MIT graduate student, Steve Russell. Bushnell's version of Russell's game, which he called Computer Space, was made of integrated circuits connected to a 19-inch black-and-white television screen. Unlike a computer, Bushnell's invention could do nothing but play the game, which meant that, unlike a computer, it could be produced cheaply.

Bushnell envisioned video games like his standing next to pinball machines in arcades. With hopes of having his invention put into production, Bushnell left Ampex to work for a small pinball company that manufactured 1,500 copies of his video game. The game never sold, primarily because the player had to read a full page of directions before he or she could play the game—way too complex for an arcade game. Bushnell left the pinball company and with a friend, Ted Dabney, put up $500 to start a company that would develop a simpler video game. They wanted to call the company Syzygy, but the name was already taken, so they settled on Atari, a Japanese word that was the equivalent of "check in the go."

In his home laboratory, Bushnell built the simplest game he could think of. People knew the rules immediately, and it could be played with one hand. The game was modeled on table tennis, and players batted a ball back and forth with paddles that could be moved up and down sides of a court by twisting knobs. He named the game "Pong" after the sonar-like sound that was emitted every time the ball connected with a paddle.

In the fall of 1972, Bushnell installed his prototype for Pong in Andy Capp's tavern in Sunnyvale, California. The only instructions were "avoid missing the ball for a high score." In the first week, 1,200 quarters were deposited in the casserole dish that served as a coin box in Bushnell's prototype. Bushnell was ecstatic; his simple game had brought in $300 in a week. The pinball machine that stood next to it averaged $35 a week.

Lacking the capital to mass-produce the game, Bushnell approached established amusement game companies, only to be repeatedly shown the door. Down but hardly out, Bushnell cut his hair, put on a suit, and talked his way into a $50,000 line of credit from a local bank. He set up a production line in an abandoned roller skating rink and hired people to assemble machines while Led Zeppelin and the Rolling Stones played at full volume over the speaker system of the rink. Among his first batch of employees was a skinny 17-year-old named Steve Jobs, who would later found a few companies of his own, including Apple Computer, NeXT, and Pixar. Like others, Jobs had been attracted by a classified ad that read "Have Fun and Make Money."

In no time at all, Bushnell was selling all the machines that his small staff could make—about

---

This case was prepared by Charles W. L. Hill, the University of Washington. This case is intended to be used as a basis for class discussion rather than as an illustration of either effective or ineffective handling of the situation. Reprinted by permission of Charles W. L. Hill.

10 per day; to grow, however, he needed additional capital. The ambience at the rink, with its mix of rock music and marijuana fumes, put off most potential investors, but Don Valentine, one of the country's most astute and credible venture capitalists, was impressed with the growth story. Armed with Valentine's money, Atari began to increase production and expand its range of games. New games included Tank and Breakout; the latter was designed by Jobs and a friend of his, Steve Wozniak, who had left HP to work at Atari.

By 1974, 100,000 Pong-like games were sold worldwide. Although Atari manufactured only 10% of the games, the company still made $3.2 million that year. With the Pong clones coming on strong, Bushnell decided to make a Pong system for the home. In fact, Magnavox had been marketing a similar game for the home since 1972, although sales had been modest.[2] Bushnell's team managed to compress Atari's coin-operated Pong game down to a few inexpensive circuits that were contained in the game console. Atari's Pong had a sharper picture and more sensitive controllers than Magnavox's machine. It also cost less. Bushnell then went on a road show, demonstrating Pong to toy buyers, but he received an indifferent response and no sales. A dejected Bushnell returned to Atari with no idea of what to do next. Then the buyer for the sporting goods department at Sears came to see Bushnell, reviewed the machine, and offered to buy every home Pong game Atari could make. With Sears's backing, Bushnell boosted production. Sears ran a major television ad campaign to sell home Pong, and Atari's sales soared, hitting $450 million in 1975. The home video game had arrived.

BOOM AND BUST

Nothing attracts competitors like success, and by 1976 about 20 different companies were crowding into the home video game market, including National Semiconductor, RCA, Coleco, and Fairchild. Recognizing the limitations of existing home video game designs, in 1976, Fairchild came out with a home video game system capable of playing multiple games. The Fairchild system consisted of three components—a console, controllers, and cartridges. The console was a small computer optimized for

graphics processing capabilities. It was designed to receive information from the controllers, process it, and send signals to a television monitor. The controllers were handheld devices used to direct on-screen action. The cartridges contained chips encoding the instructions for a game. The cartridges were designed to be inserted into the console.

In 1976, Bushnell sold Atari to Warner Communications for $28 million. Bushnell stayed on to run Atari. Backed by Warner's capital, in 1977, Atari developed and brought out its own cartridge-based system, the Atari 2600. The 2600 system was sold for $200, and associated cartridges retailed for $25 to $35. Sales surged during the 1977 Christmas season. However, a lack of manufacturing capacity on the part of market-leader Atari and a very cautious approach to inventory by Fairchild led to shortages and kept sales significantly below what they could have been. Fairchild's cautious approach was the result of prior experience in consumer electronics. A year earlier, it had increased demand for its digital watches, only to accumulate a buildup of excess inventory that had caused the company to take a $24.5 million write-off.[3]

After the 1977 Christmas season, Atari claimed to have sold about 400,000 units of the 2600 VCA, about 50% of all cartridge-based systems in American homes. Atari had also earned more than $100 million in sales of game cartridges. By this point, second-place Fairchild sold about 250,000 units of its system. Cartridge sales for the year totaled about 1.2 million units, with an average selling price of about $20. Fresh from this success and fortified by market forecasts predicting sales of 33 million cartridges and an installed base of 16 million machines by 1980, Bushnell committed Atari to manufacturing 1 million units of the 2600 for the 1978 Christmas season. Atari estimated that total demand would reach 2 million units. Bushnell was also encouraged by signals from Fairchild that it would again be limiting production to approximately 200,000 units. At this point, Atari had a library of nine games, while Fairchild had 17 games.[4]

Atari was not the only company to be excited by the growth forecasts. In 1978, a host of other companies, including Coleco, National Semiconductor, Magnavox, General Instrument, and a dozen other companies, entered the market with incompatible cartridge-based home systems. The multitude of choices did not seem to entice consumers, however, and the 1978 Christmas season brought unexpectedly low sales. Only Atari and Coleco survived an industry shakeout. Atari lost Bushnell, who was ousted by Warner executives. (Bushnell went on to start Chuck E. Cheese Pizza Time Theater, a restaurant chain that had 278 outlets by 1981.) Bushnell later stated that part of the problem was a disagreement over strategy. Bushnell wanted Atari to price the 2600 at cost and make money on sales of software; Warner wanted to continue making profits on hardware sales.[5]

Several important developments occurred in 1979. First, several game producers and programmers defected from Atari to set up their own firm, Activision, and to make games compatible with the Atari 2600. Their success encouraged others to follow suit. Second, Coleco developed an expansion module that allowed its machine to play Atari games. Atari and Mattel (who entered the market in 1979) did likewise. Third, the year 1979 saw the introduction of three new games to the home market—Space Invaders, Asteroids, and Pac Man. All three were adapted from popular arcade games and all three helped drive demand for players.

Demand recovered strongly in late 1979 and kept growing for the next three years. In 1981, United States sales of home video games and cartridges hit $1 billion. In 1982, they surged to $3 billion, with Atari accounting for half of this amount. It seemed as if Atari could do no wrong; the 2600 was everywhere. About 20 million units were sold, and by late 1982, a large number of independent companies, including Activision, Imagic, and Epyx, were now producing hundreds of games for the 2600. Second-place Coleco was also doing well, partly because of a popular arcade game, Donkey Kong, which it had licensed from a Japanese company called Nintendo.

Atari was also in contact with Nintendo. In 1982, the company very nearly licensed the rights to Nintendo's Famicom, a cartridge-based video game system machine that was a big hit in Japan. Atari's successor to the 2600, the 5200, was not selling well, and the Famicom seemed like a good substitute. The negotiations broke down, however, when Atari discovered that Nintendo had extended its Donkey Kong license to Coleco. This allowed Coleco to port a version of the game to its home computer, which was a direct competitor to Atari's 800 home computer.[6]

After a strong 1982 season, the industry hoped for continued growth in 1983. Then the bottom dropped

out of the market. Sales of home video games plunged to $100 million. Atari lost $500 million in the first nine months of the year, causing the stock of parent company Warner Communications to drop by half. Part of the blame for the collapse was laid at the feet of an enormous inventory overhang of unsold games. About 15 to 20 million surplus game cartridges were left over from the 1982 Christmas season (in 1981, there were none). On top of this, approximately 500 new games hit the market in 1993. The average price of a cartridge plunged from $30 in 1979 to $16 in 1982 and then to $4 in 1983. As sales slowed, retailers cut back on the shelf space allocated to video games. It proved difficult for new games to make a splash in a crowded market. Atari had to dispose of 6 million ET: The Extraterrestrial games. Meanwhile, big hits from previous years, such as Pac Man, were bundled with game players and given away free to try to encourage system sales.[7]

Surveying the rubble, commentators claimed that the video game industry was dead. The era of dedicated game machines was over, they claimed. Personal computers were taking their place.[8] It seemed to be true. Mattel sold off its game business, Fairchild moved on to other things, Coleco folded, and Warner decided to break up Atari and sell its constituent pieces—at least, those pieces for which it could find a buyer. No one in America seemed to want to have anything to do with the home video game business; no one, that is, except for Minoru Arakawa, the head of Nintendo's United States subsidiary, Nintendo of America (NOA). Picking through the rubble of the industry, Arakawa noticed that there were people who still packed video arcades, bringing in $7 billion a year, more money than the entire movie industry. Perhaps it was not a lack of interest in home video games that had killed the industry. Perhaps it was bad business practice.

The Nintendo Monopoly

Nintendo was a century-old Japanese company that had built up a profitable business making playing cards before diversifying into the video game business. Based in Kyoto and still run by the founding Yamauchi family, the company started to diversify into the video game business in the late 1970s. The first step was to license video game technology from Magnavox. In 1977, Nintendo introduced a home video game system in Japan based on this technology that played a variation of Pong. In 1978, the company began to sell coin-operated video games. It had its first hit with Donkey Kong, designed by Sigeru Miyamoto.

The Famicom

In the early 1980s, the company's boss, Hiroshi Yamauchi, decided that Nintendo had to develop its own video game machine. He pushed the company's engineers to develop a machine that combined superior graphics-processing capabilities and low cost. Yamauchi wanted a machine that could sell for $75, less than half the price of competing machines at the time. He dubbed the machine the Family Computer, or Famicom. The machine that his engineers designed was based on the controller, console, and plug-in cartridge format pioneered by Fairchild. It contained two custom chips—an 8-bit central processing unit and a graphics-processing unit. Both chips had been scaled down to perform only essential functions. A 16-bit processor was available at the time, but to keep costs down, Yamauchi refused to use it.

Nintendo approached Ricoh, the electronics giant, which had spare semiconductor capacity. Employees at Ricoh said that the chips had to cost no more that 2,000 yen. Ricoh thought that the 2,000-yen price point was absurd. Yamauchi's response was to guarantee Ricoh a 3-million-chip order within two years. Since the leading companies in Japan were selling, at most, 30,000 video games per year at the time, many within the company viewed this as an outrageous commitment, but Ricoh went for it.[9]

Another feature of the machine was its memory—2,000 bytes of random access memory (RAM), compared to the 256 bytes of RAM in the Atari machine. The result was a machine with superior graphics-processing capabilities and faster action that could handle far more complex games than Atari games. Nintendo's engineers also built a new set of chips into the game cartridges. In addition to chips that held the game program, Nintendo developed memory map controller (MMC) chips that took over some of the graphics-processing work from the chips in the console and enabled the system to handle more complex games. With the addition of the MMC chips, the potential for

more-sophisticated and complex games had arrived. Over time, Nintendo's engineers developed more powerful MMC chips, enabling the basic 8-bit system to do things that originally seemed out of reach. The engineers also figured out a way to include a battery backup system in cartridges that allowed some games to store information independently—to keep track of where a player had left off or track high scores.

The Games

Yamauchi recognized that great hardware would not sell itself. The key to the market, he reasoned, was great games. Yamauchi had instructed the engineers, as they were developing the hardware, to make sure that "it was appreciated by software engineers." Nintendo decided that it would become a haven for game designers. "An ordinary man," Yamauchi said, "cannot develop good games no matter how hard he tries. A handful of people in this world can develop games that everyone wants. Those are the people we want at Nintendo."[10]

Yamauchi had an advantage in the person of Sigeru Miyamoto. Miyamoto had joined Nintendo at the age of 24. Yamauchi had hired Miyamoto, a graduate of Kanazawa Munici College of Industrial Arts, as a favor to his father and an old friend, although he had little idea what he would do with an artist. For three years, Miyamoto worked as Nintendo's staff artist. Then in 1980, Yamauchi called Miyamoto into his office. Nintendo had started selling coin-operated video games, but one of the new games, Radarscope, was a disaster. Could Miyamoto come up with a new game? Miyamoto was delighted. He had always spent a lot of time drawing cartoons, and as a student, he had played video games constantly. Miyamoto believed that video games could be used to bring cartoons to life.[11]

The game Miyamoto developed was nothing short of a revelation. At a time when most coin-operated video games lacked characters or depth, Miyamoto created a game around a story that had both. Most games involved battles with space invaders or heroes shooting lasers at aliens; Miyamoto's game did neither. Based loosely on *Beauty and the Beast* and *King Kong*, Miyamoto's game involved a pet ape who runs off with his master's beautiful girlfriend. His master is an ordinary carpenter called Mario, who has a bulbous nose, a bushy mustache, a pair of large pathetic eyes, and a red cap (which Miyamoto added because he was not good at hairstyles). He does not carry a laser gun. The ape runs off with the girlfriend to get back at his master, who was not especially nice to the beast. The man, of course, has to get his girlfriend back by running up ramps, climbing ladders, jumping off elevators, and the like, while the ape throws objects at the hapless carpenter. Since the main character is an ape, Miyamoto called him Kong; because the main character is as stubborn as a donkey, he called the game Donkey Kong.

Released in 1981, Donkey Kong was a sensation in the world of coin-operated video arcades and a smash hit for Nintendo. In 1984, Yamauchi again summoned Miyamoto to his office. He needed more games, this time for Famicom. Miyamoto was made the head of a new research and development (R&D) group and told to come up with the most imaginative video games ever.

Miyamoto began with Mario from Donkey Kong. A colleague had told him that Mario looked more like a plumber than a carpenter, so a plumber he became. Miyamoto gave Mario a brother, Luigi, who was as tall and thin as Mario was short and fat. They became the Super Mario Brothers. Since plumbers spend their time working on pipes, large green sewer pipes became obstacles and doorways into secret worlds. Mario and Luigi's task was to search for the captive Princess Toadstool. Mario and Luigi are endearing bumblers, unequal to their tasks yet surviving. They shoot, squash, or evade their enemies—a potpourri of inventions that include flying turtles and stinging fish, man-eating flowers and fire-breathing dragons— while they collect gold coins, blow air bubbles, and climb vines into smiling clouds.[12]

Super Mario Brothers was introduced in 1985. For Miyamoto, this was just the beginning. Between 1985 and 1991, Miyamoto produced eight Mario games. About 60 to 70 million were sold worldwide, making Miyamoto the most successful game designer in the world. After adapting Donkey Kong for Famicom, he also went on to create other topselling games, including another classic, The Legend of Zelda. While Miyamoto drew freely from folklore, literature, and pop culture, the main source for his ideas was his own experience. The memory of being lost among a maze of sliding doors in his family's home was re-created in the labyrinths of the Zelda games. The dog that attacked him when he was a child attacks Mario in Super Mario. As a child,

Miyamoto had once climbed a tree to catch a view of far-off mountains and had become stuck. Mario gets himself in a similar fix. Once Miyamoto went hiking without a map and was surprised to stumble across a lake. In the Legend of Zelda, part of the adventure is in walking into new places without a map and being confronted by surprises.

Nintendo in Japan

Nintendo introduced Famicom into the Japanese market in May 1983. Famicom was priced at $100, more than Yamauchi wanted, but significantly less than the products of competitors. When he introduced the machine, Yamauchi urged retailers to forgo profits on the hardware because it was just a tool to sell software, and that is where they would make their money. Backed by an extensive advertising campaign, 500,000 units of Famicom were sold in the first two months. Within a year, the figure stood at 1 million, and sales were still expanding rapidly. With the hardware quickly finding its way into Japanese homes, Nintendo was besieged with calls from desperate retailers frantically demanding more games.

At this point, Yamauchi told Miyamoto to come up with the most imaginative games ever. However, Yamauchi also realized that Nintendo alone could not satisfy the growing thirst for new games, so he initiated a licensing program. To become a Nintendo licensee, companies had to agree to an unprecedented series of restrictions. Licensees could issue only five Nintendo games per year, and they could not write those titles for other platforms. The licensing fee was set at 20% of the wholesale price of each cartridge sold (game cartridges wholesaled for around $30). It typically cost $500,000 to develop a game and took around six months. Nintendo insisted that games not contain any excessively violent or sexually suggestive material and that they review every game before allowing it to be produced.[13]

Despite these restrictions, six companies (Bandai, Capcom, Konami, Namco, Taito, and Hudson) agreed to become Nintendo licensees, not least because millions of customers were now clamoring for games. Bandai was Japan's largest toy company. The others already made either coin-operated video games or computer software games. Because of these licensing agreements, they saw their sales and earnings surge. For example, Konami's earnings went from $10 million in 1987 to $300 million in 1991.

After the six licensees began selling games, reports of defective games began to reach Yamauchi. The original six licensees were allowed to manufacture their own game cartridges. Realizing that he had given away the ability to control the quality of the cartridges, Yamauchi decided to change the contract for future licensees. Future licensees were required to submit all manufacturing orders for cartridges to Nintendo. Nintendo charged licensees $14 per cartridge, required that they place a minimum order for 10,000 units (later the minimum order was raised to 30,000), and insisted on cash payment in full when the order was placed. Nintendo outsourced all manufacturing to other companies, using the volume of its orders to get rock bottom prices. The cartridges were estimated to cost Nintendo between $6 and $8 each. The licensees then picked up the cartridges from Nintendo's loading dock and were responsible for distribution. In 1985, there were 17 licensees. By 1987, there were 50. By this point, 90% of the home video game systems sold in Japan were Nintendo systems.

Nintendo in America

In 1980, Nintendo established a subsidiary in America to sell its coin-operated video games. Yamauchi's American-educated son-in-law, Minoru Arakawa, headed the subsidiary. All of the other essential employees were Americans, including Ron Judy and Al Stone. For its first two years, Nintendo of America (NOA), based originally in Seattle, struggled to sell second-rate games such as Radarscope. The subsidiary seemed on the brink of closing. NOA could not even make the rent payment on the warehouse. Then they received a large shipment from Japan: 2,000 units of a new coin-operated video game. Opening the box, they discovered Donkey Kong. After playing the game briefly, Judy proclaimed it a disaster. Stone walked out of the building, declaring that "It's over."[14] The managers were appalled. They could not imagine a game less likely to sell in video arcades. The only promising sign was that a 20-year employee, Howard Philips, rapidly became enthralled with the machine.

Arakawa, however, knew he had little choice but to try to sell the machine. Judy persuaded the owner of the Spot Tavern near Nintendo's office to take one of the machines on a trial basis. After one night, Judy discovered $30 in the coin box, a phenomenal amount. The next night there was $35, and $36 the night after that. NOA had a hit on its hands.

By the end of 1982, NOA had sold more than 60,000 copies of Donkey Kong and had booked sales in excess of $100 million. The subsidiary had outgrown its Seattle location. They moved to a new site in Redmond, a Seattle suburb, where they located next to a small but fast-growing software company run by an old school acquaintance of Howard Philips, Bill Gates.

By 1984, NOA was riding a wave of success in the coin-operated video game market. Arakawa, however, was interested in the possibilities of selling Nintendo's new Famicom system in the United States. Throughout 1984, Arakawa, Judy, and Stone met with numerous toy and department store representatives to discuss the possibilities, only to be repeatedly rebuffed. Still smarting from the 1983 debacle, the representatives wanted nothing to do with the home video game business. They also met with former managers from Atari and Coleco to gain their insights. The most common response they received was that the market collapsed because the last generation of games were awful.

Arakawa and his team decided that if they were going to sell Famicom in the United States, they would have to find a new distribution channel. The obvious choice was consumer electronics stores. Thus, Arakawa asked the R&D team in Kyoto to redesign Famicom for the United States market so that it looked less like a toy (Famicom was encased in red and white plastic), and more like a consumer electronics device. The redesigned machine was renamed the Nintendo Entertainment System (NES).

Arakawa's big fear was that illegal, low-quality Taiwanese games would flood the United States market if NES was successful. To stop counterfeit games from being played on NES, Arakawa asked Nintendo's Japanese engineers to design a security system into the U.S. version of Famicom so that only Nintendo-approved games could be played on NES. The Japanese engineers responded by designing a security chip that was embedded in the game cartridges. NES would not work unless the security chips in the cartridges unlocked, or shook hands with, a chip in NES. Since the code embedded in the security chip was proprietary, the implication of this system was that no one could manufacture games for NES without Nintendo's specific approval.

To overcome the skepticism and reluctance of retailers to stock a home video game system, Arakawa decided in late 1985 to make an extraordinary commitment. Nintendo would stock stores and set up displays and windows. Retailers would not have to pay for anything they stocked for 90 days. After that, retailers could pay Nintendo for what they sold and return the rest. NES was bundled with Nintendo's best-selling game in Japan, Super Mario Brothers. It was essentially a risk-free proposition for retailers, but even with this, most were skeptical. Ultimately, thirty Nintendo personnel descended on the New York area. Referred to as the Nintendo SWAT team, they persuaded some stores to stock NES after an extraordinary blitz that involved 18-hour days. To support the New York product launch, Nintendo also committed itself to a $5 million advertising campaign aimed at the 7- to 14-year-old boys who seemed to be Nintendo's likely core audience.

By December 1985, between 500 and 600 stores in the New York area were stocking Nintendo systems. Sales were moderate, about half of the 100,000 NES machines shipped from Japan were sold, but it was enough to justify going forward. The SWAT team moved first to Los Angeles, then to Chicago, then to Dallas. As in New York, sales started at a moderate pace, but by late 1986 they started to accelerate rapidly, and Nintendo went national with NES.

In 1986, around 1 million NES units were sold in the United States. In 1987, the figure increased to 3 million. In 1988, it jumped to over 7 million. In the same year, 33 million game cartridges were sold. Nintendo mania had arrived in the United States. To expand the supply of games, Nintendo licensed the rights to produce up to five games per year to 31 American software companies. Nintendo continued to use a restrictive licensing agreement that gave it exclusive rights to any games, required licensees to place their orders through Nintendo, and insisted on a 30,000-unit minimum order.[15]

By 1990, the home video game market was worth $5 billion worldwide. Nintendo dominated the industry, with a 90% share of the market for game equipment. The parent company was, by some measures, now the most profitable company in Japan. By 1992, it was netting over $1 billion in gross profit annually, or more than $1.5 million for each employee in Japan. The company's stock market value exceeded that of Sony, Japan's premier consumer electronics firm. Indeed, the company's net profit exceeded that of all the American movie studios combined. Nintendo games, it seemed, were bigger than the movies.

As of 1991, there were more than 100 licensees for Nintendo, and more than 450 titles were available for NES. In the United States, Nintendo products were distributed through toy stores (30% of volume), mass merchandisers (40% of volume), and department stores (10% of volume). Nintendo tightly controlled the number of game titles and games that could be sold, quickly withdrawing titles as soon as interest appeared to decline. In 1988, retailers requested 110 million cartridges from Nintendo. Market surveys suggested that perhaps 45 million could have been sold, but Nintendo allowed only 33 million to be shipped.[16] Nintendo claimed that the shortage of games was in part due to a worldwide shortage of semiconductor chips.

Several companies had tried to reverse-engineer the code embedded in Nintendo's security chip, which competitors characterized as a lockout chip. Nintendo successfully sued them. The most notable was Atari Games, one of the successors of the original Atari, which in 1987 sued Nintendo of America for anticompetitive behavior. Atari claimed that the purpose of the security chip was to monopolize the market. At the same time, Atari announced that it had found a way around Nintendo's security chip and would begin to sell unlicensed games.[17] NOA responded with a countersuit. In a March 1991 ruling, Atari was found to have obtained Nintendo's security code illegally and was ordered to stop selling NES-compatible games. However, Nintendo did not always have it all its own way. In 1990, under pressure from Congress, the Department of Justice, and several lawsuits, Nintendo rescinded its exclusivity requirements, freeing up developers to write games for other platforms. However, developers faced a real problem: what platform could they write for?

SEGA'S SONIC BOOM

Back in 1954, David Rosen, a 20-year-old American, left the U.S. Air Force after a tour of duty in Tokyo.[18] Rosen had noticed that Japanese people needed lots of photographs for ID cards, but local photo studios were slow and expensive. He formed a company, Rosen Enterprises, and went into the photo-booth business, which was a big success. By 1957, Rosen had established a successful nationwide chain. At this point, the Japanese economy was booming, so Rosen decided it was time to get into another business—entertainment. As his vehicle, he chose arcade games, which were unknown in Japan at the time. He picked up used games on the cheap from America and set up arcades in the same Japanese department stores and theaters that typically housed his photo booths. Within a few years, Rosen had 200 arcades nationwide. His only competition came from another American-owned firm, Service Games (SeGa), whose original business was jukeboxes and fruit machines.

By the early 1960s, the Japanese arcade market had caught up with the United States market. The problem was that game makers had run out of exciting new games to offer. Rosen decided that he would have to get into the business of designing and manufacturing games, but to do that he needed manufacturing facilities. SeGa manufactured its own games, so in 1965 Rosen approached the company and suggested a merger. The result was Sega Enterprise, a Japanese company with Rosen as its CEO.

Rosen designed Sega's first game, Periscope, in which the objective was to sink chain-mounted cardboard ships by firing torpedoes, represented by lines of colored lights. Periscope was a big success not only in Japan but also in the United States and Europe. It allowed Sega to build up a respectable export business. Over the years, the company continued to invest heavily in game development, always using the latest electronic technology.

Gulf and Western (G&W), a United States conglomerate, acquired Sega in 1969, with Rosen running the subsidiary. In 1975, Gulf and Western (G&W) took Sega public in the United States but kept Sega Japan as a G&W subsidiary. Hayao Nakayama, a former Sega distributor, was drafted as president. In the early 1980s, Nakayama pushed G&W to invest more in Sega Japan so that the company could enter the then-booming home video game market. When G&W refused, Nakayama suggested a management buyout. G&W agreed, and in 1984, for the price of just $38 million, Sega became a Japanese company once more. (Sega's Japanese revenues were about $700 million, but by now the company was barely profitable.)

Sega was caught off guard by the huge success of Nintendo's Famicom. Although it released its own 8-bit system in 1986, the machine never commanded more than 5% of the Japanese market. Nakayama, however, was not about to give up. From years in the arcade business, he understood that great games drove sales. Nevertheless, he also understood that more powerful technology gave game developers the tools to develop more appealing games. This philosophy underlay Nakayama's decision to develop a 16-bit game system, Genesis.

Sega took the design of its 16-bit arcade machine and adapted it for Genesis. Compared to Nintendo's 8-bit machine, the 16-bit machine featured an array of superior technological features, including high-definition graphics and animation, a full spectrum of colors, two independent scrolling backgrounds that created an impressive depth of field, and near CD quality sound. The design strategy also made it easy to port Sega's catalog of arcade hits to Genesis.

Genesis was launched in Japan in 1989 and in the United States in 1990. In the United States, the machine was priced at $199. The company hoped that sales would be boosted by the popularity of its arcade games, such as the graphically violent Altered Beast. Sega also licensed other companies to develop games for the Genesis platform. In an effort to recruit licensees, Sega asked for lower royalty rates than Nintendo, and it gave licensees the right to manufacture their own cartridges. Independent game developers were slow to climb on board, however, and the $200 price tag for the player held back sales.

One of the first independent game developers to sign up with Sega was Electronic Arts (EA). Established by Trip Hawkins, EA had focused on designing games for personal computers and consequently had missed the Nintendo 8-bit era. Now Hawkins was determined to get a presence in the home video game market, and aligning his company's wagon with Sega seemed to be the best option. The Nintendo playing field was already crowded, and Sega offered a far less restrictive licensing deal than Nintendo. EA subsequently wrote several popular games for Genesis, including John Madden football and several gory combat games.[19]

Nintendo had not been ignoring the potential of the 16-bit system. Nintendo's own 16-bit system, Super NES, was ready for market introduction in 1989—at the same time as Sega's Genesis. Nintendo introduced Super NES in Japan in 1990, where it quickly established a strong market presence and beat Sega's Genesis. In the United States, however, the company decided to hold back longer to reap the full benefits of the dominance it enjoyed with the 8-bit NES system. Yamauchi was also worried about the lack of backward compatibility between Nintendo's 8-bit and 16-bit systems. (The company had tried to make the 16-bit system so that it could play 8-bit games but concluded that the cost of doing so was prohibitive.) These concerns may have led the company to delay market introduction until the 8-bit market was saturated.

Meanwhile, in the United States, the Sega bandwagon was beginning to gain momentum. One development that gave Genesis a push was the introduction of a new Sega game, Sonic the Hedgehog. Developed by an independent team that was contracted to Sega, the game featured a cute hedgehog that impatiently tapped his paw when the player took too long to act. Impatience was Sonic's central feature—he had places to go—and quickly—and he zipped along, collecting brass rings when he could find them, before rolling into a ball and flying down slides with loops and underground tunnels. Sonic was Sega's Mario.

In mid-1991, in an attempt to jump-start slow sales, Tom Kalinske, head of Sega's American subsidiary, decided to bundle Sonic the Hedgehog with the game player. He also reduced the price for the bundled unit to $150, and he relaunched the system with an aggressive advertising campaign aimed at teenagers. The campaign was built around the slogan "Genesis does what Nintendon't." The shift in strategy worked, and sales accelerated sharply.

Sega's success prompted Nintendo to launch its own 16-bit system. Nintendo's Super NES was introduced at $200. However, Sega now had a two-year head start in games. By the end of 1991, about 125 game titles were available for Genesis, compared to 25 for Super NES. In May 1992, Nintendo reduced the price of Super NES to $150. At this time Sega was claiming a 63% share of the 16-bit market in the United States, and Nintendo claimed a 60% share. By now, Sega was cool. It began to take more chances with mass media-defined morality. When Acclaim Entertainment released its bloody *Mortal Kombat* game in September 1992, the Sega version let players rip off heads and tear out hearts. Reflecting Nintendo's image of their core market, its version was sanitized. The Sega version outsold Nintendo's two to one.[20] Therefore, the momentum continued to run in Sega's favor. By January 1993, there were 320 titles available for Sega Genesis and 130 for Super NES. In early 1994, independent estimates suggested that Sega had 60% of the United States market and Nintendo had 40%, figures that Nintendo disputed.

3DO

Trip Hawkins, whose first big success was EA, founded 3DO in 1991.[21] Hawkins's vision for 3DO was to shift the home video game business away from the existing cartridge-based format and toward a CD-ROM-based platform. The original partners in 3DO were EA, Matsushita, Time Warner, AT&T, and the venture capital firm Kleiner Perkins. Collectively, they invested more than $17 million in 3DO, making it the richest start-up in the history of the home video game industry. 3DO went public in May 1993 at $15 per share. By October of that year, the stock had risen to $48 per share, making 3DO worth $1 billion—not bad for a company that had yet to generate a single dollar in revenues.

The basis for 3DO's $1 billion market cap was a patented computer system architecture and a copyrighted operating system that allowed for much richer graphics and audio capabilities. The system was built around a 32-bit reduced instruction set computing (RISC) microprocessor and proprietary graphics processor chips. Instead of a cartridge, the 3DO system stored games on a CD-ROM that was capable of holding up to 600 megabytes of content, sharply up from the 10 megabytes of content found in the typical game cartridge of the time. The slower access time of a CD-ROM compared to a cartridge was alleviated somewhat by the use of a double-speed CD-ROM drive.[22]

The belief at 3DO—a belief apparently shared by many investors—was that the superior storage and graphics-processing capabilities of the 3DO system would prove very attractive to game developers, allowing them to be far more creative. In turn, better games would attract customers away from Nintendo and Sega. Developing games that used the capabilities of a CD-ROM system altered the economics of game development. Estimates suggested that it would cost approximately $2 million to produce a game for the 3DO system and could take as long as 24 months to develop. However, at $2 per disc, a CD-ROM cost substantially less to produce than a cartridge.

The centerpiece of 3DO's strategy was to license its hardware technology for free. Game developers paid a royalty of $3 per disc for access to the 3DO operating code. Discs typically retailed for $40 each.

Matsushita introduced the first 3DO machine into the United States market in October 1993. Priced at $700, the machine was sold through electronic retailers that carried Panasonic high-end electronics products. Sega's Tom Kalinsky noted, "It's a noble effort. Some people will buy 3DO, and they'll have a wonderful experience. It's impressive, but it's a niche. We've done the research. It does not become a large market until you go below $500. At $300, it starts to get interesting. We make no money on hardware. It's a cutthroat business. I hope Matsushita understands that."[23] CD-ROM discs for the 3DO machine retailed for about $75. The machine came bundled with Crash 'n' Burn, a high-speed combat racing game. However, only 18 3DO titles were available by the crucial Christmas period, although reports suggested that 150 titles were under development.[24]

Sales of the hardware were slow, reaching only 30,000 by January 1994.[25] In the same month, AT&T and Sanyo both announced that they would begin to manufacture the 3DO machine. In March, faced with continuing sluggish sales, 3DO announced that it would give hardware manufacturers two shares of 3DO stock for every unit sold at or below a certain retail price. Matsushita dropped the price of its machine to $500. About the same time, Toshiba, LG, and Samsung all announced that they would start to produce 3DO machines.

By June 1994, cumulative sales of 3DO machines in the United States stood at 40,000 units. Matsushita announced plans to expand distribution beyond the current 3,500 outlets to include the toy and mass merchandise channels. Hawkins and his partners announced that they would invest another $37 million in 3DO. By July, there were 750 3DO software licensees, but only 40 titles were available for the format. Despite these moves, sales continued at a very sluggish pace, and the supply of new software titles started to dry up.[26]

In September 1996, 3DO announced that it would either sell its hardware system business or move it into a joint venture.[27] The company announced that about 150 people, one-third of the workforce, would probably lose their jobs in the restructuring. According to Trip Hawkins, 3DO would now focus on developing software for online gaming. Hawkins stated that the Internet and Internet entertainment constituted a huge opportunity for 3DO. The stock dropped $1.375 to $6.75.

SEGA'S SATURN

3DO was not alone in moving to a CD-ROM-based format. Both Sega and Sony also introduced CD-ROM-based systems in the mid-1990s. Sega had, in fact, beaten 3DO to the market with its November 1992 introduction of the Sega CD, a $300 CD-ROM add-on for the 16-bit Genesis. Sega sold 100,000 units in its first month alone. Sales then slowed down, however, and by December 1993 were standing at just 250,000 units. One reason for the slowdown, according to critics, was a lack of strong games. Sega was also working on a 32-bit CD-ROM system, Saturn, which was targeted for a mid-1995 introduction in the United States. In January 1994, Sega announced that Microsoft would supply the operating system for Saturn.[28]

In March 1994, Sega announced the Genesis Super 32X, a $150 add-on cartridge designed to increase the performance of Genesis cartridge and CD-ROM games. The 32X contained the 32-bit Hitachi microprocessor that was to be used in Saturn. Sega called the 32X "the poor man's 32-bit machine" because it sold for a mere $149. Introduced in the fall of 1994, the 32X never lived up to its expectations. Most users appeared willing to wait for the real thing, Sega Saturn, promised for release the following year.

In early 1995, Sega informed the press and retailers that it would release Saturn on "Sega Saturn Saturday, Sept 2nd," but Sega released the 32-bit Saturn in May 1995. It was priced at $400 per unit and accompanied by the introduction of just 10 games. Sega apparently believed that the world would be delighted by the May release of the Saturn. However, Saturn was released without the industry fanfare that normally greets a new game machine. Only four retail chains received the Saturn in May, while the rest were told they would have to wait until September. This move alienated retailers, who responded by dropping Sega products from their stores.[29] Sega appeared to have made a marketing blunder.[30]

SONY'S PLAYSTATION

In the fall of 1995, Sony entered the fray with the introduction of the Sony PlayStation.[31] PlayStation used a 32-bit RISC microprocessor running at 33 MHz and using a double-speed CD-ROM drive. PlayStation cost an estimated $500 million to develop. The machine had actually been under development since 1991, when Sony decided that the home video game industry was getting too big to ignore. Initially, Sony was in an alliance with Nintendo to develop the machine. Nintendo walked away from the alliance in 1992, however, after a disagreement over who owned the rights to any future CD-ROM games. Sony went alone.[32]

From the start, Sony felt that it could leverage its presence in the film and music business to build a strong position in the home video game industry. A consumer electronics giant with a position in the Hollywood movie business and the music industry (Sony owned Columbia Pictures and the Columbia record label), Sony believed that it had access to significant intellectual property that could form the basis of many popular games.

In 1991, Sony established a division in New York: Sony Electronic Publishing. The division was to serve as an umbrella organization for Sony's multimedia offerings. Headed by Iceland native Olaf Olafsson, then just 28 years old, this organization ultimately took the lead role in both the market launch of Play-Station and in developing game titles.[33] In 1993, as part of this effort, Sony purchased a well-respected British game developer, Psygnosis. By the fall of 1995, this unit had 20 games ready to complement PlayStation: the Haldeman Diaries, Mickey Mania (developed in collaboration with Disney), and Johnny Mnemonic, based on the William Gibson short story. To entice independent game developers such as EA, Namco, and Acclaim Entertainment, Olafsson used the promise of low royalty rates. The standard royalty rate was set at $9 per disc, although developers that signed on early enough were given a lower royalty rate. Sony also provided approximately 4,000 game development tools to licensees in an effort to help them speed games to market.[34]

To distribute PlayStation, Sony set up a retail channel separate from Sony's consumer electronics sales force. It marketed the PlayStation as a hip and powerful alternative to the outdated Nintendo and Sega cartridge-based systems. Sony worked closely with retailers before the launch to find out how it could help them sell the PlayStation. To jump-start demand, Sony set up in-store displays to allow potential consumers to try the equipment. Just before the launch, Sony had lined up an impressive 12,000 retail outlets in the United States.[35]

Sony targeted its advertising for PlayStation at males in the 18- to 35-year age range. The targeting was evident in the content of many of the games. One of the big hits for PlayStation was Tomb Raider, whose central character, Lara Croft, combined sex

appeal with savvy and helped to recruit an older generation to PlayStation.[36] PlayStation was initially priced at $299, and games retailed for as much as $60. Sony's Tokyo-based executives had reportedly been insisting on a $350 to $400 price for PlayStation, but Olafsson pushed hard for the lower price. Because of the fallout from this internal battle, in January 1996, Olafsson resigned from Sony. By then, however, Sony was following Olafsson's script.[37]

Sony's prelaunch work was rewarded with strong early sales. More than 800,000 PlayStations and 4 million games had been sold in the United States by January 1996. In May 1996, with 1.2 million PlayStations shipped, Sony reduced the price of PlayStation to $199. Sega responded with a similar price cut for its Saturn. The prices on some of Sony's initial games were also reduced to $29.99. The weekend after the price cuts, retailers reported that PlayStation sales were up by between 350% and 1,000% over the prior week.[38] The sales surge continued through 1996. By the end of the year, sales of PlayStation and associated software amounted to $1.3 billion, out of a total for United States sales at $2.2 billion for all video game hardware and software. In March 1997, Sony cut the price of Play-Station again, this time to $149. It also reduced its suggested retail price for games by $10 to $49.99. By this point, Sony had sold 3.4 million units of PlayStation in the United States, compared to Saturn's 1.6 million units.[39] Worldwide, PlayStation had outsold Saturn by 13 million to 7.8 million units, and Saturn sales were slowing.[40] The momentum was clearly running in Sony's favor, but the company now had a new challenge to deal with: Nintendo's latest generation game machine, the N64.

NINTENDO STRIKES BACK

In July 1996, Nintendo launched Nintendo 64 (N64) in the Japanese market. This release was followed by a late fall introduction in the United States. N64 is a 64-bit machine developed in conjunction with Silicon Graphics. Originally targeted for introduction a year earlier, N64 had been under development since 1993. The machine used a plug-in cartridge format rather than a CD-ROM drive. According to Nintendo, cartridges allow for faster access time and are far more durable than CD-ROMs (an important consideration with children).[41]

The most-striking feature of the N64 machine, however, was its 3D graphics capability. N64 provides fully rounded figures that can turn on their heels and rotate through 180 degrees. Advanced ray-tracing techniques borrowed from military simulators and engineering workstations added to the sense of realism by providing proper highlighting, reflections, and shadows.

N64 was targeted at children and young teenagers. It was priced at $200 and launched with just four games. Despite the lack of games, initial sales were very strong. Indeed, 1997 turned out to be a banner year for both Sony and Nintendo. The overall United States market was strong, with sales of hardware and software combined reaching a record $5.5 billion. Estimates suggest that PlayStation accounted for 49% of machines and games by value. N64 captured a 41% share, leaving Sega trailing badly with less than 10% of the market. During the year, the average price for game machines had fallen to $150. By year-end there were 300 titles available for PlayStation, compared to 40 for N64. Games for PlayStation retailed for $40, on average, compared to more than $60 for N64.[42]

By late 1998, PlayStation was widening its lead over N64. In the crucial North American market, PlayStation was reported to be outselling N64 by a two-to-one margin, although Nintendo retained a lead in the under-12 category. At this point, there were 115 games available for N64 versus 431 for PlayStation.[43] Worldwide, Sony had now sold close to 55 million PlayStations. The success of PlayStation had a major impact on Sony's bottom line. In fiscal 1998, PlayStation business generated revenues of $5.5 billion for Sony, 10% of its worldwide revenues, but accounted for $886 million, or 22.5%, of the company's operating income.[44]

THE 128-BIT ERA

When Nintendo launched its 64-bit machine in 1996, Sony and Sega did not follow, preferring instead to focus on the development of even more powerful 128-bit machines.

Sega was the first to market a 128-bit video game console, which it launched in Japan in late 1998 and in the United States in late 1999. The Dreamcast came equipped with a 56-kilobit modem to allow for online gaming over the Internet. By late 2000, Sega had sold approximately 6 million Dreamcasts worldwide, accounting for about 15% of console sales since its launch. Sega nurtured Dreamcast sales by courting outside software developers who helped develop new games, including Crazy Taxi, Resident Evil, and Quake III Arena. The company had a goal of shipping 10 million units by March 2001, a goal it never reached.[45]

Despite its position as first mover with a 128-bit machine, and despite solid technical reviews, by late 2000 the company was struggling. Sega was handicapped first by product shortages due to constraints on the supply of component parts and then by a lack of demand as consumers waited to see whether Sony's 128 bit offering, the much anticipated PlayStation 2 (PS2), would be a more attractive machine. In September 2000, Sega responded to the impending United States launch of Sony's PS2 by cutting the price for its console from $199 to $149. Then in late October, Sega announced that, due to this price cut, it would probably lose more than $200 million for the fiscal year ending March 2001.[46]

Sony's PlayStation 2

PS2 was launched in Japan in mid-2000 and in the United States at the end of October 2000. Initially priced at $299, PS2 is a powerful machine. At its core was a 300-megahertz graphics processing chip that was jointly developed with Toshiba and consumed about $1.3 billion in R&D. Referred to as the Emotion Engine processor, the chip allows the machine to display stunning graphic images previously found only on supercomputers. The chip made the PS2 the most powerful video game machine yet.

The machine was set up to play different CD and DVD formats, as well as proprietary game titles. As is true with the original PlayStation, PS2 could play audio CDs. The system was also compatible with the original PlayStation: any PlayStation title could be played on the PS2. To help justify the initial price tag, the unit doubled as a DVD player with picture quality as good as current players. The PS2 did not come equipped with a modem, but it did have networking capabilities, and a modem could be attached using one of two USB ports.[47]

Nintendo GameCube

Nintendo had garnered a solid position in the industry with its N64 machine by focusing on its core demographic, 7- to 12-year-olds. In 1999, Nintendo took 33% of the hardware market and 28% of the game market. Nintendo's next generation video game machine, GameCube, packed a modem and a powerful 400-megahertz, 128-bit processor made by IBM into a compact cube. GameCube marked a shift away from Nintendo's traditional approach of using proprietary cartridges to hold game software. Instead, software for the new player came on 8-centimeter CDs, which are smaller than music CDs. The disks held 1.5 gigabytes of data each, far greater storage capacity than the old game cartridges. Players could control GameCube by using wireless controllers.[48]

Nintendo tried to make the GameCube easy for developers to work with rather than focusing on raw peak performance. While developers no doubt appreciated this, by the time GameCube hits store shelves in late 2001, PS2 had been on the market for 18 months and boasted a solid library of games. Despite its strong brand and instantly recognized intellectual property, which included Donkey Kong, Super Mario Brothers, and the Pokémon characters, Nintendo was playing catch-up to Sony. Moreover, another new entrant into the industry launched its 128 bit offering at about the same time: Microsoft.

Microsoft's Xbox

Microsoft was first rumored to be developing a video game console in late 1999. In March 2000, Bill Gates made it official when he announced that Microsoft would enter the home video game market in fall 2001 with a console code named Xbox. In terms of sheer computing power, the 128-bit Xbox had the edge over competitors. Xbox had a 733-megahertz Pentium III processor, a high-powered graphics chip from Nvidia Corp, a built-in broadband cable modem to allow for online game playing and high-speed Internet browsing, 64 megabytes of memory, CD and DVD drives, and an internal hard disk drive. The operating system was a stripped-down version of its popular Windows system optimized for graphics-processing capabilities. Microsoft claimed that because the Xbox was based on familiar PC technology, it would be much easier for software developers to write games for, and it would be relatively easy to convert games from the PC to run on the Xbox.[49]

Although Microsoft was a new entrant to the video game industry, it was no stranger to games. Microsoft had long participated in the PC gaming industry and was one of the largest publishers of PC games, with hits such as Microsoft Flight Simulator and Age of Empires I and II to its credit. Sales of Microsoft's PC games increased 50% annually between 1998 and 2001, and the company controlled about 10% of the PC game market in 2001. Microsoft also offered online gaming for some time, including its popular MSN Gaming Zone site. Started in 1996, by 2001 the Web site had become the largest online PC gaming hub on the Internet, with nearly 12 million subscribers paying $9.95 a month to play premium games, such as Asheron's Call or Fighter Ace. Nor was Microsoft new to hardware; its joysticks and game pads outsell all other brands, and it had an important mouse business.

To build the Xbox, Microsoft chose Flextronics, a contract manufacturer that already made computer mice for Microsoft. Realizing that it would probably have to cut Xbox prices over time, Microsoft guaranteed Flextronics a profit margin, effectively agreeing to subsidize Flextronics if selling prices fell below a specified amount. By 2003, Microsoft was thought to be losing $100 on every Xbox sold. To make that back and turn a profit, Microsoft reportedly had to sell between six and nine video games per Xbox.[50]

Analysts speculated that Microsoft's entry into the home video game market was a response to a potential threat from Sony. Microsoft was worried that Internet-ready consoles like PS2 might take over many Web-browsing functions from the personal computer. Some in the company described Internet-enabled video game terminals as Trojan horses in the living room. In Microsoft's calculation, it made sense to get in the market to try and keep Sony and others in check. With annual revenues in excess of $20 billion worldwide, the home video game market is huge and an important source of potential growth for Microsoft. Still, by moving away from its core market, Microsoft was taking a big risk, particularly given the scale of investments required to develop the Xbox, reported to run as high as $1.5 billion.

Mortal Combat:
Microsoft versus Sony

The launch of Xbox and GameCube helped propel sales of video game hardware and software to a record $9.4 billion in 2001, up from $6.58 billion in 2000. Although both Xbox and Nintendo initially racked up strong sales, the momentum started to slow significantly in 2002. Microsoft, in particular, found it very difficult to penetrate the Japanese market. By September 2002, Sony had sold 11.2 million units of PS2 in the United States versus 2.2 million units of Xbox and 2.7 million units of Nintendo's GameCube. Unable to hold onto market share in the wake of the new competition, Sega withdrew from the console market, announcing that, henceforth, it would focus just on developing games for other platforms.

In June 2002, Sony responded to the new entry by cutting the price for PS2 from $299 to $199. Microsoft quickly followed, cutting the price for Xbox from $299 to $199, while Nintendo cut its price from $299 to $149.[51] A year later, Sony cut prices again, this time to $179 a console. Again, Microsoft followed with a similar price cut, and in March 2004 it took the lead, cutting Xbox prices to $149. Sony followed suit two months later.[52]

Microsoft's strategy, however, involved far more than just cutting prices. In November 2002 Microsoft announced that it would introduce a new service for gamers, Xbox Live. For $50 a year, Xbox Live subscribers with broadband connections would be able to play online-enabled versions of Xbox games with other online subscribers. To support Xbox Live, Microsoft invested some $500 million in its own data centers to host online game playing.

Online game playing was clearly a strategic priority from the outset. Unlike the PS2 and GameCube, Xbox came with a built in broadband capability. The decision to make the Xbox broadband capable was made back in 1999 when less than 5% of United States homes were linked to the Internet with a broadband connection. Explaining the decision to build broadband capabilities into the Xbox at a time when rivals lacked them, the head of Xbox, Jay Allard, noted that "My attitude has always been to bet on the future, not against it."[53] While Sony's PS2 can be hooked up to the Internet via a broadband connection, doing so requires the purchase of a special network adapter for $40.

By mid-2003, Xbox Live had some 500,000 subscribers, versus 80,000 who had registered to play PS2 games online. By this time there were 28 online games for Xbox and 18 for PS2. By January 2004, the comparative figures stood at 50 for Microsoft and 32 for Sony. By mid-2004, Xbox Live reportedly had over one million subscribers, with Sony claiming a similar number of online players.[54] In May 2004, Microsoft struck a deal with EA, the world's largest video game publisher, to bring EA games, including its best selling Madden Football, to the Xbox Live platform. Until this point, EA had only produced live games for Sony's platform.

In spite of all these strategic moves, by late 2004, Xbox was still a distant second to PS2 in the video game market, having sold 14 million consoles against Sony's 70 million (Nintendo had sold 13 million GameCube consoles). While Sony was making good money from the business, Microsoft was registering significant losses. In fiscal 2004, Microsoft's home and entertainment division, of which Xbox is the major component, registered $2.45 billion in revenues, but lost $1.135 billion. By way of contrast, Sony's game division had $7.5 billion of sales in fiscal 2004 and generated operating profits of $640 million.

Microsoft, however, indicated that it was in the business for the long term. In late 2004, the company got a boost from the release of Halo 2, the sequel to Halo, one of its best-selling games. As first-day sales for Halo 2 were totaled, executives at Sony had to be worried. Microsoft announced that Halo 2 had sales of $125 million in its first 24 hours on the market in the United States and Canada, an industry record. These figures represented sales of 2.38 million units and put Halo 2 firmly on track to be one of the biggest video games ever with a shot at surpassing Nintendo's Super Mario 64, which had sold $308 million in the United States since its September 1996 debut. Moreover, the company was rumored to be ahead of Sony by as much as a year to bring the next generation video game console to market. In late 2004, reports suggested that Xbox 2 would be on the market in time for the 2005 Christmas season, probably a full year ahead of Sony's PlayStation 3 (PS3). Sony was rumored to be running into technical problems while developing the PS3.[55]

THE NEXT GENERATION

As the battle between PS2 and Xbox drew to a close, it was clear that Sony was the big winner. From 2001 through the fall of 2006, when PS3 hit the market, Sony had sold about 110 million PS2 consoles, versus 25 million for Microsoft's Xbox and 21 million for Nintendo's GameCube.[56] Sony's advantage in its installed base translated into a huge lead in number of games sold: approximately 1.08 billion for PS2 by mid-2006 versus 200 million for the Xbox.[57] With the console companies reportedly making an average royalty on third-party software of $8 per game sold, the financial implications of Sony's lead with PS2 are obvious.[58] Indeed, in 2005 Sony's games division contributed to 6.24% of the company's total revenue but 38% of operating profit. In contrast, Microsoft's home and entertainment division lost $4 billion between the launch of Xbox and mid-2006.

However, by 2006, this was all history. In November 2005, Microsoft introduced its next generation machine, Xbox 360, beating Sony and Nintendo to the market by a solid year. The Xbox 360 represented a big technological advance over the original Xbox. To deliver improved picture quality, the Xbox 360 could execute 500 million polygons per second: a four-fold increase over the Xbox. The main microprocessor was 13 times faster than the chip in the Xbox. Xbox 360 had 512 megabytes of memory, an 8-fold increase, and a 20-gigabyte hard drive, 2.5 times bigger than that found on the Xbox. Xbox 360 is, of course, enabled for a broadband connection to the Internet.

The machine was made by Flextronics and Wistron, two contract manufacturers (a third started production after launch). Priced at $299, Xbox 360 was sold at a loss. The cost for making Xbox 360 was estimated to be as high as $500 at launch, falling to $350 by late 2006. Microsoft's goal was to ultimately break even on sales of the hardware as manufacturing efficiencies drove down unit costs.

To seed the market with games, Microsoft took a number of steps. Taking a page out of its Windows business, Microsoft provided game developers with tools designed to automate many of the key software programming tasks and reduce development time and costs. The company had also expanded its own in-house game studios, in part by purchasing several independent game developers, including Bungie

Studios, makers of Halo. This strategy enabled Microsoft to offer exclusive content for the Xbox 360, something that third parties were reluctant to do.

With the costs of game development increasing to between $10 and $15 million for more complex games, and development time stretching out to between 24 and 36 months, Microsoft also had to provide an inducement to get third-party developers onboard. Although details of royalty terms are kept private, it is believed that Microsoft offered very low royalty rates, and perhaps even zero royalties, for a specified period of time to game developers who committed early to Xbox 360. One of those to commit early was EA, the leading independent game development company, which reportedly budgeted as much as $200 million to develop some 25 versions of its best-selling games, such as its sports games, for Xbox 360. Microsoft budgeted a similar amount to develop its own games.[59]

In the event, some 18 games were available for the November 2005 launch of Xbox 360, and by the end of 2006, this figure had increased to about 160. Halo 3, which was expected to be one of the biggest games for Xbox 360, was released in September 2007. Exclusive to the Xbox 360, Halo 3 racked in first-day sales of $170 million, which was an industry record. Grand Theft Auto 4, the most popular franchise on PS2, was also launched simultaneously for both Xbox 360 and PS3 in 2007: a major coup for Microsoft.

The initial launch of Xbox 360 was marred by shortages of key components, which limited the number of machines that Microsoft could bring to market. Had Sony been on time with its launch of PS3, this could have been a serious error, but Sony delayed its launch of PS3, first until spring of 2006 and then November 2006. By the time Sony launched PS3 in November 2006, some 6 million Xbox 360 consoles had been sold, and Microsoft was predicting sales of 10 million by the end of 2006.

As with Xbox, Microsoft pushed Xbox Live with Xbox 360. The company invested as much as $1 billion in Live from its inception. By late 2006 Microsoft was claiming that some 60% of Xbox 360 customers had also signed on for Xbox Live and that the service had 4 million subscribers. By early 2008, there were more than 10 million subscribers. Xbox Live allowed users to play against each other online and to download digital content from Xbox Live

Marketplace. Looking forward, there is little doubt that Microsoft sees Xbox Live as a critical element of its strategy, enabling Xbox owners to download any digital content—games, film, music—onto their consoles, which could become the hub of a home digital entertainment system.

The business model for Xbox 360 depends on the number of games sold per console, the percentage of console owners who sign up for Xbox Live, sales of hardware accessories (e.g., controllers, an HD-DVD drive, wireless networking adapter), and the console itself achieving break-even production costs. Reports suggest that Microsoft will break even if each console owner buys six to seven games, two to three accessories, and some 10 million sign on to Xbox Live (Microsoft splits Xbox Live revenues with game developers). By the end of 2006, it was estimated that some 33 million games had been sold for Xbox 360.[60]

Sony finally introduced PS3 on November 11, 2006 in Japan and November 17, 2006 in the United States. The delay in the launch of PS3 was due to Sony's decision to bundle a Blu-ray drive with PS3, along with problems developing the "cell" processor that sits at the core of the PS3. Blu-ray is Sony's proprietary HD-DVD format. The company is currently locked in a format war with Toshiba, which is pushing its rival HD-DVD format (which can be purchased as an accessory for the Xbox 360). Sony has argued that the combination of its cell processor and Blu-ray DVD drive will give PS3 a substantial performance edge over Xbox 360. While this is true in a technical sense (the Blu-ray discs have five times the storage capacity of the DVD discs for Xbox 360), few reviewers have noticed much in the way of difference from a game playing perspective—perhaps because few games were initially available that showed the true power of the PS3.

What is certain is that incorporating Blu-ray drives in the PS3 has significantly raised the costs of the PS3. Sony is selling its standalone Blu-ray drives for $999, which suggests that the PS3, initially priced at between $500 and $600 depending on configuration, is in a sense a subsidized Blu-ray player. Shortages of blue diodes, a critical component in HD-DVD drives, also limited supply of the PS3 after its launch. Only 93,000 PS3 players were available for the Japanese launch. At launch, there were some 20 games available for the PS3. Sony also announced its own live offering to compete with Xbox Live and stated that it would be free to PS3 users.

Nintendo is also back in the fray. In November 2006, it launched its own next generation offering, Wii. When developing the Wii, Nintendo made a number of interesting strategic decisions. First, it decided not to compete with Microsoft and Sony on graphics processing power. Instead of developing a high-powered machine crammed full of expensive custom-built components, they used off-the-shelf components to assemble a much cheaper machine that could be sold at a much lower price point (the initial price was $250). Although this machine did not offer the graphics processing capabilities of Xbox 360 or PS3, the games were cheaper to develop, about $5 million each as opposed to as much as $20 million for the PS3. Second, Nintendo decided to target a new demographic, indifferent people who had no interest in video games, as opposed to the stereotypical game player. Nintendo already had some evidence that this market could be tapped and would be extremely lucrative. In 2004, Nintendo had introduced a game for its handheld player, the DS, that was aimed not at its core 7- to 12-year-old demographic but at much wider market. The game, Brain Age, based on a brain training regime developed by a Japanese neuroscientist, was a huge hit in Japan, with sales of more than 12 million units. It made the DS a hit in such unlikely places as nursing homes. Third, rather than processing power, Nintendo decided to focus on developing a motion sensitive, wireless controller that could detect arm and hand motions and transfer them to the screen. This enabled the development of interactive games, with players physically controlling the action on screen by moving their arms, whether by swinging an imaginary bat, driving a go-kart, or slashing a sword through the air.[61]

By early 2007, it was clear that the Wii was turning into a surprise hit. The combination of low price, innovative design, and a portfolio of recognizable games based on Nintendo's long-established franchises, such as Mario Brothers and Pokémon, helped to drive sales forward. Moreover, as planned, the Wii seemed to have appeal to a broad range of age groups and both genders. Soon articles started to appear explaining how retirement homes were buying the Wii so that residents could play virtual baseball with their visiting grandchildren, and sales started to accelerate.

Exhibit 1   Cumulative Sales of Platform Through September 2008 (millions of units)

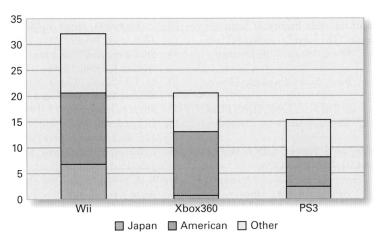

□ Japan   ▨ American   □ Other

Source: Raw data from VG Chartz at http://www.vgchartz.com/.

By 2008, Nintendo had seized the leadership position in the industry (see Exhibit 1). Cumulatively, the Wii had sold some 32 million units worldwide by September 2008, compared to 20.6 million units for Xbox 360 and 15.3 million units for the PS3. Moreover, Nintendo had established a strong position in all major markets, unlike Microsoft for example, which had been unable to garner significant Xbox

360 sales in Japan. The popularity of the Wii helped to drive Nintendo's sales and earnings to record levels, with net profits forecasted to reach a record $3.78 billion for the year ending March 2009. Nintendo's market capitalization on the Japanese stock market surpassed Sony's, and in September 2008 it was second only to Toyota. It would appear that Nintendo was back.

Endnotes

1. A good account of the early history of Bushnell and Atari can be found in S. Cohen, *Zap! The Rise and Fall of Atari*, New York: McGraw-Hill, 1984.
2. R. Isaacs, "Video Games Race to Catch a Changing Market," *Business Week*, December 26, 1977, 44B.
3. P. Pagnano, "Atari's Game Plan to Overwhelm Its Competitors," *Business Week*, May 8, 1978, 50F.
4. R. Isaacs, "Video Games Race to Catch a Changing Market," *Business Week*, December 26, 1977, 44B.
5. P. Pagnano, "Atari's Game Plan to Overwhelm Its Competitors," *Business Week*, May 8, 1978, 50F; and D. Sheff, *Game Over*, New York: Random House, 1993.
6. S. Cohen, *Zap! The Rise and Fall of Atari*, New York: McGraw-Hill, 1984.
7. L. Kehoe, "Atari Seeks Way out of Video Game Woes," *Financial Times*, December 14, 1983, 23.
8. M. Schrage, "The High Tech Dinosaurs: Video Games, Once Ascendant, Are Making Way," *Washington Post*, July 31, 1983, F1.
9. D. Sheff, *Game Over*, New York: Random House, 1993.
10. Quoted in D. Sheff, *Game Over*, New York: Random House, 1993, 38.
11. D. Sheff, *Game Over*, New York: Random House, 1993.
12. D. Golden, "In Search of Princess Toadstool," *Boston Globe*, November 20, 1988, 18.
13. N. Gross, and G. Lewis, "Here Come the Super Mario Bros.," *Business Week*, November 9, 1987, 138.
14. D. Sheff, *Game Over*, New York: Random House, 1993.
15. D. Golden, "In search of Princess Toadstool," *Boston Globe*, November 20, 1988, 18.

16. Staff Reporter, "Marketer of the Year," *Adweek*, November 27, 1989, 15.
17. C. Lazzareschi, "No Mere Child's Play," *Los Angeles Times*, December 16, 1988, 1.
18. For a good summary of the early history of Sega, see J. Battle, and B. Johnstone, "The Next Level: Sega's Plans for World Domination," *Wired*, release 1.06, December 1993.
19. D. Sheff, *Game Over*, New York: Random House, 1993.
20. J. Battle, and B. Johnstone, "The Next Level: Sega's Plans for World Domination," *Wired*, release 1.06, December 1993.
21. For background details, see J. Flower, "3DO: Hip or Hype?" *Wired*, release 1.02, May/June 1993.
22. R. Brandt, "3DO's New Game Player: Awesome or another Betamax?" *Business Week*, January 11, 1993, 38.
23. J. Flower, "3DO: Hip or Hype?" *Wired*, release 1.02, May/June 1993.
24. S. Jacobs, "Third Time's a Charm (They Hope)," *Wired*, release 2.01, January 1994.
25. A. Dunkin, "Video Games: The Next Generation," *Business Week*, January 31, 1994, 80.
26. J. Greenstein, "No Clear Winners, Though Some Losers: The Video Game Industry in 1995," *Business Week*, December 22, 1995, 42.
27. Staff Reporter, "3DO Says 'I Do' on Major Shift of Its Game Strategy," *Los Angeles Times*, September 17, 1996, 2.
28. J. Battle, and B. Johnstone, "The Next Level: Sega's Plans for World Domination," *Wired*, release 1.06, December 1993.
29. J. Greenstein, "No Clear Winners, Though Some Losers: The Video Game Industry in 1995," *Business Week*, December 22, 1995, 42.
30. D. P. Hamilton, "Sega Suddenly Finds Itself Embattled," *Wall Street Journal*, March 31, 1997, A10.
31. S. Taves, "Meet Your New Playmate," *Wired*, release 3.09, September 1995.
32. Kunni, I., "The Games Sony Plays," *Business Week*, June 15, 1998, 128.
33. C. Platt, "WordNerd," *Wired*, release 3.10, October 1995.
34. I. Kunni, "The Games Sony Plays," *Business Week*, June 15, 1998, 128.
35. J. A. Trachtenberg, "Race Quits Sony Just Before U.S. Rollout of Its PlayStation Video-Game System," *Wall Street Journal*, August 8, 1995, B3.
36. S. Beenstock, "Market Raider: How Sony Won the Console Game," *Marketing*, September 10, 1998, 26.
37. J. A. Trachtenberg, "Olafsson Calls It Quits as Chairman of Sony's Technology Strategy Group," *Wall Street Journal*, January 23, 1996, B6.
38. J. Greenstein "Price Cuts Boost Saturn, PlayStation Hardware Sales," *Video Business*, May 31, 1996, 1.
39. Greenstein, J., "Sony Cuts Prices of PlayStation Hardware," *Video Business*, March 10, 1997, 1.
40. D. Hamilton, "Sega Suddenly Finds Itself Embattled," *Wall Street Journal,* March 31, 1997, A10.
41. Staff Reporter, "Nintendo Wakes Up," *The Economist*, August 3, 1996, 55–56.
42. D. Takahashi, "Game Plan: Video Game Makers See Soaring Sales Now—And Lots of Trouble Ahead," *Wall Street Journal*, June 15, 1998, R10.
43. D. Takahashi, "Sony and Nintendo Battle for Kids under 13," *Wall Street Journal*, September 24, 1998, B4.
44. I. Kunni, "The Games Sony Plays," *Business Week*, June 15, 1998, 128.
45. R. A. Guth, "Sega Cites Dreamcast Price Cuts for Loss Amid Crucial Time for Survival of Firm," *Wall Street Journal*, October 30, 2000, A22.
46. R. Guth, "Sega Cites Dreamcast Price Cuts for Loss Amid Crucial Time for Survival of Firm," *Wall Street Journal*, October 30, 2000, A22.
47. T. Oxford, and S. Steinberg, "Ultimate Game Machine Sony's PlayStation 2 Is Due on Shelves Oct. 26. It Brims with Potential—But at This Point Sega's Dreamcast Appears a Tough Competitor," *Atlanta Journal/Atlanta Constitution*, October 1, 2000, P1.
48. R. A. Guth, "New Players from Nintendo Will Link to Web," *Wall Street Journal*, August 25, 2000, B1.
49. D. Takahashi, "Microsoft's X-Box Impresses Game Developers," *Wall Street Journal,* March 13, 2000, B12.
50. K. Powers, "Showdown," *Forbes*, August 11, 2003, 86–87.
51. *The Economist*, "Console Wars," June 22, 2002, 71.
52. R. A. Guth, "Game Gambit: Microsoft to Cut Xbox Price," *Wall Street Journal*, March 19, 2004, B1.
53. K. Powers, "Showdown," *Forbes*, August 11, 2003, 86–87.
54. E. Taub, "No Longer a Solitary Pursuit: Video Games Move Online," *New York Times,* July 5, 2004, C4.
55. J. Greene and C. Edwards, "Microsoft Plays Video Leapfrog," *Business Week*, May 10, 2004, 44–45.
56. "Playing a Long Game," *The Economist*, November 18, 2006, 63–65.
57. B. Thill, "Microsoft: Gat Game? Update on Vista, Xbox and the Tender," *Citigroup Capital Markets*, August 30, 2006.
58. Ibid.
59. D. Takahashi, *The Xbox 360 Uncloaked*, Spider Works, 2006.
60. B. Thill, "Microsoft: Gat Game? Update on Vista, Xbox and the Tender," *Citigroup Capital Markets*, August 30, 2006.
61. J. M. O'Brian and C. Tkaczyk, "Wii Will Rock You," *Fortune*, June 11, 2007, 82–92.

THE GLOBAL AUTOMOBILE INDUSTRY IN 2009

INTRODUCTION

As the first decade of the 21st century drew to a close, the global automobile industry was facing unprecedented economic challenges. A deep recession had driven automobile sales down to levels not seen since the 1960s. Many long-established companies, including General Motors (GM), Chrysler, and Toyota, sought government aid to help them survive the downturn. Ultimately, Chrysler had to seek Chapter 11 bankruptcy protection. General Motors, also went down that road. In contrast, Toyota, with $19 billion in cash on its balance sheet, looked well positioned to survive the downturn in good shape.

At the same time, two seismic shifts were taking place in the structure of global demand. First, while demand imploded in many developed nations during 2008, growth continued in some developed nations, particularly China, which experts predicted could become the world's biggest automobile market sometime between 2016 and 2020. Reflecting this, several automobile companies from developing nations were using their strong home markets as springboards to expand their global reach. These included Tata Motors of India, which purchased Jaguar and Land Rover from Ford in 2008, and China's Geely, which, in mid-2009, was reportedly bidding for General Motor's Saab unit and Ford's Volvo subsidiary, both of which were based in Sweden.[1] In addition, high fuel costs were driving a migration in demand away from large vehicles, such as the sports utility (SUVs) vehicles so beloved by Americans, toward smaller more fuel-efficient cars, including hybrids such as the Ford Focus and Toyota Prius.

BACKGROUND

Some 50 years ago, renowned management author Peter Drucker called the automobile industry the "industry of industries." In many respects, his characterization is still true today. The industry makes over 50 million cars and trucks a year, employs millions of people in factories scattered around the globe, and accounts for about 10% of the gross domestic product in many developed countries. The industry consumes nearly half the world's output of rubber, 25% of its glass, and 15% of its steel.[2] Its products are responsible for almost half of the world's oil consumption and are a major source of rising carbon dioxide levels in the atmosphere, the greenhouse gas implicated in global warming. Modern cities, with their attendant suburban sprawl, have been designed around the automobile. The automobile has shaped our landscape, changed our atmosphere, and exerted a profound influence on the global economy. It is indeed still the industry of industries—and today the industry of industries is going through wrenching changes.

The emergence of the modern industry dates back to 1913 and Henry Ford's first implementation of the production technology—the continuously moving assembly line—that would revolutionize so much of industrial capitalism over the next few decades. Ford quickly became the master of mass production, churning out thousands of black Model T Fords from his Highland Park plant in Michigan. Mass production dramatically lowered the costs of building cars and paved the way for the emergence of a mass consumer market. It was not Ford,

This case was prepared by Charles W. L. Hill, the University of Washington, as the basis for class discussion rather than to illustrate either effective or ineffective handling of an administrative situation. Reprinted by permission of Charles W. L. Hill. All rights reserved. Copyright © Charles W. L. Hill, 2009.

however, but Alfred Sloan, the CEO of General Motors, who in the mid-1920s realized that the key to success in the industry was serving customers by offering them "a car for every purse and purpose."[3] Under Sloan, GM segmented the market, producing a differentiated range of models to consumers. In doing so, the company seized market leadership from Ford and has not relinquished it since.

By the 1960s, General Motors, Ford, and Chrysler dominated the United States market; then by far the world's largest. GM at one point made more than 60% of all automobile sales in the United States, and collectively the three companies accounted for more than 90% of sales. Moreover, the companies were now multinationals, with significant operations outside of North America, particularly in Europe, the world's second-largest car market. This, however, was all about to change. Riding the wave of economic disruption caused by the OPEC oil price hikes of the 1970s, foreign manufacturers of fuel-efficient cars began to invade the United States market. First there was Volkswagen, with its revolutionary VW Beetle, followed by a slew of Japanese manufacturers, including, most notably, Honda, Nissan, and Toyota.

It was the invading Toyota that was to usher in the next revolution in car making. Faced with a small and intensely competitive home market and constrained by a lack of capital, Toyota started to tweak the mass production system first developed by Ford. Engineers tried to find ways to build cars efficiently in smaller volumes and with less capital. After years of experimentation, by the 1970s, a new production system emerged at Toyota. Later dubbed "lean production," it was based on innovations that reduced setup times for machinery and made shorter production runs economical. When coupled with the introduction of just-in-time (JIT) inventory systems, flexible work practices, an organization-wide focus on quality, and the practice of stopping the assembly line to fix defects (which was the antithesis of Ford's continually moving assembly line), the lean production system yielded significant gains in productivity and product quality. In turn, it lowered costs, improved brand equity, and gave Toyota a competitive advantage. Toyota capitalized on its lean production system to grow faster than its rivals; by 2008, the company had replaced

General Motors as the world's largest automobile manufacturer.

As was the case with mass production, Toyota's innovation of lean production was imitated, with varying degrees of success, by other volume carmakers. Japanese competitors were the first to try to adopt Toyota's innovation. During the 1990s, the American volume carmakers jumped on the bandwagon. Despite this, Toyota still enjoys an advantage in the automobile industry, based on production excellence, although the gap has closed significantly. Just as importantly, the sluggish American response to Japanese and European invasions of their home market allowed the foreigners to capture even more market share.

By the end of the first decade of the new century, America's big three (now often referred to as the Detroit Three) were rapidly losing their grip on the domestic market. Collectively, GM, Ford, and Chrysler accounted for 47.9% of car and light truck sales in the United States in 2008, down from 61.8% in 2003 and 74% in 1997 (light trucks include pickup trucks and SUVs, both segments in which the big three have traditionally been very strong).[4] The other 52.1% of sales were attributed to foreign producers, up from 26% in 1997. Moreover, in stark contrast to the situation in the 1980s when most foreign cars were imported into the United States, by 2008, most foreign nameplates were built in "transplant" factories located in North America.

What saved the Detroit Three during the 1990s and early 2000s were robust sales of light trucks, particularly SUVs. Foreign manufacturers had been caught off-guard by the American appetite for SUVs, which surged as oil prices remained low and the economy boomed. In 2003, GM, Ford, and Chrysler still accounted for 74% of light truck sales. But there, too, market share was eroding due to gains made by Japanese and European SUV models.[5] The rapid rise in oil prices between 2004 and 2008, when oil peaked at nearly $150 a barrel, up from $20 a barrel in 2001, brought an end to the two-decade boom in SUV sales, removing the main source of strength for American manufacturers. With competition in the passenger car segment intensifying, the outlook for the Detroit Three looked increasingly grim. Then the economic recession of 2008 hit the industry.

THE 2008 GLOBAL FINANCIAL CRISIS AND AUTOMOBILE SALES

The recession started in the United States housing market. Over the prior decade, mortgage lenders had been making increasingly risky loans to American homebuyers, some of whom clearly could not afford the loans that they were taking on. However, low "teaser rates" that expired after one to five years, to be replaced by much higher interest rates, persuaded many borrowers to take on mortgage debt obligations. Moreover, many believed, incorrectly as it turned out, that if they could not meet their mortgage payments, they could always sell their home and pay off the loan.

For their part, mortgage lenders were encouraged to make risky loans by the development of a market for mortgage-backed securities. This enabled them to bundle mortgages into bonds and sell them off to other financial institutions, thereby shifting the risk. The institutions that purchased these mortgage-backed securities were themselves able to buy insurance that protected them against the risk of default by mortgage payees, which would have significantly reduced the value of the bonds they held. This insurance took the form of complex derivatives, known as collateralized debt obligations, or CDOs, that were then traded between institutions. CDOs were viewed as relatively safe investments because default rates on mortgages were low.

The entire system seemed to work as long as housing prices continued to rise and defaults stayed low. But in 2007, a two-decade rise in United States housing prices came to an abrupt end. Furthermore, the interest rates were starting to rise on many adjustable rate mortgages that had been sold with low teaser rates. As rates started to rise, defaults surged, homes were foreclosed at record rates, and an increase in the supply of homes for sale drove prices down even further. At this point, the United States financial system went into a tailspin. The value of mortgage-backed securities and derivatives such as CDOs plunged, damaging the balance sheets of many financial institutions. Because financial institutions from all over the world had been purchasing American mortgage-backed securities and derivatives, the crisis immediately became global. With assets on their balance sheets, financial institutions had no choice but to dramatically reduce the new loans that they made, and after decades of easy credit, suddenly it became very difficult to borrow money.

The credit squeeze hit the automobile industry particularly hard because cars are, for many people, their second-biggest purchases after homes and are often financed with loans. Moreover, even for those people who used cash to buy cars, the financial crisis suddenly made them very nervous; they responded by putting off any purchases of big-ticket items such as automobiles as they waited for the crisis to resolve. As a consequence, demand for automobiles plunged. For 2008, United States automobile sales were down 18% from 16.1 million units in 2007 to 13.2 million units in 2008. Most of the sales fall occurred in the second half of the year, with monthly sales figures recording some of the lowest levels since the 1960s. Moreover, little relief was seen for 2009. Standard and Poor's, for example, was forecasting United States sales of 11.5 million units in 2009, a 39% drop from 2007.[6]

What complicated the situation was that at the same time the financial crisis was unfolding, oil prices surged to record highs, hitting $150 a barrel in mid-2008. As prices at the gas pump rose, people who were buying cars switched to more fuel-efficient vehicles, many of which were made not by American producers, but by smaller foreign firms such as Hyundai and Kia of Korea and Subaru of Japan. Even though oil prices subsequently fell as the recession took hold, the perception had taken hold that once the economy recovered, oil prices would again increase, and demand for pickup trucks and SUVs remained weak.

While the slump in demand was most dramatic in America, other markets also saw sharp declines, and for many of the same reasons: the global financial crisis caused credit contraction and increased uncertainty about the future, which hit automobile sales particularly hard. In France, for example, sales fell 15.8% in December 2008 compared with a year earlier. In Japan, the figure was 22%; in Italy, 13.3%; and Spain, 49.9%.[7] Looking forward, forecasts called for global automobile sales of approximately 46.6 million units in 2009, down from a peak of 54.92 million units in 2007.[8]

However, while demand declines have been the norm in developed nations, there is a different story in developing nations (see Exhibit 1). In China, India,

Exhibit 1   Global Automobile Sales: 2000, 2007, 2008, and 2009 Forecast (millions of units)

	2000	2007	2008	2009 Forecast
Total Global Sales	46.64	54.92	52.17	46.66
North America	19.77	18.83	15.85	12.80
Canada	*1.55*	*1.65*	*1.64*	*1.38*
United States	*17.35*	*16.09*	*13.19*	*10.50*
Western Europe	14.75	14.75	13.54	12.46
Eastern Europe	2.38	3.58	4.01	3.41
Asia	7.85	14.42	15.07	14.44
China	*0.61*	*5.15*	*5.04*	*5.29*
India	*0.60*	*1.18*	*1.20*	*1.23*
South America	1.89	3.34	3.70	3.55
Brazil	*1.17*	*1.98*	*2.19*	*2.24*

Source: "Auto Production Swings from Reverse into Drive," Global Auto Report, *Global Economic Research*, April 29, 2009.

and Brazil, for example, the sales declines were much smaller, and growth had already resumed by early 2009. In all of these countries, relatively low levels of automobile ownership, coupled with fast underlying economic growth rates, suggest that sales will continue to grow at a robust rate in coming years.

Two factors made the sharp sales declines particularly painful for automobile manufacturers. One was their high level of fixed costs. As sales fall below breakeven run rates, high fixed costs imply rapidly rising losses. Exacerbating the situation was the fact that between 2004 and 2008, some 19 million units of new productive capacity had been added to the global industry.

The combination of expanding global capacity, followed by a sharp drop in demand, when coupled with a demand shift to smaller cars, proved toxic for several companies. Hardest hit were General Motors and Chrysler. Both companies were forced to seek government aid in an attempt to stave off bankruptcy. In total, the United States government had committed $17.4 billion in aid to GM and Chrysler by early 2009. In contrast, Ford, who had raised significant capital from private investors in

2007, declined government aid and signaled that, despite operating losses, it would be able to survive the recession. Despite the aid both Chrysler and GM were forced into bankruptcy. Under an agreement negotiated after Chrysler's bankruptcy, the Italian company Fiat will take over management of the company's assets. Fiat itself had undergone a dramatic turnaround between 2004 and 2008 under the leadership of Sergio Marchionne, primarily through a combination of production efficiencies and new product launches, including small cars that have sold well in an environment of high fuel prices. As of May 2009, Fiat was also reported to be bidding for Opel, the European arm of General Motors.

Toyota, too, reported a loss of $3.6 billion for the financial year that ended in March 2009, its first-ever as a public company, primarily due to the sharp sales declines in the United States and Japan. However, with $19 billion in cash on its balance sheet, the result of years of high profits, Toyota was financially secure. Despite this, Toyota's finance arm had apparently sought some $2 billion in government aid from the Bank of Japan to help its finance arms survive the global credit crunch.

Other governments, eager to protect jobs, were also putting up cash to support their local producers. French government officials said that automakers could expect approximately $7.8 billion in loans and loan guarantees. Germany unveiled a similar plan. In Britain, automobile producers (which are almost entirely in foreign hands) sought about $3.3 billion in government loans. Similarly, the Swedish government provided around $3.4 billion in loan guarantees to Volvo and Saab (which at the time were owned by Ford and GM, respectively). In Brazil, where the market continued to grow, the government instructed Banco de Brasil to make $1.7 billion available to the financing units of local automakers so that they could cope with the global credit crisis.[9]

The flurry of government aid for ailing automakers prompted a caution from Pascal Lamy, the Director General of the World Trade Organization. Although he chose his words carefully, Lamy seemed to suggest that loans and loan guarantees were, in effect, subsidies to inefficient producers, and going forward they could distort world trade and discriminate against efficient producers who did not receive similar subsidies.

Most forecasts called for 2009 to be another rough year for the global automobile industry, although many believed that demand would start to recover toward the end of the year and the recovery would be sustained through 2011. During that time period, growth was predicted to be strongest in the emerging markets of China, India, and Brazil. The structure of the global industry, however, may be irreversibly altered.

INDUSTRY TRENDS

Several important trends characterized the competitive landscape of the global automobile industry in the first decade of the 21st century. Most important among these were the decline of America's big three, the shifting patterns of global demand (and particularly the growth of China as a major market and producer), and the increasing attention paid to nontraditional engines, including hybrids and fuel cells.

The Decline of America's Big Three

The decline of America's big three auto producers has been ongoing for decades. Once accounting for as much as 90% of all cars and trucks sold in the United States, by the mid-1990s the figure had fallen to 75%, and today it is about 44% (see Exhibit 2). Taking up market share have been the Japanese trio of Honda, Nissan, and Toyota and, to a lesser extent, Volkswagen, Hyundai, and Subaru. The decline has been notably steeper in the passenger car segment of the industry in which the big three saw their share decline to under 42% by 2008. In contrast, the light truck segment has long been a source of strength for the American producers, and collectively they still account for around 70% of the share in this segment. However, sales declines have been sharp in this segment due to the relatively poor fuel economy of most light trucks.

Many foreign companies now build a significant proportion of their output in North America. Japanese investments began in the early 1980s as a response to the threat of import controls on exports from Japan. By the early 2000s, foreign-owned producers had the capacity to build some 3 million automobiles in the United States, up from zero in 1981.[10] The foreign investment shows no sign of slowing down. Hyundai opened its first United States factory in Montgomery, Alabama, in 2005, making it the first Korean car company to build in North America. Meanwhile, Toyota opened its sixth North American factory in San Antonio, Texas, in 2006. Collectively, foreign-owned auto factories accounted for close to 30% United States automobile production by 2008.

Exhibit 2 U.S. Market Share, Passenger Cars and Light Trucks, February 2009

Producer	Share %
General Motors	18.9%
Toyota	16.9%
Ford	14.3%
Chrysler	10.9%
Honda	10.6%
Nissan	8%
Other Asian makers	12.8%
European makers	7.6%

Source: *Ward's Auto World*, March 2009.

Many states offered financial incentives such as tax breaks in an effort to attract inward investment by foreign producers and the associated jobs. Estimates suggest that by mid-decade the cumulative value of incentives given to attract new factories amounted to between $1.2 billion and $2 billion, which translates into an investment incentive of $1,000 for every car built by a foreign-owned factory.[11]

The addition of foreign capacity created an excess capacity situation in the American market, which became particularly evident during 2008–2009 when excess productive capacity exceeded 40%. Predictably, the result was significant price competition. This included zero rate financing, cash back on purchases, and large reductions from sticker prices, none of which was enough to prevent bankruptcy for Chrysler and General Motors.

The rise of foreign competitors in the United States market has been attributed to a number of factors, including better designs and more fuel-efficient offerings (particularly in the passenger car segment) superior product quality, higher employee and capital productivity, and lower costs due to smaller pension and health care commitments.

Quality seems to be an important factor explaining market share changes in the industry. J. D. Power and Associates produces quality rankings for automobiles sold in the United States market. Over the years, Toyota and Honda brands have consistently had among the best quality rankings in the industry. However, it is notable that American producers have made great strides, and by the mid-2000s, they were closing the gap. Nevertheless, as of 2008, foreign producers still dominated J. D. Power's vehicle dependability rankings, which measure problems per 100 vehicles within their first three years on the market. As can be seen from Exhibit 3, in March 2009, the industry average was 170 problems per 100 vehicles over three years. Although Buick and Jaguar, brands then owned by GM and Tata Motors of India topped the list, Toyota and Honda brands both scored consistently better than most major brands of Ford, Chrysler, and GM (Tata Motors purchased Jaguar from Ford in June 2008.) This being said, Ford has shown particularly strong improvement in recent years. It is clear that by 2009, the quality deficit that had longed plagued American made cars had been eliminated for some brands.[12]

With regard to productivity differences, the story is similar. American-owned plants have long had a productivity disadvantage compared to their foreign competitors. However, the gap has narrowed substantially in recent years as American-owned producers have worked to improve their productivity by implementing improved manufacturing techniques based on Toyota's model. According to the *Harbour Report*, an annual survey of manufacturing productivity in American assembly plants, although a substantial gap remained in 2003, by 2007 it had been reduced significantly (see Exhibit 4).[13] Indeed, Chrysler's plants matched those of Toyota, and General Motors outperformed Nissan.

Exhibit 3 J. D. Power Vehicle Dependability Study, 2009: Problems per 100 Vehicles over 3 Years

Brand	Rating
Buick	122
Jaguar	122
Lexus	126
Toyota	129
Acura	146
Cadillac	148
Honda	148
Ford	159
Chrysler	165
Industry Average	*170*
GM	174
Chevrolet	185
Volvo	186
Nissan	199
Dodge	202
Jeep	220
Pontiac	220
Volkswagen	260
Suzuki	263

Source: "Buick and Jaguar Tie to Rank Highest for Vehicle Dependability," J. D. Power press release, March 19, 2009.

Exhibit 4 Productivity Differences Measured by Total Labor Hours per Unit and Profit per Vehicle among U.S. Plants

Manufacturer	2003	2007	2007 Profit per Vehicle($)
Ford	38.60	33.88	−1,467
Chrysler	37.42	30.37	−412
General Motors	35.20	32.29	−729
Nissan	32.94	32.96	1,641
Honda	32.36	31.33	1,641
Toyota	30.01	30.37	922

Note: Productivity measures are for assembly, stamping, engine, and transmission combined.
Source: Oliver Wyman, *The Harbour Report, 2008,* Media Release, June 5, 2008.

Despite the closing of the productivity gap, American vehicle makers still lost money on every car they made in 2007, while their Japanese competitors made money (see Exhibit 4). The main reason was higher labor costs at the big three. This was due not just to higher wage rates but also to the pension and health care obligations that American manufacturers have long borne not just for their current employees but also for their retirees. General Motors, for example, has 2.4 pensioners for every current employee. In the early 2000s, both Ford and GM had to issue bonds worth billions of dollars to plug the holes in their pension funds. GM now has to pay out $1 billion a year in interest payments just to service these bonds. Moreover, the company has to pay out some $3 billion a year to cover health care costs for retirees. Just as troubling, GM may have to increase funds going into its pension plan if the fund does not earn a long-term return of 9% per annum.[14]

As a consequence of such factors, in 2007, the average labor cost at the American big three was $75 an hour, compared to $45 an hour at Toyota's American assembly plants. However, all three American companies have been renegotiating their contracts with the Union of Auto Workers (UAW), and trying to shift the obligations for retirees onto the union. Indeed, bankruptcy protection has enabled Chrysler and GM to accelerate this process. According to the *Harbour Report,* the implication is that by 2011, hourly labor rates for the big three may be down to $54.

Labor costs may fall still further for American manufacturers under an agreement negotiated with the UAW in early 2009. The agreement was required by the federal government as a condition for its loans to GM and Chrysler, which totaled $17.4 billion. The agreement was to cut pay for laid off workers, ease work rules to allow for greater job flexibility, and eliminate wage increases tied to the cost of living. Although Ford took no government aid, the UAW has the same agreement with all American manufacturers, so Ford also benefits from the government requirement.[15]

Among the American manufacturers, Ford seems best positioned to come out of the 2008–2009 recession in the industry. Ford raised some $23.5 billion in cash in 2006, before the recession hit, by mortgaging almost all of its plants and assets while interest rates were low. At the start of 2009, it still had $13.4 billion in cash on its balance sheet, which will be enough to see it through the recession without additional capital injections unless the recession continues well into 2010. As noted earlier, despite receiving $4 billion in government assistance, Chrysler entered bankruptcy protection in May 2009 and Fiat has taken over management of the company. GM, despite receiving $13.4 billion in federal assistance, also entered bankruptcy. The problems at GM and Chrysler seem to have been benefitting Ford, which started to pick up market share from its rivals in early 2009.

Shifting Patterns of Global Demand

While America's automobile market was in a deep recession in 2008–2009, as was most of Europe and Japan, some developing markets continued to expand. As recently as 2000, the United States market accounted for 37% of global demand. By 2008, this figure was 25%, and it was forecasted to fall to 22% in 2009 (see Exhibit 1). Leading the growth in developed nations was China. In 2002, there were just 16 vehicles per 1,000 people in this fast-growing country of 1.3 billion. This was compared to more than 800 vehicles per 1,000 people in the United States and 585 per 1,000 in Germany. By 2008, the figure for China had increased to 30 per 1,000 people, which is still very low. India, too, has a large population, fast economic growth, and a low level of car ownership (17 per 1,000 in 2008), so there, too, rapid growth in demand has been occurring.[16]

J. D. Power estimates that demand in China will climb to 14.6 million units per annum in 2013, up from a little over 5 million in 2008. By 2018, J. D. Power foresees demand for 19.9 million units per annum in China, compared with demand for 17.6 million units in the United States, which would make China the world's largest market. In fact, sales in China surged in early 2009 as their government offered subsidies on purchases of small fuel-efficient cars. For the first four months of 2009, sales in China outstripped those in the United States. J. D. Power also sees rapid growth in demand for automobiles in Brazil, India, and Russia, and by 2018 believes that demand in developing nations will outstrip demand in developed nations.

To serve the growing demand, foreign automobile makers have been investing heavily in these markets. Automobile production in China, which stood at 2 million units in 2001, was approaching 10 million units by 2009. Ironically, one of the most successful foreign companies in China has been GM, which produces cars in China through two joint ventures; a 50–50 partnership with Shanghai Automotive Industry, which makes and sells Chevrolets, Buicks, and Cadillacs in China, and a one-third stake in SAIC-GM-Wuling. China requires foreign auto manufacturers to enter into joint ventures with local producers. GM plans to double its Chinese capacity to 2 million vehicles a year and launch 30 new models tailored to the Chinese market by 2014. However, it is of note that most of GM's sales gain has come at its SAIC joint venture, in which SAIC has a controlling 51% ownership stake.[17] In May 2009, GM announced that it would start exporting cars to America from its SAIC joint venture.

China also has its own home grown industry. In addition to companies like SAIC and Shanghai Automotive, automakers include Brilliance, Geely, and Chery Automobile. While these companies are starting to export production to other developing nations, they have not yet broken into developed markets such as the United States and Western Europe. Among other constraints, their cars would not currently pass stringent United States emission requirements. In 2009, rumors swirled that these companies were considering purchasing parts of GM and Ford, including Saab, Volvo, and Hummer. Such a purchase would give them access not only to well-known global brands but also to technological know-how, which currently is the weak spot of Chinese manufacturers.[18] It would also follow the lead set by India's Tata Motors, another emerging automobile company, which, in 2008, purchased the Jaguar and Land Rover brands from Ford.

Changes in Operations

In an effort to cope with the tough competitive conditions in the North American market and elsewhere, automobile companies are looking hard at additional ways to take costs out of their system or capture more of the available demand. Among the most notable initiatives underway have been an industry-wide attempt to streamline product development, offer a wider range of niche cars, work more closely with suppliers, develop systems for building cars to order, and introduce a new breed of hybrid cars.

Historically, it took four years and cost as much as $1 billion to develop a new car model and prepare a factory for its production. To recoup those fixed costs, automobile companies needed high-volume sales, which required selling cars without a major update for four years and sometimes as long as seven years. To attain maximum economies of scale, automobile manufacturers tried to run their plants at full capacity, producing 240,000 units a year. The ideal was to have each plant produce just one model.

In recent years, the automobile market has become increasingly fragmented. Models are now updated more frequently to keep pace with changing consumer tastes and competitive pressures, shortening product life cycles. Customers have demanded more variety, and automobile companies have been willing to give it to them, bringing a wider variety of niche cars to the market. The Ford Taurus, for example, was once the best-selling passenger car in America with annual sales of approximately 500,000 (equivalent to two plants running at full capacity). As sales slipped, Ford decided to kill the Taurus and replace it with two models, one smaller than the Taurus and one bigger.

To recoup the costs of such offerings, development and manufacturing costs have to be reduced. Automobile companies are trying to do this by using a common platform and parts in a wider range of cars. An example depicting the industry's evolving philosophy is GM's 2005 roadster, the Pontiac Solstice. Under the old economics, the Solstice would never have made it off the drawing board. The car was forecasted to sell only 25,000 units a year. With a projected sticker price of $20,000, the volume was insufficient under the old paradigm to recoup costs. To make the car economically, GM revolutionized its product design philosophy. By digitalizing much of the design of the car and tools, GM was able to cut $50 million out of the design costs. It used to take 12 design engineers three months to produce a clay model, an essential step in the design process. Now a single designer can take an idea on a computer screen to an animated video of a vehicle in three weeks. GM saved another $80 million by designing the car so that it could use existing tools at its factory. More money was saved by a decision to base the car on a common platform architecture called Kappa, which would be used for other small rear-drive cars. According to GM, the company could make an almost unlimited number of bodies on the Kappa architecture, and each vehicle would be profitable with a volume of 20,000 to 25,000 a year.[19]

Using the same platform across a wide model range is fast becoming industry standard practice. As with so many other industry trends, the Japanese pioneered the practice. Honda, for example, builds its Odyssey minivan, the Pilot SUV, and the Acura MDX SUV on the same platform. In 2004, Chrysler based its vehicle fleet on 13 distinct platforms, but by 2008, the company had decreased this to just four platforms, in the process reducing the product development budget from $42 billion to $30 billion. Ford and General Motors have similar aims. The Kappa platform for GM's Pontiac Solstice will also be used for its new Saturn coupe and at least one more GM car. As GM develops its next generation Chevy Silverado and GMC Sierra pickups, it plans to reuse much of the existing platform, cutting development costs in half to nearly $3 billion. Over the next eight years, Ford plans to use its Mazda 6 sedan platform (Ford owns Mazda) as the basis for 10 new vehicles. The idea, according to Ford's head of operations, is to engineer it once and use it often.[20]

Another design goal is to try and use the same parts in a wider variety of car models and, where appropriate, use parts from old models in new cars. Detroit auto designers formerly boasted that new models were completely redesigned from the floor up with all new parts. Now that is seen as costly and time-consuming. At General Motors the current goal is to reuse 40%–60% of parts from one car generation to the next, thereby reducing design time and tooling costs. At Ford, the number of parts has been slashed. For example, Ford engineers now choose from just four steering wheels, instead of contemplating 14 different designs.

As a result of all these changes, the costs and time for bringing new cars to market is shrinking. Most of GM's new development projects are now on 24-month schedules—a far cry from the late 1980s when GM engineers celebrated because they were able to bring out the Chevrolet Corsica in *just* 45 months![21] Ford has reduced its product development time by 25% since the late 1990s and is still getting better by 10% per year.

Hand in hand with changes in design philosophy, automobile companies are retooling their factories to reduce costs and make them capable of producing several car models from the same line. By doing so, they hope to be able to reduce the break-even point for a new car model. With the Solstice, for example, GM cut design costs by using a common platform and parts. It has cut tooling and production costs by investing in flexible manufacturing technologies that can be used to produce multiple designs based on the Kappa platform from the same basic line. GM has also worked hard to get unions to agree to changes in inflexible work rules. Assembly line workers now perform several different jobs, which reduces waste and boosts productivity.

Ford hopes to have 75% of its production built on flexible assembly lines by 2010. If successful, its investments in flexible factories could reduce annual costs by some $2 billion a year.[22] Ford spent $400 million modernizing an 80-year old assembly plant in Chicago. This plant is now capable of making eight models from two different chassis.

Reengineering their plants to accommodate a wider range of models is not cheap. In 2003, GM spent some $7.3 billion on capital improvements at its automobile plants, up from an average of $5.4 billion in the early 1990s. In the early 1990s, Ford spent some $3.5 billion annually on capital improvements. More recently, its capital spending has been running at a $7.5–$8 billion annual rate. Chrysler, too, has increased its spending, while Toyota spent some $9 billion upgrading its factories in the mid-2000s.[23]

Companies are also changing the way they manage their suppliers. At one time, the American automobile companies were highly vertically integrated, producing as much as 70% of their component parts in-house. Those parts that were not made in-house were often purchased using an annual competitive bidding process. The last decade has seen enormous changes here. Both Ford and GM have sold off major chunks of their in-house suppliers. GM spun off its in-house suppliers in 1999 as Delphi Automotive. Delphi took some 200,000 former GM employees with it, about one-third of the total, many of whom were union members. Ford spun off its in-house suppliers the following year as Visteon Corporation. Delphi and Visteon are now the number one and two auto parts suppliers in the United States. In an effort to assert their independence, both companies are moving rapidly to build a more diverse set of customers.

The Detroit Three have also been reconfiguring their relationships with independent suppliers. The automobile companies are now expecting their Tier 1 or major suppliers to produce modules—larger vehicle parts that comprise several components such as fully assembled chassis, finished interiors, and "ready for the road" exterior trim. These modules are then bolted and welded together to make finished vehicles, rather like toy models being snapped together. For such an approach to work, the suppliers have to get involved earlier in the process of designing and developing new models and engineering assembly tools. To create an incentive for them to do so, the automobile manufacturers have been entering into longer-term contracts with their Tier 1 suppliers. At the same time, Tier 1 suppliers face intense price pressures and requirements for quality improvements. If they do not meet these, the automobile companies have shown a willingness to walk away from long-term deals. In 2003, for example, Chrysler pulled a $90 million contract from a supplier of interior products, Collins & Aikman, because of poor product quality.[24]

Another trend has been to encourage major suppliers to locate new facilities next to assembly plants. Ford's refurbished plant in Chicago has a supplier park located next door. The idea is to get suppliers to deliver inventory to the assembly line on a JIT basis. At the Chicago plant, the average component now needs to travel only half a mile, as compared to 450 miles in the past. The proximity has saved suppliers transportation costs, which are passed onto Ford in the form of lower prices. In addition, Ford has reduced inventory on hand at its Chicago plant from two to three days' worth to just eight hours' worth.[25]

Once a car is built, it spends between 40 and 80 days sitting in factory lots, distribution centers, and dealers' forecourts before it is actually sold. This represents a huge amount of working capital that is tied up in inventory. To make matters worse, one of the biggest problems in the automobile industry is predicting what demand will be. To a large extent, repeated rounds of price cutting (disguised as incentives) in the American automobile industry have been initiated in an attempt to move slow-selling inventory sitting on dealers' lots. If automobile companies could predict demand more accurately, they might be able to reduce the mismatch between inventories and demand—and hence the need to resort to incentives.

In an effort to improve this end of the value chain, the automobile companies have been trying to reduce the time between ordering and delivery. The ultimate goal is to have cars built to order, with cars being assembled and shipped to a dealer within days of a customer placing an order. This is similar in conception to the way that Dell sells computers, with customers ordering a computer and paying for it, online, while the machine is shipped out within days. Nissan has calculated that if it could move to a build-to-order system with a short cycle time, it could reduce costs by as much as $3,600 a vehicle.[26]

Achieving this goal, however, is easier in theory than in practice. One obvious problem is that if the flow of orders is lumpy or seasonal, so will be the output of a factory, which might result in periods where capacity is not being fully utilized. Another problem involves changing buyer behavior. In

America, at least many consumers look for instant gratification and expect to be able to purchase a car when they walk onto a dealer's lot, which is the antithesis of a build-to-order system. Still, there are some signs of a shift away from this mentality. Honda, for example, has been building its best-selling MDX SUV to order—although the delivery time is more like two months than two days. In Germany, BMW now builds some 60% of its cars to order, but once again the delivery time can be as long as two months. Toyota, too, is trying to build more cars to order. By the mid-2000s Toyota was building about 12% of the cars it sold in the United States to order, with a build time of just 14 days.[27]

New Technologies

For years, automobile companies have experimented with alternative power sources, most notably fuel cells. These investments have been driven by national and local government demands for lower emissions of carbon dioxide, carbon monoxide, and nitrogen oxides. Of particular concern has been the global buildup of carbon dioxide, the greenhouse gas implicated in global warming. In Europe, the European Commission has persuaded carmakers to agree to a voluntary deal to cut overall emissions across their car fleet by 25% by 2008 or face the imposition of strict emission rules on specific models. In California, draft regulations may require car manufacturers to reduce emissions of carbon dioxide by 30%, starting in 2009. In addition, California already has regulations in place that require 2% of car makers' fleets to be zero emission vehicles (ZEV), although this requirement is proving to be a "soft" one. In May 2009, the United States government raised the stakes by introducing tough new standards for fuel efficiency, which called for automobile manufacturers to make fleets that, on average, achieved 35.5 miles per gallon, up from 25.3 miles per gallon.

The only conceivable ZEV at this juncture is a car powered by an electric motor that runs on a fuel cell. A fuel cell combines hydrogen with oxygen from the air to produce water. The process generates an electric current strong enough to power a car. For all of their promise, however, fuel cells have drawbacks. It costs about 10 times more to produce a fuel cell than an internal combustion engine, the range of cars using fuel cells is still too limited for most customers, and replenishing hydrogen will require a network of hydrogen filling stations, which currently are not available.

Automakers have also been experimenting with modified internal combustion engines that use hydrogen rather than gasoline as a fuel. Here too, however, progress has been held back by the total absence of a network of hydrogen filling stations and serious technical problems associated with storing liquid hydrogen (which requires very cold temperatures).

More promising in the short to medium term are hybrid cars. In hybrid cars, at low speed the power comes from an electric motor that gets electricity from an onboard battery. At higher speed, the internal combustion engine kicks in and provides power, while simultaneously recharging the battery through a generator. When braking, energy from the slowing wheels is sent back through the electric motor to charge the batteries. The result can be substantial savings in fuel consumption, with little in the way of a performance penalty. Toyota's Prius hybrid can go from a standstill to 60 mph in 10 seconds and averages 60 mpg in the city and 51 mpg highway driving. This makes the Prius an ideal commuting car. The big drawback is that the hybrid propulsion system adds about $3,000 to $5,000 to a vehicle's sticker price, and the battery has to be replaced about every 100,000 miles at a cost of about $2,000. At a gas price of $2 a gallon, it takes some five years for a hybrid to repay the additional investment.

Introduced in 1997, Toyota had sold some 200,000 Prius cars by mid-2004. Sales started to increase rapidly in 2003 and 2004 as higher fuel prices made consumers more concerned about fuel economy. In 2004, sales in the United States were limited only by supply constraints to 47,000 units. By 2008, with fuel prices hitting $4 a gallon in the United States, Toyota was selling 250,000 Priuses a year. In May 2009, the company introduced its third-generation Prius in Japan, with plans to roll the car out globally over the next few months. Pre-orders in Japan were for 80,000 units, far surpassing the automaker's goal of selling 10,000 a month in its home market. In total, Toyota hopes to sell some 300,000–400,000 of the new Priuses a year.[28] In addition to the Prius, Toyota also sells hybrid versions of some of its other models, including the Lexus SUV, the Highlander SUV, and the Camry sedan. The company aims to increase its overall hybrid sales to $1 million by 2010–2012 and offer hybrid versions of all of its vehicles by 2020.

Toyota is not alone in developing hybrid technology. Most notably, both Honda and Ford have introduced hybrid models, and both are reportedly selling well. Bob Lutz, the vice chairman of GM, who was at one time well known for his resistance to alternative technologies, said that GM will aim to build about one-third of its vehicles as hybrids by 2015 and 80% by 2020.

In addition to hybrids, GM is also placing a bet on another technology, lithium ion batteries, with its Chevy Volt. Scheduled for market introduction in 2010, the Chevy Volt is a compact four-door electric car with a reserve gasoline-powered engine. The primary power source is a large lithium ion battery (lithium ion batteries are typically found in small electric appliances such as cell phones). The battery can be charged by plugging it into a wall socket for six hours, and fully charged, it will fuel the car for 40 miles, which is less than most people's daily commute. After that, a gasoline engine kicks in, providing both drive power and recharging the lithium ion battery. GM estimates fuel economy will be over 100 miles a gallon, and charging the car overnight from a power outlet would cost about 80% less than filling it with gas at $3 per gallon. The car will cost somewhere between $30,000 and $40,000; because it uses battery-powered technology, buyers will be able to take a $7,500 tax credit.

Endnotes

1. F. Balfour, "China's Geely Eyes GM's Saab, Ford's Volvo," *Business Week*, May 8, 2009, 18.
2. "A Survey of the Car Industry; Perpetual Motion," *The Economist*, September 4, 2004, 3–4.
3. The phrase first appeared in GM's 1924 Annual Report to Shareholders, and more than anything else, it captured the essence of Sloan's revolutionary marketing philosophy. For details, visit GM's Web site at http://www.gm.com/company/corp_info/history/index.html.
4. Standard & Poor's, *Industry Survey: Autos & Auto Parts*, December 25, 2008.
5. Figures from Standard & Poor's, *Industry Survey: Autos & Auto Parts*, June 24, 2004.
6. Standard & Poor's, *Industry Survey: Autos & Auto Parts*, December 25, 2008.
7. "Global Car Sales Fall by Double Digits," *CNNMoney.com*, January 5, 2009.
8. "Auto Production Swings from Reverse into Drive," Global Auto Report, *Global Economic Research*, April 29, 2009.
9. "Too Many Moving Parts," *The Economist*, February 7, 2009, 71.
10. A Survey of the Car Industry, "Detroit's Nine Lives," *The Economist*, September 4, 2004, 6–9.
11. Ibid.
12. "Buick and Jaguar Tie to Rank Highest for Vehicle Dependability," J. D. Power press release, March 19, 2009.
13. Oliver Wyman, *The Harbour Report, 2008*, Media Release, June 5, 2008.
14. D. Welch, "Has GM Outrun Its Pension Problems?" *Business Week*, January 19, 2004, 70.
15. M. Dolan, "Ford Benefits as GM and Chrysler Stumble," *Wall Street Journal*, Feburary 20, 2009, B1.
16. Standard & Poor's, *Industry Survey: Autos & Auto Parts*, December 25, 2008.
17. I. Rowley, "Would Bankruptcy Stall GM's China Growth?" *Business Week Online*, April 28, 2009, 14.
18. K. Marr, "As Detroit Crumbles, China Emerges as Auto Epicenter," *Washington Post*, May 18, 2009, A1.
19. M. Phelan, "GM Predicts Sporty Profits Even from Fewer Sales," *Knight Rider Tribune Business News*, March 13, 2004, 1.
20. D. Welch and K. Kerwin, "Detroit Tries It the Japanese Way," *Business Week*, January 26, 2004, 76; A. Taylor, "Detroit Buffs Up," *Fortune*, February 9, 2004, 90–94.
21. D. Winter, "Shrinking Product Development Time," *Ward's Auto World*, June 2003, 36–40.
22. J. Muller, "The Little Car That Could," *Forbes*, December 8, 2003, 82; "The Year of the Car," *The Economist*, January 3, 2004, 47.
23. Standard & Poor's, *Industry Survey: Autos & Auto Parts*, June 24, 2004.
24. Ibid.
25. K. Kerwin, "Ford to Suppliers: Let's Get Cozier," *Business Week*, September 20, 2004, 8.
26. A Survey of the Car Industry, "Fighting Back," *The Economist*, September 4, 2004, 14–16.
27. R. Rosmarin, "Your Custom Car Is Ready at Toyota," *Business* vol. 2 (October 2004): 150–151.
28. Y. Takahashi, "New Prius Is Set to Race Insight," *Wall Street Journal*, 2009, May 19, B2.

CASE

4

IKEA: FURNITURE RETAILER TO THE WORLD

INTRODUCTION

IKEA is one of the world's most successful global retailers. In 2007, IKEA had 300 home furnishing superstores in 35 countries and was visited by some 583 million shoppers. IKEA's low-priced, elegantly designed merchandise, displayed in large warehouse stores, generated sales of €21.2 billion in 2008, up from €4.4 billion in 1994. Although the privately held company refuses to publish figures on profitability, its net profit margins were rumored to be approximately 10%, high for a retailer. The founder, Ingvar Kamprad, now in his 80s but still an active "advisor" to the company, is rumored to be one of the world's richest men.

COMPANY BACKGROUND

IKEA was established by Ingvar Kamprad in Sweden in 1943 when he was just 17 years old. The fledgling company sold fish, Christmas magazines, and seeds from his family farm. His first business had been selling matches; the enterprising Kamprad purchased them wholesale in 100-box lots (with help from his grandmother who financed the enterprise) and then resold individually at a higher markup. The name IKEA was an acronym: I and K his initials; E stood for Elmtaryd, the name of the family farm; and A stood for Agunnaryd, the name of the village in southern Sweden where the farm was located. Before long, Kamprad had added ballpoint pens to his list and was selling his products via mail order. His

warehouse was a shed on the family farm. The customer fulfillment system used the local milk truck, which picked up goods daily and took them to the train station.

In 1948, Kamprad added furniture to his product line; in 1949, he published his first catalog, distributed then as now, for free. In 1953, Kamprad was struggling with a problem: the milk truck had changed its route, and he could no longer use it to take goods to the train station. His solution was to buy an idle factory in nearby Almhult and convert it into a warehouse. With business now growing rapidly, Kamprad hired a 22-year-old designer, Gillis Lundgren. Lundgren originally helped Kamprad do photo shoots for the early IKEA catalogs, but he started to design more and more furniture for IKEA, eventually designing as many as 400 pieces, including many best sellers.

IKEA's goal over time was to provide stylish functional designs with minimalist lines that could be cost-efficiently manufactured under contract by suppliers and priced low enough to allow most people to afford them. Kamprad's theory was that "good furniture could be priced so that the man with a flat wallet would make a place for it in his spending and could afford it."[1] Kamprad was struck by the fact that furniture in Sweden was expensive at the time, something that he attributed to a fragmented industry dominated by small retailers. Furniture was also often considered family heirlooms, passed down across the generations. He wanted to change this: to make it possible for people of modest means to buy their own furniture. Ultimately, this led to the concept of what IKEA calls "democratic design"—a design

This case was prepared by Charles W. L. Hill, School of Business, University of Washington. Reprinted by permission.

that, according to Kamprad, "was not just good, but also from the start adapted to machine production and thus cheap to assemble."[2] Gillis Lundgren was instrumental in the implementation of this concept. Time and time again, he would find ways to alter the design of furniture to save on manufacturing costs.

Gillis Lundgren also stumbled on what was to become a key feature of IKEA furniture: self-assembly. Trying to efficiently pack and ship a long-legged table, he hit upon the idea of taking the legs off and mailing them packed flat under the tabletop. Kamprad quickly realized that flat-packed furniture reduced transport and warehouse costs, and damage (IKEA had been having a lot of problems with furniture damaged during the shipping process). Moreover, customers seemed willing to take on the task of assembly in return for lower prices. By 1956, self-assembly was integral to the IKEA concept.

In 1957, IKEA started to exhibit and sell its products at home furnishing fairs in Sweden. By cutting retailers out of the equation and using the self-assembly concept, Kamprad could undercut the prices of established retail outlets, much to their chagrin. Established retailers responded by prohibiting IKEA from taking orders at the annual furniture trade in Stockholm. Established outlets claimed that IKEA was imitating their designs. This was to no avail, however, so the retailers went further, pressuring furniture manufacturers not to sell to IKEA. This had two unintended consequences. First, without access to the designs of many manufacturers, IKEA was forced to design more of its products in-house. Second, Kamprad looked for a manufacturer who would produce IKEA-designed furniture. Ultimately, he found one in Poland.

To his delight, Kamprad discovered that furniture manufactured in Poland was as much as 50% cheaper than furniture made in Sweden, allowing him to cut prices even more. Kamprad also found that doing business with the Poles required the consumption of considerable amounts of vodka to celebrate business transactions, and for the next 40 years his drinking was legendary. Alcohol consumption apart, the relationship that IKEA established with the Poles was to become the archetype for future relationships with suppliers. According to one of the Polish managers, there were three advantages of doing business with IKEA: "One concerned the decision making; it was always one man's decision, and you could rely upon what had been decided. We were given long-term

contracts, and were able to plan in peace and quiet.... A third advantage was that IKEA introduced new technology. One revolutionary idea, for instance, was a way of treating the surface of wood. They also mastered the ability to recognize cost savings that could trim the price."[3] By the early 1960s, Polish-made goods were to be found on more than half of the pages of the IKEA catalog.

By 1958, an expanded facility at the Almhult location became the first IKEA store. The original idea behind the store was to have a location where customers could come and see IKEA furniture set up. It was a supplement to IKEA's main mail-order business; but it very quickly became an important sales point in its own right. The store soon started to sell car roof racks so customers could leave with flat-packed furniture loaded on top. Noticing that a trip to an IKEA store was something of an outing for many shoppers (Almhult was not a major population center, and people often drove in from long distances), Kamprad experimented with adding a restaurant to the store so that customers could relax and refresh themselves while shopping. The restaurant was a hit, and it became an integral feature of all IKEA stores.

The response of IKEA's competitors to its success was to argue that IKEA products were of low quality. In 1964, just after 800,000 IKEA catalogs had been mailed to Swedish homes, the widely read Swedish magazine *Allt i Hemmet* (Everything for the Home) published a comparison of IKEA furniture to that sold in traditional Swedish retailers. The furniture was tested for quality in a Swedish design laboratory. The magazine's analysis, detailed in a 16-page spread, was that not only was IKEA's quality as good if not better than that from other Swedish furniture manufacturers, the prices were much lower. For example, the magazine concluded that a chair bought at IKEA for 33 kronor ($4) was better than a virtually identical one bought in a more expensive store for 168 kronor ($21). The magazine also showed how a living room furnished with IKEA products was as much as 65% less expensive than one furnished with equivalent products from four other stores. This publicity made IKEA acceptable in middle-class households, and sales began to take off.

In 1965, IKEA opened its first store in Stockholm, Sweden's capital. By now, IKEA was generating the equivalent of €25 million and had already opened a store in neighboring Norway. The Stockholm store, its third, was the largest furniture store in Europe and had an innovative circular design that was modeled on the famous Guggenheim Art Museum in New York. The location of the store was to set the pattern at IKEA for decades. The store was situated on the outskirts of the city, rather than downtown, with ample space for parking and good access roads. The new store generated a large amount of traffic, so much so that employees could not keep up with customer orders, and long lines formed at the checkouts and merchandise pick-up areas. To try and reduce the lines, IKEA experimented with a self-service pick-up solution, allowing shoppers to enter the warehouse, load flat-packed furniture onto trolleys, and then take them through the checkout. It was so successful that this soon became the company norm in all stores.

International Expansion

By 1973, IKEA was the largest furniture retailer in Scandinavia with nine stores. The company enjoyed a market share of 15% in Sweden. Kamprad, however, felt that growth opportunities were limited. Starting with a single store in Switzerland over the next 15 years, the company expanded rapidly in Western Europe. IKEA met with considerable success, particularly in West Germany, where it had 15 stores by the late 1980s. As in Scandinavia, Western European furniture markets were largely fragmented and served by high-cost retailers located in expensive downtown stores, selling relatively expensive furniture that was not always immediately available, for delivery. IKEA's elegant functional designs with their clean lines, low prices, and immediate availability, were a breath of fresh air, as was the self-service store format. The company was met with almost universal success even though, as one former manager put it: "We made every mistake in the book, but money nevertheless poured in. We lived frugally, drinking now and again, yes perhaps too much, but we were on our feet bright and cheery when the doors were open for the first customers, competing in good Ikean spirit for the cheapest solutions."[4]

The man in charge of the European expansion was Jan Aulino, Kamprad's former assistant, who was just 34 years old when the expansion started. Aulino surrounded himself with a young team. Aulino recalled that the expansion was so fast paced that the stores were rarely ready when IKEA moved in. Moreover, it was hard to get capital out of Sweden due to capital controls; the trick was to make a quick profit and get a positive cash flow going as soon as possible. In the haste to expand, Aulino and his team did not always pay attention to detail. He reportedly clashed with Kamprad on several occasions and considered himself fired at least four times, although he never was. Eventually the European business was reorganized, and tighter controls were introduced.

IKEA was slow to expand in the UK, however, where the locally grown company Habitat had built a business that was similar in many respects to IKEA, offering stylish furniture at a relatively low price. IKEA also entered North America, opening 7 stores in Canada between 1976 and 1982. Emboldened by this success, in 1985, the company entered the United States. It proved to be a challenge of an entirely different nature.

On the face of it, America looked to be fertile territory for IKEA. As in Western Europe, furniture retailing was a very fragmented business in the United States. At the low end of the market were the general discount retailers, such as Walmart, Costco, and Office Depot, who sold a limited product line of basic furniture, often at very low prices. This furniture was very functional, lacked the design elegance associated with IKEA, and was generally of a fairly low quality. Then there were higher-end retailers, such as Ethan Allen, that offered high-quality, well-designed, high-priced furniture. They sold this furniture in full-service stores staffed by knowledgeable salespeople. High-end retailers would often sell ancillary services as well, such as interior design. Typically these retailers would offer home delivery service, including set up in the home, either for free or a small additional charge. Because it was expensive to keep large inventories of high-end furniture, much of what was on display in stores was not readily available, and the client would often have to wait a few weeks before it was delivered.

IKEA opened its first United States store in 1985 in Philadelphia. The company had decided to locate on the coasts. Surveys of American consumers suggested that IKEA buyers were more likely to be people who had travelled abroad, considered themselves risk takers, and liked fine food and wine. These people were concentrated on the coasts. As one manager put it, "There are more Buicks driven in the middle than on the coasts."[5]

Although IKEA initially garnered favorable reviews, and enough sales to persuade it to start opening additional stores, by the early 1990s, it was clear that things were not going well in America. The company found that its European-style offerings did not always resonate with American consumers. Beds were measured in centimeters, not the king, queen, and twin sizes with which Americans are familiar. American sheets did not fit on IKEA beds. Sofas were not big enough, wardrobe drawers not deep enough, glasses too small, curtains too short, and kitchens did not fit American-size appliances. In a story often repeated at IKEA, managers noted that customers were buying glass vases and using them to drink out of, rather than the small glasses for sale at IKEA. The glasses were apparently too small for Americans who like to add liberal quantities of ice to their drinks. To make matters worse, IKEA was sourcing many of the goods from overseas, priced in the Swedish kronor, which was strengthening against the American dollar. This drove up the price of goods in IKEA's American stores. Moreover, some of the stores were poorly located, and not large enough to offer the full IKEA experience familiar to Europeans.

Turning around its American operations required IKEA to take some decisive actions. Many products had to be redesigned to fit with American needs. Newer and larger store locations were chosen. To bring prices down, goods were sourced from lower-cost locations and priced in dollars. IKEA also started to source some products from factories in the United States to reduce both transport costs and dependency on the value of the dollar. At the same time, IKEA noticed a change in American culture. Americans were becoming more concerned with design, and more open to the idea of disposable furniture. It used to be said that Americans changed their spouses about as often as they changed their dining room tables, about 1.5 times in a lifetime, but something was shifting in American culture. Younger people were more open to risks and more willing to experiment. There was a thirst for design elegance and quality. Starbucks was tapping into this, as was Apple Computer, and so did IKEA. According to one manager at IKEA, "Ten or 15 years ago, travelling in the United States, you couldn't eat well. You couldn't get good coffee. Now you can get good bread in the supermarket, and people think that is normal. I like that very much. That is more important to good life than the availability of expensive wines. That is what IKEA is about." [6]

To tap into America's shifting culture, IKEA reemphasized design and started promoting the brand with a series of quirky hip advertisements aimed at a younger demographic: young married couples, college students, and 20- to 30-something singles. One IKEA commercial, called "Unboring," made fun of the reluctance of Americans to part with their furniture. One famous ad featured a discarded lamp, forlorn and forsaken in some rainy American city. A man turned to the camera sympathetically. "Many of you feel bad for this lamp," he said in thick Swedish accent. "That is because you are crazy." Hip people, the commercial implied, bought furniture at IKEA. Hip people did not hang onto their furniture either; after a while they discarded it and replaced it with something else from IKEA.

The shift in tactics worked. IKEA's revenues doubled in a four-year period to $1.27 billion in 2001, up from $600 million in 1997. By 2008, the United States was IKEA's second-largest market after Germany, with 35 stores accounting for 10% of its total revenues, or around $2.4 billion, and expansion plans called for 50-plus stores in the United States by 2012.

Having learned vital lessons about competing in foreign countries outside continental Western Europe, IKEA continued to expand internationally in the 1990s and 2000s. It first entered the UK in 1987, and by 2008, it had 17 stores in the country. IKEA also acquired Britain's Habitat in the early 1990s and continued to run it under the Habitat brand name. In 1998, IKEA entered China, where it had 4 stores by 2008, followed by Russia in 2000 (11 stores by 2008), and Japan in 2006, a country where it had failed miserably 30 years earlier (by 2008 IKEA had four stores in Japan). In total, by 2008, there were 285 IKEA stores in 36 countries and territories. The company had plans to continue opening between 20 and 25 stores a year for the foreseeable future. According to one manager, an important limiting factor on the pace of expansion was building the supply network.

As with the United States, some local customization has been the order of the day. In China, for example, the store layout reflected the layout of many Chinese apartments, and because many Chinese apartments have balconies, IKEA's Chinese stores included a balcony section. IKEA also has had to adapt its locations in China, where car ownership is still not widespread. In the West, IKEA stores are generally located in suburban areas and have lots of parking space. In China, stores are located near public transportation, and IKEA offers delivery services so that Chinese customers can get their purchases home. IKEA has also adopted a deep price discounting model in China, pricing some items as much as 70% below their price in IKEA stores outside China. To make this work, IKEA has sourced a large percentage of its products sold in China from local suppliers.

The IKEA Concept and Business Model

IKEA's target market is the young, upwardly mobile global middle class who are looking for low-priced but attractively designed furniture and household items. This group is targeted with somewhat wacky, offbeat advertisements that help to drive traffic into the stores. The stores themselves are large warehouses festooned in the blue and yellow colors of the Swedish flag that offer 8,000 to 10,000 items, from kitchen cabinets to candlesticks. There is plenty of parking outside, and the stores are located with good access to major roads.

The interior of the stores is configured almost like a maze that requires customers to pass through each department to get to the checkout. The goal is simple; to get customers to make more impulse purchases as they wander through the IKEA wonderland. Customers who enter the store planning to buy a $40 coffee table can end up spending $500 on everything from storage units to kitchenware. The flow of departments is constructed with an eye to boosting sales. For example, when IKEA managers noticed that men would get bored while their wives stopped in the home textile department, they added a tool section just outside the textile department, and sales of tools skyrocketed. At the end of the maze, just before the checkout, is the warehouse where customers can pick up their flat-packed furniture. IKEA stores also have restaurants (located in the middle of the store) and child-care facilities (located at the entrance for easy drop off) so that shoppers stay as long as possible.

Products are designed to reflect the clean Swedish lines that have become IKEA's trademark. IKEA has a product strategy council, which is a group of senior managers who establish priorities for IKEA's product lineup. Once a priority is established, product developers survey the competition and then set a price point that is 30% to 50% below that of rivals. As IKEA's Web site states, "We design the price tag first, then the product." Once the price tag is set, designers work with a network of suppliers to drive down the cost of producing the unit. The goal is to identify the appropriate suppliers and the least-costly materials, a trial and error process that can take as long as three years. By 2008, IKEA had 1,380 suppliers in 54 countries. The top sourcing countries were China (21% of supplies), Poland (17%), Italy (8%), Sweden (6%), and Germany (6%).

IKEA devotes considerable attention to finding the right supplier for each item. Consider the company's best-selling Klippan love seat. Designed in 1980, the Klippan, with its clean lines, bright colors, simple legs, and compact size, has sold some 1.5 million units since its introduction. IKEA originally manufactured the product in Sweden but soon transferred production to lower-cost suppliers in Poland. As demand for the Klippan grew, IKEA then decided that it made more sense to work with suppliers in each of the company's big markets to avoid the costs associated with shipping the product all over the world. Today there are five suppliers of the frames in Europe, plus three in the United States and two in China. To reduce the cost of the cotton slipcovers, IKEA has concentrated production in four core suppliers in China and Europe. The resulting efficiencies from these global sourcing decisions enabled IKEA to reduce the price of the Klippan by some 40% between 1999 and 2005.

Although IKEA contracts out manufacturing for most of its products, since the early 1990s, a certain proportion of goods have been made internally (in 2008, about 90% of all products were sources from independent suppliers, with 10% being produced internally). The integration into manufacturing was born out of the collapse of communist governments in Eastern Europe after the fall of the Berlin Wall in 1989. By 1991, IKEA was sourcing some 25% of its goods from Eastern European manufacturers. It had invested considerable energy in building long-term relationships with these suppliers, and had often helped them to develop and purchase new technology so that they could make IKEA products at a lower cost. As communism collapsed and new bosses came in to the factories, many did not feel bound by the relationships with IKEA. They effectively tore up contracts, tried to raise prices, and underinvested in new technology.

With its supply base at risk, IKEA purchased a Swedish manufacturer, Swedwood. IKEA then used Swedwood as the vehicle to buy and run furniture manufacturers across Eastern Europe, with the largest investments being made in Poland. IKEA invested heavily in its Swedwood plants, equipping them with the most modern technology. Beyond the obvious benefits of giving IKEA a low-cost source of supply, Swedwood has also enabled IKEA to acquire knowledge about manufacturing processes that are useful both in product design and in relationships with other suppliers, giving IKEA the ability to help suppliers adopt new technology and drive down their costs.

For illustration, consider IKEA's relationship with suppliers in Vietnam. IKEA has expanded its supply base in Vietnam to help support its growing Asian presence. IKEA was attracted to Vietnam by the combination of low-cost labor and inexpensive raw materials. IKEA drives a tough bargain with its suppliers, many of whom say that they make thinner margins on their sales to IKEA than they do to other foreign buyers. IKEA demands high quality at a low price. But there is an upside; IKEA offers the prospect of forging a long-term, high-volume business relationship. Moreover, IKEA regularly advises its Vietnamese suppliers on how to seek out the best and cheapest raw materials, how to set up and expand factories, what equipment to purchase, and how to boost productivity through technology investments and management process.

Organization and Management

In many ways, IKEA's organization and management practices reflect the personal philosophy of its founder. A 2004 article in *Fortune* describes Kamprad, then one of the world's richest men, as an informal and frugal man who "insists on flying coach, takes the subway to work, drives a 10-year-old Volvo, and avoids suits of any kind. It has long been rumored in Sweden that when his self-discipline fails and he drinks an overpriced Coke out of a hotel mini bar, he will go down to a grocery store to buy a replacement."[7] Kamprad's thriftiness is attributed to his upbringing in Smaland, a traditionally poor region of Sweden. Kamprad's frugality is now part of IKEA's DNA.

Managers are forbidden to fly first class and are expected to share hotel rooms.

Under Kamprad, IKEA became mission driven. He had a cause, and those who worked with him adopted it too. It was to make life better for the masses, to democratize furniture. Kamprad's management style was informal, nonhierarchical, and team based. Titles and privileges are taboo at IKEA. There are no special perks for senior managers. Pay is not particularly high, and people generally work there because they like the atmosphere. Suits and ties have always been absent, from the head office to the loading docks. The culture is egalitarian. Offices have an open plan and are furnished with IKEA furniture; private offices are rare. Everyone is called a "co-worker," and first names are used throughout. IKEA regularly stages antibureaucracy weeks during which executives work on the store floor or tend to registers. In a 2005 *Business Week* article Andres Dahlvig, the CEO, described how he spent time earlier in the year unloading trucks and selling beds and mattresses.[8] Creativity is highly valued, and the company is replete with stories of individuals taking the initiative; from Gillis Lundgren's pioneering of the self-assemble concept to the store manager in the Stockholm store who let customers go into the warehouse to pick up their own furniture. To solidify this culture, IKEA had a preference for hiring younger people who had not worked for other enterprises and then promoting from within. IKEA has historically tended to shy away from hiring the highly educated, status-oriented elite, because they often adapted poorly to the company.

Kamprad seems to have viewed his team as extended family. Back in 1957, he bankrolled a weeklong trip to Spain for all 80 employees and their families as reward for hard work. The early team of employees all lived near each other. They worked together, played together, drank together, and talked about IKEA around the clock. When asked by an academic researcher what the fundamental key was to good leadership, Kamprad replied "Love." Recollecting the early days, he noted that "When we were working as a small family in Aluhult, we were as if in love. Nothing whatsoever to do with eroticism. We just liked each other so damn much."[9] Another manager noted that "We who wanted to join IKEA did so because the company suits our way of life. To escape thinking about status, grandeur and smart clothes."[10]

As IKEA grew, the question of taking the company public arose. While there were obvious advantages associated with doing so, including access to capital, Kamprad decided against it. His belief was that the stock market would impose short-term pressures on IKEA that would not be good for the company. The constant demands to produce profits, regardless of the business cycle, would, in Kamprad's view, make it more difficult for IKEA to take bold decisions. At the same time, as early as 1970, Kamprad started to worry about what would happen if he died. He decided that he did not want his sons to inherit the business. His worry was that they would either sell the company, or they might squabble over control of the company, and thus destroy it. All three of his sons, it should be noted, went to work at IKEA as managers.

The solution to this dilemma created one of the most unusual corporate structures in the world. In 1982, Kamprad transferred his interest in IKEA to a Dutch-based charitable foundation, Stichting Ingka Foundation. This is a tax-exempt, nonprofit legal entity that in turn owns Ingka Holding, a private Dutch firm that is the legal owner of IKEA. A five-person committee, chaired by Kamprad and including his wife, runs the foundation. In addition, the IKEA trademark and concept was transferred to IKEA Systems, another private Dutch company, whose parent company, Inter-IKEA, is based in Luxembourg. The Luxembourg company is, in turn, owned by an identically named company in the Netherlands Antilles, whose beneficial owners remain hidden from public view, but they are almost certainly the Kamprad family. Inter-IKEA earns its money from a franchise agreement it has with each IKEA store. The largest franchisee is none other than Ingka Holdings. IKEA states that franchisees pay 3% of sales to Inter-IKEA. Thus, Kamprad has effectively moved ownership of IKEA out of Sweden, although the company's identity and headquarters remain there, and established a mechanism for transferring funds to himself and his family from the franchising of the IKEA concept. Kamprad himself moved to Switzerland in the 1980s to escape Sweden's high taxes, and he has lived there ever since.

In 1986, Kamprad gave up day-to-day control of IKEA to Andres Moberg, a 36-year-old Swede who had dropped out of college to join IKEA's mail-order department. Despite relinquishing management control, Kamprad continued to exert influence over the company as an advisor to senior management and as an ambassador for IKEA, a role he was still pursuing with vigor in 2008, despite being in his 80s.

Looking Forward

In its half century, IKEA had established an enviable position for itself. It had become one of the most successful retail establishments in the world. It had expanded into numerous foreign markets (Exhibit 2), learning from its failures and building on its successes. It had bought affordable, well-designed, functional furniture to the masses, helping them to, in Kamprad's words, achieve a better everyday life. IKEA's goal was to continue to grow by opening 20 to 25 stores a year for the foreseeable future. Achieving that growth would mean expansion into non-Western markets, including most notably China where it had recently established a beachhead. Could the company continue to do so? Was its competitive advantage secure?

Exhibit 1   IKEA by the Numbers in 2008

IKEA Stores	285 in 35 countries
IKEA Sales	€21.2 billion
IKEA Suppliers	1,380 in 54 countries
The IKEA Range	9,500 products
IKEA Coworkers	127,800 in 39 countries

Source: http://franchisor.ikea.com/showContent .asp?swfld=facts9.

Exhibit 2   Sales and Suppliers

Top Five Sales Countries		Top Five Supplying Countries	
Germany	15%	China	21%
United States	10%	Poland	17%
France	10%	Italy	8%
UK	7%	Sweden	6%
Sweden	6%	Germany	6%

Source: http://www.ikea.com/ms/en_GB/about_ikea/facts_ and_figures/index.html.

References & Reading

1. Anonymous, "Furnishing the World," *The Economist*, November 19, 1995, 79–80.
2. Anonymous. "Flat pack accounting," *The Economist*, May 13, 2006, 69–70.
3. K. Capell, A. Sains, C. Lindblad, and A. T. Palmer, "IKEA," *BusinessWeek*, November 14, 2005, 96–101.
4. K. Capell et al., "What a Sweetheart of a Love Seat," *BusinessWeek*, November 14, 2005, 101.
5. C. Daniels, "Create IKEA, Make Billions, Take Bus," *Fortune*, May 3, 2004, 44.
6. J. Flynn and L. Bongiorno, "IKEA's New Game Plan," *BusinessWeek*, October 6, 1997, 99–102.
7. R. Heller, "Folk Fortune," *Forbes*, September 4, 2000, 67.
8. IKEA Documents at www.ikea.com.
9. J. Leland, "How the Disposable Sofa Conquered America," *New York Times Magazine*, October 5, 2005, 40–50.
10. P. M. Miller, "IKEA with Chinese Characteristics," *Chinese Business Review*, July–August 2004, 36–69.
11. B. Torekull, *Leading by Design: The IKEA Story* (New York: Harper Collins, 1998).

Endnotes

1. Quoted in R. Heller, "Folk Fortune," *Forbes*, September 4, 2000, 67.
2. B. Torekull, *Leading by Design: The IKEA Story* (New York: Harper Collins, 1998), 53.
3. Ibid.
4. Ibid.
5. J. Leland, "How the Disposable Sofa Conquered America," *New York Times Magazine*, October 5, 2005, 45.
6. Ibid.
7. C. Daniels and A. Edstrom, "Create IKEA, Make Billions, Take a Bus," *Fortune*, May 3, 2006, 44.
8. K. Capell et al., "Ikea," *Business Week*, November 14, 2005, 96–106.
9. B. Torekull, *Leading by Design: The IKEA Story*, 82.
10. B. Torekull, *Leading by Design: The IKEA Story*, 83.

THE RISE OF IBM

From its beginnings as a company that developed instruments to measure time, IBM grew to become the world's largest computer company. At its height in 1966, its stock was valued at $140; in 1993, its stock was trading at $42 a share, and shareholders had lost hundreds of billions of dollars of their investments. How could a giant company like IBM have fallen so low? How could the company strengths that contributed to its success have led to its fall? Why did IBM lose control of its customers and markets? To understand the problems that IBM currently faces, we need to look at IBM's past and at the way its strategy and structure developed over time.

BEFORE THE COMPUTER

In 1900, Charles Flint, a financier and arms merchant, owned, among other businesses, the International Time Recording Company (ITR), a clock manufacturer, and Computing Scale Company of America, a weighing scale and food slicing machine manufacturer.[1] These two business machine manufacturers formed the seeds of what was to become IBM. In the search for new markets for its products, ITR began to produce new kinds of time measuring machines that, among other things, permitted the rapidly expanding Bell telephone company to time its customers' long-distance calls. By 1910, ITR had become the leader in the time recording industry and had sales over $1 million. Computing Scale's main product was a scale that weighed items and calculated the cost per unit; the company also sold meat and cheese slicers to retail stores.[2]

Toward the end of the 19th century, an engineer named Herman Hollerith invented a calculating machine that sorted cards by punched holes. Any kind of data could be recorded by punching holes according to a standard procedure; and then the data could be analyzed statistically to provide a picture of the overall results. Potential customers for this device were organizations, such as government agencies, railroads, and retail establishments, that needed a way of managing and manipulating large amounts of information. The U.S. Census Bureau, for example, saw the potential of this device for handling its national data collection efforts, and Hollerith was awarded a contract for managing the data processing of the 1890 census. Holes were punched in cards to represent different census attributes, such as age, sex, and national origin. The cards were then sorted by the punched holes, and Hollerith's calculating machine supplied the requested data, such as the statistics for the percentage of people in a certain age group in a certain state.

The punch card machine required a huge number of punched cards—in the census, one for every family unit—that could be used only once, so each machine sale provided card revenue. Thus, although the machines performed quickly and accurately, they were expensive to operate. Nevertheless, the potential uses of the machine were limitless because any kind of data could be recorded on these cards. James Powers, an employee of the U.S. Census Bureau, immediately saw the potential of the calculating machine; from his experience with Hollerith's machines at the Census Bureau, he understood its strengths and weaknesses. Using this information,

For the most recent financial results of the company discussed in this case, go to http://finance.yahoo.com, input the company's stock symbol, and download the latest company report from its homepage.

Powers stole a march on Hollerith by inventing an improved calculating machine; using his contacts at the Census Bureau, he managed to get the contract for the 1910 census.[3]

Hollerith was now in a difficult position; he had lost his principal customer and lacked the resources to improve his machine and find new customers. He approached Flint to get him to invest in the business, but Flint, seeing the opportunity to broaden his company's line of business machines, decided to acquire Hollerith's Tabulating Machine Company. In 1911, Flint merged it with ITR and Computing Scale to form the Computing Tabulating & Recording Company (CTR).[4]

Although Power's machine was technologically better, Hollerith had developed the practice of only leasing his machines to customers. Customers liked this arrangement because it lowered their costs. Also, Hollerith provided a repair service for the machines, which were prone to breakdown. Using CTR's resources, the calculating machines were continually improved over time, and the new and improved machines were leased to customers. These leases provided CTR with a continuing source of revenues, but, more importantly, each of CTR's customers were required to buy their punch cards from CTR; 75% of the tabulating revenues came from the sale of the punched cards, while only 25% came from the lease of the actual machines. In 1912, CTR's profits were $541,000, with two-thirds coming from ITR. Its time machine division, however, saw profits rise to $613,000 in 1913 with most of the increase coming from the calculators. This proved very important to CTR because the next year, 1914, profits plunged to $490,000 due to a decline in the time clock sector, and the calculating business kept the company afloat.[5]

Thomas Watson Arrives at CTR

In 1914, to build CTR's business, Flint agreed to hire Thomas Watson as the general manager of CTR.[6] Watson was a former employee of National Cash Register (NCR), another major business machine company, which Watson had joined in 1895 when he was 21 years old. Watson had a passion for selling and began selling pianos, sewing machines, and organs when he was 18. However, the opportunity to earn large commissions eventually led him to NCR, where a mentor took an interest in his career and helped him develop selling skills until he became the star salesman at NCR within three years. Watson became an NCR branch manager in 1899.[7]

To exploit Watson's talents, NCR assigned him to create an independent company, called Watson's Cash Register and Secondhand Exchange, using NCR funds to beat NCR's competitors in the used cash register market. Just as NCR had a virtual monopoly over the sale of new cash registers, Watson set out to monopolize the used cash register market by deliberately undercutting competitors' prices. With their businesses failing, NCR then acquired its competitors. In 1912, Watson and 29 other NCR managers were indicted for a violation of antitrust laws. Watson was fined and sentenced to one year in jail; however, although he won an appeal, he decided to leave NCR. Watson had other offers in the boat, auto, and retail industries, but because he wanted to use his knowledge of business machines, he accepted the offer at CTR.[8]

Watson's career at NCR was significant because he implemented many of NCR's sales practices at CTR. Although NCR's competitors had higher quality cash registers than NCR, NCR consistently beat the competition because of the way it organized and rewarded its sales force. NCR had a strong sales force in which salespeople were granted exclusive territories and paid on commission. This made them aggressively pursue all sales opportunities in their territories. They continually called on customers and built strong, personal relationships with them. This sales strategy had been developed by the leader of NCR, John Patterson, who believed that a product was worthless until it was sold. Patterson insisted that NCR salespeople answer repair calls immediately and instilled in them that they were selling a *service* not just a *product*. NCR created a training school in 1894 for its salespeople; it also established the NCR "Hundred Point Club," which recognized and rewarded salespeople who had exceeded their quotas. Members of the club received bonuses and trips to conventions in big cities, coverage in the company newspaper, and congratulations from Patterson.[9] As described following, Watson took full advantage of his knowledge of NCR's sales practices at CTR. However, he also took full advantage of his entrepreneurial ability to sense unmet customer needs. He was fascinated with the potential of the punch-card calculating machine.

In 1904, Watson had seen a friend at Eastman Kodak using a Hollerith punch card calculating machine to monitor salespeople. Each time a sale was completed, all the data was entered onto a card, which was sorted and tabulated monthly to generate reports indicating what each person sold, which products were selling best in which regions, etc. The cards were permanent records that could be filed, accumulated, and printed automatically.[10] The punch card system eliminated boring jobs such as copying ledger entries and writing bills. Furthermore, the machines were relatively inexpensive compared to employing clerks to keep records, dependable, and fast. Thus as head of CTR, Watson was most interested in the calculating machine side of the business, even though the time measurement business generated the highest sales and profits.

When Watson became president of CTR in 1915 after NCR, he convinced Flint that CTR should devote most of its resources to developing the tabulator side of the business. Watson implemented a plan to develop new tabulators, recorders, and printers to print the output of the tabulating machine. To achieve this new plan, the company funded the development of a research laboratory to improve the tabulating machines and established a facility to train salespeople. His goal was to create a sales force like NCR's sales force and make better tabulating machines than CTR's competitors. To help provide the revenue to achieve this, Watson licensed foreign companies to produce and sell the tabulators in foreign markets. The licensees paid a royalty to CTR based on sales. This was the beginning of CTR's international strategy. Within two years, CTR's research laboratory created a new line of tabulators that were easier to use than competitors' models and priced below their prices, offered for lease on favorable terms. Powers was CTR's major competitor at this time.

To compete with Powers, who had tabulators as good as CTR, Watson used the strategy that NCR had developed in the cash register business: Watson, like Patterson, emphasized that the salesperson's role was to provide good quality customer service, not merely to lease and install a machine. He established the "100 Percent Club" to reward salespeople, and those who met quotas were honored at conventions. Employees were also paid on commission, and quotas were increased each year.[11] In addition,

employees received a premium salary and good benefits, and the company's policy of internal promotion made it possible for hard-working employees to advance quickly in the organization.[12] These employment practices made it easy for CTR to attract and retain good employees and gain the commitment of its workforce.[13]

By 1917, CTR's sales had increased to $8.3 million from $4.2 million in 1914. All three of its divisions were doing well. Computing Scale's products were now used in shipyards and factories throughout the United States to measure the quantity of products, such as nuts and bolts. ITR had record sales due to World War I. CTR had leased 1,400 tabulators by the end of the war. Virtually all big insurance companies, railroads, and government agencies used CTR's tabulators. In addition to leasing the machines, sales of punch cards were also increasing and contributing to company revenues. In 1919, CTR launched a new printer that displayed the data collected and analyzed in the Hollerith tabulators and card sorters. The printer was also priced less than the machine made by Powers and was so successful that CTR had a backorder for the printers. Watson planned to build a new production plant to meet the high demand.[14]

The large expenditures on research and development (R&D) and developing a skilled national sales force put a severe strain on the company's resources. It was so severe that when sales revenues dropped from a record $16 million in 1920 to $10.6 million in 1921 due to slump in the economy, CTR was in trouble and needed external funds to survive. Fortunately for the company, Guaranty Trust Bank loaned CTR the money it needed to meet current liabilities. In 1922, sales revenues rebounded, and the company made a profit. However, the company had to cut costs in every area, including sales and R&D. CTR learned not to let cash balances go too low and implemented policies of low dividends, high revenues, and careful cost controls. In addition, the company intentionally refrained from introducing new products until a mass market had developed for its new range of tabulating machines.[15]

Watson became chairman of CTR in 1924 and renamed the company International Business Machines (IBM). This new name not only presented an integrated image of the company's three main product lines but also indicated the direction Watson planned for the company: providing advanced business machines for both domestic and foreign markets.

IBM's strategy from the 1920s on was to produce and lease business machines that collected, processed, and presented large amounts of data. From 1924 to 1941, IBM's primary business was the production and lease of punch card tabulating machines, and punch cards contributed most to the revenues of the company. As the technology of punch card machines became more advanced, they could sort 400 cards a minute and print paychecks and address labels. Tabulating machines were increasingly used by large companies to keep records on their employees, suppliers, and customer accounts.[16] Companies usually leased IBM's machines; IBM developed a specific punch card system to meet the needs of each individual customer.[17] For example, IBM developed a coding system appropriate to each client's information processing needs.

The potential of punch card tabulating machines had been recognized by other companies as well. Although the Powers Accounting Machine Corporation had long been IBM's competitor, new competitors included Burroughs, NCR, Remington Rand, and Underwood Elliot Fisher. Underwood, created in 1927, ruled the typewriter industry with its Model 5 and had a sales force as good as IBM's, while Burroughs was the leader in adding machines. At this time, IBM was not interested in mass producing machines like typewriters and adding machines unless such machines could be made part of the tabulating system. Its strategy was to lease its machines and then support the machines with trained service representatives who were available to handle customers' problems and make suggestions for improving customers' information processing as their individual businesses changed. Leasing gave IBM several competitive advantages over Burroughs, NCR, and Remington Rand who all sold machines. First, it allowed the company to retain control over outdated technology that could not be resold in the used market (a problem NCR had encountered). Second, leasing made it easier for the customers because they were not committed to a large capital outlay or purchasing outmoded machines. Third, leasing provided IBM with a steady cash flow. Moreover, by leasing machines, IBM was also able to force customers to purchase the thousands of cards they used each month

from IBM. The practice of making customers buy its cards led to an antitrust law suit in 1936. The Supreme Court ruled that IBM should discontinue requiring customers to buy cards from IBM alone. However, this ruling had no impact because IBM was the only effective supplier of cards, and its sales force made sure that customers were kept happy.

During the 1920s and 1930s, IBM also began to develop specialized tabulators to handle specific types of information processing needs for customers. For example, IBM developed a proofing machine for banks that could sort and add checks, a very labor-intensive process. This proof machine, which was called the IBM 405 and launched in 1932, became IBM's most profitable product at the time. The 405 consisted of a punch, a sorter, and an accounting machine. Operators punched holes in cards to represent data. The sorter put the cards in the appropriate bins. The cards were then taken out of the bin and run through the accounting machines, which generated printouts of the data and could also print checks. Some customers rented verifiers that attached to the punch to ensure the cards were properly prepared. IBM trained its customers' employees on how to use the 405 at no cost to ensure a demand for their products.

By 1939, IBM was the biggest and most powerful business machine company in the United States. IBM owned about 80% of the keypunches, sorters, and accounting machines used for tabulating purposes. By this time, Remington Rand and Burroughs were minor competitors, and the Powers company had disappeared, unable to match IBM's strengths in sales and R&D.[18]

By 1939, Watson had also reorganized the company's business divisions. The punch card tabulating division was now the center of the company's business, and he was building the company's other divisions around this division. For example, Watson decided to keep ITR, which sold time clocks among other things, because customers bought many time cards, which were similar to punched cards. However, he sold off the largest part of the scale division because it no longer fit the company's new direction. On the other hand, Watson bought Electromatic Typewriter Company because it was working on keypunch consoles. By 1945, IBM developed this company to become the United States leader in electric typewriters, which were sold by IBM's large and well-trained sales force.[19]

In 1939, total revenues were $34.8 million, and profits were $9.1 million. Sales of punch cards were about $5 million of this total and had higher profit margins than any other product.[20] However, the start of World War II accelerated the demand for IBM's tabulating machines, and sales rose to $143.3 million by 1943. However, profits were only $9.7 million compared to $9.1 million due to the wartime excess profits tax. Higher sales were achieved because IBM created mobile punch card units that followed supply controllers across war zones, and bookkeeping was done on the battle-field.[21] For example, a mobile unit would go to a Pacific island and compute the soldiers' payrolls. The tabulators also recorded bombing results, casu-alties, prisoners, displaced persons, and supplies. A punch card record was maintained on every man drafted and followed him until he was discharged from the military.[22]

THE COMPUTER AGE

Toward the end of World War II, a research team at the University of Pennsylvania constructed a computer to solve math problems for the army; the machine, called the ENIAC, could compute ballistic tables for the big guns of World War II. In 1946, the ENIAC was the only working computer in the world. This computer was the size of a small house and had 18,000 vacuum tubes, which tended to burn out. The machine cost $3 million to build, took a long time to set up, and was very difficult to use. The inventors of the computer, J. Presper Eckert and John Mauchley, realized that computers could take the place of punch card tabulating machines and that they would eventually be used in business. They created a company to develop and manufac-ture a computer for commercial use, the Univac (standing for UNIVersal Automatic Computer). In 1948, they received an order from the U.S. Census Bureau for their computer (just as Hollerith had 60 years before), and in the same year, Prudential Insurance also ordered a Univac.[23] These organiza-tions were two of IBM's largest customers, and so IBM became interested in the new computer tech-nology.[24] However, in 1950, Remington Rand, which also sold typewriters, tabulators, filing cabinets, and electric shavers, forestalled IBM and bought Eckert

and Mauchley's company to gain entry into the new computer market. Just as Watson had realized the potential of the punch card machine, so Remington realized the potential of the computer. The race was on to become the company that would dominate the next generation of business machines—computers.

IBM had not ignored technical developments in the tabulating industry. By 1948, it had developed an electromechanical machine called the MARK I that was 51 feet long by 8 feet high and cost $1 million. This machine was more advanced than a punch card machine, but it was still not a true computer. It was slower than the Univac.[25]

Tom Watson's two sons, Tom Jr. and Arthur ("Dick"), joined IBM at the end of the war.[26] Tom Jr. convinced his father that IBM would lose everything if it did not embrace the new technology and enter the computer market.[27] Large insurance companies such as Prudential and Metropolitan Life were IBM companies that had been complaining for a long time that the punch card system required too much storage space and was becoming too slow and cumbersome to handle the volume of information these companies were generating. IBM began investigating new kinds of storage systems, such as magnetic tapes, and look-ing at computers that used new electronic circuits to sort data and handle calculations. After looking at the ENIAC computer, which used the new elec-tronic circuits, Watson Jr. encouraged IBM's research laboratory managers to recruit more electronic spe-cialists.[28] He prodded IBM to incorporate electronic circuits in punch card machines because a primitive electronic circuit could perform 5,000 additions per second compared to 4 per second for the fastest mechanism in a punch card machine.

Working quickly, and with access to the com-pany's large resource base, IBM developed a new machine in 1946 that could compute payroll in one-tenth the time a punch card machine could do it. The 603 Electronic Multiplier was not a true com-puter; numbers were processed from punch cards rather than from signals recorded in the machine's memory circuits. The machine was upgraded to the 604, which had electronic circuits that could divide. When it was introduced in mid-1948, it sold by the thousands. Both machines matched IBM's exist-ing punch card equipment, which made it easy for IBM's customers to upgrade to the new machines. The machine's success convinced Tom Watson Jr. and Senior that electronics would grow even faster. From this time on, the company committed its resources to developing an advanced new computer system, just as 30 years before Tom Sr. had bet CTR's future on advanced punch card machines.[29]

IBM began working on its first family of electronic computers, called the 701 in 1949. Tom Jr. became president of the domestic division of IBM in 1952, the same year in which the 701 was launched.[30] The 701 was a scientific computer for use in laboratories, but it was not as advanced as the Univac. However, although Remington Rand was ahead in technology, the company lacked IBM's vision, and Rand would not permit punch card salespeople to sell Univacs. Tom Jr., however, placed IBM's sales force behind its computer and required both senior executives and engineers to help train its sales force in operating the new machine. By 1953, IBM installed 32 of its 701 computer machines and had 164 on order compared to Remington Rand's 33 installations and 24 orders.

The 702, a commercial computer for general accounting applications, was launched in 1954. This machine was faster than the Univac, and with this machine, IBM took the technological lead. By 1956, IBM had 87 computers installed at various businesses and 190 on order, compared to all other competitors combined installations of 41 and combined orders of 40 computers.[31] Because all its machines were leased, it was easy for IBM to upgrade its customers to its new advanced machines. When the 705 was developed to replace the 702, and the 704 to replace the 701, IBM retained and increased its market share.[32] Between 1950 and 1956, IBM's revenues tripled from $214.9 million to $743.3 million.[33] The average growth rate of the company from 1946 to 1955 was 22%. Watson Jr. decided to expand IBM's product line as fast as the market would allow.

IBM's technological success was due to the way Watson Jr. had totally changed the company's R&D thrust. IBM's research lab had been dominated by engineers because its punch card machines operated on mechanical principles. None of its engineers understood electronics, however, so Watson Jr. hired a new lab chief and increased the staff from 500 mechanical engineers and technicians in 1950 to more than 4,000 electrical engineers by 1956. Watson Jr. also created a smaller lab in California to specialize in storage devices. In less than three years, this lab invented the computer disk that stores data

on magnetic tape that became the backbone of IBM's future computer systems.

Watson Jr. also led the development of the IBM 650 in 1956 that provided enough data processing power for most general commercial applications. The 650 was less powerful than the 700 series, but it was much cheaper. The 650 introduced thousands of punch card customers to computers. It was designed to work with ordinary punch card equipment but made the punch card system much more powerful and versatile. For example, life insurance companies compute insurance premiums from actuarial tables based upon the age, sex, and other customer factors. Using a 650, these actuarial tables could be loaded into the computer memory, and when the punch card containing information on a customer was loaded into the machine, the computer did the calculations and furnished the total.[34] Previously, a clerk had to figure the totals and record the information on a punch card for recording purposes; the 650 did everything.

IBM put its huge sales force behind the 650 machine, and as a result of its efforts, within a year almost 1,000 machines were sold. Most computers were used in administrative offices and in factories for controlling the manufacturing process.[35] By the end of the 1950s, IBM had a 75% market share. The remaining market was divided among Remington Rand, Honeywell Electronics, NCR, and a few others. Although Underwood Typewriter and NCR attempted to launch small computers, the 650 was a better performer.

The Transistor

In 1956, the transistor, developed by William Shockley at Bell Labs, weighed 100 times less than the vacuum tube. Compared to a vacuum tube, the transistor required a lot less electrical power, could perform calculations at a much faster rate, and had the potential to miniaturize computing systems. The transistor made it feasible both to design a more complex and powerful computer and sell it at a price that most companies could afford.[36]

IBM researchers had been successfully using the vacuum tube, and like the mechanical engineers before them, they were reluctant to change to a transistor-based computer technology. Watson Jr. sent a memo to development personnel stating that no more IBM machines would be designed using vacuum tubes.[37] This memo started a whole new thrust in IBM's research efforts that ultimately led to the 7000 computer series, IBM's first computers based on transistors instead of vacuum tubes.[38] However, scientists had a hard time wiring transistors together until the integrated circuit was invented in 1959 by a Fairchild Semiconductor engineer. The whole circuit board was the size of a fingernail. By the early 1960s, IBM computers guided Polaris missiles and air force jets. When integrated circuits were mass produced, their cost fell from $1,000 per circuit in 1960 to a few cents per circuit by 1970. IBM developed successive generations of more powerful machines to exploit the new technology.[39]

Redefining the Industry

By 1960, IBM's computer division was disorganized and had a product line consisting of eight newer transistor-based computers and several older vacuum tube machines. This caused several problems for IBM's customers because the computers were not compatible. For example, if a customer expanded and wanted to upgrade to a larger or newer computer, the customer had to lease a whole new range of equipment and rewrite all the programs to make the computer work in the company. The disjointed product line was also causing problems for IBM's personnel. Because IBM's product line had grown so large, Watson Jr. decided to split the data processing division into two units: one for machines that rented for over $10,000 a month and one for machines that rented for less than $10,000 a month. However, this product division caused competition between managers of the different product lines, each of whom fought to obtain resources to develop and improve their particular product line. This also led to a duplication of R&D efforts. The diverse range of computers made it more difficult for IBM's sales force to learn the different systems associated with each computer and to efficiently inform customers about their suitability for their particular business.

IBM's technological thrust had outpaced the ability of the company to adequately service its products. Its attempt to become the leader in the industry resulted in the development of a fragmented product line that was confusing its customers and employees. The company needed a new strategy to grow. Watson Jr.'s answer was that IBM needed to build

a line of computers that would cover the needs of the whole computer market. The project was called the System/360, representing 360 degrees in a circle, because IBM wanted to meet the needs of every user in both the scientific and business community. The 360 was intended to make all other computers, both IBM's and its competitor's, obsolete. All of the 360 computers would be compatible with one another. Moreover, they would all use the same operating language, software, disk drives, printers, etc. The goal of this design was to lock in customers to IBM's computer systems and make it difficult for customers to change to competing products. Their incentive would be keep buying new IBM products when they wanted to upgrade their systems. The other goal of the system was to make better use of IBM's R&D resources and make it easier for its sales force to sell an integrated package of products to customers. The project was challenging because hardware and software had to be coordinated, and IBM began producing its own electronic parts for the first time.[40] IBM opened six new plants around the world to manufacture the System/360 computers. Over a four-year period, $5 billion was invested, and 50,000 new employees were hired.[41]

The System/360 mainframe computer was launched in 1964 and captured 70% of the market.[42] The project was an immense success and put IBM way ahead of its competitors. Although before the 360, competitors such as RCA, Burroughs, Honeywell, Univac, and General Electric sold machines that performed much better than IBM computers for the same price, the compatible design and the power of the System/360 beat all competitors.[43] Moreover, marketing played as large a role in the success of the project as did technology. Although all its competitors had access to integrated circuits and could produce an advanced computer, only IBM had the capacity to sell a machine, install it correctly, and provide the quality service that allowed it to retain and lock in its customers.

Due to the success of the System/360 mainframes and the IBM sales force, IBM dominated the computer industry.[44] The 360 spurred growth in the whole industry. In 1963, there were only 11,700 computers in the United States, however; this figure doubled in 1965 and redoubled in 1969. By 1969, IBM had revenues of $7.196 billion and earnings of $934 million. Although, the situation was masked by increasing revenues from world trade and interest earned from investments, by 1970, IBM was starting to slow down. Its stock price actually declined in 1970. The company had grown at an annual rate of 22% from 1946 to 1955, but its growth was only 16% per year from 1955 to 1970 and slowed further after 1970. The reason was that IBM was beginning to face competition from other companies who had begun to produce computers for other segments of the computer market. Before we examine the new competition in the computer industry, it is useful to discuss the scope of IBM's domestic and foreign operations to understand how large and complex the company had become.

GLOBAL DEVELOPMENT

IBM's movement into global markets began in 1908 when Herman Hollerith made a licensing agreement with the British Tabulating Company (BTC) to produce and sell Hollerith tabulators throughout the British Empire. Tom Watson Sr. continued with Hollerith's vision of IBM as an international company and established IBM's foreign department. After WWI, he began to build small manufacturing plants in Germany, France, and Great Britain to evade the tariffs these countries levied on foreign imports. Sales and marketing agencies were also created throughout Europe, Latin America, and parts of Asia. The branches were called Watson Business Machines and their function, as in the United States, was to provide the high level of customer service that supported IBM's business machines. In 1935, foreign revenue was $1.6 million, with punch cards once again being the biggest contributor. By 1939, more than 12% of IBM's revenues came from foreign operations.

During WWII, IBM's plants in Europe and Japan were seized. However, even though IBM's German plant, which contributed 50% of the foreign department's revenue, was in ruins, by 1945, foreign revenues were almost $2 million. After the war, IBM's British plant became the largest facility outside North America. In 1949, IBM renegotiated the 1908 agreement with BTC whereby BTC, would receive a free, nonexclusive license on all current IBM products in exchange for letting IBM sell its new products through its own sales organization. This agreement resulted in the creation of a new subsidiary called IBM UK, which, selling IBM's new advanced computers, soon came to dominate the British and European markets.

In 1949, Dick Watson, who spoke German, French, Italian, and Spanish, was put in charge of IBM's international operations. In 1950, the foreign department was renamed the IBM World Trade Division and became an independent subsidiary that would receive product and financial support from the IBM domestic Division but would operate on its own. By 1950, the World Trade Division had 10 factories producing machines and more than 20 facilities making cards throughout the world. The World Trade Division operated in 58 countries through subsidiaries such as IBM Deutschland, IBM France, and many smaller units in Latin America and Africa.[45]

Of World Trade's 16,000 employees in 1954, only 200 were Americans because Dick Watson believed that most success would be achieved if each subsidiary was responsive to the needs of its own region or country. Dick Watson set high standards for the World Trade Division, hired good people as country managers, and was responsive to local customs. So, for example, the German subsidiary would be staffed by German nationals who could be responsive to the needs of its German customers and understand their specific problems.[46] By 1967, foreign revenues were $1.6 billion and net earnings were $209 million. World Trade sales were equal to IBM's domestic sales. Although IBM operated in 130 countries, Europe accounted for two-thirds of foreign revenue.[47] In 1970, Dick Watson resigned from IBM to become the United States ambassador to France. With his departure, the World Trade Division was further divided into world regions: Europe, the Middle East, Africa, the Americas, and the Far East. By 1970, foreign revenues had increased to $3.5 billion.[48]

DOMESTIC OPERATIONS

IBM Domestic, which was led by Tom Watson Jr., was limited to operations in the continental United States, but as the parent company, it was also responsible for R&D and financing operations for the entire company.[49] The rapid growth of the company began to produce enormous problems for the company. By 1950, not only was IBM designing and manufacturing many different models of computers, it was also designing and manufacturing many of the component parts used in the computers, such as disk drives and transistors peripheral equipment such as printers file storage, and servers. The range of the company's activities had increased enormously, and IBM's operating structure had lagged behind the growth in the company, which began to cause many problems.

Despite IBM's growth (in 1955, the company reached $500 million in revenues), it was run by Tom Watson Sr. until he retired in 1955. Watson Sr. oversaw all of IBM's operations, and a line of top managers was always waiting to see him. No formal organizational chart existed because Watson believed that people should be interested in all aspects of IBM's activities rather than focusing on specific jobs. The company had no clear chain of command, no policy of decentralization that gave lower level managers the right to make independent decisions, and no formal planning process or business policies. Knowledge was simply in employees' heads, and strategy emerged gradually over time from discussions and negotiations between Watson Sr. and his top management team.

After Watson Sr.'s retirement, Tom Watson Jr. and Al Williams, IBM's president at the time, decided to construct an organizational chart to see who reported to Watson. They found that 38 to 40 top managers had been reporting directly to him. It was obvious to them that this highly centralized management style could not continue if the rapidly growing company was going to stay on top of the computer industry. Unmade decisions were accumulating because managers lacked the authority to make decisions.

Watson Jr. wanted to break with his father's centralized, autocratic style of decision making and speed up the process, so he and Williams reorganized IBM's operating structure to decentralize control to managers who were given the responsibility of managing the different functional areas of the company. The organization chart they devised put Red Lamotte in charge of sales and R&D and Al Williams in charge of finance, while Watson Jr. would take control of the company's strategy. However, this reorganization simply divided the chaos among three people instead of one; there were still far too many managers reporting to the three top managers, and they were unable to control IBM's operations. So, in 1956, IBM was reorganized along divisional

lines. IBM Domestic was broken up into five individual divisions: the field engineering division, which primarily served commercial customers; the federal systems division, which primarily served government agencies; the systems manufacturing division, which manufactured the computers; the component manufacturing division, which manufactured the components; and the research division, which performed the basic research and design activities. In each division, a general manager would make decisions for the division. The World Trade Division would continue to operate separately from the now subdivided Domestic Division.[50]

This divisional structure ensured that each executive had clearly defined tasks. Watson Jr. created a top management team of six people, consisting of himself and the heads of the five divisions to oversee the company. Each of the five general managers was responsible for a major part of IBM, and Watson Jr. oversaw the entire company. Watson Jr. claimed that his ability to choose and retain an intelligent top management team was his greatest contribution to IBM.[51] He created a corporate staff of experts in sales and marketing, finance, manufacturing, personnel, and communications to advise him and oversee the activities of the divisions. The corporate staff was seen as staff or advisory managers, while divisional managers were seen as line managers, with responsibility for the bottom line operating results. The line managers were responsible for meeting production targets, beat sales quotas, and increase market share. The staff managers gave advice to line managers; the heads of the divisions, who were their superiors, conveyed policy from corporate headquarters to the operating divisions and ensured that the proper objectives were in place and being met. Each line manager would be evaluated solely on his or her unit's results, and each staff manager would be rated on his or her effort in making IBM a world leader.

IBM's divisional structure produced many tensions between corporate (staff) and divisional (line) personnel. For example, as a part of their roles, staff managers would often identify problems that needed to be addressed and would write memos to line managers suggesting how to solve it. Line managers, however, viewed these moves as interference and intrusions into their areas of operations. They began to guard their territories from corporate personnel who had no direct authority over divisional managers. To resolve these tensions,

Williams created a check and balance system in IBM called "contention management." This system forced both staff and line managers to meet and encouraged them to debate the merits of an idea; no operating plan became final without staff approval. When line and staff managers could not agree, the problem was sent to the corporate management committee—the top six executives. Over time, however, an increasing number of issues were sent to the top of the organization to resolve, and it became accepted that top management would resolve important strategic issues. Thus, despite Watson's claimed policy of decentralizing authority to divisional managers and their subordinates, much of IBM's decision making remained centralized at the top of the organization. Managers from IBM's mainframe division, its chief revenue earner, had the most power in shaping corporate decision making.

IBM's policy of long-term employment, commitment, and loyalty to the company's objectives became entrenched during this period, and the company became known throughout the industry for its job security and good pay.[52] With its high rate of growth, internal promotions were easy to come by, and employees rose rapidly throughout the corporate ranks. In 1955, employee stock options were offered for the first time. In 1966, managers were required to attend an in-house IBM management school, where they were trained on IBM's philosophy on communications, sales and service efforts, meetings, and employee treatment (such as visiting workers with sick spouses).[53] This policy taught employees the IBM way and helped to cement IBM's corporate culture and its style of doing business.

NEW MANAGEMENT AND NEW CHALLENGES

In 1970, Dick Watson resigned to become the United States ambassador to France, and Tom Watson Jr. suffered a heart attack that resulted in his retirement in 1971. When Tom Watson Jr. appointed T. V. Learson as CEO in 1971, the period of the Watson family's control over IBM came to an end. IBM was the largest, most successful computer company in the world and had achieved complete domination over the global computer industry. The question for Learson was, what new challenges could IBM confront? How should it use its vast resources to exploit a computer market that was growing by leaps and bounds? How could the company exploit its privileged position to dominate the computer market of the future? The answers were not long in coming.

Endnotes

1. David Mercer, *The Global IBM* (New York: Dodd, Mead & Co., 1988), 27–31.
2. Robert Sober, *IBM: Colossus In Transition*, (New York: Times Books, 1981), 11.
3. Ibid. 15–19, 21.
4. David Mercer, *The Global IBM*, 27–31.
5. Robert Sober, *IBM: Colossus in Transition*, 49–59.
6. David Mercer, *The Global IBM*, 31–42.
7. Robert Sobel, *IBM: Colossus in Transition*, 32–38.
8. Ibid. 49–59, 61.
9. Ibid. 24, 27–30.
10. Thomas Watson Jr. and Peter Petre, *Father Son & Co.: My Life At IBM And Beyond.* (New York: Bantam Books, 1990), 70.
11. Robert Sober, *IBM: Colossus in Transition*, 49–59, 61.
12. David Mercer, *The Global IBM*, 31–42.
13. Robert Sober, *IBM: Colossus in Transition*, 62.
14. Ibid. 63.
15. David Mercer, *The Global IBM*, 31–42.
16. Thomas Watson Jr. & Peter Petre, Father Son & Co., 70.
17. David Mercer, *The Global IBM* 31–42.
18. Robert Sobel, IBM: *Colossus in Transition*, 72, 75–82, 86–87, 92.
19. Ibid. 83.
20. Ibid. 84.
21. David Mercer, *The Global IBM*, 31–42.
22. Thomas Watson Jr. & Peter Petre, Father Son & Co., 112.
23. "The Machine That Changed the World."
24. Thomas Watson Jr. & Peter Petre, Father Son & Co., 192.
25. Ibid. 190.
26. David Mercer, *The Global IBM*, 41–43.
27. "The Machine That Changed the World."
28. Thomas Watson Jr. & Peter Petre, Father Son & Co., 24–35.
29. Ibid. 136–137, 189, 192.
30. Ibid. 24–35.
31. Ibid. 243.
32. Robert Sober, *IBM: Colossus in Transition*, 127–128.

33. David Mercer, *The Global IBM*, 46.
34. Thomas Watson Jr. & Peter Petre, Father Son & Co., 244.
35. "The Machine That Changed the World."
36. "The Machine That Changed the World."
37. Thomas Watson Jr. & Peter Petre, Father Son & Co., 24–35.
38. Lewis, 92-98. BW 14 Feb. 1988, 92–98.
39. "The Machine That Changed the World."
40. Thomas Watson Jr. & Peter Petre, Father Son & Co., 292, 346–350.
41. David Mercer, *The Global IBM*, 51.
42. Lewis, 92-98. BW 14 Feb. 1988, 92–98.
43. Thomas Watson Jr. & Peter Petre, Father Son & Co., 346–350.
44. Robert Sober, IBM: *Colossus in Transition*, 169.
45. Ibid. 131–137, 197–199, 202, 204.
46. David Mercer, *The Global IBM*, 251–254.
47. Robert Sober, IBM: *Colossus in Transition*, 131–137, 197–199, 202, 204.
48. Ibid. 203–204, 207.
49. "The Intimate Tale of IBM's First Family." *Fortune*, 14 June 1990, 92–132. Book Excerpt from *Father, Son & Co.: My Life at IBM and Beyond*, By Thomas Watson Jr. and Peter Petre, Bantam Books (1990).
50. David Mercer, *The Global IBM*, 52–53.
51. Thomas Watson Jr. & Peter Petre, Father Son & Co., 24–35.
52. Ibid. 288–289.
53. Ibid. 24–35.

The Fall of IBM

T. V. Learson took over as CEO of IBM after Tom Watson Jr. in 1971 and became the head of a company that had a 75% share of the world market for mainframe computers—computers powerful enough to manage the information processing needs of an entire company. Learson had made a major personal contribution to IBM's emergence as the dominant global mainframe manufacturer when he led the development of IBM's highly successful System/360 mainframe series that led to the rapid rise in the company's fortunes. IBM's 360 mainframes fully automated a company's manual information processing systems, such as payroll, accounting, and customer record keeping, making the punch card obsolete. As the former head of the 360 program, Learson understood the critical importance of research and development (R&D) in maintaining and defending IBM's preeminent position in the mainframe market. Because of this, he initiated and oversaw the development of IBM's new, more powerful System/370 computer series.

Technical advances lowered the System/370's price per calculation to 60% less than that of the System/360s, plus the 370 had a larger information storage system. The 370s still used the software of the 360s however, making them primarily an upgrade rather than a replacement. Nevertheless, the 370 machines became the backbone of IBM's mainframe product line from the early 1970s on. Most of the advances that IBM traded to its mainframe computers from this time on were designed primarily to either improve the 370 machines' processing power

or the performance of its various components, such as its software, its printers, and, especially, its storage capacity. The 370 series became the industry standard that IBM's competitors tried to match and outperform.

Under Learson's control, and then under the control of Frank Cary who became CEO when Learson retired in 1973, IBM continued to enjoy its domination of the mainframe market. By 1980, IBM had a market value of $26 billion, four times its size in 1971.

INCREASING COMPETITION

Although IBM's continued domination of the mainframe market produced record increases in revenues and profits every year, its performance masked some major problems that were developing during the 1970s and 1980s. The first major problem, which Cary had recognized as early as 1970, was that the mainframe computer market was starting to mature. Almost every large United States business possessed a mainframe computer, as did most scientific and higher education institutions. Furthermore, IBM also had saturated the international market. As a result, IBM's rate of growth was falling; even though its revenues were increasing, they were increasing at a decreasing rate. Competition was increasing from companies that were trying to find ways to attract IBM's customers and share in the

For the most recent financial results of the company discussed in this case, go to http://finance.yahoo.com, input the company's stock symbol, and download the latest company report from its homepage.

huge revenues in the mainframe computer market. Its major competitors at the time were Amdahl, Honeywell, Burroughs, Univac, NCR, and Control Data.

Many of these companies began offering IBM's customers mainframe systems at a lower cost than the expensive IBM systems. Initially, IBM faced competition only from companies selling IBM-compatible peripheral equipment such as disk drives, storage devices, and printers at lower prices than IBM's products. Its sales force had been able to ward off such threats. Now, however, the nature of competition was changing. IBM's competitors began selling cheaper, higher performing, IBM-compatible central processing units (CPUs)—the brain of the computer and the source of its processing power. For the first time, competitors were offering a low-price alternative to the IBM mainframe. At the same time, IBM was still pursuing its high-priced lease strategy, which was backed by excellent customer service. Another emerging low-price threat came from leasing companies. These leasing companies would buy old 360s from IBM and lease them on better terms than IBM offered, attracting price-conscious IBM customers. While these competitive threats were small, they nevertheless gave IBM cause for concern.

From 1970 on IBM became concerned about the threat of low-cost, foreign competition in the mainframe computer market after witnessing the decline of several United States industries, including automobiles, due to the entry of low-cost Japanese competitors. The price of integrated circuits, the heart of a mainframe computer, was plummeting at this time, and Japanese companies had the technical capability to build a powerful computer that could match or exceed the IBM 370. The existence of a low-cost global competitor was a major threat to IBM's domination of both the United States market and the global market.

In response to the threat of low-cost competition, Cary announced that IBM would spend $10 billion to build new automated plants to produce low-cost computers over a six-year period. In this way, IBM would be able to meet the challenge of low-priced computers should the threat materialize and its customers start to switch to low-cost competitors. John Opel, who became IBM's CEO in 1981, was also concerned about competition from Japan and carried on with Cary's low-cost producer strategy. Under his control IBM spent $32 billion

from 1980 to 1985 to determine ways to reduce manufacturing costs.

IBM's push to reduce manufacturing costs did not fit well with its strategy of offering excellent customer service and using its very expensive sales force to sell and service its machines. It was unlikely that IBM would ever be able to compete on price with its competitors because its customer service and support activities raised its costs so much. Moreover, competing on price had never been a part of its strategy; IBM always had competed on its unique ability to provide customers with an integrated, full-line computer service. Analysts wondered whether Opel was spending too much to lower manufacturing costs and whether the $32 billion could not be better spent in some other way.

CHANGES IN TECHNOLOGY

Changes in mainframe technology also caused a change in IBM's strategy during the 1970s. As a result of technological innovations, particularly the plunging costs of integrated circuits, the life span of a mainframe computer—the time it could be used until it was technologically outdated—was shortening rapidly, and development costs were increasing. Formerly, customers would use the same IBM mainframe for several years. Now, however, IBM was forced to replace its leased computers every two or three years. This made it difficult to recoup development costs and obtain the premium price on its machines that it was accustomed to.

Because the computer life span was getting shorter and because of the growth low-cost competition, IBM under Cary, and then Opel, decided to phase out IBM's system of leasing machines to customers. Instead they decided to begin selling machines—a major change in IBM's strategy. Although this move increased revenue in the short term, it had major repercussions for the company in the long term. First, the leasing system had tied IBM to its customers and ensured that when customers upgraded and expanded their computer systems, they would look first at IBM machines. Moreover, leasing facilitated IBM's strategy of providing customers with excellent customer service and guaranteed the company a steady cash flow and control of the used machine market. With the end of leasing, IBM would be more susceptible to fluctuations in the demand for its products because its customers would be able to shop around.

From 1980 on, IBM began to face major competition from 370 clone manufacturers, large companies like Amdahl (which had a faster 370 processor than IBM), and Hitachi Data Systems (whose low-price machine generated record sales throughout the 1980s). IBM's customers began to feel more comfortable about buying 370 clones from companies that also promised quality support and service at low cost. IBM's sales growth for its biggest mainframe dropped from 12% annually in 1984 to 5% annually in 1990 as a result of the increased competition. Increased mainframe competition with Amdahl and Hitachi Data Systems also led to price discounting, despite the fact that IBM attempted to offer its customers a unique package that included software and services via addition to hardware. The days when IBM could demand whatever price it wanted for its machines were over.

The end of its leasing program also led to increased competition from independent computer leasing companies that would buy older mainframes and then sell the older processors at a price that was frequently only 10% of the cost of IBM's newest machine. These companies also disassembled mainframes to make smaller computers; for example, they could make two smaller machines out of one larger machine. In response to this price competition, IBM was forced to reduce the price of its machines.

The end of leasing, combined with a growth in low-cost competition, changed the nature of industry competition in ways that the company did not expect. IBM's strategy was now to protect its mainframe market from competitors and hang on to its customers at all costs. IBM devoted most of its immense resources to developing technically superior mainframe products, lowering the cost of production, and supporting its very expensive but very successful sales force.

IBM's focus on protecting its mainframe market blinded it to threats from the emergence of new kinds of computers. Even when it did recognize the competitive threat, IBM's operating structure and culture, shaped by its preeminent position as the world's leading mainframe computer company, made it difficult for IBM's managers to see emerging problems in its environment and react quickly to the changes that technology was bringing about in the computer industry. The way IBM handled the emerging threat from new kinds of computers, such as minicomputers, personal computers (PCs), and workstations, illustrates many of the problems it experienced as a result of a corporate mindset that "mainframes were king."

THE MINICOMPUTER MARKET

One of the new computer markets that emerged in the 1970s was the minicomputer. Minicomputers were smaller and priced anywhere from $12,000 to $700,000, which was significantly cheaper than mainframe computers. The steadily falling price of integrated circuits during the 1960s and 1970s made it feasible to build a minicomputer that was affordable to small businesses or could be used in specialized technical or scientific applications. IBM had ignored this new market segment, preferring to focus its resources on developing and improving its profitable 360 and 370 series computers.

Two researchers from the Massachusetts Institute of Technology pioneered the development of a smaller, more powerful computer. They founded the Digital Equipment Corporation (DEC), which, in 1965, launched the PDP-8, a computer that could handle the smaller information processing needs and tasks of companies such as small businesses, offices, factories, and laboratories. The venture was very successful, and by 1968, DEC's sales reached $57 million, and its earnings were $6.8 million. DEC's computer competed with the lower end of the 360 range. The computer sold well in research facilities, but it did not do as well in business, because IBM dominated this market with its powerful sales force. However, DEC had plans to develop a more powerful machine. As it grew, it was quickly expanding its own national service network, imitating IBM's.

To meet DEC's challenge, which was still seen as a minor issue, Cary formed the General Systems Division in 1969. Its goal was to produce the System/3 which was to be IBM's small, powerful minicomputer. IBM did not, however, rethink its technology or invest resources to develop new minicomputer technology to make a product to suit this new market segment. Rather, IBM tried to adapt its existing mainframe technology to the minicomputer market.

IBM's top managers had risen up the ranks of IBM from the mainframe division and were conditioned by the idea that the level of computing power was everything. "The bigger the better" was the philosophy of these managers. Moreover, big machines meant big revenues. IBM's mainframe managers saw the potential earning power of the minicomputer as insignificant when compared to the huge revenues generated by its mainframes. More fundamentally, however, IBM's top managers did not want competition from a new computer division inside the company that would absorb large amounts of the company's resources and might change the company's future direction and strategy.

The result was that when the System/3s were developed, they were too big and too expensive to compete with DEC's machine and too small to compete with IBM's own mainframes. This caused them to fail to make much inroad into what was becoming a very big market segment. As the minicomputer segment of the market continued to grow rapidly in the 1970s, Cary tried to increase the importance of the minicomputer group inside IBM's corporate hierarchy by reorganizing IBM's Data Processing Division and splitting it into two units: General Systems to make minicomputers and Data Systems to make the mainframes. He hoped that this change would force IBM managers to change their mindset and support the company's move into the new markets.

So strong was the entrenched position of mainframe managers that Cary's change of structure created huge divisional rivalry between mainframe and minicomputer managers. The mainframe division saw itself as being in direct competition for resources with the minicomputer division. Managers in both units failed to cooperate and share technological resources to develop the new range of machines. When the General Systems Division finally produced a minicomputer called the 8100, it did not have a technological edge over the DEC machine. Nevertheless, it was successful, as many IBM customers had large sums of money invested in IBM mainframes and were reluctant to switch suppliers. Moreover, IBM's powerful sales force (although at first reluctant to push minicomputers for fear of reducing their commissions) could service the needs

of the minicomputer users. By the end of 1980, more than 100,000 minicomputers had been sold. IBM and DEC were the industry leaders, while the new companies that had sprung up, such as HP and Wang, were also increasing their market share.

In 1986, DEC introduced its new VAX 9000 minicomputer. This new minicomputer shocked IBM's mainframe managers because it had the same speed and capacity as IBM's largest 370 mainframe, the 3090, but cost only 25% as much. For the first time, mainframe managers were forced to accept the fact that minicomputers might be feasible substitutes for mainframes in many applications. Although DEC gained business with its new machine in market segments previously dominated solely by IBM, such as large financial service companies and corporate data processing centers, it still could not seize many of IBM's loyal customers who were locked into IBM systems. Nevertheless, DEC's share of the minicomputer market grew from 19% in 1984 to 25% in 1988, while IBM's share dropped from 24% to 16% in the same period.

Finally, in 1988, IBM brought out the AS/400 series, a minicomputer that was superior to DEC's VAX. The AS/400 series was based on RISC (reduced instruction set computing) technology. Fast RISC chips could equal and exceed the speed of large mainframes, including IBM's own mainframes. Many large companies that had a great deal of money invested in IBM mainframes moved to adopt the IBM minicomputer system because it was compatible with their IBM mainframe systems. As a result of the success of its new minicomputers, IBM increased its market share from about 16% in 1988 to 28% in 1992, while DEC's market share fell. DEC then planned to produce its own machines based on RISC, but in the interim, it introduced new machines to compete with IBM's AS/400s on price. IBM now had a $14 billion business in minicomputers, which have gross margins of 56%.

THE PERSONAL COMPUTER

Another technological breakthrough, the microprocessor or "computer on a chip," sparked the development of the personal computer (PC), which was developed in 1977 by Steven Jobs and Stephen Wozniak, the cofounders of Apple

Computer. By 1980, Apple's sales had grown to $117 million. Once again, IBM stood by and watched as a new market segment was created. This time, recognizing the mistakes it had made in the minicomputer market by not moving quickly enough to develop a machine to compete with the industry leader, it decided to move quickly to create its own machine to compete with Apple's.

In the mainframe market, IBM made its own chips, circuit boards, disk drives, terminals, tape drives, and printers; wrote its own proprietary software for its machines; and helped to develop software to meet the needs of its customers. As a result, its machines were not compatible with those of its rivals that used their own proprietary hardware and software. The machines of different manufacturers would not work together. In 1981, however, in an effort to enter the PC market quickly, IBM outsourced and bought the inputs it needed from other companies make its PC. For example, Intel supplied the 8088 microchip that was the heart and Microsoft delivered MS-DOS, the programming language and software applications for the new IBM machine. Finally, computer stores, not the IBM sales force, were used to sell the new IBM PCs to get the machines to individual customers quickly.

IBM's first PC, more powerful than the first Apple computer, was introduced at a price of $1,565 in 1981. Intel's 8088 chip had more main memory and was more powerful than the chip used in the Apple II computer, and Microsoft's operating system, MS-DOS, was better than the current industry standard. These features, combined with the power of the IBM brand name, made the IBM PC an immediate success; it quickly became the industry standard for all other PCs. Backed by IBM's legendary service, business users turned to the machines in the thousands. By 1984, IBM had seized 40% of the personal computer market, but the IBM PC still could not be produced or distributed fast enough to meet the enormous customer demand.

Even the runaway success of the IBM PC became a threat to the company because its competitors rapidly imitated it; soon clone manufacturers were selling IBM-compatible personal computers as powerful or more powerful than IBM's own machines. For example, Compaq, founded in 1981, began to clone IBM PCs and produced a high-powered machine that seized a large share of the high-price business market. In 1986, Compaq beat IBM to the market

with a machine using Intel's powerful new 386 chip. At the same time, other clone makers, such as Zenith and Packard Bell, attacked the low-price segment of the computer market and began producing PCs that undercut IBM's.

IBM, threatened both in the high-price and low-price end of the PC markets fought back with the PS/2. It had a proprietary hardware channel that IBM made sure could not be imitated, as its first personal computer had been. However, customers resisted buying the new PS/2. They did not want to become locked into a new IBM system that was not compatible with IBM's old system and their other software or hardware investments. In the face of hostility from its customers, and losing market share, IBM was forced to back down. In 1988 IBM began producing PS/2s that were compatible with the existing industry standard—ironically, its own older standard.

It was suddenly clear to IBM that it no longer controlled the rules of the competitive game in the personal computer industry. Nonetheless, it was still slow to change its strategy. Despite the fact that its cheaper rivals had machines that were as powerful as its own, IBM still attempted to charge a premium price for its product. In response, its customers went elsewhere. IBM's share of PC sales in the United States dropped from about 37% in 1985 to 24% in 1988. Clone makers continued to improve IBM's older standard, and IBM's market share declined to 16.5% in 1990.

In 1991, a major price war broke out in the PC market, brought on in large part by the steadily dropping price of computer hardware, such as Intel's microprocessors. IBM reduced prices three times to compete, and prices of the PS/2 were cut by as much as 25%. Partly due to price competition, a typical 386 PC, which had cost $3,500 in early 1991, cost $1,600 in late 1991 and only $1,200 in early 1992. In 1992, IBM also introduced new low-priced lines of computers such as the PS/Value Point. This computer was targeted at the fastest growing segment of the computer market, the home market, and business customers who did not need all the features of the high-end PS/2. These new models were very successful and in great demand. Nonetheless, IBM did not hold a dominant position in the PC market; in 1992, its market share was 12%, the same as its rival Apple and about twice that of rivals like Dell, Compaq, and NEC.

The PC price wars continued into 1993. In February 1993, Dell Computer, a rapidly growing clone maker, introduced price cuts of 5% to 22% across its entire product line. In response, IBM cut prices by as much as 16% on some models, including the PS/Value Point. Apple cut prices five times in 1993, for a reduction of up to 33%, on its three highest-priced computers in an effort to increase United States sales. PC makers also battled over distribution and the offering of extras, such as warranties. PCs ranged from $500 clones to $2,000 laptops to $25,000 network hubs. PCs dominated the computer industry, with world sales of $93 billion in 1993 compared to mainframe sales of $50 billion. The laptop segment of the PC market alone reached $5.67 billion in 1990. IBM, however, did not have a product for this market segment until 1991. It also faced tough competition from market leader Toshiba as well as from Apple.

By 1992, it was clear to IBM and industry analysts that IBM was just one more competitor in a very competitive market. Since 1990, IBM's PC division had yet to show a profit. This was due to intense price competition and because IBM's costs were above competitors such as Compaq, which moved quickly to slash costs in 1990 when the price of PCs began tumbling.

IBM's response to competition in the personal computer industry throughout the 1980s clearly was affected by its "mainframe mindset." Even though it was clear that new segments of the computer market were developing and that new uses for computers were being found, IBM managers still discounted the potential threat to mainframes from either the minicomputer or the personal computer. IBM was not alone in being unable to sense the significance of changes in the environment. Kenneth Olsen, one of the founders of the minicomputer maker DEC, went on record saying, "Personal computers are just toys" in discounting the challenge of PCs to minicomputers, just as IBM had discounted the threat of minicomputers to mainframes 10 years earlier. The Olsen philosophy blinded IBM's top management to the prospect that powerful PCs could become a threat to IBM's main line of business mainframes. This predicament was somewhat surprising given that the computer industry always had been dominated by technological change. IBM's success was itself the result of moving quickly and decisively to exploit the opportunities of new technology: the punch card machine, the transistor, and the integrated circuit.

Throughout the 1980s, IBM's personal computer division (which is the biggest personal computer operation in the world) could not respond quickly to the price cutting moves of its rivals and introduce new kinds of personal computers because of its centralized decision making style. Whenever a competitor reduced prices, managers of the personal computer division had to get approval from the corporate management committee to cut prices, a process that sometimes took months. As a result, the PC division was never able to forestall its rivals. Moreover, just as in the case of minicomputers, rivalry between PC and mainframe managers hampered efforts to quickly exploit the potential of the powerful new microprocessors.

IBM's competitors moved quickly to increase the power of their PCs by exploiting the power of the new generation of microprocessors. They also encouraged the development of powerful new netware software. This software could link PCs together and to a more powerful computer, such as a minicomputer or a workstation, so that a network of PCs could work as effectively as a mainframe—but more conveniently and at only a fraction of the cost.

Workstations

Workstations are the fourth wave of computers following mainframes, minicomputers, and PCs. While PCs are designed for individual jobs such as word processing and financial analysis, workstations essentially are very powerful PCs designed to be connected to each other and to a mainframe through software. Workstations can analyze financial results and track inventories much faster than PCs and much more cheaply than minicomputers or mainframes. A network of workstations can also be linked to an even more powerful workstation (or minicomputer) called a file server, which contains a company's files and databases or which can retrieve them from a company's mainframe computer. Workstations, usually priced from $5,000 to $100,000, were first developed for scientists and engineers but increasingly were utilized by business professionals. New network software links workstations so that many people can work together simultaneously on the same project. These desktop machines have "user friendly" graphic displays and allow people at different machines to share data and software. By 1988, the workstation market was $4.7 billion. Workstations have a 45% profit margin compared to 58% for minicomputers.

Prior to 1989, IBM was a small player in this segment. Underestimating the potential power of personal computers and slow to develop powerful minicomputers (its AS/400 series was not introduced until 1988), IBM managers once again failed to see the potential of an emerging market. IBM had only a 3.9% market share in 1987, compared to Sun Microsystems's 29% and Apollo's 21%, the two upstart companies that were the innovators of the workstation. Once they realized the importance of this market segment, both IBM and DEC introduced workstations based on RISC processors, which make machines two to three times faster by eliminating all insignificant instructions. IBM introduced the IBM RT PC workstation in 1986, but the machine failed due to an underpowered microprocessor. Notwithstanding its problems, IBM launched the RS/6000 workstation in 1989 and captured 18% of the market by the end of 1991.

Competition in the workstation market was increasing as a result of market growth. This segment was growing 27% annually by 1992, compared to 5% for the computer industry as a whole. As the price of workstations fell, more and more small businesses, which could not afford to use mainframe or minicomputers, could afford workstations. The workstation market also was very important to large computer makers because workstations could be used in networks with larger mainframe computers. Thus, controlling the workstation market protected a company's mainframe market. By the end of 1991, the workstation market was $11.3 billion, and IBM was facing severe competition from DEC, Sun, Apollo, and HP, all of which sold RISC workstations.

SOFTWARE AND SERVICES

Designing software (the instructions that allow computers to perform tasks) and providing customer service, particularly assistance in the design of programs to manage company-specific databases and systems, have been rapidly expanding segments of the computer industry for the past 20 years. IBM has always realized the importance of developing proprietary software that can link and join its mainframes,

minicomputers, workstations, and personal computers to provide customers with a completely integrated computer package. It failed, however, to recognize the developing market for more general operating language and software applications.

By 1981, 33% of the total computer industry revenue came from software and services, a figure that rose to an estimated 50% in 1993. Although software and services accounted for 33% of IBM's total revenues by 1990, 68% of this revenue came from supporting customers' IBM mainframe computer systems, which represented a declining share of the computer market. Thus IBM, tied to software that supports mainframes, was not in a strong position to compete in the new software and services market.

IBM's failure to realize the potential for software seems surprising given that it had outsourced the operating language for its personal computer to Microsoft and saw the success of the MS-DOS operating system. IBM's focus was mainframes and its continuing belief that its own proprietary hardware and software would become the industry standard seems to have been the source of its reluctance to enlarge and expand its software operations. In 1980, when IBM had the opportunity to indirectly control the software market by purchasing a large chunk of Microsoft stock at a low price, it declined to do so.

IBM soon found that developing new applications software was a difficult business to be in. First, IBM had a hard time recruiting talented programmers. They were not attracted to IBM's bureaucratic and conservative corporate culture, in which centralized decision making limited their opportunities to be creative and take risks. Second, talented software programmers found they could make more money in business for themselves; any programmer who could develop a new system generally started his or her own company. Microsoft recognized this problem early on; consequently, Bill Gates, Microsoft's chairman, gives his top programmers large stock options to encourage their best performance. Many of them have become millionaires as a result.

In today's computer market, developing better and more advanced software is crucial to selling more hardware or computers of all kinds. So, late as usual, IBM embarked on a program to forge alliances with many small, independent software companies to develop software for IBM machines quickly: mainframes, minicomputers, workstations, and PCs. One of IBM's goals was to rejuvenate sales of its mainframe by encouraging software companies to write programs that make mainframes the key part of a computer network that links personal computers and workstations. IBM spent $100 million in 1989 to acquire equity stakes in 12 software developers, including Interactive Images for Graphics, Inc.; Polygen Corporation for scientific software; and American Management Systems, Inc., for mainframe software. Marketing agreements were also made with several other firms. IBM loaned software developers up to $50,000 for startup costs and took a seat on the developer's board. For example, IBM was working on a project called Systems Application Architecture (SAA), which is a set of rules for links between programs and computers. SAA would facilitate the creation of networks with all types of machines, including mainframes and PCs.

In 1988, IBM created a new unit to launch applications software and established a position called "complementary resource marketing manager," responsible for connecting software "business partners" with IBM customers. Salespeople were expected to sell the products of these software partners as well as IBM products. Although most of the programs were for mainframes, many could be adapted to work with networks based on PCs. Software and services accounted for 40% of IBM's revenue in 1992. IBM wanted to achieve 50% of revenues from software and services by the year 2000.

SYSTEMS INTEGRATION AND OUTSOURCING

Traditionally, IBM limited its service activities to providing support for its own proprietary software and hardware. It did not use its skills to analyze various aspects of a customer's business, such as its inventory control or warehousing operations, and then custom design and install an appropriate mix of hardware and software to meet the customer's needs, a service known as systems integration. Moreover, it had not recognized the developing market for outsourcing data processing, whereby one company agrees to take over and manage all aspects of the data processing function for another company in return for a fee. By 1992, however, the systems integration and outsourcing market generated more revenues than the mainframe market.

IBM's failure to see the developing market segment for systems integration and outsourcing had not been lost on one of IBM's star salesmen, Ross Perot. When IBM capped the amount of money that Perot could earn from commissions in selling computers and ignored his plan to start an IBM division whose function would be to provide data management services to customers to advise them on ways to manage their data files and systems, Perot left IBM and started Electronic Data Services (EDS).

The systems integration market and outsourcing market were now growing at 19% annually. IBM's failure to enter this market early allowed its competitors—principally EDS and Andersen Consulting, the accounting firm that early on established a computer consulting division—to gain a first-mover advantage and dominate the market. At the time, EDS had 50% of the outsourcing business of managing a company's data storage and management needs, compared to IBM's 6%. Andersen dominated the market for advising companies on their software and hardware needs. IBM led primarily in the market for government contracts.

To quickly develop a presence in this lucrative market, IBM began developing alliances with various organizations. It formed a joint venture with Coopers & Lybrand to provide management consulting in selected industries. IBM also teamed with AT&T to make IBM's mainframes work better with AT&T's network management systems. IBM established the Integrated Systems Solutions Corporation subsidiary in 1991 to provide a platform for IBM to enter the data processing outsourcing market. Its business was increasing; for example, in 1992, it received a 10-year, $3 billion agreement to run the computer systems for McDonnell Douglas Corporation. The subsidiary did outsourcing for 30 companies, including Continental Bank. IBM would run all of a client company's systems, from mainframes and workstations to voice and data telecommunication. It was aggressively advertising its strengths and services in this area.

THE NEW COMPUTER INDUSTRY

By 1990, IBM received about 50% of its gross profit from mainframe hardware, software, peripherals, and maintenance; 6% from minicomputers; 18.5%

from PCs and workstations; and 12.4% from non-maintenance software and services. However, the future revenue-generating potential of each of these market segments was uncertain as the boundaries between the segments grew less clear. Would workstations replace minicomputers? Would workstations and minicomputers replace mainframes? Would a network of PCs linked by advanced software to a mainframe eliminate the need for minicomputers or workstations? Obviously, IBM had the most to gain from making mainframes the center of a computer network, while its competitors had as much to gain from making minicomputers and powerful workstations the wave of the future.

By 1990, IBM was facing stiff competition in all the developing segments of the computer market, from companies that were mainly specialized in one market niche, for example, Microsoft in the software segment or Sun Computer in the workstation niche. IBM was fighting to increase its market share in each market segment but was suffering because of tough competition from strong competitors that had developed their own loyal customer following.

Moreover, the market for mainframe computers, IBM's principal source of revenue, was declining as machines such as PCs and workstations were able to perform mainframe tasks at lower cost. It had been estimated that, while 80% of 1986 computer industry profits were attributable to mainframe computer sales, by 1991, sales of mainframe computer systems accounted for only 20%. The PC revolution had reduced costs and allowed customers to buy much cheaper computer systems to do work previously performed by expensive mainframes and minicomputers.

As a result of this shift, suppliers of computer components such as chips and software were the winners, as their share of industry profits rose from 20% in 1986 to 31% in 1991. Thus, for example, the share prices of Microsoft and Intel, which control the software and microprocessor markets, respectively, soared. Similar growth occurred in the share prices of Conner, Quantum, and Seagate, which dominated disk drives, as well as Andersen Consulting and EDS, which were the leaders in system integration. IBM's share price, however, fell dramatically from a high of $160 in 1987 to less than $50 in 1992.

To fight the trend toward PCs and workstations, IBM attempted to make its 370 computer the central component of a network of computers that link individual users to the mainframe. It did not succeed, however, as sales growth for its biggest mainframe, the 370, dropped from 4% per year in 1990 to less than 2% per year in 1992. Even many of IBM's 370 users began switching to IBM AS/400 minicomputers because they could perform the same task more easily and cheaply. The mainframe market was now the third-largest market behind PCs and minicomputers.

IBM FIGHTS BACK

In 1985, John Akers became CEO and was charged with the task of using IBM's vast resources to make it the market leader in the new lucrative market segments of the computer industry and reduce IBM's dependence on mainframes. He took over a company in which managers were still arrogant and complacent and believed completely in IBM's preeminence despite all the warning signs that it had lost its competitive edge. Its top management committee, staffed primarily by managers from its mainframe division, seemed unable to make the type of innovative decisions that would allow IBM to respond quickly to the rapidly changing computer environment. The result was a failure to develop products fast enough and a mistaken commitment to the mainframe computer. Even its renowned salespeople had become a problem for the company. Committed to the IBM product, they had become oriented to selling and servicing the mainframe; they were not oriented toward satisfying customer needs, which might be for a minicomputer or a workstation.

Akers launched a "year of the customer" in 1987 to refocus the sales force on meeting the needs of the customer rather than the needs of the mainframe. Most importantly, Akers realized the need to restructure the company and change IBM's highly centralized style of decision making if it was to innovate the next generation of products and emerge as a market leader in the new market segments. Akers recognized that the biggest problem for IBM was its highly bureaucratic organizational structure that slowed decision making and continually frustrated attempts to be innovative and entrepreneurial.

The 1998 Restructuring

To speed decision making, in January 1998, Akers reorganized IBM into seven divisions based on the main product market segments in which the company was competing: personal computer systems, mid-range systems, mainframes, information systems and communications, technology development (such as microchips), programming, and software. The idea behind the reorganization was to demolish the mainframe mindset by giving the managers of each division the autonomy and responsibility for developing new products for their respective markets. No longer would mainframe managers be able to stifle the pace of change and discourage the development of products that threatened the dominance of the mainframe. The sales force, however, was to remain a separate entity whose job would still be to sell the whole line of IBM products. The logic for this was that the sales force could sell customers integrated IBM computer systems: networks of PCs, file servers, and mainframes and provide the computer software, service, and systems consulting to tailor the system to customers' individual needs.

The disadvantage of the single sales force was that each division would not be able to devise a sales strategy specific to its own competitive environment, and salespeople would not be able to focus on a single product line. IBM felt that the economies of scale and scope provided by a unified sales force outweighed these disadvantages. Twenty-thousand employees were transferred from staff and lab positions to the sales force, and the commission system was revamped so that salespeople were evaluated on total revenue, not on the number of units rented or sold.

IBM's Contention System

If the first purpose of the reorganization was to focus IBM's activities more closely on the main segments of the computer market, the second purpose was to shorten the product development cycle and speed products to market. Since the early 1970s, IBM had taken advantage of its dominance in the market to use a "contention" system to control new product development. In this system, two or more project teams designed competing product prototypes, and a series of committees at both the divisional level and the corporate level met over a period of months to debate the merits of each project. A project would be approved after six committee members rated the two processes, which could take months or years; then the committee met to finalize the product plan. During this process, if any committee member said,

"I non-concur," meaning that he or she disagreed with the project, it would be sent back for further review or scrapped.

The result of the contention system was that the projects that were approved were generally successful. However, the time frame associated with making the decision was generally so long that products were late to market, putting IBM at a competitive disadvantage. For example, the small, independent team charged with the development of the first IBM PC launched the product in one year. However, once the PC group was put into the Information Systems and Communication Division and decision making became constrained by IBM's contention system, the speed of the development process slowed significantly. For example, the PS/2 was not introduced until 1987, missing the 1985 target. This delay allowed clone makers of the older PCs to gain 33% of the market share in PCs. Other symptoms of IBM's overly bureaucratic approach to decision making included its failure to enter new market segments quickly. For example, IBM entered the PC market four years late; it was also a laggard in workstations. Similarly, IBM's top managers refused to recognize the importance of the growth of minicomputers and were hesitant to launch products that would compete with the mainframes.

The reorganization was designed to shorten the time it took to get a product to market and overcome the hurdles to product development. In the 1980s, IBM no longer had the luxury of taking a long time to make competitive decisions, as smaller and more agile competitors were forging ahead and the product life cycle of computers was shortening.

In an attempt to cut costs, increase profitability, get close to the customers, and reduce bureaucracy, Akers embarked on a major campaign to downsize the organization. The 1985 workforce of 405,000 was reduced to 389,300 in 1988 through early retirement and attrition. In addition, overtime and temporary employees, equivalent to 12,500 full-time employees, were cut. Despite the fact that IBM closed plants, cut spending, and reduced capital outlays, costs grew faster than revenues during most of the reorganization. Moreover, analysts could not discern any noticeable change in IBM's strategy or the way it made decisions. Products were still late to market.

The 1988 reorganization was a failure. Although each division was supposed to become more autonomous, in reality, most decisions still required approval by IBM's corporate headquarters managers—managers who had risen through the ranks from the powerful mainframe computer division. Products that might have cannibalized the sale of mainframes were still discouraged by corporate managers, who, having achieved their success during the mainframe era, were hesitant to introduce products to compete with mainframes. One example of the mainframe mindset involved the PC unit's push to get into the laptop market in 1989 by competitively pricing their laptop at $4,995. Corporate headquarters insisted on a price of $5,995 to meet corporate profit in margin targets. As a result, many competitors were able to price their products lower than IBM's machines. Even though IBM later priced the machine lower, it never regained lost market share.

To allow the personal computer division to respond faster to the quickly changing PC market, Akers decided to place the PC business in a separate operating unit. In 1991, Akers formed the IBM Personal Computer Company and gave it control over the design, production, distribution, and marketing of IBM PCs. Prior to this change, distribution was performed by IBM's large sales and marketing division. After the change, 1,200 former marketing and sales employees were transferred to the new PC unit, which also was to handle telephone sales. The corporate sales force was to continue to sell to big corporate customers. In decentralizing authority to managers in the PC division, Akers was showing managers his plans for the IBM of the future.

The 1991 Restructuring

IBM announced another restructuring at the end of 1991, which was aimed at decentralizing decision making authority to the divisions and reducing the role of IBM corporate headquarters in setting divisional strategy. Akers divided IBM into 13 separate divisions: nine divisions were based on the company's main product lines, and four divisions were to be marketing and service operations organized geographically. The nine manufacturing divisions were to supply the four marketing divisions. The goal of the restructuring effort was to make the divisions independent units operating under a broad IBM umbrella, thus freeing them from corporate control.

Aker's plan was that each division would be an autonomous operating unit that could freely negotiate transfer prices of inputs with other divisions and, if a division wanted to, buy from and sell to outside companies. The divisions were to treat each other as they would outside companies; no favorable prices were to be granted to IBM divisions. Moreover, the performance of each division would be reported separately, and each division would be accountable for its individual profits and losses. The heads of the divisions were responsible for developing annual business plans and were to guarantee IBM a certain return on money invested in their division. In the past, most managers did not know the details, such as profit and loss statements, of an individual division's financial performance. Each divisional manager signed a contract to meet objectives in revenue growth, profit, ROA (return on assets), cash flow, customer satisfaction, quality, and morale. If the divisional heads were successful, they would get a share of the profits. If they failed, their jobs were on the line. Financial results for all 13 units were to be made public by 1994.

The goal of this restructuring was to free up IBM's powerful resources and make it more competitive. Division heads would have control over long-term development and business level strategy. For example, the Personal Systems Division's manager could decide how PCs and workstations were produced and designed, and the PC division's R&D function would not compete directly with the mainframe division for resources. The hope was that the divisions would be able to compete with their smaller, more entrepreneurial rivals once they were freed from corporate bureaucracy.

The sales divisions would still be responsible for selling the whole range of IBM products, however, and control over sales would be centralized at corporate headquarters. The logic, once again, was that customers wanted a sales force that could handle their entire computer needs, and there were synergies from having one sales force provide a full set of products and services. IBM's traditional focus on service was still a strong competitive advantage. Analysts were skeptical however, of having only one sales force, especially one in which representatives were still biased toward mainframes. Many analysts felt that one sales force was a mistake; giving each division its own sales force would be a better source of competitive advantage. Moreover, the huge costs of operating the sales force could be hard to allocate between divisions, causing rivalry among them.

To demonstrate the commitment of IBM's thirteen operating divisions top management to IBM's more autonomous and entrepreneurial approach to doing business, IBM's PC division was given total control over its own sales and named an independent unit in 1992. James Cannavino, the head of the PC unit, took total control over the PC division's strategy and organized the PC division around products instead of functions. The five product groups of the PC division were the low cost Value Points; PS/2; PS/1, aimed at home and small business users; portable products; and Ambra, a line of PCs built by an Asian contractor and sold in Europe. Each product group was in charge of its own brand development, manufacturing, pricing, and marketing. This change was designed to allow the product groups to respond much more quickly to changes in the PC market, where products may have a life span of only six months to a year. In addition, Cannavino met with 32 CEOs of Silicon Valley startups and told them that he wanted to form alliances with them to speed the development of new hardware and software products, such as multimedia and CD-ROM products. The IBM PC division was the world's largest company.

NEW MANAGEMENT AND NEW PLANS

Despite the 1991 organization, IBM's profits and revenues continued to decline; 1991 revenues fell 5% from 1990, the first decline since 1946. The company's 1991 loss of $2.8 billion was the first loss in IBM's history. In 1992, IBM's losses increased to $5 billion on $65 billion in revenues. In January 1993, the stock fell below $46, the lowest price in 17 years. Pressure for change at the top was increasing.

Under pressure from investors and the public, John Akers resigned in January 1993. Although Akers reorganized and restructured, critics claimed that he never went far enough in implementing the reforms that would really turn around IBM. For example, despite the fact that between 1985 to 1992 a total of 100,000 IBM workers were cut mainly through early retirement and that Akers had removed the whole of IBM's former top management team to try to rid IBM of the "mainframe mindset," critics

claimed that Akers had avoided initiating the major layoffs that were needed to restore profitability.

In 1993, the board of directors searched for a replacement for Akers. Shunning an insider for fear that he could not bring a fresh perspective to IBM's problems, they chose an outsider to be the CEO of IBM, marking the first time an outsider had occupied the top job. Louis Gerstner, former CEO of RJR Nabisco, was recruited in March 1993. Gerstner had no experience in the computer industry, and IBM's stock price dropped $3 to a new low when he took over.

Gerstner immediately hired outsiders to form a new top management team to run the company. Jerry York, former chief financial officer (CFO) at Chrysler was recruited as IBM's CFO. Gerry Czarnecki, who was in charge of cutbacks at Honolulu's Honfed Bank, became a vice president. These outsiders were tough cost cutters, experienced at restructuring large companies. Gerstner hired another outsider, Abby Kohnstamm, a former senior vice president of cardmember marketing at American Express, to be vice president of corporate marketing.

Gerstner and his top management team spent all of 1993 analyzing how IBM worked as a prelude to "reengineering the corporation." Reengineering refers to a two-step process whereby an organization first identifies and analyzes each of the core business processes—manufacturing, marketing, R&D, and so on—that make a business work and then changes or reengineers them from the bottom up to improve the way they function. Gerstner formed an 11-person "corporate executive committee" of IBM's top managers to spearhead the reengineering effort. Gerstner then gave each manager responsibility for heading a task force. Eleven task forces were formed to analyze IBM's main processes, which were modeled on the reengineering effort that Cannavino had performed in the PC division. As discussed previously, the result of that effort led to the move to a product group structure, in which each group took control over its own manufacturing and marketing—a change that had been very successful. Gerstner hoped that a corporate-wide effort would also prove successful.

Despite the fact that most analysts felt Gerstner would continue with Akers' approach of decentralizing decision making to the divisions, and even spinning off IBM's businesses into independent companies, Gerstner showed no sign of following this strategy. Gerstner preferred to restructure the relationship between the corporate center and the divisions. Moreover, Gerstner announced his belief that IBM should continue to follow its traditional strategy of providing customers with a full line of hardware and software products and services and announced his support for the mainframe division.

As a part of this full-line strategy, and despite expectations that he would decentralize IBM's sales force and give each division responsibility for its own sales, Gerstner announced in 1993 that he would not change the current companywide sales force structure. The current sales force of 40,000 salespeople would still pursue the strategy of one face to a customer because customers "do not want to be bothered by several salespeople." Apparently, Gerstner and his top management team believed that IBM's core strategy of being a full service company was appropriate. They believed the company's main problem was that it was too big. To reduce size in 1992, Gerstner announced plans to shed 115,000 more jobs in 1993 and 1994, reducing the workforce to 250,000 from a peak of 405,000 in 1985. Announcing in 1993 that "the last thing that IBM needs now is a corporate vision," Gerstner nevertheless identified four goals he had for IBM: (1) to get the company to the right size; (2) to spend more time with customers; (3) to determine the strategic issues by process reengineering; and (4) to build employee morale in the face of the huge layoffs.

Analysts wondered how Gerstner's strategy would work. They wondered whether Gerstner understood the divisional rivalries that led to IBM's problems and how he expected his new strategy to result in faster product development and the greater sharing of ideas and resources between divisions. Some critics argued that Gerstner should have aggressively pursued a strategy of breaking up IBM into fully independent operating units and that his new policy of encouraging the sharing of skills and resources between divisions would not work and was no break from the past. Moreover, they claimed he had been slow to reduce IBM's operating costs and the lavish way in which it spent its resources. For example, IBM operated one of the largest fleets of private jets in the corporate world, maintaining three country clubs for its employees, with its own management school complete with skeet shooting and tennis courts.

Had Gerstner, in the first six months of his reign as IBM's CEO, bought into IBM's culture in which the mainframe mindset still controlled the corporation? Gerstner contended that no amount of cost cutting would solve IBM's problems unless IBM could change from the inside out. IBM still spent 10% of its revenues on R&D and had many good ideas continually pouring from its development labs. According to Gerstner, the problem for the company was to use those ideas effectively, and the start of this was to reengineer the company to make better use of its resources. IBM also needed to increase integration among divisions so that they could share skills and resources more effectively. Gerstner believed that continuing Aker's strategy of breaking IBM up into 13 separate companies would do nothing to ensure the survival of the company in the long run.

On September 26, 1993, IBM announced a loss of $46 million for the third quarter, compared to a $40 million loss in 1992, bringing its total loss in 1993 to $8.37 billion. Was Gerstner's strategy working, and when could IBM's investors and employees expect to see the results?

IBM IN 2009

Since he became CEO of IBM in 2003, Sam Palmisano has worked hard to build a new global computer services company, which in 2009 was the largest and one of the most profitable in the world. In 2009, IBM had a market capitalization of more than $119 billion and employed more than 319,000 people worldwide in more than 150 countries. What kind of business model and strategies has Palmisano and his top management team pursued that allowed IBM to regain its position as an industry leader and wiped out memories of its disastrous performance in the 1980s? In addition, what challenges lie ahead if the company is to retain its competitive advantage and leading position in the global business computer services and consulting industry and keep rivals such as HP, Accenture, Dell, and Oracle at bay? That was the question Palmisano was grappling with in the spring of 2009 as the effects of the recession that started in 2008 started to bite into IBM's revenues and profits.

AKERS'S LAST STAND

As discussed in "The Fall of IBM," John Akers' vision of IBM's future was for the corporation to be broken up into 13 different companies that would be spun off to operate independently—essentially dismantling the IBM empire. While IBM's top managers developed a timetable to do this, Akers still faced the problem of how to keep it afloat in the short run. In his final desperate attempt to keep IBM viable, Akers continued to make drastic cost reductions, and between 1991 and 1993 an additional 80,000 employees were laid off as IBM sought to lower its cost structure. Its workforce was now less than half at its peak. The restructuring charges associated with these layoffs resulted in record losses of more than $15 billion for IBM, and its stock price plunged to record lows as investors decided the future lay not in mainframe computers but in networks of servers and client PCs. Moreover, by this time, its personal systems group that manufactured its PCs and the servers it was developing had become a liability. Competitors such as Dell, Gateway, and Sun had gained a major low-cost advantage over IBM's PCs and servers, and the PC division was losing money.

By 1993, IBM's performance still showed no signs of improvement, so Akers resigned; the board of directors searched for a successor with the strategic skills necessary to find the right business model to turnaround the declining company. They chose Louis Gerstner, an ex-management consultant who had engineered a major turnaround in the performance of American Express and Nabisco, as the new CEO. Gerstner had no background in the computing industry and his appointment was viewed by many analysts—and by many of IBM's powerful top managers—as an enormous mistake. How could an outsider with no knowledge of the way IBM operated, develop a business model to compete against rivals in the rapidly changing computer sector?

For the most recent financial results of the company discussed in this case, go to http://finance.yahoo.com, input the company's stock symbol, and download the latest company report from its homepage.

GERSTNER'S IMMEDIATE MOVES

IBM's board chose Gerstner because they wanted a new CEO who would have a fresh perspective on the company's problems—one who had not been a part of IBM's slow-moving bureaucratic culture characterized by slow, centralized decision-making and power struggles between divisions. Gerstner's task was to build the right business model for IBM— what kinds of products, customers, and distinctive competencies should IBM develop in the future if it was to remain as one company—or should IBM be broken up?

The major argument Akers had made in support of breaking up IBM into 13 different and independent companies was that the managers of each new company would be free to decide what business model to pursue to best compete against rivals in its particular industry. While this was one path to increasing returns to stockholders, before making this decision, Gerstner decided to closely study IBM's different business groups, search out their strengths and weaknesses, and examine the fit between them—what was the rationale for keeping IBM as a whole versus breaking it up into parts? Gerstner had a reputation for "hands-on" management involving frequent visits to talk to managers at all levels and in all divisions. He spent his first months as CEO on a whistle-stop tour interviewing IBM's managers; he also visited many of IBM's largest corporate customers to discover what they wanted from IBM now and in the future.

Gerstner soon announced that he intended to keep IBM as a single united company. His strategic analysis led him to conclude that IBM's ability to provide clients with a complete and comprehensive computing or information technology (IT) solution that could be customized to each client's particular needs was the source of its future competitive advantage. IBM's principal problem was to find a better way to integrate the activities of its hardware, software, and service (HS&S) groups to create more value for customers. In other words, Gerstner decided that IBM needed to work toward offering clients an improved, more comprehensive IT package.

Once he made the decision to keep IBM intact, Gerstner's main challenge was how to speed innovation and decision making both within and across IBM's HS&S groups. He quickly found that IBM's top managers, accustomed to a slow-moving culture based on consensus decision making, could not respond to his demands fast enough. One IBM manager described the old IBM's decision-making process as like "wading through a jar of peanut butter." Gerstner announced IBM's managers "just didn't have what it takes." He began to replace many senior IBM executives with managers from lower down its ranks. To reduce costs, however, he was forced to continue to lay off large numbers of employees in product areas that he felt could not compete successfully in the new advanced competitive IT industry.

GERSTNER'S NEW BUSINESS MODEL

Over the next three years, Gerstner spent his time identifying IBM's core set of distinctive competences and deciding what strategies to develop to build these competences and provide a solid foundation for IBM's new integrated business model. What was Gerstner's vision to rebuild IBM? His business model was that IBM should (1) provide a complete package of state-of-the-art computing solutions HS&S, especially outsourcing and consulting) that could be customized to a particular client's needs and (2) to take advantage of the possibilities created by the Internet to create new markets for IBM's products and services. Gerstner focused on making IBM a customer-driven company, by which he meant that every manager and employee had the responsibility to design, make, or sell those products or services that could best meet the needs of IBM's clients. Given that sales of mainframes were declining and PCs and servers were becoming commodity products with low-profit margins, what IBM had to do was to provide something *unique* so that customers would be willing to pay a premium price for its products and services. The challenge facing IBM was to learn how to customize products to the needs of customers if it was to be able to succeed in the new highly competitive computing environment.

Changes in Computer Hardware

Gerstner instructed his top managers to begin initiatives in all its IT groups to meet clients' changing IT needs. In its traditional hardware business, it faced two major problems. First, because mainframe sales were declining because of the growing popularity of lower-cost network servers and PCs, Gerstner instructed hardware managers to do everything possible to reduce the costs of mainframe computing while increasing the scalability of its computers. Scalability means that a computer can be customized and designed and built to suit the needs of different-sized companies or different-sized computing tasks from managing global databases to operating a small chain of restaurants. IBM began to position its smaller mainframes as "enterprise servers." Sales reps were told to emphasize to clients that computers could be made at a size and price to suit their unique needs, but a large powerful mainframe computer was still needed at the hub of a large company's IT system. In addition, IBM wanted to sell its clients software and services such as maintaining and upgrading their software and managing their databases, so it deliberately set the price of its hardware low, knowing it could make more money later in providing the new software and services.

Changes in Computer Software

The rapid pace of change in computer software resulted in a major challenge for Gerstner and his managers. Before IBM made the mistake of allowing Microsoft to provide the MS-DOS operating system for its own PC, it had been the largest seller of computer software (principally for mainframes and mainframe applications) in the world. Now Microsoft had usurped its position, but there were many other challenges as well from makers of specialized applications software such as Oracle, which is the market leader in database management software, and SAP, the German company whose Enterprise Resource Planning (ERP) software was soaring in popularity. ERP software allows a company to link its value-chain activities and connects mainframes to servers and servers to PCs. It gives a company's managers at all levels extensive real-time information about a company's activities; ERP software has become the backbone of most IT systems in large companies. IBM had little to offer clients in these software applications areas; these companies had gained a first-mover advantage that was difficult for IBM to challenge.

Gerstner instructed the software division to focus its efforts on developing new business applications software that would improve a company's value-chain performance, along with "middleware" software that is designed to link all the different pieces of a company's hardware—mainframes, servers, PCs, and laptops together. To catch up with competitors in these areas, Gerstner acquired software companies that possessed unique solutions to provide clients with valuable new business applications and allow them to make better use of their computer networks. One of the companies IBM acquired at a cost of more than $3 billion in 1995 was Lotus, which had developed the popular Lotus Notes collaborative software. This software created a corporate intranet, an information network inside a company that allows managers at all levels to share information quickly both inside their own department and division and between divisions.

In his push to develop expertise in middleware, Gerstner also bought software companies that had the "middleware" software necessary to link the hardware and software provided by *any* computer company across *all* the levels of computing. In other words, he wanted IBM to control the middleware necessary to provide customers with a "seamless" solution to their computing needs regardless of their legacy system. A *legacy system* is a company's current IT system at any point in time. If IBM had the middleware necessary to link any kind of IT hardware and software, it would be able to upgrade any client that wished to improve its legacy system to take advantage of new and advanced IT applications offered by any company. This revolutionary approach was part of Gerstner's "open standards" strategy designed to make IBM's own services available to *all* kinds of customers.

Changes in Services and Consulting

Gerstner's drive to focus the efforts of all IBM employees on satisfying the needs of clients had been strongly influenced by the continued success of IBM's computer services group, which contributed about 20% to IBM's revenues in 1995. Gerstner recognized that this division possessed the customer-focused business model that IBM needed to grow its revenues in the future, especially if sales of its hardware and software declined. Moreover, Gerstner was familiar with the business model that Jack Welsh, former CEO of General Electric (GE), had developed for his company. GE would sell a product such as a turbine or aircraft or diesel engine at a relatively low price to increase sales because each sale would result in a profitable stream of future income from servicing and maintaining the complex equipment it sold. Gerstner recognized that this model was viable in the new IT environment; he also recognized that in the IT sector, clients need expert help to decide which kind of computer solution best meets their current and future business needs. In IT, companies such as Electronic Data Services (EDS) and Accenture were the leaders and earned huge profits by providing companies with expert help; the market was increasing by double digits each year. For example, SAP could not satisfy the demand of large global clients to install its ERP software in its client's companies. Clients were paying billions of dollars to consulting companies such as Accenture and Cap Gemini for their expert help.

In 1996, Gerstner renamed the services division to Global Services and charged it with the task of spearheading IBM's push into the outsourcing and value-chain management business to go head-to-head with competitors such as EDS and Accenture. Gerstner's business model was now that Global Services would offer clients an outsourcing and business consultancy service based on assessing a customer's current legacy system and its future computing needs. IBM consultants would then design, plan, implement, maintain, and upgrade the client's IT system over time to help reduce the client's cost structure, improve its products, and build its competitive advantage. Gerstner also hoped that providing such expert services would once again build up switching costs and keep IBM's clients loyal on a long-term basis because of its ability to show them how its comprehensive, customized computing solution could help increase their profitability over time. Global services experienced continuing success throughout the 1990s and into the 2000s.

THE NEW GLOBAL SERVICES DIVISION

Gerstner's strategy was now focused on strengthening the global services division, led by Sam Palmisano, because he believed this was the new foundation on which IBM's future success lay. Global services had three main lines of business: (1) strategic outsourcing services that provide customers with competitive cost advantages by outsourcing customers' processes and operations; (2) integrated technology services designs, implements, and maintains customers' technology infrastructures; and (3) business consulting services deliver value to customers through business process innovation, application enablement, and integration services.

Gerstner's business model for IBM was that the company would build such a broad and sophisticated range of computer hardware and software, backed by the best consulting and service competencies in the industry, that it would overwhelm its competitors in the future. EDS and Accenture provide consultancy and service, for example, and HP, Dell, Sun, Oracle, and Microsoft produce computer hardware and software, but none of them had the capability to match the breadth and depth of IBM's growing computer offerings. By the late 1990s, the ability to bundle products together was becoming a major advantage to clients seeking a seamless and cost-effective way of managing their IT systems; it has only become more important since.

In implementing this business model, Gerstner recognized that in many specific computer hardware and software product areas IBM was no longer the industry leader. So he and Palmisano embarked on a strategy of offering IBM's clients the best or "leading-edge" products currently available, such as SAP's ERP software, Peoplesoft's HRM software, Sun's servers, or Dell's PCs when they were either clearly better or lower priced than those supplied by IBM's own divisions. Then, and crucially, IBM's consultants, as a result of its focus on developing expertise in middleware that links any computer products together, were able to guarantee clients that they could install, maintain, and integrate them so that they worked together seamlessly.

In adopting this strategy, IBM was strengthening its commitment to "open standards" in the computer industry by announcing publicly that in the future it would continue to work to make all the *future* software and hardware of all producers—its competitors—compatible by strengthening its expertise in middleware. In doing so, Gerstner and IBM were also assuring clients that when they used IBM's computer consulting services, they would not become locked into IBM's proprietary hardware and software—no switching costs would arise from this source. However, Gerstner hoped at the same time that clients would be impressed by IBM's ability to provide such a complete service that they would become "locked in" because of the high quality of the service that it could provide.

An additional advantage of the open standards approach was that as IBM's consultants went from client to client assessing their needs, they were able to provide detailed feedback to IBM's other divisions about whether their products were adequately meeting clients' needs. So, if a consultant decided that a competitor's software was more appropriate than that offered by IBM, the division making the software could now clearly recognize why its product was not meeting customer needs—and what was necessary to improve its software to make it the "best of breed" or leading-edge product. Thus, Gerstner's strong focus on being close to clients had the additional advantage of spurring innovation throughout the organization; managers had a clear goal to achieve; and they knew Gerstner and his top management team were watching their performance. If a division did not meet customer needs, its managers might lose their jobs, or the division might be sold off or shut down.

E-Business at IBM

Another indicator of how well Gerstner was attuned to the changing IT environment was his early recognition that the growth of the Internet and e-commerce would become a dominant force dictating which kinds of IT would be most necessary in the future. IBM coined the term *e-business*, and Gerstner established an Internet division in IBM in 1995 before most other IT companies. IBM's early recognition of the future possibilities of e-business allowed its engineers to adapt its software and hardware to serve Internet-related value-chain transactions before its competitors. Once again, being close to its clients helped IBM understand their changing needs and built its competitive advantage. Also, the acquisition of Lotus helped IBM understand the potential of the Internet. Lotus Notes was a company-specific or internal software collaboration application, while the Internet provided a major channel for collaboration between different companies. It was by chance that IBM's acquisition of Lotus revealed how the power of the Internet could shape supply-chain transactions between companies and their suppliers

and distributors. The Lotus collaborative software provided a model for making IBM's middleware software "Internet compatible."

IBM embarked on its e-business initiative in 1996 with a global marketing campaign aimed at showing companies how value-chain transactions with other companies and clients could be carried out online. Soon companies recognized that its competency in e-business gave it a competitive advantage over companies such as SAP, Oracle, and HP, who now raced to catch up. As a result, it attracted a growing number of e-business clients, which resulted in a major increase in its global computer services revenue. First in line to adopt IBM's e-business software were large corporations that needed to manage transactions with hundreds or even thousands of suppliers and distributors. Companies such as Walmart and Goodyear formed contracts with IBM to use its immense computing resources to manage their huge volume of online transactions.

IBM, however, also recognized that small and medium-sized businesses (SMBs) were another important customer group for its computer services—especially as it had developed scaleable computer hardware and software that could be sold at a price that meets a client's budget. IBM had developed less-expensive software targeted at the needs of SMB clients. It now worked with the thousands of new dot.com start-ups, such as Internet Web-design and Web-hosting companies, to teach these companies how to install and maintain its software in SMBs. IBM hoped that once SMBs had made the connection with IBM, they would start to buy other kinds of its software, for example, to manage their databases and functional, value-chain tasks such as bookkeeping and inventory control.

Palmisano Takes Over

In 2003, Lou Gerstner stepped down, and Sam Palmisano became IBM's new CEO. Since then, IBM has continued to modify its strategies and reorganize the activities of its operating groups to strengthen its business model. Indeed, IBM's growing global strength has forced its major competitors to alter their business models to compete more effectively with IBM. For example, HP merged with

Compaq and took over EDS in 2008 to be able to provide a combination of HS&S to compete with IBM. Oracle has spent more than $50 billion in the 2000s taking over software and consulting companies such as PeopleSoft and BEA Systems for the same reasons. All major IT providers have had to adjust their business models to deal with the threat that IBM's expanding global presence and IT offerings have created.

Nevertheless, after years of growth, by 2005, IBM's performance had started to fall. The problem Palmisano soon realized was that its now dominant global technology services group that had grown like wildfire and provided the largest proportion of IBM's revenues and profits had run into trouble. As discussed following, its global outsourcing business had come under intense competition from low-priced overseas outsourcing companies, particularly Indian companies, at a time when its cost structure was quickly rising because of the rapid growth in the number of its employees, now more than 150,000 people worldwide. With the revenues of global services group plateauing, Palmisano had to search for new strategies to grow IBM's revenues and profits and solve the problems of its global services group.

Palmisano decided to change IBM's business model and strategies in several ways. First, he decided to cut the cost structure of its global services group. Second, to make up for slowing revenues and profits, he accelerated the strategy he had begun in 2003—changing IBM's business model so that all its operating groups focused on investing resources to move into higher profit-margin IT businesses in which the specialized skills of IBM's workforce could be used to develop higher value-added IT services, based on some combination of research, software, and services that would offer its customers greater value. Third, he decided to exit any hardware businesses in which profit margins were thin and focus resources on strengthening and growing its core mainframe business. Finally, he made globalization and the drive to increase IBM's presence in every country in which it operated a major priority across the company. All IBM's business groups were instructed to focus on cooperating to grow global sales of the HS&S package they offered customers, not just in the advanced G7 countries in North America, Europe, and Japan, but across all world regions, especially in the rapidly growing economies of India and China.

To achieve all these strategies, and especially to expand its global customer base quickly, Palmisano also changed IBM's structure. In the early 2000s, IBM's overseas divisions had operated independently on a country-by-country basis; there was little cooperation between them. Palmisano built a more streamlined global structure in which IBM technical experts who specialized in certain business functions or industries were organized into "clusters of business expertise." These clusters might be in any country of the world but are connected to each other and to IBM's HS&S groups through its own proprietary Lotus high-speed communications Intranet. Project managers can search worldwide for the HS&S experts with the right skills for a job located in different countries around the world and form teams of experts quickly to meet the needs of clients in any country. For example, IBM created global and regional teams of skilled experts in particular industries, from airlines to utilities, who travel as needed to consult on projects.

The many changes its new global structure brought about in the operations of its HS&S groups are discussed following, but one of the most important changes was that in 2007 Palmisano decided to split the global services group into two parts: the global technology services (GTS) group that was to specialize in IBM's traditional kinds of IT services such as outsourcing maintenance and database management; and the global business services (GBS) group that was to specialize in developing high-margin business and industry IT solutions customized to the needs of individual clients.

The Global Technology Services Group

Palmisano assigned all of IBM's more traditional "routine" lower-margin IT services to the global technology services (GTS) group. The GTS group handles value-chain infrastructure services and uses IBM's global scale and its expertise in standardizing and automating transactions to manage outsourcing, integrated technology services such as logistics and data center management, and maintenance services for its global clients.

As noted previously, IBM was experiencing increasing low-cost competition in its outsourcing services business that provided it with billions of dollars of revenues from contracts with large global companies to manage their "non-core" business functions such as distribution, logistics, and data center management. This intense competitive pressure was coming from low-cost Indian companies such as Infosys, Tata Consulting Services, and Wipro, which had grown enormously in the 2000s because of their lower labor costs. Indeed, their profit margins were more than 20%, while margins at IBM were half that and shrinking because of the competition. These companies gained such an advantage because labor costs were still about 70% to 80% of the total cost of traditional technology service contracts involving activities such as maintaining and updating software and data centers for corporate clients. They were taking away billions of dollars in revenues from IBM.

IBM had to compete more effectively in this IT services segment, which had been a main source of the increasing revenues that had allowed it to rebuild its competitive advantage. Like most manufacturing companies, IBM was forced to eliminate 20,000 GTS jobs in Europe and the United States and move these jobs to India. Its Indian workforce grew from 30,000 in 2004 to 45,000 in 2006. Then in June 2006, IBM announced it would triple its investment in India to $6 billion over the next three years to take advantage of its growing importance as a market for technology products and a source of high-technology workers. By 2009, it had more than 75,000 Indian employees.

IBM made the investment to establish huge, low-cost service delivery centers for its global clients, improve the software necessary to automate the management of networks and data centers, and develop IT to improve telecommunications, especially Internet services. From India, IBM runs a whole range of IT services for its global customers, including software delivery services such as upgrading and maintaining client software and managing and protecting database centers. For example, in Bangalore, IBM has a command center that monitors the operation of the database server networks of more than 16,000 different clients, including the way thousands of its outsourcing software applications are performing around the world. It is the largest of IBM's three global IT services centers; the other two that are growing in size are in Brazil and China. Palmisano's goal was to expand the scope of IBM's traditional outsourcing operations and attract more and more global clients to compensate for reduced profit margins so it can still increase profits from this group. And IBM has the global reputation necessary to convince customers it will be able to reduce their cost structure and improve their profitability.

However, IBM moved to India not only to take advantage of lower labor costs but also because the country has a huge pool of talented software engineers that IBM recruited to develop new, advanced software that can *automate* the IT jobs currently performed by its Indian employees in logistics and data center management. In other words, IBM's long-term goal is not simply to replace skilled labor with lower-cost skilled labor but to use that skilled labor in combination with advanced automated software. This means that over time, although IBM's Indian workforce will continue to increase in size, engineers will be able to manage a much higher volume of global customer accounts more efficiently, which will significantly increase IBM's profit margins in its traditional services business. IBM has made dozens of acquisitions in the 2000s to help improve its skills in software automation and develop smarter, more customized software that allows it to maintain its clients', value-chain functions at lower cost to compete with its Indian rivals.

Global Business Services Group

If the goal in its GTS group was to increase profit margins and the number of customer accounts by being able to offer global customers lower prices and high-quality customer service, the goal of its global business services (GBS) group is to offer customers state-of-the-art value-creating software services that can be customized to their needs, albeit at a premium price. In other words, in creating the GBS group, Palmisano's goal was accelerate its move into higher-margin service activities, especially consulting and business transformation in which IBM could use the specialized skills of its United States software engineers to offer customers IT services that increase their competitive advantage. Specifically, the GBS group's strategy is to offer its customers professional, innovative services that deliver value by providing them with state-of-the-art solutions that leverage IBM's industry and business process expertise.

Such services include consulting, systems integration, and application management services that tap into IBM's expertise in IT and apply it to fields such as utility grid optimization and energy conservation, genetics-based personalized medicine, fraud detection and prediction, and even traffic management. For example, one of IBM's projects involved working with a Texas utility, CenterPoint Energy, to install computerized electric meters, sensors, and software in a "smart grid" IT project to improve service and conserve energy. Dozens of IBM's industry experts from around the country moved to work on the project to design and build advanced software tailored to the needs of a utility company. Because some of the programming work can be done in India, engineers are on the project team as well.

IBM plans to use the valuable skills learned and software written for the Texas smart-grid project in new projects with utility clients around the world, thus leveraging its skills in a high-profit margin business. In 2008, IBM announced it was entering into a new agreement with CenterPoint to develop the software platform necessary to supply the utilities rural customers with high-speed Internet connections through the power grid. By connecting their PCs to any electrical socket in their homes, they will be able to obtain broadband Internet service. Also, in 2008, IBM announced hundreds of new global services contracts with diverse companies around the world, such as Philippines PSBank, the second-largest savings bank in the country, PTT Chemical Public Company of Thailand, and Skynet in Lithuania to provide Internet protocol television. This was growing evidence of its increasing expertise in specialized IT services.

Building up its repertoire of skills across industries and across business functions is a key way in which IBM intends to grow its revenues and profits over time. And, its competitors recognizing its growing competitive advantage were forced to expand their capabilities to provide customers with a competitive HS&S package. For example, in 2008, HP acquired EDS, the third-largest IT services company in the United States for $14 billion to add its 140,000 employees to the IT services group and improve its repertoire of IT skills and clients to compete better with IBM for global customers. HP, following IBM's lead, has also divided its service activities into those that improve the efficiency of companies' value-chain operations through outsourcing and logistics management and those that involve using its IT expertise to help companies innovate and find new ways to improve their value-creation skills. Of course, IBM continues to emphasize that its combination of vast experience and IT expertise is unmatched on a global scale.

Another competitor that has also been aggressively expanding the breadth of its IT service and software lineup is the database management software leader, Oracle. Oracle has spent more than $50 billion since 2004 to acquire companies such as PeopleSoft and BEA Systems to widen its ERP lineup and better compete with its ERP archrival SAP. At the same time, however, Oracle's new product lineup has resulted in more competition with IBM, especially in the server market. Increasing competition here has prompted IBM to develop closer ties with SAP. In 2009, IBM and SAP announced an agreement with British retailer Marks & Spencer (M&S) to implement a suite of SAP Retail applications. The program aims to provide M&S with accurate business intelligence data and state-of-the-art functional and industry IT solutions that will allow it to discover business improvement initiatives that will increase operating efficiency and responsiveness to customers. IBM will draw on its expertise in organization, process, and technology to provide end-to-end program management, including change management and business process consulting services. SAP will provide its "Industry Solution for Retail," a suite of business applications designed specifically to meet the unique requirements of large and sophisticated retailers. Also in 2009, IBM announced it would be the first global IT company to fully adopt the Run SAP(R) methodology and that it would become a launch partner for SAP(R) Business Suite 7 software, SAP's new flexible and modular software suite. As global partners, SAP and IBM will jointly help customers reduce the total cost of running SAP's ERP software.

Software Group

Clearly, the ability of IBM's two global services groups to provide customers either low-cost traditional IT services or value-creating, customized consulting solutions depends on it having the distinctive competence to develop state-of-the-art software applications across business processes and industries. Since 2005, Palmisano has emphasized the central role advanced software development must play in IBM's future business model to offset the slowing revenues from global services because of low-cost global competition. To spur its efforts in software development, and especially to increase its share of the high-margin services business, IBM began to make many acquisitions. By 2007, had IBM spent $11.8 billion to acquire 36 software and 18 service companies in fields such as security, data management, and Web commerce.

One particularly important acquisition occurred in 2008 when IBM announced it had acquired Cognos, a leading maker of business intelligence software, for $4.9 billion. IBM's acquisition came after SAP's acquisition of Business Objects and Oracle's takeover of Hyperion, the other two leading makers of business intelligence software in 2007. Business intelligence software sifts through huge masses of data and uses sophisticated problem solving procedures to identify and discover crucial events such as changes in the buying habits of a customer group or the "hidden" factors reducing the efficiency of a company's value-chain functions or business processes. Cognos software is used by many retailers, including Home Depot, Amazon.com, American Eagle Outfitters, and 7-Eleven. Recent advances in IT have increased the power of business intelligence software to identify ongoing changes and forecast likely future events, an area in which IBM had no expertise. So, to prevent its competitors from gaining a possible future competitive advantage, IBM decided to make this acquisition, just as it had made the important decision to acquire Lotus Notes over a decade earlier. IBM will be able to incorporate Cognos software into all its software/service packages and hence strengthen its competitive advantage.

In October 2008, IBM unveiled new Express Advantage products aimed at SMBs, including HS&S packages specifically customized to the needs of SMB clients. For example, its new packages help SMB clients improve operational efficiency, increase customer responsiveness, and continuously lower risk. In 2008, in a deal worth as much as $800 million over eight years, Amgen, the biotech company hired IBM to provide a HS&S package that will provide computer networks, software, messaging systems, helpdesk support, and other services.

In 2009, IBM announced a new "virtual world" IT initiative to make it easier for geographically dispersed people to interact and collaborate without the time and expense of in-person meetings. Virtual worlds are interactive, immersive Web sites based on the use of three-dimensional graphics. IBM was using selected clients to test its "Sametime 3D" virtual technology, which allows people inside and between companies to exchange instant messages, chat verbally, share real-time presentations and ideas in private, virtual meeting spaces that exist permanently in real time so people can meet on regular, periodic, or impromptu bases.

In 2009, IBM also announced a new agreement with Amazon Web Services (AWS), a subsidiary of Amazon.com, to deliver IBM's software to clients and developers via cloud computing. The new "pay-as-you-go" model provides clients with access to development and production instances of IBM DB2, Informix Dynamic Server, WebSphere Portal, Lotus Web Content Management, WebSphere sMash, and Novell's SUSE Linux operating system software in the Amazon Elastic Compute Cloud (Amazon EC2) environment, providing a comprehensive portfolio of products available on AWS.

In May 2009, IBM announced it had acquired Exeros, a privately held data discovery software maker and will wrap Exeros' technology into its business intelligence or analytics unit. Exeros software includes Discover X-Profiler, an application that profiles data; Discovery Unified Schema Builder, which allows users to prototype the combination of various data; and the Discovery Transformation Analyzer, which scans business rules and spots anomalies.

Systems and Technology Group

In its hardware division, Palmisano continued his strategy of focusing on high–profit margin products that directly complemented its service and software offerings. As noted earlier, IBM had sold off its PC business to Lenovo for $1.25 billion and its disk drive business Hitachi for $2 billion. In 2007, IBM decided to spin off its printer business, which was suffering from intense competition from HP and Xerox, to Ricoh for $725 million.

Palmisano directed the systems and technology group to put its resources into developing new kinds of mainframes and servers that would appeal to a wider number of customers groups and expand global sales. IBM still receives about 25% of its $100 billion in annual revenue from sales, software, services, and financing related to its mainframes and servers.

Mainframes, the hub of a large company's IT system, crunch the massive amounts of data that are generated, for example, every time someone withdraws money from an automated teller machine, uses a credit card, or buys a product from a large retailer. Since 2005, IBM has been pursuing the strategy of constantly upgrading the performance of its large mainframes to offer its customers a better value prospection, that is, to give them more and more power and flexibility for each IT dollar they spend. And, beginning in 2006, it began to offer customers the option of buying smaller and much-less expensive mainframes to drive sales to medium-sized global customers. In 2007, for example, it introduced its latest generation of mainframes, the powerful z10 Enterprise Class (z10EC) mainframe that retails for about $1 million and the smaller z10 Business Class (z10BC) mainframe that retails for about $100,000. The larger mainframe is twice as powerful as its predecessor; the smaller one is 40% faster, has more than 50% more total systems capacity, and up to four times the maximum main memory compared to the previous "mini-mainframe" IBM introduced in 2005. At a fraction of the cost of its large mainframe, the z10BC is also a way for IBM to offer more machines to more market segments. Priced at $100,000, the machine is not directed at small businesses that would use more inexpensive server rack configurations; it is highly attractive to smaller enterprises and midmarket companies looking to consolidate multiple server racks in many data centers with one large machine.

IBM sells its large mainframes directly to customers through its own salesforce to protect the lucrative software and service revenues that accompany these sales. The smaller mainframe, however, is sold through its 20 global channel partners, who also provide the software and service package customized to each client's needs. IBM pursued this strategy to accelerate the adoption of the machines throughout the world because global customers, particularly those in India and China, are the main targets for these $100,000 machines. Its strategy worked. IBM's mainframe installed base doubled from 2005 to 2009 because of IBM's ability to deliver increasing amounts of processing power to customers at a decreasing cost. In addition, the new mainframes used far less energy, something that is becoming increasingly important throughout the IT hardware industry.

In 2009, IBM was accused of purchasing software maker Platform Solutions to stifle competition in the mainframe market and protect its franchise. Platform Solutions had developed software that turned racks of servers into a linked system that could mimic the performance of IBM's expensive mainframes. IBM announced it would refuse to license its mainframe software to Platform that would allow its software to work. But when its legal attempt to stop Platform from gaining access to its software failed, IBM bought it for $150 million and then shut down work on the software. The Computer and Communications Industry Association, a trade group backed by Google, Oracle, and Microsoft, described the Platform deal as an attempt by IBM to purchase a company solely to foreclose competition in the mainframe marketplace and protect its cash cow at the expense of consumers. IBM contends the continued popularity of its mainframes stems from its continuous efforts to modernize them so that they can run more contemporary business software. Other competitors, such as Sun, HP, and Microsoft, have also attempted to develop software for connected racks of linked servers to enable them to handle the huge number-crunching tasks mainframes can perform, but their efforts have had only limited success.

New software called virtualization technology is currently being developed, however, that may result in linked server racks being able to emulate the power of mainframes. This may be one reason that prompted IBM in 2009 to announce it would acquire Sun, still a leading maker of server HS&S for about $7 billion; the deal would also give IBM control over the key storage systems used for mainframes. In the end, however, the deal fell through when Oracle made a higher offer for Sun to gain control of all its server HS&S assets, including its Java software. It appears that Sun's goal will be to expand the role of servers to also mimic the power of IBM's mainframes, something that will intensify the competition between the two companies.

IBM has always been interested in the idea of hosting its client's data on its own network of mainframes and developed an IT service called "business on demand" to offer them this option. By the mid-2000s, however, the cost of linked racks of servers (which might contain 10,000 powerful individual servers) was falling sharply as Intel and AMD introduced ever-more advanced microprocessors, which when combined with Oracle's database management software, made them low-cost alternatives to renting space on IBM's mainframes. Also in the mid-2000s, the idea of cloud computing had been pioneered by Internet companies such as Google, Yahoo!, and Microsoft, and the concept was gaining in popularity. In the cloud computing business model, Internet and other companies design their own customized data centers to store vast amounts of information that can be accessed and processed from afar using PCs, netbooks, cell phones, or other devices. For example, Google pioneered an online document hosting service in which both individuals and companies can upload documents that are stored in Google's data centers on server racks and then can be accessed using word processing or spreadsheet software programs and so on. Once again, these data centers are composed of tens or even hundreds of thousands of servers linked into racks, which are in turn connected together to provide immense amounts of storage and processing power.

What is unique about the cloud computing model, however, is that, cloud data centers require server racks that have been configured with the right HS&S to meet the needs of each individual company. These data centers are not "off-the-shelf" standardized products, such as IBM's mainframes. Even more unique, the growing number of companies that are competing to offer these integrated server racks have developed a new business model in which these racks are housed in portable storage platforms that are housed in shipping containers similar to those used to deliver products around the world on ships and trucks. These storage platforms are then integrated into a company's physical data center using networking hardware and software. This business is growing fast; it is expected to be a multibillion-dollar business in the future.

Given that its business on demand initiative was not working, IBM was anxious to enter this market. It also is a major maker of server racks, and in 2008, IBM bought the cloud computing platform maker, Platform Systems, to provide new portable computing data centers. IBM calls its new product iDataPlex; it is a self-contained data center housed in different-sized shipping containers that can hold 1,000 to 10,000 server computers powered by Intel or AMD chips. One of its platforms offers customers the option of placing 1,500 server computers into 40-foot semi-trailers that are ready to plug in from parking lots.

Developing hardware platforms that have to be customized to the needs of individual companies is a new strategy for IBM; however, its army of IT services and software experts provide it with the competence necessary to do this. IBM claims its new cloud computer container platform costs only half as much in real estate, set-up, and construction costs than a similar physical data center. In addition, compared to the platform systems offered by competitors such as Dell, HP, and Rackable Systems, IBM claims its trailers have innovative water-cooling mechanisms so that the servers do not heat up the data centers. This eliminates the need for most air-conditioning. As a result, IBM claims its systems consume 40% less power than standard servers and can pack more than twice as many computers into the same space.

Companies trying out its platforms include Yahoo! and other Internet companies; companies in finance and other traditional industries are also testing them. In 2009, Google for the first time publicly showed the design of its own cloud computing data centers, which are also technologically advanced, especially cooling wise. Clearly there is competition ahead.

Finally, in April 2009, IBM announced it was strengthening its strategic alliance with network equipment maker Brocade Communication. IBM sold its own networking equipment business to Cisco Systems in the early 2000s. However, innovations such as its cloud computing data center trailers, as well as the growing need to connect all the different kinds of IT hardware used by its clients seamlessly to the Internet and especially to remote data centers means IBM must have access to state-of-the-art networking products to align perfectly with its own software. In the future, IBM will rebrand Ethernet switching and Internet routing products made by Brocade as IBM products and sell them as a part of its complete IT HS&S package to its global customers. One more reason for this partnership is that rivalry with Cisco increased in 2009 after Cisco announced it was entering the server data center market and planned a "revolutionary" new kind of self-contained rack server that would possess a huge amount of database storage capacity and processing power linked to its own network communication hardware and software. Such a self-contained server would eliminate the need for expensive IT consulting and service; it would offer companies with a low-cost alternative, and, over time, companies could simply order as many of Cisco's server racks as needed to operate or expand their business. Presumably Cisco will also offer a portable container-based platform solution.

IBM's Recent Performance

By 2006, IBM's performance was recovering as a result of Palmisano's strategic initiatives, especially his decision to split apart the old global services group. Trimming its service workforce had significantly reduced its cost structure, and sales of its new mainframes were up by 25%. Software revenue rose 5%, helped by increasing sales of its popular WebSphere software package that improves the performance of a company's electronic commerce and business applications. In addition, its shift toward higher profit-margin services and automating traditional business processes such as procurement, finance, and human resources was leading to increasing numbers of long-term service contracts. In particular, its higher-profit business transformation outsourcing grew by 45%. Palmisano commented that "the strength of our business model across hardware, software and services is paying off." Geographically, IBM enjoyed solid growth of 5% in the G7 countries, but more rapid growth was occurring in emerging markets. For example, sales in India were up by 50%.

IBM's performance continued to improve through 2007 into 2008. IBM reported profit rising 12% on strong growth in software and services. Due to its success in selling higher-margin software and services, its profit margins were steadily improving. Indeed, by 2008, IBM software's revenue showed the biggest gain and had become the largest contributor to IBM's profits. Palmisano announced that software would be the driving force behind IBM's future growth. Obviously, the ability to develop state-of-the-art business software drives up IBM's service revenues and the sales of mainframes that are optimized to use its new software.

By May 2008, IBM stock was trading near its six-year high level, and it seemed as though Palmisano's new strategies had worked. However, then came the recession in the summer of 2008. Although, as expected, revenues from its hardware group fell sharply as large companies reduced their spending on mainframes and servers, IBM was not hurt as badly as its competitors because of its major push to globalization. In 2007, for example, it had reported that it enjoyed more than 10% growth in revenues in more than 50 countries.

In October 2008, analysts were surprised when IBM reported strong third-quarter profits despite the financial services industry meltdown. As IBM's CFO explained, although financial services is IBM's biggest customer segment contributing 28% to its revenues, and the one hit hardest by the economic downturn, 75% of that revenue came from outside the United States. Also, only 15% of those financial institutions that had been severely impacted were IBM clients, so the company was not highly exposed to the meltdown. Moreover, even in the United States, IBM benefitted from many new short-term contracts with financial companies such

as banks and brokers that increased their spending on risk analysis and compliance tools to try to weather the downturn. In fact, globally, IBM had signed more than $12.7 billion in new long-term services contracts in the last quarter of 2008, while short-term contract signings were up 13% to $6.1 billion. This showed IBM was able to generate new business despite tough economic times.

In April 2009, Palmisano expressed more confidence that the company was on track to achieve its projected earnings target for the full year despite uncertain markets worldwide. The company reported solid performance in a period of economic turmoil, helped by cost-cutting and its strategy of moving into higher profit margin software and services businesses. Like most other large companies, in March 2009, IBM announced 5,000 job cuts in the United States, which accounted for more than 4% of its United States workforce—115,000 by the end of 2008. The cuts were mostly in IBM's global services business and, as noted earlier, IBM has greatly expanded its business and employment in fast-growing markets such as India, China, Brazil, and Russia. At the beginning of 2009, IBM had 75,000 workers in India and 13,000 in China.

Similarly, the improving profit margins IBM was enjoying in its expanding services and software businesses were significantly boosted by the 100 acquisitions IBM had made since 2000, which had cost $20 billion, and its moves to aggressively pursue opportunities in faster-growing markets abroad such as India and China. Also, of course, 40% to 60% of its profits come from its long-term contracts with customers who pay a fixed yearly fee for its value-chain management software and services. It is difficult to reduce this spending even in a recession. Indeed, the recession had sparked a lot of interest in the cost-saving outsourcing deals offered by its GTS group. One example is a $500 million, seven-year contract IBM signed in March 2009 to manage data centers and software for Kaiser Permanente, a large hospital and managed health care company. In fact, in 2009, the market offering the strongest possibilities for revenue growth was the public sector, with government and state organizations, in which contracts were up 50% as countries around the world announced *$5 trillion* in economic stimulus programs to increase customer demand for technology and other goods to increase spending and boost economic growth.

INDEX

A

Absolute cost advantage, 59–60
ACE system, 196–197
Acquisition, 174
  restructuring strategy and, 188, 192
  strategic change and, 212–215
Activity ratios, C10
Advanced Micro Devices (AMD), 65
Agency problem, 33, 34
Agency relationship, 34
Agency theory, 34
Agent, 33, 34
Airline industry
  in decline stage, 72
  deregulation of, 76
  price wars in, 72
Alcan, 182
Alcoa, 182
Allard, Jay, 13
Aluminum industry, 182
Amazon.com
  consolidation and, 131
  customization at, 107
AMD, 65
Analogy, reasoning by, 18
Analyses. See External analysis;
  Internal analysis; and SWOT
  analysis
Andreesen, Mark, 13
Anticompetitive behavior, 43
Antitrust law, 42, 178
Apple Computer
  innovation at, 104
  vertical integration at, 180
Arthur Andersen, 41
Asset, specialized, 182
Astra Zeneca, 220
AT&T, 193
Auditors, financial statements and,
  40–41
Auto industry
  bargaining power in, 64
  competitive advantage in, 85
  local responsiveness and, 154, 159
Autonomous action, 12
Average collection period, C10

B

Baby boomers, 76
Backward vertical integration, 180, 184
Banana industry, 184
Bankruptcy regulations, 63
Bargaining power
  of buyers, 63–64
  horizontal integration and, 177–178

of Intel, 65
of suppliers, 64–65
of Walmart, 67
Barriers
  to entry, 58, 182, 212
  to exit, 63, 138
  to imitation, 110
  to mobility, 69
Bartz, Carol, 233
BEA Systems, 223
Behavior, anticompetitive, 43
Behavior control, 252
Bell, Alexander Graham, 13
Bias
  cognitive, 17–18
  prior hypothesis, 17–18
Bidding strategy, 215
Board of directors, 34, 38–39, 49
Boeing
  ethics at, 44
  globalization of production at, 147
  stock options and, 40
Bombardier, 155
Bottom-up change, 205
Bowerman, Bill, 141
Brand loyalty, 58–59, 124
Breen, Edward, 35
Broad differentiator, 123
Budget, operating, 252
Buffet, Warren, 40
Burgelman, Robert, 12
Burns, Larry, 23
Business, defining, 30
Business ethics, 42
Business-level managers, 6
Business-level strategy, 10
  competitive positioning and, 118–119,
    129–140
  distinctive competence and, 119, 120,
    124, 127
  at Nike, 141–142
  types of, 120–129
  at Walmart, 120
Business practice officer, 48
Business process, 201
Business unit, 6
Buyers' bargaining power, 63–64

C

Cambridge Antibody Technology, 220
Canon, 206, 207
Capabilities, 108–109
Capacity, excess, 63, 133–134
Capital
  productivity, 87
  relational, 220

return on invested, 2
risk, 33
structure, C10
Carrefour, 151
Case study
  analyzing, C2–C6
Case study analysis
  explanation of, C1–C2
  financial analysis role in, C8–C12
  writing, C6–C8
Cash flow, C12
Caterpillar
  customer responsiveness at, 92, 107
Cellular phone industry, 70
Centralization, 232–233
CEOs, 6
  agency problem and, 34–38
  board of directors and, 39
  characteristics of good, 19–21
Cereal industry, 133
Chaining strategy, 130
Chevy Volt, 23–24
Chief executive officers. See CEOs
Cifera, 150
Cisco Systems
  information systems at, 98
  innovation at, 89
Citicorp, 190
Citigroup, 190–191
Coca-Cola
  business definition and, 56–57
  entry barriers and, 59
  imitation at, 110
  product development at, 136
Code of ethics, 47
Cognitive bias, 17–18
Commitment
  credible, 220
  escalating, 18
Communication problems, 235
Company infrastructure, 93, 100
Compaq, 174, 178
Compensation
  pay for performance, 98
  stock-based, 39–40
Competence, distinctive. See Distinctive
  competence
Competition, nonprice, 135–137
Competitive advantage, 2. See also
  Competitive positioning
  building blocks of, 86–90. See also
    Value chain
  business-level strategies and, 118–119
  distinctive competencies and, 108–111
  functional-level strategies and, 93–107
  superior performance and, 2, 4
  sustained, 4
  of Walmart, 3–4

Competitive positioning. *See also* Business-level strategy
  in different industry environments, 129–140
  nature of, 118–119
  of Nike, 141–142
  at Walmart, 120
Competitive structure, of industry, 61–62
Competitors. *See also* Five forces model
  definition of, 56
  potential, 58–60
Concentration on a single industry, 173–180
Conglomerate, 192, 196
Consolidated industry, 61, 62
Contract law, 42
Control
  illusion of, 18
  organizational, 244–255
  span of, 229
Convergys, 179
Cooper, Robert, 104
Cooperative outsourcing relationships, 186
Core competence. *See* Distinctive competence
Corporate governance, 28. *See also* Board of directors; CEOs
  ethics and, 49
  strategy and, 33–41
Corporate-level managers, 6, 201, 204, 210. *See also* CEOs
Corporate-level strategy, 10, 201
  concentration on single industry, 173–180
  related vs. unrelated diversification, 191–192
  restructuring and downsizing, 192–194
  value creation through diversification, 187–191
  vertical integration, 173, 180–186
Corruption, 44, 46
Cost advantage, absolute, 59–60
Cost conditions, industry, 62
Cost-leadership strategy, 121–122, 124–125
Cost reductions, pressures for, 153–154, 156, 167–168
Costco, 3, 4
Costs
  fixed, 62, 94, 138
  operating, 175, 243–244
  switching, 60
Cott Corporation, 59
Coyne, William, 190
Credible commitment, 220
Cross-functional product development teams, 105
Culture, organizational, 32, 46, 47–48
Currency exchange rates, 73–74
Current ratio, C10
Customer defection rates, 96–97
Customer needs, 56, 107, 118–119, 154
Customer-oriented business definition, 31, 56
Customer response time, 90

Customer responsiveness, 90, 106–107, 108
Customization, 96, 107

D

David, George, 192, 196, 197
Davidson, Dick, 233
Days Sales Outstanding (DSO), C10
Debt-to-assets ratio, C10–C11
Debt-to-equity ratio, C11
Decentralization, 232–233
Decentralized planning, 16–17
Decision making, strategic, 17–19, 48
Declining industry, 72, 137–140
Defection rates, customer, 96–97
Delegation, 20–21
Deliberate strategy, 14
Dell, Michael, 257–258
Dell Computers, 235, 236, 257–258
Dell versus SGI (Silicon Graphics International)
  competition in server and cloud computing, case on, C13–C20
Demand, industry, 62
Demographic forces, 75–76
Devil's advocacy, 18
Dialectic inquiry, 19
Differentiation, 228. *See also* Product differentiation
  horizontal, 228, 234–244
  integration and, 247
  vertical, 228, 229–233
Differentiation strategy
  cost leadership and, 124–125
  explanation of, 122–124
Differentiator, broad, 123
Digital Equipment, 182
Directors, 34, 38–39, 49
Discount, diversification, 193
Disney, Walt, 255
Distinctive competence
  business-level strategy and, 119, 120, 124, 127
  competitive advantage and, 108–111
  diversification and, 188–189
  entry mode and, 166–167
  strategic change and, 205–208
Diversification
  creating value through, 187–191
  discount, 193
  as entry mode, 173, 186
  internal governance and, 187–188
  related vs. unrelated, 191–192
  restructuring and, 192–194
  at 3M, 189, 190
Diversified company, 187
Divestment, 194
  strategy, 138, 140
Dividend yield, C12
Divisional-level strategy. *See* Business-level strategy
Domino's Pizza, 106
Downsizing, 192–194
DuPont, 247
Dyment, Roy, 107

E

eBay, 131
Economies, location, 149, 151
Economies of scale, 58, 94, 149
Economies of scope, 189–191
EDS, 179
Efficiency, 87, 93–100
Electronic Data Systems (EDS), 179
Elevonic 401, 196
Ellison, Larry, 222, 223
Embryonic industry, 70
Emergent strategy, 14–15
Emotional intelligence, 21
Empire building, 36
Employee productivity, 87, 97–98
Empowerment, 20–21
Enron, 37, 38, 41
Entry
  barriers to, 58, 75, 212
  modes of, 161–168
Environment
  industry, 9
  macro-, 9, 73–77
  national, 9
Environmental degradation, 44
Escalating commitment, 18
Ethical dilemmas
  definition of, 42
  exercises, 9, 33, 66, 86, 129, 154, 178, 220, 232
Ethics, 42
  business, 42
  code of, 47
  officer, 48
Excess capacity, 63, 133–134
Exchange rates, currency, 73–74
Exit barrier, 63, 138
Exit strategies, 194
Exploitation, opportunistic, 44
Exporting, 161–162
Express mail delivery industry
  exit barriers in, 63
  fixed costs in, 62
External analysis, 7, 8, 9, 56
  of industry life cycle, 69–73
  of industry structure, 56–66
  of macroenvironment, 73–77
  strategic groups and, 66–69
External stakeholders, 28, 205
Exxon, 36

F

Federal Trade Commission (FTC), 178
FedEx
  excess capacity and, 63
  fixed costs of, 62
  vertical differentiation and, 231
Feedback loop, 11
Fiat-Chrysler, 125
Fill in the blanks, 206–207
Financial control, 241, 250–251
Financial statements, and auditors, 40–41

Fiorina, Carly, 178
Five forces model, 57–66, 122
Fixed costs, 62, 94, 138
Flat structure, 229
Flexible manufacturing technology, 96
Focus strategy, 120, 125–127
Ford, 220, 250
Forward vertical integration, 180, 181
Four Seasons hotel chain, 107
"48 Hours," 42
Fragmented industry, 61, 129–131
Franchising, 130–131, 163–164
FTC, 178
Fuji, 164
Full integration, 185
Functional-level managers, 5, 7
Functional-level strategy, 10
   competitive advantage and, 93–107
   obstacles to change and, 204
Functional structure, 234–236

G

GAAP, 35
Galvin, Christopher, 210
Gates, Bill, 11, 13, 19, 254
GE. *See* General Electric
General Electric (GE), 20
   ivory tower approach and, 16
   managers of, 6
   strategic alliance and, 219
General managers, 5. *See also*
   specific types
General Motors (GM), 23, 36
   imitation at, 110
   innovation at, 105
   market segmentation and, 119
   multidivisional structure of, 242
   vs. Toyota, 85, 86
   vertical integration at, 184
Generally agreed-on accounting
   principles (GAAP), 35
Geographic structure, 238–239
Gillette, 136
Global automobile industry, in 2009
   case on, C40–C51
Global environment, 75, 146–148
   choosing strategy for, 156–161
   competitive pressures in, 152–155
   entry modes in, 161–168
   increasing profitability through,
      148–152
Global standardization strategy,
   10, 156–157
Global strategy. *See* Global environment
GM. *See* General Motors
Goal, 32–33. *See also specific control*
   systems
Goldman, Daniel, 21
Google's mission
   ethical principles, and involvement
      in China, 51–52
Governance mechanisms, 34, 38–41,
   187–188
Government regulation, 60
Grove, Andy, 12, 111

Growth industry, 70–71, 129–131
Growth rate, 37

H

Hallmark Cards, 201
Hamel, Gary, 205, 206, 207–208
Hanson PLC, 215
Harvest strategy, 138, 139–140, 194
Heavyweight project manager, 105–106
Heinz, H. J., 122
Hewlett, Bill, 46
Hewlett-Packard
   working conditions at, 46
Hiring, and ethics, 47
Holdup, risk of, 183
Home Depot, 36
Home video game industry
   Atari Pong to Nintendo Wii, case on,
      C21–C37
Horizontal differentiation, 228, 234–244
Horizontal integration, 174–178
Horizontal merger, 131
HP Way, The, 46
HTML, 13
Hubris hypothesis, 18
Human resources strategy, 93, 97–98
Hypertext markup language (HTML), 13

I

IBM, 214
   fall of, case on, C71–C83
   location economies and, 151
   mission of, 31
   rise of, case on, C60–C69
   in 2009, case on, C84–C95
   vertical integration at, 180, 182
IKEA, 169
   case on, C52–C58
Illusion of control, 18
Imitation, barriers to, 110
Immelt, Jeffrey, 6, 251
Industry, 56
   analyzing structure of, 56–66
   competitive structure of, 61–62
   concentration on a single, 173–180
   consolidated, 61, 62
   cost conditions of, 62
   declining, 72, 137–140
   demand in, 62
   environment of, 73–77
   fragmented, 61, 129–131
   growth, 70–71, 129–131
   life cycle of, 69–73
Inflation, price, 74
Information asymmetry, 34
Information distortion, 231, 243
Information manipulation, 43
Information systems, 93, 98, 100
Infrastructure, company, 93, 100
Innovation, 89–90
   increasing, 103–106
   process, 89
   product, 89, 103–104
   at 3M, 108

Inputs, 87
Inside directors, 38–39
Intangible resources, 108, 110
Integration, 228
   acquisition and, 215
   differentiation and, 247
   full, 185
   horizontal, 174–178
   managers and, 247
   organizational control and, 244–247
   postacquisition, 213–214
   taper, 185
   vertical, 173, 180–186
Intel, 12
   bargaining power of, 65
   innovation in, 89
Intellectual property law, 42
Intelligence, emotional, 21
Intended strategy, 14–15
Internal analysis, 7, 8, 9–10
Internal governance, 187–188
Internal new ventures, 208–212
Internal stakeholders, 28, 205
International licensing, 162
International strategy, 159–160
Internet, and fragmented industries, 131
Internet Explorer, 13, 44
Inventory system, JIT, 97, 102
Inventory turnover, C10
Iridium project, 210
Ito, Yuzuru, 196
Iverson, Ken, 20
Ivory tower approach, 16–17

J

Java, 13
JIT inventory system, 97, 102
Joint venture, 164–165, 215
Joseph Schlitz Brewing Company, 122
Just-in-time (JIT) inventory system,
   97, 102

K

Kahneman, Daniel, 19
Kamprad, Ingvar, 169
Kelleher, Herb, 20
Klippan love seat, 169
Kmart, 67
Knight, Phil, 141
Kodak
   mission of, 30, 31
   vertical integration at, 184
Kozlowski, Dennis, 35
Kroc, Ray, 20

L

Laws, business, 42, 178
Leadership
   price, 134–135
   strategic, 19–21, 47–48, 100. *See also*
      specific leaders

Leadership strategy, 138–139
Lean production, 89–90, 96
Learning effects, 94–95
Legal/political forces, 76–77
Leverage ratios, C10–C11
Liaison role, of manager, 245
Licensing, 162–163
Life cycle, industry, 69–73
Liquidation strategy, 194
Liquidity ratios, C9–C10
Loblaws, 59
Local responsiveness, pressures
    for, 152–153, 154–155, 156
Localization strategy, 157–159, 160
Location
    economies, 149, 151
    and organization structure, 236
Logistics, 92, 97
Long-term contracting, 194
Low cost structure, 86, 96
Lutz, Bob, 23–24

M

Macroeconomic forces, 73–74
Macroenvironment, 9, 73–77
Managers
    business-level, 6
    corporate-level, 6, 201, 204, 210.
        See also CEOs
    functional-level, 5, 7
    heavyweight project, 105–106
    integration and, 248
    liaison role of, 245
    motivation of, 231
Market development, 136–137
Market niche, 125. *See also* Focus
    strategy
Market penetration, 136
Market segmentation, 119, 120
Market-to-book value, C11
Marketing, 92, 96–97
    strategy, 96–97
Mass customization, 96
Materials management, 92, 97
Matsushita, TQM at, 196
Mature industry, 72, 131–137
Maytag, 237
Mazda, 220
MBO, 194
McDonald's
    franchising and, 163
    global expansion at, 149, 152
    strategic leadership at, 20
    vertical integration at, 184
McKinnell, Hank, 36
Measurement systems, 235
Mega-opportunities, 206, 207–208
Merger, 131, 174, 233. *See also specific*
    mergers
Microsoft, 19
    economies of scale and, 94, 149
    ethics at, 44
    flexible strategic planning at, 11, 13
    international strategy and, 160

mission of, 9
    organizational values at, 254
    permanent teams at, 246
    stock options and, 40
    strategic alliance and, 217
Mintzberg, Henry, 14, 15, 245
Mission, 30–31
Mission statement, 9, 29–32
Mobility barriers, 69
Model T Ford, 94
Monaghan, Tom, 106
Monsanto, 207, 208
Moral courage, 49
Mosaic, 13
Motivation, and organization
    structure, 231
Motorola, 204, 210, 217, 220
MTV, 158
Mulally, Alan, 250
Multidivisional company, 5, 240–244
Murdock, Rupert, 174

N

Nardelli, Bob, 36
National environment, 9
Naval, 139
Needs, customer, 56, 107, 118–119,
    154
Neiman Marcus, 238–239
Netscape Navigator, 13
News Corp, 174, 216
News industry
    acquisition strategy and, 216
    horizontal integration and, 174
    technical change in, 75
Niche strategy, 138, 139
Nike
    business-level strategies at, 141–142
    ethics at, 42
    outsourcing and, 179
Noblesse oblige, 43
Nonprice competition, 135–137
Nordstrom, 86
Norms, organizational, 254
Nucor Steel
    distinctive competencies of, 109
    human resources at, 97, 98
    leadership of, 20
    values of, 32

O

Odle, Stephanie, 45
On-the-job consumption, 35–36
Operating budget, 252
Operating costs
    horizontal integration and, 175
    organization structure and, 243–244
Operating responsibility, 241
Opportunistic exploitation, 44
Opportunities, 56, 207–208. *See also*
    specific opportunities
Oracle, 177
Oracle Corporation, 222–223

Organizational control, 32
    behavior controls and, 252
    ethics and, 46, 47–48
    integration and, 244–247
    leadership, 254–255
    nature of, 247–255
    at Walmart, 255–256
Organizational design, 227. *See*
    also Organizational structure;
    Organizational control
Organizational norms, 254
Organizational structure, 227
    building blocks of, 228–229
    horizontal differentiation
        in, 234–244
    operating costs and, 243–244
    role of, 227–229
    vertical differentiation in, 229–233
Organizational values, 254
Output, 87
Output control, 251–252
Outside directors, 38, 39
Outside view, 19
Outsourcing, 178–180, 186, 202

P

Packard, David, 46
Palm, 89
Partner selection, 218–219
Patents, 110
Pay for performance compensation, 98
PeopleSoft, 222
PepsiCo
    entry barriers and, 59
    product development at, 136
Permanent teams, 245–246
Perrier, 92
Personal computer industry
    bargaining power in, 65
    price signaling in, 134
    value-added chain in, 181
    vertical integration in, 180
Personal ethics, 46, 47
Pfeffer, Jeffery, 21
Pfizer, 36
Pharmaceutical industry
    bargaining power in, 64
    closing case of, 78–79
    global expansion in, 155
    strategic groups in, 66–67, 68
Philip Morris, 76, 138, 188–189
Planning
    scenario, 15–16
    strategic, 7–11, 13, 16, 17, 236, 241
Polaroid, 108
Political/legal forces, 76–77
Porsche, 126
Porter, Michael E., 57, 86. *See also* Five
    forces model
Portfolio of core competences,
    205–208
Positioning strategy, 104
Postacquisition integration, 213–214
Prahalad, C. K., 205, 206, 207–208

Premier plus 10, 206, 207
Premium price, 123
Price
    cutting of, 133
    inflation of, 74
    reservation, 84
    stock, 250
Price-earnings ratio, C11
Price leadership, 134–135
Price signaling, 134
Price war, 61, 71, 72
Pricing, transfer, 243
Primary activities, 91–92
Principal, 34–35, 37–38
Principle of the minimum chain
    of command, 231
Prior hypothesis bias, 17–18
Process, business, 201
Process innovation, 89
Procter & Gamble
    economies of scope at, 189, 191
    global expansion at, 148, 157,
        158, 160
    market penetration and, 136
    vertical differentiation and, 231
Product
    bundling of, 176–177
    development of, 136. See also
        Innovation; Research and
        development
    quality of. See Quality, product
    structure of, 236–237
    substitute, 65–66
Product development team, 105
Product differentiation, 86, 89, 100, 103,
    118–119, 120, 176–177
Product innovation, 89, 103–104
Product-oriented business definition,
    30–31
Product proliferation, 132–133, 137
Product-team structure, 237–238
Production, in value chain, 92
    efficiency and, 94–95, 96
    globalization of, 147
Productivity
    capital, 87
    employee, 87, 97–98
Profit ratios, C8–C9
Profitability, 2, 39
    global expansion and, 148–152
    long-run. See specific strategies
    revenue growth rates and, 37
    scale of entry and, 209–210
Promotion, 47

Q

Quality, product, 88, 89, 137
    franchising and, 164
    increasing, 100–103
    vertical integration and, 184
Quality as excellence, 88–89, 103
Quality as reliability, 88–89, 100–102
Quantum Corporation, 106
Quick ratio, C10

R

Raymond, Lee, 36
RCA, 163
Realized strategy, 14
Reasoning by analogy, 18
Reengineering, 201–202
Related diversification, 191–192
Relational capital, 220
Representativeness, 19
Research and development, 91, 94, 211
    efficiency and, 94
    organization structure and, 243
Reservation price, customer's, 84
Resources
    competition for, 243
    intangible, 108, 110
    tangible, 108
Responsibility, strategic, 241
Restructuring, 192–194, 202
Retail industry
    competitive advantage in, 84
    strategic groups in, 68
Return on invested capital (ROIC),
    2, C9
Return on investment (ROI), 250
Return on stockholders equity (ROE), C9
Return on total assets (ROA), C9
Risk capital, 33
Risk of holdup, 183
Rivalry, 61–63, 177
ROI, 250
ROIC, 2
Roll, Richard, 18
Royal Crown Cola, 59, 136
Royal Dutch Shell, 15

S

Sales, in value chain, 92
Sam's Choice, 59
Sam's Club, 4
SAP, 222–223
Sarbanes-Oxley Act, 39, 41
Scale, economies of, 58, 94
Scale of entry, 209–210
Scenario planning, 15–16
Scenarios, "what if," 15
Schultz, Howard, 112
Scope, economies of, 189–191
Screening, 214–215
SEC, 35, 40
Securities and Exchange Commission
    (SEC), 35, 40
Securities law, 42
Segmentation, market, 118–119, 120
Self-dealing, 43
Self-managing team, 98
SGI (Silicon Graphics International)
    versus Dell
        competition in server and cloud
            computing, case on, C13–C20
Shakeout stage, of industry, 71
Shareholder-return ratios, C11–C12
Siebel Systems, 222
Signaling, price, 134

Singapore Airlines, 103
Sinofsky, Steve, 13
Six Sigma methodology, 100–102
SKUs, 67
Sloan, Alfred, 242
Smith Corona, 31
Snecma, 219
Social forces, 76
Soft drink industry
    entry barriers in, 59
    structure of, 56
Southwest Airlines, 20, 97
Span of control, 229
Specialization, 94
Specialized asset, 182
Spinoff, 194
Stakeholders, 28
    rights of, 42
    types of, 28–29. See also specific types
Standardization, 253
Starbucks, 112–113, 149
Steel industry, 72, 137, 138
Stock-based compensation, 39–40
Stock keeping units (SKUs), 67
Stock options, 39–40
Stock price, 250
Stockholders, 28, 29, 33, 34, 42
Strategic alliances, 215–220
Strategic change, 201–205
    distinctive competences and, 205–208
    through acquisitions, 212–215
    through internal new ventures, 208–212
    through strategic alliances, 215–220
Strategic control systems, 248–250
Strategic groups, 66–69
Strategic leadership, 19–21. See also
    specific leaders
    customer focus and, 106–107
    ethics and, 47–48
Strategic managers, 5–7. See also specific
    types
Strategic planning, 7–11
    at Microsoft, 11, 12
    organization structure and, 236, 241
Strategic responsibility, 241
Strategy, 2. See also specific strategies
    corporate governance and, 33–41
    in declining industries, 137–140
    as emergent process, 11–15
    ethics and, 42–49
    process for planning, 7–11
Strategy formulation, 8
Strategy implementation, 8, 10–11
Structure(s)
    analyzing industry, 56–66. See also
        specific types
    flat, 229
    functional, 234–236
    geographic, 238–239
    low cost, 86, 89, 100, 104
    multidivisional, 5, 240–244
    product, 236–237
    product-team, 237–238
    tall, 229–231
Stuck in the middle, 128
Substandard working conditions, 44

Substitute products, 65–66
Sun Microsystems, 13
Sunderstrand, 197
Sundown rule, Walmart's, 99
Suppliers' bargaining power, 64–65
Support activities, 92–93
Sustained competitive advantage, 4, 84
Swartz, Mark, 35
Switching costs, 60
SWOT analysis, 8, 10, 203, C3

T

Takeover constraint, 41
Tall structure, 229–231
Tangible resources, 108
Taper integration, 185
Target, 3, 4
Task force, 245
Teams
    permanent, 245–246
    self-managing, 98
Technological change, 75
Telephone industry, 60
Texas Instruments, 94
ThinkPad, 151
Threats, 56, 203. *See also specific threats*
3M, 12
    diversification at, 189, 190
    innovation at, 108
Tie in sales, 44
Time Warner, 213
Times-covered ratio, C11
Titanium Metals Corp, 44
Tit-for-tat strategy, 134
Tobacco industry
    in decline stage, 137
    social forces and, 76
Top-down change, 205
Tort laws, 42
Toshiba, 217, 219, 220
Total quality management (TQM),
    100–101, 202
Total shareholder returns, C11
Toyota, 23, 24
    bargaining power of, 64
    global expansion at, 148, 149,
        154, 156
    vs. GM, 85, 86
    lean production system of, 89

market segmentation and, 119
    quality and, 88
TQM, 100–101, 202
Transfer pricing, 243
Transnational strategy, 159
Travelers, 190
TRW Systems, 220
Tyco, 35, 37

U

Unilever
    code of ethics at, 47–48, 49
Union Pacific (UP), 233
Unit, business, 6
United States Steel Industry
    Association, 77
United Technologies Corporation (UTC),
    192, 196–197
Universal needs, 154
Unrelated diversification, 191–192
UPS, 63

V

Vacuum tube industry, 138
Value chain, 90–93, 180, 181
Value creation, 84–86. *See also specific
    functions*
Value creation through diversification,
    187–191
    through horizontal integration,
        174–178
    through vertical integration, 173,
        180–186
Values, 32, 254
Verizon Wireless
    customer defection rates and, 96
Vertical differentiation, 229–233
Vertical integration, 173, 180–186
Virtual corporation, 179
Vision, 31
Volvo, 103

W

Walmart
    bargaining power of, 67
    competitive advantage of, 3–4

and competitive positioning, 120
    efficiency at, 97
    employees of, 99
    entry barriers and, 59
    global expansion at, 149, 150–151,
        152, 153
    leadership of, 19, 20. *See also*
        Walton, Sam
    organizational culture of, 255–256
    profitability of, 2
    support activities in, 92, 93
    working conditions at, 45
Walton, Sam, 3–4, 19, 20, 45, 67, 99,
    120, 255–256
Wang, Jerry, 233
Welch, Jack, 19, 20
Western Union, 13
What if" scenarios, 15
White space, 206, 207
Wholly owned subsidiary, 165
Wilson, Charles, 36
Windows, 44, 45, 67, 99
Wireless telecommunications industry
    customer defection rates in,
        96–97
    infrastructure differences in, 155
Wookey, John, 222, 223
Working conditions
    at Hewlett-Packard, 46
    at Nike, 42, 44
    substandard, 44
    at Unilever, 47
    at Walmart, 45
World cars, 154
Wrapp, Edward, 21

X

Xbox, 12
Xerox
    international strategy and,
        160, 164

Y

Yahoo!, 189, 233

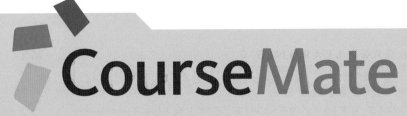

CourseMate

ENGAGING. TRACKABLE. AFFORDABLE.

Cengage Learning's Management **Course**Mate provides instructors with all of the reporting tools needed to track student engagement, while students can access interactive study tools in a dynamic, online learning environment.

Course Mate **features include:**

- **Engagement Tracker,** a Web-based reporting and tracking tool, allows you to monitor your students' use of course material and assess their engagement and preparation.

- An **Interactive eBook** provides students with an interactive, online-only version of the printed textbook.

- **Interactive Teaching & Learning Tools** including quizzes, flashcards, videos, and more—all online with **Course**Mate.

- It's **Affordable**—about half the cost of a traditional printed textbook.

About Engagement Tracker

Engagement Tracker, available within every **Course**Mate product, allows you to assess your students' preparation and engagement. This intuitive, online reporting tool makes it easy for you to evaluate use of study resources, monitor time-on-task and track progress for the entire class or for individual students. Instantly see what concepts are the most difficult for your class and identify which students are at risk throughout the semester.

To access additional course materials including **Course**Mate, please visit **www.cengagebrain.com**. At the CengageBrain.com home page, enter the ISBN of your title (from the back cover of your book) using the search box at the top of the page. This will take you to the product page where these resources can be found.

SOUTH-WESTERN
CENGAGE Learning™

**Strategic Management Essentials,
Third Edition**
Gareth R. Jones, Charles W. L. Hill

Vice President of Editorial, Business:
Jack W. Calhoun

Acquisitions Editor: Michele Rhoades

Developmental Editor: Suzanna Bainbridge

Senior Editorial Assistant: Ruth Belanger

Marketing Manager: Jon Monahan

Associate Content Project Manager:
Jana Lewis

Media Editor: Rob Ellington

Frontlist Buyer, Manufacturing:
Arethea Thomas

Marketing Communications Manager:
Jim Overly

Production Service:
S4Carlisle Publishing Services

Art Director: Tippy McIntosh

Internal Designer: Mike Stratton,
Stratton Design

Cover Designer: Patti Hudepohl

Cover Photo Credits:
B/W Image: iStockphoto
Color Image: Shutterstock Images / dicogm

Rights Acquisitions Specialist: John Hill

For permission to use material from this text or product, submit all requests online at **www.cengage.com/permissions**
Further permissions questions can be emailed to
permissionrequest@cengage.com

ExamView® is a registered trademark of eInstruction Corp. Windows is a registered trademark of the Microsoft Corporation used herein under license. Macintosh and Power Macintosh are registered trademarks of Apple Computer, Inc. used herein under license.
© 2008 Cengage Learning. All Rights Reserved.

Cengage Learning WebTutor™ is a trademark of Cengage Learning.

Library of Congress Control Number: 2011925165

International Edition:

ISBN-13: 978-1-111-52520-0

ISBN-10: 1-111-52520-X

Asia
www.cengageasia.com
tel: (65) 6410 1200

Australia/New Zealand
www.cengage.com.au
tel: (61) 3 9685 4111

Brazil
www.cengage.com.br
tel: (55) 11 3665 9900

India
www.cengage.co.in
tel: (91) 11 4364 1111

Latin America
www.cengage.com.mx
tel: (52) 55 1500 6000

UK/Europe/Middle East/Africa
www.cengage.co.uk
tel: (44) 0 1264 332 424

**Represented in Canada by Nelson
Education, Ltd.**
tel: (416) 752 9100/(800) 668 0671
www.nelson.com

Cengage Learning is a leading provider of customized learning solutions with office locations around the globe, including Singapore, the United Kingdom, Australia, Mexico, Brazil, and Japan. Locate your local office at: **www.cengage.com/global**

For product information: **www.cengage.com/international**
Visit your local office: **www.cengage.com/global**
Visit our corporate website: **www.cengage.com**

Printed in China by China Translation &
Printing Services Limited

1 2 3 4 5 6 7 15 14 13 12 11